Previous books by
David M. Rubenstein

How to Invest
The American Experiment
How to Lead
The American Story

THE
HIGHEST
CALLING

Conversations on the
AMERICAN PRESIDENCY

DAVID M.
RUBENSTEIN

SIMON & SCHUSTER
New York   London   Toronto   Sydney   New Delhi

Simon & Schuster
1230 Avenue of the Americas
New York, NY 10020
Copyright © 2024 by David Rubenstein

All rights reserved, including the right to reproduce this book
or portions thereof in any form whatsoever. For information,
address Simon & Schuster Subsidiary Rights Department,
1230 Avenue of the Americas, New York, NY 10020.

First Simon & Schuster hardcover edition September 2024

SIMON & SCHUSTER and colophon are registered
trademarks of Simon & Schuster, LLC

Simon & Schuster: Celebrating 100 Years of Publishing in 2024

For information about special discounts for bulk purchases,
please contact Simon & Schuster Special Sales at
1-866-506-1949 or business@simonandschuster.com.

The Simon & Schuster Speakers Bureau can bring authors to
your live event. For more information or to book an event, contact
the Simon & Schuster Speakers Bureau at 1-866-248-3049
or visit our website at www.simonspeakers.com.

Interior design by Lewelin Polanco

Manufactured in the United States of America

1 3 5 7 9 10 8 6 4 2

Library of Congress Cataloging-in-Publication Data is available.

ISBN 978-1-6680-6762-8
ISBN 978-1-6680-6773-4 (ebook)

*To Ted Sorensen, who inspired me to work for a president,
and Stu Eizenstat, who gave me the chance to do so.*

CONTENTS

PREFACE

Whenever I interview an author who has written a book about George Washington or Abraham Lincoln, my first question is always "Why do you think the world really needs another book on this president?"

Someone interviewing me about this book might, fairly, ask the same type of question: "Why does the world really need another book on the U.S. presidency?"

There are plenty of books on the presidency. What I wanted to do with this one, however, is to provide some hopefully unique insights into the accomplishments, failures, personalities, and characters of many of our best-known presidents, through interviews I have conducted with many of these presidents' biographers and with some of the presidents themselves.

My hope is to remind readers how truly different our presidents have been in their backgrounds, personalities, goals, and perspectives, and how these differences can really shape, for the good or bad, the country and the world. Although a president is just one person, an entire country (and indeed the world) can be moved in one direction or another by what that one person decides.

And thus, I would like readers to think about the significance of the decision to vote, since about a third of eligible voters do not even vote in presidential elections.

In June 2024, as this is written, the differences between the two main candidates for president—Presidents Joe Biden and Donald Trump—are stark. And the country is likely to go forward in vastly different directions depending on who wins the election. A small number of votes in a few of the "swing" states can decide the election.

Every American has a real interest in how the country proceeds, and those eligible should exercise their right to vote, and in doing so exercise the right that so many Americans have died protecting for almost 250 years.

INTRODUCTION

For the past hundred years, the position of the American presidency could well be argued to have been (and continue to be) the single most important position in the world.

Despite its importance, most Americans seem to know a good deal less about the position—its history, strengths, and weaknesses—and about the 45 individuals who have held this position—and who have thereby played a major role in shaping the United States and the world—than might be desired by an informed citizenry.

As the country approaches its 250th anniversary, a worthwhile goal for America is for citizens to learn more about the country's history and government, including the position that has become the central one in the U.S. government in so many ways: the presidency. I have tried, through interviews with living presidents as well as scholars and journalists on particular presidents, along with my own perspectives on the office and personal experiences with it, to contribute toward this goal of providing a better understanding of our presidency.

Over the last few years, in public speeches and interviews, I have often said, obviously tongue-in-cheek, that my career path—private equity—is humankind's highest calling. In truth, the U.S. presidency deserves that appellation—an incredibly difficult job done in the service of the country and, in many ways, large parts of the world.

The Presidency of the Last Century

When President Woodrow Wilson went to Paris in 1918 to negotiate the treaty designed to end the Great War, he was received with public adulation and acclaim that exceeded anything even Julius Caesar experienced upon returning to Rome after a conquest.

In that moment, the world saw for the first time just how large a colossus the U.S. president had become on the global stage. That stood in stark contrast to when Thomas Jefferson walked by himself—no security, staff, or family—from his boardinghouse to his first inauguration. What was once intended by the Founding Fathers to be a position heading one of three essentially equal branches of a republican government had clearly become, by Wilson's tenure, the most powerful office on the planet, with its occupant seen as the undisputed leader of the Western world.

That larger-than-life presence shrank not long after Wilson came back from Paris. He was unable to get his beloved creation in the treaty, a League of Nations, approved by the Senate, despite a train tour throughout the country designed to develop public support for the concept. During that railroad trip, Wilson suffered a stroke, which, when followed by at least one more severe stroke, essentially ended his visibility (and viability) as president, as he became a complete recluse at the White House during the remainder of his second term. Wilson's wife, Edith, acted as his eyes and ears and essentially became the de facto president.

Wilson was succeeded by the charming but ineffectual (and less than honest) Warren Harding, who died in office and was followed by the most laconic and low-key of American presidents, Calvin Coolidge. He was succeeded by Herbert Hoover, who had an impressive and global reputation as a gifted engineer and public servant; but the Great Depression ultimately overwhelmed him, and he came to be seen as a helpless, if not clueless, leader in dealing with the Depression. So the office of the American president was no longer seen as the behemoth it had once seemed when Wilson entered Paris.

And then came Franklin Delano Roosevelt, stricken by polio in midlife, not considered much of an intellect by his peers, and indeed widely viewed as an effete, born-to-the-manner patrician still heavily influenced by his domineering mother. But, in time, Roosevelt, like Wilson, became larger than life, due to his reinvention of what the federal government could do to get the country out of the Depression. And by serving an unprecedented third term, during which Pearl Harbor occurred and the U.S. fought and largely won (by the time of his death) the greatest war the world had ever seen, Roosevelt clearly surpassed Wilson as the undisputed leader of the Western world, reinstating the position of the American president.

Roosevelt's death brought the relatively unknown, though quite decisive, Harry Truman into the White House, a turn of events few had once imagined as possible and even fewer thought desirable (including his mother-in-law). While Truman has in recent years come to be appreciated by scholars, he left office with a low approval rating; indeed, the man who made the bold, historic decision to drop two atomic bombs was not seen during his tenure as a larger-than-life figure. Maybe a bit of a smaller-than-life figure.

Truman was followed by the hero of D-Day, Dwight D. Eisenhower. Despite the worldwide acclaim that Eisenhower had achieved in his military service, his presidency was, by his design, a low-key affair. He was no Douglas MacArthur in his desire for public attention, and he was pleased with serving his country in this role; but he did not seek the glory or fame that he could have readily attained by virtue of his prior accomplishments (or by the unprecedented growth of the federal government's power from the time of World War II).

In the Public Eye

A fair question might be asked: Why did a man like Eisenhower, who did not relish the limelight, and who had already devoted his life to his country, want to be president? And indeed, it might well be asked, why would anyone want to be president? Just look at what has happened to presidents over the past hundred years. Hoover was blamed for the Great Depression and decisively lost his reelection bid. Roosevelt died in office at 63, his health no doubt harmed by the considerable pressures of the job. Truman left office after deciding not to seek reelection (his approval ratings having gone as low as 22 percent). Kennedy was assassinated. Johnson was largely driven from office by the unpopularity of the Vietnam War. Nixon was forced to resign. Ford survived two assassination attempts and was defeated for reelection. Carter was defeated for reelection. George H. W. Bush was defeated for reelection. Clinton was impeached. George W. Bush fought two unpopular wars and was barely reelected. And Trump was impeached twice, lost his reelection bid, and was later indicted multiple times by the very government he once led.

Three presidents since World War II who were reelected left office with no lasting damage to their personal reputation: Eisenhower, Reagan, and Obama. But Eisenhower will likely be remembered more for his pre-presidential reputation, having led the D-Day invasion and winning the war in Europe. While Reagan almost died because of an assassination attempt early in his time in office, he later also had a major scandal—the

Iran-Contra affair. His staff had illegally sold weapons to Iran, using the profits to fund the contra forces against the leftist government in Nicaragua, and for a few weeks at least it was not clear if his reputation could ever recover from it. However, Reagan did survive because the public didn't think that he paid enough attention to details to have actually known what was happening. And he ultimately left office with relatively high approval ratings.

Obama may be a rare president who came to office with a comparatively unknown public reputation and left with an enhanced public reputation (hard-core Republicans notwithstanding)—even though he had relatively few epic or transformative accomplishments other than the Obamacare legislation. Obama will always be remembered most for having been the first African American to have been elected president—no small feat in a country where African Americans are about 14 percent of the population and the legacies of slavery and Jim Crow made the election of a Black president seem unlikely.

With few exceptions, the odds of becoming president and emerging after eight years alive, healthy, and with an unscathed reputation are modest. The greater prospect, unfortunately, is that a president will die in office or will leave either disgraced in some way or defeated for reelection—which, while not exactly a disgrace, does impair one's public reputation and perhaps future effectiveness. (Jimmy Carter spent more than forty years working on global peace and health challenges, won a Nobel Peace Prize, and was generally able to rehabilitate his public image—but it took more than four decades.)

Despite this record, people still line up years in advance to run for president, committing themselves for at least two years to relentless travel, constant fundraising, essentially no family time, often inedible food, reduced sleep and exercise, and the abandonment, for some time, of an existing position or career.

The presidency is the ultimate job in the world that one can hold (and can seek) without having to work one's way up a ladder over 30 to 40 years. Anyone who is a native-born citizen and is 35 years of age can serve, and the fact that previous long shots—like Carter, Obama, or Trump—made it encourages others to run. The opportunity to be at the center of the universe, with the power to affect the lives of so many fellow citizens and so many individuals around the world, is like a drug, and a normal cost-benefit analysis is thrown aside. And, if one survives the rigors and challenges of the presidency, being a former president can be better in many ways than actually being president—no national responsibilities, popularity tends to increase, compensation (through speeches and books) can be extraordinary, and there is lifetime Secret Service protection.

Traditionally, individuals who have contemplated seeking the presidency tended to have a reasonably well-known public reputation and some level of meaningful accomplishment. Of course, there were always exceptions: Lincoln had only served one term in Congress, was later defeated for the Senate, and outside of the Lincoln-Douglas Senate debates of 1858 was little known in much of the country until he secured his party's nomination in 1860.

The opening of access to the nominating process in the 1960s and 1970s—making a lack of traditional qualifications less relevant—has made many individuals believe that they could become president by directly appealing to voters. John Kennedy probably initiated that thought process in modern times. Although the son of a wealthy businessman, he was young and relatively unaccomplished as a representative and senator. But he went on the road, built a strong grassroots organization, appealed directly to voters rather than the backroom political bosses (with some exceptions), and managed to capture the nomination and the presidency in what seemed like an almost effortless manner. (His father's money—there were no spending or reporting requirements then—no doubt helped a great deal. But if a father's wealth were enough to make one president, there would be more presidents, rather than just one, whose father was a Forbes 400 member.)

The concept of going on the road, taking one's case to the American voters, and being a force for change in Washington no doubt propelled Jimmy Carter into the presidency. Although he had not been an overly popular governor of Georgia, he did attract a fair amount of national attention for being a New South governor. Reelection was not then permitted in Georgia, and thus Carter, with no reelection prospects, considered his future political options and thought a long-shot run for president was not so ridiculous. He had met others who were thinking of running and he felt he was as competent as all of them, if not more so. And what was the downside? His peanut farm and warehouse businesses were not going anywhere. So Carter began the ultimate bare-bones campaign, surrounded by a group of young Georgians, and developed a novel concept—running as someone who was not from Washington (and not a lawyer), who was not part of the Watergate mess in Washington, who could bring the South back into the Democratic Party mainstream, and who would change Washington in a way that only a true outsider could do. And it worked. He essentially won the Iowa caucuses and the New Hampshire primary, and the rest is history.

Since then, every fresh face in the political world thinks he or she can do what Carter did. And some have. Obama is the best example. But Trump essentially had the same idea—a fresh political face with business experience who could clean up the Washington "swamp." And Trump's march toward the nomination in 2016—anticipated by virtually no one at the campaign's outset—worked almost flawlessly, despite campaign staff infighting and Trump's at times incendiary comments and unusual behavior.

That someone with no government experience could get elected does show the problems of a system where anyone can run and traditional qualifications are not really a prerequisite. On the other hand, my sense is the American people like to believe that any person has a chance to rise up and run (in part because of the "American Dream" mythology), and that the American people should have the widest possible selection of candidates.

The job does not come without its challenges. Congress might be controlled by another party. Even if not, Congress may well not support a president's programs. Foreign leaders are no longer as willing to follow the U.S. lead on geopolitical and military matters. The job has health risks—aside from possible assassinations, every president seems to age considerably—and that is not surprising, for they have to deal with the toughest problems, the ones that cannot be solved by anyone else in the government.

And the press exposure, especially with the advent of around-the-clock television news, the internet, and social media, essentially means that every mistake is magnified and transmitted instantly around the world. The minute-by-minute exposure to the media, and thus the public in the U.S. and around the world, places so much pressure on a president that it is a wonder anyone really wants the job. But we're lucky that some talented people still strive for the highest office.

A Lifelong Interest in the Office

My first memory of hearing about a president directly was Eisenhower. I was born in 1949, and I am not sure if my memory is accurate, but I vaguely remember watching what must have been the 1956 Republican National Convention on a small black-and-white television in our modest row house in Baltimore. I realized, even then, that the U.S. president was an important person—maybe the most important person.

In a few short years came John F. Kennedy, the charismatic, handsome young senator from Massachusetts, candidate for the 1960 Democratic nomination, and a person that my blue-collar, dedicated Democratic parents thought was the ideal candidate. I was delighted when he won, and followed my sixth-grade teacher's instructions to watch the inauguration. School was even closed for the occasion. I am not sure that I honestly recognized Kennedy's inaugural address as the most eloquent of the twentieth century at the time, or a model of speech craftsmanship the likes of which we have not really seen since. But the day after the inauguration, my teacher took two hours to go through the speech line by line, and I got it—this was truly a masterpiece of oratory.

Perhaps the memory of "Ask not what your country can do for you, but what you can do for your country" is what led me several decades later to want to work for the man who helped to author that speech: Kennedy's former special counsel, Ted Sorensen, who later became a partner at a New York law firm, Paul, Weiss, Rifkind, Wharton & Garrison. And I did precisely that in 1973 upon graduating from the University of Chicago Law School. (My admiration for Kennedy has remained: since then, I have served for fourteen years as chairman of the John F. Kennedy Center for the Performing Arts in Washington, the living memorial to our 35th president. I have also been deeply involved with the Kennedy School at Harvard, serving as its capital campaign chair and longtime chair of its executive council. And I have been a large donor to the John F. Kennedy Presidential Library in Boston, as well as to the organization started by Jacqueline Kennedy, the White House Historical Association.)

The Kennedy speech and Sorensen experiences focused my interest in pursuing a career in government, though not in politics as a candidate (I didn't have enough charm, good looks, money, or self-confidence for that). After two years with Paul, Weiss, where I quickly concluded I was not going to be a great corporate lawyer, Ted Sorensen helped with a recommendation, and I got a position as chief counsel for a Senate subcommittee being chaired by Senator Birch Bayh of Indiana, who was about to launch his presidential campaign in 1976. Disappointingly, Bayh dropped out five months later, after poor showings in the Democratic primaries, having joined the campaign too late to attract the required field and fundraising talent. Yet this brief taste of being around a presidential candidate (even on his Senate staff) made me think about actually joining a presidential campaign.

Inside the White House

In a lucky twist of fate, Milton Gwirtzman, a friend of Senator Ted Kennedy and Ted Sorensen, asked if I would be interested in interviewing for a position on the general election policy staff of Governor Carter. Carter was seen as the likely Democratic nominee, defying almost everyone's expectations, given his long-shot, shoestring campaign. As noted earlier, he was a one-term Southern governor, who had no national profile at his campaign's beginning, when it was widely viewed that Southerners could not lead the Democratic Party ticket. It was generally believed they would not be able to sufficiently juggle their state political bases with the more progressive views of Northern Democrats.

I interviewed with Stu Eizenstat, a lawyer from Atlanta and former speechwriter in the Lyndon Johnson White House, who had been Carter's principal (really only) policy advisor during the Democratic primaries. I got the job. The two of us and the other policy staff that Stu hired were all twenty- and thirty-year-olds with some Capitol Hill experience (almost all had more than I did), and we had a single-minded view—not really shared by Carter—that he could win the election by having well-reasoned policy positions and papers (written by us) to support his programs.

The outcome is now known: Carter won the election, but barely. Had just a few states (i.e., Texas and Hawaii) voted differently, Carter would have lost the Electoral College vote (he won the popular vote by just 50 percent to 48 percent). Had the election gone on another week—Ford was surging toward the end—it was widely thought by many independent observers that he could have won. A one-term Southern governor, not all that popular in his own state, had defeated an incumbent president and was going to the White House. It was actually harder for me to believe that I was going to the White House, the place that our presidents from John Adams onward had lived.

Normally, many of the winning presidential campaign staff members wind up drifting over to the White House staff, though it is typically supplemented by more experienced policy professionals or distinguished citizens. Carter had a novel idea: instead of waiting until he was in office to put together this team, he did so during the campaign (and used precious campaign funds to support the effort). Designed to enable him to govern from day one, his pre-election transition team would have thought through the various policy decisions he would have to make as president early in the term. But this transition team was not designed to include many campaign types like me.

In the end, Carter's two closest campaign advisors—his chief of staff, Hamilton Jordan, and his communications advisor, Jody Powell—convinced Carter not to dismiss the campaign people so readily, because we were not just political types but also had credentials qualifying us for government service as well. For instance, my boss Stu Eizenstat had worked in the Johnson White House. Stu was my ticket to any White House position, and ultimately he was tasked to run domestic policy in the postelection transition effort. But Carter did not actually ask Stu to be his senior White House domestic policy advisor until about two weeks before the inauguration.

Stu then asked me to serve as his deputy, which I was of course thrilled to do—Deputy Assistant to the President for Domestic Policy, at age 27, three years out of law school. Life could not get much better, I thought. A slight problem arose quickly, when Walter Mondale, the incoming vice president, requested that Stu hire Mondale's domestic policy advisor to be his deputy. Stu said he had already selected a deputy. Mondale suggested then that Stu have two deputies, and he did. Bert Carp, an experienced, Stanford-educated Hill veteran who knew the ins and outs of the Democratic policy world infinitely better than I did, essentially ran the staff day-to-day and focused on policy. I substituted for Stu when he could not do something (often including meetings with the president), helped review various staff papers for him, wrote papers that he would edit or rewrite before they would go to the president, and served as Stu's eyes and ears in the West Wing, where my office was, next to his. I was probably more interested in the politics of the West Wing and the trappings (and history) of the presidency and the White House than Bert was, and he cared more about the intricacies of the Democratic interest group positions than I did. So it worked—though we did not get reelected, so maybe it did not.

Although I was not that experienced in domestic policy matters, had not known Carter, and was not part of the Georgia clan that was so prominent at the White House, I carved out a role for myself that led to a reasonable amount of impact for a junior White House aide. That was helped by the fact that (1) I was willing to work essentially around the clock (*Newsweek* ran a story about how I was in the White House so much that the cleaning ladies at night were complaining that they could never get access to my office); (2) I knew Carter's positions as well as anyone (I had been tasked in the transition with compiling all the positions he had taken during the long campaign—pre-internet, it was not easy to gather all this information—and came to be known as someone who knew the president's views as well as anyone but his most senior advisors); and (3) my boss, Stu Eizenstat, was also a wonkish workaholic, and he had enormous influence on matters in the domestic arena, and as his deputy, I benefited from his reputation. That said, everything was a team effort; I'm not sure I can cite one thing that I was solely responsible for that helped the country get better. No one at the White House has an idea that gets very far without others weighing in and modifying it somewhat.

The president's popularity declined a fair bit while in office. We struggled with inflation, unclear presidential directives and policy statements, a fractious Congress (even though controlled by the Democrats, many of whom felt no particular loyalty to Carter), gas station lines, the Iranian hostage crisis (and a failed rescue mission), an intraparty nomination fight from Senator Kennedy, and ultimately the decisive loss to a person whom few in the White House thought the American people would want to lead the country. In our obviously myopic view, Ronald Reagan was an ex-actor who seemed uninterested in most policy matters, and we believed would be seen at the time as dangerously old. (He was 69, which I no longer see as quite so old.)

Early in 1981 within Democratic circles, Reagan was considered way beyond his depth, and it was assumed that he would inevitably falter and the throne would be reclaimed by the next Democratic presidential nominee, one without Carter's flaws. To those who had worked in the Carter administration, that was going to be Walter Mondale, someone thought to be so different from Carter in approach and personality that the association with Carter would not prevent his election. That, of course, proved to be unrealistic. Mondale struggled to get the nomination, and then lost 49 states (all but his home state) in the general election.

Before all that unfolded, I considered going back into the political world with Mondale, and then going back to the White House in a more senior position when he inevitably won. But I ultimately came to my senses—luck had already struck once. I would have to spend a few years working for Mondale, while also practicing law to pay the rent, before joining his campaign full time; I might not actually get offered a better job than I had already had in the Carter White House; and I was really not likely to become part of Mondale's inner circle, which was already set with many who had worked a decade or more for him. So I stayed in the private sector, and ultimately left the practice of law to start a private equity firm, The Carlyle Group, that grew to be one of the largest in the world.

Since then, I have still done my best to keep up with what was going on with my great interest, the presidency. I knew reasonably well a great many people who served in the Clinton, Obama, and Biden administrations, and actually came to know those presidents a bit, though I have never been a close advisor to any of them. I also have not made any political contributions to presidential candidates or presidents, trying to be reasonably apolitical in that regard (and to avoid the buying-access criticisms often leveled at wealthy campaign donors). Too, when I later chaired the boards of organizations like the Kennedy Center, the Smithsonian Institution, the National Gallery of Art, and the Library of Congress, I felt it was better to not be seen as political in order to ensure bipartisan support for these organizations, and campaign donations might have foiled that goal.

Through my post-Carter activities, I also came to know a number of Republican presidents. At one point after he left the presidency, George Herbert Walker Bush was an advisor to Carlyle, which primarily meant he made some speeches to investors for us. I found him to be a friendly and gracious individual, and probably knew him better than I knew any of the Democratic presidents. Through him, I met his son, who had briefly served on a Carlyle portfolio company board. And I came to know Donald Trump a bit before he was elected and saw him from time to time while he was president, typically in connection with the Kennedy Center or White House Historical Association matters.

My hope is that my interest in the presidency will be infectious to readers. Since leaving the White House about four decades ago, I have devoted time and effort to honoring the special leadership role that presidents play in our country and the world. For instance, in addition to the Kennedy-related donations, I helped with the funds needed to repair the Washington Monument after earthquake damage, led the efforts to rehabilitate the Lincoln and Jefferson Memorials, supported building the Presidential Library building at Mount Vernon (George Washington's home), and led the renovation efforts at Monticello (Thomas Jefferson's home) and Montpelier (James Madison's home). I have thought that by writing this book, I might help educate readers about the presidency, and thereby incent them to vote in presidential elections. As with my previous books, the interviews that I conducted—with leading presidential scholars and journalists and with presidents—have been edited for length and clarity and updated in consultation with the interviewees.

Finally, to some extent, I suppose my lifelong interest in the presidency is due to my pride in being an American. The presidency is perhaps the most visible, regular symbol of the country. Like many others from modest circumstances who have lived the "American Dream," I feel that achieving what I have been able to do would not have readily happened in other countries—because this country encourages upward mobility as part of its ethos, and because my last name would probably be a bit of a barrier in some other countries (particularly in the countries from which my forebears came, Ukraine and Russia). We still have work to do to make this country more equitable and a beacon to freedom for all. But the progress toward that goal is more realistic in this country than almost any other.

David M. Rubenstein
June 2024

THE
HIGHEST
CALLING

1

DOUGLAS BRADBURN
on George Washington

(1732–1799; president from 1789 to 1797)

When the Constitution was being drafted in Philadelphia in 1787, perhaps the greatest debate involved representation in Congress. Should it be by population or by state? Should enslaved people be represented in some way, and how? Should there be two legislative bodies (as in England) or just one? These issues were resolved with equal representation in the Senate and representation by population in the House, with enslaved people being counted only as three-fifths of a white person for representation purposes.

That the shape and nature of the legislature was foremost in the mind of the delegates is perhaps best illustrated by the fact that the legislative branch of government is in Article One. The discussion over how the chief executive position would operate and function—contained in Article Two—received a fair bit of discussion. The delegates did not want a king, queen, or an aristocratic figure, but instead someone who was elected, and whose powers could be checked, if necessary, by the other two branches of the federal government.

During the Convention, there were more than a few heated discussions about the powers and authority of the chief executive, to be called a president. But there probably would have been much more debate had it not been widely accepted that the first president would be none other than the man who presided over the Convention, the hero of the Revolutionary War—George Washington.

After the Convention and the ratification process, Washington was really the only person considered for the presidency. He was not universally admired during the Revolutionary War, when he lost more battles than he won, in part because he had insufficient troops and ammunition. By the war's successful conclusion, Washington became godlike, and was the one person whom all thirteen states seemed to feel comfortable supporting for president.

But Washington was reluctant to serve. He had left Mount Vernon for eight years to fight the war, and he allowed himself to be persuaded to attend the Constitutional Convention—and to help with the ratification process—yet he wanted to stay out of further public service. Neither his father nor grandfather had lived past 50, and he was already 55.

Washington was ultimately persuaded to be a candidate, and he was elected twice unanimously, a record that will surely never be matched again. As president, he established many of the traditions that we still use today. He left office extremely popular as well—a bit of a rare occurrence now.

Had he wanted to, Washington could have been elected to a third term or more. However, he decided eight years was enough. That became the unofficial limit on presidential service until Roosevelt broke it during World War II. (Now a constitutional amendment, the Twenty-Second Amendment, enshrines the two-term limit. Upset that Roosevelt broke the unwritten two-term limit, Republicans worked hard to get that amendment approved by Congress and ratified by the states. Ironically, many Republicans did not like the amendment as much when they realized that Eisenhower could have easily won a third term but was prohibited from seeking it.)

There are a large number of outstanding books on Washington, and it is hard to narrow it to one definitive book that everyone should read. In recent years, one won the Pulitzer Prize—the biography written by Ron Chernow, who has become better known for writing a book on Washington's Revolutionary War aide and later secretary of the Treasury, Alexander Hamilton. (His book on Hamilton inspired Lin-Manuel Miranda to write his award-winning musical *Hamilton*.) For this book, though, I decided to interview Doug Bradburn, the director at Mount Vernon, the historic home of George Washington that was purchased by the Mount Vernon Ladies' Association in 1858 and restored to its current, excellent condition. He is an American history scholar who previously ran the George Washington Presidential Library. I interviewed him on July 5, 2023.

*   *   *   *

DAVID M. RUBENSTEIN (DR): What is your responsibility as president and CEO of George Washington's Mount Vernon?

DOUGLAS BRADBURN (DB): I am charged with maintaining the mission of the Mount Vernon Ladies' Association, which is our corporate name, and the mission is to preserve this estate to the highest standards and educate people around the world about the life, leadership, and legacy of George Washington. I oversee a staff of about 600 employees and 300 volunteers. Our annual budget is around $60 million.

DR: When was Mount Vernon originally built?

DB: The original estate house, the Mansion House, was built in 1734. It was about a story and a half tall, and George Washington expanded it over his time running Mount Vernon in the 1750s, and then into the 1770s. The final mansion was completed by 1789.

DR: For whom is Mount Vernon actually named?

DB: It's named for an English admiral named Edward Vernon. George Washington's half brother Lawrence Washington served on the same ship with Admiral Vernon while he was the commander of British forces attempting to conquer the Spanish Main. Lawrence Washington came to greatly admire him, and changed the name of the estate from Little Hunting Creek to Mount Vernon in honor of Admiral Vernon.

DR: How did George Washington come into ownership of it?

DB: Lawrence Washington died, and George Washington started renting it from his widow in 1754. Essentially, he came into full ownership in 1761, when Lawrence Washington's widow and daughter died.

DR: What was Mount Vernon during Washington's lifetime? Was it a plantation, a farm?

DB: George Washington's Mount Vernon was a plantation. It was a combined agricultural business, which had outlying farms producing crops for market as well as mills, distillery, ultimately fisheries. It had multiple economic purposes, all of which were agricultural.

DR: How big was it?

DB: By the time he died in 1799, it was 8,000 acres. When he inherited it, it was 2,200 acres. He expanded it over the course of his lifetime.

DR: Was it a place where the work was essentially done by enslaved people, and if so, how many slaves were there?

DB: Yes, in line with every other eighteenth-century Virginia agricultural plantation, the labor was enslaved. Over the course of his lifetime, over 540 people were enslaved there. When he died, there were 317 at Mount Vernon. When he started at Mount Vernon, there were probably about 70.

DR: What happened to Mount Vernon when Washington died in 1799?

DB: The 8,000 acres were divided up in three ways among different family members. Many of the enslaved people were freed; others moved with the Custis family (the relatives of Martha Washington's first husband), whom they were owned by.

DR: Who was Miss Cunningham?

DB: Ann Pamela Cunningham was a South Carolina woman of some distinction, that is to say, some wealth, some family recognition, and she was the first regent of the Mount Vernon Ladies' Association. She created the organization that purchased this place from the last descendants of the Washington family and made it public for visitation.

DR: Where did she get the money to purchase Mount Vernon? How much did she spend on it?

DB: She created the association, which in 1858 began a national fundraising campaign to raise the money. Ultimately, they raised $200,000, which in the nineteenth century was a substantial amount of money. They got it from a variety of sources. It came from schoolkids, it came from volunteer firefighter associations, it came from Masonic organizations. It came from all over the country. It really is the first national fundraising campaign in American history. Together, they used that money to purchase the estate.

DR: Is it still owned by the same organization?

DB: It is.

DR: Does the government currently support Mount Vernon?

DB: No, we do not receive any tax dollars from the federal, state, or local governments. About 70 percent of our annual revenue comes from our business operations of ticket sales for visitors, food sales, or retail sales. The rest are donor-supported funds, which means we have membership programs, people who give generously every year, a small endowment that we draw off of, and we raise money through other means.

DR: How many visitors does Mount Vernon get in a typical year?

DB: Before the COVID pandemic, we got typically a million visitors a year. Last year we had 800,000. This year we're on pace to beat that. We'll be back to a million a year very soon.

DR: Do presidents of the United States still visit Mount Vernon?

DB: Absolutely. Twenty-seven presidents have visited Mount Vernon. The last one to come was President Biden. He was here in 2022.

DR: Let's start with George Washington's early years. Where was Washington born?

DB: He was born in a place called the Pope's Creek, which is on a branch of the Potomac River in what's called the Northern Neck of Virginia. It's currently Stafford County. He grew up in a place called Fairy Farm, which is right across the river from Fredericksburg, Virginia. That is mostly where he spent his youth.

DR: Who were his parents?

DB: His mother was Mary Ball Washington, who was a woman from a notable Virginia family, although she was adopted into that family, and his father was Augustine Washington, who went by Gus.

DR: Did he have any siblings?

DB: He had two half brothers from Gus's previous marriage, and then he had three younger brothers and two sisters. One of his sisters, Mildred, died when she was very young. The other one lived a long life. George was the oldest of the second family of Augustine Washington.

DR: What did Washington do in his youth, when he wasn't chopping down cherry trees?

DB: His youth is still quite a mystery in many ways. His father died when he was 11 years old, and that shaped him a lot because George Washington didn't get a formal education. His two older half brothers did. They were sent to an English boarding school, the same school that his father had gone to, and so he likely was going to go to that school and get a proper classical gentlemanly education. He didn't get that. He had reading, writing, and arithmetic from tutors. Essentially, he was self-educated. He became an autodidact. He was reading a lot when he was young. He became a great horseman at an early age. He was out and about in the farms of Virginia quite a bit. Clearly, his great passion in life was farming, so that must have been a big part of his job.

DR: What was he best known for as a teenager or young adult?

DB: I don't think he was known for much. He had the reputation of a quiet, thoughtful, but very athletic child. We know that he had his "Rules of Civility." He copied out 110 rules of polite behavior, which, I think, speaks to his desire to know how to behave without a father to guide him in society in nineteenth-century Virginia, which was based on manners. He always had that reputation of someone who was trying to do things the right way.

DR: Was he interested as a youth in joining the British army?

DB: He was. His brother's experience in the War of Jenkins' Ear with Admiral Vernon clearly had an impact on him. The army was also a potential route for him, because he really wasn't going to inherit much property by the standards of Virginia gentry. The British military seemed like the way. His brother thought he should become a midshipman in the Navy, but his mother stopped that from happening when he was 16 years old. One thing his brother did assure is that he learned how to become a surveyor. Surveying is one of the professions you could do as a Virginian to make money and also have the opportunity to do so out West.

DR: How did he get involved with the French and Indian War?

DB: That comes directly through his surveying efforts, because he became the surveyor for the Fairfax interest of Northern Virginia. The Fairfaxes had land in what's now the Shenandoah Valley, and they were concerned with the Ohio River Valley as well, an area that Virginians claimed. Washington was nominated for a volunteer post by his great patron here, Colonel William Fairfax, to do a diplomatic mission into the Ohio Valley to tell the French there that it was Virginian property and get them to leave. That led to Washington ultimately getting a commission in the Virginia regiment, a regiment that the colony of Virginia raised to fight the French in the Ohio Valley. That was the beginning of his military career.

DR: Was he working for the British or working for the Virginians? What did he do in that war?

DB: He was the commander in chief of the Virginia forces involved in that war. They all fell under British authority, but they weren't formally in the British establishment, so he didn't have, for instance, a commission from the king. He had a commission from the colony of Virginia, which was considered by the mainline British army as second-rate. They were sort of the local bumpkins. His role was to defend the frontier. With hundreds of men under his command, he was instructed to defend the frontier from Indian and French incursions.

DR: Did he get captured and almost killed during the war?

DB: He did surrender his first command at the very beginning. It wasn't an official war yet, so he never really was an official prisoner of war. That was the loss of the Battle of Fort Necessity at the beginning of the war. In fact, he can be credited with helping to start the Seven Years' War, which, of course, would go on to be fought between the allies of Great Britain and the allies of France. Washington's early claim to fame is that he started a world war.

DR: Was he not in a situation where he could have been killed?

DB: He was, absolutely. He was often in harm's way. In fact, famously, General Edward Braddock took a mission out to capture a French fort at what is now Pittsburgh, and that whole expeditionary force essentially got destroyed. Washington was there as a volunteer in Braddock's military family. He helped with the retreat, and during that battle his horse was shot from under him two times. He had bullet holes in his coat, but he never had been wounded himself in battle. He was in harm's way quite a bit in the French and Indian War, but fortunately for the future of America he wasn't killed.

DR: What did he do after the war?

DB: After the war he resigned his commission in Virginia. He was frustrated by his experience in the war, because he never got the recognition from the British military establishment that he craved. They never made him an officer. They never recognized his regiment as a British regiment. He resigned in 1759, and married Martha Washington. It's a major turning point in his career. He basically thought his military career was over. He was going to focus his efforts on becoming a Virginian businessman, a planter, and a political leader. He went from trying to be a British imperial military figure to becoming a Virginian of renown. By marrying Martha Custis, he was able to do that, because she brought a lot of wealth into his life.

DR: She was married before. Is that where she got her wealth?

DB: She was married to Daniel Parke Custis. The Custis family was one of the first families of Virginia, going back into the seventeenth century. They had massive wealth, not only in land and slaves, which is where most of the wealth was in the eighteenth century, but they even held things like Bank of England stock and British securities. They had real wealth. She, as the widow of Custis, was able to control a third of that wealth until she died. Washington himself was also in charge of the wealth of her children, who would ultimately inherit most of the Custis estate. So Washington was in a prime position to be able to make investments and expand Mount Vernon.

DR: Did he have any children with Martha? Did she have any children before they got married?

DB: She had children from her first marriage. She and George did not have any of their own. We don't know exactly why. He wrote a letter saying that they were resigned to the fact that they weren't going to have children. Some historians believe that Washington might have become infertile when he got smallpox in Barbados when he was 19 years old. Either way, George and Martha never had any children.

Martha had two surviving children from her first marriage—a daughter, Patsy, and a son, Jack—who became George's stepchildren, though Patsy was an epileptic and died at 17. The son went on to have four children of his own. Two of these—George Washington Parke Custis and Nellie Custis—were raised by George and Martha Washington at Mount Vernon. There were children around Mount Vernon, in the family, but they were Martha's grandchildren, and George's stepgrandchildren.

DR: How would you describe George Washington's personality?

DB: He was quite reserved. He had a reputation for being taciturn, and quiet in company. He also clearly was the type who didn't suffer fools at all. I think he was a commanding presence from an early age. Now, with people who were intimate with him, close friends who'd been around him his whole life, it's clear that he was much more agreeable. But with strangers he was not one to talk constantly at a dinner party.

DR: Let's talk about the Revolutionary War. Was Washington very upset with the British imposition of taxes on the colonies after the French and Indian War?

DB: He was. George Washington had three major economic grievances toward the British system. One was the mercantilist system itself, which required Virginia planters to sell all their tobacco through British merchants. They couldn't sell it anywhere in the world; they couldn't try to get the highest bidder for it, and they had to go through English brokers. He always thought he was being cheated by that whole system. Then, when they imposed taxes, he felt like it was a double tax, because the system required him to sell his main product through the British and then taxed him to purchase the things he needed from the British. Finally, he had a strong interest in Western land investments. He had land that he believed he earned in the French and Indian War. It was part of the bounties that were offered to him to become an officer, yet the British Empire was denying access to this land. Washington's grievances against the taxes were part of a broader economic frustration with the constraints placed on him.

DR: Was he involved in politics at that time in Virginia?

DB: He was. He became a leader in the local community. He was a justice for the county court, which was essentially made up of the people who ran the county. He was in the House of Burgesses, which was the main assembly of the colony of Virginia. He was a vestryman in his church, which was in charge of all the poor in the county. Then, when the opposition to Parliament's taxes started, he was one of the leaders in that opposition. He and George Mason locally drafted something called the Fairfax Resolves, which argued that it was unconstitutional to tax the colonies, and helped create a nonimportation agreement. Because of that, he was very actively involved. In fact, he was ultimately selected to be one of the Virginians to go to the First Continental Congress.

DR: He was at the First Continental Congress in 1774.

DB: That's right. It met in the fall of 1774, a direct response to the destruction of the tea in Boston in December 1773. The British had passed the Intolerable Acts, closing the port of Boston. That led to the gathering of the first Congress in Philadelphia.

DR: Was he also a member of the Second Continental Congress?

DB: He was, and that's the Congress that appointed him as the first commander in chief for the American army. The First Continental Congress issued their protests and sent a petition. The Second Continental Congress actually came together after fighting had broken out at Lexington and Concord. They started to become a quasi-government. They took over that army and started to figure out how to support it. That was the beginning of the creation of the American system.

DR: Is it true that he wore his military uniform at the Second Continental Congress, more or less advertising his military background?

DB: He did, yes. It's an important story. He wore his uniform in part because he had already been named the commander in chief of Virginia's forces. That was really his expertise. Of all the men of the Continental Congress, very few had any military service. He was certainly in his uniform, and that would have reminded people if they didn't already know.

DR: Did he want to command the American troops in the Revolutionary War? Who proposed him for that position?

DB: He was proposed by John Adams. Adams was an interesting person to propose him, because the army was largely a New England army. These are the people who had surrounded General Gage in Boston. But Adams wanted to make sure that Virginia was a big part of this cause for independence. He thought, politically, they needed a Virginian, and Washington fit the bill there. Did Washington want to command the troops? I think he would have absolutely wanted some kind of commission, if there was going to be an army. Would he want to be commander in chief? That's hard to say. He claims he didn't. That was part of what you were supposed to say. He might have thought he didn't quite have the background yet to be the commander in chief. None of the forces he commanded in the French and Indian War were bigger than a brigade. Now, all of a sudden, he was in charge of a whole army and the navy and the operations and the strategic planning. It was a daunting effort, and any failure would be placed on him.

DR: Once he got the assignment of commanding all the American troops, what did he do? Where did he visit? What did he wear? Was he a great military tactician? What was his strength as a military leader?

DB: The first thing you do when you're created a general officer, you go shopping. He went to Philadelphia to get a tent and get all the stuff you need, because he didn't have any of it. The whole beginning of the army is one of creations. He's establishing the first way to organize the army, the first way to discipline the army. He doesn't have any maps when he gets to Boston, he doesn't have a quartermaster staff, he doesn't have a proper modern army. The first effort is really to get everything organized, to create some proper logistics to work with Congress.

When we think about Washington's successes and failures in command, we always have to remember that he is the one who built the whole culture of the American army from the beginning. What is remarkable is that they not only survive but win the war. His strength as a military leader was logistics and politics, and as a strategic leader as well, thinking in broad strokes about how to make sure the cause could survive. Tactically, he had some failures early on. Some people say he wasn't a great tactician. The reality is, in some cases, his failures had to do with the fact that the people he was commanding were completely untrained. In many of the early losses, he was dealing with an army that wasn't an army at all, fighting against the British army, one of the most experienced professional armies in the world.

But it's true there were times he failed on the battlefield. The Battle of Brandywine comes to mind. He didn't protect his flank, and that's a tactical failure. He did have some tactical brilliance. He crossed the Delaware, and beat the Hessians at Trenton. He beat the British at Princeton, which Frederick the Great, the great German general, said were the best 10 days in military history. Washington had his moments, but I think his real strength was logistics, strategy, and politics. Did he have troops that were well trained and equipped? No. The United States did not have any capacity to create clothing on any scale, let alone arms and armaments. Gunpowder was always scarce, so the troops, who were supposed to be supported by the states, oftentimes arrived with nothing—what Washington would describe as naked. Over time, the troops got better and better trained, and that's one of the great successes of Washington's Continental Army. It did, by the end, become an effective fighting force.

DR: What was the size and armament advantage of the British?

DB: The British army itself, at the beginning of the American Revolutionary War, was fairly modest, about 50,000 troops total. They would expand their establishment to 190,000 by the end of the war. This included a lot of what we call foreign fighters, the Hessians or the German mercenary troops. The British also had the largest navy in the world. It was the most successful and most professional navy in the world, with over 500 ships at a time, when the Americans had none. They had no navy at all.

The American army was never really more than 16,000 to 20,000 in the field at any time. Over the course of the war, over 250,000 Americans would serve in the Army, but never more than 40,000 at a time. George

Washington never commanded more than 16,000 healthy troops at one time. For instance, in the early battles at Long Island, when he was trying to defend New York City, he was outnumbered two-to-one by the British. That's a typical ratio throughout the war.

DR: How many battles did Washington win in the Revolutionary War? How many did he lose?

DB: He fought 17 battles. I think he won 6 and lost 7. There were four draws. Some people argue about the draws. You could claim the Battle of Monmouth was a victory. He lost more than he won, as people famously say, but in war you have to win the last battle, and that was critical. The other great thing about his losses was that they always kept the army intact. He never surrendered it. The Army would oftentimes have these sort of brilliant retreats. Of course, brilliant retreats don't win a war, but they allowed him to keep fighting until opportunity gave him the chance to make a decisive victory.

DR: Was it so bad at some points that he thought winning was impossible?

DB: He regularly invoked divine authority to help, because he thought it was impossible. It needed a miracle. In fact, he wrote a letter to his brother at the end of 1776, when he was being chased by the British across New Jersey and his army had dwindled from 20,000 to about 3,000 men, in which he said the game was pretty well up. He felt he needed to strike a blow like crossing the Delaware on Christmas night. Otherwise, they would definitely lose the war.

DR: He managed to win the battle at Yorktown. Was it brilliant tactics or the French navy that made the difference?

DB: The French navy made it possible for the combined American and French armies to win at Yorktown, because it kept the British from escaping from the York River and kept them from being reinforced by other British forces. The French navy was there because Washington was working with the French expeditionary force in America. The leader of that force, General Rochambeau, and others were communicating with Washington, trying to figure out how to have a decisive victory. The French navy was going to be in the Capes of the Chesapeake to help contain

Cornwallis. What was brilliant about Washington's role in that siege was his ability to get the Army there without the British even knowing that he had left New York for the first month of the campaign. That was critical, because getting from New York to the outskirts of Yorktown, Virginia, was much more difficult in the eighteenth century than today. It had to be done by land and sea, and you had to bring everything along by hand, by foot, by horseback. It was an incredible logistical success, and a great success of the allies working in concert.

DR: What happened after Yorktown? What did Washington do?

DB: The critical thing Washington did after Yorktown was he kept the Army together. The Army mutinied in Pennsylvania, it complained and almost mutinied in New York, and he was still the commander in chief, who constantly worked with Congress to try to make sure that the troops were mollified, that they were paid, that they were kept under control. After Yorktown the challenge was that it was clear the war was ending, and the Army wasn't getting paid. They insisted. How do you keep people calm and at peace in that situation? It was a challenge for him, but he successfully did it.

DR: What did Washington do during the two-year period it took to get a peace treaty? Was he just holding down the fort, in effect?

DB: Essentially holding down the fort. He was stationed largely at West Point, at Verplanck's Point on the Hudson River, on the north side of Manhattan. The British main army was in Manhattan. He was there, making sure they weren't making any moves to go anywhere else. In the meantime, he was making sure the Army was getting paid and that there was a plan for officers after the war. That came to a head in 1783, when there was a near rebellion of the officers, called the Newburgh conspiracy, which happened at Newburgh, New York. He was able to convince them not to march on Congress and demand their pay. He was able to demobilize that army successfully, one of his first great gifts to the United States after the victories.

DR: At Newburgh, he gave a famous talk to his troops. To their surprise, he took out his eyeglasses, which people hadn't seen him wear before. What did he say about that?

DB: That was a powerful moment. George Washington came into this meeting of officers unannounced—they didn't know he was coming—and he told them: you can't do this, you can't go to Congress, we have to wait, we have to be patient. Then, to finally try to convince them, he pulled a letter out of his pocket from one of the members of the Continental Congress, and he said: "Excuse me, I've not only gone gray but also blind in the service of the country" as he put on these spectacles, which is an incredible true story. He had not before been seen wearing spectacles. That dissipated any kind of resistance to Washington, and it was a great theatrical moment. He was a wonderful performer. He had been there through the whole war, and he had sacrificed as much as anyone, so I think that was powerful and moving.

DR: Let's talk about the postrevolutionary period. Why did Washington not take over the whole government, as military leaders overseas had frequently done when they won a war?

DB: Great revolutions often end with the army taking over because they haven't been paid. That's what Oliver Cromwell did when he kicked out Parliament and became a dictator, because he felt like there was still too much to be done and he was the only one to do it. George Washington had promised that he would give up his commission once the job was done. He was a member of the Continental Congress. He kept his word, despite believing that there was much to be done and that the country was in danger of breaking apart. He did it because he promised he would do it. Ultimately he did it, I think, because he believed that this experiment in self-governance needed to be civilian-led, have popular representation, and not be led by military figures, because the military would ultimately lead to dictatorship and destroy the very liberty they were fighting for.

DR: Where did he say farewell to his troops and resign his commission?

DB: He said farewell to his troops and officers at Fraunces Tavern in New York City, which is still there, one of the rare survivors of the eighteenth-century New York world. He resigned his commission at the State Capitol in Annapolis, which is also still there. You can see him in statue form in that wonderful old chamber at the Statehouse, nicely restored.

DR: What did he do next? How long had he been gone from Mount Vernon at that point?

DB: He resigned his commission and rode to Mount Vernon to return on Christmas Eve. He'd only been in Mount Vernon a handful of days in the eight years of the war, which is really remarkable. Usually eighteenth-century field generals, in the wintertime, go on long furloughs. They go somewhere much more comfortable. Washington had stayed with the troops. If he hadn't stayed with the army, it probably would have fallen apart, because it was oftentimes desperate to survive. He was finally back at Mount Vernon, and he began turning his attention to his great passion: agriculture. He had not only seen many estates and different ways of farming across North America, but he was also a deep reader of English literature on agricultural reform. He was a man of the Enlightenment. He believed that human beings can improve the world that they've inherited, that they can use the latest technologies and techniques to make and do things better. He thought that his major contribution was going to be helping this newly independent country to become the breadbasket of the world, to become an agricultural powerhouse. To do that he thought they needed to reform many practices.

DR: Why was it, at that time, that when the winter came, soldiers would just not fight? They would just stay in their camps. Didn't anybody attack them in the wintertime?

DB: Winter campaigns were notoriously challenging in the eighteenth century because you didn't have modern ways to move a lot of troops, or easy ways to feed them and carry resources. Resources were harder to come by. Horses died quickly. In the eighteenth century, traditionally, you didn't have winter campaigns. Armies essentially hunkered down and tried to get through to the spring. That's what's so remarkable about some of Washington's early winter campaigns, the Battle of Trenton and the Battle of Princeton, when it was almost impossible to move these armies around and be sure that they would still be there when you actually wanted to fight.

DR: At that time, did Washington have any interest in serving further in government?

DB: He did not. He thought his resignation was his big goodbye. His last "Circular to the Governors of all the States" was a political statement—"I won't be here, but here are the things we should focus on"—and a promise to the public that he would take no more role in any office.

DR: Who persuaded him to get involved with the Constitutional Convention?

DB: A lot of people did. One of the critical figures is James Madison, because he saw that Washington was interested in the future of the country, interested in the West. Washington had land out west. He wanted to figure out what to do with his land. He also knew that tens of thousands of people were moving west of the Appalachian Mountains. He visited, he went out there and saw that it was chaos. He was concerned that they were going to leave the country, and wondered, "How can we make sure that these Westerners are connected to the East?" He believed that the Potomac River, which is closely connected to the Ohio River Valley, could be improved and become a great commercial highway into the West. He created the first corporation in the United States, incorporated in multiple states, called the Potomac Navigation Company, which intended to improve the Potomac River and make it navigable.

To do that, they had to create a special agreement between Virginia and Maryland. It was done at Mount Vernon, and it's called the Mount Vernon Compact. It's still in existence today. It's a treaty between the two states about how to share the river. This was so successful, they said, "We should have another convention next year in Annapolis." That was a failure, but they said, "Let's meet again next year in Philadelphia." The Philadelphia Constitutional Convention came directly out of Washington's efforts to create the Potomac Navigation Company. Madison and Hamilton were of the opinion that if George Washington didn't go to Philadelphia, this constitutional convention wouldn't succeed. It wouldn't have the reputation to do what it needed to do.

DR: What was his role at the Constitutional Convention?

DB: Washington was ultimately made the president of the Convention, the formal chair. He sat as the chair for almost the entirety of the convention.

DR: Did he speak up much to let others know his views?

DB: He did not. He was very quiet at the Convention itself. He was active outside of chambers. He would often have dinner with different members. He met with the Virginia delegation often. He voted with the Virginia delegation when he wasn't in the chair. He was not trying to use his influence to shape debate, but it is highly likely, and I think provable in some cases, that he was orchestrating some of the great compromises behind the scenes. In fact, he often had dinner with people who would be the first speaker the next day, at a time when the delegates were starting to figure out some of the great compromises.

DR: Would the Constitution have been adopted without Washington's support?

DB: I don't think it would have. It was very controversial. We can just take the example of Virginia. James Monroe said that it was Washington's interest that carried the day. Virginia almost didn't ratify the Constitution, even with James Madison there at the ratification convention. Washington wasn't there in person, but everybody knew he supported the Constitution. In fact, when it circulated in newspapers around the country, it was always with a preamble, which was a letter that George Washington wrote introducing the Constitution and saying that he believed that it was a great opportunity, a great thing.

DR: What did Washington propose at the end of the convention? Did he not talk at the end?

DB: He did talk at the end. One of the things he advocated for was to increase the number of people represented by a member of the House of Representatives, to make it more democratic than it was. Then there were only 30,000 citizens that were represented by one congressperson. Today it's much more than that. In some ways it's less democratic in the House than it was.

DR: What did he do upon returning from the Constitution Convention to Mount Vernon? Did he get back into being a farmer?

DB: They were in the process of getting the Constitution ratified. Mount Vernon became a center of political intelligence for the Federalists' movement to ratify. Washington was regularly sending, for instance, copies of the *Federalist Papers* around the country to his political allies.

DR: Did he want to be the leader of the new government and just feign a lack of interest? Or did he really not want to be the leader?

DB: This is always hard to get at. I don't think he really wanted to. I do think he wanted the union to survive and ultimately came to believe that without him in the presidential chair, the union might fail, and that they had a better chance with him, for he had a strong reputation across the United States. For that reason he was the unanimous choice for the first president of the United States, because he had been commander in chief, because he won the war, because he was beloved and popular. That was the deciding factor for him.

DR: Who persuaded him in the end to be a candidate for president?

DB: A number of people. Henry Knox was a good friend from the war. Madison, Hamilton, John Jay, the great jurist from New York — they were all saying, "Without you, this thing won't work."

DR: What was the vote for him in the end? Was it close or not?

DB: The vote in the Electoral College was unanimous. In that first election, many of the electors were chosen by assemblies, not by direct ballot from the people, but there were a couple of cases in which it was a popular election that chose the electors. He won unanimously in both his first and second elections.

DR: Where did he move to lead the government?

DB: He had to move to New York. The first place the government met was in New York. As the Constitution called for, one of the first things they had to do was figure out what the permanent seat of the national government would be. That could have been New York, it could have been Philadelphia, it could have been somewhere else.

DR: Was he very popular in the country at that time, because he was the winning general of the war?

DB: He was extremely popular, beloved. When he was going to his inauguration as president, he was greeted by thousands of people, women and men, in parades. They would write poems and songs about him. He was the one indispensable national figure, maybe with the exception of Benjamin Franklin, who probably wasn't as well-known by the general citizenry as Washington was but was still similarly thought of as one of the fathers of the country.

DR: Who did Washington appoint to his cabinet, and how big was the cabinet in those days?

DB: The cabinet was small. The secretary of war was Henry Knox from Massachusetts, who was great. George Washington had made him the head of the artillery. Alexander Hamilton from New York was ultimately appointed the secretary of the Treasury. Washington had been trying to get Robert Morris to do it. Morris was the great financier of the American Revolution, but he didn't want to and recommended Hamilton. Thomas Jefferson, a Virginian, was made Washington's first secretary of state. Edmund Randolph was the first attorney general. He was also Virginian, a former governor of Virginia, and, in fact, had been one of Washington's personal attorneys in some cases there.

The cabinet was regionally diverse. You had New England, New York, the middle colonies, and the South represented. That was one of the critical things Washington was trying to assure, that the cabinet could represent the geographic diversity of interests in the Union itself. John Adams was vice president, but Washington considered him part of the legislature, not part of the cabinet, because Adams also served as the president pro tem of the Senate. So Washington often kept Adams away from cabinet discussions.

DR: What were Washington's major initiatives during his first term as president?

DB: The first term was about setting up the government and trying to make sure that it could run. He was also dealing with Native American problems in the West, and also figuring out how to make trade come back with the British. He had to appoint every officer of the country. There was no civil list, there was no civil test, and so he had to make over 4,000 appointments with people all over the United States. He had to appoint all the first Supreme Court justices, he had to get the government up and running. That meant creating the departments of the executive branch that would execute the laws passed in Congress. You had the first patent laws passed during that time, you had a number of lighthouses created. You had the Naturalization Acts to figure out how to naturalize people. You had the Native American policy. The first treaty of the United States was with the Creek Federation in the Southeast, which established peace with the Native Americans in that region for many years. The first U.S. census had to be managed. Then the taxes, of course. One of the critical things of Washington's administration was Alexander Hamilton's efforts to establish the credit of the United States. The United States had borrowed a lot of money from Europe and from a lot of Americans. It hadn't paid any of its bills on time. The full faith and credit of the United States was a nonexistent thing. Interest rates were extremely high, so to establish a proper national debt that could be funded and managed was the major administrative success, I think, of his administration.

DR: Did he enjoy being president? Did he consider quitting before the term was over?

DB: He did not enjoy it. He tried to quit after his first two years. He mentioned that going to his inauguration he felt like a prisoner going to the gallows, which is maybe a little hyperbolic, but it was, again, another challenging role. He had a lot to lose by taking it on. He tried to quit after two years. Thomas Jefferson, Alexander Hamilton, and many others, including his family friend Elizabeth Powel, convinced him the government was too unstable, he couldn't go anywhere. He wanted to leave after his first term, but at that point, the country started to get really polarized. This major war, the French Revolution, had exploded in the world, and navigating those waters became very treacherous. He was convinced that he was the only one to do it. He did resign after his second full term, even though he could have been elected for the rest of his life, probably unanimously.

DR: What did he accomplish in his second term?

DB: The second term was critical, because he kept the United States out of war. It seems easy to stay out of war, but in fact it was very popular to try to get involved in the French Revolution on the side of the French people. He didn't want to do that at all. In the second term, he expanded the U.S. Navy. The creation of the first six frigates of the United States Navy was done during that time. The Naturalization Act was critical. He established peace in the Ohio Valley by defeating a coalition of Native Americans who had been receiving support from the British. They had been at war with the United States for a long time.

One thing I didn't mention about his first term, which is important, is that he traveled to every state in the union. The next president to do that was James Monroe. It helped Washington understand what people thought of this new form of government. As he said, he walked on untrodden ground, and everything he was doing was establishing a precedent. He also understood that this was government based on popular opinion, and he needed to have a way to directly reach people.

During those visits, he also established the role of the presidency as an aspirational voice for what America is about. For instance, on his famous visit to the Touro Synagogue in Rhode Island, he assured the Jews of Newport that they not only would be tolerated, but they had freedom of conscience. They had the right to exercise their religion. Washington advocated over 18 times the principle of religious freedom throughout the country before the First Amendment to the Constitution was passed. As president, he was establishing not only the institutions of office but some of the aspirational values of what it means to be American.

DR: Why is his farewell address so well-known?

DB: The farewell address was circulated widely at the time. Throughout the nineteenth century, it was memorized by school kids and taught in various forms. The Senate still reads it every year on Presidents' Day. I don't know if they're paying attention when they read it, but it's a critical warning to the citizenry of the United States of the things they need to do to make sure that their great experiment in democracy will survive.

DR: Was it written by Alexander Hamilton?

DB: It was written largely by Hamilton with pieces from Madison that Washington had asked for when he tried to resign the first time. These are themes that Washington had been hammering on his whole life, including a call for a national university, something that Hamilton never supported. So Hamilton is the speechwriter, but Washington is the author.

DR: How much time did Washington put into designing and helping to build the new nation's capital?

DB: A lot. He was named by Congress the head of the commission that helped create the Federal District. That not only meant laying it out but hiring the architects and picking the plans. Washington laid the cornerstone of the Capitol Building in 1792 in a Masonic ritual, which included a big barbecue. He was associated with the planning and the creation of the capital. In typical congressional fashion, Congress didn't fund any of the buildings. Washington had to raise money privately to build the Capitol Building and the White House itself. We must be the only great nation in the world whose major public buildings were built through private efforts. To do that, Washington had to sell land, he had to borrow money. He had to get those buildings built, at least started and almost finished, when he was president. Otherwise, it was likely that the capital would never move to what became known as Washington, D.C.

DR: Washington retired after two terms, but he never actually served as president in Washington?

DB: That's right. He's the only president never to have served in Washington, D.C.

DR: What did he do upon returning to Mount Vernon?

DB: He once again jumped into his agricultural projects with enthusiasm. He was one of the most famous men in the world, so people were constantly coming to see him and get his advice. But even then he started new businesses. He started a distillery when he came back after the presidency. By the time he died, it was producing over 11,000 gallons of whiskey a year, one of the largest distilleries we can identify at the end of the eighteenth century. He was still very much engaged in business. He was also planning for his own future, and struggling to figure out how to deal with his estate. He'd been trying to figure out a way to free the people he held in slavery for years, which he began in earnest while president. In 1793, he wrote to some English agricultural reformers about his desire to try to figure out a way to emancipate the people he owned. It's clear that he tried to purchase the people who were enslaved here by the Custis family, whom he couldn't legally free. That's a really interesting part of his history, because his reputation was on the line as much as his feelings of humanity.

DR: But in the end, he did free the enslaved people on his property upon his death and was the only founding father to do so, is that correct?

DB: That's absolutely correct. He freed them in his will, and not only freed them, he provided for education for the ones who were too young to have professional work on their own. He established pensions for the ones who were too old. These pensions were paid out from his estate into the 1840s.

DR: How did Washington die?

DB: Washington died of an infection of the throat. His epiglottis eventually swelled up and kept him from being able to breathe, something like strep throat. It's not clear when or how he got it. It is clear that the day he felt ill, he had been out on his horse all morning, in the snow and sleet and rain, then came back to Mount Vernon to dine with some visitors in the afternoon, at three o'clock. He didn't change out of his wet clothes until after that, and that evening he had a sore throat. That was the beginning of the end.

DR: He used a technique that was common then, as I understand it, to let blood out of your veins. Theoretically, bad spirits go away.

DB: Medicine in the eighteenth century was still dependent on the Galenic system, tracing back to ancient Greece. There was an idea of humors that needed to be drained out, and so you bled people to do that. Washington was a great proponent of bleeding, asking to be bled before his physicians arrived. When his physicians arrived, they felt like he'd been bled enough. They did do other things like blister him. They gave him enemas. It sounds like an awful last 24 hours. He wasn't getting better. He asked to get dressed, get out of bed, then he got back into bed. It was a long death. His final words were "'Tis well." He asked Martha to bring up multiple wills from his study, and asked her to throw the ones he didn't want into the fire and make sure that the latest will—which is critical, because it's the will that freed all of his enslaved people — was the one that was recognized as the legal will.

DR: Where is Washington buried?

DB: He is entombed here at Mount Vernon, in a new tomb in a location that he asked for in his will. It is an interesting story, though, because Congress voted to have him entombed at the site of the new Capitol Building in Washington. John Adams wrote Martha and asked if Washington could be entombed there. Her only condition was that when she passed, she'd be able to be next to him. That was the plan. He was going to be moved to the Capitol. In fact, the Capitol vault was a tomb that was built for Washington and Martha, directly underneath the dome, which has that incredible mural of Washington floating up into heaven. He would have been buried in our Capitol. But the Capitol was burned by the British during the War of 1812. Congress later never got its act together. Ultimately, the executors of Washington's estate would build his tomb here at Mount Vernon in the 1820s and '30s, and he was entombed here then.

DR: Has his coffin ever been open since he was buried?

DB: Between when he was first laid to rest in 1799 in the old tomb here, and then moved to his new location, his coffin was opened. There's an oral history of a boy who claims that when he saw Washington, he looked as fresh as the day he was buried. Whether or not that was imagined or real, who knows, but it certainly hasn't been opened since. But I think one of the reasons that Mount Vernon exists today is because he's here. If the body had been moved to the Capitol, this place would have fallen apart. It's made of wood. It wouldn't have been preserved. It wouldn't be the pilgrimage site that it became because people visited Mount Vernon to pay their respects to the father of their country and his tomb. That's the reason this place became the birthplace of American preservation. The house itself was kind of an afterthought.

DR: What do you see as George Washington's greatest legacy?

DB: The great experiment, democracy, the country that we have today is his legacy. Our independence was won by him, with help. He was the first president of the United States. He was an indispensable leader for us, and those institutions that are still governed by the Constitution would not exist without his leadership. The institutions he created are still with us. That's a basic point. Another that bears talking about is that he gave us a model of republican leadership, that is to say nonmonarchical, noncorrupt leadership based in public service, with leaders who serve the public good and then go back into the citizenry. This is a model that we want our politicians to aspire to. When we complain about our presidents and say they're not acting presidential, in some ways we're thinking of the kind of president that Washington established in that office.

DR: Finally, what would you like to ask George Washington? If he were to come back at some point, what would you like to interview him and say?

DB: I have too many questions. As the head of Mount Vernon, I have all kinds of technical questions about how the house looks now, and what kind of wallpaper he had here and there. But aside from that, there are two things I'd want to know. One, who did he want to be the second president of the United States? If he could have chosen anybody, who would he have chosen? Because I don't think he wanted Adams per se. Nobody had anything against Adams. I think Washington originally wanted Jefferson, but that became untenable when Jefferson became too much of an enthusiast for the French. The question is, would Washington have wanted Hamilton? Did he love Hamilton, like Hamilton claimed he did? Or was Hamilton a useful, powerful figure who would have been a bad president? I don't know. So I want to know who would Washington have chosen as his next president.

A more modern question would be to understand his attitudes toward slavery and how they evolved over his lifetime. Why didn't he free his slaves earlier? Was it impossible, was it political? Did he not want to do it? We might need to give him a truth serum first to answer that question.

2

GORDON WOOD
on John Adams and
Thomas Jefferson

Thomas Jefferson (1743–1826; president from 1801 to 1809);
John Adams (1735–1826; president from 1797 to 1801)

If George Washington was the most prominent of the Founding Fathers responsible for the break from England and the successful fight against the British, clearly John Adams and Thomas Jefferson were second and third. But is that the right order?

John Adams, Washington's vice president and the second U.S. president, was one of the strongest advocates for cutting ties with England at the Second Continental Congress, which ultimately voted on a motion proposed by Richard Henry Lee to split from England. And it was Adams who wanted to have Thomas Jefferson, his junior by eight years, serve on the committee that drafted the explanation for this withdrawal, now known as the Declaration of Independence. Adams later asked Jefferson to draft that Declaration.

To the surprise and consternation of Adams for the rest of his life, the Declaration became the symbol of the break from England. While Jefferson initially thought that the Second Continental Congress had "mutilated" what he had written, he later basked in the glory of the Declaration's words. And indeed, on his tombstone, he wanted the authorship to be the first of his accomplishments to be listed.

Shortly after the war, cracks began to form in the relationship between these two towering figures of the Revolutionary era, but that did not prevent them from working together as representatives of the United

States immediately after the war was won, when the U.S. government, operating under the Articles of Confederation, asked Adams and Jefferson to negotiate various trade and diplomatic agreements while they were both living in Europe. But those initial cracks later resurfaced when Adams and Jefferson served in the government created under the Constitution.

Most visibly, they disagreed on the all-important issue of who should be president. Jefferson served as Adams's vice president, but then ran against Adams when Adams sought reelection, and—with the help of Alexander Hamilton—Jefferson beat Adams and effectively humiliated him. Adams had thought he was entitled to two terms, like Washington, and could not believe that his once good friend had run against him and defeated him.

That began a long period of estrangement between Adams and Jefferson. They barely had any contact for years. But ultimately, with the help of a mutual friend and fellow Revolutionary-era leader, Dr. Benjamin Rush, these two strong-willed leaders began a correspondence that brought the two historic figures together. And that lasted until they both died on July 4, 1826—fifty years to the day of the Declaration of Independence— an occurrence widely seen at the time as a sign from providence of the unique status of these two men.

The story of how Adams and Jefferson went from good friends to bitter enemies to good friends again was brought to life by Gordon Wood, one of the country's leading scholars of the Revolutionary era, in *Friends Divided*, his 2017 book about their complicated relationship. I had a chance to interview this extraordinary scholar at a Congressional Dialogues session at the Library of Congress on February 14, 2018.

*   *   *   *

DAVID M. RUBENSTEIN (DR): You're probably the country's most eminent scholar on the Revolution. What could the British have done to prevent the colonies from trying to withdraw from the Union?

GORDON WOOD (GW): If the British had offered in 1775 what they did as part of the Carlisle Peace Commission in 1778—which would have given the colonists everything they wanted, essentially a commonwealth status with no parliamentary authority over them—that would have undercut the radical position. Those seeking independence would have lost support. Eventually, America was growing so fast in population that there would have been some adjustment in the empire. America's population had twice the growth rate of Britain's. We would have surpassed them sometime in the early or mid-nineteenth century, and something would have had to have been done by then. But the actual break could have been postponed if the British had offered earlier what they ended up offering as part of the Carlisle Commission's proposed peace deal. It was a desperate act by Prime Minister North's government, which feared an American alliance with France. It was too late.

DR: If they had not withdrawn and there hadn't been a Revolutionary War, your view is that eventually we would have broken away?

GW: We were so much bigger. Some adjustment would have had to be made, because we couldn't be ruled by a small island.

DR: As schoolchildren in the United States, we were often taught that King George was a little crazy. Was he crazy or not?

GW: He suffered from a disease—porphyria, it was thought, though some are now suggesting that he was manic-depressive—but he didn't show any of the symptoms while he was running the war. He was a hard-liner. He was certainly a hawk, and he certainly was the last person to give up. Prime Minister North simply tried to retire, to resign many times. Finally, Yorktown did it and the government fell, and George had to accept the results.

DR: It is often said that George Washington was the indispensable man in the Revolutionary War. If Washington had not existed, would we have won the war? Was he indispensable?

GW: I think if he had died, say, at Brooklyn Heights in 1776, another general would have emerged—someone, maybe Nathanael Greene. But by the time we get to the end of the war, Washington had taken on such iconic status that he seemed almost indispensable. And as president, he was indispensable in the sense that the country could not have held together without his presence. We would have been torn apart sectionally and every other way. He really was indispensable by the time you get to 1789–90. But during the war, somebody else would have emerged. It was very difficult for the British to put down a rebellion 3,000 miles away. We know about that; we've tried it in Vietnam. It's very difficult to deal with situations so far away from your source of supply.

DR: Had we stayed with the Articles of Confederation and not gone to the Constitution, could the colonies have survived with that form of government?

GW: Jefferson's presidential administration acted as if it was under the Articles of Confederation, with only the addition of the power to levy tariffs. Jefferson didn't like the new Constitution. He thought that the Articles with the addition of a couple of amendments would be entirely satisfactory, and in effect he governed as if he were under the Articles. In the antebellum period, the federal government was very weak. Except for the delivery of the mail, people didn't really know that they were living under a federal government. Since all they had were customs duties as indirect taxes, they could scarcely feel the presence of the national government.

DR: Let's talk about Adams and Jefferson. They both died on July the 4th, 1826, exactly fifty years after the signing of the Declaration of Independence. They died within five hours of each other. What did people say about it?

GW: Most people thought it was providential, and they certainly thought it was too coincidental. It simply was beyond their imaginations. And of course there was a little maneuvering. They knew that they were dying, and they tried to stay alive to make it to the 4th, but they didn't know—they were 500 miles apart—that each of them was dying on the same day. It was treated by the country as a miracle of some sort, as you can well imagine. It still boggles the mind to think about it.

DR: Jefferson and Adams had a complicated relationship. As history was unfolding, when they both died, who was the greater figure, Adams or Jefferson?

GW: By the time they die, Jefferson is an international superstar. Adams is not. Adams was very jealous of Jefferson. Jefferson had emerged as the author of the Declaration of Independence, and was publicly credited as such, and by the 18-teens, he realized that that Declaration was important to the nation. Indeed, he told his son-in-law to save the desk on which he had written the Declaration. It would become a relic, he said. When he died, he listed on his tombstone "Author of the Declaration" as the first of his three great accomplishments.

Adams is appalled at that idea. Author? He was a draftsman of a committee report! How could he be the author? Poor John Adams never recovered from the acclaim given Jefferson for the writing of the Declaration. He felt that he had given this young Virginian kid the job because he had arrived at the Continental Congress and wasn't doing anything else in the Congress. Adams was on at least 24 committees and was chairing many of them, including the Board of War—that is, he was managing the war in 1776. It seemed an incidental matter, this drafting of the Declaration, and it contained nothing that was original, as Jefferson himself later admitted. Jefferson said that he simply put down on paper the enlightened conventional wisdom of the day, although he did it with unusual grace. So it's no wonder that Adams was jealous and upset by the praise Jefferson was getting.

DR: During the Second Continental Congress, when Congress voted to separate from England, on July the 2nd, Adams wrote to his wife. What did he say?

GW: He thought that July 2nd, the day the Congress voted independence, would be the important date and that would be the one celebrated by bonfires and fireworks and so on. Only later did he come to realize that he was mistaken and that the day the Congress accepted the Declaration would be the one the country would celebrate.

DR: When the Declaration was being put together, it was a committee of five people who were assigned to write it. Who were those people?

GW: Roger Sherman (Connecticut), Benjamin Franklin (Pennsylvania), John Adams (Massachusetts), Robert Livingston (New York), and Thomas Jefferson (Virginia). It was distributed sectionally. They wanted to involve each part of the continental United States.

DR: The most famous line in the Declaration, and perhaps the most famous sentence in the English language, is "We hold these truths to be self-evident," ending with "all men are created equal." Did Jefferson really believe all men, or people, were created equal? Did Adams believe that? What did Jefferson mean?

GW: Jefferson believed that all men were created equal, except for Black Africans. He voiced his suspicions about the inferiority of Blacks in the only book he ever wrote, his *Notes on Virginia*, published in the 1780s. But conventional liberal wisdom, enlightened wisdom, shared by most educated people said that all men, including Africans, were indeed created equal. Most enlightened men believed that everyone was born with the same blank slate on which the environment and experience operating through the senses carved out the different and unequal adult personalities and characters that made up the society. In other words, nurture, not nature, was what mattered. Even a slaveholding Virginian as aristocratic as William Byrd believed that all men, even men of different ethnicities and races, were born equal and that, as Byrd said, "the principal difference between one people and another proceeds only from the different opportunities for improvement."

Even climate was important in shaping people. Some thought that Africans' blackness came from their skin being scorched by the hot African sun and that their skin would eventually lighten in the more temperate climate of North America.

This emphasis on the environment operating on the blank slates of newborns and working to distinguish one person from another is something that I think we Americans deeply believe in. We put a lot of stress on education of the young, and despite all the modern talk of DNA and genes, we continue to believe that a proper education and the right upbringing can level out the differences between people. No one believed more devoutly in education than Jefferson.

Although Adams as a young man shared the enlightened belief that all were born equal, he came to believe that any talk of equality was hogwash. He ended up believing that we were born unequal and we remain unequal, and he put very little stock in education. He didn't repudiate education, but he said, it's not going to make much difference. He delighted in telling people that when he was in Paris he went to a foundling hospital and saw babies who were less than four days old. Some were smart. Some were stupid. Some were beautiful. Some were ugly. He believed in nature, not nurture. So they differed in that fundamental belief.

In that respect, and in others too, Adams took on the American myth that everyone was equal. The other myth he challenged was American exceptionalism. Jefferson created the idea of American exceptionalism. We are a special country, he said. We have a special role, to bring democracy to the rest of the world. Adams thought that Jefferson's view of American exceptionalism was crazy. We are just as sinful, just as corrupt, just as vicious as other nations, he said. There's no special providence for the United States. So Adams is odd in this respect. He challenges these myths by which many Americans currently live. It's understandable why Jefferson is celebrated and Adams is not.

DR: The Library of Congress has Jefferson's draft of the Declaration. But the copy that was used by the printer, with the corrections or additions resulting from the internal debate on the Declaration, does not exist any longer. Is that right?

GW: Right.

DR: If you go to the National Archives, you see the Declaration of Independence signed in August, not July. The delegates came back and signed it in August of 1776. Later it was fading so much that John Quincy Adams, as secretary of state, wanted everybody to see what the Declaration originally looked like. As a result, 200 perfect copies were made by a printing process that took a lot of the ink off the original. When the *New York Times* on the 4th of July runs a copy of the Declaration of Independence, what you're seeing is a copy of a so-called Stone copy, named for Willian Stone, the printer. Now there are maybe 40 to 50 Stone copies left. The original broadside printed after the text was agreed to by the delegates of the Second Continental Congress and given to people in July of 1776 is called a Dunlap copy. Dunlaps were printed on July the 5th and those broadsides were the document sent to George Washington to read to the troops, to each of the colonies, and to King George. (There are about 25 Dunlap copies extant.)

Back to Adams and Jefferson. Let's talk about their background briefly. Jefferson was from a wealthy family, Adams from not a wealthy family?

GW: Jefferson inherited slaves and land from his father but also many more slaves and land from his father-in-law, so he became one of the wealthiest members of the Virginia aristocracy. Adams was different. He came from a middling background, and the wealth that he acquired came almost entirely from his law practice. He was a very successful attorney, certainly the most successful attorney in Boston by 1770. He was the top lawyer in the colony of Massachusetts.

DR: Who was the better writer?

GW: It depends on what you want to read. Adams's diary is unbelievably rich and is well worth reading. There is nothing like it from Jefferson. But in their public documents, Adams is turgid and heavy and Jefferson is smooth and graceful. So Jefferson is by far the better stylist in public writings.

DR: Who was the better talker?

GW: Adams. Jefferson was not good at public speaking, and he did not speak in public very often. Adams did, and he was the leading advocate for independence in the Congress. That's why the two men bonded, because they were both radicals in favor of independence. Jefferson became ill and couldn't make the First Continental Congress, but he sent a document along that was published without his approval. This *Summary View of the Rights of British Americans* (1774) became the most radical pamphlet written by any American until Thomas Paine's *Common Sense* two years later. So when Jefferson showed up in the Second Continental Congress, Adams knew he had a fellow radical, and one who could write well. They bonded in their enthusiasm for breaking from the British.

DR: At that time, who was more famous?

GW: Adams was by far more famous.

DR: And Adams was roughly seven years older?

GW: Eight years older. He treated Jefferson as a kind of son, a protégé, and Jefferson played that role. That made the friendship work.

DR: The first time they ever met was during the Second Continental Congress. They had never met before.

GW: That's right.

DR: After the Declaration of Independence is issued and we go to war, what does each man do?

GW: Adams went abroad as a diplomatic commissioner in Paris to try to negotiate peace and also to raise money from the Dutch for the war effort. Jefferson went back to Virginia. He retired, and his Virginian colleagues don't understand what he's doing. He claimed that he had to study philosophy. It was more important than public service. But then his colleagues elected him governor to get him back into politics, and his governorship was something of a disaster. He was actually censured by the legislature of Virginia. It's an embarrassing moment, the most embarrassing moment in his career. So he's only reluctantly brought back into government while Adams is abroad. When Jefferson's wife dies, he's free to go abroad, himself, and he joined Adams in the early 1780s as a commissioner to arrange treaties of trade with the various European states.

DR: Jefferson's wife dies when Jefferson is 39 years old, and he then goes to Europe. Both he and Adams are in France with Benjamin Franklin. What are they all doing there?

GW: The treaty of peace has already been signed by the time Jefferson gets to Paris. The commissioners had been assigned by the Congress to negotiate treaties of commerce with various states in Europe. The Americans, especially Jefferson, have a very naïve notion of the willingness of European nations to open their borders to free trade and the free movement of people. Jefferson is an enlightened radical. He wants open borders. He wants to do away with monarchy, because monarchs were the source of war and republics were naturally pacific. Although Adams had written the model treaty which the commissioners were supposed to promote, he had become increasingly conservative and doubtful of their mission. "No facts are believed, but defensive military conquests," he said. "No arguments are attended to in Europe but force." He would be a hard-liner in the context of our politics now. By contrast, Jefferson was the ultraliberal, dreaming of revolutions overthrowing monarchs everywhere and people opening up their states to everyone.

DR: Under the Articles of Confederation, Adams becomes our ambassador to England?

GW: Not ambassador, but minister to Great Britain, the former mother country. We didn't have ambassadors until the 1880s. We sent only ministers abroad. We thought the rank of ambassador was too expensive. Having the lesser rank of minister was often embarrassing to our diplomats.

DR: Did King George receive him?

GW: He did receive him. Adams made a wonderful speech about how much he loved England and its constitution. But he told George III that he was now a patriotic American. The king responded warmly, telling Adams that he was impressed by his devotion to his country. Later, Jefferson joined Adams for a little vacation in England, and the two of them attended the king's court, where we're told King George turned his back on them.

DR: Jefferson and Adams at that time were close?

GW: Very close.

DR: Ultimately the Constitutional Convention is held. Jefferson and Adams are still overseas?

GW: They're abroad.

DR: So they have nothing to do with the Constitution.

GW: Except indirectly. Adams in 1776 had written his *Thoughts on Government* that had a profound effect on the state constitution-making in 1776–77. These state constitutions create separation of powers which barred members of the legislature from holding executive office, the prerequisite for parliamentary cabinet government. Adams believed in checks and balances. In some respects these revolutionary state constitutions are more important than the later federal Constitution, which was derived from them. Adams also wrote an earlier document, the Massachusetts Constitution of 1780, which created a strong senate and a governor who had a limited veto. Adams wanted an absolute veto, but the limited veto that could be overridden by two-thirds of the legislature is adopted by the Constitutional Convention in 1787. So Adams is very important in constitution-making. Although he was not physically present, he had an influence on the people in Philadelphia in '87.

DR: While Adams is liking the British constitution and many of the checks and balances there, Jefferson falls in love with France?

GW: Jefferson was a complete Francophile, and he was totally supportive of the French Revolution in all of its stages. As the minister to France, he committed all kinds of improprieties. With French radical aristocrats plotting changes in France's constitution, Jefferson as the American minister got involved. He invited the liberal French aristocrats to his quarters where they sit around and plot revolution. This activity is very inappropriate for a minister from another country, to say the least, and Jefferson has to apologize to the French foreign minister for his behavior. He became an enthusiast for the French Revolution, naïvely thinking it was over with the fall of the Bastille. But he came to accept the Terror of 1793 as a necessary stage in the Revolution.

Adams is doubtful of the French from the beginning. He predicted that the Revolution would be a disaster. The French, he thought, weren't up to democracy or republicanism. And of course Adams turns out to be more correct than Jefferson.

DR: Speaking of improprieties, at this point Jefferson has his youngest daughter sent to France. Who brought her over?

GW: Sally Hemings is supposed to be attending her. She's only about fourteen at this point, in charge of a nine-year-old. I accept the argument that Annette Gordon-Reed has made—a sophisticated argument, very persuasive—that Sally became Thomas Jefferson's concubine. Sally's brother James accompanied her with the aim of learning how to become a French chef in order to make French food for Mr. Jefferson at Monticello. But both siblings realize they could walk out and be free in France, where there was no basis for slavery. Under that threat, James Hemings agrees to go back with Jefferson to America and train another slave in French cooking if in return Jefferson would free him. The agreement worked out and Jefferson did indeed free James. According to the later account of one of Sally's children, Jefferson made the same type of deal with Sally. In return for her becoming Jefferson's concubine, her children would be freed when they reached maturity. Jefferson fulfilled that bargain too. It was not a love relationship. It seems to have been strictly a physical relationship to meet Jefferson's sexual needs, a tough relationship.

Jefferson certainly didn't treat Sally's children (his children) with any kindness or affection. When the children were born, he entered their births in his Farm Book as "child born of Sally Hemings." These births were listed along with the births of new heifers and new hogs. As the children later lamented, Jefferson paid no attention to his offspring. This was unusual, because many of the other planters who had mixed-race offspring often gave them gifts at Christmas and showed them some kind of attention and affection. Jefferson did none of that. For him the relationship seems to have simply been physical.

DR: The Constitution is ratified. George Washington is elected president of the United States. Who's elected vice president?

GW: Adams. He was the most famous Northerner. And since the electors could not vote for more than one person from a state, they couldn't vote for both Jefferson and Washington, so Adams is elected as vice president.

DR: Does he think he's deserving of that position?

GW: Oh, yes. He understood that Washington had a superior rank in the eyes of the public, but he thought he was second in status.

DR: What about Jefferson? What happens to him?

GW: Jefferson was appointed secretary of state by Washington even before he arrived back from France. He was surprised because he thought he was coming back to the States for just a short time and would return to France. Alexander Hamilton was appointed secretary of the Treasury, a more powerful office in Washington's administration. That's one other thing that Jefferson and Adams later had in common—their bitter hatred of Alexander Hamilton.

DR: When Adams is vice president, he's presiding over the Senate. Does he spend a lot of time doing that? Does he spend a lot of time in Washington?

GW: He took being president of the Senate very seriously. Unlike vice presidents today, who occasionally show up in the Senate to cast a tie-breaking vote, Adams not only voted in many cases where there were ties, but he participated fully in the debates. He was very eager to have a monocratic-type title given to the president, something like "His Benign Highness."

DR: What does Jefferson do that begins the end of his relationship, for a while, with Adams?

GW: He's sparring with Hamilton in Washington's cabinet at the very time he was emerging as the leader of an opposition group organized by Jefferson's close friend James Madison. It was a republican interest at first, and then it became a Republican Party contesting the administration of the Federalists. By 1792, Jefferson's position as the leader of the Republican opposition while sitting in Washington's cabinet became impossible, and he finally resigned and returned to Monticello.

DR: Before it became impossible, was he not hiring agents to write negative articles about George Washington?

GW: He hired the poet Philip Freneau to organize a newspaper in opposition to the Federalist-dominated newspaper. Jefferson plotted with Madison to oppose the Federalist government, which he sincerely believed was being run by Hamilton and his fellow monocrats that were trying to reverse the Revolution and take us back to something resembling the English monarchy. To him it's a very frightening prospect.

DR: So he resigns as secretary of state and he goes back to Monticello and starts writing letters. Then George Washington decides after two terms he's had enough, and an election is held. Who is the favorite candidate?

GW: Adams beat Jefferson in the presidential election of 1796, but he won by only three electoral votes, which he found horribly humiliating. Adams expected to get the kind of unanimity that Washington had gotten. Washington of course is the only president who has received all possible electoral votes. Adams saw himself as the heir to the throne, as it were, and he expected to come into the presidency with the same kind of strength and acclaim as Washington had. He's appalled that he only beat Jefferson by three votes. In those days, the person who came in second in electoral votes became vice president. So we had the curious situation of a president who was a Federalist and a vice president who was a Republican, the leader of the opposition party. Because parties weren't really acceptable yet, the Federalists never saw themselves as a party; they were just the administration. Jefferson, however, did see himself as leading a party, but it was just a temporary one that would go out of existence once the monocrats were eliminated. It was a very unusual situation.

DR: As vice president, does Jefferson preside over the Senate? Does he stay in Monticello? Does he talk to Adams much?

GW: He sometimes talked to Adams, but the relationship was very cool. Jefferson thought that his being vice president might be good for the country. People were tense and anxious about having the party division and yearned for harmony and stability. Parties suggested partiality and were not what people had expected. Many hoped that the two revolutionaries who had once been friends might somehow collaborate and bring the country together. Jefferson actually wanted to reconcile the parties, and he drafted a letter to Adams suggesting something along the lines of a collaboration. He showed the draft to Madison, who advised Jefferson not to send the letter. We don't know what's going to happen in the future, said Madison, and if the situation became more divisive, the letter could become embarrassing. So Jefferson never sent the letter, and the two former friends remain estranged through the whole period.

DR: Adams is getting ready to run for reelection. I presume that he thinks he's going to win?

GW: Yes; 1798–99 is one of the crucial moments in our history. We came as close to a civil war as we ever have, except for the actual Civil War in 1860. The Federalists thought the French were going to invade the United States, which helps explain the enactment of the Alien and Sedition Acts. The fear was real. The only other time we've been so fearful was in 1942, when we thought the Japanese were going to invade the United States. Many otherwise high-minded people, including Earl Warren, attorney general of California, and President Roosevelt, signed off on the internment of over 100,000 Japanese, the majority of whom were American citizens. In explaining the Alien and Sedition Acts we have to understand the real fear of the French invading. Napoleon was setting up puppet republics all over Europe, in the Netherlands, in northern Italy, in Switzerland, and why not the United States? Especially since the French believed that there were all those Republican Party quislings in America who presumably would welcome a French takeover. Fortunately, the British under Admiral Nelson beat Napoleon in the Battle of the Nile in October of 1798, destroying the French fleet. That eliminated the threat, and the whole idea of an invasion collapsed. The United States and France remained in a quasi-war, which Adams courageously sought to end by sending a delegate to negotiate a peace with France. A convention of peace was signed, but word of peace came after the election. Otherwise, I think he might have been reelected.

DR: When you ran for election or reelection in those days, did you campaign?

GW: Neither man left his home. Adams stayed in Quincy, Jefferson stayed at Monticello. They never spoke publicly. But they had followers who spoke for them. The followers expressed a scurrility that has never been matched, attacking each of these men in the press.

DR: Adams loses to Jefferson. They had been great friends, but strained now because one man had defeated another.

GW: Yes. Adams doesn't show up for the inauguration. He gets on a 4 a.m. stagecoach to Quincy. His son, John Quincy, did not attend the inauguration of his successor, Andrew Jackson.

DR: How long does it take to go by coach to Massachusetts?

GW: It would have taken a week at least, depending on how many hours a day they traveled.

DR: Jefferson is sworn in. Does he walk to the swearing in?

GW: Yes. He's a man of the people—sort of like what Jimmy Carter wanted to do. No chariot, no six horses. He walks to his inauguration. His speech to the Congress is written and not delivered in person. That remained the practice until Woodrow Wilson reestablished the oral delivery of the inaugural address.

DR: Jefferson is president of the United States. Adams is back in Massachusetts. Are they corresponding?

GW: No, not at all. They're bitter, both of them. Adams feels humiliated, because somehow it seemed natural that he should have served two terms the way Washington had.

DR: What about the relationship between Abigail Adams and Jefferson? They were friendly when they were in Europe. What happened to that relationship?

GW: Both Abigail and Jefferson thought the world of each other in the 1780s and they even flirted a bit in their letters. In 1804 Abigail broke the estrangement by writing a letter of condolence to Jefferson, whose daughter had died, the daughter whom Abigail had hosted in London in 1787. Jefferson responded eagerly to her letter, perhaps thinking that this might be an opening to a reconciliation. He was warm enough and recalled their friendship, but then he made the mistake of trying to explain why he and Abigail's husband were at odds. He said that there was only one thing that Adams as president did that bothered him—all those midnight judges that he appointed. After Adams had lost the election in November 1800—the new president didn't take office until March 1801, so from November to March we had a lame-duck president—in accordance with a new Federalist Judiciary Act he appointed a whole lot of judges, including Chief Justice John Marshall. Jefferson was appalled and angry at this, and he told Abigail so. She comes back harshly in defense of her husband. Jefferson tried to respond, to defend himself, and Abigail comes back even more harshly. And that was it. Jefferson said, "Uh oh," and just lets it go.

DR: Explain this to me. Adams appoints a lot of people right at the end—midnight appointments. I thought you said in your book that Jefferson got rid of those people. But they were judges. Weren't they appointed for life?

GW: Yes, the new federal appellate judges presumably had lifetime appointments.

DR: How did they lose them?

GW: The new Republican-dominated Congress came into power and in the Judiciary Act of 1802 did away with the Judiciary Act of 1801, and in the process eliminated the 16 new appellate judges. It could easily have been seen as a violation of the Constitution.

DR: Jefferson serves eight years as president. He goes back to Monticello. He has no relationship with Adams. They don't write anymore?

GW: That's right. No letters.

DR: There was a man who tried to bring them back in touch with each other. Who was that?

GW: Dr. Benjamin Rush, the most famous physician of the period, a resident of Philadelphia. He knew both of them. He knew both men but Adams better. He believed that these two Revolutionary leaders represented the two parts of the American Revolution, the North and the South, and that their reconciliation was important for posterity. He worked for two years to bring them together, telling each that the other one loved him. Finally he convinced Adams that Jefferson was open to a reconciliation, and Adams sent a letter to Jefferson along with what he calls a piece of Massachusetts manufacturing. It was actually two volumes of his son's lectures at Harvard. But Jefferson, a literal-minded guy, without much of a sense of humor, took Adams at his word, and in his response to Adams he launched into a long discussion of manufacturing in Virginia. Because the two volumes didn't accompany Adams's letter and came later, Jefferson was embarrassed when they arrived and apologized to Adams. Adams was delighted at the resumption of the friendship, and from that moment on the ice is broken and they begin exchanging letters.

DR: How many did they write between each other?

GW: A hundred and fifty-eight letters, with Adams writing at least twice as many as Jefferson. But that's understandable. Adams was embarrassed by his volubility and wondered whether Jefferson had many more correspondents than he. So he asked Jefferson, in 1820 or so, how many letters he had received during the previous year. Jefferson told him 1,267, most of which he answered. Adams was stunned. He had received only 123, a tenth

of Jefferson's total. Jefferson was an international superstar, corresponding with everyone from the czar of Russia to the great German naturalist
Alexander Humboldt. By comparison, Adams was small potatoes. He was
not in the same celebrity league with Jefferson. And he's still not, as we
know from the lack of a memorial to him in Washington.

DR: They didn't have a Xerox machine. How do we know what they wrote
in their letters?

GW: They saved everything.

DR: They wrote two copies of each letter?

GW: They copied most of them. Jefferson especially was scrupulous about
keeping copies of his papers. Adams kept copies too. He had people copy
for him. In his old age, he was going blind, and he would dictate the letters.

DR: When Adams would write to Jefferson, he would sometimes write
insulting things. Did Jefferson respond?

GW: Adams loved to razz his friends. By 1815, Napoleon was defeated and
the Bourbons were back on the throne of France. And Adams would say to
Jefferson something like, "Mr. Jefferson, what do you think of the French
Revolution now?" This kind of teasing, this kind of taunting, Adams loved
to do that. He was taking risks, because any normal person might have
cut him off. But Jefferson valued the relationship and just swallowed that
kind of teasing. He was very polite. It's one of the secrets of Jefferson's
success. He was utterly polite to everyone. Of course, when you're polite
to your enemies, that can seem two-faced, and Jefferson had a reputation
for being hypocritical and disingenuous. Adams never had that reputation.
He was very frank with people.

DR: When they both die on July the 4th, 1826, are both equally celebrated,
or does Jefferson get more attention?

GW: It's interesting to look at the eulogies. The ones from the South barely
mention Adams, sometimes ignoring his death entirely. Jefferson is the
Southern hero, keeping the dangerous federal government at bay. There's
no doubt that by 1826 Jefferson was by far the more famous of the two

men, largely because of the Declaration of Independence and his leadership of the Democratic-Republican Party. Still, he was not yet the Founder that he became. It's Abraham Lincoln who really establishes the modern reputation of the Founders. In the Antebellum period, when people talked about the Founders, they didn't mean Jefferson and Adams and Hamilton. They meant the seventeenth-century founders, John Smith, William Bradford, and William Penn. But Lincoln in a series of speeches in the 1850s gave honor to Mr. Jefferson, and used his phrase "All men are created equal" to mobilize the North for the struggle over slavery that lay ahead.

DR: But Jefferson was not against slavery. Is that correct?

GW: No. As a young man, Jefferson knew that slavery violated what America stood for, and he tried to abolish it in Virginia. He was way out ahead of his fellow planters. He pushed for a number of enlightened reforms in the Virginia legislature, including the abolition of slavery, but his colleagues accepted a few of his reforms but not the abolition of slavery. His fellow planters admired him because he knew so much, more than any other single person in North America, and I include Benjamin Franklin in that. But as he aged, Jefferson became much more defensive about the South and slavery. His letters from his later years reveal Jefferson as a Southern fire-eater in his attitudes, frightened by what was coming and envious of New England where his granddaughter had settled. He and Adams both knew that slavery was creating a sectional crisis that threatened to break up the Union.

So the sectional issue, especially after the Missouri Crisis of 1819–20, created some tension in their relationship. They don't talk about slavery much. Adams hated slavery and never owned a slave. But he realized that this was one issue that he dared not tease Jefferson about. He thought it was a Southern problem and that Jefferson and his fellow southerners would have to solve it. Adams avoided the issue, but Jefferson mentioned it briefly over the Missouri crisis. He was apprehensive about what it meant for the South. In his last years Jefferson, Pollyanna that he was, was far less happy than Adams. Adams the cynic and pessimist had never expected much of the future and thus was less surprised than Jefferson by what was happening.

DR: If you could have dinner with only one of these two men, who would you have dinner with?

GW: That's a tough one. Jefferson would have been a gracious and fascinating dinner companion because he knew everything, and he would regale you with his knowledge. Adams had a good sense of humor and with his sarcastic take on the world would have been very entertaining. As a New Englander, I guess I have to go with Adams.

DR: If you had the chance to ask a question each of Jefferson and Adams, what would you ask them?

GW: I'd ask Jefferson why he didn't take a stronger stand late in his life against slavery. And Adams? I'd ask him why he, who had done so much for the country, was so jealous of everyone else.

3

ANNETTE GORDON-REED
on Thomas Jefferson

(1743–1826; president from 1801 to 1809)

For most who serve as president, it is the highlight of their lives. For generals who led the country to victory in a major war, like Washington, Ulysses S. Grant, and Dwight D. Eisenhower, perhaps being president was the second most important professional accomplishment. For one president, however, it was not even in his top three achievements. That was made clear by Thomas Jefferson when he indicated that his epitaph should include three accomplishments, in this order: author of the Declaration of American Independence; author of the Virginia Statute for Religious Freedom; and father of the University of Virginia.

In Jefferson's mind, his presidency might not have ranked with the enduring value of those other three accomplishments, but it was not an insignificant eight-year period. He did consummate the Louisiana Purchase, which more than doubled the size of the United States (providing resources and opportunities that paved the way for the country to eventually encompass all the land leading to the Pacific Ocean, as well as all the land needed to help make the United States the economic and geopolitical power that it became). And Jefferson brought to the presidency an intellectual mind, recognized years later by President Kennedy when hosting a dinner for Nobel Prize winners: "I think this is the most extraordinary collection of talent, of human knowledge, that has ever been gathered together at the White House, with the possible exception of when Thomas Jefferson dined alone."

For most Americans, the Declaration of Independence ensures Jefferson's memory lives forever, as he correctly surmised in his epitaph.

Ironically, he probably spent no more than a few days writing his draft Declaration; and he was bitterly upset that the delegates to the Second Continental Congress made many changes (more than 60) to his draft ("mutilating" it, in his view).

But Jefferson ultimately took pride in the document, for it was the most complete statement about why the colonies made their historic decision to separate from England. In the Preamble, he wrote a sentence that did not receive much attention then but which has probably become one of the most famous sentences in the English language: "We hold these truths to be self-evident, that all men are created equal, that they are endowed by their Creator with certain unalienable Rights, that among these are Life, Liberty and the pursuit of Happiness. . . ." (He initially wrote "sacred and undeniable," and Benjamin Franklin, always the editor, substituted "self-evident.")

It can fairly be asked how Jefferson could write that all men are created equal when slavery was permitted in the U.S. and he owned more than 600 slaves during his lifetime (and had a slave with him in Philadelphia). And why did he not include women in his statement?

There are, of course, answers to these questions. In brief, Jefferson did not regard slaves or even freed Blacks as equals to whites, and women were not considered then to be equal to men in any undertaking. But that one sentence could be said to have become in time the creed of the U.S.: that all *people* are equal—that is, for men and women, all races, to have equal opportunities and equal legal treatment. While the U.S. has struggled from its start to live up to them, Jefferson's words are what the country, certainly in more recent times, is committed to achieving.

That Jefferson wrote this statement is paradoxical because of his commitment to slavery. While he recognized its immorality, he stopped early in his political career from trying to do much about it, as he believed it should be gradually abolished. Indeed, Jefferson had a large estate that he recognized was economically viable only because of slavery. He understood and precisely calculated the economic value to him of each slave. And he developed a sexual relationship with an enslaved person at Monticello, Sally Hemings.

This relationship was made public by one of his political enemies at the time, and Jefferson never publicly denied or admitted to it. (It has been interpreted that he later denied its existence in a private letter.) But it has widely been thought that he fathered six children with Sally

Hemings, whom he probably first met when she was 14 and bringing Jefferson's youngest daughter to France.

Many who had worshipped Thomas Jefferson were troubled that the great intellect and author of the Declaration of Independence could have had a relationship with an enslaved person. And for several centuries the relationship with Sally Hemings was not widely accepted by his admirers, or by those who worked to shape his public image.

But DNA evidence has changed all that. Historian, legal scholar, and Harvard professor Annette Gordon-Reed wrote the Pulitzer Prize–winning book *The Hemingses of Monticello*, in which she provided essentially incontrovertible evidence that Thomas Jefferson was indeed the father of six of Sally Hemings's children, four of whom lived to adulthood. Those four were freed by Jefferson through the terms of his will, consistent with a promise that he apparently made to Hemings upon the beginning of their relationship in France. He did not free her in his will, supposedly because she wanted to remain in Virginia. Under Virginia law in those days, a freed slave needed permission from the state legislature to remain in the state if freed, and Jefferson presumably did not want the legislature discussing her even after his death. (Jefferson's daughter effectively later freed Sally Hemings, who lived the remainder of her life in the Charlottesville area.)

We know little about Sally Hemings. She may have been illiterate, because enslaved people were generally not allowed to learn how to read and write. But we do know one fact that may have attracted Jefferson to her. Sally's father, John Wayles, had impregnated one of his slaves. Wayles was also the father of Thomas Jefferson's wife, Martha. And so it seems that the 44-year-old Jefferson saw a 14-year-old version of his wife (who died at 33) when he first saw Sally Hemings, who was herself apparently three-quarters white.

That Jefferson was a slave owner has attracted much criticism in recent years from those who think he should not be lionized by monuments and memorials. My own view is that, unlike certain Confederate generals, he is not being lionized for his active support of slavery. So I have thought that, in light of Jefferson's having written the Declaration of Independence, among many other accomplishments, that it is still appropriate to honor him. In my own case, I decided to do so in three ways. First, I provided the lead funding to refurbish Monticello, Jefferson's home, as long as the slave area, Mulberry Row, was rebuilt and that the visitors would be reminded about this aspect of his life. Second, I provided the lead funding to refurbish the Jefferson Memorial in Washington, provided that more information about Jefferson's life—the good and bad—would be made available to visitors. And third, I have bought and put on public display more than a dozen rare copies of the Declaration of Independence, including the one now at Monticello.

I interviewed Annette Gordon-Reed about her book at the New-York Historical Society on March 19, 2017. Jefferson's life was extraordinary in many ways, and while there are many interesting books on Jefferson, this one is so significant that it seemed important to include it and its author in this book.

* * * *

DAVID M. RUBENSTEIN (DR): You've written two books so far about Jefferson. One was the original book you wrote about him and Sally Hemings. The other one builds upon the first, *The Hemingses of Monticello*, which won the Pulitzer Prize. For people who may not be familiar with the background, who was Sally Hemings and when did Thomas Jefferson first meet her?

ANNETTE GORDON-REED (AGR): Sally Hemings was the daughter of Elizabeth Hemings, an enslaved woman who belonged to a man named John Wayles, who also happened to be Jefferson's father-in-law. When Jefferson married Martha Wayles, she brought with her to Monticello Elizabeth Hemings and the six children that Elizabeth Hemings had with John Wayles. One of them was Sally Hemings. So Jefferson would have met Sally Hemings when she was two or three.

DR: Thomas Jefferson's wife dies when he's 39. She has given him two children who survived. On her deathbed she said, "I want you to promise me you'll never marry again." And he says?

AGR: "Yes." He promised that. This is the story that's told by the members of the Hemings family. Martha Jefferson had difficulty with childbearing and she died as the result of complications from childbirth.

DR: So she died. Thomas Jefferson had already written the Declaration of Independence, and we'll get to that in a moment. He's 39. His wife dies.

He's very distraught. Ultimately he gets an assignment to go to France to more or less serve as our ambassador, and he brought one of his daughters over?

AGR: He went to Paris in 1784 with his eldest daughter, Martha, and he takes along with him a man named James Hemings, who was Sally Hemings's older brother. James is going to be taught to become a French chef. Jefferson liked French cooking, and he wanted a French chef for Monticello. He's left two younger daughters with his sister-in-law, in the company of Sally Hemings as sort of a companion. They are at his sister-in-law's home. Now, in this convoluted story, the sister-in-law is Sally's half sister.

So they're all there at Eppington, and one of the girls dies, and Jefferson at this point says, "I want my other daughter with me." He wants to have his daughter Polly brought over by, as he says, "a careful Negro woman, such as Isabel." Isabel Hern was about 28 years old at that point. But instead, Elizabeth—another Elizabeth, all these people have the same names—his sister-in-law, sends Sally Hemings over with the younger daughter. She's 14, and she's the minder for a 9-year-old. Abigail Adams is aghast. They go to London to the Adamses' house before they go to Paris and she's like, "What is this kid doing with this other kid?"

DR: Sally Hemings's father was also Jefferson's wife's father. So Sally Hemings was the half sister of his wife. When Sally Hemings came over to Paris, she was then 14 years old?

AGR: Yes.

DR: He never actually saw his wife at 14, but he could imagine that's what she might have looked like?

AGR: We don't know. Sally Hemings could have looked like her. A half sister sometimes does.

DR: Sally Hemings was three-quarters white.

AGR: Yes.

DR: Okay. So Sally Hemings ultimately connects with Thomas Jefferson.

AGR: That's a way to put it. What happens is that instead of going to get his daughter, Jefferson sends one of his servants, Adrien Petit, to London to pick up the girls, and Abigail Adams is furious.

DR: That he didn't show up.

AGR: "You made her come over here and now you're not even going to come to get her." So Abigail was not happy with him. In Virginia, they had actually tricked the daughter onto the boat. They had Sally Hemings go on the ship with her, and then they said to the young daughter, "Oh, we're just going to play a game." And then the daughter falls asleep, and when she wakes up, they're out to sea. So Abigail was not happy with him.

DR: So Sally Hemings shows up in Paris. Thomas Jefferson doesn't like living in Paris, or he loves living in Paris?

AGR: He loves living in Paris. He likes the music. He likes the architecture, the civilization. He was a little frightened of the women.

DR: Was he fairly flirtatious?

AGR: Fairly, but Ben Franklin was sort of a bon vivant. He was all out in Paris.

DR: Franklin was in a league by himself.

AGR: He was in a league by himself. Jefferson was more a homebody. He went to salons, but he went to English-speaking salons, and he really didn't like the women, whom he thought were a little forward. In Jefferson's view, they're prostitutes, almost, out in the streets seeking pleasure and talking politics.

DR: There's no slavery in France then, is that right?

AGR: There's slavery in the French colonies. There's not supposed to be slavery in Paris. There are no slaves in France, they said, but sometimes French colonials did bring their slaves to Paris. And when they did, very often people would petition for freedom, and every petition for freedom that was made in Paris during that time was granted. It was pretty much a pro forma thing.

DR: So at some point Thomas Jefferson decides to go back to Monticello in Virginia. He says to James Hemings, "You're free, more or less. You could be free. I can't force you back, but you should come back." And what does he say to Sally Hemings?

AGR: By this time she is going to have a baby, and Madison Hemings (another Jefferson-Hemings child who later gave an account of his life) said the baby is Jefferson's baby. She did not want to go back to the United States, because if she had a child in the United States, the child would be enslaved, because slavery followed the mother. Whatever your mother was, you were. And Jefferson promises her that if she comes back with him, she will have a good life at Monticello. Any children they had would be freed when they were 21. And she agreed to that.

I should say at the time nobody really wanted to go. Jefferson was the only person who wanted to come back to the United States. His daughters didn't want to come back. His secretary, William Short, did not want to come back. James Hemings didn't want to come back. They were having the time of their lives there. And Jefferson was like, "I'm losing control of all these people." He was the one who was keen on getting everybody home.

DR: You indicated that Madison Hemings said the deal was, "You come back, our children will be freed at the age of 21." Who was Madison Hemings, and when did he say this?

AGR: Madison Hemings was the third child of Sally Hemings and Thomas Jefferson. Beverly, male, was the oldest. Then there was Harriet. And then there's James. His name was James Madison Hemings. He was born in 1805. He gave an interview to a reporter in 1873, a Pike County, Ohio, Republican, in which he was talking about his life at Monticello and mentioned this in passing, but not as the main point of the recollections that he gives. It's annoying in a way, because you want them to say, "All the stuff about you is interesting, but we really want to know about your mother and father." But he's talking about his life in Ohio and life at Monticello.

DR: They go back to Monticello. Sally Hemings delivers six children?

AGR: Yes. Four survived.

DR: Of those children, most were conceived presumably when Thomas Jefferson was there at Monticello?

AGR: Yes.

DR: At the time the children were born, he was at Monticello?

AGR: Not for every one. I think only for two of the four who survived: Harriet and Eston. The other ones, Beverly and Madison, he was away at Washington.

DR: Was it common for slave owners to have affairs—if *affair* is the right word—with their slaves?

AGR: To have children with, yes, it was common. It was very common, and you can see that now in the DNA testing. You can see it in the family histories of African American people. But now it's been confirmed, using DNA, by population geneticists who go around and test people and find European Y male chromosomes in almost half of African American men.

DR: Thomas Jefferson, when he comes back, gets back into government matters. When he comes back from France he's made secretary of state under George Washington. Ultimately he quits, goes back to Virginia, then becomes vice president under John Adams. Then he's elected our third president. At the time he's running for president, does anybody mention Sally Hemings?

AGR: Yes, but not by name. The rumors about him began around 1798–99. They're blind items, if you know Page Six of the *New York Post*. "What senior statesman is known for his interest in yellow-skin women?" Those kinds of things started appearing, and poems and so forth that people were writing about it. But not her name. Nobody mentioned Sally until James Callender, after Jefferson is president.

DR: Who is James Callender?

AGR: James Callender was a Scottish émigré who came to the United States. I guess you could call him a journalist. Jefferson was interested in his talents and paid him, actually supported him as he was writing some pretty rough things about John Adams in the 1790s during a very, very contentious time.

DR: Because Jefferson and Adams might be competitors to be president?

AGR: Absolutely. And the Federalists were giving as good as they got. Callender had supported Jefferson in the 1790s. Then, under the Alien and Sedition Act, he was put in jail by Adams's people under the laws that he supported. Jefferson promised to pardon everybody who was put in jail for writing allegedly seditious things about the president. And once he got to the presidency, he did. He lets Callender out. Callender then wants to be paid back for all of the work that he had done.

DR: He wanted to be paid hundreds of dollars?

AGR: No. He wanted to be the postmaster of Richmond. He wanted a patronage job. It happens to people who are sort of attack dogs during a campaign and then come and want to be a secretary or something, and people say, "No, you're an attack dog. We don't make you the postmaster of Richmond. We want responsible people opening the mail." And Jefferson said, "No, I'm not going to give it to you."

That's when James Callender says, "I know all of these things about you that people have told me in Charlottesville and Richmond." He actually went to Charlottesville and Richmond and asked around among Jefferson's neighbors. And he wrote a story in 1802 called "The President, Again." "By this wench Sally he has five children," and so forth. That's when the news broke on not just the national scene but also the international scene. People wrote about it.

DR: If somebody's accused of having children with a slave, which was not considered to be socially appropriate for whites in those days, certainly not for the president of the United States, the accused presumably would respond. What did Jefferson say?

AGR: Nothing. He said nothing. First of all, Jefferson was not a fool. He was many things, but not that. Not to say that Alexander Hamilton was, but just a few years before, he had gotten into trouble because people assumed that he was stealing from the Treasury. He said, "I'm not stealing from the Treasury. All those payments that I'm giving, they're for some other reason." And he basically admitted in a pamphlet that he was being extorted by the husband of a woman with whom he was sleeping. He was carrying out an adulterous affair, thinking, "If I'm okay on the public side, this private stuff isn't anybody's business." It was the worst thing for him to have done.

So Jefferson, who was a very savvy politician, just shut up. His surrogates came out and said, "Oh, this didn't happen."

DR: Jefferson never admitted it, never denied it.

AGR: He did say things like, "All these things they're saying about me are untrue." And so what people say is, "Aha. That's a denial." Except it's really not, because they were saying lots of things about him. And some of them were true.

DR: When he was president, did Sally Hemings ever come to the White House?

AGR: We don't know. People went back and forth between Monticello and the White House, or the President's House as it was called, all the time.

DR: So when Jefferson is finished being president, he goes back to Monticello. He's got his oldest daughter, Martha, the only surviving child from his marriage, living there. And she has 11 children?

AGR: She had 12, but one died.

DR: So the scene at Monticello is there are 11 children of Martha's living there, his grandchildren. He's got his children from Sally Hemings living there. What was it like with all these kids?

AGR: Madison Hemings describes Jefferson as being kind, but he says, "He was not in the habit of showing us partiality or fatherly affection." He was affectionate with his grandchildren, meaning he bounced them on his knee and was playful. But he was not in the habit of doing that with children.

There are several letters where he writes to his overseer at Poplar Forest, his retreat, and he says, "I'm coming up with Johnny Hemings and his two assistants." Now all of the sons were apprenticed to John Hemings, who was the master carpenter. So he and Madison Hemings and Beverly and Eston would be at Poplar Forest for weeks at a time. It's not a sense of him not being around them. It's that he's not acting toward them like they are his legitimate white children, which he wouldn't have done.

DR: Why didn't Thomas Jefferson just say, "I'm in love with you. I'm with you for 38 years of my life. Why don't we get married?" Why couldn't they just get married? It was against the law?

AGR: It was against the law. They couldn't marry. You couldn't marry someone from a different race in Virginia until 1967 and *Loving v. Virginia*, the Supreme Court decision.

DR: Sally Hemings had a sister who lived with a man in Charlottesville. They were not married but living together openly. Why couldn't Thomas Jefferson be more open about it? Or why do you think he wasn't?

AGR: Well, she was living there with him. I don't know what else she could do besides what they were doing. The neighbors were saying, "They're living together, they cohabit." It was Mary Hemings who lived with Thomas Bell, a merchant and a friend of Jefferson's. And they corresponded, visited each other, and so forth. When he died, he actually left Mary Hemings the house and property, which you can't do for a slave, but you can do it if people in the community go along with it.

DR: So people often ask you, I'm sure, "How did Sally Hemings slip in to his bedroom?" You might describe how he set up his house so that nobody could actually go in to his bedroom unless they knew a certain code to the lock or they came in through a certain door.

AGR: Sally Hemings's job, Madison Hemings and other people said, was to take care of Jefferson's rooms. She was his chambermaid. She took care of his wardrobe and his room. So she was supposed to be there. There would be a reason to be coming in and out. But he had, in the early 1800s when he was president, built on to his bedroom—you can see it now if you go to Monticello—a sort of covered porch and steps. You could get in to Jefferson's room from the outside. There are multiple ways to get in from the outside or from the inside. He could leave without people inside knowing that he had gone.

It's an interesting setting up of his life. Very, very private. He had special locks on his door that could be locked remotely, and double blinds, and a sort of panel next to his bed. Extreme privacy. Margaret Bayard Smith, an author and historian of this period, said that nobody could get in to his room unless he let them in, because he was the person who had the key, and presumably Sally Hemings.

DR: His room was his bedroom. He had a little bathroom, and then he had his library.

AGR: The study. He conceived of this when he was in Paris. It's built for maximum comfort for himself, not so much for other people. People talk about the narrow staircases at Monticello, but those rooms were built just for visitors. He didn't know in the 1790s that his daughter was going to get married and that her husband was going to fail and that they would all have to move in to the house in 1809. That was not his thought. So it's very private. Bachelor quarters. He's pretty clearly not going to get married again.

DR: After Thomas Jefferson dies in 1826, historians begin to write about him. Do they mention Sally Hemings, or does that just go away, or do people assume that the father of her children was somebody else?

AGR: They mention it to suggest that it's not true. Then one historian, Henry Randall, who was the most famous early biographer of Jefferson, tells another Jefferson biographer that he had seen a letter and talked to one of Jefferson's grandchildren, who said, "The reason Sally Hemings's children look just like Jefferson is that they are the children of his nephew." One of the Carrs. Cousins look like one another. That's the story they tell, so historians believed that. Part of my first book was to ask, "Why do you believe this?" If you're looking at documents, in the course of telling this story, the grandchildren say multiple things that are not true. Typically that makes you distrust people. But it didn't with earlier Jeffersonian historians. All they were focusing on was that he said he didn't do it. An alternative story that was accepted in history then was that it was Jefferson's nephew who fathered the children, even though there's no connection with Sally Hemings.

DR: When you're writing your first book, you go through documentary evidence. You do a lot of research and you say, "This seems unlikely that the historical acceptance of Carr as the father is true. It's probably Thomas Jefferson." But then the DNA evidence becomes available and shows what?

AGR: It shows a connection between the Hemings descendant that they tested and the Jefferson descendants. The Carrs are a totally different group of people.

Another family, a Black family, the Woodsons, had claimed descent from Jefferson and Sally Hemings, which I denied in my first book. I had some very sharp conversations with a member of that family about it. But DNA analysis showed that there was in fact no connection between the two of them.

DR: The DNA evidence comes out, and I guess that's case closed. All the white descendants of Thomas Jefferson agree?

AGR: No, they didn't agree. And many of them still don't agree.

DR: Even today?

AGR: Even today, they say, "No, it must have been another Jefferson." First it was the Carrs. When they picked the Carrs, of course Jefferson's grandchildren couldn't know that there would one day be a time when you could differentiate between maternal relatives and paternal relatives. So they picked the most convenient people. And the people who had been writing to me saying, "It's the Carrs, it's the Carrs," the day after the DNA came out, they started saying, "Oh, it must be another Jefferson relative, because it just cannot be he who did this."

DR: There are people who write books that say it was Jefferson's brother, but based on other evidence that also seems unlikely.

AGR: The DNA evidence killed the Carr story, which is the story that the family had been telling. But it's the other stuff as well—the pattern of her conceptions, the names of the children. They're all named for Thomas Jefferson's friends and favorite relatives. There are diary entries from some of his friends about all of it.

DR: Does the Thomas Jefferson Foundation, which now owns Monticello, agree with your analysis?

AGR: Yes, they do. Now when you go to Monticello, in the film that they show it says, "Most historians believe that he was the father of all of her children." That's a part of the story. They are now going to be interpreting what they take to be her room for a particular time at Monticello. That is something they accept.

And I think most people in America, strangely enough, believed the original story (i.e., that it could not be the great man Thomas Jefferson) before my book and before the DNA evidence came out. I don't think the foundation had much of a problem with it. It was mainly historians with an exalted view of Jefferson who were really upset about it.

DR: Thomas Jefferson wrote the famous sentence "All men are created equal," and yet was a slave owner, and impregnated a slave and so forth. Is it because Thomas Jefferson was the author of the Declaration of Independence that his having children with an enslaved person gets so much attention?

AGR: I think so, because of what he symbolizes. He is a symbol of America. And if you say that a symbol of America had children with an African American woman, a person who, even though she's mainly white, would have been considered African American, then in a way it's like saying the country is not really white. And that's a lot for some people to take. The Founding Fathers are typically looked to as a way to justify excluding people. "Well, they weren't talking about you." These are our fathers, but if you have somebody who was an actual father of people who were nonwhite, that messes the story up.

DR: Thomas Jefferson died on July 4th, the same day as John Adams, on the 50th anniversary of the date of the Declaration. Did he honor his commitment to free the children of Sally Hemings?

AGR: Yes, he did. The two eldest, William Beverly and Harriet, he writes in the Farm Book that they ran away, but actually they left. He put Harriet on a stagecoach. Beverly left a few months before her. They go to Washington, and we don't really know what happened to them. That's something I would like to try to find out. Madison and Eston are freed in his will. Sally Hemings is not formally freed.

DR: Why?

AGR: He didn't say why, but if you think of what would have happened if he did free her, you might understand why he wouldn't do it. In 1806 a law was passed in Virginia saying that any enslaved person who was freed had to get permission from the legislature to remain in the state. So he would have had to write to the legislature — he did for the sons, but not for her — and he'd have to say, "Gentlemen of the legislature, would you allow Sally Hemings to stay in Virginia?" And, because she was over 45, he would have had to detail how he planned to take care of her. So then he would say, "And here's the money and the land that I'm going to provide for her." It would be a total admission that the affair had happened.

And I think he would have thought it would have been humiliating. Martha Randolph, his daughter, was the most important person in Jefferson's life. There's no question about it. And to humiliate her and her children by making these public statements when all he had to do was to say to Sally, "Go in to town and live the rest of your life," which is what happened. In the 1830 census Hemings is listed as a free white woman. In the 1833 census she's listed as a free colored woman. So there's law on the books and there's law in the way it works. And in that community, everybody knew who she was.

DR: Do we know much about her? Do we know what she looked like? Was she literate? Could she read and write?

AGR: We don't know if she was literate. We know her brothers Robert and James were literate. There's a long list of French cooking utensils that James wrote about in his own hand. Robert and Jefferson corresponded. All those letters are missing.

DR: Jefferson was fastidious about keeping track of all of his letters. He had a special machine, so he wrote a letter and there was another pen writing the same thing. We have copies of 14,000 or so of his letters?

AGR: About 19,000.

DR: Does he ever mention Sally Hemings?

AGR: Oh, yes.

DR: And what does he say about her?

AGR: Just mundane things, but not many things at all. Giving instructions about firewood to be taken to her place and other people's places as well. She comes back from France and she pretty much disappears from the family records.

DR: His children by her passed as white. They were seven-eighths white.

AGR: By Virginia law they were white. It was not the one-drop rule. If you were seven-eighths white, you were considered to be white. The two eldest, as I said, go off to live as white people. The two youngest stay in the Black community, until Eston, the absolute youngest, doesn't feel that his children can have many opportunities in Ohio. He was a violinist. He made his living as a musician. There are articles about him and his daughter who was a pianist and so forth. But there was only so far they could go. So he takes his family and moves to Madison, Wisconsin, changes his name from Eston Hemings to E. H. Eston Hemings Jefferson, and he goes by E. H. Jefferson. They become white. His sons become prominent in the Madison community.

DR: This is getting to the great paradox of America. We have a country where we started by saying that all men are created equal and everyone's supposed to be able to pursue happiness. Yet the people who enslaved some of these people were the Founding Fathers. So how could people as intelligent as Thomas Jefferson, brilliant in so many different areas, how could they have been slave owners? How do you square those two things?

AGR: I don't know that we have to. Jefferson knew slavery was wrong, but there are many things that we believe about our lives, intellectual ideas, that we can't live up to, for emotional reasons, let's say lack of character, lack of strength, or whatever. The people who freed slaves in the eighteenth century during Jefferson's time were under the influence of religion, mainly. And he was not, not in the way that the Quakers were, or Evangelicals, Methodists, and Baptists.

DR: Some people question whether he was really Christian.

AGR: I think he was a Christian. He was a Christian in his own way.

DR: Didn't he make his own Bible where he took out some of the miracles of Christ? He took out things that he didn't believe?

AGR: He did do that. He left what he thought were Jesus's pure teachings but not the things that people had put on to Jesus, that Jesus had never said he did.

DR: Jefferson's view was that whites and Blacks, if they were equal, could not live together in society. His early view was that slavery was wrong but that Blacks should leave the country?

AGR: The liberal position for Jefferson, John Marshall, James Madison, and people of that time was that there should be emancipation and expatriation. At first, Jefferson thought that Blacks should go out West, and then, once it was clear that the West was going to be for white people, that there should be some other place. He said whites would never give up their prejudices against Blacks, Blacks would never forgive whites for what they had done, and there would be a race war. We kind of laugh at that except we kind of have had one. Racial conflict. We congratulate ourselves. We have come very far but it hasn't been easy. It's not easy now.

DR: You've studied Jefferson for many years. Do you admire him more now that you have researched him as much as you have, or do you admire him less now that you know more about him?

AGR: I admire things about him. As I get older, I realize how hard it is to do anything in the world. It's tough to accomplish something. And he accomplished a lot. There was a lot that he didn't accomplish. And I feel much more humbled thinking, "What is it that I've done in comparison?" He helped start a country. The idea was that the next generation of people would carry things forward. But to say, "All right, you start a country, you're a vice president, you're a president, you found a university, how come you didn't end slavery?" is a bit much for me.

That's our passion, and it should be our passion to think about race and slavery and all those things. But his passion was "We have started a country," and he was always fearful that it wasn't going to work. I was about to say, "We know it worked."

DR: It has worked.

AGR: It has definitely worked. But he didn't know that it was going to work. It's clearer to me now how paranoid he was and how intent he was on making the experiment go. And all these other things he thought— "Okay, the slavery thing will take care of itself"—but how many times in life have I or other people thought, "If I could just get here, that other thing will take care of itself"?

DR: Suppose Thomas Jefferson were here and you had a chance to interview him. Would you say, "Is it true about Sally Hemings?" What would be the question you would ask him?

AGR: If he were here now, I would say, "What do you think about all this?" No, seriously, a question that he could answer on his own? I'd ask him if he was going to make white men send their slave children back to Africa. What would be the basis for it? Because when he's writing the will, and he's doing the petition to the legislature about letting the men that he is freeing stay in Virginia, he says, "This is where their family and their connections are."

And that's the answer to why every African American should stay in the United States. He knew that about the people in his life. "I'm not going to send Burwell Colbert and John Hemings back to Africa, because their mother's and their father's land is where they belong." He understood that in his day-to-day life.

DR: Let's talk about a few other facets of Jefferson's life not related to Sally Hemings and slavery. He wrote the Declaration of Independence at the age of 33. Did he put a lot of time in to it? Some people say he sort of plagiarized what other people had written. What do you think?

AGR: He put a lot of time into it, and he didn't commit plagiarism in the sense that we think of it today. He's very clear in saying, "These are not ideas that I thought up myself." What he was trying to do was to get the common sense of the people at that time, how they felt about things. Sure, there were influences. He didn't see himself as an oracle bringing forth something new. This was stating principles that he thought were universal and would be clear.

DR: He said the Continental Congress mutilated what he had written, and he was very upset about their changes, though he sat mute and didn't really object to what they were doing. But he didn't admit that he was the author for many years. Is that right?

AGR: His authorship wasn't really known until the 1790s, well after the Declaration was written in 1776. When we got parties, actual political parties, his authorship became a way of standing up to the idea that he was as good as George Washington, who was the head of the Federalist Party, that Jefferson was responsible for the Declaration. So it was useful at that time.

DR: On his tombstone, what does he choose to put as the first thing—Author of the Declaration of Independence?

AGR: That, and then the Virginia Statute for Religious Freedom, and the founding of the University of Virginia.

DR: Because of the *Hamilton* musical, we hear more about Jefferson than maybe we did before. Was he really an archenemy of Hamilton's? What was the basis for that?

AGR: At first, they were not enemies. But then he became an archenemy because he believed that Hamilton and the Federalist party were counter-revolutionaries. After you have a revolution, there's a counterrevolution. These people, including Hamilton, wanted a president to serve for life, a senate that served for life. Jefferson thought, after we've gotten rid of a king, why would we do that? And Hamilton talked about the British constitution as the greatest thing ever. So they became enemies.

DR: In the first cabinet, Thomas Jefferson served as secretary of state under George Washington. But then Jefferson was getting people to stay negative things about George Washington while he was secretary of state. Wasn't that not good to do?

AGR: Jefferson was a modern politician. He had a newspaper that was devoted to criticizing the administration. Right now he would be one of those unnamed sources in the *New York Times* that are trying to, they think, save the union in some way. People saw him as underhanded and deceptive, but he was really practicing tactics that we do quite openly today.

DR: Washington got mad at him and they stopped talking?

AGR: Washington got mad at him because Jefferson kept trying to convince him that Alexander Hamilton was the devil. And Washington didn't believe that. And he didn't like the bickering, because people didn't think, strangely enough, that you should have parties. They thought that there shouldn't be factions. In the "Federalist 10" essay, Madison talks about the problem with factions. People should get together and find out what the public interest was. Washington certainly didn't like partisan bickering.

DR: In hindsight, one of the greatest things Jefferson did when he was president, in my view at least, was the Louisiana Purchase. How could he justify that when he was a small-government person and there's no authority in the Constitution for buying half of the country?

AGR: He thought you might need a constitutional amendment. So he drafted one, then put it in a drawer and considered he really didn't need it. The first law is self-preservation, and he thought that expanding the country by taking the entire continent was the safest thing to do. If you had part of the landmass of the country under the control of other countries, there would always be an attempt to pull people back into European power politics. So he justified it by saying that this is something that will ultimately be for the safety of the United States.

DR: In terms of his intellect, you've had a chance to read his letters and so forth. Would you say, on the IQ scale, would he do 800 SATs? Was he a pretty smart person?

AGR: He was a pretty smart person. If he were alive today, he probably would be an engineer or an architect or something like that. He was mechanical.

DR: Pauline Maier, who was a distinguished historian at MIT, said that he was the most overrated person in American history.

AGR: I love Pauline but I think she's wrong.

DR: You would say he deserves his memorial in Washington, D.C.?

AGR: Absolutely. The grid of the country is a Jefferson grid. There are just too many things that he was involved in, whether you like him or not. History's not just about all the people you like. It's about people who have done things that are important and helped shape the country, and he did.

4

TED WIDMER
on Abraham Lincoln

Abraham Lincoln (1809–1865; president from 1861 to 1865)

Without George Washington, it is unlikely that the history of the United States would have occurred as it did. The Revolutionary War would likely have been lost, the Constitution (which saved the country from the unworkable Articles of Confederation) would never have been written or ratified, and the strength and dignity of the presidency might have never occurred. But for all of Washington's contributions to the country and to the office, it is still difficult to say that anyone other than Abraham Lincoln was the country's greatest president.

Lincoln kept the Union together when most other Northerners would likely have allowed the Confederacy to go its own way. He was determined to hold the country together, and in the process felt it was necessary to issue the Emancipation Proclamation, freeing some slaves during the war. Then, at the war's end, he helped ensure passage of the Thirteenth Amendment, permanently ending slavery in the United States. And he accomplished those goals with a humility and eloquence unmatched by any other president. His Gettysburg Address and Second Inaugural Address, both of which he wrote himself, are still among the gold standards of presidential speeches.

So it comes as no surprise that more books (over 16,000) have been written about Abraham Lincoln than any other American, each with a slightly different take or nuanced perspective on our sixteenth president. For instance, Doris Kearns Goodwin's well-known *Team of Rivals* emphasized the unique nature of Lincoln's cabinet, which was largely composed of his competitors for the presidency. (That book was the basis for Steven Spielberg's award-winning *Lincoln*.) Since *Team of Rivals*, one particular Lincoln book stood out to me as really providing new information.

In *Lincoln on the Verge: Thirteen Days to Washington*, historian Ted Widmer follows the circuitous, dangerous route Lincoln took from Springfield, Illinois, to Washington, D.C., for his first inauguration. The trip, by train, had to be careful not to go through Confederate territory, and to be on the lookout for possible assassins. During this journey, Lincoln stopped at 70 cities and made many speeches, including one at Independence Hall in Philadelphia. It was the first time that most Americans had a chance to see Lincoln in person, and they generally liked what they saw. Of course, he was elected because of his support in the North. He received no electoral votes in the Southern — later Confederate — states, and was not even on the ballot in many of them.

Upon arriving in Washington, Lincoln was not disguised as a woman, as has often been written, but he was wearing clothing that hid his identity, for there was a real fear that assassins were waiting for him. (The most serious assassination effort was to occur in Baltimore, but Lincoln's security team was alerted to it, and managed to use an unexpected train for the final leg of the trip.) From the train station, he was taken by his security team to the Willard Hotel, where he stayed during the remaining 10 days before his inauguration. It was felt that keeping Lincoln there was the most sensible way to protect him.

I am often asked who I would most like to interview, dead or alive, and I invariably say Lincoln. He had intellect, humility, wisdom, and a self-deprecating sense of humor. The significance of being president during the country's worst period would easily make for the most interesting of interviews. Yet no Lincoln interviews exist. In his day, the interview was not a format that really existed.

Lincoln was a truly unique individual, and the country is fortunate that he served as president when he did. Without him, the United States probably would have broken into two countries, making impossible so many of the creations and outcomes which have made the country the envy of so much of the world for so long.

I interviewed Ted Widmer at the New-York Historical Society on Feb. 5, 2021.

*   *   *   *

DAVID RUBENSTEIN (DR): So what prompted you to want to write a book about the 13 days that Abe Lincoln took to go from Springfield to Washington, D.C., in 1861?

TED WIDMER (TW): I've loved Lincoln since I was a little kid. I also was a bit of a train buff, so it seemed like a natural marriage of two topics I cared a lot about. Lincoln on a train—I thought it was an interesting way to see him moving across the landscape. The moving part was good because we always think of him as still, in a photograph or a statue. And I wanted the reader to get an experience of the landscape, of seeing what America looked like in 1861.

DR: It's said that there are more books written about Abraham Lincoln than any other American. I've read my fair share, but I honestly had never read or known about a book on just the trip to Washington. Have there been other books?

TW: Yes. In 1960 a guy named Victor Searcher wrote a book that's a little hard to find now, about this trip. It didn't have footnotes, which made it very hard for me to fact-check to make sure what he was saying was true. The journey has crept into other books about Lincoln. In a lot of them, it's a couple of paragraphs here and there, maybe more than that in some other books. But I think this is by far the longest book on just these 13 days.

DR: How many years of research and writing did it take you?

TW: When I finished it, I realized it had taken me nine years. I'm a little embarrassed. I realized that was twice the length of the Lincoln administration, just to cover 13 days. But I dropped down very deeply into the research, and I hope that shows.

DR: It does. You spent nine years with Abraham Lincoln. Did you emerge feeling better about him than you had before, not as good, or about the same as when you started the research?

TW: That's a really good question, and it produces a complicated answer, which is that he was like a close friend for nine years. I would wake up and go spend time with this friendly presence. Of course he's not living, but you get to know someone pretty well. He was a comforting presence, and I looked forward to being with him. I often worried about my objectivity as a historian, because I was admiring or worried about admiring him too much. But I really thought hard about it and I saw him under incredible duress, growing every day of this trip and surviving great adversity and then saving the country. So I felt okay. When I considered "Am I too pro Lincoln?" I felt good about where I landed.

DR: Abraham Lincoln is elected president in 1860. Does he have an overwhelming mandate in his election victory?

TW: No. He wins the Electoral College by a fair amount. He has 180. There are four candidates running. The next closest has 72. But because there were four candidates, his percentage of the overall vote is very small. It's under 40 percent, which is tiny. It's 39.8 percent, the second-smallest margin of victory or plurality any president has ever had. John Quincy Adams had less. But when you think about how famous Lincoln is, it's shocking to think he won with such a small percentage of the vote. So he wasn't that solid as he was thinking about forming his government.

DR: Did he win any Southern states?

TW: No, he didn't even come close. He got about 1 percent, and no votes in some states. He was not allowed on the ballot in many Southern states. But in Virginia, Maryland, and Kentucky he got like 1 or 2 percent. He got a few votes in the German American section of St. Louis, if you want to call that a Southern place. It was a striking election because all of his support came from the North and the Midwest.

DR: In my home state of Maryland, he got 4 percent of the vote or something like that.

TW: Maryland was always a headache for him, including the difficulty of crossing Maryland to get to Washington.

DR: So today we have elaborate situations for presidential transitions. Once somebody is elected president, that person gets staff. They go through elaborate efforts to figure out who their cabinet's going to be. They are surrounded by press all the time. Was that the case in 1860? Did

Lincoln have a big staff to help him with his transition? Who was advising him on appointments and things like that?

TW: His staff was basically two young men: John Nicolay, his first secretary, and John Hay, his second secretary. He was lucky they were incredibly talented. And we are lucky because they wrote beautifully about him and about their time with him. But he only really had those two young men, and they could barely keep up with the correspondence. I think they didn't keep up with it, and they had the overwhelming difficulty of forming the cabinet and figuring out, delicately, the things he had to say to try to keep the South in the country. That was hard. He was also very far away. Springfield, Illinois, was and is far away from Washington, D.C. And the Republican Party was so new, they had no federal strategy. It wasn't like a party that had been in power once and then came back. They were in power for the very first time.

DR: Had the American people ever seen him in person much outside of Illinois? What was the perception of him?

TW: With only a couple of exceptions, and they're not that impressive, no one had ever seen Lincoln. He was a one-term congressman, from 1847 to 1849, just two years. And he did not leave a deep or good impression after his one term in Congress. A few people remembered him from Washington, from Congress in the late 1840s. And he'd gone on a couple of isolated trips around the Midwest, to Cincinnati, Wisconsin, and Kansas, mostly speaking before modest crowds. He had one significant trip. He came to New York in February 1860, only a couple of months before he got the nomination, and gave a famous speech at the Cooper Union. But that's just one trip, one speech, one city. There are a few other little speeches. So most Americans had never seen Lincoln.

DR: In those days the elections were held in November but the inauguration was held when?

TW: March 4th back then.

DR: So you had from November to February, a long time. In the 1930s, the inauguration was moved to January. Once Lincoln's elected, what does he decide to do? Does he prepare? Why did he decide not to come to

Washington until right before the inauguration, and what does he do for all those months he's sitting around Springfield?

TW: He doesn't do a whole lot for a while. He wins on November 6th, and then a couple of weeks later he goes on a short trip to Chicago. And it's an important trip. He barely knows his running mate, Hannibal Hamlin. He remembers Hamlin from the late 1840s, but Hamlin does not remember him, which says a lot about Lincoln's stature. But Hamlin comes out to meet him and they see Chicago, and the press is around and reports on him. Then he goes back to Springfield and attends to his correspondence, walking to his office every day. It's understood that he's beginning to write his inaugural address, but it's very slow. He's also sitting for a sculpture, and people can just come around and walk right in to say hello to him.

A lot of curious people are coming to Springfield from Illinois or even other states. One time a Southerner comes in and walks away pleased to have met Lincoln. But it's a kind of dicey time where he's not saying much and the country is obviously falling apart. In South Carolina they're saying they're going to secede. And they do in late December, and he doesn't really have a strategy. He's not the president yet. President James Buchanan is falling apart personally, but Lincoln can't intervene. He's just a private citizen in Springfield, Illinois. So it's a scary time for the United States.

DR: South Carolina secedes first and other states follow. Jefferson Davis resigns from the Senate to become the president of the Confederacy. But why? Lincoln did not say he was going to eliminate slavery. He specifically said he was going keep slavery as long as it was only in the states that had been around at the time of the Constitution being signed. Why did people fear that he was going to get rid of slavery? Those in the South feared it.

TW: You're absolutely right. He goes to great lengths to say that he will not interfere with slavery where it already exists, which is actually a problem for Lincoln's reputation today. Because there are all kinds of different opinions in the world of history, and many people dislike Lincoln from the left. They feel like he wasn't abolitionist enough.

If he had been more abolitionist, there's no way he could have gotten the nomination. It just would not have happened. So he was just in the right spot. He'd said things that were antislavery but he'd also expressed a desire to work with the South, to keep them in the country, to protect their institutions, meaning slavery, where they already existed. Where he drew a line—and it was an important line—was the expansion of slavery into the West, where the slave states had over and over again promised they would not try to expand slavery. Then they kept sneaking back and trying to do that. And Lincoln said, "No, you can't do that." They were very worried about that, because they felt they were losing influence in Congress as the North grew much faster than the South. The North was getting more House members, more senators as new states came in. Eighteen sixty is a census year too, and it's counting overwhelming population growth in the North and not in the South. But there were things going on under the radar. I think the South was pretty excited to go its own way. There's evidence that they were having meetings to plan it even before the election. They were interested in acquiring Cuba and even more of Mexico than already had come in. They wanted to make a bigger version of the South that sort of spread around the Gulf of Mexico.

DR: Put it in context, because it may be hard for people to believe: the Thirteenth Amendment ultimately ended slavery. James Buchanan as president was proposing a Thirteenth Amendment which was reaffirming slavery.

TW: Absolutely right. It's shocking. There were two Thirteenth Amendments. I believe that the first one is still technically on the books, unratified. It's been in limbo ever since then. There was an amendment proposed that would have been the Thirteenth Amendment, and Lincoln approved it in his first inaugural address. He said that if it was approved, he would go along with it. Later, what is now the real Thirteenth Amendment comes along. It's the exact opposite. It abolishes slavery forever.

DR: So let's go through the trip. When does Lincoln leave Springfield to head to Washington?

TW: February 11th, 1861.

DR: And who organized the trip for him?

TW: I studied that question and there is no clear answer, but there is a strong suggestion that it was his former rival William Henry Seward, who's a senator from New York and a former governor. Most people thought he would be the Republican nominee a year earlier. He's friends with a political boss based in Albany named Thurlow Weed, and they had extensive railroad connections and friendships. They send out some railroad people to meet with Lincoln and begin to plan the trip.

DR: Now if I were going to take a train today from Chicago to Washington, it wouldn't take 13 days. Even if trains are quicker now, why did it take 13 days to go from Springfield to Washington then?

TW: He could not take the direct route. It was a little bit embarrassing to him that he couldn't go through the state of his birth, Kentucky. That would have been the most direct route, to go through Kentucky and Virginia right into Washington. He wrote a letter to a close friend in Kentucky and said that if he went into the state of his birth, he was in danger of being lynched. So that's how dangerous it was. But then, when he understood that he had to go the long way around, he turned it into a virtue. He met with a lot of Northern governors and legislatures. He went to every capital city. It was a kind of democracy tour from one state capitol to the next. They were all these little Greek Revival capitols. And Lincoln is going from one to the next. He's based in Springfield, which is a capital. He goes to Indianapolis, makes it eventually to Columbus and then Albany. Trenton in New Jersey. Harrisburg is an important stop. Stopping at the state capitols was a good agenda for him. He picked up political strength from meeting with the governors. He also could express himself to the people of each state.

Governors and state capitals were very important in 1860. If a war was going to come, it would be the governors who would call up the troops, not a president, or that's what they thought in 1861.

DR: When did Lincoln realize that people wanted to kill him? Was it right after the election? You mentioned the possible lynching if he'd gone to Kentucky. But Kentucky wasn't the only state where people were saying, "We've got to kill this person." When did he begin to realize it, and was he afraid of this?

TW: He's getting hate mail. You can see some of the letters that were coming into Lincoln, thanks to the Library of Congress, which has digitized all of them. There were drawings sent of him with a noose around his neck, and very ugly letters with swear words. Other people who were working with him said he threw out a lot of the hate mail, so probably even more was coming in than we have.

There's no evidence that he was upset by it. There's a little bit of evidence that Mary Todd Lincoln, his wife, was upset by it. He did bring four military officers on the train with him. They had been writing to him, warning him of certain dangers along the route. So that shows that he was paying attention.

DR: On the day that he begins the trip, he makes a farewell speech in Springfield. What does he say there?

TW: It's a beautiful speech. It's very short, but extremely important. Only about nine sentences, it probably took about two minutes to say. Crowd estimates have varied over the years, but I would guess about 200 people were standing there, and there was a light drizzle. Some people said snow. It's like the movie *Rashomon*. Every person there remembered it a little differently. Lincoln spoke with great poignancy about what it meant to him to be from this place that he was leaving, and how he'd lived there for 25 years and raised his children there and buried one child there. He continued that with God's help, a task was before him that was greater than any president had faced since George Washington. He said that with God's help he could not fail, without God's help he could not succeed. And then he asked for their prayers and got on the train.

What is so significant is it was a personal expression from one citizen to his fellow citizens. It was all about small-town democracy. And that is how Americans experienced democracy in 1861. It was instantly transcribed by reporters and then telegraphed, in a way not so different from how a speech goes around very fast today. People around the country got a feeling for Lincoln that they'd never had, that this is a guy we can understand. He's like a neighbor. I think he helped himself a lot with that speech.

DR: Who went with him on the trip from his family? Did all of his sons and his wife go?

TW: They did, but they met him the second day. They were not on the first leg of the trip from Springfield to Indianapolis.

DR: Each leg of the trip he gets a different train car, is that right? There are different cars available for him, and they're outfitted as appropriate for a future president of the United States. They're reasonably nice.

TW: Very nice, usually.

DR: Was he a person attentive to his clothing? Did he make certain that he was neat every day and looked fastidious as the next president of the United States?

TW: He was the absolute opposite of that. He was famous for paying no attention to his clothing at all. His tie was often coming undone. Some people had raised collars. His was usually flatter. Everything about it was relaxed. It wasn't just how tall he was and how skinny. He had very long arms but his legs were not that long for his height. So, he often had clothes that didn't fit him properly.

He'd wear a hat that was starting to cave in from overuse and he wouldn't even notice it. He barely acknowledged how he looked. So other people were always trying to help him. There were moments along the trip where either his wife or one of the younger people around would subtly bring out a new hat and ask him to wear it, and he would look a lot better.

DR: Everywhere he goes, he travels during the day, gets off at night, stays in a hotel, makes a speech, a different speech each time. He goes from Springfield to where?

TW: Indianapolis, Cincinnati and Columbus, Pittsburgh, Cleveland.

DR: And then?

TW: Buffalo, Albany, New York City, Trenton, Philadelphia, Harrisburg, and then a complicated, all-night secret train route back through Philadelphia, then Baltimore to Washington.

DR: You point out in your book that a lot of famous people met him. Former presidents of the United States like Millard Fillmore, future presidents of the United States like Grover Cleveland. How did you find out these famous people were there during these various visits? Can you talk about one young woman he met, who had suggested to him in a letter that he grow a beard?

TW: Yes, that's the lovely Grace Bedell, who I think was 14 at the time. She lived near Buffalo in Westfield, New York. She wrote an adorable letter to Lincoln saying she had a lot of older brothers and she thought she could get them all to vote for him—she's like a ward boss—if he would work with her and upgrade his appearance a little bit. She wrote, "If you grow a beard, I think you won't look so skinny," and sent the letter. Lincoln obviously liked the letter. He wrote her back. He didn't write back to that many people, but he wrote her. He said, "Don't you think people would think it was a bit of affectation?" if he were to change his look. So it sounded like he was saying no. But then he went ahead and grew the beard. That's a great scene when he gets to Westfield, New York. The train stops and he meets her, and it changed her life. She never stopped talking about it.

DR: Before he gets to New York City, of all the stops, where was the biggest crowd?

TW: They're a lot in a row. In Cincinnati it's huge. In Buffalo it's absolutely huge. And then in New York City itself, it's about 100,000 people in the streets. You have to trust the reporters. They do exaggerate, so it's hard to be exact. But people were often saying that about 100,000 people came out to see Lincoln, which is a mind-boggling crowd. We don't see crowds anywhere near that large today.

DR: The train would stop. He'd get off, a carriage would meet him, he'd make a speech and the crowd would envelop him. He would have a hard time getting through the crowd, but eventually he'd go to the hotel. He stayed at a hotel each night.

TW: That's right.

DR: In those days, in the 1860s, if you stayed at good hotels, did they have showers? Did they have bathrooms with indoor plumbing?

TW: That is the kind of question I was often trying to solve, and it's hard to find in a Lincoln biography. You have to do a lot of sleuthing to find out. Most of them did not. It's possible there was hot water he could use in some way, that someone would carry up some hot water that was heated over a fire for him, maybe. The one exception was the fanciest hotel in America, a hotel called the Astor House in New York City on lower

Broadway. They had indoor plumbing, which was a revolution. No one could believe it. When he got there, there was real plumbing.

DR: He gets to New York City, which at that time is the biggest city in the United States?

TW: Yes. It's got a little over 800,000 people, which is way bigger than any other city.

DR: Why did so many people want to greet him, just to see him?

TW: There was almost no way to visualize Lincoln. You might see a campaign pin. You could mail a letter in an envelope that was printed with an image of Lincoln. They were trying to get his image around, but it was hard. And daily newspapers had no visuals. There were weekly newspapers, kind of like *Time* magazine, that could do primitive images. The weekly newspapers, which mostly came out of New York City, were important in getting people a sense of what he looked like. They went out by train all around the country. But for an overwhelming number of people, it was the first time they'd ever seen him. And everybody knew the country was going to change forever because of this guy. They didn't quite know what was going to happen, but they knew a big change was coming.

DR: He had reporters covering him on the train, traveling with him. What was the general impression in the articles they wrote? That he was a distinguished person, a little unusual-looking but a great speaker? How many speeches did he give before he got to New York?

TW: That's one of the most fascinating aspects of the trip for me. The trip was hard and there was a constant demand on him to speak. Every time the train pulled into a little village—there are a lot of little villages in America—he would go out and speak, and those speeches were unscripted. He generally wrote out a scripted speech, one per day, which was the formal big event, like going to Ohio and speaking to the governor and legislature.

And he would write out some formal, a little bit boring speech for a situation like that. What was not boring at all were these informal human encounters where he's just going to the platform on the back of the train and saying hello to people. He was funny. Sometimes he was a little bit emotional. Everyone who knew him said he varied a lot, from a kind of lower register where he seemed depressed to an upper register where he seemed buoyant. You didn't know which Lincoln you were going to get. It's dynamic and unpredictable.

DR: How old is he at this time?

TW: He turned 52 on the second day of the trip.

DR: After New York, he goes to the heart of American history—Philadelphia, a place that is almost religious to him, because that's where the Declaration of Independence and the Constitution were drafted. He goes to Independence Hall, where they were actually drafted. Can you talk about the speeches that he gave there and why they were so emotional? They may have been the most uplifting speeches he gave during the entire trip.

TW: It's funny you use the word *religious*. I really agree with that. He felt that this was where America's secular scripture came from, almost like the Ten Commandments, but it's the Declaration and the Constitution. All came out of this building, which was sacred to Americans then. It still is. But now, in a way, Washington is—we hear this phrase a lot—the soul of America, around the Lincoln Memorial. But back then, it was more Independence Hall. He'd grown up loving American history. He read the famous childhood books, just like I read childhood books about Lincoln. He was reading about George Washington, reading Mason Weems's biography of Washington, which is filled with stories we don't believe, like cutting down the cherry tree. Lincoln read those books and loved them.

As he was coming out of New York and going into New Jersey, he remembers the struggles of George Washington in New Jersey—the crossing of the Delaware to take Trenton from the Hessians, and just how hard it was. In the New Jersey State House he gives a beautiful speech about what the American Revolution meant to him and how they must have been fighting for some bigger cause than just their independence, something that would mean a lot to all people everywhere, someday.

He gets to Philadelphia and he goes into Independence Hall. And he can feel the emanations coming out of Independence Hall. He's talking about its teachings, almost like the building is alive and talking to him. It's unusual and sort of spiritual. He says, "If I ever forget its teachings," meaning the Declaration, "may my tongue cleave to the roof of my mouth and may my right hand forget its cunning," which is right out of the Old Testament.

He goes in the next morning and he's overwhelmed. It's his first time ever in Independence Hall. He'd been to Philadelphia but not in the building. And he gets very emotional again. He says, "Every political sentiment I have ever had comes from the Declaration of Independence."

He adds, "I would rather be assassinated than ever forget what I know to be the truth of this document." He's just been told there's a good chance he will be assassinated. So a moment freighted with emotion. But it's also very sophisticated politics. I'm sure it's sincere and it's coming out of his memory of his life and childhood. But it's also really good politics, because he's reminding Americans that the Declaration of Independence is an antislavery document. It promises these human rights, these freedoms—"Life, Liberty and the pursuit of Happiness"—to every person, and that means African Americans. So he's using a beautiful and familiar document to promote the cause of antislavery.

At the same time, Jefferson Davis is trying to start his government. He has a stronger claim to the memory of the American Revolution. His family and his wife's family fought in a more distinguished way, but he doesn't say anything. So Lincoln gets an advantage.

DR: From Philadelphia, he goes to Harrisburg to meet with the governor. After, he gets on a very small train, smaller than normal, and it's kept secret. Why?

TW: So all along, there's another drama. My first drama is the difficulty of a guy on a train where everyone in America is trying to get at him. He's trying to speak in a compelling way and succeeding. That's the second big drama. And then there's a third drama, which is they're beginning to figure out a lot of people are trying to kill him when he comes through Baltimore.

There have been spies on the ground, very effectively going around the bars and restaurants, picking up intelligence and conveying it to Lincoln's entourage that this is a serious threat. The news of the threat, by the way, came to them from a woman, Dorothea Dix, a mental health advocate traveling through the South, who heard verifiable stories about an assassination conspiracy.

He's trying to ignore it. He doesn't want to have to change his route.

But finally he's persuaded. They put him on an all-night commuter train with ordinary passengers, in a passenger compartment, leaving Philadelphia late at night, going through Baltimore, with a change. They would change the locomotive and move the passenger cars by horse. The horse would pull the car along the streetcar tracks of downtown Baltimore, from one train station to another, and they would hitch that car to the southbound train that would go to Washington. They'd do all that about 11:00 at night in Philadelphia. They come into Baltimore about 3:30 in the morning, leave about 4:00, and get into D.C. at about 6:00 in the morning. And he made it. No one knew he was on the train.

DR: There have been reports over the years that he snuck into Washington dressed as a woman. Where did those reports come from?

TW: That's an interesting story about how the press was a little unreliable in his time. Lincoln's got all kinds of headaches to deal with. The whole time he's on this trip, the South is attacking him every moment they can, criticizing his speeches and saying, "He's uncouth, he's physically repellent. He's the least qualified person who's ever been elected." He has hardly any education and very little political experience, so let's just give them credit for that one. It's probably true. But then, after all his speeches, they say, "You cannot read his speeches without howling with laughter, because they're so bad." Which is the opposite of how we think of Lincoln today. And he's got problems with the Northern press too, though he's got some papers behind him. There's a Republican media network, not really organized, it's just city by city. But there are Republican papers in most of the Northern cities. There are also Stephen Douglas papers, Northern Democrats who don't like him very much and are kind of mad that he got elected.

The night he takes the secret train, they shut down Harrisburg. They actually cut the wires so no one could send a telegram out of Harrisburg, and they locked all of the reporters into the hotel they were staying in and waited a few hours until Lincoln was safely far enough away that they couldn't spoil the secret. Then they told them. A reporter for the *New York Times*, which was one of Lincoln's relatively sympathetic papers, was so mad that as a result he concocted a totally fake story that ran.

Then as now, the *New York Times* considered itself a very reliable newspaper. But the story was filled with false information that said Lincoln had dressed up in Scottish clothes, whatever those are. That was enough for editorial cartoonists in weekly and monthly newspapers and magazines to draw Lincoln in a kilt or a tam. They didn't really know what Scottish clothes looked like, often making them look sort of Irish. Either way Lincoln looked ridiculous, and it was a real black eye for him as he was trying to be the dignified new president of the United States.

DR: So when he does arrive in Washington, not in a dress and not in a kilt, he is driven to the Willard Hotel, where he stays until he's inaugurated. How long is he there before the inauguration?

TW: He comes in on the morning of the 23rd of February, and he stays there until March 4th. Nine days.

DR: The people in Baltimore who wanted to assassinate him missed him because he came through on a conventional train. They didn't realize he was on it. Why didn't they go to his hotel and assassinate him there?

TW: It's a really good question. I don't have a very good answer, except I think he was in a kind of security bubble once he made it to a hotel filled with famous politicians. And presumably there was security in a well-known, genteel establishment in Washington. I would imagine he also had his own security. Allan Pinkerton rides with him. Pinkerton's a railroad detective then and later works for the U.S. government. He gets Lincoln into the hotel, and I would imagine he stayed pretty close for the days that followed.

DR: During the trip, one person who does see him, as you report in your book, is a man named John Wilkes Booth. Did he have any contact with Lincoln during this trip?

TW: John Wilkes Booth is performing in a play in Albany, New York. Lincoln comes into Albany on the train and speaks. As usual, huge crowds come out, and Booth was reported to be denouncing Lincoln loudly within earshot of anyone who was close to him, to the point that people were telling him to cool it. I wondered if he had actor's jealousy, because Lincoln was getting huge crowds. His crowds were okay but nothing like what Lincoln had.

DR: Final question for you. Let's suppose you had an opportunity to interview Abraham Lincoln. What one question would you like to ask him?

TW: I'd love to ask him about his mother. He almost never talked about his mother. She died when he was very young, about nine years old. That may be where his depression comes from. There's this pain inside of him. I think overcoming trauma helped him to be a great man and a great president, and it helped him to be a president during a time of trauma. The Civil War is like a body that's being torn apart. The two halves of the country are being ripped apart, and hundreds of thousands of young men are being killed. He survived the deaths of his mother and his sister and probably a young woman he loved named Ann Rutledge.

His survival made him strong. You feel that steel inside of Abraham Lincoln. I'm pretty sure he wouldn't want to talk about it, but it's fascinating from the point of view of a historian. He spoke so little about himself. He was incredibly modest. He rarely used the word *I* in any of his speeches, which is unusual. Most politicians say the opposite. I'd love to try to understand a little bit more about who he was as a child, as a young man, and the adversity he overcame to become Abraham Lincoln.

5

RON CHERNOW
on Ulysses S. Grant

(1822–1885; president from 1868 to 1877)

Many presidents have had midcareer turnarounds that took them from near oblivion to the presidency. But surely none can rival that of Ulysses S. Grant.

He had been a West Point graduate and fought with some distinction in the Mexican-American War (ironically not far from his later rival Robert E. Lee); but Grant resigned from the military in circumstances that suggest he was pushed to do so for having had, on more than a few occasions, too much alcohol while on duty. (Grant seemed to have had a near-lifelong addiction to alcohol, though rarely had it interfered with his military duties.) Out of the military with no commercial skills, Grant worked for a while, unhappily, under his two younger brothers in their father's leather business in Illinois, and essentially tried to become a farmer on his brother-in-law's and father-in-law's land in Missouri. That did not work well either. To support his family, he chopped trees on his land and personally sold the resulting firewood on street corners in nearby St. Louis.

Amazingly, the Civil War began in 1861 and seven years later Grant was elected president of the United States at age 46. How could such a turnaround occur—selling firewood to make ends meet and then becoming president of the United States?

Because of his military experience, Grant volunteered to help the Illinois militia and ultimately became its leader. When he proved successful in his militia-led attacks on the Confederate Army, he was brought back into the Union Army to lead further attacks against Confederate forces. Grant seemed more willing than other Union generals to fight Confederate forces directly. He was criticized at the time by some who said that his battle successes were due to his willingness to throw his large forces into battle, even if that resulted in substantial Union deaths and casualties (which it did).

But Lincoln was more concerned with victories than casualties, and with none of his other generals willing to be as bold—or able to be as successful—as Grant, the president eventually made him the lieutenant general of the Union Army (its most senior position). And while the result was a good deal more Union casualties, Grant took the fighting directly to Lee and his forces, until Lee felt compelled to surrender at Appomattox Court House, effectively ending the war and making Grant a national hero.

Because of his affection for what Grant had done for him and for the country, Lincoln invited him and his wife, Julia, to Ford's Theatre on the night of April 14, 1865. But the Grants declined (apparently because Mrs. Grant did not want to spend an evening with Mrs. Lincoln, whom she regarded as quite unpleasant). The Grants decided to take a train to visit their children in New Jersey instead. If Grant had attended the play, *Our American Cousin*, that evening, would his military entourage have been able to stop John Wilkes Booth from assassinating Lincoln? One can never know.

With Lincoln's assassination, Andrew Johnson became president, but he turned out to be not as committed to Reconstruction in the South as Lincoln had been. Grant had a number of disputes with Johnson, and left government and became a candidate for president in 1868. In part because of Johnson's clashes with Grant and Congress over Reconstruction, the House impeached Johnson, but the Senate failed to convict by one vote.

Because of his military hero status, Grant was asked to serve as the Republican nominee for president in 1868. He decided to do so, and was elected relatively easily, defeating a former governor of New York, Horatio Seymour. Unfortunately, Grant's presidency was not as successful as his military efforts. He was too trusting of some businessmen and his own officials, and a number of scandals tarnished his reputation. And economic problems in the country—the Panic of 1873—prompted Grant to not seek a third term.

After leaving office, and following a well-received tour around the world, Grant entrusted almost all his money to his son's investment company. But that company turned out to be fraudulent due to the son's partner's actions. So Grant was essentially broke. To rebuild his wealth, he changed his mind on writing a memoir, and published it with a company owned by the family of Samuel Clemens (Mark Twain). Grant finished his memoir just as he died from throat cancer. But the book was very well written (scholars often say it is one of the best memoirs written by a president, though it deals only with Grant's life up to the presidency). The family's finances were restored by the book's commercial success.

Ron Chernow is one of America's finest biographers, and I had a chance to interview him about his book *Grant* for a Congressional Dialogues session at the Library of Congress on February 12, 2019.

*   *   *   *

DAVID M. RUBENSTEIN (DR): Your books on the House of Morgan, Rockefeller, the Warburgs, they're epic books, so it must take a long time to write them. How did you get trained to do that?

RON CHERNOW (RC): My dirty little secret is that I never took a history class. Everything I've written about in my adult life has been self-taught. I did two degrees in English literature, one at Yale and one at Cambridge. I thought that I wanted to be a novelist. So for 10 years after I got out of school, I was a freelance magazine writer. I was constantly scribbling short stories that were never published, and then I started writing these books in my midthirties, and I suddenly realized that God had created much better stories and situations and characters than I could ever invent. But all of that training and narrative from the magazine writing and from studying literature and writing stories flowed into the work.

DR: When you write a book, do you do the research for five years and then you write for five years?

RC: *Grant* took six years. It was four solid years of research, two solid years of writing. Strangely enough, the two years of writing coincided with the opening of the *Hamilton* musical, so I was telling people that I had two full-time jobs. Mornings and afternoons during the week I was writing *Grant*, and then evenings and weekends I was at the show. I was going round the clock. I'm amazed that the book is as coherent as it is, because I wasn't during that period.

DR: Let's talk about Grant. In the twentieth century, when you saw surveys of presidents of the United States, he was typically near the bottom—Buchanan, Grant, and so forth. Why did you pick him as a topic, and do you think it's unfair he was so poorly rated?

RC: In the first survey of presidential historians, back in 1948, Grant ranked next to last. The only president who ranked lower was Warren Harding. It was the two corruption presidents. Three years ago, Grant had risen to number 28. In the most recent poll he'd risen to 21, so he's now in the upper half. This is the fun of history. History's an argument without an end. We're always reevaluating people, and I think that Grant's reputation will rise higher. And so I felt that Grant, as a president but also as a general, was ripe for rehabilitation.

DR: Some people said that as a general he won battles by just having more bodies to throw into them, and lots of people got slaughtered on his side. Is that a fair criticism of his generalship?

RC: It doesn't really stand up to analysis. If you look at the percentage of soldiers who died in Grant's battles, it's pretty much the same as with Robert E. Lee's or anybody's Confederate army. It's interesting that Ulysses S. Grant, during the Civil War, captured three entire Confederate armies. He captured an army of 13,000 at Fort Donelson in Tennessee in 1862. He captured the Confederate army at Vicksburg in 1863—31,000 soldiers. And then, of course, he captured Lee's army at Appomattox Court House. Robert E. Lee never captured a single Union army, so why has there been all of this glorification of Lee, and why is Grant denigrated as the butcher?

DR: He's also widely thought to be an alcoholic. Is that a fair criticism of him?

RC: Yes. When I started the book, it always seemed the conversation about Grant was whether he was a drunkard or not. But *drunkard* is a loaded word. It has this moralistic sense that this is an unscrupulous person who's gleefully indulging his habit. What I found was that Grant was a binge drinker who would and could go for two or three months without touching a drop, and then he would have a two- or three-day bender. He had a tremendous sense of responsibility. He never drank on the eve of battles. He certainly never drank during battles. But then after the battles were over, when the pressure was off, he would slip away to a little town where his soldiers wouldn't see him, and he would go off on a spree, as they called it.

DR: Did he know Robert E. Lee before the war?

RC: They had met during the Mexican War. Now remember that Robert E. Lee was 15 years older than Ulysses S. Grant. During the Mexican War, Lee was on General Winfield Scott's staff, and he came over to Grant's brigade. Grant vividly remembered meeting Lee. Lee told Grant at Appomattox Court House that throughout the war he had tried to remember meeting Grant and couldn't. But Grant said that meeting Lee during the Mexican War was very important, because there was a mystique of Lee that he was this invincible general. Grant said that having actually met Lee, he knew that he was a mortal and that he could beat him.

DR: When Lincoln was assassinated that night, the Grants were invited to go. It is said that Julia Grant didn't like Mrs. Lincoln and didn't want to go. Had General Grant been there, do you think Lincoln might not have been assassinated?

RC: The story was this. A few weeks before Lincoln was assassinated, Abraham and Mary Lincoln visited the Grants in City Point, Virginia, where Grant had his headquarters. There was a military review where Mary Lincoln and Julia Grant rode out together. When they arrived at the parade ground, Mary Lincoln saw the beautiful young wife of Major General Edward Ord on horseback next to Lincoln. Mary Lincoln was having severe psychological problems at that point, flew into a jealous rage, started berating Mrs. Ord, who burst into tears, having no idea what this tirade was about. Julia Grant then intervened to try to protect Mrs. Ord, and as often happens when you intervene in an argument, Mary Lincoln turned on Julia. So the night the Lincolns went to Ford's Theatre, Lincoln felt that the country wanted to see the victorious president and the victorious general. Julia Grant refused to go because Mary Lincoln was going, so the Grants made an excuse. They went up to a house they owned in Burlington, New Jersey. It's one of the great ifs of history. If Grant had been there, one possibility is that he would have been killed. Grant also, with his great military instincts, might have sensed danger. Grant probably would have had an entourage of military aides there, so Julia Grant's refusal to spend the evening with Mary Lincoln may have changed history.

DR: You might tell the story about Mrs. Grant's eyes and her desire to fix them and what her husband said.

RC: She was squint-eyed. She had strabismus (i.e., where one eye is not aligned with the other), and she was so self-conscious about it as First Lady, she always had pictures taken in profile, on her good side. But there's a very touching story that during the war, while Grant was off fighting, Julia Grant consulted a doctor to see whether the eye problem could be surgically corrected, and the doctor said that it was too late in her life to do it. When Ulysses found out that Julia had consulted a doctor about this, he said to her, "Julia, why did you do that? Didn't I fall in love with these very eyes? And I never want you to change them." He was at bottom a very romantic man, and he was repaying a love that was no less unconditional.

Because during the 1850s, when Grant is down and out and failing at one thing after another, selling firewood on street corners in St. Louis, Julia Grant has a dream one night. She has a dream that her husband will become president of the United States. And when she wakes up and tells people the dream, everyone laughs. Nothing could have seemed more ridiculous than that this man selling firewood on street corners would someday be president of the United States.

DR: When presidents get ready to write their autobiographies, they're always told that the gold standard is the memoir written by Ulysses S. Grant at the end of his life. It became the gold standard because it was so eloquent, so forceful and well written. How did somebody who had never written a book before write such a wonderful book? And is there any truth to the rumor that his publisher, Samuel Clemens, might have actually written it?

RC: The answer to the first question is that, for those who knew Grant, it was not surprising that he wrote such a brilliant book, because he'd always prided himself on his writing. During the war he was famous for the terseness and the clarity of his orders. As a two-term president, he wrote all his own speeches and papers and took tremendous pride in it. So he was very gifted verbally throughout his life.

There's an interesting Library of Congress angle to the question "Did Mark Twain ghost write the famous memoir?" I got that question so much when I was writing the book that I came here to the Library of Congress and I insisted that the archivists show me the original manuscript. The manuscript is in five dark-blue leather-bound volumes. They wheeled it out. It was the most poignant day of my research. I leafed through every page. Grant was dying of cancer of the throat and tongue as he was writing, and you could see he starts out writing in a very clear, firm hand, but by the end of the manuscript it's starting to slant and wobble. Except for a few straight paragraphs toward the end, it was all in Grant's handwriting, so I was able to say conclusively that Grant wrote the memoirs. Twain himself said that his only help with the manuscript was relatively trivial matters of grammar and punctuation.

DR: Let's go back to the beginning of Grant's life. Where was he born, and what did his parents do?

RC: He was born in the southwestern corner of Ohio, south of where Cincinnati is. He was born on a bucolic stretch of the Ohio River. This is significant for his later life, because on winter evenings the Ohio River would be frozen and slaves would sprint to freedom from slave-owning Kentucky to the free state of Ohio. In a way, he was living in this border area that straddled North and South.

DR: What was his name at birth?

RC: His name at birth was Hiram Ulysses Grant, which sounded nice except that it saddled him with the unfortunate initials H.U.G. He finally tired of all the teasing from his friends and he dropped the Hiram, become plain Ulysses, and then, when the local congressman nominated him for West Point, he mistakenly added the *S*. As Grant liked to say in later life, the *S* stood for absolutely nothing.

DR: His father was very antislavery?

RC: Yes. He came from an abolitionist family. He married into a slave-owning family from Missouri, and the abolitionist Grants felt so strongly about their Ulysses marrying into a slave-owning family that, when they got married in St. Louis in 1848, not a single member of the Grant family attended, as a protest.

DR: Because her family were slave owners.

RC: Yes. Her family owned about 20 to 30 slaves.

DR: So, he grows up on Ohio, and his father is—?

RC: He's a tanner.

DR: Did Grant like that business? Did he want to be in that business?

RC: No, Grant was revolted by the business. In fact, his father's tannery was across the street from the house. Grant had a second-floor bedroom window, and fumes from the tannery would waft into his bedroom. He was so sickened by the fumes that for the rest of his life, he could not stand to eat meat swimming in its own juices. The meat had to be burnt to a dry crisp. During the Civil War, his favorite breakfast was oysters soaked in vinegar, washed down with a cup of black coffee and finished off with a fine cigar. That was Grant.

DR: As a young man, he gets nominated to go to West Point. Did he want to go to West Point?

RC: No, his father wanted him to go, not because he wanted Ulysses to be a general someday, but his father was a real skinflint and he saw West Point as a free form of vocational education. So Grant, quite unwillingly, went. He later said that during the time he was at West Point, there was a debate going on in Congress to abolish the academy. He said he read the newspaper every day and was rooting that Congress would abolish West Point so that he could go home.

DR: When he's there, he's not a great academic superstar, is he?

RC: No, he's lackluster. He graduates 21 out of a class of 39. Quite unlike all the other people that I've written about, Grant completely lacked ambition. In fact, his highest aim when he graduated was to be an assistant math professor at the academy. Not a full professor, mind you, but an assistant professor. That was the height of his ambition.

DR: But he decided to stay in the military. He had to. What was his assignment?

RC: He was assigned to the Jefferson Barracks in St. Louis. He fought for four years in the Mexican War. He was a quartermaster in commissary, which meant that he mastered logistics. That turned out to be extremely important during the Civil War, where he was the head of the Union Army across a 1,300 mile front.

DR: The woman he marries, Julia Grant, was the sister of one of his roommates? Is that how he met her?

RC: Yes, that's right. At his wedding, James Longstreet and Simon Buckner and these other future Confederate generals are there. Again, it's one reason why Grant has an understanding of the Confederate generals, because so many of them had been his friends. He had known so many of them at West Point. That's one of the fascinating things about the Civil War. These people who knew each other intimately were fighting against each other.

DR: Ultimately there's a gold rush in California in the late 1840s, and the military, I guess to protect the peace out there, sends some people. Grant gets sent there. Why does his military service end?

RC: He's assigned to a couple of bleak, remote garrisons on the West Coast. The second was near Eureka, California, up in the redwood country there. On his meager army pay, he could not afford to bring his wife and children out. Grant got very depressed, started drinking heavily, and then in 1854 is drummed out of the military when he shows up drunk.

DR: Was he court-martialed? Or he just voluntarily quit?

RC: He was threatened with court-martial, so he quit ahead of being court-martialed.

DR: He goes back to Ohio?

RC: No, to St. Louis. Julia had gotten 60 acres of land as a wedding gift from her father, so Grant handcrafts a log cabin that he nicknamed Hardscrabble, facetiously. Then he tries to make a go of it at farming, and he can't. He's so desperate that he begins to sell firewood on street corners in St. Louis. From their farm, he would have to trudge 10 miles each way alongside the cart loaded with wood. He was seedy and unshaved, and he was very depressed. One day when he was selling firewood, one of his old army buddies ran into him and said, "My God, Grant, what are you doing?" And Grant said, "I'm trying to solve the problem of poverty." He was so poor that winter of 1857, he pawned his watch in order to buy Christmas gifts for his children.

DR: Is he selling firewood in 1861?

RC: In 1860, finally, in complete desperation, he goes to his overbearing father, who lives in the small town of Galena, Illinois, on the Mississippi. Grant begs for a job in his father's leather goods store, where he goes to work as a clerk, junior to his two younger brothers. You can imagine what a comeuppance that was. So that's where Grant is one year before the Civil War.

DR: So he's drummed out of the military for alcoholism, more or less, and he's selling firewood on the streets, without any real money. How did he wind up in the military in the Civil War?

RC: After the attack by the Confederacy on Fort Sumter, there was a desperate shortage of officers. About one-third of the officers of the regular army were from the South and defected to the Confederacy. Grant still had all the old West Point lore in his mind. He had fought with distinction in the Mexican War for four years. So the governor of Illinois, Richard Yates, makes him a colonel, two months after the outbreak of war. Four months after the outbreak, he's a brigadier general. Twelve months after the outbreak he's a major general, and by the end of the war he's the first lieutenant general since George Washington. He's the general in chief of the victorious Union army. This man who had never had a single person working for him before suddenly has a million soldiers under his command.

DR: Initially he's in what's called the volunteer army. In other words, it wasn't the regular army.

RC: They were a volunteer regiment.

DR: How does he distinguish himself in the volunteer army so much that the regular army asks him to join them?

RC: His discipline, his fairness, his toughness, his knowledge. Grant was a complete professional. As I was saying, he had mastered logistics. Also, in the Mexican War, as quartermaster he was not obligated to engage in any fighting, but he made a point of fighting in every battle. So he had practical battlefield experience. He knew the Army from top to bottom.

DR: He eventually gets in the regular Army, and then he's commanding the Union troops in Shiloh and in Vicksburg. Those are two gigantic victories. Why were they so significant to the Union?

RC: Shiloh because it stopped the northern march of the Southern army. Vicksburg was arguably the most important victory for Grant or of the war. It occurred the same week as Gettysburg, so is often overshadowed by that. But Union forces had captured New Orleans, Baton Rouge, and Memphis, so the only remaining Confederate stronghold on the Mississippi River was Vicksburg. Vicksburg was located at a hairpin bend of the river. It had seven miles of elaborate fortification, so it was considered virtually impregnable. Grant runs his ships past the big guns at Vicksburg and marches his soldiers down the west bank of the Mississippi. They cross over, and then he has this lightning campaign of five dazzling victories in three weeks. Instead of going north to Vicksburg, he goes northeast, throws himself between Vicksburg and any possible Confederate reinforcement. When Vicksburg surrenders, this cuts the Confederacy in half. You have to realize that a lot of the cattle and livestock for the Confederacy were west of the Mississippi River.

DR: That was such a big victory that ultimately Lincoln said, "You must be pretty good, why don't you come east?" Is that what happened?

RC: Finally, in February 1864, Congress revives the rank of lieutenant general. In early March 1864, Grant comes to Washington to become general in chief, checking into the Willard Hotel. Coincidentally there was a reception going on in the White House that night. He goes around the corner to the White House, walks into the Blue Room, and there's Lincoln in a packed reception of people. It was the first time that Lincoln had ever set eyes on Grant. There was such pandemonium in the room that they had Grant, who was relatively short, get up on a sofa so the crowd could see him. He was a very bashful man. He was sweating heavily, and Grant later said that the hottest campaign he ever fought was standing on the couch in the White House that night.

DR: People complained to Lincoln about Grant, said he was an alcoholic. What was Lincoln's response to that?

RC: There's a famous story, which is a true story, that a group of congressmen went to him to complain about Grant's drinking. Lincoln had all these procrastinating, do-nothing generals, and he said to the congressmen, "If you find out what brand of whiskey Grant drinks, I'd like to send a barrel to all of my other generals." But had it not been for all of the stories about the drinking, I think that Grant probably would have been named general in chief sooner in the war.

DR: In the end, it comes down to the effort to win the South. Grant sends General Sherman to go through the South, and then he decides to go against Lee in Richmond. How does he outmaneuver Lee in Richmond?

RC: Grant was a master of logistics. If you look at the campaign in Richmond and Petersburg that finally ends the war, Grant has Lee and his Army of Northern Virginia pinned down in defensive positions at Richmond and Petersburg. What Grant does is he systematically cuts off every single railroad and canal linking Lee to food and other supplies. He essentially starves him out. When Lee takes his army and flees west to Appomattox Court House, it's because his army is starving. They're hoping there will be supplies when they arrive there. That was really how Grant won.

DR: Ultimately, Lee sends word that he'd like to surrender. They meet at Appomattox Court House. U. S. Grant used to stand, in the view of some, for Unconditional Surrender Grant. Why was he so polite at this surrender?

RC: The most beautiful passage in Grant's memoirs is when he's talking about Appomattox. When he first got the letter from Lee saying that he's going to surrender, Grant said that he was jubilant, but then very quickly his mood changed. He writes in the memoirs, "I felt like anything other than rejoicing over the downfall of a foe who had fought so long and so valiantly, and had suffered so much for a cause, even though that cause was the worst for which I could imagine an army fighting." Grant realized that only by being magnanimous was there any possibility of North/South reconciliation. It was fascinating because he not only fed the famished

Confederate soldiers, he refused to enter Richmond, the Confederate capital that fell. Julia wanted him to go and Grant said to Julia, "Don't you realize how bitter defeat is to these people? Would you have me make it worse?" There was a proposal after the Civil War for a large historical painting in the Capitol Rotunda that would show Lee surrendering to Grant, and Grant vetoed the idea, because he felt that it would only embitter and humiliate the South.

DR: After Appomattox, the war's essentially over. Not too long after, Lincoln is assassinated. What did President Johnson think about Grant, and what role did he give him?

RC: The first year of the relationship wasn't too bad. Grant said that President Andrew Johnson was, as he put it, vengeful, passionate, and opinionated. They clashed over Reconstruction. Andrew Johnson was violently opposed to Reconstruction, had very little sympathy with the aspirations of the four million former slaves who were now citizens. Andrew Johnson, as president, said, "This is a white man's country, and by God, as long as I'm president, it's going to be a white man's government." Grant was a strong supporter of the Civil Rights Act of 1866, a strong supporter of the Thirteenth, Fourteenth, and Fifteenth Amendments. So he and Andrew Johnson were bound to clash.

DR: Johnson is impeached but not convicted in the Senate by one vote. A groundswell forms to keep him from being president again. He doesn't get the nomination. Did Grant want to be the nominee of the Republican Party?

RC: Grant's funny. As I said, he was always very uncomfortable overtly showing ambition. He said that he had regrets about giving up the job as general in chief, which he loved, although he seemed happy enough becoming president. But the situation that happened in 1868 was not unlike the situation that happened in 1952 with Eisenhower, the war hero who had been studiously nonpartisan. Everyone was guessing what party Grant belonged to in 1868, the same way that everyone was guessing which party Ike belonged to in 1952.

DR: So Grant didn't campaign for the job?

RC: No, he didn't, again because of Appomattox. Grant had a symbolic value where he stayed above the fray. He was a symbol of national reconciliation. And he won narrowly in the popular vote but in the Electoral College overwhelmingly.

DR: But in those days, he didn't go to the convention?

RC: No. He was in Galena, Illinois. At that time, it was still considered unseemly to campaign. You didn't go to the convention. Then, in 1872, he won reelection by the biggest landslide between the elections of Andrew Jackson and Teddy Roosevelt.

DR: As president of the United States, Grant served for eight years. But it was widely thought at the time that his administration had a lot of corruption. Was he personally corrupt, or he just couldn't figure out who was worth keeping, who was honest or not?

RC: That's the strange thing about Grant's presidency, because he himself was almost prudishly honest. Throughout the Civil War, he was prosecuting war profiteers. He was not involved in the scandals. He prosecuted all of them vigorously. But Grant was strangely and almost incurably blind to unscrupulous people around him. One of the worst rascals turned out to be a man named Orville Babcock, who was effectively his chief of staff. And this blindness of Grant, this fatal innocence, is something that didn't change throughout his life.

DR: Despite these problems, could he have been reelected for a third term?

RC: I argue in the book that the corruption scandals were the minor story of the administration, however unfortunate. The big story that I spent a lot of time on is that Grant crushed the original Ku Klux Klan. At the time that Grant became president, the Klan was killing thousands of Blacks who were registering to vote for the first time under the Fifteenth Amendment. Grant hires a crusading attorney general from Georgia named Amos Akerman. The Justice Department was created in 1870. Akerman brings 3,000 indictments, gets a thousand convictions against the Klan, and that original Klan is destroyed. The Klan that we know, that unfortunately is still with us, was from the revival of the group in the 1910s and 1920s. Grant doing this, and his campaign against the Klan, seems to me one of the great acts in presidential history, and I felt that this was, in many ways, a forgotten story.

DR: He could have been reelected. In those days, you could run for a third term. Why did he decide not to run?

RC: He said that, from the time at Fort Sumter to the end of his second term, for 16 years he had been essentially carrying the weight of the nation on his shoulders. He said he was under constant strain, he was worn-out, he was burned-out. His last day in the White House, he said he never wanted to get out of any place as much as he wanted to get out of there. He said he felt like a boy who had been let out of school.

DR: He was elected president when he was 46. Eight years later, at 54, a relatively young age, he leaves the White House. What does he do immediately when he leaves?

RC: Grant always had a romantic longing for travel, so he takes a trip around the world that lasts for two years and four months. He meets with every head of state. He meets with Queen Victoria, Bismarck, the pope, the czar, the emperor of Japan. I should mention that he traveled with his own personal journalist, John Russell Young, who was the Librarian of Congress when this building was built. Young wrote a beautiful book called *Around the World with General Grant*. Grant pioneered a new role, postpresidential diplomacy. He ended on this around-the-world tour arbitrating an offshore dispute between Japan and China. He was traveling on a warship provided by the government, and he was really an unofficial representative of the country.

DR: When he finally gets back after two and a half years, does he say, "I might like to be president again"?

RC: Julia was interested in getting back into the game. She was, in many ways, more ambitious than he was, and so he very nearly got a third Republican nomination. He felt that after this around-the-world tour he was much more cosmopolitan and worldly. He felt that he could contribute a lot in terms of foreign policy. He also felt strongly that the so-called redeemer governments were coming into power in the South. These were governments that were bent upon repealing all of Reconstruction, which bothered him, because he had been such an instrumental force in Reconstruction. But he very narrowly lost the Republication nomination to James Garfield, who of course became president.

DR: So he goes to New York and he decides to get into the investment business. Does he have any acumen for business?

RC: Zero. And Grant was cheated once again. I should mention that in giving up his job as general in chief, he sacrificed his military pension. There was no presidential pension at the time. So his son Buck knew a young financier named Ferdinand Ward, who'd been lionized as the young Napoleon of Wall Street. Grant formed this partnership with him, Grant and Ward. Unfortunately, Ferdinand Ward was the Bernie Madoff of his day. The whole thing was a big Ponzi scheme. Grant in his innocence imagined that he was a multimillionaire, and he woke up one morning in 1884 and discovered that he was worth $80 and Julia was worth $130.

DR: So he borrows money from William Henry Vanderbilt, and then he loses that investment.

RC: Yes, and two things happened almost simultaneously. He and his wife and all his children were wiped out financially. At the same time, he was diagnosed with what would be terminal cancer of the throat and tongue, so he did something that he had vowed he would not do. He wrote his Civil War memoirs.

DR: He was a gigantic cigar smoker, 19 a day or something like that.

RC: Twenty a day during the war. He felt very virtuous after the war when he cut down to 10.

DR: So he smoked a lot of cigars and the doctor said he had cancer. He had previously not been willing to write any memoirs. He thought it was not a good thing to write memoirs. Why was he against it initially?

RC: He thought that there was something very egotistical about the way that all these Civil War generals rushed to cash in on it, rushed to give their point of view of how wonderful they'd been as generals. So he swore he wouldn't do it. But he had cancer of the throat and tongue. He was petrified that when he died, which he knew was imminent, that Julia would be left destitute. So he wrote these now-famous memoirs in terrible pain. He said that even to swallow a glass of water felt like swallowing a glass of molten lava.

What he would do when he was writing the book was that he would not eat or drink for four or five hours at a time, because when he ate or drank, he was in such excruciating pain, he would then have to take the opiates or some painkiller that would fog his brain. The fact that he did this magnificent memoir in unbearable pain, under these conditions, is nothing short of miraculous. He finished the memoirs just three days before he died in July 1885. He had willed himself to stay alive to finish them.

DR: While they're the most famous presidential memoirs, they don't deal with the presidency. Why did he not write about the presidency?

RC: Number one, I think he wanted to relive his glory days as a general. Two, he was really doing this for money, and it was the Civil War that sold. His presidency was a much more mixed record, and he would not have had the time or energy to go into it.

DR: When he dies, he's given enormous honors by the federal government.

RC: He's buried in New York, in Grant's Tomb. Do you know where that joke comes from?

DR: Groucho Marx.

RC: Groucho Marx, that's right. For those of you who don't know the story, Groucho, in the 1950s, had the quiz show *You Bet Your Life*. The contestants would come out and Groucho would mercilessly ridicule them. But even Groucho began to feel sorry for them, that so few of them knew a single answer. So he decided to ask each a question that everyone would know the answer to, and that question was, who's buried in Grant's tomb? And to Groucho's astonishment, half the contestants got it wrong.

Grant's Tomb, for those of you who visit it, is gigantic. It's the largest mausoleum in North America. And if you want to see the regard in which Ulysses S. Grant was held in in the nineteenth century, go to Grant's Tomb. It's really magnificent.

6

CANDICE MILLARD
on James A. Garfield

(1831–1881; president from January 1881 to September 1881)

One of the most talented individuals to have ever been elected president, James Garfield, is one of the least known, in no small part because he served such a short time. Four months into his administration, which began in 1881, Garfield was shot by a deranged office seeker, Charles Guiteau. Sadly, Garfield died not so much because of the bullet that remained in his abdomen for several months but because a not very competent physician, Willard Bliss, appointed himself as the doctor in charge of the recovery and kept other doctors away from Garfield. The concept of maintaining sanitary medical conditions was not widely accepted at the time, and as a result Dr. Bliss and others often used their bare fingers to probe for the bullet that was lodged in Garfield's abdomen. The inevitable result was infections throughout Garfield's body, and he died three months after being shot.

Interestingly, in the effort to locate the bullet, in an era where X-rays and CT scans did not exist, the inventor of the telephone, Alexander Graham Bell, developed a metal-detecting device that could have located the bullet, and he did use it on Garfield. But because the doctor thought the bullet was on Garfield's right side, Bell was not allowed to use his device on the left side (where the eventual autopsy showed the bullet was lodged). Had Bell been able to help find the actual bullet, and had it been removed in a safe and sanitary way, it is possible Garfield could have lived. Sadly, he was succeeded by his vice president, Chester Arthur, a former machine politician who had been a New York customs official and was not someone widely admired for his intellect or honesty.

Because Garfield did not serve very long, it is difficult to say he was a consequential president. But his potential certainly seemed high. He had been born into poverty but came to be an excellent student and ultimately a college president, a distinguished scholar, a Civil War general and hero, a ten-term member of Congress, and was about to become a senator when he was nominated for president against his wishes. Garfield had actually nominated another senator from Ohio, John Sherman, to be the Republican nominee, but the convention eventually decided, on the 36th ballot, that Garfield was the best candidate. In the tradition of those days, he did not campaign in the general election. He stayed home in Ohio and managed to beat another former Civil War general, Winfield Scott Hancock, closely (via the popular vote) and decisively (via the Electoral College).

Garfield's assassin believed that he was responsible for Garfield's election, having made a halting and largely ignored speech for him in the campaign. Guiteau's efforts to get Garfield and his secretary of state to appoint him as a consul in Paris were never taken seriously, and Guiteau felt he was being treated shabbily and sought to avenge this insult. So he positioned himself at a train station on what is now the Mall in Washington, knowing that Garfield was scheduled to take a train on that particular day. Guiteau ultimately was tried and sentenced to death, and was executed by hanging about one year after the assassination occurred.

This unfortunate story has been recounted in *Destiny of the Republic*, written by Candice Millard, a former writer for *National Geographic* and a talented author of histories. I had a chance to interview her about the book at the New-York Historical Society on April 11, 2023.

*   *   *   *

DAVID M. RUBENSTEIN (DM): Let's talk about James Garfield, the subject of your book *Destiny of the Republic: A Tale of Madness, Medicine, and the Murder of a President.* Garfield was only president for a few months, so not that distinguished and long a record, but it's a very interesting story about how he became president and what happened in the couple of months that he was president. Let's go back to the beginning. Who was James Garfield? Where was he from?

CANDICE MILLARD (CM): James Garfield was from Ohio. He was our last president born in a log cabin. He was incredibly poor. His father died when he was just two years old. He didn't have shoes until he was four. But his mother and his older brother realized that he was special, that he was absolutely brilliant. And they saved and saved. They saved $17 to be able to send him to college. He went to what's now known as Hiram University in Ohio.

But he still needed to help pay for his tuition. He was a janitor and a carpenter his first year to help pay his tuition. But then, by his second year, he was so brilliant—when he was still a sophomore in college, still a student—they made him a professor of literature, mathematics, and ancient languages. By the time he was 26, he was a university president. He was an incredible classicist. He knew the entire *Aeneid* by heart in Latin. And while he was in Congress, he wrote an original proof of the Pythagorean theorem. If you know any other congressman who can do that, I would love to know.

DR: He also graduated from Williams College?

CM: He did. He went to Williams after Hiram.

DR: He was a very distinguished person. How did he get into politics? Did he always want to be in politics?

CM: He was incredibly charismatic and a talented speaker, and that became clear early on. He was a strong abolitionist. He really wanted to fight in the Civil War, and he did. He obviously fought for the Union, and was a real hero in that war.

He was encouraged to go into politics. He never campaigned for himself. He said, "If people want me, these are my values, these are my interests, and then they can vote for me or not."

DR: In the Civil War, he rose up to be a general because he was so good at what he was doing. How did he learn military tactics, and how did he become so accomplished as a military leader?

CM: It was reading. That really defined his life, studying. He was a scholar. And so he studied military tactics and military strategy, and he was very good at it. But then, while in the military, he won a seat in Congress and Lincoln asked him to come to Washington and take that seat and serve, because he needed him.

DR: He's in Congress. How does he rise up? Is he the chairman of any committees that do anything important?

CM: One of the things he cared a lot about was hard money. That was important to him. Also education. And he was instrumental in bringing about Black suffrage. He gave a speech on the floor of Congress on that subject which would tear your heart out. It was incredibly moving and powerful.

DR: Let's set the context. Lincoln is assassinated. Andrew Johnson becomes president, is impeached but not convicted, doesn't run for reelection. General Grant runs and is elected for eight years. He doesn't run for a third term. The next president elected is Rutherford B. Hayes. He doesn't run for reelection because he promised to run for only one term, and he nobly decided to honor his promise. This is in 1880, and there are several people who want to be the nominee of the Republican Party. Who are those people?

CM: Ulysses S. Grant is hoping for a third term. Everyone assumes that he's going to win. John Sherman, from Ohio, is also hoping he will get the nomination. He's William Tecumseh Sherman's brother and he's secretary of the Treasury. He's worried about Grant, but he's also worried about Garfield. Garfield is not running but everybody is fascinated with him and they want him to run, and there has been a lot of murmuring. Sherman thinks, "The best way to make him not be a threat to me is to ask him to give my nominating address at the convention."

DR: He's asked to go ahead and make the nominating speech. He wants to do that?

CM: He does not want to but he feels like he can't say no.

DR: The convention is held in Chicago in 1880. On the first ballot, what happens?

CM: What happens first is they give these nominating addresses and there's this man named Roscoe Conkling, who is a famous, powerful senior senator from New York. He wants Grant to win, because he's going to be the man behind the power and he's going to be running things.

He's a flamboyant guy. He has a great spit curl, and he would wear these fancy coats, and he would write with lavender ink. He gives a stirring speech and the whole crowd is going crazy. It's 15,000 people. Garfield has to go up next to give the nominating speech for Sherman, and he's obviously very different—he's quiet, wise. He stands up and he starts speaking, and most of it is extemporaneous, because he took ideas from the other speeches. And everyone is mesmerized or fascinated. At one point, he says, "Gentlemen, I ask you, what do we want?" And someone in the crowd shouts, "We want Garfield."

Everybody starts going crazy, and he's trying to get them to settle down and listen to him. He finishes his speech and he sits down, and they start the ballots. Each state stands up. James Blaine was also running, the magnetic man from Maine. These ballots are coming in, and John Sherman is somewhere else, nervously following the results coming in by telegraph.

Then at one point someone stands up and says, "We give our vote to Garfield." And Garfield stands up and he says, "I'm not a candidate. I refuse it." They shout him down. He thinks, "Well, it's just one vote."

But they don't have anybody who's won it, so they do another round. There are a few more votes for Garfield, and a few more. Other people change their vote and send it to Garfield, and more and more and more. He's trying to stop it but he can't, and it becomes this flood of votes. He wasn't even a candidate, didn't want to be a candidate, and he finds himself the Republican nominee for president of the United States.

DR: They had 36 ballots or something?

CM: 36 ballots. The most ballots ever at that point.

DR: He honestly didn't want to be the nominee, but he is the nominee. In those days, when you're the nominee of the party, do you go campaign or just sit on your porch?

CM: No, they told him, "Just sit cross-legged and look wise." He was very happy to go back to his farm in Ohio, where his children and his wife were. But people would come to him. He spoke German, and he actually gave the first presidential campaign speech in a foreign language on his front porch.

DR: In the election, who was his main opponent?

CM: A man named Winfield Scott Hancock.

DR: Who was a military person?

CM: Yes.

DR: What did the election results show?

CM: It was very, very close. They didn't find out until the wee hours of the morning, but Garfield ended up winning. It's interesting, his reaction to it. He said he felt this overwhelming sense of sorrow because he understood all that he was going to lose, and he understood all the pressure that he would now be under.

DR: Did Sherman ever think that maybe Garfield really wanted it?

CM: He didn't. Garfield said, "Make sure Sherman knows that I don't want this and that my vote is going to go to him." But Sherman at some point said, "It's okay, he should have it. He should be the nominee."

DR: Sherman is the brother of the famous Civil War general who went through Georgia, and he's also the author of the Sherman Antitrust Act, which for lawyers is a big deal. So Sherman is pacified. He's not going to be the nominee of the party. Garfield gets elected. Between the election in November and inauguration in March, he puts together a distinguished cabinet?

CM: It's a pretty distinguished cabinet. The only problem is Roscoe Conkling, whom I was talking about earlier. Conkling is furious that Grant didn't win, and he's apoplectic at the thought that he can't control Garfield. So he thinks, "What I need to do is start picking off Garfield's nominees." When Garfield would announce that he's going to nominate somebody to his cabinet, Conkling would make them come to his apartment, which was nicknamed the Morgue, and threaten them, scare them. Then they would sell Garfield out. Garfield had already had his vice president forced on him. There was a division in the Republican Party between the "stalwarts" and the "half-breeds." The stalwarts were all for controlling the government and the half-breeds were for reform.

Conkling had this man named Chester Arthur, who was kind of his puppet. Arthur was one of these guys who liked the good life. He liked to show up for work around noon, he liked fine wine, he liked nice dinner parties. He moved his birth date back a year so he'd appear more youthful. And the only job he ever had was as the collector of the New York Customs House, which Conkling had given him through Grant. The party says to Garfield, "We need Conkling's power to help us get you elected, so you have to take Chester Arthur. He has to be your vice president."

DR: Chester Arthur's elected vice president. Garfield comes to Washington. He's married and has children?

CM: Garfield is married to Lucretia. Yes, he has children. He's lost a couple to illness, sadly.

DR: He comes to Washington, is sworn in. What does he want to do right away? Does he have reforms he wants to do?

CM: He has a lot of things that he had planned. Again, he's been forced into this position, but he thinks, "If I have to do it, then I'm going to use it for good." Again, education is important to him, and foreign issues are important, and equality for Black citizens.

DR: Let's go to what happens at the assassination attempt. Can you explain who the assailant is and why he thinks he's owed a job and why Garfield didn't want to give him the job?

CM: Charles Guiteau was Garfield's opposite in every way. He had had a difficult childhood, and he had thrown himself into every opportunity he could, but would fail at every opportunity. He was a failed lawyer. He was a failed journalist. He had joined a free-love commune and he had failed even there. The women nicknamed him Charles Get-out.

But he believed that he was meant for greatness. One night, just before the presidential election, he's on a steamship on Long Island Sound. He's on the deck thinking about what great things he's going to do in his life. The steamship crashes into another steamship and dozens of people die. Guiteau is saved, but he believes that it's not just accidental, that God has chosen to save him for a great purpose. So when Garfield gets the nomination, Guiteau thinks, "I'm going to personally make sure that

Garfield is elected president. And then, to thank me, he's going to make me the ambassador to France."

DR: What does Guiteau do for Garfield? Does he make speeches for him?

CM: He wrote a speech that was originally called "Grant versus Hancock" because he thought Grant was going to be the nominee. Then he just crossed out "Grant" and wrote "Garfield versus Hancock." He begged them and begged them during the campaign to let him give a speech. They finally say, "Okay, go ahead." He goes onstage and mumbles through a little bit and then runs off. But then, when Garfield is elected, Guiteau said to the secretary of state, "You're welcome. Now make me ambassador to France."

DR: What did the secretary of state say?

CM:. "No, absolutely not." But Guiteau doesn't give up. He keeps going to the secretary of state's office. He keeps going to the White House. You have to remember this is the height of the spoils system. Garfield, the president of the United States, is expected to meet with office seekers personally, people who want things like "Can you put me in charge of this post office?" every day from 9:30 a.m. to 1:30 p.m. Guiteau is all for the spoils system and he thinks, "I asked first, so I'm first in line. If I just don't give up, if I just keep going every day, I'm going to wear them down." He's clutching the speech that he wrote, to prove that he made Garfield president.

DR: Did he ever meet with Garfield himself?

CM: He did. This is 16 years after Lincoln's been assassinated and there's still no protection for the president of the United States. Garfield has an aging police officer and his 23-year-old personal secretary. One day Guiteau just walks into the president's office while Garfield is in there.

DR: He just walks in?

CM: He just walks in and hands him his speech. Garfield says, "Okay, thank you. I'll consider it." But then Guiteau starts to stalk the president.

DR: He thinks about maybe killing him, or he's just stalking him to put pressure on to get the job?

CM: He's frustrated. Finally the secretary of state tells him, "You need to stop. This is not going to happen." Guiteau goes home—he's living in a boardinghouse—and he has what he believes is a divine inspiration that God wants him to kill the president. He says, "It's nothing personal. It's just what God wants to happen."

He sits outside the White House on a bench for days, waiting for the president to come out. He follows him to church, where he thinks about killing him. One night he is sitting across from the White House and Garfield walks out. Garfield, again, has no protection at all. He walks down the street to his secretary of state's house and then the two men walk through the streets of Washington. Guiteau is following them the entire way holding a loaded gun.

DR: Where did he get a gun?

CM: He had a family friend that he went to and asked, because he has no money. He's moving from boardinghouse to boardinghouse, when rent is due. He never pays his bill. He sometimes works as a bill collector, and he just keeps whatever he manages to collect. He has no money, and he's becoming more and more obsessed, more and more desperate and deranged. He goes to this family friend, he gets some money, and he buys a gun. He's never shot a gun, and he goes to the banks of the Potomac to practice.

DR: Did he actually pay for the gun with money or did he say, "I will pay you when I get some money"?

CM: He paid with money that he had borrowed from this family friend.

DR: He has a gun. He decides he's going to kill Garfield. It's announced publicly that Garfield is going to be taking a train ride somewhere?

CM: That's right. Lucretia, his wife, had been very sick. She nearly died. She had gone to New Jersey to recuperate. He's going to go meet her, and then they're going to go to a reunion at Williams.

DR: One of the train stations in Washington was where the Mall and the National Archives are now. Guiteau goes there to wait for Garfield to show up?

CM: That's right. It was the Baltimore and Potomac train station and it was just a disaster. The tracks ran along the Mall, and trains would regularly skip the tracks and kill people on the Mall. In fact, Theodore Roosevelt in the end razes the train station. But it's there at this time in 1881. Garfield goes with his secretary of state in a carriage, and he steps inside the station where Guiteau is waiting.

DR: Guiteau sees him. Does he shoot him once or twice?

CM: He shoots him and hits him in the arm, and then he shoots him a second time in the back.

DR: Do people rush to Garfield's defense? Do they try to get the assassin?

CM: It's just chaos, as you might imagine. People are screaming. Garfield has fallen. They grab Guiteau right away. They capture him immediately.

DR: Also present at the time of the shooting is Robert Todd Lincoln?

CM: That's right. Lincoln's son was there. He was Garfield's secretary of the interior, and he was going to be traveling with him. I always say that if you were a president around that time, you would send Robert Todd Lincoln to China or somewhere far away, because he was with his father when he died, he was with Garfield when Garfield was shot, and then he ended up being with McKinley when McKinley was shot 20 years later.

DR: Garfield is shot. Is there a doctor right there who says, "I can take care of you"?

CM: Robert Todd Lincoln sends for one of the doctors who had been at his father's deathbed, Dr. Doctor Willard Bliss. His first name was Doctor. His parents had named him Doctor. He was sort of a controversial character. He had sold something called cundurango, which was supposed to cure cancer and syphilis and anything that ailed you. He had gotten in trouble for taking bribes. He had been in prison for a brief amount of time.

But Robert Todd Lincoln knew him and trusted him, and he calls for him and Bliss comes to the train station.

Several doctors descend on Garfield. He is on the floor of this train station—you can't imagine a more germ-infested environment—with these two bullet holes in him. They immediately start probing the wound with unsterilized, unwashed hands and instruments on the floor of the train station. They finally get a horsehair-and-hay mattress and take him upstairs, but continue probing for the bullet.

DR: Do they finally take him to a hospital?

CM: No. At that time, the last place you'd want to go would be a hospital, for they were not sanitary. They ended up taking him back to the White House.

DR: He goes back to the White House. Garfield has his own personal doctors, I assume. Did they rush to help or what happens?

CM: They do. Garfield has his own doctor and Lucretia has a doctor too, a woman, which is very rare at that time. Susan Edson. They used to call her Mrs. Dr. Susan Edson. They didn't know what to do with a female doctor. She is there as well. But Bliss immediately takes over and he pushes everybody out. He says, "This is my patient." He saw in this horrible national tragedy an opportunity for personal fame and power.

DR: By now the bleeding has presumably stopped, but how seriously is Garfield injured? The shot in the arm is not a fatal shot. The shot that goes into his back, how bad was that?

CM: It's this incredible stroke of luck, actually. The bullet goes through his back but it doesn't hit any vital organs and it doesn't hit his spinal cord. It goes in on the right and then to the left, and it's behind his pancreas. The problem is they won't stop probing the wound for the bullet. Today he would have spent, at most, a night in the hospital.

DR: The bullet goes in through the right side initially and then it winds up on the left side?

CM: Correct.

DR: How do they probe? They put a finger in and just kind of look for the bullet?

CM: They do. They put fingers in. They also have these instruments, these long metal sticks that they use. No anesthesia, no painkillers for him, nothing.

DR: They can't find the bullet?

CM: They can't find it.

DR: They can't find the bullet, but how is Garfield kept alive? Is he in a lot of pain? What happens?

CM: He's in extraordinary amounts of pain. Bliss decides that he should give his gunshot victim rich foods and alcohol, and continue to probe for the bullet. He refuses to use what to him is this brand-new, untested, and unsafe method of sterilization.

Joseph Lister, who had been a renowned surgeon in England, had discovered antisepsis 16 years earlier. He had come to the United States. He had gone around the world, explaining the importance of it and warning doctors that if they didn't sterilize their hands and instruments, they were risking killing their patients.

DR: Dr. Lister and Listerine.

CM: That's right. But Bliss doesn't want any part of that.

DR: Let's talk about another person who shows up. Alexander Graham Bell, better known for inventing the telephone, has an idea.

CM: Bell is only 34 years old at this point. He had invented the telephone just five years earlier, and it had made him famous, and it gained him a little bit of money. He has all these ideas, all these things he wants to work on. But when he finds out that Garfield has been shot, he drops everything he's working on, and he works night and day to develop something called the induction balance. This is before the invention of the medical X-ray. Basically it's the first metal detector. It's a metal detector connected to a telephone receiver.

DR: His idea is, "I can come over and put the metal detector on the body of Garfield and figure out where the bullet is, because I'll detect where the metal is." Is that right?

CM: That's right.

DR: Is the machine ready to go, or does he have to perfect it before he takes it?

CM: He's perfecting it. He's very much aware the world is watching while he's trying to perfect it. He's testing it. He's getting big chunks of meat and shooting into them and then trying to make sure he can find the bullets in the meat. He goes to a home for Civil War veterans and tries it out on them, and it absolutely works. He tells the White House, "I'm ready." They have him come over, but two things happen.

One, they have Garfield on something that's very rare at that time, which was a mattress with metal springs in it, which obviously is going to interfere with the metal detector. But also Bliss had publicly stated that the bullet was on the right side of the president's body, and he doesn't want anything to show that he's wrong. So he will only let Bell test the right side.

DR: It's very hot in Washington at the time. How do they air-condition the situation so Garfield is not sweating to death?

CM: A lot of people proposed ideas. People are writing to them from everywhere, wanting to donate things. They're worried. Finally the Navy hooks up the very first air-conditioning system in the White House to cool it—because it's July in Washington, D.C.—to try to alleviate some of his suffering.

DR: What about his diet? What is he able to eat in this environment?

CM: He's able to eat very little. He was this big, handsome guy. He's 49 years old, and he loses 50 pounds. He has enemas, which is why he can't keep anything down.

DR: Graham Bell comes and he's told he can only look at the president's right side. What happens?

CM: He thinks it doesn't work and he's very discouraged. Bliss just has him go. At first everyone thinks Garfield's going to die. Then he survives. Months are going by, and he seems to be getting better. Then he takes a terrible turn, because he's just riddled with infection. And at some point Garfield says, "I know I'm going to die."

DR: No other doctor comes in or is allowed to do anything. What does Mrs. Garfield say? Is she relying on this Dr. Bliss?

CM: She is. I think like many people, even today, when somebody you love is sick, you're terrified and you're trusting the people who are in charge. She put her trust in him.

DR: Garfield's in bed. Who's running the country? Chester Arthur or Mrs. Garfield or who?

CM: Everyone expects Chester Arthur to just jump on this. People are coming from Ohio to try to prevent him from taking over the presidency. But he surprises everyone and stays in New York. He refuses even to go to Washington. He doesn't want it to look like he's waiting in the wings for Garfield to die. He's grief-stricken by what's happened to Garfield, and he cuts ties with Conkling and refuses to go to Washington. So he's not running anything. It's Garfield's poor 23-year-old personal secretary who's trying to keep things going while Garfield's so sick.

DR: Do members of Congress go to visit him and say, "What do you want us to do? We want some direction"?

CM: Bliss won't let anybody see him. He's completely isolated him in the White House. Occasionally he'll let his wife come, but no one else is allowed to see the president.

DR: What is the press saying?

CM: They're writing a million articles. That was really central to my research about it. Bliss is issuing bulletins that they put up on giant boards in New York and other places, and news is going out by telegraph, so there are many, many articles. People didn't really understand. At first they thought he was going to die. Then Garfield seems to be getting better, and now he's getting worse. People are starting to ask questions about Bliss, but it's too late at that point.

DR: Does Alexander Graham Bell get a chance to come back with his machine and look a second time?

CM: He doesn't, no.

DR: He's not invited back? The machine will actually work, but it wasn't allowed to be used on the correct side.

CM: It does work. And then they use it in the Boer War and the Russo-Japanese War.

DR: How many months are we now talking about? Garfield has been in this bed for a month or two months?

CM: He's shot on July 2nd and he lives until mid-September—September 19th.

DR: He wants to go to see the water. How do they arrange for him to go to see the ocean, and why does he want to go?

CM: Even though he grew up in Ohio, he had worked on the Erie Canal, and he loved the water, he loved the ocean. He says, "I know I'm going to die. I want to see the ocean." There's a wealthy man, who's actually British, who has a home in New Jersey, and he offers his home. So they take a train car and they gut it. They take all the chairs out, and they put in a false ceiling to help keep it cool. They try to cushion it for Garfield, and they put his bed in it.

People in this town where he's going work night and day to build the train tracks up this hill to where this house is. When the train gets there, though, it can't go the last distance to the house. So all these people who have been waiting go and physically lift the train to take it to the house.

DR: How does Garfield get out of the White House? He's in a stretcher and they take him downstairs, and take him by horse to the train station?

CM: That's right. They get him into the train station and then they lift him.

DR: Does his wife go with him?

CM: Yes.

DR: Finally he gets to the New Jersey shore. How long does he live while he's there?

CM: He's alive for just a few more days.

DR: He dies and everybody is shocked and saddened by this, I assume?

CM: At this point, they're not shocked. He ended up having an aneurysm of the spleen and heart.

DR: An autopsy is done, and what does the autopsy show?

CM: The autopsy showed that he had septic shock and septicemia.

DR: And where was the bullet?

CM: The bullet was on the left side.

DR: So the doctor was wrong?

CM: The doctor was wrong. And when the autopsy report is sent out and made public, the American people realize right away that their president didn't have to die, and they understand why he did, and Bliss is publicly disgraced.

DR: But he asked to be paid for his services, right?

CM: He did. He hands Congress a bill for $25,000, which is about half a million dollars in today's money. They are, as you can imagine, outraged.

DR: Is he paid anything?

CM: They pay him $6,000, just to get rid of him.

DR: Does he lose his medical license?

CM: He doesn't, but he loses his practice. He's publicly disgraced. He says he lost his health at the same time. His life is never the same.

DR: What happened to the assassin?

CM: Charles Guiteau is put on trial. He had one of the first insanity defenses. Because Garfield was president for such a short time, we forget. People at that time knew this would be an additional tragedy—that Garfield would be forgotten. But at the time, it was a horrible national tragedy, and the American people were devastated and enraged, and they were determined to see Guiteau hanged. They do have this trial, and he is found guilty and sentenced to death.

DR: Does he represent himself in the trial?

CM: He had a sister who basically raised him and loved him very much. She had known that he was ill and that he needed help. But at that time, you could just leave and nobody could find you. They would try to get him help and then he would leave. Her husband was a lawyer, but he was just a tax attorney. However, he's the only one in the country willing to represent Guiteau. So he takes it on, but Guiteau keeps shouting things during the trial and belittling him, so it doesn't go well.

DR: Guiteau is found guilty?

CM: He's found guilty.

DR: Does he have any last wishes? How long does it take before they sentence him to death?

CM: It's just a matter of about a month. He makes an unusual request of his executioner. He's written this poem called "Going to the Lordy," and he wants to deliver this poem on the gallows. At first he asked to do it in his underwear, for some reason. And they say, "You can't do in your underwear, but you can recite this poem." And he says, "I'm going to recite the poem and when I'm done, I'm going to drop it, and that's when you can hang me."

DR: Is that what they do?

CM: And that's what they do.

DR: That occurs how long after Garfield dies?

CM: Not long after.

DR: So this is the story of how the doctor in charge really didn't do a very good job. Had he done a better job, presumably they could have found the bullet. Do people think today they could have saved Garfield?

CM: Absolutely. I don't think there's any question. In fact, the man who captured Guiteau after he shot Garfield had a bullet in his brain from the Civil War and was doing fine. And the bullet that hit Garfield was behind his pancreas; it wasn't going to do any more damage if they had just left him alone. His injuries were far less severe than Reagan's when Reagan was shot. If they'd just left him alone, he almost certainly would have survived.

7

A. SCOTT BERG
on Woodrow Wilson

(1856-1924; president from 1913 to 1921)

Many presidents' reputations improve as scholars review their administrations with time—the emotions and politics of an era having passed—and with access to more documents than were originally available, as with Ulysses S. Grant, Harry Truman, and possibly Jimmy Carter. The reputation of one president, however, has declined considerably in recent years from the lofty status he once enjoyed. Woodrow Wilson was seen as a godlike figure when entering Paris to negotiate the end of the Great War. He was viewed as the leader who had helped ensure victory in the war. That he failed to get his beloved League of Nations approved by the Senate was seen, at the time, as a political act by the Republicans who had been beaten by Wilson in the two most recent presidential elections (after they had won the four prior elections).

But recently, historians and scholars have learned more about Wilson. The stroke he suffered in 1919 left him so incapacitated that he really could not make informed or intelligent decisions, allowing his wife, Edith, to effectively become president of the United States for 18 months. Neither the public nor other government officials, in Congress or the administration, were told about the seriousness of the stroke (though some members of Congress and cabinet members did see him).

Further, while not hidden from public view during his presidency, Wilson restored the racial segregation of the federal workforce and also essentially allowed the reimposition of Jim Crow laws.

As a result of this second look at Wilson, he is no longer an icon of the Democratic Party; the Woodrow Wilson School at Princeton no longer carries the Wilson name (even though he was also a president of Princeton); and Wilson College at Princeton has also been renamed.

Given this new context, it's worth revisiting Wilson's time in office, especially since he was a consequential president. An accomplished biographer, A. Scott Berg, thought so, and spent ten years researching and writing *Wilson*, perhaps the most definitive biography of our 28th president. I interviewed Scott Berg about this book at a Congressional Dialogues session at the Library of Congress on April 3, 2014, which was before some of the reassessment of Wilson.

✳   ✳   ✳   ✳

DAVID M. RUBENSTEIN (DR): About a hundred years ago Woodrow Wilson came onto the scene. He got elected from a place where he didn't grow up. He was an academic. He got elected to his first statewide office the first time he ran. And as soon as he got elected, he ran for president and he won the first time. He served two terms, winning the second one more narrowly than the first. He was a great speechmaker and he loved to play golf. Do you think that could ever happen again?

A. SCOTT BERG (ASB): I'm not sure it can happen yet again.

DR: Let's talk about one of the most significant parts of his presidency. He was trying to get the treaty for the League of Nations approved by Congress, and to do that he went on a kind of whistle-stop tour out west, but then he had a health problem. What happened?

ASB: I think this is the most quixotic journey a United States president has ever taken. Wilson came back from Paris, where he had been for six months. Now, imagine the president of the United States left the country for a half year because he felt that the negotiation of this treaty was so important. He felt it was going to change the future of the world.

He came back and he found an increasingly hostile Republican Congress, and in that moment he began to realize he was not going to get the treaty passed. Presidents can negotiate all they want in a treaty, but the Senate must ratify it. Wilson realized that Henry Cabot Lodge, who was the chair of the Foreign Relations Committee in the Senate, was not about to pass this thing. So Wilson decided, "I will take my case to the people."

He put together a 29-city tour. He was in very fragile health, more fragile than his doctor had let him know.

But Wilson embarked, in the late summer of 1919, and went around the country. Halfway through, he was winning the hearts and minds of America. I should add here that President Wilson was the last president to write all his own speeches. Wilson could speak for an hour—without notes, without a grammatical error, without a paragraph out of place; and he was winning this country over, when, suddenly, he exhibited the first signs of a stroke. The doctor said, "This tour is over. We're taking the train directly back to Washington."

Wilson was able to walk, think, do everything. He got home three days later. Then he suffered a paralyzing stroke. And for the next year and a half, virtually nobody saw the president of the United States.

As a result of the stroke, his wife, Edith Bolling Galt Wilson, was told by the doctors that any stress would kill him. When she asked what could be done, one of the doctors said, "Well, perhaps you could run the day-to-day operations around here. You've been included on everything." For all intents and purposes other than making policy decisions, Edith Bolling Galt Wilson—remember her name—became the first female president of the United States.

DR: It has been called the "petticoat presidency."

ASB: It was the "petticoat presidency" behind everyone's backs. Nobody really knew what was going on. It was kept a secret, as you could do a hundred years ago. And it was quite spectacular.

Wilson could still speak and think, but he was paralyzed on one side. He had, as we now know often attends strokes, wild mood swings. Sometimes he'd be petulant, even more than he had been as president, sometimes kind of exuberant with emotion. He was all over the map, and it was Mrs. Wilson who, day-to-day, ran the operations. Nobody saw this man.

The League fight is still going on, which Wilson is losing, and the Republicans think, "Now is the time to come in for the kill. We insist on seeing the president. We are going to send a committee over to see him." When they asked to send somebody, he agreed.

Wilson staged the visit. He had the lights brought up very bright in his bedroom. He buried his left side under blankets and quilts. He planted some props on his good side so that he could demonstrate dexterity. And in came this little committee—just two senators. One of them, one of his rivals, said, "Mr. President, it's so good to see you. I just want you to know we've all been praying for your health." And Wilson said, "Which way, Senator?"

The meeting was over. Clearly he had his wit and his wits.

"And by the way," he said, "Senator, what's going on with that deal you have in Mexico?" which nobody was supposed to know about. Something under the table. This senator could not get out of there fast enough. He went down and told the press, "The president is doing very well. His mind is shipshape."

DR: Wilson has two strokes. In Pueblo, Colorado, he has the first stroke, and doctors say, "We've got to take him home." When he returns to D.C., he has another stroke that affects the left side of his body. From the time that he got back to the White House, he never again really recovered his health?

ASB: He never fully recovered. The last stop on the tour, before he really crumbled, was in Pueblo. It's one of the most moving scenes in the life of a president, in which maybe the greatest orator we've ever had in the White House—certainly the greatest orator of his day—is giving his umpteenth speech, and each one is a little different. In Pueblo, for the first time he starts to drop words and the thread of his talk. He's stumbling. Something is clearly going on. The Secret Service guard is standing right there, ready to run in and catch him. It's right after that that they get him on the train, and that night he has a throbbing headache. That's when the doctor comes in and says, "The tour is over."

So that was the first sign. This is an interesting thing about presidential incapacity and how we elect our presidents and what we know about them. This I got from going through his doctor's records, some of which have just been made public and can be found in Staunton, Virginia, at the Woodrow Wilson Presidential Library. And you will see in these papers, as I did, that Woodrow Wilson was suffering minor cerebral incidents as far back as the 1890s, when he was a college professor at Princeton. So there was this long, gradual progression. If we had known the status of Woodrow Wilson's health when he ran for public office—and certainly in today's world—he never would have been elected.

DR: He was in his second term when this happened. But for a while, he was so delusional that he thought he could get elected to a third term. How could he think that?

ASB: Exactly. How could he think that? One of the things that often accompanies strokes is a kind of euphoric thinking. Wilson was all over the place in his thought patterns. Mostly bedridden, he had been removed from the news, because Edith and his doctors kept that from him. After his second term, he retired to a house on S Street in Washington, where there's a wonderful museum now.

A condition called anosognosia often accompanies right-brain strokes, by which the patient is so sick he doesn't realize it—sometimes becoming delusional. In retirement, and, indeed, in the final days in the White House, he makes lists of his third cabinet and decides, "Yes, they're going to need me. When the Democrats convene in 1920 to nominate the president, there's going to be a stalemate and there's going to be a great hue and cry, there's going to be a demand for Wilson to come back." He was, in many ways, out of his mind.

DR: Woodrow Wilson's first wife, Ellen, was the love of his life. He met her in the South?

ASB: Woodrow Wilson met his first wife when he was practicing law in Atlanta, which he did briefly. He was in Atlanta for about a year and a half, when it dawned on him that he wasn't very good at it. It dawned on him mostly because he had no clients. None.

I exaggerate. He had one client. His mother got him a client . . . and the client was his mother. She hired him to do some legal work in a little town called Rome, Georgia.

While he was working in Rome, this very straitlaced Presbyterian minister's son met the local Presbyterian minister's daughter. I don't have to tell you what's going to happen to two Presbyterian ministers' children when they meet. Indeed, they instantly fell in love with each other. Wilson was dying to marry her, but he realized he still didn't have a sustainable career that he cared about. So, he went to graduate school because he wanted to have a life in academia. Once he got his first job, which was teaching at Bryn Mawr College, he finally had enough money to marry. (He ultimately went from Bryn Mawr to Wesleyan and then finally to Princeton, where he became president of the university.) And he married Ellen Axson from Georgia. They had, for the most part, a rather idyllic marriage. Wilson got elected president in 1912. They moved into the White House, and they were there a year and a half when Ellen Wilson, the love of his life, suddenly died of what we call Bright's disease.

DR: Kidney disease?

ASB: It's nephritis, basically. Woodrow Wilson was despondent. He could barely get out of bed. He literally thought about giving up the presidency. He didn't know how he could go on. And they were all but pulling him out of bed each day.

The very week that Ellen Wilson died, a war broke out in Europe, which we now call World War I. And everyone is knocking on the door, saying, "Mr. President, we've got to do something here. You've got to attend to this." Being a man of great duty, he did.

DR: You're saying that by presidential marriage standards, it was a pretty good marriage?

ASB: It was an excellent marriage. There was a reputed love affair in his early days as a college professor, which I parse in the book. I lay out all the facts for each side and that it was most likely not a physical love affair, but an emotional one.

DR: As president, one of Wilson's closest advisors was a doctor, Dr. Grayson. Dr. Grayson met a young woman, and he decided to marry this young woman, and then his wife-to-be introduced Wilson to a woman named Mrs. Galt, who was a widow. And she became the second Mrs. Wilson?

ASB: She did, indeed. Longtime citizens of Washington will remember Galt and Bro. Jewelers, which was started by her first husband's family in 1802. Wilson was 16 years older than Edith Bolling Galt. Edith was a direct descendant of Pocahontas, so she liked to say she was the "most American" First Lady we ever had. And it's hard to deny that.

Her first husband was older and died, leaving her a somewhat reclusive but attractive young widow, who wanted nothing to do with the government or anybody who worked for it.

But then she was introduced to Wilson. It was kind of a meet-cute in a 1930s movie—a real setup by Wilson's doctor, Cary Grayson. They did meet and Wilson fell in love at first sight—for the second time. He spent the next year courting her through letters. If you can picture Woodrow Wilson, it may be hard for you to imagine what I'm about to tell you—but this man wrote some of the most passionate, romantic love letters I have ever read in my life. I'm not forgetting the Brownings, the Adamses, anybody you can come up with. These Wilson letters will just knock your socks off.

DR: With his first wife, he did not get her deeply involved in public affairs.

ASB: Not at all—though she did become the first activist First Lady, who went to Congress to lobby for funds to clean up the slums in D.C.

DR: But with his second wife, all of a sudden he's teaching her everything about what he's doing. Why?

ASB: Wilson would tell you the answer is "providence," as he felt providence was the answer to everything. But it's curious that they get married at the end of 1915, when the Great War was raging. We were not yet in the war, but there was a lot of activity that involved America and what our role might be during the war.

Wilson brought his wife up to speed on everything. He had Mrs. Wilson decoding secret messages being sent from Europe. He had her listening to every important speech that he was going to give and parsing it. He would often take her to meetings with cabinet members. It's almost as though he knew that something was going on with his body and something might happen and she would have to know everything that was going on.

The more realistic answer is simply that he was so in love with this woman, so grateful that she married him. He had to talk her into marrying him. As I said, she was rather shy, removed from government, unschooled not just in politics but really in anything. And here was our only PhD president, a college professor, who had written a dozen books on the workings of the government. He knew all this stuff, and he educated her in many ways, just so he could have her by his side at all times. You think the Reagans were close? Read about the Wilsons.

DR: Let's go back to the subject that he was trying to address at the time of the stroke. At the peace agreement at the end of World War I, most important to him was to have a League of Nations. First, where did he get this idea for a League of Nations? And second, had he not had his stroke, do you think he could have persuaded Congress to approve it?

ASB: Let me start with the second first. I don't do crystal-ball history, so I can't tell you what could have happened. I will tell you what did happen. Wilson had an international vision from the moment he hit the White House, and he had a definite point of view about what role the United States should play in the modern world. And it was becoming a modern world.

This is just a small thing, but it will set the table for what happened in Paris. When Wilson came into office, the Panama Canal had just been completed—Teddy Roosevelt's great canal. He had stolen the isthmus and built the canal. There was, in its treaty, a stipulation that said the United States would be exempt from certain tolls from certain boats going through the Panama Canal—because we built the canal.

One of Wilson's first actions as president was to say, "We've got to get rid of this exemption." The Republicans couldn't believe it. Teddy Roosevelt thought, "This is just the end." Even Wilson's party members thought, "Why? This is a mistake. We are America. We are exceptional, and we built this thing."

Wilson's point was he believed in a different form of American exceptionalism. He believed we were an exceptional nation, but that exceptions should not be made for the United States. Why shouldn't we pay the same toll that every other country does? He muscled this change through the Congress. I take that back: he reasoned it through the Congress, because he had a real gift for talking to the legislature. Wilson, perhaps because of all he had written about Congress and just because of who he was, had this funny notion about American government. He believed the executive branch and the legislative branch—get ready, wait for it—should cooperate.

I mean this quite literally. He believed these two branches should co-operate the government. That's why Wilson, in his time in the presidency, called an extraordinary 25 joint sessions of Congress. Because he wanted to have a conversation with the Congress—really a conversation with the country, but through the Congress.

Wilson would not only show up for a joint session, he would show up the next day and go to the President's Room—a room you still have to find a janitor to open for you. It has become such an obscure room, at least obscure from what its real purpose was. It was for the president to come and talk to the legislators. And it's beautiful. It may be the most beautiful room in the Capitol.

The League was always on his mind. He got to the League because he had this international vision. One of the reasons he led the United States into the war was he thought he could help dictate the peace. That's why he sacrificed 100,000 American lives. I was going to say it was quixotic, but this is more like King Arthur believing that there should be a round table where everyone is equal, where every nation of the peaceful world could gather. And they would agree to a collective security, that there would be an army of a kind, that if you attacked any one of our members, we'd all go after you, and it would be such a formidable force that no country would go to war.

DR: Why would Henry Cabot Lodge and others be against that?

ASB: Who could be against that? There were a lot of people who were, like Teddy Roosevelt, a little more bellicose than others, who believed that war is sometimes a most effective solution.

Those six months while Wilson was away in Paris, the Republicans were having secret meetings at night, and they finally decided, "Whatever Wilson brings back from Paris, we don't care what's in that treaty. Whatever it is, we're against it. Wilson and the Democrats won the war. We're going to win the peace. We will come up with our own peace plan, our own treaty, whatever it takes." That was a large reason that Henry Cabot Lodge was against it. Pure politics.

DR: To go back to Wilson's earlier career, he was the governor of New Jersey and president of Princeton, but he was not from New Jersey or the Northeast. He was from the South. How did he migrate up to New Jersey, and how did his upbringing in the South, where he apparently at one point met Robert E. Lee, affect his views?

ASB: In so many ways. He was born in Staunton, Virginia. He was raised in Augusta, Georgia; Columbia, South Carolina; and Wilmington, North Carolina. He went to Davidson College for a year, where he didn't do very well. He was a little too young, a little too immature. He came home, where his Presbyterian minister of a father met one of the great Presbyterian ministers in this country, James McCosh, who was president of Princeton. President McCosh was touring the South, where he met Reverend Wilson and his son, young Tommy Wilson as he was known, and he said, "The boy'll be coming to Princeton, no doubt." And indeed, Wilson went north to go to Princeton, which was a great bastion of Presbyterianism.

DR: He goes to Princeton. He's an okay student.

ASB: Better than okay.

DR: He comes back to Princeton as a professor. He writes a lot. Then, all of a sudden, he's elected president of the university?

ASB: He is elected president of Princeton in 1902. And he put his hand in everything. Princeton had been sliding into a long period of mediocrity, and the trustees decided, "We need some fresh blood. We need Wilson." Practically overnight, he not only reformed Princeton education, he reformed college education in this country.

If you went to a college in which you majored in something, in which you had perhaps two lectures and a small class a week, in which you had core education requirements, and maybe some electives on top of that, maybe an honor code as well, you studied under the Wilson model. Those were all elements Woodrow Wilson introduced at Princeton. They became so successful they mushroomed everywhere.

DR: He was very popular as president of Princeton. He got a lot of attention. He was lecturing all over the country. But then there was a dispute over the future of the graduate school, and ultimately it led to his feeling disaffected and not being upset to leave Princeton?

ASB: That is correct. After Wilson had taken on the educational model, he wanted to go after the social model. He felt, correctly, that Princeton was this playground for the sons of the very rich. This is where the sons of J. P. Morgan and so forth went to school. Wilson didn't like this. He remembered being a poor Presbyterian minister's son when he went to Princeton. He wanted to get rid of the rich-playground mindset.

There were a couple of social structures, one of which had to do with the location of the graduate college, which really was about something bigger than that. It was about what graduate education meant in this country. Wilson lost that and another big social battle, and the trustees were about to fire him, in fact.

DR: He all of a sudden got the attention of some political person, and they said, "We're going to nominate you to be governor of New Jersey."

ASB: He got the attention of a man named "Sugar Jim" Smith. Beware of anyone named Sugar Jim. I don't care if it's politics, business, whatever. In any case, Sugar Jim was, to be kind about it, maybe the most corrupt political boss in America. Sugar Jim was so corrupt he realized how corrupt he was. So he thought, "What I really need is a puppet. Who is the squeaky-cleanest guy in the state of New Jersey? What about Professor Wilson at Princeton, who's writing all these speeches and books about education? He's a professor, so we know we can push him around."

So Sugar Jim says, "Would you like to run for governor? I can pretty much assure you're going to win this election."

Wilson won in a landslide. After being handpicked by possibly the most corrupt machine to be its puppet, Wilson's first action as governor of New Jersey in 1911 was to kick out the machine. He literally barred the machine from entering government buildings. Now everybody in the country is looking to New Jersey, saying, "Who is this man that broke this machine?" And the Democratic Party is saying, "We have an election in about a year and a half. Maybe we have somebody of presidential timber here."

DR: The governorship then was a two-year term?

ASB: It was a four-year term. He served only two of his four years, and in that time introduced the most progressive legislation of any state in the country.

DR: So in those days you didn't go out and campaign for the nomination. You had people do it for you, and you didn't physically campaign. But he was not against being the presidential nominee of the party in 1912?

ASB: Correct.

DR: How did he get the nomination?

ASB: It was a little more like the parliamentary system, which he rather loved. He didn't run for office, he would stand for office. "If everyone insists I become president, well, what can I do?"

He did travel around and gave some speeches. He was in some primaries, which were not the way primaries work today. But he made himself quite visible and made it known he was available.

DR: So they go to 46 ballots at the Democratic Convention.

ASB: Forty-six ballots. And by the 46th he was helped enormously by the man who was the face of the Democratic Party then, a man maligned by history, a three-time loser for the White House named William Jennings Bryan, from Nebraska. Bryan threw all his weight behind Wilson, because he felt Wilson was the purest progressive of all the Democrats.

DR: So in 1912 Wilson is the Democratic nominee. He's running against one person who is president of the United States, William Howard Taft, and one person who was president, Teddy Roosevelt. How did he beat those two people?

ASB: It's one of the glorious elections in American history. You've got this starchy college professor, Woodrow Wilson, running against William Howard Taft, a really decent man, the Republican incumbent, who didn't want to be president, and had taken the Republican Party further to the right than his predecessor, Theodore Roosevelt.

Theodore Roosevelt was so incensed at what Taft had done, he ran as a Bull Moose candidate, a Republican progressive, and became the greatest third-party candidate the country has ever had. He came in second. The incumbent, William Howard Taft, came in third. As if that wasn't enough, there was a fourth candidate, Eugene Debs, the great socialist. There was never a chance of Debs's winning, but he really contributed a lot to the discussion. Even people who didn't agree with Debs at least admired his sincerity.

DR: Wilson gets to be president of the United States, just two years after elected governor. What does he decide to do at the beginning of his term?

ASB: Until that time, Woodrow Wilson enjoyed arguably the most meteoric rise in American history. In October of 1910 Woodrow Wilson was the president of a small college in New Jersey. In November of 1912 he's elected president of the United States. It's just stunning. It's staggering. And you think he didn't have political elbows, you know? He came in and showed the country how it could be done.

A lot of it was by stagecraft, the way he chose to do things. But when he came in, the first thing on his mind was the economy. We had suffered economically. In 1907 there had been a crippling panic, and what freaked

Wilson out the most was that J. P. Morgan almost single-handedly had bailed out the United States. This was just unbelievable to Wilson, that a man could bail out a country.

So the first thing Wilson did was a major reform of the tariff system, which he felt had been benefiting big business and was hurting lower- and middle-class Americans. It was a very tough fight, but he called a joint session of Congress. In the summer of 1913 he brought Congress back into session. He said, "What I have to offer is so important you've all got to come here and stay here. We've got to do this." He showed up in the President's Room every day and got that done.

After phase one, he wanted to start something he called a Federal Reserve System. And indeed this may be his most important legacy. The Federal Reserve System, now a hundred years old, was Woodrow Wilson's second measure. He believed that wealth should not be concentrated among a few New York bankers but be spread out across the country, an archipelago of banks that would answer to the federal government, which would have some oversight.

Then he quickly moved us into the 40-hour workweek. Lots of labor laws. We got into the modern income tax—a graduated income tax to make up for the funds we weren't getting from the tariffs. He put the first Jew—Louis Brandeis—on the Supreme Court, which was a controversial shattering of a glass ceiling. There's a through-line that starts with Wilson as president of Princeton, through the governorship, and through his entire presidency: It was always about leveling the playing field.

DR: He was the first Democratic president since Grover Cleveland?

ASB: Yes.

DR: The workforce of the federal government had been integrated before him. He then segregated the workforce, upsetting part of his constituency and backsliding on racial equality in this country. That seems counter to his otherwise progressive ideals. Why would he have done that?

ASB: Woodrow Wilson was a Southerner. He was raised in the Old South. He remembered the Civil War. As a result, he grew up in a deeply segregated society. When Wilson came into office, he had another first, at the behest, largely, of two cabinet members: his postmaster general, former congressman Albert Burleson of Texas, and his secretary of the Treasury,

William Gibbs McAdoo of California, who also became his son-in-law shortly thereafter. They were both Southern racists. And I mean rather virulent racists. Most of Wilson's cabinet was from the South, and they were racist and they were pro-segregation.

Now, make no mistake about it. Woodrow Wilson appointed all these people to the cabinet. These were the people he was comfortable with, the kind of people he grew up with. Where it really began to come to a head, though, was the Treasury Department and the Post Office, the two areas in which integration was just starting to happen. And the postmaster general and the secretary of the Treasury said, "We cannot have Blacks and whites eating together, as the logical progression will be that someday perhaps a white person will have to work under a Black person, and that simply cannot be allowed."

There was already huge racial tension around the country. Yes, integration was starting, but not everywhere. There were fights breaking out in the Post Office and the Treasury Department. Wilson did not want this on his watch. He kept his door open to African Americans for six and a half of his eight years, before his stroke. He listened to all the petitioners, promised to make some inroads, to do the best he could. I don't think he did, but he promised that.

But the bigger point is, he felt the country was not ready for it. He felt that in the South, among the people he grew up with, there were still Civil War veterans alive and well, and he said, "There's just no way this country will allow it."

DR: So he tolerated the resegregation?

ASB: He tolerated it, though he never encouraged it. But he did allow it. He did not stop it. He must own it.

DR: We talked about the women's suffrage movement. Under his administration, the Nineteenth Amendment, which allowed women to vote, was approved. But he wasn't really a supporter of it initially?

ASB: Initially, he was not a supporter of the amendment. Wilson, from the time he was in government, was for the enfranchisement of women. He did think it was a states' rights issue. Now, we know from the modern civil rights movement that "states' rights" is often code for something else. In Wilson's case, he very publicly went to New Jersey, to vote for his state to give women the right to vote. But he really did hold back when it came time to a Nineteenth Amendment—until we went to war. And then he became an active and vocal supporter.

DR: Let's get to the Great War in Europe. His position his entire first term was to keep us out of the war. In fact, he got reelected saying, "I kept us out of the war." Why did he want to stay out so much, and how did he change his mind?

ASB: He felt we should stay out of this war largely because it was primarily a European war. Up until our entry into the war, we were an isolationist country. We had armed forces, we had an army, and a navy of sorts, which numbered 100,000. Our military was the size of Portugal's. We were not ready to go to war, by any means. We had Teddy Roosevelt saying, "We've got to go to war, let's start building up a big army." A lot of jingoist talk.

Wilson was very reluctant. He didn't think it was America's place. He felt the best thing we could do was to stay out of it. He even called on Americans to remain "neutral in thought." But conditions kept changing. German militarism was not diminishing. They were torpedoing ships, most famously the *Lusitania*. American lives were being lost. Wilson tried every diplomatic measure he could think of—diplomatic notes back and forth, conferences, using anybody who might be able to reason with the other parties.

He finally realized, above all, that the Germans were not going to back down, and Wilson, a lifelong Anglophile, could finally admit, to himself anyway, that he was not neutral in thought. And then he learned of the Zimmermann Telegram—which, if you don't remember your history books, was this discovered note from Germany to Mexico, saying "Come on into the war, and we'll give you Texas and California back."

DR: Zimmermann was the German ambassador to Mexico, and we intercepted a telegram that essentially encouraged the Mexicans to attack us. So Wilson goes to Congress and says, "Let's go to war." Congress approves. We send four million soldiers over. We lose 100,000. Ultimately, there is an armistice. Why does Wilson think he needs to go to Paris—the first president to ever leave the United States and go to Europe—and negotiate the peace agreement himself?

ASB: I want to back up one step. On April 2nd, 1917, what did Woodrow Wilson do? He called a joint session of Congress, and he delivered what has to be his most important speech. It is, I believe, the most important foreign policy speech in the history of this country, because at the heart of this speech is one deathless sentence: "The world must be made safe for democracy."

Now, whether you like that sentence or not, whether you believe in it or not, doesn't matter. All American foreign policy to this day stems from that one sentence. We have become, some say, the police force of the world, some say the minister spreading democracy.

Wilson remembered the Civil War. Wilson is the only president we ever had who grew up in a country that had lost a war—the Confederate States of America. He saw the devastation to the Southern states. He saw the deprivation. He didn't want to go through that again for the country at large. He didn't want any mother ever to have to lose her son to war.

So, he kept us out. And then he got us in. And he made a contract with himself. Okay, 100,000 Americans lost their lives. He really worried about that. He thought about those men every day. And he thought—this is Wilson, some say with a Christ complex—that he was the only man on Earth who could guarantee a proper peace.

So he went to Paris, largely because he had 14 points, the fourteenth of which was a League of Nations, but also because he felt all the other countries had big agendas. They wanted Alsace-Lorraine back, or they wanted big reparations paid. Wilson went over with one item on his agenda: that there should be this roundtable where every country could come and sit. It was his vision, and he believed that only he could communicate it to the others.

DR: He goes there for six months, coming back once, only to return to Europe. He spends six months there, and ultimately an agreement is reached. He comes back home but then can't get it through the Congress. After the stroke, he is incapacitated. Things don't really work out, he loses power. What happens when he leaves the White House?

ASB: Wilson became the first president of the United States to leave the White House and remain in Washington, D.C.—at what's now the Wilson House on S Street. There, physically compromised, mentally and emotionally compromised, he's thinking about writing a book. He gets as far as one paragraph. He's not capable of doing it. He begins to lose his sight. And he just starts to fade away.

DR: He ultimately dies, at the age of 67. His wife lives in the house until 1961.

ASB: Woodrow Wilson dies in 1924. In 1961 John F. Kennedy is inaugurated as president of the United States, and outside the Capitol are the risers for the special guests. And there, in the third row, is a little old lady. Nobody had a clue who she was. She was Mrs. Woodrow Wilson. Kennedy specifically wanted her there for the inauguration.

DR: You spent 13 years of your life on this book. If you could ask one question of Woodrow Wilson, what would you want to know that you don't know as a result of 13 years of research?

ASB: The question I would ask—though I know the answer that he would give—I would shake him by the lapels and say, "Why didn't you give an inch? Why didn't you practice so much of what you preached to Congress about compromise when it is important? Why not get at least half a loaf, get your treaty, get your League of Nations?" At the very end, Republican Henry Cabot Lodge counteroffered one final version, which did not change much. But he knew Wilson would never accept it, which is why he offered it. And Wilson, of course, didn't accept it. He ended up getting nothing.

I would like to hear him articulate his feelings. His answer, I think, would be, as I suggest in the book, that he owed it to those 100,000 soldiers who didn't come home to their mothers.

8

AMITY SHLAES
on Calvin Coolidge

(1872–1933; president from 1923 to 1929)

Not all presidents sought the job of president. Not all enjoyed politics. Not all liked public attention or to talk publicly. But one seems to lead the pack in not seeking to be president, not liking politics, not talking publicly (especially about himself), and in not seeking or enjoying public acclaim: President Calvin Coolidge.

Elected as Warren Harding's vice president, Coolidge assumed office upon Harding's untimely death from a heart attack. From that point forward, Coolidge maintained a flinty, New England approach to the presidency, as he had in previous parts of his life: do not talk more than absolutely necessary, do not spend more money than you have, do not brag about yourself or your accomplishments, and do not see or promise government as the solution to all of society's ills.

The result was a low-key presidency, with a program of reducing federal indebtedness, without trying to become the most visible, important person in the world, or even the country.

This approach seemed to work for Coolidge. He finished Harding's term, ran for election on his own, won overwhelmingly, and ultimately chose not to run for another term, allowing his secretary of commerce, Herbert Hoover, to run as the Republican nominee. Hoover won handily, no doubt reflecting citizens' satisfaction with Coolidge policies. (The 1920s, often called the Roaring Twenties, were a generally robust time for the U.S., with the Great Depression not beginning until Hoover's term.)

Coolidge returned to his native New England, and lived a low-key postpresidency with his wife, Grace.

Most historians do not rank Coolidge all that high—in part because he did not seem too interested in using the powers of the office. In the conservative political world, however, he has been seen as a bit of a hero, for with the help of his Treasury secretary, Andrew Mellon, he was focused on paying down debt, keeping the government out of everyone's lives, and embodying the virtues of modesty, frugality, and down-home New England values. Such appreciation showed up even many decades later, including when Ronald Reagan, the embodiment of modern-day conservative Republican values, placed Calvin Coolidge's portrait in the Cabinet Room at the White House.

In recent years, a few conservative writers and historians have worked to revive Coolidge's image. One of those is Amity Shlaes, the chairperson of the Calvin Coolidge Presidential Foundation and the author of *Coolidge*, a biography of the 30th U.S. president. I interviewed her at a New-York Historical Society event on August 14, 2023.

*   *   *   *

DAVID M. RUBENSTEIN (DR): When did Calvin Coolidge become a person of interest to you?

AMITY SHLAES (AS): I was at work on a book about the 1930s and the Great Depression, and the headline of that book was that "they broke it," or "it broke." The "it" behind that pronoun was the U.S. economy. Before it was broken, who made the economy in the twenties? I next turned to writing a book about the 1920s economy, and came to know President Coolidge, the big president of that period. He was so interesting, I decided to attempt a full-length biography of him instead of writing a book about the twenties.

DR: What was it about him that you most admire?

AS: His awareness of the importance of markets for U.S. prosperity and for America's future. And of the importance of the health of the U.S. economy. Most presidents, when they're admired, are admired for wars. They go abroad and do something. Or they are admired as progressives for giant reforms. There are very few presidents who are admired for keeping the economy going. It sounds kind of boring, right? And yet it is hard to do, and Coolidge did it well.

He's also a certain American type, the agricultural-lawyer type, more like a nineteenth-century mayor or the judge in a local town or a farmer, and has those values. We don't see that as much today. I'm from the Midwest. These values may be historically more familiar in the Chicago area because of the surrounding farmland. In short, Coolidge didn't show off, didn't talk about his money, never marketed himself.

DR: How long did it take you to research and write this book?

AS: Several years. Coolidge didn't make it easy. He does not have a presidential library as the presidents who succeeded him do. One gets the impression he wasn't sure he wanted a federally funded library, which was a bit of sanctimony and virtue on his part. He didn't want the federal government to pay for him postpresidency. But he also hurt his own legacy by not allowing his papers to be put into a systematic collection at a presidential library.

So his papers were scattered, and that deterred historians. He also hid some papers or got rid of them. I'm not sure why. To research Coolidge, you have to go to the Vermont Historical Society, or the Forbes Library of Northampton, Massachusetts, where he practiced law most of his career. The Library of Congress has some of his papers too. And we have papers at the Coolidge Foundation in Plymouth Notch, Vermont, the birthplace of President Coolidge. I have also digitized his entire press-conference set of records, in an effort to get as much as I could of Coolidge online.

DR: Has anything occurred since your book appeared that has changed or reinforced your view about Calvin Coolidge?

AS: I like the people who are attracted to him. He attracts a certain type, more quiet people. He was a refraining president. He believed inaction was a virtue. That's very rare too. So he attracts that kind of person, and I got to know a lot of them, including members of the Coolidge family. They are second-impression, not first-impression, people.

I was on the editorial board of the *Wall Street Journal*; so I wrote a lot of tax editorials, and initially I came to Coolidge with an economic view. Since then, I've come more to appreciate his legal attitude and philosophy. He's not quite the same as an originalist Supreme Court judge, but he's close to that. He was a quite sincere federalist, a practicing one, and you saw that in his everyday life.

DR: Where was he born and raised? Who were his parents? Did he have any skills as a youth that would have separated him from the pack as a potential president of the United States?

AS: Not many. He was born in a place that stayed remote. Plymouth Notch, Vermont. Plymouth runs along the Green Mountains, in a kind of bowl. The grade of the incline is steep, so the train doesn't like to go there. He went to boarding school in Ludlow, Vermont.

His family were farmers, and they were very small-town. His father was sheriff, justice of the peace, and a farmer. His grandfather tried to breed animals. Very resourceful people because, agriculturally speaking, Vermont is hard to farm; the joke about that part of Vermont is that you farm rocks. Plymouth is not arable, and that's true of some of the rest of the state, which is why it's such a dairy state. His father eventually started a cheese collective. What's a cheese collective absent electricity or a train to take your milk to market? It's an exercise in economic desperation. You want to make something that's not perishable, that you might one day be able to take to market, and because you lack refrigeration. That was cheese. The cheese factory is still there.

The Coolidges were not poor like the Lincolns, but they had to scramble every year, and they didn't have a lot of cash, like most farmers at the time. Calvin Coolidge did go to boarding school, but that was because there was no secondary school in the village of Plymouth, so kids would go down the road. He sometimes walked 10 miles. He slept over and he boarded while he was in secondary school. He also went to Saint Johnsbury Academy, which still exists, and finally made it, by the skin of his teeth, into Amherst. He was not a star student. In fact, in my book I contend that no freshman seemed less likely to succeed than Calvin. He was skinny, quiet, not tall. He didn't even appear to be a good talker. Amherst was a college with plenty of good talkers, including many wealthy young men. It was a school of men from New York, and there was Coolidge, who was kind of a hayseed, as a freshman certainly.

DR: What did he do when he graduated?

AS: He ended up reading law, but did not attend law school. The Coolidges thought that was kind of expensive, so he ended up clerking, as Lincoln had. He clerked for a firm called Hammond and Field in Northampton, Massachusetts, which is a veritable metropolis compared to Plymouth.

DR: Ultimately he runs for office?

AS: Yes. His law firm was active. One of the fellows there was in the city government. Coolidge gets involved, and he starts as a runner for the party of the partner whom he worked for, the Republican Party. He clerks for the town and eventually becomes a state rep, then state senator, and mayor of Northampton, from 1900 to 1918. Then he goes back and is mayor of Northampton, then state senator, then lieutenant governor, then governor. A very gradual climb.

DR: Was being governor one of his career ambitions? Did he win the governorship the first time he ran?

AS: He won the first time he ran. He was a deliberate man. But this was in a period where party mattered more, and he did serve within the Republican Party. He was a loyal servant of the GOP. He once said, "If nobody is partisan, nobody can be independent." That is, independents are free riders on our willingness to be partisan. He was aware of the pitfalls of partisanship, being loyal to a party, right or wrong.

DR: He gets elected governor in 1918, and does one thing as governor that gets an enormous amount of attention and makes him a national figure. What is that?

AS: It was a rough year during his first term. It was 1919, coming out of World War I. There was an epidemic, influenza. Prices were going up, while wages were not. Many veterans were wounded in World War I, and there were no antibiotics. There were strikes. Among the many groups that went on strike were the Boston police, who by a quirk in the law reported through a chain to the governor of the state—Calvin Coolidge.

DR: The police go on strike and he famously says, "There's no right of anybody to strike in this kind of situation"?

AS: That's right. The police contract said no strikes. There wasn't public-sector unionism as we have it today. With the police off duty, there was looting and violence, and Coolidge as governor had to call in the National Guard to keep the peace in Boston. It was a tough decision for him to do anything about the police because Coolidge was known for getting the immigrant vote. In Boston, the police were Irish Americans, his constituency. They had voted for him in the past, and he had an election coming up, because at that time governors in Massachusetts were elected annually.

He oversaw the police commissioner and supported the commissioner's firing the police for breach of contract. He said, "There's no right to strike against the public safety by anybody, anywhere, anytime." He thought he would lose the election because of that. The police were nice people who were indeed underpaid. But President Wilson backed Coolidge up. It was a turning point as Coolidge's remarks reverberated across the country: "There's no right to strike against the public safety." And that put him in the vice presidential slot.

DR: When Warren Harding was nominated for president on the Republican Party ticket in 1920, he selected Calvin Coolidge. Did Coolidge seek that position or was he surprised to get it?

AS: I would say he made himself open to it. Coolidge was quite—I won't say coy, because that's too negative—but he believed the job had to come to you. That's what he always taught young people. But I think he was quite open to the presidency. He had a booster, Frank Stearns, who owned a big department store in Boston. Stearns published a book of Coolidge's speeches, *Have Faith in Massachusetts*, which became a campaign item. It was an example of successful campaign literature, and it inspired Republicans.

DR: Warren Harding and Coolidge are running against Governor James Cox of Ohio for president and Franklin Delano Roosevelt for vice president, and they win. Then Harding dies and Coolidge becomes president. Was he surprised that Harding died suddenly?

AS: Coolidge was vice president, which was a useful education for him. Taxes were high. With the capital gains tax rate, there was no legal clarity as to whether capital gains, this important tax for business, was ordinary income or not. So either cap gains weren't taxed at all or they were taxed in the 70 percent range, which confused businesses and chilled the markets. And they said, "We want a relatively normal environment so markets can revive after the war." Harding and Coolidge committed to a series of both tax cuts and clarifications of the code to establish more certainty, both about the nature of the tax code and about tax rates, which they promised would be down. Harding hired Andrew Mellon, one of the greatest Treasury secretaries—right up there with Alexander Hamilton. Then Harding passed away, and it was like a relay race, where Coolidge picked up the baton. Whether he wanted it or not, he was sure that finishing what Harding had started was his obligation. And that gave him confidence as well.

DR: So Coolidge gets to be president, and then he has an opportunity to run for election on his own. Does he want to run?

AS: Yes, but he wouldn't put it that way. He was a Republican, and the Republicans were losing steam. It became particularly clear after Harding's passing that there were scandalous aspects to his government, in particular the Teapot Dome scandal, where sweetheart contracts were handed out to friends of friends of the White House. Why was that so terrible? Because Harding had promised, essentially, to privatize. And if you're going to say it's better to have privatization and have oil leases, say, in private hands, you better privatize well, otherwise there's a strong argument for your opponents that the government can manage the oil reserves better. Harding besmirched his own endeavor. So Calvin Coolidge was cleaning up. And he was determined.

DR: Coolidge runs for reelection, in effect, and he gets elected on his own?

AS: He doesn't merely get elected on his own. Usually it was a three-party race. As I was saying, the Republicans were losing steam. So were the Democrats. There was this new party, the La Follette Progressives. They got 16 percent of the popular vote. Usually when that happens, it's an ugly race, and whoever wins just gets a plurality. Nonetheless Coolidge took an absolute majority of the votes, which was quite a feat.

DR: So what did he do in his first full elected term? What was his biggest accomplishment?

AS: One was to finish the tax program. He and Treasury Secretary Mellon were very close. As a team, they vowed to get the income tax rates down to 25 percent, and they did. The top marginal rate, which inspired Ronald Reagan, for example, became 25 percent. Mellon and Coolidge vowed not to betray people, and they didn't want to change tax rates a lot, because they knew how hard that was when rules change all the time. Even more than, say, having a fair tax rate, they believed in reestablishing trust with the electorate, which is a concern we have today. They did what they said, over and over again, in order to show that voters could trust them. And whether you liked or didn't like a specific policy, what people did like about Coolidge is he did what he said. He wasn't too tricky.

DR: He was famous for not talking very much. Did he take a lot of pride in not making long speeches or not speaking frequently?

AS: It's odd. It's kind of a power thing, isn't it? Powerful leaders sometimes wait for other people to talk and give their elevator pitch while the powerful person is silent. That was partly Coolidge. He was certainly capable of talking, but he didn't talk a lot. I don't think it was because he was shy. I don't think anyone who is capable of becoming U.S. president is predominantly shy. He was economical with words when it suited him.

DR: He was famous for taking naps every day. Was that a lifelong habit?

AS: Oh, yes. But all presidents have their quirks. He worked with great discipline, not only on the tax issue, but also on sustaining traditional federalism. If you look at his executive orders, they were mostly about reinforcing federalist law up to that time. Coolidge believed that states were the basis of America.

DR: He could theoretically have run for reelection again in 1928, but he chose not to do so. Why not?

AS: He was in South Dakota in the summer of '27 when he made this decision. The sculptor Gutzon Borglum was up there, beginning to lay the dynamite to put the profiles of the great presidents into Black Hills granite at Mount Rushmore. Coolidge thought about Theodore Roosevelt in particular, because Roosevelt didn't run again and then did run again in 1912 with the Bull Moose Party. And he was thinking about George Washington, who was also going up on Mount Rushmore. It's pretty clear Coolidge wanted to be more like Washington than TR.

He believed that we ought to change leadership from time to time. He also said, "It's a great advantage to the president and a major source of safety to the country for him to know he is not a great man."

DR: So he decides not to run in 1928. His secretary of commerce, Herbert Hoover, openly seeks the nomination, and he gets elected. Coolidge retires. Where does he retire?

AS: He goes back to Massachusetts, where he made his career as an attorney and young politician. What's particularly charming about the Coolidges is they never owned their own house in Northampton (up to the postpresidency period). They rented half a two-family house on Massasoit Street, which one can still see. They were modest. He owned his family land in Vermont. But he wasn't a flamboyant liver.

So they tried living in this half house, but the crowds kept coming. It's hard to imagine, but Coolidge was enormously popular. He certainly would have been reelected in '28. He got a fat magazine contract, the way one would get a book contract today, and he paid for a little bit grander house, but not very grand, called the Beeches in Northampton, with a bit of a distance from the door to the street so that the crowds couldn't come right onto his porch. But he passed away soon after, so he didn't get to enjoy the Beeches for long.

DR: How many years did he live after he left the presidency?

AS: He left the presidency in '29 and he died in January of '33.

DR: And where is he buried?

AS: He's buried in Plymouth Notch, Vermont. His grave is quite Coolidge. It's not the tallest grave in the cemetery.

DR: When Ronald Reagan was elected president, he put Coolidge's portrait in the Cabinet Room. Why was that significant?

AS: It was supposed to symbolize both the tax effort, because Reagan, too, cut taxes, and Coolidge's view that some union actions may not be good for America. Reagan had a famous strike of air traffic controllers. Again, it was a difficult strike, because the air traffic controllers were nice people who worked hard and had a difficult job, no question. But the strike jeopardized public safety. Reagan read a bio of Coolidge, former attorney general Ed Meese once told me, around that time. They were similar, Coolidge's police strike action and Reagan's decision to be tough on the air traffic controllers.

DR: Why should people learn about Calvin Coolidge, and what does he mean to America today?

AS: One, he was the president who never said anything mean about anyone else that I could find. He really did not like Louis Brandeis, but you don't find any public document. He never smeared people, and that's important to us now—that we get along and find common ground. Two, he had an economic model that worked, contrary to what's imparted by some history books. That is, the prosperity of the '20s wasn't a champagne bubble in Jay Gatsby's glass. It was an interesting period when we saw productivity getting so huge that we got Saturday off, which we hadn't had heretofore. A lot of innovations that we count as important in modern life, such as indoor plumbing and electricity and home appliances, came in under that Coolidge economy. He had 4 percent real growth. They didn't have much unemployment.

He was aware that the U.S. had to be competitive, that another currency could take away our newfound advantage. Sterling in those days could become dominant, as it had been. He knew that our advantage was tenuous, and that we must pay attention to what happened in Europe with the economies there, and that money can move around the globe.

DR: Finally, Calvin Coolidge was happily married his entire life to somebody he'd met as a young man. Did they have children?

AS: Oh, absolutely. If you want to study a marriage, the Coolidge marriage is amusing and compelling. Being a First Lady is tough, and Mrs. Coolidge wrote about that. But they stuck together. She played the extrovert to his introvert. I say played, because again, politics is theater. They had two sons, John and Calvin. The great tragedy, one he shares with Lincoln, is that one of his sons, Calvin Junior, died while he was in the White House.

This is the story some of us were told, that Calvin Junior died because of a blister he got playing tennis. He was a boy who grew fast. Probably his old sneakers did not fit. This was just before we got antibiotics. There are schools of thought that say President Coolidge was depressed ever after and was incapacitated by that grief. Calvin Junior was a very likable boy too. He worked in a tobacco field in Massachusetts. Someone said, "If my father was president, I would never work in a tobacco field." And Calvin said, "If my father were your father, you would." Coolidge insisted his sons work. It was such a loss for that family.

9

JONATHAN DARMAN
on Franklin Delano Roosevelt

(1882–1945; president from 1933 to 1945)

A perfect illustration of the difficulty of predicting successes at the outset of one's career is Franklin Delano Roosevelt.

FDR was born and raised in the idyllic setting of the Hudson Valley area, the wealthy and somewhat pampered only child of his strong-willed mother, Sara, and his father, James, a wealthy businessman who had another child from an earlier marriage.

In his youth and early adulthood, Franklin was not considered all that brilliant or athletic, or frankly even much of a leader—more of a follower and a loner. But, in time, he grew intellectually and as a leader to become the twentieth century's most consequential president, not only serving longer than any other president (a little more than 12 years) but also winning two of the most significant fights America faced in that century—the Great Depression and World War II.

So what happened? Historians have still not reached a consensus on the transformation of Franklin Roosevelt from an aristocratic, not overly successful lawyer who was a bit of a mama's boy (his mother seemed to have the most influence over him, in part because she controlled the family purse strings). A cousin, Theodore Roosevelt, lent some political allure to his last name, even though Teddy was a Republican and Franklin was a Democrat, and thus he was a bit less likely to benefit from the storied name.

Jonathan Darman, the son of the former Reagan/Bush official Richard Darman (and a former Carlyle colleague of mine), offers one theory in his book on Roosevelt, *Becoming FDR*.

In Darman's view, the polio that Roosevelt contracted at age 39 in 1921 completely transformed him. He had to learn how to function in society again after the debilitating disease struck him. It was misdiagnosed for at least a month, making a restoration of the use of his legs all but impossible. When Roosevelt realized that his life had changed permanently, he developed a stronger character as he fought to reenter the business and political worlds. He did not pity himself, but rather tried to provide a cheerful outlook to others, even though he had to struggle to get from one place to another. He tried hard to give the appearance that he could walk, with some assistance, but he was never really able to move his legs again.

Initially, Roosevelt, his family, and advisors saw little chance for him to regain a political base or opportunity. He had already been a New York state senator, Woodrow Wilson's assistant secretary of the Navy during World War I, and James Cox's running mate in the 1920 presidential election, in which they lost to Warren Harding. But after polio, a chance arose to run for governor of New York. At first he thought such a race was not practical, especially if the public realized just how debilitating the polio was for him. (The press largely chose not to cover the extent of his physical problems, and rarely showed him in a wheelchair or struggling to walk.)

Aided by the strong support of outgoing governor Al Smith, Roosevelt not only won the Democratic nomination for governor of New York in 1928 but also won the general election and returned to public life. Four years later he won the Democratic nomination for president, easily beating Herbert Hoover, who seemed unable to deal with the Great Depression and its effects on the country.

Could any of this had happened had Roosevelt never been afflicted with polio? No one can know for certain, but Jonathan Darman, whom I had a chance to interview at the New-York Historical Society on March 28, 2023, makes a compelling case that the grit and determination needed to recover from the loss of his ability to walk remade Roosevelt's personality and character, making his presidency possible.

*   *   *   *

DAVID M. RUBENSTEIN (DR): What prompted you to think that the world needed another book on FDR?

JONATHAN DARMAN (JD): I was wrestling with a question that felt urgent, which is, how does a president bring hope to the country?

Franklin Roosevelt, with his leadership of the country through the Depression and World War II, is probably the best example we have of a president who comes into office and is able to convince people not only that the future is going to be okay in a time of challenge but that together they can do big things. I wanted to look at his life with fresh eyes and see what there was to say about how he did that.

DR: The premise of your book is that, absent polio, Roosevelt might not have developed the empathy and resilience that he later showed, and his wife might not have developed some of the unique qualities that enabled them both to go to the White House and to be effective as president and First Lady. Is that right?

JD: That's right. Franklin Roosevelt had a whole career in politics before he got polio at the age of 39. You look at that person who was a young, charismatic, attractive politician and say, "What if this person had never gotten polio? Might he, if everything had gone his way, have ended up in the White House someday?" Potentially yes, but I don't think that person would have been a great president, because he needed to experience what real suffering and setback is like and come to understand how it is that you can find your way out of that.

DR: Others have written about his polio, and some people have said that had it been diagnosed properly right away, he might have been able to recover much better than he did. He didn't really get diagnosed properly for a month or so?

JD: That's right. He gets sick in early August 1921 but isn't properly diagnosed until the end of August. What if he had gotten the best medical attention right away? It's quite possible that he would have still been disabled in some way from polio, but it's also possible that his paralysis wouldn't have been as extensive, because he would have been prescribed a period of long bedrest where he was moving as little as possible, and then gotten excellent physical therapy. That might have meant less severe consequences from the infection than those he ultimately experienced.

DR: I always had thought that the country really didn't know the extent of his illness. You point out that most people who read newspapers knew he had polio. It was well described. They may not have realized how incapacitated he was. Did he try to not be photographed in a wheelchair or walking with his cane?

JD: We all have this idea that there was this code of silence and ignorance in the public about his disability. Particularly when you're talking about his life in the 1920s, in the years when he's on his rise to the presidency, there's a key distinction to be made between his being okay, essentially, with people understanding that he had a disability and his not wanting to be seen in any circumstance where he would appear weak or helpless.

That's why he was sensitive about being seen in a wheelchair or ever being in a situation where he might fall in public. There were a lot of times where he came close to that. His main concern was controlling the optics of it. He was carried by other people all the time, but he didn't want to be seen in public being carried.

DR: What about Eleanor Roosevelt? We'll talk later about their relationship. What was the result on her of his getting polio?

JD: Eleanor's transformation in these years is in a lot of ways more dramatic than her husband's. If you look at the summer of 1920, a year before FDR gets polio, he's the vice presidential nominee. A reporter finds Eleanor and asks her what she thinks about women's suffrage. Women's suffrage is a big issue in 1920. Eleanor Roosevelt's response is, "I don't have a strong feeling either way. Personally, I'm content with my husband and my children." And within just a few years, she's not only going to have an opinion about women's suffrage, she will support it. She herself is going to be one of the most significant women in either of the two political parties, and in a lot of ways Franklin's polio brings that about, because she steps forward as the representative of the family on the public stage.

DR: After he contracted polio, FDR had many different doctors talk to him, who advised this and that. What he seemed to like most was going to Warm Springs in Georgia. Why did he go there so much, and did it help?

JD: He hears about Warm Springs for the first time about three years after he gets polio. He hears that it's a miraculous place in Georgia where there are spa waters that have cured other paralysis victims. He's looking for a miracle. The conventional wisdom was that muscle recovery that wasn't coming back after one to two years probably was never going to come back. He wasn't walking, and he wasn't willing to accept that. So he was immediately drawn to Warm Springs.

I think he had imagined that it would be this big spa resort. He had spent some time in those kinds of places as a child. It's not that. It's very run-down. But he gets in the water, and he has two thoughts right away: "This does feel like magic water," and "It's a shame that it's only for me." The real miracle of Warm Springs is it unlocks this tremendous capacity for empathy in Franklin Roosevelt. It acquaints him with his own ability to help other people, which will be so essential for him going forward.

DR: But is there any evidence that the many years he spent there—and later he bought Warm Springs—improved his physical health?

JD: It was good for him because he was in warm water. In the wintertime, he was able to swim, which was good exercise. But no, he never regained the ability to walk there in the way that other polio patients did.

DR: When was FDR born?

JD: FDR was born in 1882 at his family estate in Hyde Park, New York.

DR: And who was his father?

JD: His father was James Roosevelt, who was a member of this illustrious Roosevelt family. He was an older man at the time that FDR was born, around 53 years old. It was actually his second marriage and his second family. He had had another son from his first marriage before his first wife died.

Franklin and James had this close relationship in Franklin's childhood where they're spending time together on the Hyde Park estate. That develops what's going to be a real key attribute of Franklin Roosevelt's, which is the ability to connect with people who are of an older generation from his.

DR: Who was his mother?

JD: Sara Delano Roosevelt. I think of her as the 1880s equivalent of a helicopter parent. She was involved in every single aspect of Franklin Roosevelt's upbringing, which explains a lot about what he became.

DR: When he went to Harvard, did she not rent a place there as well?

JD: Yes. She wants to be there in his life at all moments. I was reminded the other day of a moment later in his career when Franklin and Eleanor move to Washington when he's assistant secretary of the Navy, and Sara goes to visit them at their house. She writes in her diary, "Arrived in Washington, moved some tables and chairs around and beginning to feel at home."

DR: She also bought Franklin and Eleanor a home in New York, then she bought a home next door and carved little doors in between. Isn't that right?

JD: Yes. The idea was that each of them would have their separate space, but that was an illusion. Sara was the mistress of all of that.

DR: Franklin grows up in Hyde Park, and mostly he cares about the outdoors. Was he a reasonable athlete or not that good?

JD: He was not a great athlete. He goes to Groton School late, and he still is a pretty scrawny young guy. Groton School is this Episcopal academy in Massachusetts where the sons of the Protestant elite went, and everything there was about your physical prowess as an athlete. He's middling at best, so he doesn't stick out at all. In fact, he gets bullied. It's partly because of his size, but it's also partly because he spent so much time in the company of his parents. He doesn't really know how to get along with other kids yet.

DR: He has no siblings. He has stepbrothers?

JD: He has a half brother who was basically a generation older.

DR: Speaking of the word *bully*, that is a word often used by Teddy Roosevelt. How was Franklin Roosevelt related to Teddy Roosevelt?

JD: Teddy was Franklin's 5th cousin.

DR: They were distant cousins but they didn't really know each other that well?

JD: No. Franklin's parents were close to Teddy Roosevelt's siblings, but because of the circumstances of life, I don't think there was a particularly close connection between the Hyde Park Roosevelts and Teddy's branch of the family.

DR: At Harvard, he does become the head of the *Crimson*, the student newspaper. How did he do that if people didn't think he was so wonderful?

JD: He's been raised to think of himself as this special, wonderful person because he's a Roosevelt, but the problem is the rest of the world doesn't seem to agree. Then, in his sophomore year, his cousin Teddy is catapulted into the presidency after the assassination of William McKinley. All of a sudden, having the last name Roosevelt is a really big deal. That elevates Franklin's status on campus in that moment, but more importantly, it focuses Franklin Roosevelt's attention on politics as an arena where he can distinguish himself.

DR: When he graduates, what does he do?

JD: He goes to law school, because that's what Teddy had done. You hear these accounts of him as a young lawyer doing trust-and-estate work. He was bored all the time.

There's a story where he's with the other clerks, and they're talking about what they want to do with their careers. Some of them want to work in firms. He says he wants to run for the New York State Legislature, then he wants to become assistant secretary of the Navy, and then he wants to become governor of New York, and then he wants to become president of the United States. That's the path that Teddy Roosevelt had had, and I think that's not a coincidence.

DR: Franklin did run for the state legislature?

JD: He did run, and won. By that point he's basically determined that he's going to do a really good Teddy Roosevelt impersonation. He's going to be the Roosevelt in the Democratic Party for the next generation. Teddy had distinguished himself as an opponent of Tammany Hall. That's what Franklin Roosevelt does early in his political career there. It doesn't work out as well for Franklin, in part because he's in the

Democratic Party where Tammany was influential, and in part because he doesn't yet have this great ability to connect that we will see in later years.

DR: So after serving in the state legislature, does he run for another office?

JD: He runs for the state legislature twice. He then gets plucked to be in the Wilson administration.

DR: How did he come to their attention?

JD: He goes to the 1912 Democratic nominating convention, in Baltimore, and he makes a lot of noise there about his connection to Teddy Roosevelt. That's something that people pay attention to, because, of course, Teddy Roosevelt is running for president that year. So to have this Democrat who's dropping Teddy's name liberally and he supports Wilson at the convention, that makes a good impression on the Wilson people. Then, when Woodrow Wilson ultimately wins and they're thinking about who to put in the administration, they think, "We've got this Democratic Roosevelt, let's put him in the Navy Department." Which is where Teddy had been.

DR: So he had the same job as Teddy Roosevelt—assistant secretary of the Navy.

JD: Yes. I think it's the first time in Franklin Roosevelt's life where his image of himself starts getting mirrored back to him by the rest of the world. He does very well in Washington in those years. He takes to the fact that it's a small town. People there like having a charming Roosevelt around, they like the proximity to power, and he likes the attention that he's getting.

DR: How did he meet Eleanor Roosevelt?

JD: A lot of people say, "We've known each other longer than we can remember." With Franklin and Eleanor Roosevelt, that's literally true. They met for the first time as small children. They don't actually form their close bond and, ultimately, their romantic connection until a number of years later, when he's a student at Harvard and she's 18 years old, returning from Europe.

DR: Her father, who was an alcoholic, dies. That father was Teddy Roosevelt's brother?

JD: That's right.

DR: So they're fifth cousins, once removed. When they get married, Teddy Roosevelt gives away the bride?

JD: Yes. There's the famous Alice Roosevelt Longworth line about her father, which was that "he wanted to be the bride at every wedding and the corpse at every funeral." He gives away Eleanor, they have the wedding ceremony, and then Franklin and Eleanor go to receive their guests and no one comes to them because they're all crowding around Teddy, the president.

DR: After they get married, they have a nice relationship for a while, but at some point he develops a relationship with her social secretary, Lucy Mercer. How did Eleanor discover it?

DR: She starts to get a hint of it—she's intuitive—in the summers of 1916 and 1917. She was spending those summers at the Roosevelt family cottage on Campobello Island. World War I had started at that point, and Franklin was staying in Washington and he's writing her these letters about people he's spending time with, and Lucy Mercer appears in those letters. If you go back and read Eleanor's responses, there's a passive-aggressive "Well, it sounds like you're having a nice time" attitude. Then she says, "I'm much happier to be where I am."

What's really devastating for her in those early years of the relationship is that she comes back to Washington in the fall and she gets this sense that everyone else has seen this. Franklin and Lucy were not discreet. So it's not just a betrayal, it's a humiliation.

DR: Eventually she unpacks one of his suitcases and uncovers love letters that he has written to Lucy Mercer?

JD: That happens in the fall of 1918. He had been in Europe at the very end of World War I as assistant secretary of the Navy. He gets very sick on the ship back because there was pandemic influenza on the ship. He got double pneumonia. Eleanor and Sara go and get Franklin from the ship and she's unpacking his bags and finds these letters. Now Eleanor Roosevelt never talks directly in public about Franklin's affair with Lucy Mercer. She talks about it with her friends, including the biographer Joseph Lash. But if you know to look for it, she leaves little hints over the years. She wrote several memoirs in her life. She wrote a memoir in 1937 where she talks about getting Franklin from the ship and she says, "He didn't seem that sick to me." I think that's her rage from that moment coloring her recollection.

It's the great crisis in the Roosevelt marriage and the great crisis in Eleanor Roosevelt's life that gets her thinking about who does she want to be and what's her purpose.

DR: So she says to him, "Want to get a divorce?" What does he say?

JD: He wrestled with it for a while. This is important for us to remember. This isn't just a casual affair. He had a strong love attachment to Lucy Mercer, and by all accounts he did think about divorce. And there are a number of reasons why he doesn't go that way.

It's said that when his mother, who was still helping him pay his bills at that point, gets word of this she says, "Then you're going to have to make do for yourself." That's a less attractive prospect for him.

DR: Because she thinks that it's going to hurt his political career?

JD: She's of an older generation, and divorce was just getting socialized in their circles. She doesn't want him getting divorced from Eleanor. But the real thing for Franklin is his political career. This is 1918. He thinks, "I want to be president of the United States someday." Maybe it's conceivable that the public would be okay with a politician who was divorced, but not someone who's had this very public affair where he's humiliated his wife and everyone knows the story.

DR: So in 1920, the Democrats nominate James Cox from Ohio to be president. Why does he pick Franklin Roosevelt to be his vice president? Roosevelt had served as assistant secretary of the Navy and one or two terms in the New York State Legislature. Why would that qualify him to be on the ticket?

JD: Assistant secretary of the Navy doesn't sound like an impressive job now. It's the number two job in the Navy Department. But those years had been the years of World War I, so it was a high-visibility position. Franklin gets himself on the ticket that year in part because he's really good at managing what we today call optics. He goes to the convention where they're selecting the president and vice president, and he makes a big show of himself. He uses his commanding physical presence. He's tall, handsome, athletic, and he's running around, he's jumping over rows of chairs, he's starting fights. He didn't make a major speech at the convention, but he did make a big impression.

DR: He gets on the ticket, and the ticket loses overwhelmingly to the distinguished ticket of Warren Harding and Calvin Coolidge. He's somewhat humiliated. Did they lose New York State as well?

JD: Yes, they lost New York. At this point, Franklin has never won anything larger than a legislative race. During his Navy Department years, he had tried several times to get statewide office in New York and failed, and so he's worried that the taint of looking like a loser is going to stick to him and get in his way.

DR: He's out of office, no job. What is he to do for a career then?

JD: It's the first time in several years that he has to think about life in the private sector. This is a moment in that pre-polio FDR phase where he has a good instinct for where things are going. He thinks basically that the Democrats have been tossed out of office and the country is entering a material age, and he says, "I don't think the Democrats are going to come back into office again until there's some great economic calamity." Which is exactly what happens.

So he decides to make money and takes a job in a law firm, again doing work that he doesn't find particularly stimulating. Then he takes another job in finance where he makes a lot of introductions and is a social presence in the New York office of his firm.

DR: The view on him at that time in New York business and political circles was that he was a bit of a dilettante and not exactly a first-rate intellect. Is that fair?

JD: That's correct. When he would give speeches in the 1920 campaign, he would make a good impression. People would say, "What a nice man." But they couldn't remember anything that he'd said.

DR: That's a problem. So his family goes to Campobello. For 100 years, they've been going to Campobello. Is that in the United States?

JD: It's a Canadian island off the coast of Maine.

DR: So it's not easy to get there, and there's not a lot of electricity or other things at the time. His children and his wife are up there one summer and he says he's going to come up?

JD: His children had spent a lot of summers there. They loved being with their father anywhere in nature, but particularly in Campobello. They thought they were going to have this wonderful long summer holiday as a family in the summer of 1921, but then fate intervenes.

DR: Before he gets there, he goes to a Boy Scout jamboree of some type, and what happens there?

JD: He was a philanthropic benefactor of the Boy Scouts, and he goes to visit the camp, where there was a polio outbreak. He didn't know it at the time, but we think that at some point during his visit, he probably comes into contact with the polio virus, and that's the moment that his life really changes.

DR: He goes up to Campobello to spend time with his kids after?

JD: By the time he's there with his kids, he's not feeling well. He had come up there with some of his business associates on a fishing trip. At one point, when he was running around on the ship, he fell into the water. And he talks about it as this terrible cold, this really striking cold. And that was unusual. He'd been in those waters all his life.

He's not feeling well, but he still is exerting himself, like he would normally. He and his family run across the island. They go out in the boat at one point, see a forest fire, go ashore, and they put out the fire. He swims in the water and he's exerting himself quite strenuously in what are going to be the last moments that he's walking.

DR: Finally he goes to bed. And what happens then?

JD: He's complaining, he has what he calls lumbago, and he has this horrible fever that night. He gets up in the morning and tries to go about his day normally. And it's clear right away that that's not going to happen. He can barely bring a razor to his face. He feels his legs buckle underneath him, and he retreats to bed. Within 24 hours he loses the ability to walk and never gets it back again.

DR: Is there an emergency clinic or hospital in Campobello?

JD: No. It was a lovely place, but it's about the worst place that you could get seriously ill in the summer of 1921. There's no electricity, there's only one phone line on the whole island, and there's only one local doctor from the nearby town in Maine who services the whole island by boat.

DR: He has his top aide, Louis Howe, there, and Eleanor too, and they eventually find a doctor to come. Who?

JD: They go through a whole odyssey, because it's clear right away that he needs a doctor. First, the local doctor says, "I think he's just got a bad cold." But after a couple of days it's obviously not just a bad cold. Then Louis Howe, who's a wonderful character in these years and very close to the Roosevelts, gets focused on how to get a first-rate doctor there. The first doctor they get there is a famous surgeon named William Keen, who was an older gentleman at that point, in his eighties.

DR: Retired for 10 years from practicing medicine?

JD: Yes. He was not someone up to date on infantile paralysis, which is what polio was known as at that point. So he sees Franklin, and he says, "I think he's got a blood clot, and he's going to be fine. I'm very confident in this." He leaves and he sends Eleanor a bill for $600. That turns out to be a wrong diagnosis.

DR: When do they decide they need another doctor, and who do they get?

JD: Louis Howe, who's paying close attention, has a sense right away that Keen is not the right person. So he's writing letters, describing Franklin's symptoms, and some of Louis's contacts, including Franklin's uncle, piece together that he might have polio.

They start saying, "Okay, who is the leading expert in the treatment of polio?" And they find a doctor named Robert Lovett. Ultimately they get Lovett to come to the island at the end of August, and he does a quick examination of Franklin Roosevelt, and right away he knows that he has polio.

DR: And how do they tell Franklin and Eleanor?

JD: Eleanor at this point I think has an idea, because she's been aware of this whole conversation that Louis has been having about what it might be. But they've been keeping it from Franklin. Remember, he's quite ill in these weeks, so she's really worried about, "What's his reaction going be when he finally gets this verdict?"

Being told you have polio, in the summer of 1921, is about as tough a diagnosis as you can get. But when they tell Franklin, she looks at him and his face is just sort of, as she describes it, "an iceberg." He doesn't have any immediate reaction. He takes it quietly.

DR: His illness is such that he basically has no control below his waist. He can't move his legs. He decided to stay there for a while, or they bring them back to New York?

JD: They will bring him back to New York a couple of weeks later. There's this dilemma, because on the one hand what you're supposed to do when you are experiencing an acute polio infection is prolonged bed rest, trying to move as little as possible. On the other hand, being on Campobello Island, it's not a tenable situation for treating someone who's seriously ill. So they bring him back to New York, and he gets checked into a hospital here.

DR: And the hospital confirms the diagnosis?

JD: Yes, and it gets announced to the public. They announced that Franklin Roosevelt has infantile paralysis. This gets to the question of deception. In the first story that appears about this in the *New York Times*, there's a quote from Franklin's doctor saying, "No one need fear any permanent disability." That wasn't true, but they knew that if people thought he was going to be permanently disabled, they might think, "His political career is over."

DR: He gets lots of treatment. Nothing actually helps the paralysis?

JD: He's recovering in these years, but it's way too slow for him. What's hard is he doesn't see the kind of progress in regaining the ability to move his legs that he wants.

DR: He ultimately goes to work again. He has to make a living. What does he do?

JD: He brings the world to him. He's living in the Roosevelt townhouse on East 65th Street, and Louis Howe is managing his affairs. Howe was Roosevelt's closest political advisor. A lot of political consultants, if a guy they've hitched their wagon to gets a terrible disability that's going to put him out of commission for a number of years, might say, "I'm going to move on to someone else." Louis Howe moved into the Roosevelts' house because he cared about Franklin Roosevelt that much. He is managing this interface between Franklin's public and private worlds.

DR: Roosevelt goes back to work, but sometimes he falls down getting there. People see him. It's very embarrassing to him. He eventually hears about Warm Springs, spends time there, and then, amazingly, Al Smith, who was at one point the governor of New York, calls and wants him to help him. How does Al Smith want him to help?

JD: This happens in the fall of 1928. Al Smith had been governor of New York for a number of years, and he was the Democratic nominee for president in 1928, and he's thinking about what he can do to help his chances. He knows that as a governor from New York State, he needs to win New York State. That's harder for someone like Al Smith than it sounds because Al Smith was a figure of the Tammany Democratic machine.

DR: He's Catholic.

JD: Yes, he was Catholic. He's very good at getting out votes here in New York City but not great at getting votes in New York State. He gets this idea that if he can have Franklin Roosevelt on his ticket, that'll help him bring up his numbers.

DR: You mean if Roosevelt runs for governor of New York, that'll strengthen the Democratic vote coming out of New York, giving more votes to Al Smith, and therefore he could win New York and then maybe win the presidency?

JD: Exactly. He does not think that highly of Franklin Roosevelt at this point. Al Smith loved being governor of New York, and he thinks if somehow Franklin gets elected governor, that Smith can be both president and the unofficial governor of New York.

DR: Roosevelt has said many times, "I'm out of politics for a while." How does he change his mind?

JD: He's spending these years devoted to recovery. He still has this idea that he is going to walk again. His doctors have concluded at this point that he's not going to, but he's not yet ready to give up on that idea, so he wants more time before he reenters politics.

Another thing that he's gotten out of these years is this incredible strategic ability and this respect for timing. So when Smith comes to him, Franklin comes around to the idea that this is his moment. What's bittersweet is, at least in his mind, he's making a choice between having a political future and ever walking again.

DR: This is 1928. The last time he was elected to something was what year?

JD: Nineteen twelve.

DR: So 16 years later, he had never run successfully for anything statewide before, and all of a sudden, he gets the nomination easily?

JD: He gets the nomination by acclaim at the convention, and his disability is a part of the conversation from the earliest moments. If you look at the New York *Daily News* the next day, the big populist bible of the time, the first line of the news story is, "They nominated a man on crutches to be the governor of New York yesterday."

DR: What happens in the 1928 election? Does Al Smith win?

JD: Al Smith does not win. He loses in a landslide to Herbert Hoover.

DR: And what happens to FDR?

JD: Franklin Roosevelt surprises everyone. They go through this drama on election night where early on they can tell that the Smith ticket is going to do poorly, and everyone thinks if Al Smith isn't going to win, then Franklin Roosevelt definitely not going to win. Except Sara Delano Roosevelt, who stays up all night and watches the returns come in. She's one of the first people to know the great surprise that Franklin Roosevelt squeaks by, even though Al Smith at the top of the ticket loses New York State.

DR: All of a sudden FDR is elected governor. Does he now say, "I'm really not qualified to be governor. Al Smith, can you help me out"?

JD: No, he doesn't. That's a great source of resentment on Smith's part. He had never thought that highly of Franklin Roosevelt's ability, and he sees him as, in his words, "a cripple." He thinks he's going to have his people running New York State, and he's quite surprised when Franklin doesn't take any of that.

DR: One of Al Smith's people is a guy named Robert Moses, who thinks he's going to run the state because he is the top aide to Al Smith. What did FDR think about that?

JD: This is one of the first breaks between Smith and Roosevelt. Smith had only one request for FDR, to keep his two top people, Bob Moses and Belle Moskowitz. And Franklin is basically thinking, "I'm not going to keep those people, because their number one loyalty is to Al Smith and I'm never going to be an effective governor if I've got them running Al Smith's administration instead of mine."

DR: In those years, the term of governor was two years. Franklin gets elected in 1928 and already he's thinking, "I should be like Teddy Roosevelt, I should run for president." The next presidential election's going to be in 1932. What does he do in the first two years as governor to get himself ready for reelection and then get ready to run for president?

JD: It's not just him who has the idea that he should run for president in 1932. Because he has this Cinderella-story victory in 1928, from the moment that this becomes public, people start talking about him as not just someone who might run for president in four years but as the front-runner. He's focused in his first two years as governor on doing as good a job as he can, which is not an easy task because he's got a Republican legislature. He finds ways to go around them and connect directly with the public, and he wants to win reelection by as large a margin as he can to show that this is not just a one-time thing.

DR: He runs for reelection in 1930, and what happens?

JD: He wins by a huge landslide. He's running against Charles Tuttle, who had been the U.S. attorney for the Southern District. People thought this was a good anticorruption candidate. But Franklin has an easy job defeating him.

DR: So he gets reelected. Does he start gearing up to run for president?

JD: It starts from the earliest moments. They are essentially running what we would call today an inevitability campaign. They want to create this perception across the country that Franklin Roosevelt is the only person who can unite all the various factions in the Democratic Party. Remember that at this point—this is 1932—the Democratic Party had been out of power for 12 years, in part because it had been at war with itself so much. So it is a compelling story: Franklin Roosevelt, who spent all this time in Georgia but is a New Yorker, is a unique figure who can unite the various wings of the party.

DR: As governor, he spends a lot of time with people who are the underclass in some ways, people who have physical problems, people who are not that economically strong. Is that part of his image, to appeal to people who are not the upper class?

JD: Yes. This gets back to this idea of what did the public know about his illness and disability? People understood, on some level, even though they didn't have all of the details, that this was someone who had been through a serious experience that had altered his life. He was someone who, despite his privileged background, could relate to people when he talked about them as the forgotten man.

DR: Who were the main competitors for the nomination in 1932?

JD: There were a number of people running. His chief opposition was John Nance Garner, who was the Speaker of the House. He didn't want to run for president in 1932, but William Randolph Hearst told him to. Hearst was a big figure at the time in media and politics, and he was one of these people who gets this idea that he's going to do everything he can to stop Franklin Roosevelt from getting the Democratic nomination. Hearst didn't like anyone who was going to be president because it wasn't him.

DR: Roosevelt campaigns for the nomination. There are no primaries then?

JD: There were primaries but they didn't have a decisive effect in selecting delegates. So there's all this drama that gets concentrated on the convention, where it's really about the perception in the room of who seems strong as a candidate.

DR: In the end, Joe Kennedy, one of the wealthiest men in the United States and the father of John F. Kennedy, cuts a deal with William Randolph Hearst. What is that deal?

JD: Kennedy is a great operator. Hearst has effectively positioned himself as part of this stop-Roosevelt movement, and it's effective. If he wants, he can keep Franklin Roosevelt from getting the nomination that year. They go through several ballots at the convention where it looks like Roosevelt's in real trouble. Kennedy goes to Hearst and says, "If you want to pick a president, the only one you're really going to be able to give it to is Franklin Roosevelt." And Hearst, who's got a high opinion of himself, views himself as a kingmaker. So he switches, somewhat opportunistically, at the last minute. He likes the idea that he's going to be seen as the person who brings Franklin Roosevelt over the line.

DR: The condition is that John Nance Garner is going to be the vice president?

JD: That's right. Garner is at his home in Washington, totally oblivious to this. He gets woken up by the Hearst press, who inform him of what's going on.

DR: The election was against Herbert Hoover. Did Roosevelt go to the Democratic Convention and make a dramatic speech?

JD: He did, breaking with precedent. You historically wouldn't show up at the convention if you were the candidate because you didn't want to be seen as influencing things too crassly and directly.

He stayed away during the nominating process. But once he secures the nomination, he flies to Chicago to show that he's someone who can go there physically, to combat the perception of polio.

DR: How does he go to the convention and show people he can walk or give the illusion of walking?

JD: By that point, he had worked out a routine. He has someone—often his eldest son, Jimmy—holding his arm so it looks like they're walking arm in arm. Then he uses a cane to support his weight, and he swings his legs so if you're not watching too closely, he looks like someone who can walk but with a great deal of difficulty. He has on thick leg braces, which he hated.

DR: He gives a speech, he gets the nomination, and then the election against Hoover is not that difficult because Hoover had gotten us into a bit of an economic problem.

JD: In Hoover's mind, he thinks he's lucky when the Democrats nominate Franklin Roosevelt in 1932. Of all the people being talked about, he knew Franklin Roosevelt best. They had been friends in Washington a decade earlier. He doesn't rate Franklin very highly. Most people don't understand how he's been changed by these years. So Hoover's quite happy when it's Franklin Roosevelt running against him.

DR: But the election doesn't go very well for Hoover because of the Depression. It's a landslide election. Does FDR look to Hoover during the transition to learn from him?

JD: He doesn't want to too closely associate himself with Hoover. When Hoover tries to meet with him a few times, he evades him in this classically Rooseveltian fashion. There's one point where Hoover's getting concerned about what is going to be the emergent banking crisis, and he writes an urgent letter to Roosevelt: "I feel so strongly about this. I'm giving this to the Secret Service to give to you, personally." Roosevelt reads the letter and takes 10 days to respond. He says, "Oh, I think someone misplaced that letter." It's not at all believable. He doesn't want to get enmeshed in Herbert Hoover's problem.

DR: On Inauguration Day, until most recently, the new president goes to the White House for coffee or tea with the outgoing president, and then they drive up to the inauguration together. Did Roosevelt do that?

JD: They do meet. Hoover makes a generous gesture. He understood that the typical ceremony, where the incoming president goes into the White House for coffee, would put Roosevelt in an uncomfortable position where he's going to be seen having to get inside. So Hoover instead says, "I'll come out and meet you in the car." And they have just the car ride together. If you look at the pictures from that ride, Franklin Roosevelt is Franklin Roosevelt, smiling, and Hoover looks like he's having the worst day of his life.

DR: Roosevelt gives his first inaugural address, the most famous line of which is, "We have nothing to—"

JD: "—fear but fear itself."

DR: Who wrote that line?

JD: That's a good question. Authorship is always an interesting question with Franklin Roosevelt. He has other people draft his speeches, but he leads the revision process, and he's saying, "Move this here, and move that here, move that there." He's not ever really writing a speech so much as conducting it like a symphony.

But with the inaugural address, he does something in the drafting process. He writes a note saying, "This is the draft that was written by Franklin Roosevelt," and he gives the time and date. I think that's because he knows that this is an address that's going to live in history.

DR: Quite a story. After spending all this time studying Franklin Delano Roosevelt, do you come away admiring him more than you did before or less?

JD: I come away admiring him a great deal more than I did before. When you write about the years that I write about, the years that he spends in recovery and rehabilitation from polio, you get to see him at his best on an interpersonal level.

A lot of politicians have moments doing altruistic things. But is it really for an altruistic purpose or are they just trying to look like someone who cares? There's no way you can say that about Franklin Roosevelt's work at Warm Springs. There's no definition of political calculation that says that you should spend a huge chunk of your personal fortune and time getting involved in other people's recovery. He does that just because he wants to help people.

DR: During the time he's president, he doesn't have a relationship with Lucy Mercer any longer, but he has a relationship with his assistant?

JD: Missy LeHand is his assistant. People at the time thought of her as his second wife almost. They have a relationship. She's definitely in love with Franklin Roosevelt, and I think he loves her back.

But there's a big difference from the Lucy Mercer relationship, which is that the Missy LeHand one has Eleanor Roosevelt's sanction. In these years she wants to be pursuing her own independent life, and she knows that her husband has a lot of needs. He has a lot of physical needs, as someone who's disabled, and he also has a lot of needs as someone who likes to have adulation and admiration. She doesn't want to play that role and she understands that Missy LeHand can do it, so she gives it her blessing.

DR: Eleanor Roosevelt develops her own relationships, and she becomes a powerful speaker for causes. She's his eyes and ears on the road, and the relationship between the two of them, in some ways, strengthened?

JD: It strengthened, I think, because she understands how these years have changed her husband. She sees that he has deepened as a person and has this unique ability to be an effective agent of change on the causes she cares about. Her rage toward him never completely goes away.

DR: On the day he dies, in April of 1945, Lucy Mercer is with him. What was Eleanor's reaction to finding this out and not being there herself?

JD: It's an amazing and heartbreaking story. Again, in the years when they decide to stay together as a couple, one of Eleanor's conditions is that Franklin end things with Lucy and have no more connection to her, and Eleanor thinks all those years that he's abiding by that. He had, in fact, remained in touch with her.

Lucy was married to someone else in those years, Winthrop Rutherfurd. He dies in the last years of Franklin Roosevelt's presidency. By then, Franklin and Lucy are spending more time together, and it's orchestrated by Franklin and Eleanor's eldest daughter, Anna. Eleanor finds out about all of this in basically the same breath—not literally, but in the same moments—that she's learned that her husband has died. It's rewriting history right in front of her eyes.

10

JEFFREY FRANK
on Harry S. Truman

(1884–1972; president from 1945 to 1953)

Harry Truman left the presidency with a then-record low approval rating of 32 percent, and from the day he was sworn in, after the death of Franklin D. Roosevelt, on April 12, 1945, he was in Roosevelt's shadow. He was not an accomplished public speaker (his flat Missouri twang and diction contrasted poorly with FDR's friendly and resonant voice); he lacked the stature of such foreign leaders as Winston Churchill; he wasn't well educated (he did not attend college); and, all in all, he was not someone whom the American people felt was an appropriate leader for such an august position.

These views began to change even before he left office, and particularly after David McCullough published his Pulitzer Prize–winning *Truman* in 1992. The reappraisal of Truman has continued to this day. He is now widely seen as a no-nonsense man from Independence, Missouri, who was not afraid of making tough decisions. He twice ordered the use of an atomic bomb and never second-guessed that decision. He oversaw the successful completion of the European and Pacific Theaters of World War II. Overcoming his own upbringing in rural Missouri, he fought for civil rights—including integrating the military. He created the CIA; and got the United Nations, the World Bank, North Atlantic Treaty Organization, and the International Monetary Fund off the ground, and these global organizations, while far from perfect, proved to be a bedrock of international cooperation for nearly 75 years. He fought against the red-baiting of Senator Joe McCarthy. And he was honest and incorruptible, despite his roots as part of a Missouri political machine not known for its integrity.

I interviewed the late David McCullough, whom I came to know reasonably well, about many of his books, but sadly never did so about his work on Truman. But I was able to twice interview a worthy successor to him, Jeffrey Frank, who spent about seven years researching and writing *The Trials of Harry S. Truman: The Extraordinary Presidency of an Ordinary Man, 1945–1953*. This interview occurred at the New-York Historical Society on March 15, 2023.

Like most of Truman's recent biographers, Frank came away admiring Truman for many of the actions and qualities described above. I came away with the realization that a president's reputation can certainly change, and that it is probably a mistake to pass judgment only during their time in office. Some historians think that decades are needed before one can really assess a presidency. A look at Truman and what he accomplished is an eye-opening example of how history and presidential reputations can shift.

*   *   *   *

DAVID M. RUBENSTEIN (DR): What prompted you to write a book about Harry Truman?

JEFFREY FRANK (JF): When I was a kid, Truman was the president. My father worked at the Pentagon, and I was immersed in that period, drawn to it again and again. The entire modern world began to take shape during his presidency.

DR: After David McCullough wrote a book on Harry Truman, which won the Pulitzer Prize, an extraordinary book, what did you think you could add to his legacy?

JF: David McCullough's book is terrific, but it's a real cradle-to-grave biography. It was also written 30 years ago. Mine is more a biography of a presidency, so I could focus more on why I really care about Harry Truman. It also includes a lot of new stuff. The National Archives has added a lot of material, the Truman Library has a lot of new material, and there are a lot of oral histories that didn't exist before.

DR: Harry Truman left office with one of the lowest popularity ratings of recent times. Now he seems to be idolized, and people think he was a great president. What changed?

JF: Time happened. When Truman was president, he was unimpressive. He was a bad speaker. Everything was going badly. There were minor scandals. The Korean War looked like a war with no end. So he was really unpopular, with one of the historically lowest ratings ever.

But as time goes by, people begin to have a different perspective, to be able to say, "Oh, he *did* do things." Henry Steele Commager wrote a piece for *Look* magazine, just before Truman left office, commenting that people will soon forget his "venial sins" and remember his major accomplishments, such as the Marshall Plan.

DR: One of the most famous decisions that he made was to drop two atomic bombs on Hiroshima and Nagasaki. Did he ever have any second thoughts about doing that?

JF: No, he never had second thoughts. There were times when I think he had pangs of conscience. In a conversation with Reinhold Niebuhr and Arthur Schlesinger Jr., he talked about how he felt awful about all the people who had been killed, but he also said he'd never regretted it. He would do it again, he said.

DR: Did he ever have second thoughts about anything he did?

JF: Yes. The Korean War was a difficult decision. He said it was his most difficult decision, and I believe him. I don't know that he regretted having so many cronies on the White House staff, but I suspect he probably did.

DR: The State Department, and virtually everybody in his administration, advised him not to recognize the State of Israel when it was about to be created as an independent country. Truman disagreed. Why did he recognize Israel and overrule his most trusted advisors?

JF: He once said that "there are two people at this desk, the president of the United States and Harry Truman." It was a Harry Truman decision, not a presidential decision. It was an emotional decision. He was obviously influenced by what had happened during World War II. There was a ship of refugees, the former SS *President Warfield*, fleeing Europe, trying to land in Palestine. That affected Truman. His friend and former business partner, Eddie Jacobson, who was Jewish, influenced him too.

DR: Truman didn't go to college. He was very plainspoken. Did people at the time feel that the presidency was lowered by having such an uneducated person in the presidency?

JF: He followed Franklin Roosevelt, who was probably the most eloquent and magnetic speaker of the last century. Truman had none of those qualities. He had a high-pitched voice. He had a Missouri accent. He would say "b'lieve." He was not charismatic. But people got used to it, and got used to his honesty and his straightforwardness. They felt a certain affection for him.

DR: An example is that when his daughter was making her debut as a singer, Paul Hume, a *Washington Post* music critic, wrote a review saying she didn't know how to sing. Harry Truman wrote a letter to Paul Hume.

JF: He basically said, "If I run into you, you'll probably need a beefsteak for your eye, and perhaps a supporter below." He was very angry. Ordinarily, Truman would not have been able to send the letter. Someone probably would have gotten him to stop. But Truman walked to the mailbox and dropped it in.

DR: One time Truman is reported to have said something like "This is a bunch of horse manure." Somebody went to Bess Truman, his wife, and said, "Can't you get him to stop saying that?"

JF: She said, "You know how long it took me to get him to use the word *manure*?"

DR: Your book is not designed to be a comprehensive look at his entire life, but you do cover it briefly. Where was he born?

JF: He was born outside of Independence, close to Grandview, Missouri.

DR: What did his parents do?

JF: His father was basically ne'er-do-well. He made bad investments. He was a farmer. He almost lost the farm, and the family was bailed out. His mother was an impressive woman, really influential. She had gone to college. She knew music, knew literature. One of the things she gave her son Harry, her favorite, was a set of books, *The Lives of Great Men and Famous Women.*

If you see a picture of his parents, you'll see that his father was much shorter than his mother. She was a dominating woman, in the best sense. Harry never stopped writing to her. Right until the day she died, they were constant correspondents. The day that the war ended in Europe, he called his mother. Then she came to Washington and stayed at the White House, her first trip ever on an airplane.

DR: She and his father gave him the name Harry S. Truman. What did the *S* stand for?

JF: It didn't stand for anything. It was based on the names of two grandparents, but he just thought he needed a middle initial.

DR: Did he have brothers and sisters?

JF: Yes, he had two siblings whom he wasn't necessarily close to. John Vivian, called Vivian, was older. Then he had a younger sister, Mary Jane.

DR: Truman had some physical weakness relating to his eyes. He had thick glasses from the time he was a young boy?

JF: He had what he called "flat eyeball," which isn't anything unusual. He was basically nearsighted. He always wore thick glasses from the time he was a kid.

DR: Was he a good student?

JF: He was an okay student. He was a very diligent music student. You would see him carrying his music for piano lessons every day.

DR: And was he a good athlete?

JF: No, he didn't do that. In fact, he was advised not to do that because he could break his glasses.

DR: After he graduated from high school, did he go to college?

JF: No, he didn't. Later on, he attended some night classes. After high school, he worked as a timekeeper for a construction company, in the mailroom of the *Kansas City Star*. He worked at a bank. These were not very presidential jobs. Then his father called him and said, "Come help out on the farm," and he went back to live on the farm and stayed for 10 years.

When Truman became president, Roy Roberts, the managing editor of the *Kansas City Star*, said, here's a man who, not so long before, "was still looking at the rear end of a horse."

DR: When World War I broke out, Harry Truman was in the military. He was in the reserves at some point?

JF: He was called up, yes. He was later promoted to captain. Truman was a Baptist from Missouri. The men he commanded were Irish Catholics from Kansas City, and they loved him. He became a real leader there, and that stayed with him.

DR: Did he come close to getting shot at himself?

JF: No, but he saw combat. He fired artillery.

DR: When the war is over, he goes back to Missouri, and he goes into business with one of his friends from high school, Eddie Jacobson. They were in the military together?

JF: They were friends from the Army. He also went back to pursue a woman, Elizabeth Virginia Wallace—Bess. He had first met her when they were about seven years old. He was completely stuck on her from that moment. He was crazy in love with her.

I think they had a very chaste relationship. Bess agreed to marry him before the war, but Truman said, basically, "Let's wait, because if I'm wounded I don't want you to be stuck with a cripple."

DR: So he goes into a haberdashery business with Eddie Jacobson. How did that go?

JF: It went okay for about two years. Then, through no fault of his, the economy went south, and so did they. The Truman and Jacobson Haberdashery went bankrupt, but Truman did not personally go bankrupt. He paid everything off eventually. It took years and years, but he didn't want to be thought of as someone who couldn't pay his debts.

DR: How did he get into politics? What was the first electoral job he had?

JF: It was called an administrative judge. He was basically a county administrator. He was recruited as a candidate by Tom Pendergast, who was the Kansas City Democratic Party boss. Harry Truman had known his nephew Jim Pendergast while he was in Europe, and that helped bring him to Pendergast's attention. He got elected in 1927.

DR: He runs for reelection, and he loses. Why did he lose, if he was so good at it?

JF: He wasn't good at elections at that time. That was the only election he ever lost, by the way.

DR: Does he give up, or does he say, "I'm going to run again"?

JF: Pendergast said, "Let's go for it again," and Truman ran two more times. He's Judge Truman, but he never went to law school and wasn't a lawyer. He was really good at details, such as finding the right level of concrete for highways. When he was courting Bess, he had a Stafford car, and it drove him crazy. He kept being afraid of getting flat tires, so one of the first things he did was to get money for the roads.

DR: He's the county judge, and he decides he'd like to be a member of Congress?

JF: Boss Pendergast first suggested he run for Congress, then reneged and said, "No, you can't run for the House," which would have been a safe bet. Then Pendergast suggested he try for the U.S. Senate, which was a real long shot. This was 1934. Truman was 50 years old. He had a chance of being a tax collector—which would have paid a lot more, but the job didn't have a long life span—or he could run for the Senate. He talked to Bess, who said it was his choice.

DR: He runs in a primary, and he wins the primary and the general election?

JF: To the surprise of many people, including Truman himself.

DR: Does he have any real success?

JF: He got along with people. He did not have a distinguished first term. He found his crowd, mostly people from rural communities around the country, with whom he often met in what was called the "Board of Education," which was Sam Rayburn's office in the House.

    In his second term, he became more active. Before the war, he thought what was needed was a special committee to check waste, fraud, and abuse in the defense industry. The Senate voted him the authority to form the committee, which he was terrific at. He saved the country a lot of money. He was so good that he ended up on the cover of *Time* magazine. That way he became sort of a national figure.

DR: Franklin Roosevelt decides to run for a fourth term. In his first term, John Nance Garner was his vice president.

JF: First and second. Garner served two terms.

DR: Then Roosevelt had Henry Wallace. After that third term, he decided he didn't like Wallace anymore, or people thought he was too liberal?

JF: He was maybe too flaky. He was a Buddhist Catholic Jewish Rosicrucian. And he was too fond of the Soviet Union. He had very interesting beliefs.

DR: So Roosevelt says, "I've got to get somebody else." Who recommended Harry Truman? Why was he on the list?

JF: Roosevelt had promised the job to James Francis Byrnes, who had been a senator and, even though he never finished high school, was a

Supreme Court justice. Those were the days when a resume didn't mean what it does today. You could be a Supreme Court justice and not even go to high school.

Then Byrnes became what was being called the "assistant president." He was in charge of all kinds of domestic programs during the war. Roosevelt basically had promised him the vice presidency, then didn't keep his word.

DR: A politician didn't keep his word?

JF: Yes. It had never happened before. But Jimmy Byrnes had real problems.

DR: Who recommended Truman? Did Roosevelt even know him?

JF: He'd met him. Truman was a senator, he would show up at the White House for parties. Roosevelt knew him well enough to say, "Hi, Harry."

Roosevelt's advisors said, "This guy makes lots of sense." Labor didn't like Jimmy Byrnes. And Byrnes was also a rabid segregationist from South Carolina. Truman was a perfect candidate. He was from a border state, he was a big supporter of the New Deal—a sort of middle choice, and Labor liked him.

DR: The convention was in Chicago. He gets the nomination and he goes on the ticket. Does he realize how unhealthy Roosevelt is?

JF: He doesn't really talk about it. He had one private meeting with Roosevelt, that's it. Roosevelt told him nothing. They met for lunch under a tree outside the White House, and Truman noticed Roosevelt's hand was shaking. The president was clearly not well. Truman didn't think he was going to die, or didn't want to admit it to himself, but he could see that Roosevelt was enfeebled.

DR: In those days, the vice president didn't have an office in the West Wing, didn't have an office even in the Executive Office complex. The only office the vice president had was in the Senate. So they didn't actually run into each other.

JF: That's right. They had one sit-down meal. That was it, apart from cabinet meetings and such.

DR: In April, Franklin Roosevelt has a cerebral hemorrhage and dies. How did Truman get notified about this?

JF: After he was sworn in for his fourth term, Roosevelt went off to Yalta to meet with Churchill and Stalin, and didn't tell Truman where he was going. When Roosevelt returned, he spoke to Congress, then left for Warm Springs, Georgia. And that's where he died, suddenly. Truman was in Sam Rayburn's office when he got a call. "You'd better come over to the White House fast." I don't know if they told him what it was, but he knew it was serious, and he rushed over.

DR: He rushed to the White House, and who swears him in?

JF: He was told the president was dead. He was taken upstairs to meet Mrs. Roosevelt, and then he had to be sworn in as quickly as possible.

DR: What did she say to him?

JF: He said, "I'm so sorry," and she said, "All the burden is on you now." The chief justice, Harlan Stone, was hurried over, though they had to wait a little bit longer because Truman wanted his wife and his daughter, Margaret, to be there. The Trumans lived in an apartment on upper Connecticut Avenue, and Bess and Margaret had to be brought to the White House to watch him being sworn in.

DR: How many months was Roosevelt president in his fourth term?

JF: Three months.

DR: Truman is sworn in. He lets Eleanor Roosevelt stay in the White House for a while. In those days, vice presidents lived in their own home. They didn't have a government home?

JF: Yes. He stayed the night at his apartment, then moved to Blair House, which is across Lafayette Park from the White House. He was very nice to Mrs. Roosevelt.

DR: In the beginning he still had to win the war in Europe. It's getting close to being won, but it's not technically won yet. After Germany surrenders, in May, there is a conference in Potsdam, outside of Berlin. And now all of a sudden Harry Truman has to show up representing the United States government with Churchill and Stalin. How did that go?

JF: It went okay. Truman held his own, simply because he was the president of the United States. This was the period when the United States was so incredibly rich, so incredibly powerful, that everyone, particularly Churchill, deferred to him. Churchill treated him almost as if Churchill was a senator seeking aid after a hurricane had hit his state. Everyone had been devastated by the war.

Stalin was a coldblooded fellow. Truman said he liked good old Joe. He believed that the Politburo was in charge, not Stalin.

DR: He called him Uncle Joe?

JF: Only privately. Roosevelt may have also, but Stalin did not like that.

DR: Truman was surprised at how short Stalin was, wasn't he?

JF: Yes. They were all short. They were all about five-five or five-six. Truman was very sensitive about that. They were all short and sort of tubby. Truman actually wasn't. But it was a very strange conference, almost like a costume party. Churchill would dress up in a Lord of the Admiralty theme, which he was entitled to. Stalin, who had become Generalissimus Stalin—he made himself Generalissimus—would wear these fancy uniforms. Truman, in the traditional American way, would wear a business suit, but occasionally with a Stetson.

DR: In those days, it took quite a while to get to Potsdam. Did he get there on a plane or a boat?

JF: It was an eight-day trip by boat. Truman did his homework on the way, reading memos, one after another. He had a lot of preparation to do, and he was worried that he wasn't going to catch up. He studied and studied and studied. This was a very stressful time.

Averell Harriman, the American ambassador in Russia, briefed Truman on Stalin. Truman was already losing patience with Stalin. He felt he was not going to keep his word vis-à-vis the future of Poland, for example.

DR: At Potsdam, Truman hints to Stalin that we have a special weapon that's more powerful than anything anybody's ever seen. Because of espionage, didn't Stalin already know about this weapon?

JF: Yes, he did, possibly even before Truman knew, because there was so much spying going on. Truman arrived on July 15th, 1945. On the 16th, he toured Berlin and saw the wreckage. That was the day he got word that Trinity, the first test of an atomic bomb, had worked. He told Churchill.

DR: On his way back, on the boat, he gets word that the first bomb is ready. Does he have to think about it, or did he say, "Go ahead"?

JF: Let me back up briefly. There were two or three committees. One committee, the "interim committee," had basically decided, "We are going to use this thing." There was no debate, no question they were going to use the bomb. Then there was a target committee that chose the place to drop it. They chose Kyoto, which is this beautiful city that has shrines and so on. And Henry Stimson, the secretary of defense, said, "Don't do it, they'll never forgive us." So Hiroshima became the place of choice.

Truman gave the order. The bomb couldn't be dropped without his order. He wanted to be away from Potsdam, out of Germany. So on August 6th, 1945, while Truman was still aboard his ship, the bomb was dropped.

DR: And that bomb didn't quite end the war.

JF: No.

DR: So the second bomb was dropped on August 9th, and six days after that, the Japanese surrendered. They were originally supposed to surrender unconditionally, which would have meant the removal and probable execution of the emperor. Why did the U.S. government allow the emperor to stay?

JF: Because that was the only thing that really made sense. How much could you crush them? There was some debate, but Admiral Leahy, Truman's chief of staff, said, "We'll be here forever" if they didn't allow the emperor to stay.

DR: After the war is over, an amazing number of things happen in foreign policy that Truman didn't get full credit for at the time. NATO was started?

JF: Yes, that came in his second term. A lot of credit for that goes to a Republican senator named Arthur Vandenberg. The nonbinding Vandenberg Resolution offered early support for Europe.

DR: And the CIA was created?

JF: Yes, through the National Security Act of 1947.

DR: There really hadn't been anything like the CIA. The FBI had been doing some of that before?

JF: Yes. There was Wild Bill Donovan's organization, the OSS, in World War II, but the FBI wasn't really doing foreign intelligence.

DR: And the UN was created. Was Truman supportive of that?

JF: Truman was very supportive of the UN, which honored Roosevelt's commitment.

DR: During that period, the famous Marshall Plan was announced. General Marshall, then the secretary of state, announced it at a Harvard commencement. Why didn't they call it the Truman Plan?

JF: Truman said to an aide, "If they call it the Truman Plan, it's going to go belly-up right away." He was aware that he wasn't very popular. Truman personally did not have that much to do with the Marshall Plan, though he gave it his full support. But a lot of people realized that if Europe wasn't helped quickly, it was going to be a human and economic disaster. People like George Kennan, who had been the Russian expert in the State Department, and Dean Acheson, who became secretary of state, and many others realized something had to be done—something that would cost an enormous amount of money. And that led to the Marshall Plan, which is an extraordinary thing. Nothing like it had ever been done before.

DR: Truman mostly got rid of the people that Roosevelt had around him. Who did he appoint instead?

JF: Truman's cabinet and Supreme Court appointments were pretty mediocre at first. In his first term, he appointed Jimmy Byrnes, who had been close to FDR, secretary of state, almost as a consolation prize for not getting the vice presidency. Byrnes was an undistinguished secretary of state. Truman couldn't wait until he was gone; in time, he got General Marshall to replace him, and then in his second term he appointed Dean Acheson, who'd been undersecretary to Byrnes.

DR: Truman didn't have the most honest people around him. He himself was honest, but there were some minor scandals caused by some of the people around him?

JF: That's true. They were little scandals, but they kept going. There was bribery. There were certain phrases like "mink coats" and "deep freezers" (i.e., gifts given to Truman officials) that made headlines.

DR: On the domestic front, people might be surprised that Truman was an ardent believer in civil rights.

JF: Not too ardent. He and his wife came from a family that had supported the Confederacy. Nonetheless, Truman supported the desegregation, in effect, of the federal workforce. But by modern standards, Truman would probably be considered something of a racist. He used the N-word all the time. He grew up in Confederate Missouri. But as I said before—he recognized that there were two people in the office: the president and Harry Truman. The president invariably did the right thing.

DR: He was also a supporter of health care for everybody. What happened there?

JF: This is something Roosevelt couldn't accomplish. Roosevelt could get legislation creating Social Security, but he couldn't get health care through Congress. Truman tried again and again. He had a very ambitious plan that eventually would have become Medicare, but it was shot down time and again in Congress.

DR: Truman is not all that popular as he goes forward. People think he's not as good as Roosevelt; the economy has some inflation after the war; and his administration had scandals. He had never been elected. Did he ever think he shouldn't run in 1948?

JF: He had no doubt that he'd run again. But according to the polls, he was destined to lose. He had trouble recruiting a vice president. The Supreme Court justice William Douglas said no.

DR: The first couple years of Truman's presidency, he has no vice president because the Constitution did not spell out steps for a vice presidential succession. Had he died in office, who would have been the president?

JF: The secretary of state. But after Truman lost the midterm elections in 1946, a Democratic senator went so far as to suggest that Truman appoint a Republican as secretary of state and, in the interest of a smooth transition, resign. Then someone like Arthur Vandenberg, seen as a model bipartisan Republican, would be next in the line of succession.

DR: In 1948, the nominee for the Republican Party is Thomas Dewey, the governor of New York, who had been the nominee in 1944 for the Republicans. He was thought widely to be certain to win. What happened?

JF: It was a strong ticket. Earl Warren, the governor of California, was the Republican nominee for vice president. All the polls said Dewey was going to win. The polls were right, but the pollsters stopped polling about two months before the election. They probably were right when they were polling, but in the end they were very, very wrong.

DR: There's a famous *Chicago Tribune* headline that said "Dewey Defeats Truman." Truman liked to hold it up to show how wrong the press was. Did Truman think he was going to lose?

JF: He never said so. He always said he thought he was going to win. But as to the newspaper, it was only the early editions. Some of the pollsters sensed there was some movement, things were happening, but they didn't poll again.

DR: Who was his vice president?

JF: Alben Barkley, who was a terrible choice. He'd been the Senate majority leader, but he was much older than Truman. It made no sense. That was one thing I never understood: picking an older vice president after being there when Roosevelt died. But Barkley was it.

DR: Truman gets elected, or reelected. During his second term, the Korean War breaks out. The North Korean forces invaded the South Korea area?

JF: Yes. It broke out at the end of June 1950. There had been border skirmishes, but suddenly it became very serious. Truman was in Missouri at the time. His secretary of defense and others were away. When they realized the severity, and that they had to meet, they immediately started discussing what they were going to do about it.

DR: Why didn't they go to Congress and get a declaration of war?

JF: People like Senator Taft of Ohio made that very same point.

DR: But Truman called it a "police action," not a war.

JF: Actually he didn't. A reporter said, "Would you characterize this as a police action?" And that's how it became known. Truman never used the phrase himself.

DR: Who was in charge of fighting for the Americans?

JF: General Douglas MacArthur was the commander, but, at age 70, he wasn't at top form. General Dwight D. Eisenhower, who had worked with MacArthur in the Philippines, once said, "How did such an idiot ever become a general?" MacArthur was both vain and famous.

He had a very successful couple of months, after a terrifying couple of months. The North basically occupied 90 percent of Korea at first, but then MacArthur had this daring, successful idea to do an amphibious landing at Inchon, behind the North Korean lines, and come to the enemy from the rear. Then the war turned around. That's when it possibly could have ended. But MacArthur decided that he was going to unify the country, as opposed to simply pushing the North Koreans back over the 38th parallel.

DR: And maybe attack the Chinese as well.

JF: It came to that later, but he had his atomic weapon dreams. The analogy to me is the first Gulf War, pushing the Iraqis out of Kuwait. What MacArthur did was turn it into the second Gulf War—regime change and a disaster. Thirty-seven thousand Americans died. Hundreds of thousands of Koreans, possibly two million Chinese. Every single village in the North was burned. Kim Il-sung, the leader of North Korea, never forgave us. His grandson is now the leader of North Korea. That's one reason why we don't have easy relations with North Korea.

DR: MacArthur says, "Maybe we should carry the bombing into China," beyond what the president has authorized. So Truman talks to people about getting rid of MacArthur. What did his advisors tell him?

JF: Truman wasn't going to go into China, but MacArthur seemed willing to drop some atomic bombs on China. Truman said, "This is it." MacArthur basically defied orders. Truman met with the Joint Chiefs of Staff, and the decision was made.

DR: Who told MacArthur he was relieved?

JF: They sent a deputy to the secretary of defense over to meet with MacArthur. But then MacArthur heard it on the radio. These things never are kept secret.

DR: So he comes back to the United States for the first time in at least 13 years. What does he do?

JF: He was invited back by Republicans, some of whom were very devoted to MacArthur. He gave a speech to the full House of Congress, and it was considered one of the great speeches of all time. One congressman said, "It was like the voice of God in the flesh today." People were weeping. The speech ended with MacArthur saying, "Old soldiers never die, they just fade away."

People thought MacArthur had a huge future ahead of him, that maybe he'd be president. It went away quickly; but there were motions to impeach Truman over this.

DR: MacArthur was popular. How does it happen that Eisenhower, who was an assistant to MacArthur at one point, becomes the next president of the United States and not MacArthur?

JF: Eisenhower was the Supreme Commander of the Allied forces in Europe. He was a national hero. Eisenhower had this great smile. He was not the friendliest man, but he was extremely appealing.

DR: At the end of Truman's term, Truman decides not to run for reelection. Why?

JF: Bess told him, "You won't survive it, and neither will I." Truman had gotten ill just before the 1952 convention, but he had decided not to run before that. He made the announcement in March of '52. The polls were terrible and some of his answers were rambling. You could just tell the weariness had gotten to him.

DR: Who does he want to have succeed him in the Democratic Party?

JF: He wanted Fred Vinson, the chief justice of the Supreme Court, who was a buddy of his. But Vinson said no. So Truman tried to recruit the new governor of Illinois, Adlai Stevenson, and Stevenson said, "I don't want anything to do with it. I just want to be governor again." But Stevenson finally realized that maybe he might want to be president. He was a reluctant candidate, and, in his acceptance speech, he talked about how "If this cup shall pass my way, I shall sip from it."

DR: Eisenhower was reluctant as well, but he got the Republican nomination.

JF: Eisenhower became less reluctant with time. And Stevenson, as he was being recruited by Truman, talked to his friend and advisor George Ball, and said, "Why would I want to do this? Eisenhower's going to win. I would probably vote for Eisenhower."

DR: Eisenhower picks Richard Nixon as his vice president. Did he know Nixon?

JF: Yes, they'd met at the Bohemian Grove in California. There's a picture of them. Nixon was enamored of Eisenhower already. Nixon had been a lieutenant in the Navy, and Eisenhower was the Supreme Commander. He went to meet him in Paris when Eisenhower was helping to set up what became NATO. I'm not sure that Eisenhower could remember Nixon, but they did know each other.

DR: Eisenhower was 62 and Nixon 39. They win in a landslide in 1952. What's the relationship between Truman and Eisenhower? Because

Eisenhower said he would go to Korea to help solve the war, which was an insult to Truman.

JF: The campaign had been nasty. They had once liked each other. Truman really admired Eisenhower. Truman had been an artillery man in the first World War. Eisenhower was a five-star general, and Truman was impressed by military men.

Eisenhower sort of admired Truman. But Truman thought the campaign was horrible, especially when Eisenhower did not defend General Marshall, who had been Eisenhower's patron and supporter. Senator McCarthy of Wisconsin, the notorious red-hunter, had attacked Marshall, saying that Marshall "is at the heart of a conspiracy so black and so infamous" that it was basically a communist conspiracy. And Eisenhower did not defend him. Truman thought, and said, that someone who does not defend his friend has no spine and is not fit to be president. Eisenhower was thin-skinned to begin with, and Truman's view sort of crossed the line for him.

DR: Eisenhower ultimately says during the campaign that he will go to Korea, and that probably helped him win the election.

JF: Right. Eisenhower gave a speech that included a promise to go to Korea to begin to end the war. One of Stevenson's advisors said, "The election was lost tonight."

DR: During the transition period, Eisenhower does go secretly to Korea, and ultimately there is an armistice that's agreed to when he's president. When Truman leaves the White House, he's leaving with very low popularity ratings. What does he do?

JF: Yes. He had a pension of about $112 a month from his time as a soldier. He first had a happy farewell lunch with his cabinet at the Achesons' house in Georgetown. He then took the train back to Independence, where he stayed for the rest of his life. He was not broke. He quickly sold his memoirs to *Life* magazine for $600,000. So he was going to do okay.

DR: Eisenhower had earlier sold his war memoirs for $500,000, so Truman wanted to get a little bit more.

JF: That's exactly right, though Eisenhower got a special tax break on his deal. I don't know that Truman did.

DR: Truman lives to be 88. He dies in 1972. And before he dies, among other things the Medicare bill is passed, and President Johnson comes out to Independence, Missouri, to sign it there. Why did he do that?

JF: Because of all the efforts Truman had made to get a health care plan. Johnson came out to Independence and sat with Truman and Bess. By this time the Truman Library had been built. Medicare card number one went to Truman, Medicare card number two went to Bess, and Johnson signed the bill there.

DR: When Nixon's elected president in 1972, although he has a complicated relationship with Truman, he presents him with a piano for the Truman Library that Truman played at the White House. And Nixon plays what song?

JF: The "Missouri Waltz." Truman hated the "Missouri Waltz."

DR: Truman ultimately becomes frail and doesn't go out in public much toward the end of his life?

JF: Yes, he had a bad fall when he was 80 years old. He slowed down. His doctor said he maybe had a type of Parkinson's. He wanted to go to the funeral for Herbert Hoover in 1984, but couldn't. He died in the hospital in Kansas City, which cost about $59 a night and was paid for by Medicare.

DR: After doing all this work on Truman, are you more impressed with him than you were before you began, or less impressed?

JF: Truman grows on you. I thought more of him. He was a decent man who tried to do the right thing, and even when he had thoughts that he knew weren't as nice as they should be, he tried to say and do the right thing.

11

SUSAN EISENHOWER
on Dwight D. Eisenhower

(1890–1969; president from 1953 to 1961)

My first memories of a president were of Dwight Eisenhower. I was three when he was elected and eleven when he left office. As I have come to learn more about Eisenhower in recent years, I have come away as a real admirer. He was old to an eleven-year-old. But in fact, he was elected at 62 and left office at 70, relatively young by today's standards.

When I was growing up, Eisenhower was seen—by me at least—as, well, dull. He gave no great speeches or press conferences. His syntax felt garbled. And there was no excitement about his programs. Eisenhower may have led the D-Day invasion, but he seemed, in office, to be less of a leader than a follower. And as I recall, he played golf a great deal (though perhaps not by the standards of Woodrow Wilson who, pre-stroke, tried to play almost every day).

My views were in line with the accepted wisdom at the time, even in Republican circles, where Eisenhower was popular but not seen as a forceful or dynamic president. Despite the bland personality, he maintained his popularity, and he left office with quite high approval ratings, certainly compared to his predecessor.

With the benefit of several decades of perspective since he left office, I now see Eisenhower much differently, as do a great many scholars. Eisenhower may have been dull, without rousing speeches, but he kept the peace for eight years; started NASA (which led to America's eventual success in space); began the Interstate Highway System (without the use of federal income tax dollars); appointed Earl Warren as chief justice;

sent federal troops to Little Rock to enforce the *Brown v. Board of Education* decision (though he may not have really liked it); oversaw an enormous, almost unprecedented economic expansion in the U.S.; began the first series of federal investments in science and technology; and oversaw the admission of Alaska and Hawaii to the Union.

I thought it might be interesting to see how someone close to Eisenhower might provide a modern, highly personal look at him, and I therefore interviewed one of his granddaughters, Susan, who has become a scholar of American and Russian history, at a Congressional Dialogues session at the Library of Congress on March 15, 2022. She had recently written a highly enjoyable book on her grandfather. Her memories of him are still vivid, and she provides a human dimension to him that I found quite appealing.

✳   ✳   ✳   ✳

DAVID M. RUBENSTEIN (DR): Dwight Eisenhower and Mamie Eisenhower had two children. One died at the age of three of scarlet fever. The remaining child was your father?

SUSAN EISENHOWER (SE): Yes, John Eisenhower. He and his wife, Barbara, my mother, had four children: David; my older sister, Anne; I'm the middle child; and I have a younger sister named Mary.

DR: You led an effort, maybe on behalf of others in your family as well, to protest the original design by Frank Gehry of the Eisenhower Memorial. What was wrong with the original design?

SE: It seemed not monumental enough for the core of Washington. But ultimately we got a monumental backdrop to a design that had already been approved by the Fine Arts Commission, *The Beaches of Normandy in Peacetime*. What a great symbol of not just his contribution in the war but what emerged after that war. It's absolutely wonderful to drive down the street and see little kids up on the plinth kind of tugging on his coat or looking up at these paratroopers. It really means a lot.

DR: Let's talk about your relationship with your grandfather. How old were you when he was in the White House?

SE: I was about nine years old when he left the presidency.

DR: You were one, more or less, when he was elected?

SE: Yes. I was born when he was commander of NATO forces in Europe.

DR: Do you remember the White House? Did he say, "I'm going to stop everything and spend time with my grandchildren," or that didn't happen?

SE: My grandmother had a pretty good rule: Don't come home from the office unless you come home. Stay there until you get your work done, because when you're at home, you're with the family. I think it helped him a lot to gain perspective, because a job like that is so extraordinarily stressful. I was one of the great beneficiaries of my grandmother's strong rule.

DR: After he left the White House, he lived another nine years or so. You were about 18 when he passed away?

SE: Yes.

DR: What was he like when he moved to Gettysburg? Did you spend time with him? What kind of person was he?

SE: I had almost an everyday relationship with him, because we lived on an adjacent farm. That's where the grandchildren strategy comes in. We had a very normal family life, and then suddenly, somebody like Winston Churchill or Charles de Gaulle would be coming, and he'd say, "Get the kids cleaned up and over at the house shortly."

He was an extraordinary man. He was as tough as he had to be, but he had an enormous capacity to empathize with other people and to make them feel important.

DR: Let's talk about his life. Where was he born?

SE: He was born in Denison, Texas. He then moved to Abilene, Kansas. He had most of his childhood there.

DR: His parents were of German descent. Did he ever think that it was strange, later on, that he was leading the war effort against the Germans?

SE: He talked a lot about his German heritage. His father was the first of his generation to speak English only, and insisted that they all speak English in the household. There were family members who spoke German.

Could I say one more thing about our crazy family? They were all conscientious objectors too. Can you imagine a conscientious objector going off to West Point and then being asked to command forces against his native ethnic group?

DR: How many children were there in that family?

SE: There were seven boys altogether, no girls. My grandfather was the middle child. The boys had to rotate through chores, which is why my grandfather was an excellent cook. He could sew on buttons. He could iron. He could do everything. My grandmother, who was a bit of a debutante, allowed Ike to do the cooking when he had the time.

DR: Why was he interested in going into the military, coming from a family of conscientious objectors? What led him to go to West Point?

SE: He was putting his older brother through college, and he was getting older and older. In those days, if you didn't turn up for college within a certain period, you lost your opportunity. A friend of his said, "Why don't you apply to the Naval Academy?" So Ike applied but was too old to get in. He then applied to West Point.

DR: He became a five-star general. There hasn't been one since then. Was he first in his class at West Point?

SE: This is one of my favorite stories. Three great commanders—Ulysses S. Grant, John Pershing, and Dwight Eisenhower—all graduated in the middle of their classes, and all three of them had questionable disciplinary records. I love that.

DR: Did he play football at West Point?

SE: He did. He was a very good football player. He even played against Jim Thorpe in the Army-Carlisle game. What an extraordinary piece of history that is. But then he broke his knee in one of the games and was on the sidelines. Not to become discouraged, he became a cheerleader. How about that?

DR: He graduated in the famous class of 1915, which is "the class that the stars fell on," they say, because so many of them became generals. What did he do right after graduation?

SE: He went to various posts, but the most important part of his immediate post–West Point trajectory was during the First World War. He commanded our nation's first tank unit. (He and George Patton were big tank enthusiasts.) It was at Camp Colt in Gettysburg. Not only did he prepare the first unit for going to the front in tanks, he also managed the Spanish flu outbreak there. There were no rules for how to handle a pandemic. The Army wasn't even admitting that they had a problem. Ike received the Distinguished Service Medal at the age of 28 for his leadership at Camp Colt.

DR: He got in trouble, though, for proposing that tanks be able to go faster than humans could walk. Tanks were supposed to go the same speed as humans. Is that right?

SE: That's correct. There may have been some revenge in this. Ike had been outspoken about this new, exotic technology, and how surely tanks can go faster than that and be armed and be a lethal weapon of war. So what did they do? They make him the first tank commander. I think he wanted very much to go to the front but ended up in Gettysburg commanding this tank corps.

DR: He was not in combat in World War I?

SE: No, he was on his way to the front when the armistice was reached.

DR: After World War I, he meets General John Pershing and works for him?

SE: He wrote a book called *The American Battlefields of France*. When World War II rolled around, what advantage did Ike have over every other general? He knew tanks and he knew the terrain, thanks to both of those projects. They weren't exactly where he wanted to be in his career, but these projects turned out to be pivotal.

DR: Between World War I and World War II, he did many different things. One of them was being an assistant to a person named Douglas MacArthur. Did he like MacArthur because of his modesty and humility?

SE: You took the words right out of Ike's mouth, had he been alive. He said in his memoirs that he learned amateur theatrics from Douglas MacArthur. MacArthur was, some say, vain and difficult. I think that they respected each other on many levels. Eisenhower kept notes on the leaders he admired and the ones he had questions about. He said that MacArthur was a genius for giving clear instructions. But I'm pretty sure that, having worked for MacArthur, he decided he wanted to be the un-MacArthur in the Army.

DR: At the age of 50, Dwight Eisenhower is a colonel. Twelve years later, he becomes president of the United States. How did he go from a colonel with no combat experience to leading Operation Overlord? When World War II breaks out, where is Dwight Eisenhower?

SE: He was up at Fort Lewis in Washington, then he went to join the Third Army in Texas. In the Louisiana Maneuvers, the largest military maneuvers in American history, the Army took over the entire state and practiced amphibious landings and more. Ike was the chief strategist for the winning side of the Louisiana Maneuvers. This is when he comes to the attention of Chief of Staff of the Army George Marshall.

DR: This was a big maneuver, with 200,000 soldiers. Eisenhower comes to Marshall's attention. Later, when they decide we need to have a general to lead the American and Allied forces in Europe, why is Eisenhower picked and not George Marshall?

SE: There's an adage, "If it ain't broke, don't fix it." General Marshall had an extraordinary relationship with the president of the United States, Franklin Roosevelt, but there was tension between Marshall and Churchill. Eisenhower got along with Churchill very well.

DR: To give him some combat experience, they said, "Before you lead the Operation Overlord, why don't you get some combat experience in northern Africa, and then we'll go to Italy."

SE: Britain's situation in Africa was precarious. Before Ike left for Europe, his friends said he would be the fall guy in case these invasions failed. His attitude was, "I'm going to do my duty." It turns out that it was a very important learning experience. I think if Eisenhower had been in combat in World War I and had fought the way they did during that war, he would have never been as creative as he was during World War II. He reimagined a war that had not been imagined before.

DR: How did he get along with the British leading general, Field Marshal Bernard Montgomery?

SE: This is legendary, probably for good reason. When I did this research and I started looking into who ends up in the Eisenhower presidential cabinet, you have a striking resemblance to the generals who surrounded him during World War II. Dwight Eisenhower appreciated pushback. Whether he thought it was fun or not is another question, but he saw the value in it. He surrounded himself by people who pushed him to question his decision making. That's what Montgomery did for him.

DR: North Africa works out reasonably well. Italy works out. So then the decision is to have Eisenhower lead Operation Overlord. How intensive was the planning for that? How long did it take to prepare for the invasion of Normandy?

SE: The preparations went on for some period before Ike was tapped. When he was given this responsibility, he looked at the plans and said, "No way. We don't have enough force here." He believed that you better have the forces amassed before you go into a situation like this. Eisenhower was the one who took the three-beaches invasion plan and enlarged it to five, including Utah Beach—which was pivotal—so that we could get American forces to Cherbourg. That was our objective, and it turns out that that was a vital addition to the plan. The British objective was Caen.

DR: The British Airborne general said, "Given current conditions, don't use paratroopers. They could be destroyed." Eisenhower overruled that as well?

SE: Yes. The paratrooper decision around D-Day is the most moving part of the story for me. The terrible weather forecast was heart-wrenching.

He knew that his chief technical expert, Air Marshal Trafford Leigh-Mallory, had advised him against using the paratroopers. You have to have the right kind of weather for dropping paratroopers so they can find their targets. But Ike decided that paratroopers were critical for securing two causeways. Capturing those two causeways would enable people to get off the beaches and move inland. So they were critical for the operation. He was told that 70 percent of those troops would perish—50 to 70 percent, including the glider forces. He went out that night and looked each one of these men in the eyes, and you know what he said to them? He said, "Where are you from?" Sometimes he got into a chat with several of them about the Jayhawks and the Cornhuskers. In one discussion with Wally Strobel, the paratrooper in that famous picture, he said, "Where you from, son?" "From Michigan." Ike said, "Do you do any fly-fishing out there?" Wally Strobel said yes. He survived that war and told my family this story.

I asked my father, "Why would Ike be talking about fly-fishing just before the most important operation of the most important invasion?" My father said, "He wanted to remind them that people back home are supporting them, and he wanted to give them something to live for."

DR: The D-Day invasion was supposed to be on June 5. What happened on that date?

SE: Terrible weather. They had to decide to postpone, though, until the weather was better. They were heavily reliant on what the outward forecast looked like. The weather committee didn't agree on the forecast. Can you imagine how tenuous that was?

DR: The weather committee was based on observation posts in Greenland or something like that.

SE: That's right.

DR: Finally the weather looks like it's going to be clear, and Eisenhower says, "Let's go ahead on June the 6th." Did he prepare a statement in case it didn't work?

SE: After D-Day, his assistant finds this piece of paper. It had been in Ike's wallet the night of the invasion. He wrote it on June the 5th. It says, "If this operation fails, the blame is mine and mine alone." Remember, he's written that just before he goes out to look those paratroopers in the eye. This assistant says, "I want to have that piece of paper for history." And Ike said, "No, this is a personal thing. I was going to release it if it failed, but it didn't, and we don't have to make a big fuss over this."

DR: Omaha Beach didn't look good for us the first couple of hours, but it turned around. Once it was certain that they had cleared the beaches and were moving forward, did Eisenhower say, "Now I'm going to go over and show that I pulled this off"? Did he go there right away?

SE: He gave his generals a lot of leeway. He went soon thereafter to sort out some problems and to be able to talk to his generals about the rest of it, so there was no pomp and no celebration.

DR: Who were the generals leading that effort?

SE: The famed Field Marshal Montgomery and General Omar Bradley. But the most interesting thing was that George Patton, who is often associated with D-Day, was actually not involved with the breakout. He was sitting in southern England commanding a fictitious unit that featured inflatable tanks and inflatable buildings. From the air, it looked like he was amassing great forces, but he was used as the decoy.

DR: When the Allied soldiers are moving further into Germany, Eisenhower comes over to assume command of the forces. The Battle of the Bulge occurs later in the fall, when the Germans hit with their last big offensive. Was he commanding the troops at the Battle of the Bulge?

SE: Yes, he was. There's a great moment when the bad news comes in about where the German positions are at the Bulge, and Eisenhower says, "There will be no long faces in this room. As dire as it looks, this is an opportunity, because they've shown their faces. Let's go get them." The Germans had played a defensive war and we played an offensive one.

DR: In the end the Allies prevail in the Battle of the Bulge. Then, as the troops are moving closer to Berlin, Eisenhower is brought to see some of the concentration camps. What does he say, what does he think about those?

SE: This is something that always has stayed with me. He went to liberate Ohrdruf, which was a subcamp of Buchenwald. He wrote to General Marshall that evening in effect: "I want as many people to come here as possible—the news media, members of Congress. We absolutely must chronicle this, because at some point, years from now, people will say it never happened." My father, who had just graduated from West Point and was in combat near Buchenwald, was ordered there by his immediate superior and took extraordinary pictures of Buchenwald. My father wanted to be sure that we would never forget.

DR: Even in 1943, before the successful D-Day invasion, Eisenhower is being asked to run for president, and he resists. After D-Day, he's getting even more entreaties to run. What does he say?

SE: "No, thank you. I've got a job to do." As soon as the war was over, though, the Democrats and the Republicans came calling. They took turns. At one point, after hearing out a delegation eager for him to consider the presidency, he said he found the conversation so embarrassing he wanted to "dive under the table." They kept saying, "You're a national treasure, and you owe it to the country." Eisenhower was a military man. He thought he knew what his job was.

DR: But after the war's over, he does take a new job as president of Columbia University. It's hard to imagine a five-star general commanding an Ivy League university today. In that day, it was considered a big deal for Columbia, and people were happy with it?

SE: Columbia University had a lot of financial problems at that time, and I'm sure the Board of Directors thought that he might be able to help with that. He did indeed raise significant funds for Columbia. But Ike had always been intrigued by and interested in education, and he said he wanted, after the war, to work for an educational institution. So there he was.

DR: Later Harry Truman comes calling and says, "I will step down and not run in 1948 if you take the Democratic nomination." How does Eisenhower respond?

SE: Eisenhower thanks Harry Truman for this offer but says no, he's not running for president.

DR: He turns down Truman's offer. He then takes the job of Supreme Allied Commander of NATO, the first one in that position. People keep saying they want him to run for president. Why does he change his mind?

SE: It's an excellent question. Let me say that Harry Truman offered him the job twice, in '52 as well. When Ike went to be the first Supreme Commander of NATO, that job hadn't existed before. He had to create a new job, a new organization. He went to Senator Taft and said, "Do I have your support for NATO?" And Senator Taft said no. I think he realized at one point that if he didn't stand up and agree to run for president, everything he'd worked for during the war to bring peace to Europe would be lost.

DR: You point out in your book that if Taft had said he'd support NATO, Eisenhower would have not sought the nomination in '52. Prior to Eisenhower, Taft was supposedly going to be the nominee, right?

SE: That's right. It's important to remember that Taft represented a wing of the party that was isolationist. You can imagine that Dwight Eisenhower, having fought a war in Europe like that, was the ultimate internationalist.

DR: Eisenhower puts his hat in the ring and gets the nomination. Then, at the convention, he finds out he has to pick a vice president. He says, "I thought somebody else was going to do that"?

SE: In those days the party played a more active role in selecting a vice president. But Richard Nixon, the young senator from California, exemplified anticommunist sentiments.

DR: Had he met Nixon before?

SE: Yes, but I don't think they were that well acquainted.

DR: So they run for president and vice president and they win overwhelmingly against Adlai Stevenson. What were Eisenhower's highest priorities in his first term as president?

SE: His highest priority was to reestablish the Republican Party as an internationalist party. There were also lots of debates about reducing taxes.

He said, "Just hang on there. We're going to balance this budget. No tax cuts until we do." There were a lot of pretty brave things in that first term.

DR: He appoints Earl Warren as chief justice of the Supreme Court. Was there a political deal for that?

SE: No political deal with Warren, but he knew well what Warren's views were. The remarkable part of Earl Warren in *Brown v. Board of Education* and the whole civil rights movement is that Eisenhower said, even during the campaign, and in his first inaugural address and State of the Union address, that he was highly supportive of civil rights and that we were going to do it by desegregating Washington, D.C., first, which he did before *Brown v. Board of Education.*

DR: In the end, he didn't comment on *Brown v. Board.* Why not?

SE: This is a good question, and I think that historians have gotten this wrong—that he was somehow against Earl Warren or *Brown v. Board of Education.* On the contrary. This is one of the Eisenhower principles. If you have to comment on one Supreme Court ruling, you'll have to comment on them all. Or people would wonder why you didn't. So he decided that he wasn't going to comment on any of them. Ike was conscious anyway that the Supreme Court was a separate branch of government.

DR: When the Little Rock school integration crisis happened in 1957, he sent in federal troops. Did he ever second-guess himself for doing that?

SE: Many people asked me, how serious was Dwight Eisenhower about civil rights? You know what I say? He sent the 101st Airborne Division in to Little Rock, Arkansas. I'd just like to remind you that's the same group of paratroopers who did D-Day.

DR: He creates, with the help of Congress, the Interstate Highway System. Why was he so interested in it?

SE: In 1919, he went on a long trek in an Army unit across the United States, leaving from the Ellipse in Washington, D.C., and ending up in San Francisco. It took about two and a half months. Can you imagine? Then, as General Eisenhower, he's confronted with the German autobahn and sees how rapidly they can move armaments and troops. He understood that America needed this for both reasons.

DR: In those days, there was a debate about whether we should appropriate funds for the highway system or should we use gas tax revenues. Eisenhower didn't want to use appropriated funds?

SE: He thought that a gas tax was more sustainable and would not be subject to the appropriations process in the same way.

DR: When the Soviet Union launches Sputnik in 1957, Eisenhower didn't seem that concerned. Did he know things that the American people didn't know?

SE: Many things like Soviet military capability were classified, so he knew lots of things that the American people didn't know, but the fascinating thing about Sputnik is that the United States and the Soviet Union together agreed to launch artificial satellites in 1957. It was part of an agreement, little noted by many of the people who make an issue out of this. Soviet scientists were in Washington, D.C., two days before Sputnik went up, talking about the launch. It was on the front page of the *New York Times*. People were still shocked.

DR: Now he had some health problems. Did he ever consider not running for reelection?

SE: He certainly asked himself whether he should put himself through it all again after his first term.

DR: And he decided to run again.

SE: My grandmother knew perfectly well that the last thing she wanted to do was to tell him how to organize his career. But of all of his advisors, she thought that he would not find it easy to sit on the sidelines, that he still had work to do.

DR: He tried to get Nixon to be secretary of defense or something else besides vice president. How come Nixon didn't take the hint? Why didn't Eisenhower just say goodbye?

SE: That remains an interesting question. I know that from reading Eisenhower's diary that he did consider other candidates for vice president in 1956. But Nixon certainly brought, in those days, some value to the ticket. Again, the party was involved in these considerations too. And the ticket enjoyed a high approval rating.

DR: In his second term, Ike has more health problems, with his heart. Was he physically ill or had he recovered?

SE: He had a small stroke, and an ileitis problem after his heart attack. What he'd do after he recovered from these things is that he would go on a really arduous trip to see whether he had the stamina to keep up the pace. He noted he would resign if he couldn't fully execute his duties. In each of those cases, he recovered surprisingly quickly.

DR: Getting ready for the 1960 presidential election, John Kennedy says that we have a missile gap and that the Soviets are way ahead of us. Was that true, and what did Eisenhower say?

SE: The problem is that the U-2 program itself was classified, and until the U-2 was shot down in May 1960, nobody knew we had this. So by the time in the campaign the public knew we had a U-2, we did not know the details of those findings. This missile gap, of course, was absolute rubbish, because the United States had a 10-to-1 superiority over the Soviet arsenal. Eisenhower knew this, but it was classified information. Richard Nixon knew it too, but they couldn't say anything about it during the election.

DR: Kennedy was briefed about it. What did he say afterwards?

SE: He continued to say what he said. After the election, though, it was Robert McNamara who said, in effect, "There's no missile gap. Forget we said that."

DR: In a famous press conference, Eisenhower was asked, "Can you tell us something Richard Nixon did as vice president?" What was his response, and what did he really mean?

SE: His famous response was, "I'll think about it and tell you next week." In all fairness, he was leaving the press conference when he was asked that and was halfway out the door.

DR: But did he support Nixon?

SE: For president in 1960, yes.

DR: So, Kennedy gets elected. Does Ike think that Kennedy is qualified to be president?

SE: I actually was part of some of those conversations. It's amazing what got discussed on the sunporch up in Gettysburg, Pennsylvania, or even in the more informal parts of the White House. I was always listening. I think his feeling was that Kennedy was relatively inexperienced, but they did meet, and they seemed to get along well. Throughout the Kennedy presidency, Ike not only gave him advice when asked, but what moved me most in my research is I discovered that he called Kennedy about the Civil Rights Act that was being proposed. He said, "I'm with you. I will make some calls to members of my party so that we can get the Voting Rights Act finally passed." The first civil rights legislation since Reconstruction was passed during the Eisenhower administration in 1957.

DR: Eisenhower retires. The Bay of Pigs occurs. Does he criticize Kennedy in private for how we handled that?

SE: Kennedy called him, and they had discussions about it. What I find interesting about it is that Kennedy was deeply concerned that the Bay of Pigs, and even the Cuban Missile Crisis, was tied to the future of Berlin. Eisenhower wasn't quite so sure about that.

DR: Why does he go to Gettysburg to retire?

SE: My grandmother, who was really a city girl, thought she wanted some of the country life, and they had some friends up there. It was an enormously productive time for him. Remember too they had lived there before, in the Camp Colt days.

DR: Eisenhower played golf. Was he a good golfer? What was his handicap?

SE: I don't know what his handicap was, but he had a mean slice, and in his retirement, he decided that he was going to put in a golf green so he could practice. I rode his horses. We had this great bond. He loved horses, and one evening, I wasn't paying attention to what I was doing, and the horses got out of the paddock and ran right over his golf green while he was sitting on the porch, watching it happen. He was known from time to time to show a temper, and I walked around that farm about three or four times afraid to go in. And after I did, he said, "I haven't seen horses run like that since I was a kid in Abilene, Kansas." He never mentioned it again to me.

DR: What was he most proud of in his entire career?

SE: He has to have been proud of his role during World War II as the Supreme Commander of Allied Forces. He asked President Kennedy to restore his rank of general. He had given up his commission to run for president. He was reinstated as General Eisenhower, and he died as General Eisenhower.

This is a very touching story. I was there. We were saying our last goodbyes. General Heaton, the Army's surgeon general, came in and said, "General Eisenhower, your family has to leave now." From his deathbed, he said, "How many stars do you have?" And poor General Heaton had to say, "Three, sir." And he said, "I've got five. They can stay, all right?"

12

FREDRIK LOGEVALL
on John F. Kennedy

(1917–1963; president from 1961 to 1963)

President Kennedy is the person who most attracted me to politics. His style, eloquence, youth, and challenge to others to help the country or to accomplish the seemingly impossible—go to the moon by the end of the decade—resonated with me and many others in my Baby Boomer generation.

Every American alive at that time no doubt remembers where they were when they heard of Kennedy's assassination on November 22, 1963. (I was in my tenth-grade English class.) After President Kennedy's death, his closest advisor, Ted Sorensen, wrote *Kennedy*, and his in-house academic and scholar, Arthur Schlesinger Jr., wrote *A Thousand Days: John F. Kennedy in the White House*. Both books set a high standard for Kennedy books, with Schlesinger's winning the Pulitzer Prize. Since then, there have been an enormous number of other books, though the Sorensen and Schlesinger books may still be among the gold standards in the Kennedy genre.

But in recent decades, Kennedy books have had some information, like his medical records, not available to the earlier biographers. In recent years, many of the books have tried to address five basic questions: (1) Could the assassination have been readily prevented? (2) Was Kennedy too inexperienced or too politically cautious to deal with some of the crises he faced? (3) Did he have life-shortening and frequently debilitating health problems that he hid from the public and that affected his judgment or abilities? (4) Why did he take such risks with his personal life, and why did the press not report what they knew about it? (5) Would the great problem that his successor ultimately faced—Vietnam—have been handled much more deftly by Kennedy, avoiding the hundreds of thousands of American and Vietnamese deaths that today seem so senseless?

Perhaps the most recent scholarly book to address these and so many other questions was written by Harvard professor Fredrik Logevall, who in 2024, after seven years of research and writing, completed his two-volume work on Kennedy. I have had the chance to interview Professor Logevall on his books and their conclusions about Kennedy on several occasions, and have included here the conversation we had at the New-York Historical Society on May 3, 2023.

✳   ✳   ✳   ✳

DAVID M. RUBENSTEIN (DR): The world doesn't lack for books on John F. Kennedy. Why did you think it needed two more volumes on him?

FREDRIK LOGEVALL (FL): A good friend of mine suggested the title of the book should be "You Don't Know Jack." That speaks in part to what I'm wanting to do here, which is to suggest that though there have been, as you say, thousands of books on the Kennedys and on Jack Kennedy, we don't have a comprehensive biography that uses the phenomenal materials that we now have available, especially at Kennedy Library, to tell what I think is one of the great American stories.

Since my comparative advantage is the fact that I'm a historian, I'm trying to contextualize Kennedy's life and, while I'm telling the story of his rise, ultimately, to the presidency, to also tell the story of America's rise to superpowerdom, and to talk about the context in which he emerged. And maybe, if I do it right, you can not only understand Kennedy better this way but, using Kennedy as a lens, understand American and (to some extent) world history better.

DR: How long has it taken you so far in research and writing? Did you ever say, "I shouldn't have taken this project on"?

FL: I never had that thought per se. But in terms of the first volume, it was about four years from starting the project to publication. And then, of course, the pandemic hit, with closure of the archives. I had to bide my time right as I began work on the second volume, relying as much as I could on digitized materials and published sources.

But now I'm hard at work. It's going well. I'm excited about the project. But I would guess ultimately it's a 10-year project. [The interview about the second volume was based on a not-then-published draft.]

DR: Have you come away admiring John F. Kennedy more or not admiring him more than you did before you started?

FL: I think I've become more conscious of his strengths and accomplishments, his undoubted gifts, but also of his flaws. And he was a flawed individual.

DR: Unlike the rest of us, right?

FL: Exactly! I had written about Kennedy previously, especially about his foreign policy decisions as president. In these studies I gave him high marks overall, though on Vietnam the scorecard is at best mixed. Still, I think overall I am more sympathetic now than when I began this biography. I'm more conscious of the fact that from an early age he had a marvelous curiosity about the world, something he gets in part from his mother, as well as a historical sensibility. From both parents he inherited a commitment to public service, to giving back.

Already in his undergraduate days he was fascinated by the challenges of democracy and democratic leadership, and what leaders must do to reconcile their sense of the nation's interests with the fickle demands of their constituents. This task went to the heart of political courage, as he saw it. He would wrote about this topic in his 1956 book, *Profiles in Courage*, but it was central also in his Harvard senior thesis, which became his first book, *Why England Slept.*

DR: What's the biggest surprise in the research you've done?

FL: That, contrary to the common view, his old man, Joe Kennedy Sr. — a formidable figure, very important in young Jack's life — did not call the shots, at least not as much as we've been led to believe.

Jack, unlike his older brother Joe Jr., was determined to be his own man, and little by little he came to see the world differently than his father did. In the year and a half or so leading up to Pearl Harbor they parted company on the question of isolationism versus intervention in World War II.

It was a surprise to me in my research, and maybe will be to readers, that he shows that capacity for independent thinking from an early age. He doesn't really trust his father's judgments when it comes to politics. In Jack's campaigns—in '46 for the House, '52 for the Senate, '60 for the presidency—the old man is important. He's a big supporter. But I don't think he's central to making Jack Kennedy the politician he is. He saw from an early point that his father's business acumen often exceeded his political discernment.

DR: Let's talk about the beginning. Joe Kennedy made a fair amount of money, was maybe one of the 10 richest people in the United States. He had how many children?

FL: He and his wife, Rose, had nine children. Their sons were Joe Jr., Jack, Bobby, and Ted. And the daughters were Rosemary, Kathleen, Patricia, Jean, and Eunice.

DR: The oldest daughter was—

FL: Rosemary.

DR: And she was given what was then thought to be a reasonable procedure, a lobotomy of some type?

FL: It's just a heartbreaking moment. It's November of 1941. Joe in particular and to some extent Rose are fascinated by advances in medical technology. They're concerned about Rosemary. She's always been behind the other kids. She's struggling in school and is held back. They try different schools, send her to myriad specialists. He hears about a procedure that he is told—I have no reason to doubt him on this—is going to make Rosemary better. She'll be the same Rosemary that you love, he is told, and she'll be able to function well. But she'll be better. So she goes under the knife. And it's a disaster. She comes out much worse than she went in.

One of the things about the Jack Kennedy story that is just extraordinary, and hard for me to in some ways grasp, is that he loses the three siblings closest to him in age when all three are in their 20s. He loses his brother Joe Jr. in the war. He loses Kathleen, or Kick—the sibling to whom he feels closest, his soul mate—in a plane crash in 1948. And he effectively loses Rosemary to this lobotomy. What does that do to him?

DR: Growing up, Jack wasn't that close to Robert because Robert Kennedy was much younger, wasn't he?

FL: There was an eight-and-a-half-year difference.

DR: So they were not really in the same social circles.

FL: Not at all, at least until they travel together to the Far East in 1951, when Jack is getting ready to run for the Senate. It's an interesting long tour of the type that American politicians no longer take—covering 25,000 miles and lasting six weeks. It's really the first time—hard to believe now—that Bobby and Jack spend serious time together. And the experience brings them much closer. Jack realized how much he valued his brother's insights, his good humor, his energy. And they both liked having their sister Patricia along on the trip too.

DR: The most visible thing I remember about John Kennedy's youth was that he was sick all the time. He was born with a lot of ailments. He seemed to spend a lot of time in the hospital when he was in high school. He initially went to Princeton and had to drop out because of health issues. He wound up at Harvard. What was the cause of those health issues?

FL: I don't think we know. At least I have not been able to determine, despite much digging, the various causes of these myriad ailments. We do know that basically from birth, he was sickly. And he struggled with health maladies from then until the end of his life. He was better toward the end, because of various medications. To some, he never looked better than he did in those final weeks before Dallas.

DR: He wasn't that happy with the fact that his mother didn't visit him much when he was in the hospital. She didn't seem to be all that attentive to him, unlike you would expect a mother to do with sick children.

FL: Yes, that's true. One might say in her defense that she's got nine of them, so she's got her hands full. And she is influenced by parenting guides of the day that preach a stern, discipline-centered approach and warn against too much maternal affection. Nevertheless, when he is at Choate, for example—but also earlier, and later at Harvard—and spends so much time in the infirmary, one might think that a mom would come to visit at least now and then, and she didn't.

His father, Joe, in some ways, is much more attentive, more nurturing. Joe will actually visit the infirmary, if not all that often. He's just that way. When the kids have a problem, they will often go to Joe before they go to their mother.

DR: When John Kennedy is in college, his role model is his older brother Joe Kennedy Jr. He's a better athlete, he's better-looking, he's smarter. Did that give John Kennedy a sense of "I'm not going to be able to do much in life, because everything is going to focus around my brother"?

FL: Yes, though I actually don't think Joe Jr. was smarter. I think the more intellectually gifted of the two was Jack. Joe worked harder, I grant you, and he had better grades.

DR: Better grades meant you were smarter.

FL: Not necessarily. Jack was a slacker compared to his hard-charging brother. In some ways, he took comfort in that. He could be in his brother's shadow. He could pursue his own interests.

But teachers who taught them both at Choate and professors who taught them at Harvard would comment on the fact that Jack was the one who seemed to have a greater interest in ideas, to grasp them more fully. But you're right, he was in his brother's shadow, really, until Joe Jr.'s death in 1944, even if he had long since begun to outshine Joe in important respects (which Joe could see all too well).

DR: As a senior at Harvard, he writes a senior thesis, *Why England Slept*, about why England wasn't prepared for the war, which was later published. Very few people get to publish their senior thesis, and he had it published by a serious publisher. Was it that great a thesis? Or his father made sure it was published?

FL: Certainly his father had an influence. His father got Arthur Krock of the *New York Times* to do some editing. His father also got Time-Life publisher Henry Luce to write a foreword. That's some serious help. But the foreword was agreed to after the publisher had signed the book, so I don't want to overstate the importance of Luce. And Krock's edits were fairly modest.

I think Jack happened upon a topic that was perfect in its timing, basically why was England not prepared for war with Hitler? Given the experience of the First World War, given the experience of the inter-war period, it hit at just the right moment, and the publisher was smart enough to see, "I can do something with this, even though it's a kid who's written it."

DR: So it's published and it does reasonably well for a book by a unknown author. World War II breaks out, and John Kennedy, like most people his age at that time, wanted to go to war. Was it easy for him to get into military service?

FL: Anything but easy, because of his health problems. He's turned down on account of his back. The Army won't take him, the Navy won't take him. He eventually lands a desk job in Naval Intelligence in Washington. That's where he's posted in the fall of 1941, when Rosemary undergoes her lobotomy nearby, and when Pearl Harbor is attacked. He's not in harm's way, much to his father's relief, but he continues to work hard to get into harm's way, which is an interesting part of the story.

Ultimately he succeeds. Again, his father's influence helps—which is ironic, because Joe Kennedy is deathly afraid that his sons will go into battle and be killed doing so. But because he knew that both Joe Jr. and Jack want to do it, he helps make it happen, using his connections in Washington. And then Jack goes off to fight the Japanese.

DR: He finds his way to the South Pacific, and he becomes the commander of a PT boat. What is a PT boat?

FL: It's a torpedo boat. It's a small, nimble vessel, not particularly useful as a military instrument, but with undeniable flair. In people's imaginations, there was something dashing, even sexy about these PT boats, and therefore about being a PT boat commander. And that's what Jack becomes. His long experience on the water growing up, with sailing boats off Cape Cod, helps him get the assignment.

DR: Now, famously, PT-109 was cut in half by a Japanese ship. Some people say, "How can you be the commander of a PT-109 and not know a Japanese ship's about to cut you in half?" What's the reason for that?

FL: It's a moonless night. That's one thing. His boat does not have radar. Some of the other boats in the squadron do have radar, but his does not. He does not know what others know, which is that the Japanese ships that they are waiting for have already passed through, and some of them are on their way back up the passage. And as a result, when this giant destroyer comes along, almost like a skyscraper, and is bearing down on his boat, he doesn't have enough time to evade. Miraculously, only two crew members die. The rest of them are now left there, sitting there, and they have to decide what to do.

DR: He takes one of the crew members in effect on his back and swims several miles—I forget exactly how many miles it was—to an island. How does somebody do that after an accident? And swimming by yourself for a couple of miles is not easy, but swimming with somebody on your back—how did he actually do that?

FL: It's hard for me to imagine. We know that he had competed for Harvard. He had been in swim meets since he was a boy, so he's an excellent swimmer. That's part of the explanation. But still, this takes three to four hours, in shark-infested waters, with the Japanese all around. Somehow, he manages to take this wounded comrade under his care, while the others swim, if they can, and they make it to this little island.

DR: They were later rescued. He goes back to the continental United States and recovers. Does he go back in the service?

FL: Yes, but he does not see action. He goes back to the United States, and he's ultimately discharged in March 1945. By the way, we should note—and this helps him in terms of his political career—he is called a hero for those efforts in helping to save his crew. It's all over the newspapers in the United States. One of the fascinating parts of the research for me was to go and look at small newspapers and large ones. And sure enough, there are articles about the son of Ambassador Kennedy performing heroically in the South Pacific. That story, the story of Jack Kennedy and PT-109, will be very important in his political rise.

DR: He does say later, "I'm going to go back and run for office and try to use my war story."

FL: Yes, although I don't have any reason to doubt him when he says that he was reluctant to make too much of the PT-109 experience, in part because he's a little embarrassed he allowed his boat to be rammed and cut in two. Certainly expert members of the Navy were a little dubious about his allowing that to happen. But eventually he agrees with his father and others that the story is too good not to use. So they do.

DR: Originally his plan had been to be a journalist. And he does do some journalism after the war?

DR: He covers the San Francisco conference at the end of Second World War.

DR: That created the UN.

FL: It's a great coming together of the victorious nations. As the war now is wrapping up, the question on everyone's minds is, what's the new world order going to look like? Jack Kennedy is there in San Francisco, and he covers this extraordinary conference. I do quite a lot with the articles he writes while there, which show his maturing international outlook.

Then he goes to England, soon after, to cover the British election where Winston Churchill and the Tories lose. To many Americans this seems an inconceivable outcome given Churchill's heroic stature, but Kennedy predicts that they could have trouble. He's one of the few U.S. observers who say, in effect, "Even though they were victorious in this war, Churchill and his party are actually in trouble." I have no doubt he could have stuck with journalism had he wanted; he showed aptitude for that, and could write quickly and well.

DR: Churchill started out as a journalist too. Maybe he looked up to Churchill.

FL: Churchill was a bit of a lodestar for him in different ways.

DR: So, there's a congressional seat in Boston that includes Cambridge. Later, Tip O'Neill had that seat. Somebody decides, "This is a good seat for John Kennedy." Does he reluctantly get in the race or eagerly agree?

FL: It's more of the latter. That said, he is a little uncertain about his prospects. That's one thing about JFK: he was always his own best critic.

And I think he said, in so many words, "I don't have any political experience. I don't really know what I'm doing as a candidate. People will say that I'm a carpetbagger, because other than when I was in college, I've never lived in the 11th District. I'm going to be perceived as a son or privilege and an interloper. How's this going to work with Irish Catholics and Italians and others in the district?"

He's a realist about what's going to happen. But by the time he makes the decision "I'm going for this," he is really determined. He's all in.

DR: Was he good as a campaigner?

FL: Not initially. He spoke too fast, didn't seem comfortable. He seldom departed from his text, and when he did, when he extemporized, he was not good at it to start with. Later, and especially in the presidential campaign in 1960, he became a superb extemporizer; here, he was anything but.

DR: He gets elected in 1946?

FL: And takes office in '47.

DR: Richard Nixon was elected to the Congress at the same time. Do they get along? Are their offices close to each other?

FL: They did get along. Imagine being a fly on this wall: Kennedy had what we might call salons, in which he would invite people to his house in Washington, in Georgetown. His sister Eunice also lived there, so the two siblings were together under one roof. He would invite people, often as many Republicans as Democrats, for these leisurely, conversation-heavy dinners. And there would be journalists; Joe Alsop would come over, for example, and Walter Lippmann on occasion. And lawmakers. And they would sit around and talk about the issues of the day.

Richard Nixon was one of those who appeared, with some regularity. They got along well in Congress, no question, and later when Kennedy was a senator and Nixon was vice president.

DR: Kennedy gets reelected in '48 and gets reelected in '50. So, after six years in the House, he's ready to be a senator?

FL: Yes. From day one in the House, he is looking at bigger things. He is thinking about the governorship or a Senate seat. His father says, "Maybe you should think about running for governor. You're in a good position to do this now." Jack listens. He feels shackled in the House, frustrated by the fact that he is but one of 435 members, and a very junior one at that. Much of the work is drudgery—you're dealing with correspondence from constituents, you're giving people tours of the Capitol, that sort of thing. And so he decides that he's going for the Senate in '52. And of course it's an epic race against Henry Cabot Lodge Jr.

DR: Henry Cabot Lodge is a well-respected senator. Do people think that there's any chance John Kennedy could beat this incumbent?

FL: Two people think he can beat him: Jack Kennedy himself and his old man. Ambassador Kennedy says, "You can do this. If you can beat Lodge in Massachusetts, there's nothing stopping you." In other words, "The presidency, Jack, can be yours." So they launch in. And the two of them decide there is a vulnerability to Lodge. He's got a great name, he's a 10th-generation Harvard man, but he's taking this race for granted, devoting much of his time and attention to lining up Dwight Eisenhower to run for the GOP presidential nomination.

DR: Does Kennedy run on his accomplishments in the House?

FL: Not really. He didn't have many accomplishments in the House! But there are two keys to his victory. Some of this he had shown in '46 and will show again in '60, namely he starts earlier and he works harder than the competition. This is a theme in all his campaigns, and it's certainly key here in 1952.

And so when Lodge is not even thinking about this, when Lodge is busy in Washington, Jack Kennedy is out in western Massachusetts, in small towns, weekend after weekend, speaking to any group that will have him. He drives himself forward, relentlessly. He starts early, and that's key to his success.

The second key to his success in '52 is that he's turning out to be an excellent politician who works hard at it. He's not yet the fluent speaker he'll become in the fall of 1960 and as president, but he's improving, and already shows an awareness of what goes into a good speech. More than that, he shows an ability to connect with voters.

Put those two things together, then add in his father's money and the fact that the family campaigns with him, and you've got a powerful thing. He's got his mother—a formidable campaigner in her own right—out there. His sisters are out there. Young Teddy is out there, working long hours, doing what he can. Bobby, all of 26, comes on board to run the campaign. It's an astonishing thing, a true family affair. You can see why it ended up the way it did.

DR: Eisenhower is at the head of the Republican ticket that year. And he wins, overwhelmingly. He wins Massachusetts as well. What happened in the Senate race?

FL: Well, young Jack Kennedy, Congressman Kennedy, becomes Senator-elect Kennedy. He pulls off an amazing win over Lodge, and in doing so becomes one of the rare bright spots for the Democratic Party in what is otherwise a pretty miserable election. Journalists said at the time, "We don't know much about this John F. Kennedy character. But he pulled off a stunner of an upset against Henry Cabot Lodge in Massachusetts. He is somebody to watch."

DR: He's elected to the Senate when Richard Nixon's elected to the vice presidency.

FL: Yes. He and Nixon have this interesting parallel track. And of course, it will lead to their slugfest for the presidency in eight short years.

DR: So he's a senator, and as a senator, he says, "I guess the next stop is the White House." One of the things people thought you needed if you were going to run for the presidency was a wife. What did he do about that?

FL: It's true. His father says to him, in essence, "Look, Jack, you can't be a bachelor if you have these kinds of aspirations. Even if you decide to remain a senator and make the Senate your career, a man of your age—you're now in your mid-30s—needs to have a spouse. Or people will start asking questions." And Jack comes to agree with this—with how much enthusiasm, we don't know. He meets Jackie Bouvier and they begin dating in 1952, and then they marry the following year.

DR: Before that happened, did he have trouble getting dates?

FL: Quite the contrary. He was successful with women to a degree that surprised even himself. He would puzzle over it. In his college days, his roommates at Harvard would marvel at how often a new woman seemed to appear at whatever dorm he was living in. Same thing at the place he had in Georgetown with Eunice while he was in Congress. There is a charisma and a charm that draws women to him, no question—even Hollywood stars like Gene Tierney. But now, in 1953 and partly because of his father's encouragement, he thinks "I'd better get serious about this. I'd better get myself a wife."

DR: Was he well-dressed in his bachelor days? Or was he fairly sloppy?

FL: This is where Jackie is quite interesting, because before meeting her he doesn't care at all about what he's wearing, and often shows up as a congressman with mismatched socks, or his shirttail hanging out, or his tie askew. From his days at Choate right up to his wedding day, he would famously leave his clothes in a pile on the floor, and then, the next morning, would just go back to the same pile and dig out something to put on. But then along comes Jackie, and he undergoes a transformation. With her encouragement he even becomes a bit of a clotheshorse. Little by little, he begins to pay attention to the cut of his suits, to the fit of his shirts, to which shoes work with which ensemble, and so on. He develops a particular preference for navy blue suits with a single vent in the back.

DR: As a senator, he hires a young man from Nebraska to be his legislative assistant and speechwriter, Ted Sorensen. Can you describe how Sorensen got that position and how their minds kind of linked together?

FL: It's one of the great political partnerships in American history. Sorensen, idealistic, intelligent, the son of progressive parents from Nebraska, has come to Washington. He is a finalist for positions with two senators. One is "Scoop" Jackson from Washington and the other is Jack Kennedy from Massachusetts. He talks to them both, and decides—and he writes about this in his marvelous memoir *Counselor*—that he's going to cast his lot with Kennedy.

But before he does, he says to Jack Kennedy—and I give them both credit for this exchange—in the final interview, "Senator Kennedy, I've got to ask you why you were not more outspoken in opposition to Joe McCarthy."

That's a pretty bold move by this young Ted Sorensen, who wants a job with this guy. But he feels compelled to ask this question. Kennedy gives him an answer about the strength of Irish Catholics in Massachusetts and family ties to McCarthy. (It turns out McCarthy has dated Jack's sisters on occasion, and Joe Kennedy knows him and likes him.)

I'm impressed by Sorensen for raising that question and Kennedy for still hiring him. And so they start to work together. And what a match it is. In some respects, Sorensen becomes a kind of alter ego to the senator. I suggest in my book that they are the Rodgers and Hart of politics.

Kennedy will tell Sorensen, "I need to give a speech on such-and-such. Here are the points I want to make." Or, "I want to write an article on this, one stressing the following points." And then Sorensen goes off and produces a draft, which they will then go over, fine-tuning until they're happy with it. Pretty soon it's hard to tell, certainly for me, where one begins and the other ends.

DR: Kennedy's elected to the Senate in 1952. Adlai Stevenson was the Democratic nominee in '52, and he lost overwhelmingly to Dwight Eisenhower. But then in 1956, he is going to be the nominee again. Stevenson says, "I don't know who I want to have as my vice president. I'll let the party decide in the convention." Does Jack Kennedy say he wants to be vice president?

FL: Not initially. Stevenson says, "I'm going to make this really dramatic. I'm going to give the decision of the vice presidency, the decision of who will be my running mate, to the floor of the convention."

Kennedy and the other contenders have only a few hours to decide: Are we going to pursue this option? It's a big decision, with big implications. And the Kennedys, Jack and Bobby, decide, "We're going for it."

Joe Kennedy, vacationing in the south of France, goes ballistic when he finds out, uses several curse words that I won't repeat here, but essentially says "You guys are crazy. Stevenson is going to get hammered by Eisenhower. You, Jack, will be blamed for the loss, because you're a Catholic. Don't go anywhere near this thing."

But Jack, showing his independence and with his brother's encouragement, defies his father. They pursue this. And in a stunningly dramatic showdown, he comes within a whisker of being the Democratic nominee. It's a good thing for him that he loses—it's one of those points in his political life when Lady Luck smiles on him. And yet the episode makes him a national figure—and his strong showing will help him down the line.

DR: This pretty much takes us to the end of your first volume. Your second volume begins with the effort of John Kennedy to put himself in a situation where he could run for president in 1960. John Kennedy's a young senator, not that powerful. Why would he think he could get elected president or get the nomination in 1960? Who were the other people who thought they should be president, and were they much more qualified, in their view, than Kennedy was?

FL: Several others did indeed believe they were more qualified than Kennedy. By some measures, he had no business thinking about this. But his calculation went like this: "At the Democratic National Convention in '56, I almost got the second slot. I could see then that I have a lot of support. I have a lot of support in New England, of course, but I can also do well elsewhere, even in the South. When I look at the competition, I don't see anybody who's better placed to win the nomination than I am, if I start early and I work harder." And so he takes the plunge.

In 1957, long before any of the others are even thinking about it, he starts to travel around the country to get name recognition to win support. And little by little, he does.

Others who have a serious shot, hard as this is to believe, include Adlai Stevenson, even though he's lost twice. There are many people in the party, especially intellectuals, who would like nothing more than for Stevenson to be the nominee one more time. This time he won't have Eisenhower to face, which means this time he will win. He's the one that the Kennedys worry about most.

Then there's Lyndon Johnson, the powerful Senate majority leader, and Hubert Humphrey, the firebrand liberal from Minnesota, and Stuart Symington from Missouri. Some of these figures are more or less well-known to us today, but that quartet constituted the most formidable potential competitors for Kennedy.

DR: In 1960, were there a lot of primaries that you had to compete in?

FL: No. In fact, it's a very different age from what had gone on before, when there were more primaries, and different from what we're used to today. Fewer than a third of the states in 1960 had them.

One reason that 1960 is so interesting to me is that Jack Kennedy sees the primaries as his ticket to the nomination. He says repeatedly that as a Catholic and somebody who's young and relatively inexperienced, the only way he can have any hope of winning the nomination is to contest—and win—several primaries. Kennedy knows that party leaders in 1960 still hold enormous power in choosing the nominee. So he tells his associates: "They're never going to accept me if I don't show that I can win primaries."

So he enters the primaries, and Lyndon Johnson makes a disastrous strategic decision, which is not to contest them. He thinks he can rely on his power position in the Senate to get him a majority of delegates. Stevenson also is content to bide his time until the convention, as is Symington. So only Hubert Humphrey challenges Kennedy in these primaries. And the contests prove to be just as crucial as Kennedy anticipates.

DR: But Johnson was the majority leader, and had an enormous amount of power. He made the mistake of thinking that power in Washington was the same as power in the nominating process?

FL: Exactly. It was understandable in a way that Lyndon Johnson might think that having allies in Congress, both the Senate and the House, and in state party leaders would be sufficient. We can say today that he should have known better, but that's because today they've become much more important—arguably too important. But that was less clear in 1960. Still, as Kennedy starts to win these primaries, Johnson begins to think, "Uh-oh. This could be a problem."

DR: Kennedy wins the New Hampshire primary, which was then first. Then he has to enter the Wisconsin primary, which is a neighboring state of Minnesota, Hubert Humphrey's home state. Is he supposed to win there as well?

FL: This was going to be a challenge for Kennedy. Because it's next to Minnesota, Hubert Humphrey is known as the third senator from Wisconsin. This is his turf. But Kennedy takes him on—in part, by the way, because of a sophisticated use of polling. This is another area in which John F. Kennedy was a pioneer. He's not the first to use polls, but he's using them more systematically. He puts a serious professional, Louis Harris, on his payroll. So JFK gets sophisticated polling in place, including in Wisconsin, that indicates to him something dramatic: "I, John F. Kennedy, can actually win this thing. If I can defeat Hubert in Hubert's own backyard, I'll go a long way to getting this nomination." It's a crucial first battle.

DR: So what happens?

FL: It's a victory for him, but of a type that he and his aides learned a lesson from, which is that they had set expectations too high. They had even made noises to some reporters that it was going to be a landslide. It's no landslide, but a closely fought battle. And so some elements of the press interpret this as a kind of moral victory for Humphrey and a defeat for Kennedy. He wins, but not by the margin his team had anticipated.

DR: The next state is West Virginia, which is very Protestant; it has very few Catholics.

FL: About 97 percent Protestant.

DR: Kennedy wasn't happy that he had to compete in West Virginia. How did he do?

FL: He wins that one too. Initially he's optimistic, partly on the basis of Harris's polling, then he reconsiders, saying to himself, "How can I enter this Protestant state and have any hope of winning? If I lose, it'll give the party bosses all the reason they need to make sure that I don't get the nomination."

So he and his team go through a period of thinking it was a big mistake to come in. What they do, classic Kennedy-style, is they work incredibly hard for a month. They crisscross the state, flood it with volunteers. Ambassador Kennedy's money is all over the state. They work 20-hour days.

JFK makes a key decision: he decides to tackle the religion issue head-on. He basically says, "When I served this country in World War II, nobody asked me if I was a Catholic or a Protestant. Nobody asked my brother, when he took his fatal final mission, what religion he followed."

An idea takes hold: he begins to see that religion can help him, including in the general election, should he get that far, as much as it might hurt him. It's an important moment.

DR: In those days, there were no campaign finance laws, so Joe Kennedy could put money in a suitcase and distribute it to people, and that was considered kosher.

FL: Quite literally in suitcases. There was a suitcase under the bed of an aide. At key moments, out would come the suitcase, and county and municipal leaders in West Virginia would be, in effect, paid, under a quasi-legal system calling slating.

Now, we should note that the Humphrey campaign also made payments. And interestingly enough, much of the money that Humphrey paid to people came from allies of Lyndon Johnson, because poor Hubert had no money.

DR: The night of the West Virginia primary, Kennedy was going to wait it out in Washington, D.C.?

FL: Yes, because he thought he might lose. He didn't want to be in a place if he lost.

DR: He goes to a movie with his friend Ben Bradlee and their spouses. They couldn't get in the movie that they wanted to see, so where did they go?

FL: They went across the street to a theater that showed soft-porn films. I was kind of hoping we wouldn't go there.

DR: So they watch that movie, and then what happens in the election?

FL: Every 20 minutes or so, Jack Kennedy gets up from his seat and goes out to a pay phone and calls to see if there's any news from West Virginia. He tries to reach Bobby; there's no news. He goes back in, watches a little more of the movie.

DR: So they say, "You're going to win"?

FL: They get home to Georgetown, and they get the incredible news: "Not only have you won, Jack, but you won handsomely."

They pile in the plane, which they had christened the *Caroline*, for Jack and Jackie's daughter. They fly down—it takes perhaps an hour—and then they have this 2 a.m. celebration in Charleston. There's this almost idyllic scene, in which Hubert Humphrey at 2 in the morning comes out from his headquarters, his hotel, to congratulate Jack on his victory. He knows his shot at the nomination is basically over, but he makes this gallant gesture. Humphrey to me is an impressive public servant.

DR: Jack Kennedy goes on to Los Angeles, where the convention is held. It wasn't 100 percent certain that he would get the nomination, but he pretty much has it locked up when he gets there. And people increasingly recognize that the big decision is "Who's going to be vice president?" Who did John Kennedy want to have as vice president?

FL: This is a topic—as it always is for people who might be nominated—of increasing urgency. Some weeks earlier, Ted Sorensen produces a memo in which he lists various candidates, and one of the people that he lists in a prominent place on that sheet is Lyndon Johnson. Sorensen indicates that Johnson is his preferred choice.

What's interesting about this is that JFK and LBJ have not gotten along well, to say the least, in the winter and spring, leading up to the convention. Johnson is making insinuations about Kennedy's health, saying he's got Addison's disease, which the campaign denies. (Johnson is right.)

So, on some level, you think he's never going to choose Johnson. And Robert Kennedy, who had already developed an intense dislike of LBJ, is arguing against selecting him. But Jack Kennedy in fact chooses Lyndon Johnson to be his nominee.

Later, it would be suggested that the Kennedy brothers felt certain that Johnson would never accept: that he's got a much more powerful position in Washington, as the grand pooh-bah in the Senate, than he will ever have as vice president. But Johnson understands that no Southerner is going to be nominated by the Democratic Party in the 1960s. His only chance to get at the top prize is to put himself up for vice president. He also suspects that his power as majority leader will be diminished come 1961, regardless of whether Kennedy or Nixon wins the election.

I think some part of Jack Kennedy understands this, understands that Johnson may well say yes; he proceeds anyway. He chooses LBJ because the Texan helps him more than any of the other contenders. As his father tells him, in so many words, "You need help in the South. You need the Old South, you need Texas. Johnson gives you more of that than any other candidate."

DR: Robert Kennedy goes to see Johnson a few times to ask him if he wants to withdraw.

FL: "Are you sure you want this?" That kind of thing, yes.

DR: And basically Johnson says, "Are you speaking for John Kennedy, or are you speaking for yourself?" Did John Kennedy want Robert Kennedy to say, "See if you can get Lyndon out of it"?

FL: That's been much discussed by historians. It's hard to pin down on the basis of the evidence. I do think the Kennedy brothers begin to have second thoughts about the nomination after core constituencies in the Democratic coalition raise hell — organized labor, liberals, Black leaders. By the time Bobby makes his approach to Johnson, where is Jack's mind on this? I think he's coming around to the idea that, "though I have reservations about Lyndon Johnson, he helps me more than anybody else. This could be a really close election, so I want him for this, even though my brother is begging me to say that we're withdrawing this offer."

DR: They emerge from the convention, and Johnson's the vice presidential nominee. Richard Nixon is the Republican nominee. Ironically, his running mate is Henry Cabot Lodge.

There had never been presidential debates. Yet there were four presidential debates. Whose idea was that?

FL: In two previous presidential elections, there were not really debates, but in '52 and '56, both candidates would appear together in some format, and there would be some questioning of both. In '60, Hubert Humphrey and John F. Kennedy had a debate in West Virginia. That was a little bit closer to what we would see in the fall. You have a sense that this could be coming. The networks are desperate for it to happen, seeing a ratings bonanza.

Nobody perceives that the four debates in 1960 will reach the kind of audience that they do. Americans by the tens of millions are tuning in from their living rooms. Although I don't want to overstate their importance, ultimately the debates help John F. Kennedy eke out a very close victory. He shows Americans that he can go toe-to-toe with the sitting vice president and hold his own.

DR: The conventional wisdom is that John F. Kennedy looked better on television, and people who watched on television thought that he won the debates. And people who listened to radio thought that Nixon won the debates. What do you think?

FL: The evidence for the latter assertion is thin. It's based on one rather small poll. Even that poll said people who listened on the radio thought both men did well. So it wasn't even so much that they thought that Nixon had prevailed. We can go on YouTube and see this ourselves, that Kennedy looks better, looks fresher, projects better.

DR: He was tan. He was fresh. Nixon apparently said, "Are you going to wear makeup?" And Kennedy said, "No, I'm not going to wear makeup." But Kennedy did have makeup on?

FL: Yes, he did. And Nixon was lathered in something called Lazy-Shave to hide his five o'clock shadow. There's also this: in that first debate, time and again we hear Richard Nixon say, "I agree with the senator." Even when invited to disagree, he'll sometimes back down and say, "I agree with the senator."

The unwillingness of Nixon to go after Kennedy in that debate had large ramifications. The first debate had the most viewers. Nixon does much better in the later debates. He probably wins the third one; maybe the second and fourth are a draw. But the damage had been done.

DR: The election goes forward. In the end, Kennedy wins narrowly in the Electoral College vote. The popular vote he won by 150,000 or so?

FL: Slightly over 100,000 votes, out of almost 69 million cast.

DR: Nixon is importuned by some to contest the election, to say, "Some of the votes were stolen, and maybe I should do something about it." Why did he not contest the election?

FL: To a degree, he did contest it. In other words, he did not raise objections when officials in the Republican Party, including his own senior aides, raised doubts about Illinois and Texas in particular. He allowed that effort to go ahead. So this common view that he was the statesman, and somebody who did not under any circumstances wish to contest this, is not quite true, as I read the evidence.

As the days passed, I think he decided that any effort to have some kind of recount was going to take much too long. That American democracy, American national security, would suffer and that his own reputation would suffer. He also lacked confidence that it would really affect any outcome. So he decided, "I'll live to fight another day."

DR: Kennedy's inaugurated, and he gives an inaugural address that many people would say is the finest inaugural address of the twentieth century. Maybe the only competition is Roosevelt's first inaugural address. What is so special about it? President Kennedy famously said, "Victory has a hundred fathers, and defeat is an orphan."

FL: It's right up there, in my view. It's one of the top four in our nation's history—Jefferson's first, Lincoln's second, FDR's first, and then Kennedy's.

What's remarkable about it is the brevity. It's about 1,350 words. Not a word is wasted. It's an inspired message, one on which the president-elect and his team spent a lot of time. He had become at this point a very inspirational speaker, and it shows. It's ultimately also a kind of conciliatory message that he gives, less hawkish on the Cold War than is often claimed.

In terms of the drafting, it's primarily Ted Sorensen. But there's input from Arthur Schlesinger Jr. Walter Lippmann has some valuable input on a couple of sections. Kennedy himself does some revising, insists on changes to the address at key points. He's very active in the production of this address. He says to Sorensen, in effect, "I want this address to really sing. This is my one opportunity to make a first impression with the American people and the world. And we're going to do it."

DR: Hugh Sidey, a *Time* magazine correspondent, was flying up to Washington, D.C., on the plane of President-elect Kennedy, and Kennedy calls him into his office and hands him a handwritten draft of a few pages, asking what he thought of the speech. Sidey then writes an article saying, "I know he wrote it because I saw it in his own handwriting." What was that all about?

FL: I'm trying to get an answer to that question, because I know the anecdote. It's been suggested that Kennedy wanted Sidey to think that this thing was from his own pen, and only from his own pen, and produced a handwritten version of a small portion that had been drafted by committee. It's not implausible. But those who have suggested that Kennedy had little or nothing to do with the address, that's not correct. Kennedy laid out what he wanted said, and then revised. He was actively involved, as he had been with his speeches since his initial run for Congress in '46.

DR: In the early part of the administration, Kennedy agrees to support the Bay of Pigs invasion by some Cuban refugees. Why did he do that? Did he not realize that there was no chance for those refugees to win?

FL: I think he was skeptical that the Bay of Pigs invasion would work from the beginning. There's ample evidence that he thought this thing was pretty half-baked at best.

It's a plan that had originated under Eisenhower. Kennedy feels new to the office, untested. "The military, CIA, and the outgoing administration are all saying to me, 'You've got to do this. We have got to get rid of Castro, or at least destabilize his government. This is a plan that will work.'" So he feels pressure. He seeks input from his own advisors. And I give him credit for this, because he wanted input even from people he knew opposed this.

At the eleventh hour, he's still saying he's not sure that this is going to work. But he pursued it anyway. And of course it ended up being a disaster.

DR: Then he does something that all politicians with big failures have done since then, with similar results. He goes on television and says, "I take the blame. It's my fault. The buck stops here." And suddenly, his popularity goes up. Why does it go up after that failure?

FL: This is something I wonder about. Maybe we're all reluctant to admit mistakes. Politicians, time and again, underestimate the maturity of their voters to handle this kind of an admission. In other words, they should learn from John F. Kennedy. Maybe we all should. Kennedy basically said, "I blew it on this. This is my mistake." And voters gave him credit for this. It's something we see all too rarely from our leaders.

DR: A lot of politicians will say, "I made a mistake, but actually I didn't make a mistake." They want to get the benefit that Kennedy got, but they also don't want to be blamed.

So Kennedy has to deal with the Soviet leader, Nikita Khrushchev. He goes to Vienna for the first head-to-head meeting between the two of them. How does that go?

FL: It does not go well from John F. Kennedy's perspective. It's an increasingly tense time in the Cold War. The issue of Berlin, which has been a festering problem between East and West, between Moscow and Washington, is becoming more of one, for various reasons.

Kennedy is prepared for this summit meeting. Some people suggest, "He probably didn't know what was coming." No, he really prepared for this. He really boned up. He knew that Khrushchev had this tendency to be, shall we say, dogmatic and tough, and not give a person a chance to speak.

So it's not as though he was unprepared for a difficult meeting. And yet he was still taken aback by the bluster, the aggressiveness of the Soviet leader. It is a very tense meeting from start to finish.

DR: He tells people it didn't go well. He tells his friends it didn't go well, including some journalists. Khrushchev, I guess, sizes up Kennedy and says, "He's not that tough, so I can put nuclear missiles into Cuba, and Kennedy won't do anything about it." Is that what led Khrushchev to put those missiles into Cuba?

FL: That's one of the reasons. This is now about a year later when the process begins. He does not think Kennedy will respond aggressively, particularly if everything can be in place before the Americans take notice. He's also wanting to right the strategic balance, or imbalance, that he perceives, especially in terms of nuclear capability. He wants to show Castro that he's supportive of the revolution. He's also competing with China for supremacy among revolutionaries in the developing world. So Khrushchev has several motives in trying this scheme.

DR: There were no spy satellites in those days. How did we find out that there were nuclear missiles in Cuba?

FL: Through photographs taken during U-2 overflights by the United States, they are able to see that these installations are underway. That's what launches us into the Cuban Missile Crisis.

DR: Kennedy decides to bring together some of his cabinet, some of his senior advisors. The most important one turned out to be Robert Kennedy. And what does President Kennedy decide to do? Many generals are telling him to bomb, to invade. Why does he not do either of those?

FL: He comes into this, partly because of his own experience in World War II, skeptical about the utility of military solutions to problems of this nature. President Kennedy is already thinking that this could get out of hand easily. He's also indicated to various people that in the nuclear age, we cannot have the two superpowers go too far down the road toward nuclear conflagration. Those two concerns condition him, from a fairly early point in the crisis, to look for some kind of political solution.

And so, against the advice of virtually everybody on the Executive Committee, the so-called EXCOMM — including, by the way, his brother, who was more hawkish early in the crisis than he would subsequently claim, including in his book *Thirteen Days* — John F. Kennedy determines that they must pursue some kind of political solution to the crisis.

And what's interesting about it is he says, in so many words, "We've got to put ourselves in Khrushchev's shoes, see it from his perspective." So you see here an example of John F. Kennedy showing a kind of empathetic understanding that is ultimately critical to the resolution of the crisis. It's the closest we've come to a nuclear war.

DR: There was a quarantine. And ultimately, as Dean Rusk would say, "The Russians blinked," and they didn't ship more missile parts in. But we have a secret deal with the Russians. This always is surprising to me. We say to the Russians, "We will move our missiles out of Turkey. You want them out of Turkey. But don't tell anybody." We didn't tell the American people, "We're going to move the missiles out of Turkey." But we told the Russians, and we wanted them to keep it a secret. Is that surprising?

FL: It's surprising in one way. There is this secret deal, as you say, and it's very important in terms of this crisis being resolved. Kennedy insists on this being kept secret, and it remains secret for 25 years. The explanation is in part that there is a midterm election coming up just a few days after the crisis. He does not want to give Republicans an opportunity to say, "Wait, you made a deal with communists? You showed weakness with the Kremlin at this hour of tremendous tension?" Also, in the back of his mind is his own reelection, which is two years away. So it's in part for domestic political and careerist reasons that he insists that this not be publicized.

DR: Let's talk about civil rights for a moment. The *Brown v. Board* decision in 1954 said, "With all deliberate speed, we're going to desegregate."

But there wasn't so much deliberate speed. And there wasn't really any significant civil rights legislation. There had been some in '57, but nothing of any consequence. Why didn't John Kennedy, in the beginning of his administration, go ahead and, as many of the progressives wanted in his party, propose civil rights legislation, or try to get it through the Congress?

FL: That's a very good question. And I would say, not merely in hindsight but in the context of his own time, he should have done that. His civil rights record in the House and in the Senate was quite good, in terms of voting for or against legislation. He believed in Black equality. But the plight of African Americans, the discrimination they endured on a daily basis, was not an issue that moved him particularly. It was not an issue in the forefront of his mind in this period. Even though some of his statements about civil rights during the 1960 campaign were pointed and powerful, he moved cautiously on the issue, afraid of alienating white Southern voters and leaders whose backing he needed in November.

The real question, though, is why didn't he move with greater dispatch once he became president? I think it's partly the same concern. In essence: "I need to be on good terms with Senate Democrats in particular. They control the key committees in the Senate, these Southern segregationists. So if I'm going to have any hope of getting legislation passed, my own re-election will be conditioned in part by how I handle this."

What he does do, however, is come around later in '62, and especially in '63, to a very different position.

DR: But he was against the March on Washington in '63. He was invited to speak there and chose not to. He was very worried it would lead to riots. He did greet Martin Luther King Jr. and some of the other speakers afterward. Was he afraid that the South wouldn't remain Democratic if he did more for civil rights?

FL: Yes, it's not his finest hour. He still worried, probably up until he takes that fateful trip to Dallas in November, about the consequences for him politically.

But we should note that in his famous June 11 speech from the White House, which is an extraordinary address, he makes civil rights a moral issue, really for the first time, addressed by a president from the Oval Office. We shouldn't underestimate the importance of that moment.

DR: So he makes a famous speech in Berlin: "Ich bin ein Berliner." Why did he make that speech? Was he really thinking it was going to make a difference in the way Khrushchev was going to conduct himself?

FL: After the Cuban Missile Crisis, I really think he does want to reconceptualize the Cold War in a fundamental way.

One of the "what-if" questions, if Kennedy had come back from Dallas alive, is what might have been the results for the Soviet-American relationship? Can we imagine that the Cold War ends? In Berlin, he's taking steps to make that happen, as is Khrushchev. They both take these steps to improve the relationship.

In Berlin, he nevertheless wants to speak for the West, speak on behalf of Western values, and it's arguably a fairly aggressive speech. Much of it is extemporaneous. This shows how far he's come as an orator.

He has a draft that you can see at the Kennedy Library and then you can compare to what he actually delivers. Much of it is his own words, in complete paragraphs. And of course he has a rapturous response from the people in Berlin. Nobody knows that this president in six months will be gunned down.

DR: President Kennedy would have said, before Dallas, "My most significant accomplishment is the Test Ban Treaty," which limited aboveground nuclear testing. Why was it so important to him to get that?

FL: He felt deeply that nuclear war must be avoided at all costs: We must make sure, those of us who are in positions of leadership, that we never take steps that get us anywhere closer to nuclear war. It certainly can't be won. It must never be waged.

This is part of an effort that he feels more strongly about after the Cuban Missile Crisis—that we, along with the Soviets, must take steps. We begin by limiting the testing, then we can maybe move to more aggressive measures.

DR: Let's talk about his personal life. He had a very complicated personal life as president. Jackie Kennedy said that her relationship with him got better because he was home more. How would you describe his personal life, and the fact that some people would say he was doing things that might be considered dangerous?

FL: I do think that their marriage got better in the final year, especially maybe in the final months. The death of their son Patrick, soon after birth, in some ways drew them closer together.

But you ask a very large question. How can a man who was quite cautious as a policymaker, including in his policymaking, often with good effect, someone pragmatic in his pursuit in his policy goals, careful in how he waged his campaigns, act so differently in this regard?

It's a question I'm still trying to sort out as I work on this volume. I don't think it's enough to say, "This is the *Mad Men* age. This is how men behaved." Not all men behaved this way. Nor can we say that it's because his father did this, although that's true. His father was, if anything, worse in this regard.

DR: Let's talk about the final trip to Dallas. It is widely thought that he needs to win Dallas. He needs Texas. Jackie Kennedy goes with him. That, I think, is the first time she went west of the Mississippi during his presidency, and the first time she went on a political trip with him?

FL: I don't know if it's the first time west of the Mississippi, but she certainly had not been traveling with him on these kinds of trips of late.

DR: She's never really been on a political trip with him?

FL: She had traveled with him in the '52 campaign for the Senate, in his reelection campaign in 1958, and on many occasions in 1960, especially in the primaries. She made a few appearances late in the fall, though she was heavily pregnant.

DR: But not when he was president.

FL: As president, that is correct.

DR: Why did they need to go to Dallas?

FL: In part because of a dispute within the Texas Democratic Party, factions in the party. Lyndon Johnson and others want the president to come and maybe help smooth things over, help improve those relations.

He's also gearing up for a reelection campaign. He's pretty sure that he will have Barry Goldwater as an opponent, and he thinks he can beat him. But Jack Kennedy being Jack Kennedy, he's taking no chances, so this is an opportunity to lay groundwork in a state he wants to retain a year hence.

So though there are aides who have concerns about the security situation in Dallas and about him going, he of course defies them. And they go.

DR: So on November 22nd, it was supposed to be raining in Dallas. And when it rained in those days, the Secret Service had a bubble it put on the presidential limousine. Kenny O'Donnell, in effect the chief of staff, said to the Secret Service, "No, the president wants to be seen. Don't put the bubble on." In hindsight that was obviously a terrible decision. But why did they publish the route that the president was going to go on? And do you have any doubt that Lee Harvey Oswald was the sole assassin?

FL: When you think about the "what-ifs" of that day, it's dizzying: What if, as you say, the weather had been what they thought? What if the motorcade hadn't slowed down when it turned the corner right underneath the Texas School Book Depository? What if Lee Harvey Oswald hadn't been working on that particular day? What if they had not published the route in the paper, which was fairly standard in those days? It was a more innocent age, needless to say. So many of these decisions had this extraordinary effect on the country and on the world. I'm still researching the developments of that terrible day, but yes, the forensic evidence is powerful that Oswald was the only gunman.

DR: When Kennedy was hit with the last shot, there was no chance that he could survive that shot?

FL: No. But another "what-if" is this: What if he hadn't been wearing the back brace that prevented him from going over on the first shot.

DR: Which went through the neck. And had he not had the back brace, he would have presumably leaned over, and the second shot wouldn't have hit him.

FL: That's right.

13

EVAN THOMAS
on Richard M. Nixon

(1913–1994; president from 1969 to 1974)

I f only Shakespeare had been around to write about Richard Nixon. What an unforgettable tragedy he could have written.

Born in modest circumstances, unable to afford the elite school education for which his brainpower would have otherwise qualified him; elected vice president of the United States at 39; lost the presidency by a whisker eight years later to his once good friend John Kennedy; wandered in the political wilderness for eight years (including losing an election for governor of his home state of California); defeated the patrician Nelson Rockefeller for the Republican presidential nomination; was elected president at 55; opened China to Western civilization; achieved détente with the Soviet Union; enacted the country's most significant environmental legislation in history; presided over the first successful manned moon landing; was reelected with a 49-state blowout victory; then not long thereafter felled by his desire to pursue his "enemies" and forced to resign the presidency—which had never happened in the country's history—because of words on tapes that he had voluntarily recorded.

Had Nixon destroyed the tapes when it was still legal to do so, his image might have been what he had once hoped. His political opponents—who never forgave his early-career red-baiting and his pugnacious personality—would not have had the political power to force a resignation or achieve a Senate conviction after a House impeachment, if one would have even occurred. And in the fullness of time, Richard Nixon could well have gone down in history as one of the country's most "historic" and successful presidents.

I did not know Richard Nixon. I only met him once, at a retirement party I hosted for the "Father of the Nuclear Navy," Admiral Hyman Rickover, whom Nixon greatly admired. But like so many in my Baby Boomer generation, I felt that I "knew" Nixon reasonably well. His decisions on the Vietnam War obviously affected many young men in my generation. (I had a standard student deferment through most of college; when those deferments were ending and Nixon imposed a lottery system, I drew a high number and was never called for enlistment.)

But my generation, and those older as well, came to know Nixon intimately through Watergate, with the *Washington Post*'s seemingly unbelievable daily revelations, the televised hearings, and the trials and convictions of his closest advisors. The intense and almost hourly press coverage was something the country had never seen. Not until Donald Trump came into office, and investigations of him began, did the country see and learn so much about a president.

After Watergate there followed a flurry of books about it and really about Richard Nixon. Everyone in the administration seemed to write a book. Most were published within a decade or so of his administration. But few have been written in recent years, with a bit more perspective to the achievements and failures of Richard Nixon.

One such book, *Being Nixon: A Man Divided*, was written by Evan Thomas, former editor of *Newsweek* and author of other bestselling biographies of Robert Kennedy, Edward Bennett Williams, John Paul Jones, and Sandra Day O'Connor, among other works relating to American history. I had a chance to interview Evan at a Congressional Dialogues session at the Library of Congress on April 26, 2016.

*   *   *   *

DAVID M. RUBENSTEIN (DR): When people write biographies, they tend to admire their subjects more than before. Do you admire Richard Nixon more now?

EVAN THOMAS (ET): Yes, but I thought he was pretty terrible at first. I worked for the Washington Post Company for 24 years, so I thought he was the devil. One reason I wrote the book was to see what it would be like to be on his side.

DR: Richard Nixon was, as you describe in your book, one of the most introverted persons you ever could imagine. How did he get into politics?

ET: It's one of the great mysteries. Richard Nixon was one of the most successful political figures in the twentieth century. He was on five national tickets. He won four times in a huge landslide. How did he do it? He was painfully shy. In some ways, he did it because he liked power. He was good at politics. Even though he was shy, he made a point of remembering people's names. He really worked at it. And he loved politics. He just loved the power game. He studied it. He mastered it. He understood what it was like to be on the outside looking in. Even when he was in the establishment, he was always on the outside, on the side of the outsiders.

DR: Some of that came from his background. He grew up relatively poor in Whittier, California. Tell us about his mother and father.

ET: His mother was a saintly Quaker but not actually the most lovable person in the world. His father was a bully. He was uncomfortable with his parents and did not have a happy childhood. But he had incredible drive. His insecurity drove him. It destroyed him too, but it drove him.

DR: He went to Whittier College. Did he do well there?

ET: Yes. He was an unpopular kid who became the president of his class this way. Whittier College was a little Quaker school, and very uptight. Richard Nixon's platform when he was running for student body president was to bring dancing to Whittier, which the authorities did not like.

Now, Nixon himself could not dance, and he hated dancing. But he understood that at Whittier the rich kids could dance any time they wanted, at the country club or at a hotel. It was the poor kids who couldn't dance. At Whittier in 1931 there were a lot of poor kids. He won in an overwhelming landslide.

DR: He was student body president, and he wanted to go to law school. Did he apply to Harvard Law School or schools like that?

ET: He went to Duke, which was a brand-new law school with a lot of money. It exposed him some fancy professors and very smart kids, mostly Phi Beta Kappa kids. Nixon did well there, mostly by being a grind.

DR: He finished third in his class or something like that. He wanted a job on Wall Street. Did he get one?

ET: He tried big Wall Street law firms. His enduring memory was sitting outside at Sullivan and Cromwell or Cravath, I forget which one, looking at the fancy oriental rug when they did not offer him a job.

DR: He got no job offers and he went back to California, practiced in Whittier as a lawyer, and then the war broke out. Did he volunteer to go into the service?

ET: He did. He was a Quaker, but as soon as Pearl Harbor happened, he went into the Navy. He wanted to be in combat, and he was sent to an airfield in the middle of Nebraska. He ended up in the South Pacific as a supply officer. He was a good officer. His men compared him to Mr. Roberts. He was loyal to his men. He was a good leader.

DR: He comes back and all of a sudden somebody asked him if he wants to run for Congress. How did that come about?

ET: They were looking for cannon fodder, basically, some guy to lose to a guy named Jerry Voorhis, who was the incumbent congressman. Voorhis ran a really stupid campaign against him. Nixon was nimble, challenged him to a debate. Voorhis should not have taken the challenge. And Nixon, partly by being slightly underhanded, got to him. Voorhis panicked and Nixon won.

DR: He gets to Congress. Who else was in that class in 1946?

ET: Jack Kennedy. Weirdly, one of Nixon's good friends was John F. Kennedy. Although they were in different parties, they were both internationalists. They were Navy veterans who believed that America had to do something about the world. They were both shy, and that bonded them. They stayed good friends until 1960, when they ran against each other and hated each other.

DR: When they were members of Congress, Nixon got a chance to go to Europe to see Dwight D. Eisenhower. Did Kennedy help him with the trip?

ET: Jack Kennedy gave Nixon a list of three girls to call in Paris. Nixon deliberately forgot the list.

DR: In the House of Representatives, Nixon was put on the House Un-American Affairs Committee, which was then a very controversial committee. What did he do there that made him famous?

ET: He unmasked Alger Hiss. Hiss was a popular, East Coast establishment, Harvard Law School guy, the head of the Carnegie Foundation. He was also a Soviet spy. But he thought he could get away with it, and conned a lot of people into thinking that he was innocent. And Nixon, who was persistent, just stayed after Hiss and exposed him as the spy he was. This was a great thing for Republicans because it made the Truman administration look bad, rightfully so. Nixon, although an obscure congressman, became an instant national hero.

DR: He decides to run for the Senate in 1950. Who did he run against?

ET: Helen Gahagan Douglas, who was a congresswoman from California. A very attractive woman, she was having an affair with LBJ at the time. She ran a bad campaign. When addressing a Black audience, she would say, "Oh, I just love the Negro people." She was kind of a limousine liberal. She was condescending and off-putting. Nixon ran a smart campaign against her and won.

DR: During that campaign he also accused her of being "pink." What does that mean?

ET: He insinuated that she was to the left. In those days, in 1950, being red was the worst thing you could be. Being pink was almost as bad. And so he called her "the pink lady," a name that stuck. She also came up with a name for him, "Tricky Dick."

DR: I guess that stuck too. So he gets elected in 1950. John Kennedy is still in the House. In 1952 Dwight D. Eisenhower is looking for a vice president. How did he pick Nixon, a person who'd only been in the Senate two years?

ET: Nixon was close to the right wing, young, and attractive. Eisenhower barely met Nixon, but he went down a political checklist with his advisors. Nixon brought him a lot and so he put him on the ticket.

DR: The recommendation was made by Tom Dewey, who was advising Eisenhower?

ET: Tom Dewey was Mr. Republican, and saw that a young anticommunist Californian could help deflect the right with Joe McCarthy, who was a kind of terrifying figure on the right for the Republican party.

DR: Nixon at the time was only 39. Eisenhower was 62 or so. Nixon's on the ticket, and things go forward. Then, all of a sudden, a scandal broke. What happened?

ET: Nixon supposedly had a slush fund of about $20,000 for his nonpolitical expenses. It was a phony scandal. It was nothing. In fact, Adlai Stevenson, who was running for president as a Democrat, had a much bigger slush fund. But it took off in the press, and it became this hot-button issue. And Eisenhower, instead of standing by Nixon, tried to dump him from the ticket. Nixon was alone.

DR: You say "tried" to dump him. Eisenhower is the Supreme Allied Commander. He was in charge of D-Day. If he wants to dump somebody, why doesn't he say, "You're dumped"?

ET: He said to Nixon, "You should fall on your sword. You should resign." Nixon instead said, "Give me a chance," and gave a famous televised speech called the "Checkers Speech." It seemed, to many East Coast types, a sentimental speech. He talked about his dog, Checkers, given to him by a contributor, and about his wife's Republican cloth coat.

But the telling thing was that when Eisenhower was watching with his buddies, commenting, "This is kind of a maudlin speech," Eisenhower's wife, Mamie, was weeping. Nixon reached a lot of people with that speech. They sympathized with him. They sensed that he was being unfairly dealt with. It turned things around. He stayed on the ticket and was a good vice president.

DR: Eisenhower said later in the campaign, "You're always my boy, and I never really wanted to dump you"?

ET: Right. Which was not true.

DR: They get elected in a big victory over Stevenson and Sparkman in '52. What job did Eisenhower give Nixon as vice president?

ET: Vice presidents often did nothing in those days, but in this case, Eisenhower sent Nixon abroad to deal with foreign leaders, and Nixon was good at it. He did his homework, studied up, cared about the world, and was good with the leaders. He was very loyal. Eisenhower had a big heart attack. It was a difficult situation. Nixon held himself really well. He was a good vice president.

DR: As they were getting ready to run for a second term, did Eisenhower consider dumping Nixon?

ET: I wrote a book about Eisenhower, and I asked John Eisenhower, Eisenhower's son, "What did your father think of Nixon?" And he said, "My father gave himself an order to like Dick Nixon."

Nixon was not that likable. And Eisenhower thought that Nixon had a drinking problem. He had a little drinking problem, not a big one. But Eisenhower just didn't like him, and he thought that he wasn't an attractive figure.

DR: So he suggested Nixon be secretary of defense in the second term, or get some experience?

ET: Yes. Which was not a bad idea. To Eisenhower, thinking like a military guy, season yourself, become secretary of defense. It's a good job, you'll learn how to manage things. All Nixon could see was that Ike was trying to dump him, that the headline was going to be "Ike Dumps Nixon." So Nixon refused to quit, and it worked. He became the nominee.

DR: At one point as vice president he's asked by Eisenhower to go down to Latin America, to Venezuela, where he almost got killed?

ET: Left-wing mobs stoned and mobbed his car—the car of the vice president of the United States. They started rocking it, they smashed the windows, and the Secret Service guy sitting next to Nixon pulled out his pistol and said, "I'm going to shoot one of those bastards." Nixon said, "Put the gun away. Don't do anything unless they actually come through and pull me out." Nixon was physically brave.

DR: And when he comes back, Eisenhower goes out to the airport to greet him.

ET: He was a hero.

DR: So Nixon decides he wants to run for president. Who were his competitors in 1960?

ET: There really were none on the Republican side. He was the heir apparent. He had the machine. Nixon was very good about campaigning for congressmen. He did it in 1954, '56, '58. In those days, there were primaries, but party machinery ran the show, and if you had a lot of congressmen on your side you were in. And he did.

DR: At one point, in a press conference, Eisenhower is asked, "What did Richard Nixon do as vice president?" What did Eisenhower say?

ET: "If you give me a week, I'll think of something." How cruel was that? It was really wounding.

Someone truthfully said Eisenhower was irritated at the reporters who were bugging him, and he was peevish. Eisenhower was old, playing a lot of golf, sick of it, and he just had an outburst. But it looked terrible for Nixon, and in the first debate in '60, the very first question from the NBC reporter was, "President Eisenhower was asked about this and said, 'If you give me a week, I'll think of something.'"

DR: Let's talk about the debates. Kennedy gets the Democratic nomination. Nixon watches Kennedy and says, "This guy's not such a great speaker. Maybe I should debate him." Was it Nixon's idea to do a debate?

ET: Yes. Totally stupid.

DR: Had there ever been a presidential debate before?

ET: No. He didn't have to debate him. Nixon had more credibility. He was older. It was a mistake.

DR: There are four debates. The first one is in Chicago?

ET: In Chicago, in the early days of TV. The producer comes up to Kennedy and says, "Would you like some makeup?" Kennedy says no. Then he goes back to his dressing room and is professionally made up. The producer says to Nixon, "Do you want makeup?" And Nixon says no, because Kennedy hadn't. Then Nixon sends his guy down to Michigan Avenue to buy some shave stick, this horrible gray grease you put on five o'clock shadow, and Nixon smears it on. If you look at the video, Nixon is sweating through this gray grease and his eyes are darting around, and Kennedy looks tan and handsome, cool. It's just sort of an unfair fight.

DR: Nixon had also been ill during the campaign, and he made a promise that seemed silly—to go to every state?

ET: To go to 50 states. Bad idea. Nixon made the mistake of being his own campaign manager.

DR: It's widely thought, in political history and political lore, that because Nixon looked so bad, Kennedy won the first debate. But people who listened on radio weren't so sure.

ET: Yes, because Nixon was pretty good on foreign policies, quite substantive, and Kennedy was a little thin. On radio, the polls show that Nixon won.

DR: The three other debates were a draw?

ET: Pretty much. The damage was done in the first.

DR: The day of the election, it turns out that it's very close. Mayor Daley calls John Kennedy and says, "With the help of a few friends, I think you're going to win Illinois." What did he mean?

ET: He meant that he stole the election. At least a lot of scholars think that in Illinois there was voter fraud. In one precinct more people voted for Kennedy than lived there.

DR: If that was the case, why did Nixon not contest the election?

ET: Because Nixon was a good guy about this. It was the Cold War. We were locked in this terrible fight with the Soviet Union. Nixon knew that it would be disruptive to put the country through a protracted challenge. And so, even though he was the presiding officer in the Senate, he had to certify his own defeat, and he was graceful about it.

DR: He's out as vice president. He decides to move back to California?

ET: To make money as a lawyer. But he can't resist getting back into politics.

DR: He's asked to run for governor in 1962, and he decides to do it even though he doesn't care about state issues?

ET: Correct. It's a mistake. He wants to get back on the stage. He misses politics.

DR: He was beaten by Pat Brown?

ET: He was. Pretty badly.

DR: And then he has a press conference. What does he say?

ET: "You won't have Dick Nixon to kick around anymore." People thought that was it, that he was finished. In fact, *Time* magazine wrote his political obituary. ABC News said, "You're right. You won't have Dick Nixon to kick around anymore."

DR: He decides to move out of L.A. and to go to—?

ET: To New York to be a lawyer, and he made a bunch of money. He was a good rainmaker. But he missed politics.

DR: In New York, they put his name on the law firm. He argues a case in front of the Supreme Court. Did he win?

ET: No, he lost. He blamed it on a liberal bias of the Supreme Court. But apparently he argued the case pretty well.

DR: In 1962 he's out of politics. How does he manage to make himself, in 1968, the nominee of the party?

ET: He helps a lot in the '66 off-year elections. The Republicans do well. LBJ's Great Society is losing out, and Nixon campaigns for 43 congressmen. Forty-one of them win. So he has a lot of IOUs. It's 1968. It is a hot, angry time. Cities and campuses are burning. And Nixon decides to get low key and moderate and be the grown-up in the room, setting himself apart from the Democrats who are being too hot. George Wallace is off to his right, getting the "angry vote." And Nixon positions himself as moderate, low-key, and experienced.

DR: During that year, Martin Luther King Jr. was killed and also Robert Kennedy was killed, so the Democratic nominee is Hubert Humphrey, and George Wallace also runs.

ET: It looked like it was Nixon's to win, but Humphrey was closing on him toward the end.

DR: How did Nixon pick Spiro Agnew as his vice president?

ET: It was purely expedient. In those days there was such a thing as an Atlantic Coast moderate Republican, which was pretty much Agnew. He was personable and had a good presence. Despite being young and inexperienced, he had given a speech standing up to some Black militants in Baltimore. Nixon liked that, even though he barely knew Agnew.

Then when Agnew became vice president, Nixon ignored him. He kicked him out of his office and gave him a worse one, refused to take any substantive advice from him, and basically ignored him until he wanted a hit man to go after the press. Then Nixon gave his best speechwriters, Pat Buchanan and Bill Safire, to Agnew and sent him out.

DR: Nixon is elected. He's got Agnew as his vice president, who later has to make appointments a couple of months ahead just to meet with Nixon. How did Henry Kissinger, who was advisor to Rockefeller and John Kennedy, wind up as a national security advisor to Nixon?

ET: To Nixon's credit, he liked talent. He loved to confound his enemies. He loved the idea of stealing away Rockefeller's advisor, making him his guy. But he also understood that Kissinger was brilliant and that he understood Nixon's realpolitik view of foreign policy, and that they would work together well.

DR: Nixon picks Haldeman as his chief of staff. Was that a good decision, in the end?

ET: Haldeman was a great chief of staff who made one mistake, called Watergate. Big mistake. Oddly, Haldeman ran a very tight ship at the White House. But he did isolate Nixon, and Haldeman lost control of the White House during Watergate, for a lot of reasons.

DR: Before that, did Nixon like to meet with members of Congress?

ET: Initially, because he thought it was his duty, and he had friends there, he did okay at first. He had good congressional liaison guys, Bryce Harlow and Tom Korologos. He had some smart guys working for him. But, as time went on, he became more isolated and stupidly got himself disconnected from Congress, and by the time he needed them, by the time Watergate happened, he didn't have many friends left.

DR: The idea to go and open up China, was that Kissinger's idea or Nixon's?

ET: Kissinger went around claiming it was his idea, but it was actually Nixon's.

DR: When they went over to China, Nixon met Mao Tse-tung. Did he know he was going to meet Mao?

ET: He hoped he was going to meet Mao. It was going to be a pretty bad trip if he didn't. But they weren't sure Mao was going to meet with him. Mao was old and sick and weird and kept from seeing many others, but he did meet with Nixon. We remember Nixon from the tapes, profane and kind of ugly. But he was good with foreign leaders. He was quiet. He didn't preach at them about how great America was. He talked about Soviet interests, Chinese interests, and American interests. Foreign leaders liked Nixon.

DR: When they arrived, Mao said, "Come meet us." How did they forget to bring Bill Rogers, the secretary of state, to that meeting?

ET: Kissinger cut him out. Kissinger was always concentrating power in Kissinger.

DR: Let's talk about Russia for a moment. The idea of meeting with Russian leaders was relatively novel at the time. How did Nixon pull that off?

ET: Nixon was the first president to go to Moscow, and he personally, with Kissinger, negotiated the first-ever arms control treaty. Nixon was a great student of the physics of politics. He understood that, precisely because he had been a red hunter himself, an anticommunist, he was exactly the guy who could go to Moscow and Beijing and make a deal. Because who was going to attack him?

DR: At one point Brezhnev came over to visit Nixon as well?

ET: He did. Brezhnev stayed with Nixon and brought his airline stewardess/masseuse, and poor Pat Nixon ran into her in the hallway as she was making her way to Brezhnev's room.

DR: Let's talk about Pat Nixon for a moment. How did he meet her, and what was the nature of that relationship?

ET: One of the saddest things is Pat Nixon. You're familiar with the images of her looking sad and tired and thin. I use a picture in my book taken in 1953. She looks fantastic. She's about 15 pounds heavier, she's beautiful. She's a knockout. And Nixon is standing there with his goofy smile. He can't believe his good luck that he married this beautiful girl.

They had a good marriage initially. Over time, Nixon, a strange guy and lonely, starts drinking a little bit too much. Haldeman bears some blame in this. As chief of staff he's isolating Nixon. He actually isolated him partly from his own wife.

DR: Did Pat Nixon ever say to her husband, "You're being isolated from me by Haldeman"?

ET: Yes, but not loud enough. Not firmly enough. The daughters did, but Nixon couldn't quite hear it.

DR: So Nixon was pretty liberal on certain things. The EPA was created then. The Clean Water Act. How do you explain a conservative Republican, as he viewed himself, having a lot of policies that liberal Democrats liked?

14

RICHARD NORTON SMITH
on Gerald R. Ford

(1913–2006; president from 1974 to 1977)

O nly one person has served as president without having been elected to that office or to the vice presidency: Gerald Ford.

Throughout much of the country's history, if a president died—four died naturally and four were assassinated—the vice president immediately succeeded to the presidency (the swearing-in occurred later but was not really necessary). Interestingly, the Founding Fathers had not included a provision in the Constitution to have a successor vice president serve out the prior vice president's term. Eighteen presidents have at least served part of their term without a vice president.

Similarly, the Founding Fathers made no provision for a successor if the vice president (rather than the president) died, was incapacitated, was impeached and convicted, or resigned. But Congress did eventually make a provision for someone to become president if one left office without having a vice president in place. Until 1948, cabinet officers would succeed a president in the order in which their departments had been created (the State Department had been created first). In 1947, Congress passed legislation providing that if there was no vice president, the Speaker of the House of Representatives and then the president pro tempore of the Senate would succeed a departed president (the reasoning being that they had been elected to office and thus had some public support). If those individuals were not available, then the cabinet officers would succeed in the order in which their departments had been created. And that is still the law of the land.

But presidential succession changed with the Twenty-Fifth Amendment to the Constitution, ratified in 1967. It provided that a vice president who succeeds to the presidency (because a president dies, is incapacitated, or is removed from office through a House impeachment and Senate conviction) can designate someone to serve as vice president and that person assumes the position upon a majority vote of both the House and the Senate. And a president may similarly designate someone as vice president, subject to confirmation by both Houses, if the incumbent vice president should leave the office.

This first became relevant with President Nixon. His twice-elected vice president, the former governor of Maryland, Spiro Agnew, resigned his office to forestall a possible jail sentence for having taken cash bribes while governor and while vice president. So President Nixon had to designate another person to serve.

His first choice apparently was his former secretary of the treasury, John Connally, also a former Texas governor known to many Americans for having been in the car with President Kennedy when he was assassinated (Connally was also wounded by a bullet). But members of Congress convinced Nixon that Connally would not be confirmed by the Democratic Congress because Democrats saw it giving Connally a leg up in getting elected president in 1980.

Gerald Ford, the House Republican leader and a widely admired member of Congress, was known to be interested in retiring from politics and was not seen as a likely presidential candidate. And he had relatively few enemies in Congress and was assured of being confirmed. So President Nixon selected him—he had known him initially from their days in the House together. And the confirmation went smoothly. (It was also believed at the time that Nixon selected Ford because he was *not* seen as presidential, so Nixon did not think he would be forced from office if his successor was someone widely regarded as not really presidential material.)

As often happens in Washington, events did not proceed as anticipated. At the time Ford was confirmed, few in the country—including Richard Nixon—expected that the unfolding Watergate scandal would likely lead to Nixon being forced to resign. Shortly after the once-unanticipated resignation did occur, President Ford felt he needed to pardon Nixon, which produced a firestorm of criticism from both parties and the public (resulting in Ford's having to defend his action in testimony before Congress—the first congressional testimony for a president he say it? He said it because Gerald Ford, as the Republican leader of the House, had a unique capacity to get under Lyndon Johnson's skin and make him say things that even he later regretted.

The last weekend of the Johnson presidency, LBJ calls Ford at home in Alexandria, invites him to the White House, and they have this amazing meeting. He says, "We've said some pretty rough things about each other, but I never questioned your integrity." Ford said the same. And they left friends. When LBJ had his first heart attack in 1970, one of the first people he heard from was Gerald Ford. The Johnson family and the Ford family became very close.

DR: Where was Ford born?

RNS: Gerald Ford was born in Omaha, Nebraska. He was born Leslie King Jr. Leslie King Sr. was a scoundrel. When I looked at Gerald Ford's baby book, there's a very poignant entry, "Baby's first automobile ride." He was two weeks old. His father had walked into his wife's bedroom with a butcher knife, threatening to kill mother and child. And baby's first automobile ride was his mother sneaking out of the house and slipping across the Missouri River to the Iowa side to take a train for Chicago. Eventually, she moved to Grand Rapids. She met a man named Gerald Ford, who became Gerald Ford Sr.

DR: Did he ever meet his biological father?

RNS: He did, under bizarre circumstances. Ford was an adolescent, working the lunch beat at a hamburger joint to earn a little bit of cash. And then one day, out of the blue, this stranger walks in, and Ford noticed he was kind of eyeing him. After ten minutes or so, he walked up and he said, "You're Leslie King." He said, "No, I'm Gerald Ford." He said, "No, you're Leslie King. I'm your father." That was his introduction. They went to lunch. He gave him $25 and disappeared. He saw him once more. He never paid the court-ordered child support payments. So the first thing Ford did when he became congressman was introduce legislation to federalize child support payments.

DR: Gerald Ford grew up in Grand Rapids, and was he a football star in high school?

RNS: Yes, he was a football star in high school. He was a football star at the University of Michigan. It was football that paid his way. In the Great Depression, they had no money, and there were no scholarships. Football scholarships were unheard of.

DR: So how did it pay his way?

RNS: He got a job waiting on tables in the nurses' dining room and as a dishwasher. He said later on he was probably the only American president who suffered simultaneously from football knee and dishpan hands.

DR: They won a national championship twice at the University of Michigan when he was playing there. Was he good enough to play in the pros?

RNS: He was approached by the Detroit Lions, the Green Bay Packers, and the Chicago Bears. But he already knew he wanted to be a lawyer. I think he knew he wanted to be a politician. So he went to Yale as an assistant football coach who also took a full-time course of law school classes.

DR: While he's at Yale Law School he leads an America First group. What was that?

RNS: The term "America First" meant something different in 1940 than it does today. The post–World War I generation was disillusioned by the promises made, and also by seeing Europe heading down the road to another war. So it stood for isolationism against American entry into World War II. Young John F. Kennedy, young Gore Vidal, not so young Walt Disney, Frank Lloyd Wright—they all joined this organization that started at Yale Law School.

In the summer of 1940, Ford discovered something he liked better than America First. It was Wendell Willkie, the Republican candidate running against FDR, who stood for joining the fight against fascism. Ford was in Philadelphia, in the convention hall crowd, shouting, "We want Willkie, we want Willkie." And needless to say, Wendell Willkie was not an American Firster. Ford resigned from America First. Unfortunately for him, in 1941, when he applied to be an FBI agent, he was personally blackballed by J. Edgar Hoover, who had discovered this connection. And I think Ford went to his grave not knowing the reason for his FBI rejection.

DR: In 1941, Pearl Harbor happens. Did Gerald Ford decide to enlist?

RNS: Yes. He signed up, and the first year he spent back at the University of North Carolina. The Air Force had a training program. They hired a lot of football players, a lot of jocks, to get future pilots into shape. Ford did that for a year. He wanted to get in on the action. So he wrote Arthur Vandenberg, who was his hometown U.S. senator and his political role model in many ways, and he pulled every string he could to get into the war. And he did. He was on the *Monterey*, an improvised quasi–aircraft carrier in the Pacific.

DR: He served from 1944 or so.

RNS: Yes. The worst part of the war for them was the great typhoon in December of 1944. The *Monterey* almost capsized. Nearby ships did capsize. Ford was up on the bridge. The ship was on fire. Two of the engines were out. And somehow they managed to bring it through.

DR: Richard Nixon, John Kennedy, and Gerald Ford all come back from the war and run for Congress. Why?

RNS: Ford ran for Congress in 1948 as an internationalist. He ran against an entrenched mossback Republican incumbent who was a fervent isolationist, and he beat him. And he won in the fall. He never had any trouble getting reelected.

DR: Was he a moderate, or conservative, or liberal?

RNS: He was elected with the endorsement of the United Auto Workers. What does that tell you? He was an unconventional Republican. His next-door neighbor in the House office building was John F. Kennedy. They used to ride the House subway together. Usually their votes canceled each other out on domestic policy, but not foreign policy.

DR: At one point Ford decided to take on the House Republican leadership. How did he get enough support to beat Charlie Halleck, who was the incumbent Republican leader?

RNS: Five years into his congressional tenure, Ford had been put on the supersecret, supersensitive Intelligence Oversight Committee, with five members—four old boys and one promising up-and-coming member. No staff, no notes. And he demonstrated his talent for discretion. That's why he was also on the Warren Commission—his ability to keep secrets. The proverbial workhorse. And so in 1964 comes the Goldwater debacle. Ford was able to keep his distance because of his work on the Warren Commission. In the wake of that election, Republicans, younger Republicans especially, and newly elected Republicans, many of them Southerners, said, "We need a new face. Everett Dirksen is great, but he's old and he hogged the stage. And Charlie Halleck is not a television figure." Ford took on Halleck, again an insurgency. He won by four votes. The four votes were supplied by Bob Dole's Kansas delegation. I always said he returned the favor a dozen years later with somewhat higher stakes. (Ford picked Dole as his running mate in 1976.)

DR: So he becomes the House minority leader. But his real goal was to be Speaker of the House, but in those days, in the 1970s, the House didn't look like it was going to go Republican. So he tells his wife, "I think I'm going to retire in 1976."

RNS: He tells his wife, "I'll be 63 in 1976. Young enough to have another career." He felt guilt, I think, over those years when he was on the road 200 nights a year, fundraising for other candidates and basically trying to become Speaker.

DR: So he realizes he's not going to be Speaker. Then Spiro Agnew was forced to resign, and Nixon, under the Twenty-Fifth Amendment, now has a chance to pick a new person to be vice president of the United States. Why does he pick Ford?

RNS: Ford knew about Agnew's problem six months before he ever acknowledged it, and he was interested in replacing Agnew. One of the things you've got to remember about good old Jerry is that he was a lot more ambitious than he let on. Nixon wanted John Connolly, a swaggering Texan who had a larger-than-life self-confidence that Nixon envied. The problem was that, among other things, Connolly had switched parties and the Democrats had hefty majorities on Capitol Hill in those days. There was no way that they were going to confirm John Connolly.

The one person who enjoyed bipartisan support was Ford, and in the end you could say it was Democrats in Congress who made Gerald Ford vice president. Nixon described Ford to someone at that time as an honest Truman. I don't think he meant it as a compliment.

DR: But is it true that Nixon said at the time, "If I pick Ford, that's my insurance policy. Nobody will ever get rid of me because they wouldn't want Ford to be president"?

RNS: Which is only the latest example of terrible judgment on Nixon's part throughout Watergate. Every mistake that could be made, he made. The people who had the highest opinion of Gerald Ford were the people who worked with him, who knew him the best. And Nixon had lost touch with those people.

DR: Under the Twenty-Fifth Amendment, you have to be confirmed by both the House and the Senate. And Ford did pretty well. He got only three votes against him in the Senate and perhaps 35 in the House. So he was overwhelmingly confirmed and gets the job. Does he expect that he's going to be president, though?

RNS: No, here's the irony. Eight days after Ford's nomination is announced comes the Saturday Night Massacre, in which Attorney General Elliot Richardson and his deputy quit rather than fire the Watergate special prosecutor. Overnight Ford's position is transformed. Instead of a caretaker to fill out Agnew's term, Congress is looking at a potential president.

DR: When the existence of the Nixon White House tapes is revealed, the Supreme Court says they have to be handed over to Congress. They contain the so-called smoking-gun evidence of Nixon's involvement in the cover-up of Watergate. Al Haig, then the chief of staff, says "Gerald Ford, you should get ready to maybe become president." That's around August of '74.

RNS: Haig had a strategy. I believe Al Haig had decided Nixon had to go, but he had to go in such a way that it did not further polarize the country. So Haig wanted to enlist people that Nixon would listen to, beginning with his vice president. And that's what Haig had in mind on August 1st, when he went over to see Ford to tell him about the smoking-gun tape and—oh, by the way—raised the option of a presidential pardon.

DR: And what did Ford say about a presidential pardon?

RNS: Ford primarily is trying to digest the fact that he'd been denying for a year—that he was going to be president. As far as everything else, it's typical Ford. He said, "You're going to have to give me time to think about this. I'm going to have to talk it over with Betty." And he said, "I also want to talk to Jim St. Clair," who was Nixon's White House lawyer. Mrs. Ford said Jerry came home that night and said Al Haig had offered him a deal, and she said, "You know you can't do that." And he said, "I know I can't." Before he went to bed that night, he called Haig and said, "That conversation we had this afternoon, no agreements, no deals." Haig was sufficiently frazzled that he called Fred Buzhardt, the man who drew up the option list including the pardon, at 2:30 in the morning and said, "What the hell have you done to me?"

DR: Did he ever regret doing the pardon?

RNS: No.

DR: Later he carried around a piece of paper that says a getting pardon means that you are admitting you've made a mistake.

RNS: It was a legalistic explanation from a 1914 Supreme Court case, which established the principle that if you accept the pardon, it is tantamount to acknowledging guilt.

DR: Ford becomes president in August of '74, and he has a famous line, "Our long national nightmare is over." Who wrote that line?

RNS: Publicly, the speechwriter Bob Hartman. What I discovered in another oral history that had not been opened previously was that there was another speechwriter named Milton Friedman, not to be confused with the economist. He wrote the line.

DR: Ford becomes president. Does he want to keep Al Haig as chief of staff?

RNS: No. But you couldn't appoint Al Haig to anything that required congressional confirmation. So Ford found him the perfect job as the military head of NATO.

DR: Who does he make his chief of staff?

RNS: He brings in Don Rumsfeld, who was his campaign manager in the campaign against Charlie Halleck back in 1965. Rumsfeld made it very clear, when we talked to him, that he was more conservative than Ford. He thought Nelson Rockefeller was the wrong pick for vice president. He thought that Henry Kissinger shouldn't be given carte blanche.

DR: Henry Kissinger was operating then as national security advisor and secretary of state.

RNS: Which Ford thought was a mistake from day one, and eventually he took Kissinger's national security hat away from him.

DR: Did he sit down with Kissinger and say, "Henry, you've got to give up one job"?

RNS: No. Jim Schlesinger was his secretary of defense and Ford said later on — I heard him say this — that Schlesinger thought Ford was a dummy. Schlesinger, like Henry Kissinger, went to Harvard, was an academic star, brilliant. The difference is that Kissinger was the consummate courtier — kiss up, kick down. Schlesinger treated everyone the same. And that included the president of the United States. Ford got sick of it and fired him, replacing him with Donald Rumsfeld. At the same time, he took Kissinger's second hat away and he made Brent Scowcroft national security advisor. Most people would think that's one of the premier foreign policy teams.

DR: Who became chief of staff after Rumsfeld?

RNS: Rumsfeld's assistant, a 34-year-old named Dick Cheney. The youngest chief of staff in White House history.

DR: Does Ford immediately say, "I really like this job. I want to run for president"?

RNS: It took him a couple of months. Originally, he thought he would not run. It's easy to think of all the burdens that he brought into the office, but he thought how liberated he was. He had never run for the office.

He made no promises, no commitments. He thought—he was naïve in so thinking—that we could put Watergate behind us, and then move on and address big issues.

DR: Let's talk about some of the issues. The economy, as you pointed out, was terrible, with high inflation and low growth. They came up with a strategy called WIN—Whip Inflation Now. What was that?

RNS: That came out of the speechwriter shop. It was terrible PR. This is in the shakedown phase of Ford's presidency. He was still thinking like a congressman with a constituency that you could address in a day. To succeed, Ford had to learn to be an executive.

DR: Under Ford, we pulled out of Vietnam. But we still have these images of the helicopter going off the roof of the embassy. Did Ford recognize he made a mistake in the exit?

RNS: Talk about a thankless position to be in. They had to pretend for the last couple of weeks that they weren't pulling out. There was a big debate going on between Schlesinger and Kissinger about when and how openly to pull out. The concern was that if you were open about it, you could start rioting, and the remaining Americans could be in physical danger. So you had that balancing act. There was not supposed to be a helicopter evacuation. The airfield was being shelled, so they had to go to plan B, which involved helicopters instead of fixed-wing aircraft. It was supposed to be a three-hour operation. It took 18 hours.

But here's the sequel. Two days after Saigon fell, Ron Nessen, the press secretary, came in with a report off the wire services. Congress had pulled the plug on resettlement money for Vietnamese refugees. Nessen said it's the only time he ever heard Ford swear. He was livid. He said, "We didn't do it after the Hungarian Revolution. We certainly didn't do it with the Cubans. And we're not going to do it with the Vietnamese." It was the one instance in his presidency where he really effectively used the bully pulpit. He went to the country. He put together this crazy-quilt coalition. The American Jewish Congress. Pope Paul weighed in. The World Council of Churches. A number of Democratic state governors. They pressured Congress to change its mind, and 120,000 Vietnamese were brought over to the U.S. That I think is his finest hour as president.

DR: The president has the opportunity to pick his own vice president. Why does Ford pick Nelson Rockefeller?

RNS: There were there were three names submitted to the FBI. George H. W. Bush was a very close runner-up. Don Rumsfeld was also on that list. Ford picked Nelson Rockefeller. Classic opposites attract. Gerald Ford had spent a life on Capitol Hill, so didn't want someone from Capitol Hill. Nelson Rockefeller had been governor of New York State for 15 years. He had unlimited access to talent. There was an exodus, some voluntary, some not so voluntary, from the Nixon White House staff. What Ford miscalculated was just how much of a red flag Rockefeller would be to the right wing of his party.

DR: He runs for election, and his opponent is Jimmy Carter, the Democratic nominee. Why does Ford get rid of Rockefeller in favor of Bob Dole?

RNS: Because he wanted to get renominated, and he'd become convinced that his renomination against Ronald Reagan was seriously in doubt if he kept Nelson Rockefeller as his VP.

DR: Who does he pick as his campaign manager to beat Reagan?

RNS: He went through several people and then finally settled on Jim Baker, who had been a junior-level official with the Commerce Department and then distinguished himself as the chief delegate counter. It was a very hard-fought convention. Then Baker took over the fall campaign. Ford was 30 points behind going into the general election race. He finished two points behind on election day.

DR: Did Reagan promise to campaign for Ford?

RNS: Let's say there was no love lost between the two or their wives. One thing that contributed to the bad blood between the two men was Ford's belief that Reagan did not fulfill promises to campaign for Ford.

DR: Carter wins the election. Is there any chance that had Ford's voice not given out and he could have talked for the last week, it would have made a difference?

RNS: Let me tell you my theory. There was a Gallup poll on the Friday before the election that showed Ford had caught up. Against all odds, he actually had a one-point lead. My theory—and I'm not alone, the late, great campaign strategist Doug Bailey is my source for this—we both felt instinctively that this poll hurt Ford.

During the campaign the assumption was that Carter's going to win in a walk. Bailey's theory was that if the question on Election Day is "Do we know enough about Jimmy Carter? Are we comfortable with Jimmy Carter?" then Ford will win. If, however, the question is "Does Gerald Ford deserve a full term?" then Jimmy Carter would win. The exit polls showed two-thirds of undecided voters broke for Carter.

DR: During the campaign, Carter and Ford debate three times. In the second one, Ford is asked, "Do you think the Soviets are dominating the Poles?" And he said, "No, the Poles are not dominated by the Soviets." Why did he say that? And why did he take so long to correct that?

RNS: By all the polls, he won the first debate. The second debate was on foreign policy, and the assumption was that this would be Ford's strong suit. He was programmed to answer another question. I won't get into that, but the fact is the problem wasn't so much what he said. Because the snap poll right afterwards showed Ford won the debate. What happened was that TV kept repeating the clip overnight. And by next morning, the poll showed Ford lost.

DR: What Ford meant to say was what?

RNS: What Ford meant to say was, "I've been to Poland, I've been to Romania, I've been to Yugoslavia. I've looked into these people's eyes. They don't think they're dominated by the Soviet Union." But he didn't say that.

DR: And he didn't want to correct it for a while.

RNS: Ford was a very stubborn guy. It took him three days to correct what could have been corrected the next morning.

DR: So he loses the election.

RNS: Nine thousand votes in two states would have changed the outcome. Ford says to a weeping admirer, "I've got to give him the White House in better shape than I got it." No talk about resisting. Or recounts. That day he gave orders to his entire administration: "This is going to be the smoothest transition in American history, by contrast with what I had to go through." And that's what they did. On Inauguration Day, as they're in the helicopter on the way to the airport, Ford asked the pilot to circle back around the Capitol Dome, and he pointed down and said, "That's my real home."

DR: He goes to California and Colorado, and he builds a library and so forth. But then, four years later, does he think about running for president again?

RNS: He thinks about it, briefly. But Mrs. Ford had had her addiction intervention and was embarking on this wonderful new life, was beginning planning for the Betty Ford Center. He felt guilty. I don't think he seriously thought about it. Ronald Reagan comes to see him in the desert and asked him—this is three weeks before the Republican Convention in 1980—to be his running mate. And Ford hears him out, but he says all the reasons why it's not a good idea, and he recommends George H. W. Bush instead.

At the convention, the idea resurfaces. Ford agrees to negotiate. There are two negotiating teams. Now, I can't prove this, but I believe this, based on what he told me. He has the famous interview with Walter Cronkite, and it's not Ford who talks about a copresidency, it's Walter Cronkite who characterizes it like that. And Ford didn't stop him. By that time, it was Wednesday night. It was late. Basically, the convention was getting out of control. The rumor was spreading on the floor that there was a Reagan-Ford ticket. Ford had decided once and for all it wouldn't work. He went to see Governor Reagan. They agreed. They shook hands. They parted, genuinely friends.

Time's run out. So Reagan picks up the phone and calls George H. W. Bush. Two days later, Ford is getting on the plane with staffers, one of whom says, "What do you think?" Ford said, "All in all I'd say it was a pretty good convention. I gave a good speech and we got Bush for vice president." For the staffer, suddenly a light went off. He said, "Were you playing games?" In other words, were you stringing this along with the desired result of forcing Reagan to pick Ford's candidate for vice president? And Ford never gave him an answer.

DR: Ford then retires for good in Rancho Mirage, and also in Beaver Creek.

RNS: He helped out Jimmy Carter on the Panama Canal treaties. Carter needed Republican votes to pass them and Ford, rather graciously, got on the phone and lobbied his fellow Republicans. But they were not friends until the Anwar Sadat funeral. Ronald Reagan sent the three living former presidents to Cairo, and on the flight back, Nixon had an itinerary of his own. So it's just Ford and Carter flying all the way back to Washington. They discovered many things they had in common. It was the start of a friendship that is akin to that of Adams and Jefferson in their later years. They also had an understanding that whichever one survived would eulogize his friend at his funeral. Which is what happened in Grand Rapids.

15

KAI BIRD
on Jimmy Carter

(b. 1924; president from 1977 to 1981)

J immy Carter might best be remembered for reinventing the post-presidency. Rather than stay out of the way of a current president, relax, write a memoir, and build a presidential library, Carter stayed actively engaged in solving health-care and democracy-related problems. As a result, he worked to eliminate the scourge of river blindness in Africa, and essentially eradicate the Guinea worm disease that has afflicted so many in Africa and other parts of the world; he monitored elections around the world; he tried to negotiate solutions to geopolitical challenges in places like Haiti and North Korea; and he became a prolific author of 32 books. He did all this while maintaining the simple lifestyle of a Plains, Georgia, resident, living in the house he built in 1960, and avoiding the effort to make large sums of money or be something other than the plainspoken, Sunday school–teaching proselytizer for Christian values, peace, humility, and sacrifice.

Jimmy Carter had many years to do all that he did, since he left the presidency in 1981. He has been a former president for a longer period than any other president—forty-three years. He has also lived longer than any other president—99 years and counting.

Prior to his presidency, Carter also broke the mold in many ways. He ran a campaign for president that defied the odds. He was a Southerner; a former governor who did not leave office that popular in Georgia; more conservative than the base of the Democratic Party; had no real money (and thus had to stay in supporters' homes when campaigning, hotels being beyond the budget); not liked by the Democratic Party establishment in Washington; not a favorite of organized labor; and had a staff that included a number of young, inexperienced Georgians. But it clicked, as the party's more liberal base was unable to unify behind a candidate who could beat him for the nomination. By the time liberals united behind Congressman Mo Udall, it was too late to stop Carter.

Although Carter started the general election campaign way ahead of Ford, the election of 1976 was essentially a tossup toward the end, as a result of the increasing public uneasiness with someone not well-known throughout the country and sufficiently experienced in the ways of Washington. But Ford's pardon of Nixon, and mistakenly saying that Poland was not under the domination of the Soviet Union in a debate, helped Carter achieve a narrow victory.

As president, Carter seemed to have an enormous amount of bad luck, which lowered his approval ratings and made him unpopular both in his party and the country. Within the party, he was seen as insufficiently liberal and unwilling to adopt many of the traditional Democratic Party programs, like a form of national health care. His failure to support such a program prompted Senator Ted Kennedy to challenge him for the Democratic Party nomination in 1980, and while Carter won the nomination, he was never able to subsequently unite the party or bring Kennedy and his supporters into the fold.

Outside of his party, he had other problems, not all of his own making. The inflation inherited from the Ford years worsened, forcing Carter to appoint Paul Volcker as chairman of the Federal Reserve; Volcker dramatically increased interest rates, slowing the economy significantly. Despite his preference, Carter allowed the former shah of Iran into the U.S. for medical treatment, resulting in the capture of 66 hostages from within the U.S. Embassy in Tehran and a more than yearlong struggle to free them (and, as well, a more than yearlong reminder of Carter's inability to do so). And long gas lines and high energy prices throughout the country reminded everyone of our dependence on foreign oil and our inability to become energy-independent, despite Carter's repeated efforts to do so.

In addition to these problems, Carter was widely seen as overmatched for the job—a micromanager when the job called for a visionary leader. He was also seen as someone who did not select priorities well. He was so interested in doing so many things, and tried to get them all done, that he overwhelmed Congress, which could not process and approve everything that he wanted. And failing to get Congress to approve all his programs made him seem weak and not quite in command of the government.

The irony was that Carter was able to get an enormous number of his programs approved. (Today, getting a debt limit bill and twelve appropriations bills passed is seen as a mammoth undertaking.) Carter got Congress to approve the Panama Canal Treaty; civil service reform; much of his energy program; airline and trucking deregulation; and the creation of the Departments of Energy and Education.

But that was not enough to give citizens a sense that Carter was firmly in control and taking the country to the right place. Indeed, he delayed a proposed energy speech for nearly two weeks as he brought leaders to Camp David to talk about the country's ills and needs. That confused the public, as did his subsequent request for the resignation letters of his entire cabinet (and accepting a few of them).

Carter loved Camp David, in part because it allowed him to escape from Washington. It was also the scene of his greatest diplomatic achievement—the peace agreement between Israel and Egypt that he painstakingly negotiated for nearly two weeks in near isolation from the rest of the world. That agreement is still in place.

I witnessed all this firsthand, as a young policy aide not sure what to make of it. Carter was highly intelligent, a workaholic and truly self-made, and in many ways also a Renaissance man (poet, artisan, author, fly-fishing expert, woodworker, classical music aficionado). He knew a great deal about almost every subject, and at times that may have been his undoing. He felt he was smart enough to understand every issue and would, like an engineer, try to develop the perfect solution. But in doing so he often ignored the politics of his perfect solution, for he abhorred the idea that he would be seen as doing something for political benefit. (Telling him something would help him politically absolutely ensured that he would not take that action.)

While I was a junior White House aide and not in Carter's Georgia inner circle, I often traveled with him outside of Washington, and interacted with him a fair amount as the deputy to my boss, Stu Eizenstat, whom Carter relied on for advice in the domestic policy arena. I admired Carter's ability to process enormous amounts of information, and his willingness to take on so many issues at once in order to develop a workable solution. But my admiration was not enough, of course, to ensure reelection. The country saw someone unable to tackle the country's biggest problems, and felt a change was needed.

In recent years, Carter's postpresidency has increasingly been recognized as significant. Too, many scholars and historians have written that the administration made more than a few unforced errors but that it achieved more than might have been appreciated at the time. The defeat of Carter by Reagan was so lopsided that he felt a bit disgraced, and the later success of the Reagan presidency seemed to further diminish Carter in the public's view. But four decades later, there has been something of a reassessment. One of the books providing such a reassessment is *The Outlier*, by Kai Bird, a distinguished biographer and historian. I had a chance to interview him at the New-York Historical Society on June 11, 2021.

✳   ✳   ✳   ✳

DAVID M. RUBENSTEIN (DM): I worked in the Carter White House, so I have some experience with President Carter myself, but I didn't know as many things as I now know after reading your book.

KAI BIRD (KB): I worked on it for six years, so my job was to unearth a few stories that you didn't know.

DR: What prompted you to want to write a book about Jimmy Carter now that his presidency is more than 40 years past?

KB: I had been thinking about Jimmy Carter for 30 years. When I finished my first biography, about John J. McCloy, an elusive Wall Street banker and lawyer, I had written a lot in that book about the Iran hostage crisis. That's a dramatic chapter, which is filled with Jimmy Carter. It made me curious about Carter and his handling of the hostage crisis in the Iranian Revolution, so I dug into it.

This was 1990, only 10 years after he'd left the White House. I went down to Atlanta and interviewed a bunch of his aides. He had just begun building the Carter Center. I had an interview with him, and I wrote a magazine article about all the great things he was doing with his ex-presidency. I came away from that experience thinking that I was the wrong guy to do this, because I didn't understand the South. It seemed like a foreign country to me, and I didn't understand Southern Baptists. I thought I didn't understand race in America, all the big issues that would be involved with Jimmy Carter, and I also realized that his papers were still closed.

But I continued to think about it. I went on to some other projects, and in 2015 I finally came back to it and sat down and wrote a proposal and sold it to a publisher. By that time, the presidential papers in the Carter Library had opened up, and it was a rich source of material.

DR: Did President Carter cooperate with you?

KB: He cooperated in that he would see me. We had a number of good interviews. In our very first interview, I asked him about the papers of his personal lawyer, Charlie Kirbo, who was a sort of mysterious behind-the-scenes character in the Carter White House. Kirbo was the closest adviser Carter had. They were the closest in age. Kirbo had known him since 1962, and I knew that Kirbo had written him hundreds of memos and letters, but they weren't in the archive.

Carter was surprised when he heard this, and he ordered his aide to look around and see if he could find them. Three days later, I got a phone call saying that they'd found five boxes of Charlie Kirbo's papers in the attic of his widow. And they gave me access to them. It's a fantastic trove of material to give you an insight into Jimmy Carter's mind.

DR: The conventional wisdom today is that Jimmy Carter was a failed president but an extraordinarily successful former president. Understandably, he doesn't like that, because he doesn't feel he was a failed president. You make the point that he was pretty successful in many things he did, not at everything. Is that a fair summary?

KB: That's a fair summary. I argue that if you want to understand Jimmy Carter, it's a seamless story from before the presidency, through the White House, to his ex-presidency. He's this driven, committed individual who's relentless and intelligent and slightly arrogant. He knows that he's the smartest guy in the room, and this explains how he managed to come from nowhere to win the presidency. It also explains some of his political failings.

DR: Why did you pick *The Outlier* as your book title?

KB: I like punchy, short titles, and that seemed to describe Carter. He's a political outlier. He was a liberal Southern white man from a small town—Plains, Georgia, population 680—and he was the only liberal in Plains, the only man who had a twenty-first-century sensibility about race. He was always sort of the odd duck, the outlier. When he came to Washington, he was the outlier. He was the president, but he routinely turned down dinner invitations from Katharine Graham, the publisher of the *Washington Post*. He just didn't think it was worth his time, socializing with the Georgetown set. So he was an outlier in his personal dealings with the Washington political establishment as well.

DR: Jimmy Carter grows up on a farm. He goes to the Naval Academy. When his father dies, he comes back to run the family business. Why did he feel compelled, after being a naval officer and hoping to rise to admiral, to come back to Plains and run the family business? What was his wife Rosalynn's attitude about that?

KB: The story is that Rosie, as he called her, hated the idea of leaving the Navy and was shocked at the idea of going back to Plains, Georgia. She refused to talk to him on the long drive back from their base in Connecticut down to Plains. She didn't want to go back to this small town where she too had grown up. She had loved the Navy life and living in Hawaii and in other parts of America, and she thought going back to Plains was a step backwards. Carter loves Plains. He loves South Georgia, he loves the people, it's his roots. He's very proud of where he came from. And when his father died, rather early in Carter's life, he felt compelled to save the family business.

But there's also another answer that I discovered that surprised me. Carter, in his Navy career, was on a successful route to maybe becoming an admiral someday, but he disliked the notion of spending the rest of his life on weapons of war armed with nuclear missiles that could have killed tens of thousands of people. He was not a military man at heart.

DR: With the help of a lawsuit filed by Charlie Kirbo, Carter overcomes what would have been a fraud-induced election loss and wins a state Senate seat in '62, and then he later decides to run for governor in 1966 against Lester Maddox. What happens in that race?

KB: He lost. He thought for sure that he was going to win that race against this archsegregationist. It was, for him, a personal humiliation. He spent the next four years relentlessly campaigning to get that governorship.

DR: He runs again in 1970. Does he run as a civil rights advocate, somebody on the left side of the Democratic Party?

KB: Not at all. He realized, in '66, that he had failed to connect with white, rural Southern voters in Georgia, and he made sure that this time he navigated that minefield. His opponents accused him of making all the dog whistles, edging right up to the line of appealing to white supremacists, but not quite crossing the line. He was pragmatic and ruthless in his campaigning, and determined to win.

DR: He wins. It is said that every senator who looks in the mirror sees a potential president, and I suspect that's probably true of most governors. Why did Jimmy Carter, though, think that a one-term governor of Georgia, not that popular, could become president of the United States in 1976? Where did that idea come from?

KB: He knew that he couldn't run again for governor. It was a one-term office. In the course of being governor, he met some of the other potential presidential candidates, including, for instance, Ted Kennedy, who came to give a speech at the University of Georgia, and Carter had a chance to size him up. Kennedy was clearly the front-runner, and Carter thought that he was shallow, not full of substance, didn't have the gravitas that was necessary for the office. That gave him a belief that he could take it. Then Kennedy dropped out before the race really got going, and Carter was left as the sort of dark-horse liberal Southerner from the new South.

He had a talented political strategist named Hamilton Jordan, a young man in his early 30s, who wrote a brilliant memo on how to campaign for and win the Democratic nomination. And, against all odds, Carter did it. Oddly enough, when Carter met with Ted Kennedy, gonzo journalist Hunter Thompson was there; he was blown away by Carter's speech at the time and thought that Carter had, in an arrogant and brilliant way, dismissed Kennedy. Thompson wrote that he had just seen the meanest politician in America.

Now, this is not the public perception, the liberal perception we have of the humanitarian Jimmy Carter, but there is a side to him that was politically ambitious and ruthless and pragmatic and determined. Hunter Thompson saw that in this encounter between Carter and Ted Kennedy. And I think it explains the '76 campaign and how he won.

DR: Carter wins the nomination in 1976 and he runs against the incumbent, Gerald Ford. They have three debates. Carter's not that experienced in foreign policy or federal matters at the time. How did he do against Ford?

KB: The first debate, he didn't do very well. The second one, he did a lot better. Ford made a mistake that really helped Carter, who had positioned himself as the new face, in the wake of Watergate and the Vietnam War and the scandals associated with the Nixon presidency. He won that race narrowly. It came down to the wire in the end, but he was successful. It was an amazing race.

DR: When Carter wins, does he say, "I really don't know Washington that well, so I'm going to bring a lot of experienced people to help me run the government"?

KB: Yes and no. He surrounded himself with Georgia boys, his own Georgia mafia, people like Hamilton Jordan and Jerry Rafshoon (his public relations/advertising advisor) and Jody Powell, his press secretary. But he did, in fact, recruit a bunch of people from the outside like Joe Califano, people considered to be part of the establishment. He made Cy Vance his secretary of state; and he appointed Zbigniew Brzezinski, a New York–based foreign policy insider, to be his national security advisor. But he governed as an outsider.

DR: The Congress of the United States, at that time, is overwhelmingly Democratic. You have a Democratic president for the first time in eight years. Was it easy for a Democratic president to get his agenda through this Democratic Congress?

KB: Partly, but it was more difficult than you would have thought. The Democrats had a substantial majority in both the House and Senate, yet Carter had a lot of trouble because he was trying to pass a great deal of liberal social legislation and regulatory initiatives, like auto safety, mandatory safety belts, and airbags. He was trying to deregulate natural gas and the airlines. He was trying to expand food stamps for the working poor. But he got pushback from conservative, largely Southern Democrats, and he got pushback from liberal Democrats who thought he wasn't going far enough.

DR: Let's talk about one of the problems that he had: inflation. It seemed to be out of control, rising to double digits. Did he not have a solution for it? Where did the inflation come from?

KB: Inflation came about, I think most economists would agree, before Carter even walked into the White House. It was brewing because of expenditures on the Vietnam War that hadn't been paid for, but largely because of the explosion in energy prices from the 1971 energy crisis and the 1973 Arab oil embargo. This ratcheted up the price of gasoline and oil, and it trickled down throughout the economy, and led to double-digit, 13, 14, 16 percent inflation rates.

Carter was really concerned about this. He campaigned as a sort of traditional liberal in '76. Once he got into office, he looked at the figures and was concerned about the federal deficit. He wanted to balance the budget. He was a small-town fiscal conservative on economic policy and a liberal on social issues. But he really wanted to do something about inflation, and he found it very difficult.

Finally, in 1979, out of great frustration, he appointed Paul Volcker to be head of the Fed. He'd been warned by his aides that Volcker was going to do drastic things to interest rates and that this was going to harm Carter politically, just as he was running for reelection, but he did it anyway. Carter doesn't get the credit he should for appointing Volcker, who by the early '80s had killed inflation.

DR: It's amazing, when you think about it, that a one-term governor gets elected president the first time he runs. He must be very skilled politically. Yet you point out in your book that if you told Carter something was good politically for him, he would almost do the opposite, a good example being Volcker. Is that what his aides would tell you—that if you wanted to convince Carter, don't tell him it was a good thing for him to do politically?

KB: Yes. I had people from the White House, who worked with him repeatedly, tell me exactly that—that he hated to be told the right thing to do politically. He wanted to know what the right thing to do was, period. This explains a lot about Carter's presidency. I talked earlier about how ruthless he could be campaigning and in trying to win power. But he had this philosophy that he got from Reinhold Niebuhr, the elite East Coast Protestant theologian, who argued that the world was full of sin but that politicians, leaders, had to use power to be able to do good.

Carter used the philosophy of Niebuhr to justify his own political ambitions, and then rationalize that once he was in the Oval Office. Then he could forget about politics and simply use his intelligence to figure out what was the right policy and do it, regardless of the politics. This explains his success, in many ways, but it also explains his political failure.

DR: Since the creation of the State of Israel in 1948, there had been war between Israel and its neighbors. There had been two hot wars, between Egypt and Israel, in 1967 and 1973. Why did Jimmy Carter, a relatively inexperienced foreign policy person, think that he could bring peace to the Middle East, at least between Israel and Egypt, and why did he think bringing them to Camp David was a good idea? And why did it work out?

KB: That's a mystery too, because as you say, Carter had no foreign policy experience. He'd made one trip to Israel as governor, where he toured around in a station wagon for a week with Jody Powell. But he was a Southern Baptist. He'd read the Bible. He'd read about Palestine and the Holy Land all his life. And when he got into the Oval Office, really from day one, in January of '77, he's telling Brzezinski—over Brzezinski's objections, by the way—that he wanted to make peace in the Middle East a priority.

Brzezinski had briefed Carter from his days on the Trilateral Commission, where they first met, about the Middle East, and Brzezinski knew how thorny the Israeli-Palestinian issue was. But Carter thought that this was an area where he could achieve some real good, and he made it a priority. It was difficult and it got him into a lot of trouble, but in the end, he decided that the best way to get the two major adversaries, Anwar Sadat of Egypt and Menachem Begin of Israel, together was to bring them to a rural setting like Camp David, which he loved, and to then isolate them and engage in the most personal of diplomacy.

Strangely, it wasn't, in many ways, a political triumph for Jimmy Carter. While Camp David took Egypt off the battlefield, it gave him no political brownie points with the Jewish American community. It got him into more trouble, in fact.

DR: You point out that Jimmy Carter loved Camp David. He went there almost every weekend. Why did he like it so much?

KB: He loved the countryside, the rural setting, being outdoors, going fishing. He loved just going on long walks with Rosie. He hated the Washington cocktail party scene. He hated socializing, making small talk, and Camp David was a way to escape from Washington. So he spent a lot of time up there.

DR: The biggest problem with getting reelected that Jimmy Carter had, in my view, occurred when the Iranian hostages were taken. Did President Carter have a good relationship with the Shah before the Shah was forced off his throne?

KB: He had met him once. In November of '77, the Shah visits Washington and is famously greeted by protesters, including anti-Shah Iranian students, making a lot of noise and throwing beer cans and whatnot outside the White House fence. Tear gas is released. It was that serious a protest. It got a little violent, and the tear gas wafted over the White House grounds and interrupted the press conference they were having on the South Lawn, and the Shah and Jimmy Carter had to wipe their eyes.

But Carter had no personal relationship with the Shah. He inherited this political alliance, over objections from his own aides who were pushing human rights and saying, "This Shah is not exactly an exemplar, and we ought to distance ourselves from him." Carter had no real reason to back off. But as it happens, the Shah, in 1977, was beginning to face real dissent inside Iran, and it snowballed, and by 1978, there was a revolution going on.

DR: The Ayatollah Khomeini and his supporters force the Shah to leave what is called the Peacock Throne. The Shah is then trying to find a place to live. Does Carter help him?

KB: Many of his aides, like Zbigniew Brzezinski, argued that the Shah should be given political asylum. Carter rejected that. His secretary of state, Cy Vance, said, "You shouldn't allow the Shah to come, because that's going to provoke the revolutionary regime in Iran." Carter had serious qualms about the symbolic notion of the Shah getting asylum in America. He worried that maybe the embassy will be taken over. So he pushes back. He refuses to give the Shah political asylum.

And in response, Henry Kissinger, David Rockefeller, and John J.

McCloy form a lobbying effort. They even give it a code name, Project Alpha, they allocate money from Chase Manhattan Bank and the powerful law firm that McCloy was running, and they set up a program where, every week, some major official in the Carter administration from the president on down was lobbied vociferously to give the Shah asylum. This went on for six months. Finally, Carter reluctantly gives in when he's told that the Shah has cancer and needs medical treatment in New York. So on humanitarian grounds, he agrees to let the Shah in.

DR: But as you point out, the truth is that the medical procedures and help that he needed could have been provided elsewhere, right?

KB: Exactly. But Carter wasn't told that.

DR: So the hostages are taken from the U.S. Embassy in Tehran. Jimmy Carter and others think that this is going to be a couple-day episode. Why did it last so long? Were Iranian government or the Ayatollah in favor of keeping the hostages that long?

KB: Yes. There was good reason for Carter to think it would be a few days or a week, because the embassy, in fact, had been stormed and taken over right after the revolution in February of 1979. Then the embassy was shortly given back to the Americans. So they thought it would be a two- or three-day affair.

But when this happened on November 4th, 1979, Khomeini was trying to consolidate the revolution and turn it into a hard-line Islamic Republic, and he wanted to get rid of the moderate political allies that had supported the revolution initially. The hostage crisis, he saw, was an excuse to purge his government of the moderates. So it went on for 444 days.

DR: Why didn't Carter just send in troops and rescue as many hostages as possible?

KB: That was discussed, but he was very concerned about the lives of the hostages. He didn't want to lose a single American life. Cy Vance was telling him, "This is going to be solved with diplomacy. It's a political crisis. The Ayatollah Khomeini is using this to consolidate his revolution. But in a few weeks or a few months, it'll be over and we'll bring all the hostages home alive." Carter had a real aversion to the use of military force. Zbigniew Brzezinski suggested that he should mine the harbors off the coast of Iran, but Carter rejected that. He believed in diplomacy, and he was determined to bring home every hostage alive.

DR: At some point, Carter agrees to have a rescue mission, not a military confrontation. Why does that not work?

KB: In my view, and I think in the view of anyone who looks at the plan, it was ridiculous. It had so many moving parts. It was so complicated that if it had succeeded in landing military troops to rescue the hostages, probably many of them and many of the rescuers would have been killed.

Two of the helicopters failed when they got to the landing zone, or had to turn back, and the whole mission was aborted. Even then, when they left, one of the helicopters ran into one of the airplanes on the ground and U.S. servicemen lost their lives as a result. The mission was put together in a hasty way. It was so complicated that it's hard to imagine why anyone thought it would succeed.

DR: While this was going on, Jimmy Carter is running in a primary campaign for the Democratic nomination against his old nemesis, Ted Kennedy. Initially that goes well. Carter is pretty popular in the Democratic Party because he's trying to get the hostages back, but eventually that fades and his popularity goes down. How close was it for Kennedy to get the nomination?

KB: Early on, Carter defeated him pretty handily, but it was a major challenge, and Kennedy refused to drop out even after losing many early primaries. He stuck it out into the late spring and then won a few primaries, like in New York, and gave Carter a real race and weakened him. Carter and Kennedy had one big issue that they disagreed about. They were both liberals on most issues, but Ted Kennedy had made national health insurance his major issue. That was the thing he really ran on, saying Carter wasn't liberal enough because he had not favored Kennedy's health care bill.

Carter himself had run in favor of national health insurance in 1976; but once in office, he pragmatically looked at the cost, and he didn't think Kennedy's bill had the votes to even get out of Kennedy's own committee.

So he proposed a compromise for national health insurance to cover just catastrophic events. Kennedy wouldn't go for it; neither would compromise, and this gave the excuse for Kennedy to run.

A strong faction of the liberal wing of the Democratic Party thought that Carter wasn't liberal enough. Even though he had appointed all sorts of Ralph Nader acolytes to office, and even though he had passed a lot of liberal legislation, they came to loggerheads. Labor unions and others fell away from Carter, and Kennedy gave him a real run for the nomination.

DR: Carter gets the nomination, but he's running against Ronald Reagan. Is Carter or his administration worried about running against Reagan?

KB: Initially not so much. He looked at him and thought, "This man is a former B-movie star, a right-wing idealogue from California, who's very old." He thought that would be an easy Republican to defeat. But by the late summer of 1980, his advisors were telling him that this was going to be a serious race, and the polls were showing that too. Carter had been weakened by Ayatollah Khomeini and the hostage crisis and inflation rates and long gas lines and Ted Kennedy running against him. And it was a tough race.

DR: There was one debate, a week before the election in Cleveland. Carter is much more experienced on national issues than Reagan, so Carter doesn't prepare that much for it. Reagan is pretty well prepared. How did the debate go?

KB: The debate was a disaster. A shock. Carter was overconfident. Reagan was folksy. He got out that line "There you go again," and it was kind of over after that. Carter stumbled a bit. He was never a very good debater. He was good on the stump in small crowds. He was good in small living-room sessions with voters. But Reagan came off as sunny, and Carter is not a sunny politician, coming back to his Niebuhrian Southern Baptist view of politics. He knew the world was sinful and he was there to make it a better place. And a lot of people sort of squirmed at his religiosity.

By contrast, Reagan seemed to validate the notion that America could do anything and go anywhere, that America was exceptional. Carter didn't believe that. He didn't believe in American exceptionalism. In many ways, he's been proven to be right about some of these larger issues on climate control and energy and race, but Ronald Reagan appealed to voters at a time where a lot of people were tired of high interest rates and high gasoline prices and all.

DR: When Reagan wins overwhelmingly, what does Carter do in the transition time of November through January?

KB: He was without a doubt the hardest-working president we've had in the twentieth century. He read 200 or 300 pages of memos every day, and, after his defeat he continued to work very hard. He, for instance, got passed the Alaska Land Act, which put 57 million acres back into the Federal Wilderness Area. It was a very popular bill with environmentalists and extremely unpopular with most Alaskans, but he got it through. He also worked very hard to get the hostages out. He was deeply involved in those negotiations right up to the day of inauguration.

DR: The hostages are not released until Carter is no longer president. In hindsight, why were the Iranians so determined not to give Carter the pleasure of releasing the hostages?

KB: It was obvious that Ayatollah Khomeini had a personal animus with Carter. He got it into his head that Carter was responsible for the Shah clinging to power. There's also something called the October Surprise, where Bill Casey, the Republican national campaign manager for Ronald Reagan, left the country in late July of 1980, went to London, and then flew secretly to Madrid, Spain, where he met with the representative of the Ayatollah Khomeini and promised him that his candidate, Ronald Reagan, would give the Iranians a better deal.

And if this happened—and I believe it happened, because I found some documents that showed that, despite all the denials, Casey did appear in Madrid, Spain, in late July—this may have prolonged the hostage crisis until the day of inauguration, when the deal was all set: we unfroze the Iranian assets that Carter had frozen in exchange for the hostages being released.

DR: After you spent six years researching and writing about Jimmy Carter, did you come away admiring him more than you had before, or did you come away more concerned about the person he was than you had been before?

KB: As a biographer, it was both. I really do admire him. I think he is, without a doubt, the most intelligent man who's occupied the Oval Office in the twentieth century, and I'm including Jack Kennedy and Franklin Roosevelt. He's the most relentless and dedicated and hardworking, but he also had a certain self-righteousness and arrogance to him that helps to explain his political failings.

So it's a mixed story. It's a very human story. But I admire him. I think most people who admire Carter's ex-presidency, what he's done as an ex-president with the Carter Center, should remind themselves that it's the same man who occupied the Oval Office, and he was trying very hard to make this world a better place.

16

TIMOTHY J. NAFTALI
on George H. W. Bush

(1924–2018; president from 1989 to 1993)

Although I worked for four years in the White House of Jimmy Carter, the president I came to know best was actually someone with whom I might seem to have little in common—George H. W. Bush. He was the vice president on Ronald Reagan's ticket that defeated Jimmy Carter in 1980. He was a lifelong Republican, a prep school graduate from a wealthy Connecticut family, the son of a U.S. senator, a transplanted Texan, an oil wildcatter, and an outstanding athlete—in short, a background with which I was not really familiar.

Yet, at Carlyle, I recruited George Bush's friend and former secretary of State, James A. Baker III, to join my investment firm in 1993, following Bill Clinton's defeat of President Bush. Subsequently, the former president began making speeches at Carlyle's events and eventually became an advisor to our Asian operations while also helping with advice in other parts of the world. And I traveled extensively around the world with President Bush as he began to increasingly speak at various Carlyle events.

As he did this, I came to know him reasonably well and also came to know his wife, former First Lady Barbara Bush, quite well, for she often accompanied him on our trips. I visited him a good many times at his summer home in Kennebunkport, Maine, and he visited my home in Nantucket a few times as well. (Maybe I developed a good relationship with President Bush because he recognized—as I liked to tell him—that he would not have become president without me. Without my helping to get inflation to record levels, thus helping to ensure Carter's loss, Reagan would not have been elected president and Bush would not have been elected vice president. Without that base, he would not have been elected in 1988. I am not sure President Bush accepted this logic, but we nonetheless developed a close relationship.)

From all these contacts and our many conversations, I came away feeling that he was one of the most gracious, polite, and kind individuals that I have ever met. He was typically concerned about other individuals' views and feelings, and rarely focused on his own perspectives. The modesty drilled into him by his legendary mother—he was trained not to use the word *I*, so as to not focus on himself—became apparent, and that manner of relating to others was not an artifice. Indeed, I could certainly see how George Bush had charmed so many others early in his life and career, and could see why he was driven to give back to society by serving in government rather than pursuing, for very long, the far easier course of making money in the Texas energy world. And he had a wonderful and playful sense of humor, at times quite self-deprecating, often relatively rare among those who reach the heights of power and success.

Getting to know and become friendly with a person who helped defeat my former boss and thereby helped unemploy me may seem a bit improbable. But that is probably no more improbable than Bush's ascent to the presidency and his later unanticipated descent from it.

On the ascent, George Bush had lost his two statewide races for the Senate and was later given three positions by President Richard Nixon, none of which seemed likely to build a political base: ambassador to the UN, representative to China, and Republican Party chairman during the Watergate days. Bush also ran a losing campaign for the Republican nomination in 1980 (and in doing so alienated Ronald and Nancy Reagan by calling Reagan's supply-side economic policies "voodoo economics")— all actions that would not have seemed likely to propel him to the presidency.

To his surprise, Bush was picked at the last minute as Reagan's running mate (when the Reagan flirtation with former president Ford for that position seemed less attractive to both Reagan and Ford upon reflection). And while he served two terms as vice president, and met with Reagan regularly, Bush was not really able to win the loyalty of the Reagan political base, even failing to get Reagan's endorsement as his successor until very late in the primary process. Still, Bush was able to defeat a popular Democratic governor of Massachusetts for the presidency, even after being behind Michael Dukakis for much of the campaign.

Once in office, Bush seemed to show why many felt he was the most prepared person in decades to actually become president. Indeed, he led a global coalition to push Saddam Hussein and his army out of Kuwait, achieving as a result the second-highest presidential approval ratings in modern times. But despite that achievement, economic challenges and a third-party challenge from businessman H. Ross Perot caused Bush to lose his once all-but-certain reelection to a very young governor, Bill Clinton of Arkansas, who had lacked any of the Washington or foreign policy experience that Bush had in spades.

The election result and the rapid descent from the presidency was something no one would have expected right after the Persian Gulf War. Indeed, many leading Democrats at the time passed on running against Bush in 1992. But the bitter, unanticipated loss to Governor Clinton was handled with grace by President Bush (and so forgiving was he that he later became quite friendly with President Clinton when both were out of office and working on humanitarian missions together).

Tim Naftali is a well-known presidential scholar and commentator who wrote a book on George H. W. Bush in 2007 titled *George H. W. Bush: The American Presidents Series: The 41st President, 1989–1993*, and I had a chance to interview him about his book and President Bush on March 25, 2024.

✳   ✳   ✳   ✳

DR: What led you to want to write a book about George Herbert Walker Bush?

TN: Arthur Schlesinger was editing a series for *Times Books* about the American presidency. He offered me the opportunity to write a book about a president of my choice. It seemed to me that to be a successful biographer, whether you're a presidential biographer or literary biographer, you needed to have some empathy for the world in which your subject had lived. I thought that I could connect with and understand some of the worlds that had shaped George Herbert Walker Bush.

The first world was Yale. I'm a graduate of Yale and I had written a little bit about the mid-twentieth-century history of the university in my senior essay there. The second of George Herbert Walker Bush's worlds that I thought I could understand was the world of the CIA. That first undergraduate project at Yale had involved studying Yalies who had gone into intelligence in World War II. Later, as a graduate student, I wrote a dissertation on World War II espionage. The third world of George H. W. Bush was that he had been president of the United States at the end of the Cold War, and my first books, coauthored with Aleksandr Fursenko, had been about the Cold War. In those three different worlds, I felt that I understood some of what he faced, and therefore could bring a certain knowledge to the project.

DR: What do you see as President Bush's legacy today?

TN: He made tough decisions at the end of the Cold War that helped create the soft landing that occurred. Historically, when great empires collapse, the consequences are war and global disruption. That was not the immediate effect of the collapse of the Cold War, in part because of George Herbert Walker Bush. Mikhail Gorbachev deserves the greatest amount of credit. But to a significant extent Gorbachev needed an American partner, and Bush played that key role superbly as head of the healthy superpower as the Soviet Union and its European empire were collapsing. That's one of his great legacies. The other is a legacy of decency, prudence, and pragmatism as an American president. Thinking purely of politics, his presidential legacy is a two-edged sword, because he wasn't reelected. George Herbert Walker Bush would have been appreciated earlier had he decided willingly that he was going to be a one-term president. His defeat in 1992 had several factors—the appeal of both Bill Clinton and Ross Perot, for example—but the lack of enthusiasm for the president among his base cannot be separated from his presidential legacy of tough, pragmatic decisions at home. He deserves a great deal of credit for reversing his "no new taxes" pledge from the 1988 campaign but it came at great political cost. His willingness to sacrifice his own political standing to do what he thought was the right thing for the country in handling the budget challenges of the early 1990s— that took a lot of political courage. We don't see that very often from politicians, even less so from presidents. And, in 1992, he wasn't rewarded for it.

DR: Bush was famously not a person who liked to brag about himself. His mother always said, "Don't use the word *I*—don't brag about yourself." If you were to ask him what was he most proud of having accomplished as president, what do you think it would have been?

TN: He was proud of the role he played at the end of the Cold War. He was proud of the leadership he provided the country in the Gulf War. He was disappointed that Saddam Hussein did not fall of his own accord. But in ridding Kuwait of the Iraqis and restoring Kuwaiti sovereignty, he had achieved the goal he had set out for the coalition. I think he was proud of the seriousness of purpose that he brought to the office. He died at a time when we saw the office under enormous stress, when we saw a president who was violating long-standing norms that had been set by Republicans and Democrats alike. I think George Herbert Walker Bush was very proud of the dignity that he had maintained in the office of president of the United States.

DR: Other than losing the reelection, what do you think he would say was his biggest disappointment in his presidency?

TN: You can't underestimate the disappointment he felt in 1992. He had come to believe he was on a path to being reelected. I think Bush felt he might have handled the budget crisis better.

DR: Let's start at the beginning. Where was George Herbert Walker Bush born and raised, and who were his parents?

TN: He was born in Milton, Massachusetts. His parents were Dorothy Walker Bush and Prescott Bush. Both instilled in him a sense of service. The Bushes were moderate Republicans, later referred to as "Eisenhower Republicans." They were uncomfortable with extremism. They were liberal on social issues and internationalists in foreign policy. From his parents, George Bush learned to be patriotic with a powerful sense of noblesse oblige. He had this sense of calling, from his earliest days to the end of his long life, and it really shaped the way he acted politically, privately, and personally.

DR: What would you say his skills and talents were as a young man?

TN: He was personable, he knew how to listen, he inspired loyalty and respect because he gave it in return. Until the last year of his presidency, he was energetic, seemed younger than his age, and people were drawn to him. That's why he was the captain of athletic teams and political teams. He was the person in a group that people naturally looked up to and respected. Those characteristics largely defined him throughout his life.

From his earliest days, he lacked a taste for introspection or self-explanation, making him a challenge for historians. He didn't write a traditional presidential memoir; he did not participate in his own oral history project at the Miller Center for his presidential library. He did, however, keep a diary, which has been helpful. One possible reason for the lack of self-examination, besides his mother's lasting admonition about "I, I, I," was that from his earliest days, he was also emotional. This was a part of Bush that he was taught not to reveal.

DR: When did he volunteer to go into the military? Did he want to leave Andover and enlist? Did he wait till after he graduated?

TN: He was 17 years old when Pearl Harbor happened, too young to join the military. You had to be 18. But he passionately wanted to join the war effort. His parents, however, wanted him to wait. On his own, he decided to sign up the day he turned 18, which was in June of 1942. He entered the Naval Air Corps, and he would become among the youngest Navy pilots in 1943 when he got his wings.

DR: How did he almost die during the war as a Navy fighter pilot?

TN: He and his crew had the mission of knocking out a Japanese radio tower on Chichijima Island. This was not his first bombing run. In this case, however, Japanese antiaircraft guns hit his plane. After completing their mission, he and one of his crew were able to bail out. Bush, who piloted the plane, hit his head trying to jump, and tore his parachute. He hit the water hard but was young and agile, and regained consciousness. A U.S. submarine eventually saw him and rescued him. The key part of this story is that, however dazed and bloody he was, and absolutely devastated by what turned out to be the loss of his two crewmates (the other crewman's parachute didn't deploy and the third man was lost), George Bush stayed in the Pacific Theater and continued to fly missions over the Japanese-occupied Philippines, showing the toughness of this man.

DR: When the war was over, he went to Yale. Was he a star student and athlete?

TN: He was a good student. He was a star athlete. He was captain of the Yale baseball team.

DR: Upon graduation, George Bush decided not to go to Wall Street, where his family was well-connected. Why did he go into the energy world and go to West Texas?

TN: Key to understanding the Bush family is a sense of familial competitiveness and a desire to make it on your own, or at least to create a space that is your own. George Bush passed up an opportunity to work on Wall Street. Instead he took a job with Dresser Industries, which produced oil field supplies, and he went out to Odessa, Texas. It's not like he went completely outside of the family bubble, because Dresser was owned by a friend of his father's. He wanted to work for himself. Out in Texas — and this is how he ended up in Midland — he raises capital with the help of his family connections. He and some friends started something called the Zapata Oil Company, which traded in oil field rights. He would stay in the oil business until he decides to run for office.

DR: After he went into politics, Zapata became a gigantic company in the oil business. Had he stayed, he would have been a wealthy man. He never regretted that?

TN: It became Pennzoil. The partners became very famous and very rich. The Bushes were well-off. They were never hugely wealthy. The money that allowed the Bushes to have the compound in Kennebunkport came from George Herbert Walker Bush's mother's family, the Walkers. By the way, George H. W. Bush was called "Poppy" because his grandfather was known as "Pop."

DR: George and Barbara Bush's first son was George W. Bush, and they had another child named Robin. What happened to her?

TN: Robin contracted leukemia, and she would die in 1953. Robin's death was a horrible event for the family, and in many ways they never got over it, which I think is true in any family that loses a child.

DR: George Herbert Walker Bush is reasonably successful in the oil business. Why does he decide to run for the United States Senate in 1964, when he never ran for anything before? How did he do in that race?

TN: Texas politics were changing. Young Republicans had a sense that there was an opportunity to knock off a liberal Democratic senator named Ralph Yarborough. Bush by then had moved to Houston. Moving to Houston was part of his calculations about running for office. He helped create the Republican machine in Houston. Even though he didn't like to brag, George Bush had deep self-confidence. He almost seemed Kennedyesque—handsome, vital. He seemed to be the face of the new Republican power in the South. Part of it was a little delusional. The Republicans had won statewide once, but in 1963–64 it was still very difficult to fight the traditional Democratic Party in Texas.

What's important about the 1964 election is that George Bush violated his own sense of what was right and wrong in politics. He let his ambition get away with him. He ran as a Goldwater Republican, which meant he ran against the Test Ban Treaty that President Kennedy had signed with the Soviets just before Dallas. And Bush ran against the Civil Rights Act that was passed in 1964. Now, he didn't run against the Civil Rights Act because he was a racist. Young George thought that the only way to win in Texas was to make a libertarian argument about civil rights—not that Black citizens didn't deserve equal rights, but that the federal government had taken too large a role. But that was not the family's position at all. In the end, this moral compromise for political gain didn't succeed. He would get more votes statewide than any other Republican, but the fact of the matter is he lost. And what made it worse was that he knew he had acted in defiance of what believed.

When he decides to run for the House in 1966, he runs as a moderate Republican. When he finally made it to Washington as an elected official in 1967, Bush would line up with the kinds of people that he had opposed in 1964. George Bush was a key vote for the 1968 Civil Rights Act, the housing rights act. He realized that Americans could not deny African American servicemen the opportunity to buy a home for their families. He made the point that we can't ask people to defend our country abroad and then mistreat them when they come home. It was a matter of right and wrong. Many of his supporters were bitterly disappointed in him. He did it because he thought it was the right thing to do.

DR: He decides to run for the United States Senate in 1970. Why did he think he could win that race?

TN: Bush thought, given that Richard Nixon had won the presidency, that in a rematch against Ralph Yarborough he could beat the liberal Democrat. What Bush didn't count on was that Yarborough would be primaried and beaten by the more conservative Lloyd Bentsen. Nixon, however, sent money (which like so much of the Nixon political system was tainted) Bush's way and backstopped him. Richard Nixon wanted attractive young Republicans like Bush to win. Bush understood that if he lost the Senate race in 1970, there was going to be some kind of job waiting for him with the Nixon administration. The chief of his campaign was his good friend and tennis buddy James Baker.

DR: After the election loss he goes to Richard Nixon and says, I'm ready for the soft landing, what have you got for me? What does Bush actually want and when does Richard Nixon decide to give it to him?

TN: President Nixon offers Bush the chance to be the U.S. permanent representative to the United Nations, after Daniel Patrick Moynihan, a Nixon domestic advisor and future Democratic senator from New York, declines. Bush has no foreign policy experience whatsoever. He's not completely deaf to foreign policy, but he didn't have any particular expertise in it. He understood quickly, however, how some of his native talents, his inherent abilities, could be quite useful in New York—his ability to listen, his natural empathy, his willingness to work with leaders of all countries. It put him in great stead for the future, because he made friendships and developed allies with people from various countries who would move on to be even more powerful as the years went by. At the UN, Bush shows hints of the diplomatic gifts that he would use to great effect as president.

The problem for George Bush was that though Nixon promised him a job, he didn't promise him any influence. Secretly, Kissinger and Nixon were opening the door to relations with China that would involve the United States ultimately turning its back on Taiwan being in the United Nations, but Bush didn't know anything about this.

DR: Despite that, George Bush does like being UN ambassador. At one point, when Richard Nixon has some political problems, he asked Bush to come down and become the chairman of the Republican National Committee, replacing Bob Dole. Did George Bush really want to go back to Washington in that role?

TN: George Bush, I think, was ready for a change. And he didn't realize that he was accepting a poison chalice when he agreed to become the head of the RNC. The current RNC chief, Senator Bob Dole, was critiquing some of the political activities that Nixon's henchmen like Charles Colson or Chuck Colson were engaged in. It isn't clear how much Bush knew of Dole's concerns. In general at the time, Bush thought that Nixon's enemies were exaggerating Nixon's dark qualities. Bush, who had just lost his father to cancer, was too trusting of Nixon, who had superficially been very helpful to him professionally. With Dole unwilling to accept every order he received from the White House, Nixon wanted a more dependable head of the RNC. Bush also had a useful reputation as a clean politician, a good guy. The White House desperately needed that, too. The Watergate break-in had already occurred.

In sum, as 1973 starts, Nixon very much wants someone with a good-guy reputation to be the head of the RNC, but most of all he wants a lap-dog. Bush's opinion of the president would shift over the course of his time at the RNC, and he turns out not to be the lapdog that Richard Nixon had hoped him to be. In the summer of 1974, when the so-called smoking-gun tape transcript is released—which proved that Nixon not only knew about the cover-up but was an architect and had lied to the American people and elected Republicans about it all—George Bush decides that Nixon has to resign. He doesn't go public with it. He provides this advice to the president.

DR: Gerald Ford becomes president. Does Bush want a job from President Ford? What job does he actually get?

TN: He thought he had a chance to be vice president. Bush viewed the vice presidency as a stepping-stone to the presidency and Bush had an ill-concealed desire to be president. He had thought the vice presidency was a possibility as far back as 1968 and that ambition burned brightly in the Ford years. Instead Ford offered him any ambassadorship that he wanted in Europe, and George Bush surprised him by saying no. He wanted to go to China. It was a good place for him to decompress. He was also very personable there. He had July Fourth parties, had hot dogs. He made the American presence in China more approachable.

DR: Whose idea was it to send him to what was seen as a political dead end, the CIA?

TN: Gerald Ford was surrounded by a number of very ambitious young men: Dick Cheney, Don Rumsfeld. Rumsfeld played a role, using Kissinger a little, to maneuver Bush into the open CIA position, on the assumption that nobody who was the head of the CIA could ever be a viable presidential candidate. To understand that, you have to know a little bit about the ill-repute the CIA had fallen into in the '70s, largely because of the Church Committee investigations of attempted assassinations against foreign leaders, but these came in an ocean of dramatic revelations that came out in the mid-1970s about a secret world that Americans didn't know about. Despite the CIA being in great disrepute, Bush was a good soldier despite the potential cost to his political future. Besides, Bush didn't share the public image of the CIA. He knew people who had gone into the agency. He took the job and loved it. Next to being president, George Bush was proudest of and loved most his time as CIA director.

DR: He wasn't there that long, but he was so well regarded that the CIA building in Langley, Virginia, was named after him.

TN: The left was attacking the CIA for its bungled plots and for secret activities that seemed to be beyond the pale morally. The right was attacking the CIA for being too supportive of detente with the Soviets. Bush thought he could come up with a way to satisfy the right without destroying the agency. He supported a plan to have these far-right analysts get access to the same intelligence the in-house Soviet experts had. The Soviets were on an unexpected, unpredicted strategic missile–building spree. Bush approves a team A/team B approach to try to mitigate these pressures that the agency was under.

DR: Gerald Ford runs for election in 1976, loses to Jimmy Carter. Did Bush want to stay at the CIA under Carter?

TN: I believe that George Bush wanted to stay. Bush believed that the way to depoliticize the agency was to depoliticize how presidents selected the head of the CIA. He had this idea that the CIA director should be able to work for presidents of different parties. But Jimmy Carter didn't think twice about removing Bush. First of all, Bush had been head of the RNC. Second, Jimmy Carter had deep misgivings about the CIA. Initially he wanted a liberal Democrat, John F. Kennedy's celebrated speechwriter Theodore Sorensen, to run the CIA.

DR: Bush goes back to Texas. Does he start running for president in 1980 right away?

TN: Bush is impatient and restless, and he wants to grasp the brass ring almost immediately. So yes, he is thinking about 1980. Nobody else in Washington, let alone the country, is thinking seriously about George Bush for 1980. He was well regarded, but many politicos thought him quite weak. He had lost two Senate races. He had been ignored by the national security team at the Nixon White House when he was at the UN. He had been put at the RNC at the worst possible time. He goes out to China and gets some good press, but he's certainly not part of the Washington scene. He comes back, and is rewarded for his loyalty by leading what was viewed by many Americans as a disreputable organization. He wanted to stay and was told by a new president that he had to leave. Despite his stellar CV, he was not seen as a man of conviction. Yet he was convinced that he could be president, which made him seem like an eccentric candidate until he began to win votes in early 1980, and surprised the political elites in the United States.

DR: It was said that his base was his Christmas card list. Ronald Reagan is the presumed favorite. To the shock of the political world, George Herbert Walker Bush wins Iowa. What happens next in New Hampshire?

TN: The loss in Iowa was a great shock to the Reagan campaign. In New Hampshire, the Bush team wanted it to be Reagan versus Bush. The Bush people thought that if you went man-to-man with Reagan, there were enough traditional Republicans, Eisenhower Republicans, to beat him. Reagan's genius was not to give Bush a chance to make it a two-person race. George Bush's mishandling of the debate in Manchester, New Hampshire, undermined whatever momentum he had developed in Iowa. He says to Reagan, "I'm not going to debate the other candidates. I'm only going to debate you." Reagan then says, "I paid for this microphone, and they're staying." Bush loses the primary and never recovers politically from New Hampshire.

DR: The result is that Reagan goes on to win the nomination. Bush pulls out reluctantly. Does he really think he is going to be picked as vice president at the convention?

TN: No. George Bush does not think he's going to be picked as Reagan's running mate. Ronald Reagan didn't really want to pick George Bush as vice president either, but James Baker and others made the argument that to pull the party together, the second-most-successful candidate in the primaries should be the running mate. Even though Reagan didn't trust Bush's instincts—he didn't really think Bush was a conservative—he agreed. Bush accepted the offer but also understood that, publicly at least, his position on social issues had to change.

DR: Ronald Reagan asked him, could he support the Republican platform? And Bush said yes. Which meant he had to support the position on abortion, which was a pro-life position. Is that correct?

TN: That's completely correct. George Bush in 1968 had supported legislation that decriminalized the use of contraceptives. He supported family planning, supported Planned Parenthood. But to demonstrate his loyalty to the top of the ticket, he had to take a position on abortion that was against the position his family had long taken on the subject.

DR: Bush and Reagan win in 1980. In eight years as vice president, did Bush develop a closer relationship with Reagan? Did Reagan really want George Bush to succeed him?

TN: Ronald Reagan developed respect for Bush. The Bushes and the Reagans, however, never developed a close personal relationship. The Reagans never invited the Bushes upstairs to the residence of the White House, for example. But Reagan was willing to give his political support to George Bush.

DR: Bush runs for president in 1988. Who does he run against?

TN: Bob Dole is his major opponent. Bush has to fight for the nomination, because regardless of what the president is saying, Reaganites do not view him as the successor to Ronald Reagan. This is essential to understanding the challenges that Bush would face as president. He is not beloved by the base of his party, which has changed over the course of the Reagan presidency. In many ways, Bush is a pragmatist. He is not an ideologue, he does not believe in fixed positions. It's not that he was a flip-flopper, it's that the world changed, and he changed with it. People in the Reagan core of the party want him to make clear that he will not alter the Reagan approach to taxes, and they want him to do it publicly, in a very humiliating way. He does it for the first time in New Hampshire. At the convention, he then says: "Read my lips, no new taxes." Now, the irony about this is that Ronald Reagan had raised taxes. But Reagan's team had been clever about hiding these taxes as so-called revenue enhancements. To this day, Reagan has a reputation as being a staunch tax cutter. Bush didn't enjoy the same trust with Republicans. In order to win the nomination, let alone the election, Bush basically handcuffed himself, saying, "I won't raise taxes."

DR: Who does he pick at the convention to be his vice president?

TN: He picks Dan Quayle, senator from Indiana. Dan Quayle is considered a dedicated conservative. No one doubts his conservative bona fides. In many ways Bush is choosing him because he's young, full of energy. Let's face it, Quayle is not going to be a real challenger to Bush, who is hoping for two terms.

DR: They get elected. How was the campaign against the Democratic nominee, Michael Dukakis? Dukakis was actually ahead until the end.

TN: At the beginning of the campaign, Dukakis is ahead. The Reagan presidency was hobbled at the end by the Iran-Contra scandal. As an unusually active vice president, Bush is involved in the scandal. He never faces criminal proceedings, but Reagan did seek his advice, particularly on the Iran side of it. The Cold War has not ended, but it seems to be moving in that direction. Many Americans were beginning to think, okay, it's time to move on. It's time to rebuild the country. The Democrats choose Michael Dukakis, in many ways a perfect foil for George Bush, because Dukakis has his own awkwardnesses, which weaken his appeal. In an era when a few bad pictures can alter a public's view of a political candidate, the fact that Dukakis appears in a tank with a helmet on makes him look silly, rather than defiant and strong.

The most infamous of the Republican tactics was only used once, but even before social media it sort of went viral. A group supportive of George Bush, but not an arm of the Republican Party, takes advantage of a furlough program that Governor Dukakis had supported in Massachusetts, which allowed felons to leave for the weekend. During one such furlough, a man named Willie Horton had killed a person. Willie Horton was

African American, and this group featured him in an ad. It seemed like a Reaganite dog whistle. The Bush campaign is attacked for it. In being attacked, the ad gets more and more currency. It's a stain on the Bush effort. Bush went low to beat Dukakis.

DR: Bush gets elected president and, early in his administration, Saddam Hussein invades Kuwait.

TN: That's not the most important thing that happens early. The Berlin Wall falls. Bush's strengths were called upon during this potentially dangerous moment in world history when the Soviet Empire collapses. Bush understands how important Gorbachev is to a soft landing of the Cold War. The U.S. government and Bush recognize that Gorbachev had let loose forces he could not control, but he was the only one who could manage how the Soviet Union responded to these forces. When the Berlin Wall falls, there are many commentators who were expecting George Bush to announce that the United States has triumphed in the Cold War. Instead he says, in effect, "I'm not going to dance on the Berlin Wall." He recognized that what you don't do with a failing adversary is to humiliate them.

The Berlin Wall falls in late 1989, and it's in 1990 that Bush has to make a series of tough decisions that show remarkable leadership. Bush understood that there were a number of key changes that the world needed to be a safer place, and one was the unification of Germany. In addition, if you find a way to get the Russians to allow a reunified Germany to ally with the West, you've eliminated the greatest cause of the Cold War. In actively seeking these two goals, Bush not only had to face skeptics on his own team, he faced skeptics in London and Paris. What Bush had to do in 1990 was to manage these two contradictory things simultaneously: one, a good relationship with Gorbachev that did not undermine him as the Soviets were losing power, and two, supporting West German chancellor Helmut Kohl in his bid to unify Germany. These are absolutely contradictory objectives, unless you can convince Gorbachev that what Kohl is doing is inevitable. That's what Bush did.

Then, in the summer of 1990, Saddam Hussein invades Kuwait. Bush believed that if Saddam were successful in Kuwait, that would give the green light to all kinds of Saddams around the world who would respond to the end of the Cold War by seeking to revise borders through the use of force. What was at stake was not just Iraqi control of Kuwaiti oil fields but the future of the international system. What Bush does is he decides that the United States is going to put together a coalition to liberate Kuwait.

DR: Is there any truth to the idea that Bush himself was not initially determined to go in militarily, or that Margaret Thatcher made him do it?

TN: I think the challenge for George Bush was working through the idea of sending men into battle. He had seen the consequences for the country of Vietnam. He had been in battle himself in World War II. Before making a decision about how to react to Saddam's aggression, he had to come to terms with the implications of an invasion of Iraqi-occupied Kuwait. I don't think the British could have forced him to send Americans into battle.

DR: He and Jim Baker and Dick Cheney put together an international coalition. It's approved by Congress. What happens in the war, and why, when the war is won so quickly, does Bush not go into Iraq to get rid of Saddam Hussein?

TN: George Bush's time at the UN had shaped him. He wanted the world—not just the Western powers—to lay down a marker in this new era that aggression didn't pay. He had UN support for liberating Kuwait; he did not have support for going into Baghdad and toppling Saddam and occupying Iraq. He hoped Saddam would be overthrown. He knew that it was a vicious dictatorship. He hoped that Saddam's military would turn on Saddam because of the stupidity of going into Kuwait. Bush definitely wanted Saddam Hussein gone. But he knew he did not have international support, nor really American political support, for toppling Saddam and occupying Iraq. It was not in the interest of the United States, or of the world Bush hoped to build, to look like it was exceeding its international authority.

DR: Bush's popularity gets almost as high as any post–World War II president has ever seen. How did he lose his reelection effort in 1992?

TN: Something else happens in 1990 that shapes Bush's presidency. I think it was another act of great presidential leadership, but it was controversial. Bush understood, early on in his presidency, that he was going to have to break his campaign promise not to raise taxes. George Bush thought that supply-side economics was fanciful. He never agreed that if you cut taxes, the economy will grow to such an extent that whatever tax revenue you lost due to the tax cut would be more than compensated for by all the economic activity you would create. But tax cuts were popular. Now, as president, he faced the problem of the federal budget deficit that he had inherited from the Reagan-Bush administration. As a consequence of some budget bills passed in the '80s, most notably Gramm-Rudman, there was going to be an automatic 40 percent federal budget cut if some progress hadn't been made on the deficit by 1991. Meanwhile, Democrats, who were in the majority in the House and Senate, preferred raising revenues to cutting federal programs. A pragmatist, Bush knew that tax rates had to go up.

Meanwhile, Republicans in that Congress were in no mood for pragmatic problem-solving. A new generation of Republican members of Congress was led by Newt Gingrich, a history professor from Georgia, who thought of himself as a Reagan populist. He saw a path to future power for Republicans in Congress, especially in the House, which had been under Democratic control since 1955, by not compromising on the budget. While Bush was seeking a prudent compromise with a Democratic majority, which would raise taxes and reduce the trendline on the budget deficit and the national deficit, Gingrich saw this as a political loser. Gingrich actively worked against Bush's efforts to compromise, depriving him of Republican votes, and the budget that is ultimately passed reflects most of the Democrats' wish list. From the summer of 1990, despite his achievements abroad, Bush would be on the defensive in his own party.

And there is another legacy of the Reaganomics that Bush has to fix. Bush recognizes that the country has to get past the savings-and-loan crisis. He recognizes that the degree of banking deregulation that occurred under Reagan had been a mistake. Bad loans were made, bad mortgages were issued, and Bush knows he has to do something about it. So he approves a bailout of the savings-and-loan industry. That also didn't put him in good stead with fellow Republicans.

DR: Bush runs for reelection. Is he healthy physically and mentally as he goes into the campaign?

TN: He isn't as healthy as he was. In May of 1991 he suffers shortness of breath while jogging. It turns out he has a thyroid deficiency, something called Graves' disease. This is the wrong time for it to occur, because this is precisely the moment when he should project vitality and provide the country with a reason why he should be reelected in 1992. The Baby Boomers felt that it was their turn. They were the same age as George Bush's children. You were seeing a cultural shift in the United States and a political shift. People were ready for something new, and George Bush had nothing new to offer.

DR: In 1992, a Baby Boomer, Bill Clinton, gets the Democratic nomination, but an independent third-party candidate, Ross Perot, also runs. What is his animus against George Herbert Walker Bush?

TN: In part, Perot hated him because one of George Bush's tasks as vice president was serving as an intermediary with those concerned about POWs and soldiers missing in action in Vietnam. Ross Perot was a leader in that cause. The U.S. military found no evidence that these people were still alive, but Perot and his inner circle believed that this was a cover-up by the Reagan-Bush team. The 1992 election became a real three-person race, which hadn't happened in the country since 1912.

DR: Perot gets about 19 percent of the popular vote but no electoral votes. If he hadn't been in the race, would it have changed the outcome?

TN: I think Clinton still would have won. It's not just that Bush was defeated, he was humiliated, winning only 37.5 percent of the vote. No incumbent president had fared as poorly in a reelection bid since Bush's fellow Yalie William Howard Taft garnered 23 percent support in 1912. Bush's bitter view of his defeat would change with time, but in 1992 Bush didn't believe that Clinton deserved to be president. Clinton got under his skin. If anybody was going to deny him reelection, he thought, it shouldn't be this upstart from Arkansas.

DR: Barbara Bush and George Herbert Walker Bush were married for over 65 years. What was the nature of that relationship?

TN: They were remarkable helpmates. Barbara Bush had points of view, which she made clear to her husband. She was up-front on the AIDS issue, for example. She had her own views on abortion, but understood that for her husband to be president, she had to keep those views to herself. She saw herself as an advisor and a supporter. She also saw herself creating a stable world around the president. Barbara was a great partner, essential, I think, to George Bush's sense of self and self-confidence.

DR: If you had a chance to interview George Herbert Walker Bush today, what one question would you like to ask him? And do you admire him today more or less than you did before you began your research on him?

TN: The process of writing the book deepened and broadened my respect for George Bush. I did not fully appreciate, until I put the pieces together for the book, the extent of his political courage. I remember listening to his inaugural speech on the radio in 1989. When you become president, you're still the head of a party, but you're also a head of state, not just the president of the people who elected you. George Bush's inaugural speech in 1989 is a perfect example of how you transition from being the head of a party to becoming head of state. He was addressing some of the harsher elements of conservatism head-on, and was saying he wanted to be a president for more people. It was an invitation to people who didn't vote for him to support his presidency. It was superb.

What I did not fully appreciate until I wrote about the first President Bush was how determined and successful he had been to make those words a reality. His presidency came between those of two charismatic men, and Bush's lack of drama and his occasional awkwardness on stage detracted, unfairly, from his historic achievements offstage.

My question for him would be about extremism in American political life, because he recognized extremism and tried to mitigate it in the Republican Party. He couldn't. I would ask him what lessons he might have learned. Is it possible to contain extremism in our country? Where does it come from? His generation had to face it, and our generation has to face it again. So that's the question I would ask him about.

Presidential greatness involves making decisions for the country that are likely to come at a personal political cost. At the height of his presidency, George H. W. Bush made decisions that he thought were right for the country, even though he knew they were risky, internationally and politically. He didn't always show political courage in his political life. But once he had the power that he had sought his entire life, he wanted to use that power in the right way for the right reasons, whatever the cost, and that's why I think George Bush deserves to be considered among our best presidents.

17

WILLIAM JEFFERSON (BILL) CLINTON AND HILLARY RODHAM CLINTON

(Bill Clinton, b. 1946, president from 1993 to 2001;
Hillary Rodham Clinton, b. 1947)

From the days of George and Martha Washington forward, the press and the public have always been interested in just how influential a First Lady might be alongside her husband. In the early days of the republic, and well into the twentieth century, first ladies have been seen as having various levels of influence on their husband's social activities, if not their political and policy stances.

Without doubt, though, the most powerful presidential–First Lady combination, in terms of political and governmental impact, has been Bill and Hillary Clinton. Not only was Hillary Clinton as knowledgeable about political and governmental matters as her husband, but she was actively involved in developing policies for his administration, both when he was governor and when he was president. Bill and Hillary Clinton were quite willing to portray themselves as a unique couple, and, in fact, in the country's history they were indeed unique—and that would have been true had Hillary not run for the Senate (and been elected) while still First Lady, served as secretary of state, and, in time, became the nominee of her party for president (becoming the first major-party female nominee for that position).

Because the Clintons have been on the national scene now for more than three decades, we tend to accept the rare combination, and forget how unique they were and still are.

At the country's inception, when women were not allowed to be involved overtly in politics (or even vote), first ladies tended to assert their influence publicly through the way they organized their husband's social lives, with White House receptions and dinners being a vital way to signal presidential support or disfavor. Dolley Madison personified this type of influence, with her active and visible socializing activities, for her husband, James Madison (and earlier, at times, for her friend the widowed Thomas Jefferson).

But first ladies tended not to openly discuss political or governmental matters, and their husbands did not want to appear to be influenced on those matters by their wives.

That changed in the twentieth century. Edith Wilson effectively became president when she made vital decisions for President Wilson following his serious stroke. But that was not publicly known at the time. What was known, less than two decades later, was the influence of Eleanor Roosevelt on her husband. Because his polio made traveling a bit more complicated, FDR was content to allow his wife to travel the country as his "eyes, ears, and legs" and report back to him on what was occurring. Eleanor Roosevelt staked out her own public positions on issues, which presumably impacted, in time, her husband's decisions on those issues.

Although Eleanor Roosevelt's immediate successors, Bess Truman and Mamie Eisenhower, did not seem interested in having their own public policy positions or trying to influence their husbands on policies, their successors did, typically in one of two ways. Some first ladies developed their own projects or causes—Jackie Kennedy focused on restoring the White House and preserving historic buildings in the area, Lady Bird Johnson focused her energies on environmental issues, and Rosalynn Carter worked on mental health policy. Other first ladies, while having their own pet projects, seemed to focus on influencing their husbands on policy or personnel matters. Nancy Reagan, for instance, famously served as her husband's chief personnel advisor (while also focusing on reducing illegal drug use). Michelle Obama—a Harvard-educated lawyer—had projects like children's health and nutrition, though she was also seen as a close advisor to her husband on a number of policy and personnel matters.

But one First Lady, Hillary Clinton, seemed to be more active than others in influencing the regular policy conversations within her husband's administration. She was the first First Lady who had been educated as a lawyer, and she developed her own distinguished career in the law and public policy as her husband was developing his political career. Indeed, it was said by the supporters of Bill Clinton's campaign for president in 1992 that by electing him, the voters would "get two for the price of one" (i.e., the Clintons were both intellectual and policy powerhouses and would both be involved in the presidency's workings).

That indeed occurred when Bill Clinton was elected president at age 46 in 1992, after serving five terms as governor of Arkansas, defeating the incumbent George H. W. Bush and the independent H. Ross Perot, an extraordinarily wealthy Texas entrepreneur.

How did Bill Clinton come from a small state governorship at such a young age to become president of the United States? He had been marked as a political comer from the time he was selected as a Rhodes scholar and returned to Arkansas to become a political leader. While he failed, shortly after graduating from Yale Law School, to get elected to Congress against an incumbent Republican, Clinton was subsequently elected attorney general of the state at age 30, and then governor at age 32. His initial re-election effort failed, in part because he was running in the same year that President Carter was running for reelection, and a Republican landslide seemed to impact even a rising star like Bill Clinton. (That Carter temporarily placed some of the Mariel "boat people" leaving Cuba in Arkansas, despite assurances to Clinton that this would not occur, surely impacted the voters' decision that year. But Clinton regained the governorship two years later, and then served another three terms before running for president for the first time in 1992, after aborting a possible run in 1988.)

Bill Clinton's political ascent and his successes as president were due to several factors. He had an infectious, likable personality, and he actually seemed to enjoy what politicians have to do in meeting and greeting countless people. Also, Bill Clinton had a beautiful mind when it came to public policy. He seemed to relish detailed public policy discussions and had a rare gift for connecting the many diverse dots of various policy matters, and he had a spouse who relished developing public policy solutions and who could match (if not better) him intellectually. (Her passion was developing solutions to help individuals from lower income families get the benefits of better education, health care, and legal services.)

As president, Bill Clinton had a rocky start. He seemed too liberal to gain Republican support for his programs and too conservative for the core of the Democratic Party; he gave the task of developing a health care program to the First Lady, but what she developed did not gain traction in

Congress and really went nowhere (though it bore a great deal of resemblance to what later became the Affordable Care Act).

That the First Lady played such a visible and active role in developing the president's health care program seemed to offend some of the public and many members of Congress, particularly Republicans. There really had not been any precedent for a First Lady being so publicly involved in developing such a major part of her husband's legislative agenda.

The result of some of the unstructured and undisciplined early years of the Clinton administration was a large setback in the midterm elections of 1994 and the beginning of the perception that Clinton would have a difficult time getting reelected. But President Clinton moved to more moderate public policy decisions—known to some as "triangulating"—and he, in time, developed legislative victories and a steadier, more focused public presence. The result was an overwhelming reelection victory in 1996 against former Senate Majority Leader Robert Dole.

The second term had its challenges for sure—most visibly the Monica Lewinsky affair and the subsequent impeachment. But Bill Clinton never gave up his focus on policy and on working as hard as possible to get his economic and foreign policy priorities through Congress. Among them were budget and tax policies that enabled the U.S. government to show budget surpluses for three of his last four years in office—the last time the U.S. budget has had surpluses.

And toward the end of the Clinton administration, an unprecedented occurrence took place: the First Lady decided to run for the Senate from New York. No First Lady had ever undertaken such an activity, but Hillary Clinton won overwhelmingly, becoming the first and only former First Lady to serve as a U.S. senator.

And she also became the only former First Lady to run for president and was thought to have had an excellent chance of winning in 2008, but Barack Obama beat Senator Clinton for the Democratic nomination. A return to the Senate seemed to be Hillary Clinton's likely career path until President-elect Obama offered her the position of secretary of state, an offer she attempted to turn down several times before ultimately accepting. After four years in that position, Secretary Clinton decided to run again for president, and this time she won the Democratic nomination against Vermont senator Bernie Sanders. And a return to the White House seemed inevitable to many.

All she had to do was beat a real estate developer/TV reality show star, Donald Trump, though earlier he had beaten sixteen other Republican rivals to get the party's nomination, thereby shocking the political world. But the seemingly impossible happened, and Donald Trump beat Hillary Clinton by winning a number of traditionally Democratic states.

That returned Hillary Clinton to private life, where she worked with her husband and their daughter, Chelsea, on a variety of Clinton Foundation projects, while continuing to advise and support Democratic officials and candidates.

Over many years, I have come to know both Bill and Hillary Clinton through various social settings, and I have interviewed them both separately on more than a few occasions. At the 92nd Street Y in New York, I had a rare chance to interview both of them together on May 4, 2023.

*   *   *   *

DAVID M. RUBENSTEIN (DR): Both of you have had incredible careers. Perhaps no couple has ever had as much political power and impact in our country together as you. I wanted to ask you, President Clinton, how do you compare the pleasure and challenge of holding high office with the pleasure and challenge of being a grandfather?

PRESIDENT WILLIAM JEFFERSON (BILL) CLINTON (BC): I don't. Hillary and I, as the world knows, only had one child, so we probably never had to make some changes. But when I was governor, I was flying home from towns in faraway Arkansas to spend the night with Chelsea so I could get up and take her to school every day. When she graduated from high school, she could count on one hand the number of things I'd missed. But she also knew when I missed something that my job required me to do something important. And she knew the same about her mother.

With the grandkids, it is a great gig. But I told Chelsea once, "You will never hear me say that being their grandfather is more important than being your father, because that was the greatest honor and maybe the most important job of my life."

DR: What do your grandchildren call you? Mr. President?

BC: Lord, no. They can hardly imagine I was president. They weren't alive. They call me Pop Pop.

DR: Okay. And what do your grandchildren call you?

HILLARY RODHAM CLINTON (HRC): Grandma.

DR: And how do you compare the pleasure of being secretary of state, senator, and First Lady with being a grandmother?

HRC: There are similarities. Negotiating with three-year-olds is about as hard as anything I did as secretary of state. There was a point where Charlotte, our granddaughter, now eight, was born, and when we would take care of her, Bill and I outnumbered her. And so that worked. Then along came Aiden, who's now six, and it was so much harder. And now with Jasper, who's three, we're just exhausted. It's like, let me fly a million miles around the world, talking to dictators. I'll get more worn out chasing the three-year-old around.

They lived with us during COVID, which was the only silver lining of that dark, dark cloud. That was a gift, having that time with them.

DR: Since you've left Washington, there's been an increase in divisiveness. It's much worse than when you were there, and it wasn't great then. But now the Democrats and Republicans don't even want to talk to each other, let alone think about bipartisan legislation. What do you think causes this, and do you see any solution in the near term?

BC: You'll say I'm being a partisan Democrat, but I'm going to say it anyway: it's because the Republicans have been rewarded for being divisive. They're great branders, better than we are. They convince people that our most left-wing members, about 10 percent of our caucus, represent 100 percent of us, to cause people in the middle to get scared; to try to get swing voters to forget that their most right-wing members represent over 90 percent of them in the House and about 60 percent in the Senate.

And the political media like binary choices. But the real world—the world all of you live in, raising your kids, running your businesses, making your decisions—is seldom black or white. You want somebody running things who can make hard judgments and realizes what the practical impact of the decision will be on real people.

But if you move to a politics where you reward people for whether they've assumed the right posture, in the right way, with the right words, turning their opponents into two-dimensional cartoons instead of three-dimensional people, and eventually turning yourself into a two-dimensional cartoon, you're not going to get very good results. That's basically what happened.

I have a lot of Republican friends still who just pretend it's not going on, or who don't like it and don't support it. But you can't blame people in politics who covet power for doing what works. And it's been working for them, except when they get in and do things people don't agree with.

They took over the Supreme Court, repealed *Roe v. Wade*. They took over the Congress and the White House, and President Trump did not keep his promise to repeal the Affordable Care Act, or even his promise to submit something better, because you couldn't protect people with preexisting conditions from higher rates unless you had the other things in the Affordable Care Act. And so they promptly lost the Congress.

But voters forget about it. Every election, it's like they're starting all over again. And it's still working for them. People like them when they're criticizing and not when they're governing.

HRC: I agree with that completely. People complain about divisiveness and wish that we could work together more. When I represented New York for eight years in the Senate, I worked across the aisle with practically every Republican on something of significance. And you're right—now they barely talk to each other, and it's a lot harder to find common ground.

The other element is the change in our information ecosystem. It was tough with talk radio and the kinds of things that we put up with in the '90s. It was unfortunate for our country and democracy when Fox News started and began to make its profit, basically, by keeping people in a lather of anger and fear and insecurity. But social media has put that on steroids. The amount of misinformation and attacks that go on, on a second-by-second basis, have pushed people even further into their own corners. It's much more difficult today.

DR: Had you not been at Yale Law School at the same time as Bill, how do you think your life would be different?

HRC: It would have been more boring. I think I would have continued what I had started doing. I wanted to be an advocate, particularly for children. I was working for the Children's Defense Fund, and with its founder, Marian Wright Edelman. I was very committed to that pathway. I never thought I would run for office myself, but I wanted to be involved in helping make policy, particularly to help kids.

DR: When you told your parents you were moving to Arkansas, what did they say?

HRC: When I was growing up, my father was a very big supporter of Republicans. He loved Dwight Eisenhower. He was a World War II vet. And so, when I brought Bill home the first time, it wasn't so much that he was from Arkansas, it was that he was a Democrat.

BC: Hillary came from the town—Park Ridge, Illinois—where Goldwater beat Johnson 80 percent to 20 percent, and the 20 percent thought Goldwater was too liberal. But I loved her father and her mother, who was a liberal Democrat. She was more liberal than Hillary and I were. It was interesting listening to their marriage unfold in terms of raising their children and advice, and everything was different. But he was a really good guy and smart, and he wound up working as a volunteer in my campaign for Congress in 1974. I ruined him.

DR: When you ran for Congress the first time, the only time you ran for Congress, you lost. Had you won, do you think you would ever have become president of the United States?

BC: Not a chance. Maybe I could have been elected to the Senate someday, but I wasn't really thinking about that. It was 1974, the Watergate year, and it was Vietnam. I was a young law professor. I'd only been home from law school six or seven months. I went to six different people and asked them to run, and none of them would run. That's the only reason I ran.

DR: You lost that race, then you became attorney general. Then you ran for governor and won, then ran for reelection and lost. Did you think you would ever have a political career again?

BC: I thought I would go on somehow, but I had no idea how. I just knew that it was a fluke. It was Reagan's big year, and everything that could go wrong in Arkansas did. We had the worst drought in 50 years. We had a missile silo with a Titan missile in it that exploded and blew the two-ton top off the silo and the nuclear warhead out into a cow pasture. And we had Cuban refugees sent to Fort Chaffee in Arkansas rioting. I did the best I could, but I got beat, fair and square.

DR: Secretary Clinton, what job is more enjoyable, First Lady, senator, or secretary of state?

HRC: They're so different. I felt so fortunate to be able to serve in those different ways. Being a First Lady, there's no job description. You kind of decide what you're going to do and how are you going to do it, and it is really up to the individual. Being a senator was just an absolute joy and privilege in every way. I loved that work. Being secretary of state in the Obama administration gave me a great chance to not just travel the world on behalf of our country but to be involved in some of the most meaningful events of that time.

DR: It's 1998. You're First Lady and your husband is going to be retiring as second-term president. Charlie Rangel and others come to you and say, "You should run for the Senate." Did you tell them they were crazy?

HRC: I did, yes. What happened was after the midterm election in November of that year, Senator Daniel Patrick Moynihan announced he was going to retire. He wasn't going to run in two years. His announcement was not even completed before Charlie Rangel, our friend, called me and said, "I really think you need to run." I said, "I love you, Charlie. That's crazy. I'm not going to run for Senate in New York."

I said no; I kept saying no. He kept sending delegations of people. It was in large measure the worry of the Democrats that Giuliani was going to run. They were trying to find somebody with enough name recognition to go up against him and be able to raise the money to defeat him.

I just kept saying no, and I would come home and somebody would call me and say, "Did you see so-and-so on this TV show, saying that you're going to run?"

Fast-forward, I'm in New York City at a high school in Chelsea to promote a documentary about women's sports called *Dare to Compete*. Billie

Jean King was there, and other great women athletes. I was First Lady, promoting women in sports. I was introduced by a student who was the captain of her basketball team at the school. I looked up at her to thank her because she was a lot taller than I am, and she bent over and whispered in my ear, "Dare to compete, Mrs. Clinton. Dare to compete," and walked away.

I kind of stumbled through my speech about the documentary, and I thought, "Maybe I'm not doing this because I'm afraid to do it. I've gone around my entire life encouraging women and girls to take risks, to do things that are hard, to get out of our comfort zone." Then I had to really think about it. And about a month later, I decided I'd do it.

DR: You ran for the presidential nomination. Barack Obama became the nominee. And to your surprise, he offered you the position of secretary of state. You turned that down initially. Why?

BC: She turns everything down. She turned me down three times when I asked her to marry me.

HRC: Eventually, I do say yes to these charming men, like Bill Clinton and Barack Obama.

Bill and I were out for a walk the Sunday after the election, and incredibly relieved. We'd worked really, really hard to get Barack Obama elected, and he was now president-elect. We're in the middle of a forest preserve on a walk, and the phone rings.

It's Bill's phone. He answers it. It's Barack Obama. And Obama says, "I want to talk to you about some of my cabinet appointees." Bill said, "We're in the middle of a forest. I'll call you back when I get home." Then Obama said, "I also want to talk to Hillary."

We get home. Bill talks to him about cabinet appointments and then hands the phone to me, and he says, "I want you to come see me in Chicago." I had no idea why, but of course I said, "Yes, I will be there." I get there, he says he wants me to be secretary of state. I said, "I love being in the Senate. I think I can help you there. I want to work on health care and these other things that we talked about in the campaign and that you've advocated."

And he said, "No, I've thought about this. I want you to be secretary of state." And I said, "Thank you so much, but I don't think I'm the right person." I gave him like five names of people. He said, "I'm not taking no for an answer. I want you to think about it."

I call him back and I say, "I've thought about it, and I'm flattered and honored, but I think it's the best decision for me to say no." He goes, "I don't want to hear from you again until you tell me yes." It was life repeating itself, because that's what Bill had said to me when I said no twice to him.

Here's what I finally decided. I said, "If it had been reversed, and I'd had ended up winning, and I wanted him to be in my cabinet, wanted him to be secretary of state, send that message to the world, I would have wanted him to say yes." And so, after talking to Bill and my daughter and others, I called him back and said, "Thank you, Mr. President-elect."

DR: Well, it worked out. Let's talk about some current affairs. What do you think is the likely outcome of the war in Ukraine? Do you see any resolution of that in the near term?

BC: I don't expect it to be resolved in the near term unless Putin has a change of heart or unless the United States and others walk away from Ukraine and it can't get enough arms and ammunition to continue. They've been amazing. They've fought and fought and fought. They haven't asked any Americans or anybody else to come and fight with them. A lot of people have volunteered and showed up.

I think they have a good chance to prevail, if we continue to give them the necessary arms and ammunition. The Russians are overloading on arms and killing a lot of civilians again, trying to intimidate them. I think Ukraine will win if we stay with them, and that we should not push them into giving up big parts of their country.

Vladimir Putin told me in 2011, three years before he took Crimea, that he did not agree with the agreement I made with Boris Yeltsin that they would respect Ukraine's territory if they gave up their nuclear weapons. Ukraine did a good thing when they gave up their nuclear weapons, and it got Brazil and South Africa to end their nuclear programs, and I was trying desperately to drive down the number of nuclear weapons in the world.

Then Putin said to me one night, "I know you did that. I know Boris agreed to go along with you and John Major and NATO." But he said, "He never got it through the Duma. I don't agree with it, and I do not support it. And I'm not bound by it." And I knew from that day forward it was just a matter of time.

DR: Boris Yeltsin and you once were together, and you whispered something in his ear, and he couldn't stop laughing. What was the joke you must have told him?

BC: What he laughed about was what I said in public, and then I whispered to him. We were doing a press conference, and he had had too much wine at lunch. He wouldn't eat at meals. He ate at other times. He was an interesting man, and I loved him. Whatever his problems were, I remember the now-apocryphal story about Lincoln and Grant, how Lincoln's officers were upset, saying, "He's such a drunk." And Lincoln said, "Find out what he drinks and give it to the other officers." That's how I felt about Yeltsin. He was better drunk than any alternative was sober.

When we were talking, he got impatient because he made some funny remark. He looked at the press crowd, and he said, "You think we're ridiculous, don't you?" He said, "We're not ridiculous, you're ridiculous." I leaned over, and I said, "Boris, don't get mad." Then I went to the microphone, and I said, "I want you all to be sure you got the attribution of that quote properly. I didn't say it." He thought it was really funny.

DR: Secretary Clinton, you've met with Putin many times. Is there any way out of the war? What is your view on how this might be resolved?

HRC: First, I think it's imperative that we continue and I would even argue increase our support for Ukraine because, as Bill just said, the Russians are back to indiscriminate bombing in cities, aiming at apartment buildings, hospitals, other civilian sites. They have committed war crimes. They are in the midst of committing genocide, particularly with respect to how they're kidnapping children and forcing Ukrainians into Russia.

It is, for me, very much in our interest. I admire the courage of the Ukrainian people. I want to see them prevail, but I also think I know Putin well enough to understand that any success he might have with this aggression will not satisfy him. He will continue to do what he has been doing.

Remember, he invaded Georgia, seized two provinces there, invaded Ukraine, seized Crimea and the Donbas region. He has funded political parties, candidates, and media to destabilize European countries. He's interfered in our elections. He is in what he views as a righteous struggle to undermine Western democracy and to reinstitute as much as he can of the Russian Empire. He's not going to stop.

Go talk to a Pole, go talk to an Estonian or a Lithuanian or a Latvian.

Talk to a Finn. Talk to people who have dealt with historic Russian aggression, who have dealt with Putin.

The only potential possible end to the hostilities is either a victory by Ukraine, including being able to take back the territory seized in 2014, or pushing Russia out of what they have seized since February 2022. That could give us breathing room to perhaps have an opportunity to protect Ukraine's legitimate borders, with the exception of what they lost in 2014, and to move them forward with reconstruction in the face of such devastation. But it's ultimately up to them. They have to decide. They've been the ones sacrificing. They've seen the terrible consequences of this barbaric aggression.

I would stand with them and support them as long as it takes for them to feel like they'd get to a stopping point where they have an advantage, because they need leverage over Putin. I wouldn't trust him at a negotiating table under any circumstances, unless the Ukrainians, backed by us, have enough leverage.

DR: Let's talk about China for a moment. President Clinton, when you were president, China became a member of the WTO because of your support. Are you surprised that the U.S.-China relationship now is as bad as it's been since Tiananmen Square? What do you think could be done to improve it?

BC: It's difficult. And it'll get harder if we walk away from Ukraine, because I think it will increase the willingness of China to attack Taiwan. Putin at least has been intellectually honest. He said he thought the loss of the Soviet Union was a tragedy for civilization. He believes there should be authoritarian dictatorships that are ideologically homogeneous running big swaths of the world.

And now President Xi has clearly decided to stay for life, or at least for an indefinite amount of time. He said that he can't pass Taiwan on to his successor, he went back on his commitment to Hong Kong that there would be one country and two systems, he has a million Uyghurs in camps in northwest China, and a litany of other things.

It's a real dilemma for me because I worked hard with China, and I tried to build a relationship. We desperately need a cooperative relationship with them to deal with things like COVID, climate change, North Korea. There's a whole lot of things that we ought to be doing together, but they make it virtually impossible because, again, if you decide to stay for life, whether your name is Putin or Xi or Smith, your number one priority has got to be crushing all dissent, eliminating any source of alternative power in your country, and then keeping people lathered up by being angry at somebody somewhere else.

I believe the best thing to do is to keep talking to them, even while we have to disagree with them publicly, and just keep looking for things we can do together that don't make us hypocritical in our defense of human rights in China and throughout the world.

DR: Secretary Clinton, are you worried about a possible invasion by China of Taiwan? And what would you recommend that the president do to improve the relationship?

HRC: I agree with Bill's analysis of Xi's decision, after there had been an agreement among prior Chinese leaders to peacefully transfer power, to decide that he was not transferring power. He was going to stay. Humiliating his predecessor, Hu Jintao, at the Chinese Communist Party meeting sent a real signal that this is someone who has consolidated power and is going to be a dangerous leader, unless he's convinced that the costs of risk taking and aggression are too much, and therefore backs off.

Xi saw that Putin's invasion didn't work as fast and smoothly as Putin apparently thought it would, and that the world united, with a few exceptions, to impose sanctions that are taking a toll on the Russian economy. Before the Russian invasion, there was a good chance he would have moved on Taiwan within two to three years. I think that timetable has been pushed back.

President Biden doesn't get the credit he deserves for what the U.S. is now building in Asia. Trump had no policy; he had tariffs. That was it. What Biden has done is to create an ongoing relationship in defense of the other nations, in defense of the Pacific and the freedom of navigation, by giving Australia nuclear-powered submarines, a big, big deal; working with Japan to, for the first time, increase their defense budget; working with South Korea to shore them up; convincing the Philippines to allow American military bases there again; working with Australia, Japan, and India so that India, which fights border skirmishes with China on a weekly/monthly basis, is now much more attuned to what needs to be done to stand up to Chinese aggression. Those were long overdue and smart moves.

But having said that, we're in a real ongoing competition with China for influence, for determining who will have the most power within some of the other parts of the world, like Africa and Latin America. It needs a lot of attention, and it needs some strategic patience.

DR: Secretary Clinton, there's a famous photo of you sitting in the Situation Room looking at the effort to capture Osama bin Laden. What were you all looking at? Everybody's mouth was open. Were you were afraid it wasn't going to work? When did you realize it actually did work?

HRC: We were all afraid that something would go wrong. I was part of the small group that studied the intelligence to make recommendations to the president about whether to do something and, if so, what. It was the most intense public service deliberation I've ever been part of, and it was secret. I couldn't tell Bill. I couldn't talk to anybody.

So we all made our recommendations to the president, and he decided to go with a raid, which meant bringing helicopters across the border from Afghanistan through Pakistan airspace into a town called Abbottabad, which happened to house the West Point of Pakistan, about a mile away from the compound where we believed that bin Laden was living. There were a million things that could go wrong.

Obviously, this had been practiced, and every angle that we could think about had been reviewed. We were in that small Situation Room, and we were watching a screen because we had video from a drone above. We had video of what was happening as the helicopters came in to land. One of the helicopters, its tail clipped the wire on the wall surrounding a little area where animals were kept. Once the helicopter tail hit, we knew it was disabled. And that was the moment, I think, that the picture was taken. We all had flashbacks to what happened when President Carter tried to rescue the hostages in Iran. It also meant that we'd have to send in another helicopter that was in hiding, to get it in there quickly enough.

We had to do all of this literally within 20–30 minutes, because people were starting to wake up and we had helicopters landing. There was obviously noise. People were living in homes around the compound. It was a hot night. People were sleeping out on their roofs. We were aware that people were waking up and starting to wonder what the heck was going on.

When the helicopters landed and the Navy SEAL Team Six got out to go into the compound, we couldn't see. We were all holding our breaths. We had to wait till we got news from inside the compound.

There was a firefight. The guards and one of bin Laden's adult sons were shooting. Eventually bin Laden was shot and then his body had to be taken out of the compound, loaded onto one of the helicopters, because we had to be sure about identification to have credibility with the world. And we had to blow up the helicopter, because it was an advanced helicopter with a lot of advanced electronics that we didn't want the Pakistanis to get. We thought the Pakistanis might very well give it to either the Russians or most likely the Chinese.

It was just so intense. Thankfully, President Obama made the right decision, and it worked.

DR: When something like that's happening, and you know about it, you can't say to your husband, "Bill, I have a secret, I just can't tell you"?

BC: If there was ever even a millimeter of doubt in Barack Obama's mind that he could trust Hillary, because of the tough fight they'd been in, I think this blew it away, because he called me as soon as it was over, and he said, "Bill, we got him." And I said, "Who?" He knew how hard I tried to get bin Laden when I was president, and nearly did once. So he said, "Bin Laden. Hillary didn't tell you?" I said, "Now, Mr. President, didn't you tell her not to tell anybody?" He said, "Sure." I said, "She didn't tell anybody."

DR: President Clinton, when you were growing up, you were a musician, and you thought briefly of being a professional musician. Any regrets about not pursuing that?

BC: When I was young, I don't think I did anything that made me happier, once I got fairly proficient on the saxophone. I looked older than I was, and I'd go in these places, and if there was a group playing, they'd give me a horn and let me play. I had a great time, but I decided when I was 16 that I could never be as great as John Coltrane.

I know, it's laughable today, but you have no idea what sacrifices were required to be a professional jazz musician in the '50s and '60s. In other words, you couldn't make enough money selling records. If you wanted to be a great jazz player, you had to do the clubs, which means you had to stay up all night, sleep half the day. And your chances of becoming addicted to some narcotic were two or three times greater than your chances of having a successful family.

And it was very important to me, having lost my own father before I was born, to try to build a family. I wanted to be a father, and I knew over the long run that people are normally happy doing what they're best at. I was absolutely sure I could be a better musician than I was, and that I could be good enough to make a decent living and maybe even achieve some fame. I had nine college scholarship offers in music. But I knew, I just felt somehow, that I belonged in politics somehow.

DR: President Clinton, you went to Georgetown University. I read that you only applied to one college?

BC: Georgetown. That's the only place I applied.

DR: If you didn't get in, were you worried about what you were going to do?

BC: Thank God, the University of Arkansas had an open admissions program for natives, so I could have just showed up. But I decided that I wanted to go to Washington, where a lot of action was. That's where all the civil rights action was taking place, all the Vietnam action was taking place.

Georgetown's School of Foreign Service, at the time, was the most highly regarded undergraduate program academically. I loved what I knew about the Jesuits and the fact that they organized the whole curriculum as a modern version of their ancient Russian city, Orem. You didn't get an elective till the second semester of your junior year. The first two years, you had to take 18 or 19 credits every semester. You had to take six classes. It was like a boot camp, and I actually lost a student election defending it.

But I wanted to go to Georgetown because it was hard. They didn't let me in until May or June. I didn't know what was going to happen, but they let me in. Then I showed up and the priest in charge of the freshman orientation said, "What is a Southern Baptist from a landlocked state doing coming to the School of Foreign Service?" I said, "Father, let's just wait a year or two and we'll both figure it out."

It was the greatest decision I ever made. It changed my life. I loved it and I still love it.

DR: President Clinton, when you were president, we had a budget surplus three times. At one point, it was thought that maybe we would run out of having any new federal Treasury bills to sell because we weren't going to have any debt, and there would thus be no benchmark around which corporate or other government debt could be priced. Any ideas about how we can get back to that?

BC: First, I did have a big argument with Alan Greenspan. He was to my left. He said, "We're not going to be able to set interest rates. We can't. How do we set interest rates on federal securities if we have no debt?" I said, "Alan, that's a high-class problem. Let's deal with that when we get to it."

But let me say, I supported President Obama's stimulus program, I supported the bill President Trump passed, and I supported the stimulus bill President Biden passed. When you have severe economic problems—like those caused by the Great Recession or COVID—you can't run a balanced budget, and you can't start cutting spending without making the economy worse.

On a related matter, I think it's nuts to make a big issue of the debt limit. It's a stupid rule we have in America that Congress has to approve twice paying for something; they've already voted to spend money on something, and the associated debt cannot be ignored by refusing to pass a debt limit bill. A lot of these people who are opposing raising the debt ceiling voted for most of the spending that is embedded there.

On the other hand, I think that President Biden has more than he can say grace over now, in a positive way, to implement the infrastructure bill, the CHIPS bill, the Inflation Reduction Act with all the climate change projects that are in it. All of it is job-creating stuff. All of it will create enormous numbers of income-tax payers and sales-tax payers. And we are now in what will be the second, maybe next year will be the third year, in a row where the deficit is going down. The aggregate debt will still go up a little bit.

But once we get to where the annual deficit is going down, then if we have appropriate growth, we should move back to a balanced budget and start paying some of the aggregate debt down, until at least this $30 trillion–plus of debt will reach a more modest percentage of our annual national income. I did dream that maybe I could get rid of it altogether for the first time since Andrew Jackson was president, but I could not do that; and then (after I left office) the Iraq War came along, and 9/11 came along, and we had to do what we did in Afghanistan.

And at one point the House leader, Tom DeLay, said, "In wartime, there is nothing more important than cutting taxes." Not since George Washington, in all the conflicts we've been in, did we ever cut taxes in wartime, and no other country ever did. We did it for the first time during the

Iraq War, and that reflected "tax cuts as theology" perspective. President Reagan had a similar theology, but he clawed back about 40 percent of his tax cuts. He tried to make it so we only tripled the debt when he was president. But the debt was then still small compared to now.

Bottom line, we should bring the deficit down as much as we can, but we ought to pay our debts. You can't spend money, borrow it, and then refuse to pay the people that loaned it to you, not if you want to be a great country.

DR: Secretary Clinton, is there anything about the 2016 campaign you might have done differently?

HRC: I wrote a whole book about it called *What Happened?*, because I couldn't figure out what happened. I think it was a perfect storm of a lot of unprecedented actions. I don't want to plow old ground, because it's obviously important to look to the future and move on, but I will say that it is important that we learned some lessons from 2016 that were applied in 2018, applied in 2020.

There is no doubt that there was interference in the 2016 election unlike we'd ever seen. There's no doubt that Vladimir Putin really didn't want me as president, and therefore ordered the Russian intelligence service, the GRU, to interfere. We had indictments that were made against the Russians that will never go to trial, because they're all Russian military intelligence operatives, but there was a line intercepted from the Russians which said, "Just don't do any damage to Trump or Bernie Sanders. We support them. Go do everything you can to destroy Hillary Clinton."

Once that became known after the election, we did a much better job protecting our elections in 2018 and 2020. And we have to keep protecting our elections, from both those inside our own country who want to suppress the vote, and from foreign actors, largely the Russians. But we also had some evidence in 2020 of a little byplay by the Chinese and the Iranians. So, this is an ongoing challenge.

DR: Would you consider ever running for office again, even though you're a bit young?

HRC: No, but I'll come back here every week to be told I'm too young to do something.

DR: President Clinton, you were elected twice, so you probably are reasonably happy with the method, but do you think the popular vote would be preferable to the Electoral College method?

BC: I do. We adopted the Electoral College when we were 13 states. We had a couple of really big states and some really small states that had distinct differences, but it also helped to load up the electoral votes of the Southern states that had slaves. Now we know that the effect of the Electoral College is to give about 36 extra votes to the most culturally conservative and furthest right American states.

I have no objection to those states voting. I want every eligible person to vote. Unlike some of the Republicans, I'd never try to make it harder for people to vote. I'd make it easier for them to vote. I want the votes counted, and I want them all to count.

Now, if you did go to direct election, the first question you've got to ask yourself is whether would we have more three-party or four-party national elections? And if so, would we have to have a runoff? That is, should you at least require a president to have, I don't know, 40 percent of the vote, 45 percent of the vote? Lincoln got elected in 1860 with 39 percent. Ross Perot got 19 percent in '92. I won the election by, I think, five and a half points, 5.8 points, something like that. But I only got 43.8 percent of the vote.

I think we should get rid of the Electoral College, but doing so might unleash even more parties. Should there be a minimum? A lot of countries have this, by the way. You have to get a majority or you have to get something over a minimal amount to be president.

DR: Secretary Clinton, I assume you prefer direct election as well?

HRC: I definitely prefer direct election.

DR: You met an enormous number of foreign leaders in your time as secretary of state. Are there one or two whom you really admire, whom you think have done a terrific job for their country?

HRC: There are so many in every category. I, to this day, am hugely grateful to and admiring of Nelson Mandela and what he did under such difficult circumstances. Knowing what he was going through and how he was able to maneuver, I'm incredibly grateful to him.

I'm a big fan of Ellen Johnson-Sirleaf of Liberia, the first woman elected a president of any African country. She was elected not once but twice. I went as secretary of state to her second inauguration. I really admired her and think she set an amazing example.

I also, as you might expect, enjoyed working with Angela Merkel. I had known Angela going back to the '90s, and I remember—I think it was like 1994 when we were in Germany—when Helmut Kohl said, "I want you to meet this young woman." She was the minister for children or sports or family, something like that. I watched her being a masterful politician, the way that she was able to maneuver and try to keep Germany together and focused.

DR: The health care system that you were trying to promote when you were First Lady is largely what we have now. I don't know if other people thank you for it. Do you think that at the time having a First Lady so involved in policy was upsetting to some male members of Congress?

HRC: I think so. I would have been shocked to think so when Bill asked me if I wanted to work on health care, because I had, at his request, worked on reforming public education in Arkansas. And one thinks of Arkansas at that time as being much more conservative than Washington, D.C. But maybe it was because I knew people on a first-name basis there and I had worked with them, and he'd been governor for a long time. We had a very respectful relationship with the legislature.

It was, I think, somewhat of a shock to the system for a First Lady to take a public role on a major initiative of her husband's. It's not that other First Ladies had not been very influential, had even testified, on a few occasions, on things that mattered to them and mattered to the administration, but my role in the health care reform effort was a bit of a shock to the system.

BC: I was at a cabinet meeting one day with congressional leadership, and Bob Dole was the Republican leader. We then had about a 55-to-45 advantage in the Senate, but the filibuster was alive and well. We knew we had to get 60 votes to pass health care.

I talked to Dole, whom I liked, and said, "Look, I know you care about health care." He had an aide, Sheila Burke, who was a nurse, who really cared about it. I said, "Why don't we just write a bill together? Because if you don't like it, you can hold 41 of your senators till hell freezes over, and we'll never get anything done. So let's just do a bill together." And he said no. He said, "You put in a bill, and I'll put in a bill to show our differences, and then we'll get together and work it out." But it never happened. Dole was generally good about keeping his word. It's the only time that didn't happen. He got a letter from a prominent Republican maven, who said, "If you let President Clinton sign any kind of health care bill, you can't be elected president in 1996. And they'll have the Congress for a generation. Convince people that it's the worst thing since the *Titanic* sank, and we'll win the Congress. And then you can win in '96." And he was halfway right.

But we tried. We tried everything we knew to do.

HRC: I'll tell you a little funny story about that too, because Bill is absolutely right. We worked on a bill that was going to require individuals to have health insurance and employers to pay. The Republicans worked on a bill that was going to lessen the employer mandate but have individuals carry the responsibility.

I met with then-senator John Chafee from Rhode Island, another honorable person. He and Dole were working on the bill. I went up to the Republican Senate caucus to present the bill at Dole's request, the bill that we were working on. At that point, Strom Thurmond was still in the Senate. He'd been there since the Civil War. He was sitting front and center in the meeting where I was telling them what we were going to put in the bill. Strom Thurmond kept saying, "That sounds really good. I like that." And all the other Republicans are saying, "Shut up, shut up, Strom. Don't say anything." That's when I went back to Bill and I said, "I think there's something at work here, because they were trying to prevent Strom Thurmond, of all people, from endorsing our bill." So, yes, there was a lot of backroom maneuvering.

But you're right, we eventually got the Affordable Care Act. We've gotten close to insuring everybody. I wish we could keep going and make sure we don't drop people from Medicaid and all the other stuff that the Republicans are doing across the states, because health care is a basic human right, and it should be delivered to everybody on an affordable, quality basis.

DR: Speaking of health, how is your health, President Clinton? You look pretty good to me.

BC: I feel good. I'm the oldest man in my family for three generations, and I'm still kicking around.

DR: When there was a tsunami in Southeast Asia, President Bush 43 asked you to do something with Bush 41. The two of you had been bitter rivals in the '92 election, yet you seem to have bonded with him. How did you get to be so close to the man you bitterly fought in the election?

BC: I think he deserves more credit than I do, because it's a lot easier to be friends with somebody you defeated than somebody who defeated you, right? It just is. But I always liked him. Hillary and I, in 1983—when he was President Reagan's vice president—went to Maine to a governors' conference, and Vice President Bush hosted all the governors and their families at his home in Kennebunkport and introduced us to his mother. She was 90-something, I think.

Hillary and I were standing there, and George came up. I took Chelsea by the hand, and I said, "Chelsea, this is Vice President Bush." He said, "How are you, Chelsea?" And she said, "Where's the bathroom?" She was three. And he took her by the hand and took her to the bathroom.

He was a very good guy, and I always liked him, even though they tried to play me pretty hard in 1992. It doesn't bother me, what other politicians do. People do what they think they can make work in a campaign.

After the election, I invited him back to the White House several times, when we announced the Middle East peace signing and when we kicked off NAFTA and other times. Then, when his son asked us to work on the tsunami together, I was thrilled. After that, we worked on Hurricane Katrina together. I also did some work with George W. Bush after he left office.

I felt close to President Bush 41. I got pretty close to Barbara too, who was a tougher nut to crack and was very shrewd. I miss him. I miss the summers when I used to go visit him every year.

DR: Final question for both of you. Secretary Clinton, in your long, distinguished career, what would you say you're most proud of having accomplished?

HRC: Taking the personal out of it—because obviously, as Bill said, we're very proud of our daughter and grateful for our family—in terms of the political and public, there are three things that really stay with me.

I'd been senator from New York for about eight months when 9/11 happened, and it was the most devastating, horrible experience for our city and our country. But it was also an absolute mandate to act to help people who'd been directly affected, to help victims' families, to help re-build New York. And it was so bipartisan.

I just want to tell a little story here. Chuck Schumer and I literally were in the only plane in the sky on September 12th, because we were flown to New York to meet with then-governor Pataki and Mayor Giuliani to survey what had happened. It was overwhelming to have seen it firsthand like that. The television could not capture it. We spent the day in meetings talking about what we were going to do. That night, around eight, nine o'clock, Chuck and I were in a meeting with all these state, local, and fed-eral officials, and we were each handed a note from our staffs who were with us that said, "The White House has just sent a budget request to deal with 9/11 for $20 billion and there's not a penny for New York in it." Our mouths dropped.

We got up and left the room. Chuck hadn't seen his family yet. He had a daughter who'd been at Stuyvesant High School and had been evacu-ated across the river, and he had another daughter who was in school at the time, so he needed to go home and see his family.

I took the last train out of Grand Central back to Washington, and I literally showed up at the door of the office of Robert Byrd, who at that time was the chair of the Appropriations Committee, at six o'clock in the morning. I said, "Senator, we need your help. The White House has sent this bill and it has not a penny for New York." This was now Thursday. And I said, "You just have to imagine what has happened. You haven't been there, but you should go. We should take a delegation. But we need money, and we need support right now."

He said, "Well, what do you need?" I said, "We need $20 billion." He said, "On top of the $20 billion?" I said, "Yes, on top of the $20 billion." And he goes, "All right, if that's what you need." By this time, Chuck was back and I go to the floor of the Senate and say, "We need $20 billion. Senator Byrd has said he would support that."

Then that afternoon, we go to the White House. It's the two senators from Virginia, Senator Allen and Senator John Warner. Chuck and I were in with the president. I could see on his face this was a devastating crisis, obviously, that had to be dealt with. And he says to us, "I'm with you. What do you need?" And I said, "We need $20 billion, Mr. President." And he said, "You got it." His staff nearly fell off their chairs.

We were going to the Cabinet Room, which is next to the Oval Office, and we got up to leave. John Warner, one of my favorite colleagues of all time, stopped me and said, "Hillary, have him make that commitment in public in this meeting." We go in. It's members of Congress from New York, Connecticut, New Jersey, but mostly New York and Virginia. The president's talking about how we're going to protect the country, and we're going to do this, and all that. He finishes talking and then I say, "And I just want to thank you, Mr. President, for committing $20 billion to New York."

And literally, by the time Chuck and I got back to the Senate, his staff was trying to undo that and telling the Republican leaders, "Don't put it in the appropriations bill." We just kept calling the White House. Bush said, "I gave my word and I'm going to follow through." That was an amazing moment for me.

DR: President Clinton, when you look back on your distinguished and long service to our country, what are you most proud of having achieved?

BC: Can I just add one thing to what Hillary said? One thing I like about George W. Bush. We have fought. We have disagreed. He started out more conservative than his father. We do speeches together that are funny because we bad-mouth each other in a funny way, but he will listen. And if he thinks you're right, he'll switch. If he thinks you're wrong, he'll argue. That's all you can ever ask.

When he passed this PEPFAR bill—the president's emergency plan for AIDS—it was more money than I could get through because he got the Christian evangelicals to support him. The Republicans were reflexively against anything I wanted to do. He got this big AIDS program, and I was, meanwhile, working as a former president with Mandela to get AIDS medication to people and get the prices down.

He invited me in 2005, a couple of years after, to Pope John Paul's funeral. I flew with his dad and him to the pope's funeral. He calls me up to his cabin and he says, "Tell me about what you're doing with AIDS." I explained what we were doing: "We're getting the medicine out there. We're getting the supply chains worked out. We're doing all these things we're supposed to be doing to fix the system. And we're working with your people" in the seven countries I think they were working in then. I said, "I'm very grateful to you, Mr. President, but you could save six times as many lives if you would just let your people in these countries use the generic drugs" that were made in India, primarily, rather than Big Pharma drugs, which they were requiring.

He said, "The pharmaceutical companies tell me they're not as good," and this is a big deal because they were big supporters of his. Al Gore had said in the 2020 election—and they all went nuts—that he thought these AIDS-ridden countries should be able to use generic drugs, and it shouldn't have anything to do with the patent rights. That was agreed in an international treaty.

I said, "I'll tell you what. What if I submitted every drug we use anywhere in the world to the FDA in America? If they approve the drug, would you then tell these countries it was okay with you if they got the generic drugs?" And Bush didn't blink. He said, "Yes."

Before you knew it, the FDA approved 22 of the 24 drugs. Instead of seven countries, PEPFAR was in 15 countries. With that one little decision to go against the polarizing grain that dominates American politics, millions of people's lives were saved. And I think that's what you should remember.

When you asked me in the beginning and I said that polarization was partly because the right had been rewarded, but it is also true that the left too easily gives up on people. We shouldn't talk down to people. The one thing I loved about Elijah Cummings and John Lewis was they treated people respectfully, and they just kept trying. They kept knocking on the door.

And so I guess one of the things I'm proudest of is that in the face of the torrent of almost life-threatening opposition I received, I just kept knocking on the door, and the results were pretty good. Specifically, we had the broadest, most widely shared prosperity that our country has had in more than 50 years. And it mattered to me that those in the bottom of 20 percent of income increased their income in percentage terms more than the top 20 percent.

I'm proud of that, and I'm proud of the fact that we basically kept marching toward peace in a world that was full of potential conflicts. And I'm sad that in the twenty-first century, a lot of the people who once thought cooperation was better than conflict have apparently gone to the other side, but they can be brought back.

18

PRESIDENT GEORGE W. BUSH

(b. 1946; president from 2001 to 2009)

I t did not seem likely that lightning would strike twice for the Bush family, and that George W. would also become president.

But it did, probably aided by former secretary of state James A. Baker III (who was then a partner at Carlyle). After the dispute on the Florida vote total in the 2000 election, Secretary Baker was asked by then-governor Bush to represent him in the recount effort. And that effort ultimately resulted in the *Bush v. Gore* decision, which led to George W. Bush becoming president. (I once asked President George H. W. Bush why he did not give his son George the same middle initials and have him be a junior. He told me that when he was growing up in Greenwich, Connecticut, his friends made fun of him for having two middle names, and he did not want to subject his son to the same taunting. So it was just *W.*)

Although George W. might have been expected to know a fair bit about the White House and governing because his father had been president, he did not spend much time in Washington during his father's time in office, and was not all that interested in the intricacies of policy at the time. He did come to the White House from time to time to see how his parents were doing and to serve as "eyes and ears" for his father and sometimes as an "enforcer." (He was the one who told President Bush's first chief of staff, former New Hampshire governor John Sununu, that he had to leave that position.)

At the time of his election to the presidency, Governor Bush was really not steeped in the intricacies of U.S. foreign policy or the workings of Washington, D.C. That was, presumably, one of the reasons he chose his father's former secretary of defense, Dick Cheney, as his vice president. Cheney knew Washington inside and out, having been President Ford's chief of staff and a six-term member of the House of Representatives, and could be president if need be.

As president, George W. dealt with two extraordinary challenges that largely defined his presidency. The first was the 9/11 hijacked plane crashes in New York, Washington, D.C., and Pennsylvania. The second was the Great Recession, the greatest economic calamity faced by the country since the Great Depression.

His initial response to 9/11—to send troops to Afghanistan to capture Osama bin Laden (and others involved in the attack)—was not controversial in the United States. President Bush, once he got his bearings after the first few days, was widely seen as a decisive leader, with sky-high approval ratings.

But the subsequent response split the country (and the world) down the middle when he decided to invade Iraq, which had no direct 9/11 connection, to destroy its presumed "weapons of mass destruction." In one of our country's greatest intelligence failures, there were no such weapons, and Iraq descended into chaos, with many thousands of Iraqis and American soldiers losing their lives until President Bush ordered what became known as "The Surge" in 2007.

That war began in the latter part of the first Bush administration, and Bush's popularity, which had soared after 9/11, descended rapidly as the war went poorly. Nonetheless he was reelected, narrowly defeating Senator John Kerry. To compound the war's challenges, during Bush's second term the U.S. financial system essentially collapsed, due initially to the failure of the home mortgage market. Only with the most extraordinary and unprecedented of measures by the Bush administration, Congress, and the Federal Reserve did the economy stabilize and start to recover.

Although I came to know his father, George H. W. Bush, reasonably well after his presidency, I did not know George W. even though our paths briefly overlapped earlier at my company. Before running for governor, when he was a private citizen, George W. served on a Carlyle portfolio company board, though I was not on that board and had essentially no interaction with George W. After he became president, I saw George W. Bush on a few occasions at the White House at various Kennedy Center Honors (I was appointed to the Kennedy Center Board by him) and other social events at the White House. When President Bush left office, I interviewed him on several occasions, and saw up close his self-deprecating sense of humor (not seen quite as much in public while he was president); his close affinity for the veterans who had returned from the Iraq War with serious injuries; his great pride in the PEPFAR program he developed to provide medicine to Africa (and other emerging markets) to reduce the spread of AIDS and save tens of thousands of lives; and his newfound passion for painting, which surprised many of his friends and relatives.

What follows is the edited transcript of an interview I conducted on stage with President Bush in Washington, D.C., at a Carlyle Group event on September 19, 2023.

*   *   *   *

DAVID M. RUBENSTEIN (DR): What's more fun, being president or a former president?

PRESIDENT GEORGE W. BUSH (GWB): They're both delightful. I really don't miss being president. I enjoyed it when I was there, but I don't miss the power; I don't miss the fame; and I don't miss Washington, D.C. I live in the "promised land," as you know. Laura and I are Texans, proud Texans, and we like living in Texas. So, I'm having a good life. I enjoy it. I really don't miss power.

DR: Since you left the presidency, you've taken up painting. Why?

GWB: Because I was bored. (Laughter.) Yes, it surprised me. I read Winston Churchill's essay "Painting as a Pastime." I'm a big Churchill admirer. It kind of harkens to today. We're becoming isolationist as a nation, and it requires certain courage in order to fight off tyrants, like Ukrainian president Volodymyr Zelenskyy is doing.

I always admired Churchill's leadership, so when I read his essay, I went home and told Laura, "If Churchill can paint, I can paint." I know it sounds cocky, but you've got to be pretty cocky to run for president in the first place, right?

DR: How many paintings have you done?

GWB: A lot. That's like asking a rancher, "How many cows you got?" (Laughter.)

DR: But you don't sell them, right?

GWB: I don't sell them, no. But it's changed my life. Every brushstroke is a learning experience. As a result of my desire to raise money for invisible wounds of war, I painted 98 veterans who got hurt. My favorite story about that is I painted a guy named Todd Domerese, who wrote me a compelling letter about the horrors of war. He also told me he had night sweats. And so I'm thinking about a guy having night sweats, and I painted a very dark painting. I was selling the book in Tampa, Florida, and I was a little worried about him seeing his portrait. But I said, "You want to see the portrait I painted?" And he looked at it and went, "That's how I used to feel." And that is the whole purpose of the book.

Then I painted immigrants. That's how I weighed into the immigration debate, trying to remind the country of the importance of immigration, not only for the present but for the future of our country.

DR: Do you think if you had taken up painting when you were in college and been a painter instead of president, you'd be happier or not?

GWB: Well, I'd have been better than a C student, that's for sure. (Laughter.) Did you ever hear about the time I gave the Yale graduation speech? Yale doesn't have graduation speakers unless you're president. My buddy, the head of the board of trustees, convinced me to go down there, and I got up and said, "To you parents of students who got honors, congratulations. To you summa cum laude students, congratulations. And to you C students: you, too, can be president." (Laughter.)

DR: Did you think at the time you were going to get into politics?

GWB: No, I wasn't very political.

DR: You grew up in Texas. Your father grew up in Connecticut. You were much more Texan than he was, right?

GWB: Yes. The best inheritance I had was being raised in West Texas and not in Greenwich, Connecticut—with all due respect to Greenwich. I was raised in the desert, basically. You get to know independent-thinking, free-enterprise-thinking people.

DR: And you went to Andover.

GWB: I didn't volunteer to go to Andover, I got shipped to Andover. (Laughter.) As a matter of fact, that's the kind of school that people where I was raised say, *What did you do wrong?*

DR: Well, you went to Yale, so you must have done reasonably well at Andover. Then you went to Harvard Business School?

GWB: I did that as well, yes. Went into the military in the meantime. You know what I learned at Harvard Business School? Not to trust Wall Street. (Laughter.)

DR: So you weren't trying to be a Baker Scholar (the top 5 percent of HBS students)?

GWB: No, no, I wasn't.

DR: You were going to be in the energy business, right?

GWB: I had been helping run a poverty program in Houston and realized that there's no money in poverty. (Laughter.) So I decided that I wanted to redirect my thinking, and Harvard Business School helped.

DR: After Harvard Business School and some work in the energy industry, you had an opportunity to buy a baseball team. Why did you want to be an owner of a baseball team?

GWB: Because I love baseball. My uncle Herbie owned 13 percent of the Mets. Joan Payson was a majority owner; I remember going up to Maine, and he had a dog named Go Go and a dog named Metsy. He would listen to the games, and he really seemed to love it. An opportunity presented itself, and I put together a group along with Richard Rainwater and Rusty Rose, and we bought the Texas Rangers.

DR: And the team did reasonably well and you sold it for a profit?

GWB: Sold it for a profit. Selling a team is the only way you make a profit in baseball. (Laughter.)

DR: After you sold it, you decided to run for governor.

GWB: Not true. I decided to run for governor before we sold it. The reason why is that the public schools in Texas were lousy. I thought, frankly, it was a civil rights issue, to challenge what I call the soft bigotry of low expectations. In other words, if you're a Black kid in a big urban school district, it's almost like, *You can't learn, let's just move you through.* I ran on a campaign to put accountability in the public school system. And I won.

DR: What did your mother and father say when you told them you were going to run for governor?

GWB: My mother said, "You won't beat her." I was running against Anne Richards, a seemingly unbeatable woman. But I had a reason to run, and I explained the reason to run. I treated her with respect. I didn't fall prey to all this kind of name-calling and stuff, and Texans bought it.

Plus, we're the tort reform state. The largest growth industry in Texas at the time was trial lawyers. I thought that was not very conducive to accumulation of capital, and so we got tort reform through.

DR: The night of the election, your brother was also running for governor in Florida. Your parents chartered a plane to fly to Florida for his victory celebration. Did you ask them about planning for your victory?

GWB: No, I didn't. But unfortunately they made a bad bet. I won, and he lost. (Laughter.)

DR: You're governor of Texas for four years and you get reelected. And then all of a sudden, people think you should be the Republican nominee. Did you want to run for president?

GWB: You know, I wasn't sure at the time. I didn't run for governor to become president. By the way, being governor of Texas is an awesome job. Our legislature meets four months out of every two years—seriously—and the governor decides if they meet more than that. And so it's a hell of a job and I really enjoyed it.

The party was looking for a new leader, and I kind of got swept up in it, and I knew exactly what I was getting into. I watched a good man become president, get beat, get pilloried in the press, but it didn't diminish my appetite for serving the country.

DR: When you ran for president, that famous election night, it came down to Florida. Al Gore called you and said, "I'm conceding the election." Then he called you back and said, "I'm not conceding anymore." Did you think that you would win at that point? And were you preparing for a transition?

GWB: We were preparing for a transition. But my attitude was that I'd run the race as hard as I could. I gave it my absolute best shot. If it turned out that I won, I was ready. And if not, that's life. And so we were preparing a transition, but I was uncertain as to what was going to happen. I knew this: if it was a legal matter, I put the best lawyers in place starting with Jim Baker.

DR: How did you pick Dick Cheney to be your vice president?

GWB: I realized he'd be the best selection. Here's the thing about selecting a vice president. Some candidates have done a lousy job. Some have done a decent job. Ronald Reagan did a really good job. (Laughter.) I think I did a good job. It's a deliberative process where you go through a lot of iterations before you pick someone to be your vice presidential nominee. The person you pick has to be able to be president. It also sent a signal that I was comfortable in my own skin, that I knew where I was weak and where my strengths were. I was pretty weak in terms of Washington, D.C., politics. Cheney had been around Washington a long time and that was comforting, I think, to some people.

DR: On your first year in office, the 9/11 terror attacks happened. You were reading books to schoolchildren at that time. What did you think was happening? Did you know immediately it was an attack?

GWB: Right before I went in the classroom in Sarasota, Florida, I saw the first plane hit the tower, and I thought it was an accident. I just couldn't believe that anything other than an accident had taken place. Then Andy Card whispered in my ear, "A second plane has hit the second tower. We're under attack." And I wasn't sure what it meant, but I knew this: that I needed to project a sense of calm, because the eyes of the nation were focused on me. And it was obvious, because there were probably 20 TV cameras in this classroom. So I waited for the appropriate moment to leave and hurriedly wrote up a statement, and I went in front of a group of parents and children who had not yet heard the news. I basically said, "We're under attack and we're going deal with it." I had no idea what "it" meant, but I knew we were going to deal with it. And from that point forward, I got whisked around the country until I finally made it back to D.C.

DR: A lot of your advisors said not to go back to Washington, D.C. Why did you want to come back?

GWB: First, because I was the commander in chief in a time of war, and I needed to be in the White House. Second, I was in a bunker in Omaha, Nebraska, and they said, "You need to give a speech to the nation." And I said, "You're right. I need to, but I'm damn sure not going to give it from a bunker. I'm going to give it from the Oval Office."

DR: So you came back to D.C., you made the speech, and then you sent troops over to Afghanistan to capture Osama bin Laden.

GWB: Well, no, I said to the Taliban, "Cough up Al Qaeda or you're going to face serious consequences." So the choice was theirs, not ours. I said, "These bastards came and killed people on our soil and we want them." The Taliban were providing safe haven for them in Afghanistan, and refused to comply. And I meant what I said. We put together a good plan and in we went.

DR: Do you think if you had sent more troops over, you would have captured Osama bin Laden at that time?

GWB: We got him eventually.

DR: Did President Obama call you right before the actual killing of bin Laden?

GWB: Yes, I was eating a souffle. (Laughter.) It's kind of out of character, I know, but there's a restaurant in Dallas called Rise. Get it? I got a call and skipped the dessert and went home, and he called and told me.

DR: During your presidency, we went through what's called the Great Recession.

GWB: Yes, we did. Wall Street got drunk.

DR: Did the secretary of the Treasury and the chairman of the Federal Reserve come to you and say, "Look, the economy is collapsing because of mortgage defaults" and so forth? Did they say, "We have to do something or the entire economy will collapse"?

GWB: Yes, that is exactly what they said. And this is after the financial markets were kind of pitching and bailing for maybe five weeks. The short sellers were just bombing weak stocks, and these stocks started collapsing right and left. And eventually they said, "Look, if you don't do something big, we're going to have a Great Depression." Which is a seminal moment, because you basically say, "Do I trust my advisors and do something about it, or do I adhere to my principle, which is let the market sort it out?" I couldn't think of anything worse than bailing out Wall Street. But these guys were saying, "You've got to bail out Wall Street or we're going to have a depression." So I listened to Paulson and Bernanke and spent your money to bail out the guys who created the instruments in the first place, which is an absolute political disaster.

You wonder why populism is on the rise. It starts with taking taxpayers' money and giving it to the powerful. It really irritated a lot of Americans, and they haven't gotten over it yet. That's just part of it; there's a lot of other reasons why. But we've had candidates say, "You're mad, I'm going to make you madder." As opposed to, "You're mad, I have some solutions to make you less mad." We're kind of in the madder stage, where people are exploiting the anger as opposed to dealing with it like leaders should.

DR: The legislation proposed at the time, known as TARP (Troubled Asset Relief Program), failed in the House on the first vote.

GWB: Yes, then the market corrected by losing $1.4 trillion in value—kind of the ultimate focus group. We ran TARP back up on Capitol Hill, and it passed. But the interesting thing is after it passed, Paulson said, "What we proposed and passed is not going work." I said, "You've got to be kidding me." He said, "It's not going work. We don't have enough time, because we weren't sure how to auction off troubled assets." And that's when he decided to dole out the money to companies like Goldman Sachs, where Paulson used to work. But you know what? It worked. We didn't have a Great Depression. The problem is, you can't prove a negative. Anyway, it was a tough moment.

DR: During your presidency, you decided to invade Iraq because it had weapons of mass destruction, we believed.

GWB: Actually, Saddam Hussein made that decision.

DR: What do you mean?

GWB: Well, I went to the UN and said, "Disclose, disarm, or face serious consequences," and he refused to disclose, which led the world to believe he wouldn't disarm—otherwise, why not disclose? It was his choice to make, and he made a fateful choice.

DR: In hindsight, if you had known there were no weapons of mass destruction, would you have still invaded?

GWB: Probably not, but you don't get the luxury of that when you're president. You've got to make the decisions that you have at hand. And remember—I don't want to sound defensive, but I will—Congress overwhelmingly gave me the authority to take any measures necessary. That includes the current president (Joe Biden), Hillary Clinton, John Kerry—on and on with these fiery speeches from the Senate floor. That's not why I did what I did. I'm just telling you there was a major consensus that Saddam Hussein had to go since he would not disclose whether or not he had weapons of mass destruction. And I can't think of anything worse than for a president to say "Disclose" and not mean it. It sends signals to the enemy that we're weak and it sends signals to our allies that you can't trust America. I was the kind of guy who, when I said something, I meant it.

DR: During your administration, you started the President's Emergency Plan for AIDS Relief (PEPFAR), which was designed to eliminate AIDS, to the extent possible, in Africa and other parts of the emerging world. Is that one of your proudest accomplishments?

GWB: It's a big accomplishment. My proudest accomplishment is that I didn't lie, cheat, or steal, and my kids love me. The American people ought to be proud of this, but nobody has any clue what I'm talking about when I say PEPFAR—they think it's deodorant or something. (Laughter.) I told the American people that a principle I believe in is that all life is precious and we're all God's children. And Condoleezza Rice tells me there's a pandemic destroying an entire generation of people on the continent of Africa.

I also believe that to whom much is given, much is required. I know this has a little religious connotation to it, but I happen to think it's important. I believe we're a blessed nation, and to sit down and do nothing when a pandemic was destroying an entire generation of people was unconscionable in my mind.

So we put together a business plan with clear goals, aligned authority and responsibility, and meaningful objectives, and we went after it. And 25 million people are alive now who would have died, thanks to the generosity of the American people. The question is: Is this in our national interest? I think a lot of Americans would say, "Not really," in this day and age. Or "Who cares about African women and children? Let somebody else worry about it."

I think it is in our interest. I think it's what great nations do. And the problem is we can't now get the reauthorization through Congress. It's so divided and so bitter that they can't pass a reauthorization on a government program that clearly works. Most government programs don't work. This one measurably works: 25 million people living who would have died. The American people ought to be very proud of that.

DR: When you were president, the first time you met Vladimir Putin, you said you looked into his eyes and you saw his soul. What did you mean?

GWB: Do you want to know why I said that? It was in Slovenia. He was nervous, and I was trying to befriend the guy. He just had gotten into office and so had I, and he wanted to talk about Soviet-era debt saddling the Russian Federation. I wasn't interested in that. I was interested in getting to know the guy.

Well, the CIA had prepared a brief that said his mother had given him a cross that she had had blessed in Jerusalem, and when the dacha where he hung the cross burnt down, all he wanted was the cross. So I said, "Is it true your mother gave you a cross she had blessed in Jerusalem?" And his whole countenance changed. Then I asked him about his daughters, and then I asked him about his exercise regime.

Anyway, we got to know each other and we agreed to work on missile reduction. You probably don't know this, but thanks to Putin and me, we reduced the number of nuclear warheads by 1,700 per nation, and we didn't need a treaty; we didn't need a bunch of experts. We just did it.

And so a reporter asked me, "Do you trust Putin?" at a press conference in Slovenia. And I started running through the possible answers. *No*—that's no good. *Trust but verify*—that would be plagiarism. (Laughter.) And so I said, "Yes," hoping the reporter move on, but he didn't. "Why?" And that's when I said, "I looked in his eyes and saw his soul." It was such a befuddling answer that they moved on. But later I looked in his eyes and saw a different soul after eight years in power. This guy had changed.

I have a great Putin story for you. I introduced Putin to Barney, my little Scottish terrier, and Putin dissed him. This is the stage where Putin looked like he was in *Lethal Force 2*; he had the black body shirt on. (Laughter.) It kind of hurt my feelings, but I didn't let him know. So a year later we're at his dacha in Moscow. This is before he had discarded his wife of many years, Lyudmilla, for a water gymnast who was like 30 years younger than he is. (Laughter.) And he said, "Would you like to meet my dog?" I said yes. I'd forgotten about the Barney diss. And out bounds this huge Russian hound, loping across the birch-lined yard, and Putin looked at me and said "Bigger, stronger, and faster than Barney." (Laughter.)

I told that to Canadian prime minister Jonathan Harper. You may think he's kind of a droll guy, but he's not. He said, "At least he only showed you his dog." (Laughter.) At any rate, the guy's got a huge chip on his shoulder. "My dog's bigger than your dog"—please.

And so you've got to ask why. The demise of the Soviet Union, in Putin's mind, diminished Russia in the eyes of history. What you're watching is him trying to reinstate Russian glory—not Stalinist glory but Russian glory. And he's lost his balance. The guy needs to be stopped, and the United States needs to hang with Zelenskyy no matter how tough it gets, because if we can't support a young democracy under attack by an autocrat, then we have a problem as a nation knowing what we're all about.

DR: Are you surprised that some people in the Republican Party think that we should reduce our overseas commitments?

GWB: I'm disappointed. I'm not surprised. The Republican Party is a little different than when I was in office. We used to be the party of freedom and working with allies to shape the world.

DR: The Republican Party has moved further to the right, some people would say.

GWB: I'm not sure. It's moved. But I think it's moved isolationist and protectionist and nativist, which is different from left and right. It's definitely moved away from conservative economic orthodoxy when you run up deficits and debts the way we've been doing as if there's no tomorrow. Not just this administration but the administration prior. There is no concern about the future when it comes to money, no desire to reform Social Security or Medicare. To me that is not fiscally sound policy.

DR: When you're president, do you get a lot of people coming to the Oval Office telling you how great you are, or do you get people who are complaining a lot?

GWB: I didn't have sycophants. Anybody who knows the people in my administration would know that they'd walk in and say, "You're not so great." And that's what you want. You want people to give you their honest advice, and once you make up your mind, if they can't accept it, they can go find a job elsewhere. But there wasn't a lot of that.

DR: Virtually nobody has ever had the chance to say to both parents, "I just got elected president of the United States." Your father came into the Oval Office the first time you were there. What was that like?

GWB: Andy Card, my friend and chief of staff, went upstairs to the residence and got my dad when I had gone to the Oval Office. I was sitting there just getting a sense of what it was like to be in the Oval Office as a newly sworn-in president, and there's a shadow outside the door. I look up and see my dad and say, "Come on in, Mr. President." He said, "Thank you, Mr. President." It was a sweet moment.

You knew him well. George H. W. Bush was a remarkable guy. First of all, he was a fabulous father. He was a busy man all his life, but he made it abundantly clear that we were his priority. And he was a kind man. Watching him get beat by Bill Clinton, who's now my buddy, was really painful. But he handled it with such grace. It was an unbelievable lesson.

I'm the only president whose dad was alive during his entire presidency. And he just happened to be president eight years prior, which made it unbelievably interesting from this aspect: "Son, I know what you're going through. I'm proud of you and I love you." And those words—I can't tell you how important it is in the midst of the drama of the presidency to have a father say, "I'm proud of you and I love you," having gone through the exact kind of things I was going through. I'm really fortunate to have had him as a father. And my mother—she was a piece of work. (Laughter.) You knew my mother.

DR: She was tough. Remember when you were running in a marathon?

GWB: Oh yes. So after Dad got beat, I decided I was going to take out my frustrations by running the Houston Marathon. Mile 20 was by the church they go to. It was a Sunday, and out come the parishioners. Dad comes out: "There's my boy!" And Mother yells out, "There's three fat women ahead of you!" (Laughter.)

DR: When you were president of the United States, you went to Camp David sometimes. Most people haven't seen it. What is it like? Why do people like it so much?

GWB: I liked it because one, it's a 20-minute helicopter ride away. Two, it's a Marine base and a Navy CB base, but Marines really man it for the president, and it's got all kinds of accommodations. It's got gyms and a movie theater. I love exercise; they built mountain-biking trails, and I used to ride with the Marines. It's rustic but comfortable. I used it a lot to court foreign leaders. I used the ranch as well as Camp David. It's a good chance to get to know people and find common ground on issues.

DR: When you look back on your presidency, what would you say you're most proud of having accomplished during your eight years in office?

GWB: Well, I told you, my girls love me—and that was in doubt for a while when I decided to run.

DR: They didn't want you to run?

GWB: No. Jenna, the TV star, said, "You're not as cool as you think you are." (Laughter.) And I said, "I know." She said, "You're going to lose." I said, "I'm still going to run." She said, "Fine, run and ruin our lives." I don't know if you've ever dealt with teenage girls.

DR: And now they're happy you were president, right?

GWB: They learned to get comfortable with Camp David, for example. (Laughter.) Anyway, our family came out strong. Laura was a great First Lady, and she was unbelievably comforting and nurturing. It was a wonderful family experience.

I'm proud of the fact that I put together a team that stayed intact, a team of very smart, very capable people who served not me or the Republican Party but served our country, and they did a noble job of serving.

DR: When you were running for president, you talked about your Christian faith in a way that many candidates hadn't done before. Was that always part of your life?

GWB: No, it wasn't. It helped me quit drinking. I was drinking too much, and I realized I was more in love with alcohol than I was with my wife and kids. And so I quit with a little help from religion—a lot of help from religion. It keeps you humble and it gives you perspective.

One of the problems with power is you lose sight of reality. You think you're "it," and religion helps keep balance in life. I'm often asked about leadership traits. We ought to look for humility as the number one trait. You have to know what you don't know, surround yourself with people who know what you don't know, and listen to them. Because power is corrupting. I've seen it firsthand: "I'm powerful, therefore I'm all-knowing." That's very dangerous for those who have positions of responsibility.

DR: When U.S. presidents are out of office, they usually build a library or a presidential center. What does your presidential center do?

GWB: Our presidential center works on domestic and international issues. We fight off isolationism. We're big free traders in our hemisphere. We believe it is necessary to have free trade between Canada, Mexico, and the United States in order to compete globally with a place like China. We're advocates for immigration reform and do pretty good work in terms of influencing Congress. Overseas we're continuing the PEPFAR legacy with work on cervical cancer in Africa. We've got a presidential leadership program with the Clinton Library, the Bush 41 Library, and the LBJ Library, where we take young leaders, 35- to 45-year-olds, and bring them down to the respective libraries and give them leadership lessons on presidential decision making. It has been unbelievably successful. We do the same thing with veterans and people running veterans programs. We're engaged, active, and making a difference.

DR: In a typical week for you, are you at the Bush Library? Are you out traveling and making a speech or two?

GWB: A fair bit. I like doing this. I don't like going to speak at Yale. But I like doing this because my mission is to say that better days are coming. There's a despondency in the country, and it's disturbing. People can't see beyond the moment. I'm not saying I'm clairvoyant, but I've studied enough American history to know that better days are coming. Most Americans are sick and tired of the noise.

Let me give you an example. One of the beautiful things about our system is the institutions that keep the ship of state afloat. On January 6th, an abysmal moment in American history, our institutions came under serious assault. The legislative body ended up meeting and ratifying the election; courts all around the country said the elections were fair; and I watched a peaceful transfer of power shortly thereafter. So the institutions got rocked, but they came out strong, and that's essential for the American people to understand. Because once you have institutional stability, like we do, democracy eventually cures itself.

As long as people take their roles seriously as voters, we're going to be just fine. It may not happen instantly, but people are sick and tired of the noise, the recrimination, the finger-pointing, the ugliness, the diminution; they want better. They want somebody to elevate our sights, and it'll happen. It'll happen.

19

PETER BAKER
on Barack Obama

(b. 1961; president from 2009 to 2017)

I t is tempting to wonder just what about the U.S. government, over the past two hundred and forty-plus years, would have most surprised the Founding Fathers as they observed their creation from a well-deserved perch in heaven. That the government survived this long? Possibly. Jefferson and others had thought the government might survive just a few decades at best. Or that there was a Civil War over slavery? Probably not. That actually had been predicted by many from the country's early days. Or that the U.S. became the largest economy and military power in the world? Certainly, few would have predicted in 1787 the extent of the U.S.'s power by the second half of the twentieth century. But many in our early days thought that the U.S., with its landmass and natural resources and growing population, would no doubt emerge a quite important nation.

My own answer to the biggest-surprise question is that an African American man was actually twice elected the president of the United States and left the office after eight years with his reputation intact (and many might say greatly enhanced), and that he produced one of the most transformative pieces of social legislation—the Affordable Care Act— the country had ever seen, something to potentially rival other landmark pieces of social legislation such as Social Security and Medicare.

The reason why the Founding Fathers would have been so surprised is that they gave the country a government that allowed, indeed facilitated, slavery for humans imported from Africa for that purpose. How, they might wonder, could any such person or descendant rise to the nation's highest office?

To be sure, following the Civil War, many freed slaves were elected to important federal and state government positions. But when Southern whites regained control of their state governments in the late 1800s and Jim Crow laws were imposed, and the Ku Klux Klan sprung up, there were few Blacks being elected to office, and this was true well into the twentieth century. In 1950, Congress had two Black members, and there were no Black senators or governors. Fifty years later, decades after the civil rights legislation of the 1960s, Blacks were increasingly getting elected to important government jobs. By 2000, there were 39 Blacks in the House, but only four Blacks have ever been elected to the Senate, and only two Blacks have even been elected governor (not counting Reconstruction elections). All of these are small numbers compared to the Black proportion of the population, but these numbers are still a vast improvement over the prior two centuries.

But a Black president? Not even in 2000 would such a prospect be seen as likely any time soon. Civil rights leader Jesse Jackson had made serious efforts to compete in the Democratic primaries in 1984 and 1988, but he was seen largely as a candidate with modest appeal outside the Black community, and even he really did not expect to get the Democratic Party nomination in those years—though he did want to advance issues of interest to Blacks by highlighting those issues to others in the Democratic Party.

And well into the early part of the twenty-first century, the prospect of a Black person becoming president of the United States was just not seen by almost everyone in the political world as realistic in their lifetimes. The conventional wisdom was that a woman (or even someone who was Jewish) would be likely to be elected before an African American.

Then, in 2004, a state senator from Illinois, Barack Hussein Obama II, electrified the Democratic Convention (and a nationwide television audience) with his keynote address. He was elected later that year to the U.S. Senate, just the second Black man to serve in the Senate since Reconstruction.

The expectations were high for Senator Obama, but probably few (including Senator Obama himself) imagined that during his first term, he would not only run a serious presidential primary campaign but beat the favored Senator Hillary Clinton and then go on to a relatively easy victory in the 2008 presidential election against the Vietnam War hero and longtime U.S. senator John McCain. But that is exactly what happened, to the surprise of almost everyone in the political world (and maybe everywhere else).

And to show that his initial presidential election was not a fluke, President Obama was handily reelected against the Republican nominee in 2012, former Massachusetts governor and future senator from Utah Mitt Romney.

Barack Obama did not emerge from the traditional civil rights movement, which had been an early home to many African American political leaders in the twentieth century. Still, Obama—the son of a white Kansas woman and a Black Kenyan man—had been a community organizer in Chicago before law school and was committed to a career in social justice of some type. But that goal was sidelined a bit when he came to some national attention after having been elected the first Black president of the *Harvard Law Review*.

That position enabled Barack Obama to pursue just about any avenue he wanted, and he chose initially a dual-track career—practicing law at a small Chicago civil justice law firm and teaching at the University of Chicago Law School. Eventually he ran for the state legislature in Illinois, was elected, and was settling into the career of a state legislator when an opportunity came to run for an open U.S. Senate seat. While that was thought by many to be an unattainable goal for a relatively unknown Black legislator with a funny-sounding name, Barack Obama did manage to get elected, helped in part by his main Democratic and Republican opponents having scandals which forced them from the race.

In the Senate, Barack Obama made a good impression on his colleagues, but he was bored with the slow pace of Senate work, and took a leap into the presidential race of 2008—against the odds, for Hillary Clinton was seen as the presumptive Democratic nominee (in the view of most political observers).

But the odds are often defied in politics, and the result was an election that the Founding Fathers almost certainly could never have foreseen.

I did come to know President Obama a bit while he served, as a result of some Kennedy Center, and other, social interactions. And those direct contacts showed me up close why those who knew him well had such a high regard for him—very smart, quite focused and disciplined, well aware of his place in history (and the great expectations for him), and a gifted speaker and writer—perhaps the best presidential writer since Woodrow Wilson.

Because President Obama left office at 55, he recognized that he likely has a long career as a former president ahead of him, and has focused much of his postpresidential years on creating the Obama Presidential Center in Chicago to carry forward his legacy and passions. When it opens in late 2025, it will be the largest (and most expensive) of all the presidential centers. (There is no library, for all papers are now digitized and there is no longer a need to store presidential papers in a physical site outside Washington.)

Peter Baker covered the Obama White House for the *New York Times* and wrote a book about President Obama, titled *Obama: The Call of History*. I interviewed him on February 25, 2024.

* * * *

DAVID M. RUBENSTEIN (DR): What prompted you to want to write a book about Barack Obama? Did you cover him at the White House when he was president?

PETER BAKER (PB:): I did. I covered all eight years. Obama was a fascinating character, maybe one of the most fascinating presidents we've had in modern times. Since then, events have proven to be even more extraordinary. But he was a singular figure in history. He had enormous challenges as a president. He was the third president I covered. I had written books about the other two, but I found Obama particularly gripping as an individual in terms of shaping our history.

DR: What is the main message in your book about President Obama?

PB: I wanted to convey that it was complicated. People tend to oversimplify these historical figures. In Obama's case, it was either he was the great hero of the left or he was the great villain of the right. But in fact, he was far more complex than people understood. When we elected him, we as a people didn't really know who he was because he hadn't had much time on the national stage. A lot of people imputed to him their idea of who he was. He once told us at the *New York Times* that he was a Rorschach test, people saw in him what they wanted to see. In some cases, they saw him as the great liberal champion of activist government, a new-era version of LBJ. Other people saw him as a bridge builder, somebody who would be bipartisan, work across the aisle. In fact, he was always much more multifaceted than any of those simplistic constructions.

DR: When history is written 10 or 20 years from now, do you think Barack Obama will be remembered most for being the first African American elected to the presidency or for things that he accomplished in office?

PB: The first line in his obituary is always going to be that he was the first African American president. Because of our history, which is marked by slavery, and Jim Crow, and racism, that by itself is just too enormous a moment not to be the focus of that obituary. That doesn't mean he didn't also achieve important things. He had to deal with a climactic moment with the economy on the edge of a worldwide meltdown—not just a recession, but a depression. He had a lot of major events take place, including the killing of Osama bin Laden and the rise of the Tea Party movement. Toward the end of his presidency there was the disappointment that settled in that we didn't solve our race issues, even though he had been elected twice; and the rise of Donald Trump reminded us that the country had not suddenly moved into this Kumbaya era that some people imagined or hoped for when Obama was first elected.

DR: Of all of his legislative accomplishments, is anything even close to the Affordable Care Act? Why did he push that so early in his administration when he campaigned on so many other issues, at least in the first campaign?

PB: As a legislative matter it's clearly his most important legacy. He tried to accomplish something that presidents going back more than a century, all the way back to Teddy Roosevelt, had talked about and tried to get, and he's the only one who came close to getting there. That stands out. I think he decided to go for that because he recognized that in a presidency, your moment of opportunity fades awfully quickly. You have a chance at the very beginning when you have momentum, you have the imprimatur of the electorate, you have relatively high approval ratings, maybe the highest you're going to get. That's your moment of maximum impact on Congress to wield your will and to get something big done. If he had waited, for instance, until the second or third year—some people thought maybe he should—if he had tried a more incremental approach, I think his calculation was that it wouldn't get done. There's reason to think that perspective is true.

I think he also took the measure of other issues, like immigration or climate change, and decided that health care came first, in part, because it had such a wide effect on so many Americans, especially at time of great economic dislocation, and that he could affect more of the economy. It was more the idea of rebuilding a different kind of economy after the upheaval of the financial crash, not just simply restoring the old version. This would be the way he could have that maximum impact.

DR: Internationally, do you think Obama will be best remembered for having captured and killed Osama bin Laden and ending the war in Iraq? Are there any international accomplishments more significant than those?

PB: Those are up there. Those are the ones he came to office promising to do and that he achieved. The killing of bin Laden especially is a pretty clean accomplishment. Nobody can really question that, nobody disagrees with that. On the withdrawal from Iraq, I think most people were happy he did that; but there's obviously the follow-up, which is that he had to go back into Iraq to some extent because of the rise of ISIS. It wasn't as clean as he might have liked, and he never quite got out of Afghanistan, which he wanted to do by the end of his term as well. People will remember the killing of bin Laden. His poll numbers went way back up again, although just temporarily. It stands out because it's such a moment of catharsis for a country ten years out from 9/11.

DR: From almost the moment Obama was elected president, it seemed as if the Republicans in Congress said, "Anything you propose we're going to be against. We don't really care about bipartisanship." Do you think some of that was racism, or they just wanted to block anything any Democratic president would do?

PB: You can't rule out racism as at least a factor for some of the opposition to him, but I think it would be wrong to say that's the entirety of it. We're in a more polarized moment, a moment where the incentive structure of politics has changed. You are not rewarded for bipartisanship anymore. At least that's the perception. A lot of people in both parties have taken the lesson from the last decade that you risk political trouble by being bipartisan. If you make a deal with the other side, you're accused of compromising values or principles or of being soft, whether conservative or liberal. So you don't have the motivation to move to the middle as much as you might have once had. Obama tried at first to make bipartisan deals; some of his own staff thought he tried too much and for too long, while some Republicans thought he didn't make a genuine effort. Either way, it didn't work. Of course, when you have the first Black president, you can't rule out race as a factor with some people, but there was a larger change in society happening at the same time that we've seen play out with the two presidents who followed.

DR: Obama seemed to be perpetually calm and a bit reserved. Was he that way in private as well? What got him excited and angry?

PB: He's a very reserved guy. He is the antithesis of the common view of what a politician is like. He's not a backslapper and a baby kisser. It's just not his nature. He was kind of an introvert, much like Jimmy Carter in some ways. He wasn't somebody who got energy from other people. With Bill Clinton, you put him in a room with other people and he came out of it all charged up. With Obama, his aides knew to give him a little space after an event in the East Room, for instance, to make sure that there was at least five minutes he could have before his next event, so he could recharge his batteries. He was reserved even with his staff. They found him hard to read at times.

But he did get upset about things, or angry or worked up. I remember the time we were in the briefing room and he came in after the shootings up at Sandy Hook Elementary School in Connecticut. He was clearly distraught at a very human moment. He had tears on his face, he could hardly speak, he had to pause for, like, nine, ten, fifteen seconds, because he couldn't get out the words. He was thinking about what happened there as a father. We think of him as a Mr. Spock–like figure because he is reserved and controlled, but there are moments during his presidency when you see the human side.

DR: Do you admire Obama more or less than when you started covering him?

PB: Admiration is not my job as a journalist. I hope I understand him a little bit better. I think he had complicated motives for things. He wanted to do what he thought was the right thing to make the country better, but he came to disdain Washington, he came to disdain the political process, and maybe that hurt his ability to get some things done. What you learn from writing a book about him is that he is different from a lot of other presidents. He wanted to be president, obviously, but it didn't seem like something that was a life ambition for him. He did it and then when he was done, he was done with it. He was ready to move on.

DR: As somebody who covered him and knows him reasonably well, what would you say were his greatest strengths and weaknesses as a chief executive?

PB: His strengths include his ability to inspire millions of people with a powerful speech. His oratory is clearly among the best of our lifetime. You have to put him up there with John F. Kennedy and Ronald Reagan and Martin Luther King Jr. as somebody who can move large numbers of people through the spoken word. You can't underestimate the importance of that in presidential leadership. His other strengths would be that he had a certain calmness—a Zen-like quality is what his staff would say. He didn't get too flustered by the ups and downs of everyday politics. He was logical. He was analytical. He examined things intellectually and carefully, mixing politics as well as policy.

But as always, your strengths can also be your weaknesses. What his staff would tell you is that he examined things sometimes too much. There was no problem that another meeting couldn't be scheduled to address. At times, they would have loved him to just make a decision and move on, but he wanted to keep thinking about things. Sometimes he did what George W. Bush didn't do, or what Obama felt like Bush didn't do, and try to think through the second, third, fourth order of implications of a decision: If this, then that, what happens then? You can do that to the point that you paralyze yourself with inaction. You can talk yourself out of doing something by asking all the things that can go wrong. I think a lot of people around him felt, at times, that he wrapped himself up too much in thinking about the consequences.

DR: If you could ask him one question, after everything that's happened since he left office, what would you like to ask?

PB: I would like to ask him about what role, if any, he thinks his presidency played in the rise of Donald Trump. The country moved so jarringly in the opposite direction by electing a guy after him who was different on every level, not just ideologically and personally, but who literally had questioned Obama's very birth, had profited off of racial animosity as a political tool. I would like to explore Obama's own thoughts about what his presidency meant in that regard, or was that always going to be the natural backlash to the eight years he spent in office?

DR: Let's talk for a moment about his early years. Who really raised Obama, his mother or his grandparents? Did he ever meet his father more than one time?

PB: It sounds like his grandparents were more instrumental in raising him. He spent some time with his mother, particularly in Indonesia, but she then sent him back to Hawaii, where he spent a lot of his childhood with his grandparents. From the stories that came out over the years, his father left home when Barack was about a year old to go to Harvard, and then returned to Kenya when Barack was three years old. After that, the father only returned once. Obama saw him during this period of a few weeks, maybe a month, and that was the only time. It weighed on him. That's why he ends up traveling to Kenya as a young man and meeting his family there after his father died, and writing the book that he writes, which is so evocative and lyrical. He didn't know his father, and he was not his father's son. His father had very little to do with shaping who he became except for the idea of him.

DR: Let me tell you one Obama story. Once, at the Kennedy Center Honors, we honored Dave Brubeck. Obama spoke to the honorees at the White House. He was supposed to read scripted remarks about Brubeck, but he kind of wandered away from those, and he said, "I only met my father once, and when my father came to visit me in Hawaii he said, 'I'm not going to be around your life very much, but I want you to learn something about music and jazz in particular, so tonight I'm going to take you to see Dave Brubeck.' Tonight, for the first time, I'm getting a chance to meet this man who my father thought was so important, and who I first saw and heard when I was a boy, in the only concert I ever attended with my father." It was pretty emotional. I thought it was well done.

PB: If you only know your father for basically a few weeks of your life, everything that happened during those few weeks would stand out and be especially important, right?

DR: Was Obama a particularly good student or athlete? Did people say when he was a young boy, "You're destined to be president of the United States"?

PB: It doesn't sound like it, no. Of course, a lot of people would have a hard time imagining in that era a Black man becoming president of United States. He was, when he wanted to be, a good student. He became the president of the *Harvard Law Review*. That became his first flash of national fame. He gets in the *New York Times* for becoming the first Black president of the law review at Harvard, and it really begins to mark his emergence as a public figure. Until then, I don't think he was a standout student. In high school, by his own account, he goofed off with his friends, even did a few recreational things that he wouldn't encourage his children to do. He did not get into Columbia right away. He had to transfer there; but then he went to Harvard for law school, and so he did better as he got older, as a lot of people do.

DR: He initially went to Occidental College, which is a very good school, but not maybe the school he originally wanted to go to, before transferring to Columbia. At either Occidental or Columbia, is there any evidence that he was a great or average student?

PB: I don't remember anything that made him stand out one way or the other, and as I recall, they never released the grades. He strikes you as somebody who would do the homework, a diligent kind of guy, but I don't know that he stood out for his academic brilliance, at least until Harvard Law, when he graduated magna cum laude.

DR: He went to Harvard and became the first African American to be the president of the *Harvard Law Review*. When he graduated, rather than go get a Supreme Court clerkship or something like that, he returned to Chicago to practice law at a civil rights–oriented law firm, a relatively small firm. Was he seen then as a potential political figure because he'd been the president of the *Harvard Law Review*?

PB: People at that time assumed that if you were a young, successful Black lawyer, you would go into civil rights law. I think he did that because that's what you were expected to do. He found that he really wasn't into practicing law that much. The law just didn't engage him in the same way that other things did. He believes he can make more of a difference than just working for some big institutional corporate law firm.

DR: He did get elected to the state legislature. Then he decided to run against Bobby Rush, the incumbent African American congressman from his district, and he lost two-to-one. Why did he decide to take on an incumbent congressman and, after losing, thought he had a chance to get elected to the Senate the next time an election was held?

PB: He was a man in a hurry. He was looking for the next opportunity, and the congressional seat where he lived was occupied. He decided to do something about it and run against the incumbent. He didn't understand that Rush had a real connection to the people in the district. It was a moment of hubris for a young politician. For a lot of presidents, an early defeat becomes important later in life. You learn from defeat as much as you do from victory. I think he learned a little bit there. But you're right, it is not like he then went back to his state Senate seat and decided to stick it out there for a while. He aims even higher. He sees an open U.S. Senate seat in a mostly Democratic state, and he ends up being very lucky. He had a series of opponents who end up sort of self-destructing.

DR: His biggest Democratic opponent and the Republican in the general election both had sex scandals. As a result Obama won. But he became nationally known earlier that year, 2004, when he spoke at the Democratic National Convention. He gave a speech that got a lot more attention than John Kerry's speech. What was so great about it?

PB: It was an accumulation of things he had been saying before, but outside of Illinois, nobody would have heard it. It was an electrifying moment. He gave voice to this idea of a greater America and personified it. He personified it both by his look—he was an African American who was up there and incredibly impressive—and by the words that he chose, the words we all remember: this appeal to American unity, the idea that there's not a red America or a blue America but a United States of America. He says that people in blue states worship an awesome God too just as people in red states also have gay friends. He's trying to get at this idea that we emphasize differences too much, and that we are one people. It is so appealing that it crosses boundaries. It's not just the Democrats who are thrilled. A lot of Republicans are impressed by him. That doesn't mean they're going to vote for him, necessarily, but they find him very impressive. Suddenly this guy, who at that point was a state senator, who hadn't even been elected to the United States Senate yet, is a national figure overnight.

DR: So many times in life people want something and when they get it, they're not sure why they wanted it. When he's elected to the Senate, did he enjoy being a senator?

PB: Not really, no. First of all, the United States Senate was different than the Illinois State Senate. In the state senate he was able to work with Republicans and get some stuff done. He felt some satisfaction from that. He discovered that the United States Senate wasn't the same way. He was naïve, perhaps, about how much impact you could have as a senator. He didn't try it for very long, only for about two years, until he begins running for president of the United States. That's a pretty full-time job.

DR: Did people think it was presumptuous for a senator of only two years to run for president?

PB: Hillary Clinton thought so, and so did many others; they thought it was preposterous for a guy who hadn't gotten anything done yet to run for president. He hadn't passed a major piece of legislation. He hadn't done anything on a national stage. Obama's a fairly self-aware guy. He himself thought it was presumptuous at first to even talk about it. Then he heard from people like Tom Daschle, the former Senate Democratic leader, who said to him, "In politics, when you have a moment like this, you just have to seize it, because you can't assume it's going to be there again in four years. The country is hungry for a person like you." He was encouraged by people like Daschle, Harry Reid, and eventually Ted Kennedy, some of these old bulls, who would normally be the kind of people who say, "Wait in line." Instead they said, "Jump the line, get up there, because you're something different and this moment is different. Don't pass up this opportunity." And he agreed to do it.

DR: Did he think "I'll put my toe in the water, get some experience, then run again in four years"? Or he really thought he had a chance to get the nomination and get elected?

PB: He is a supremely confident guy, to the point where when I asked one of his top people what's his biggest weakness, the answer was, "Cockiness." I think Obama believed strongly that he could do it. He had that sort of confidence bordering on cockiness throughout that primary process, even though you would think that Hillary Clinton was the obvious front-runner. He believed all along that he could do it.

DR: Iowa is a reasonably white state, and yet Obama won the caucuses there. How? And then how did Hillary Clinton manage to come back against him in New Hampshire?

PB: The Clintons didn't have a history in Iowa. Bill Clinton didn't compete there in 1992, because Tom Harkin was running against him. Harkin was the Iowa senator, so Bill Clinton skipped that. Second, Obama was in the next-door state, and had a bit of a connection as a result. More importantly, he just inspired Democrats there who were looking for change. Even though it's a pretty homogeneous white electorate, they found him so compelling. He managed to outmaneuver Hillary Clinton partly on the war, because Democrats were very upset about the Iraq War at that time. Obama had been against it, and Hillary Clinton voted for it. She couldn't give a good answer as to where she was at that moment, at least not an answer that was persuasive to a lot of people. I think that he did a better job of organizing. There was a certain overconfidence on the part of the Clintons that they were going to march to the nomination.

It swings back in New Hampshire, as politics often does. There's a natural tendency for New Hampshire to say, "We're not obligated to do what Iowa did." And the Clintons did have a history in New Hampshire, with a lot of people there from the 1992 race, when Bill Clinton had come in second but spun it as a comeback win given the scandals he was weathering at the time. Likewise, the Clintons managed to turn New Hampshire into a comeback win for Hillary Clinton.

DR: When Obama gets the nomination against Hillary Clinton, does he worry about losing the general election to John McCain, or did he feel fairly confident about winning?

PB: He was pretty confident from the beginning that he had a good shot. He understood the forces at work against being elected the first Black president. That wasn't something to take lightly. But the issues of the day were working in his favor: first, because of the Iraq War, which was very unpopular at the time, and McCain was as strong a supporter of the war as existed; and second, because of the economic collapse under President Bush, especially in the fall, when McCain seemed out of touch and unable to find a good response. There were one or two weeks where Obama and his team worried maybe they weren't going to win, but for the most part, they felt optimistic throughout the race.

DR: Do you think there was any overt racism in the general election? The fact that we might have an African American president, do you think that was a big factor?

PB: It's a good question. Obama has said to people that, in some ways, he feels like whatever benefit he got by being African American outweighed whatever cost there was as a matter of politics. In other words, Obama felt that he gained a lot of support from people who were excited about the idea of a Black president. It's hard to say. There were certain places he didn't campaign much and obviously some people would never vote for a person of color. But the idea of a historic breakthrough, the idea that the country could kind of purge its past, was appealing not just to people of color but to a lot of white voters, who saw him as a vehicle for that.

DR: Who came up with the idea after the election of offering the secretary of state position to his opponent, Hillary Clinton? Did he offer it the way John Kennedy offered the vice presidency to Lyndon Johnson, thinking it would be turned down?

PB: I think it was all him. His staff was a little nervous about that. They had just spent all these months competing against the Clinton people, convincing themselves as well as voters that the Clintons were not to be trusted with power anymore. Then Obama comes around and says, "No, let's give it to her." It's part of his ruthless, unsentimental logic. He decided that she had credibility on the world stage from her time as a senator and First Lady that he didn't have, and that he could use that. She would be the person who would go out to the world and hold people's hands while he made the decisions in the White House. It wasn't like he was handing over foreign policy to her. But I think he thought, in a cold, calculated way, that she could be useful to him, and he wasn't going to let their competition stand in the way of that.

DR: When he became president, we were in the middle of the Great Recession. How did Obama, who didn't have a big economics background, address that? Did he delegate it to people, or was he intimately involved in the solutions that were developed?

PB: He was intimately involved. Another indication of the way he governed was that he kept some of the key people who had been working on this under George W. Bush—even though he had just run against Bush, in effect, by saying it was time to send the Bush people home. He kept Tim Geithner, who led the New York branch of the Federal Reserve, and made him Treasury secretary. He worked closely with Ben Bernanke at the Federal Reserve. He consulted a lot with Hank Paulson, Bush's Treasury secretary. He had a lot of respect for Paulson, and vice versa. He brought in people like Larry Summers, who had been a Clinton Treasury secretary, not an Obama person, to help guide him as well. He was willing to reach out to people outside of his circle, looking for any advice he could get on how to handle that crisis.

DR: How did he organize his White House staff? Was he the kind of president who wanted to be isolated from the staff or he wanted people to come to see him all the time?

PB: He believed in a very disciplined way of running a White House. He did not want the sort of free-for-all jam sessions that were the Bill Clinton way of doing things. He wanted to have a meeting, he wanted that meeting to begin at a certain time and end at certain time. He wanted to hear from a lot of people, including those who may not agree with his view. In fact, he made a point at meetings of calling on people who weren't speaking up, because he assumed they had something to say that he didn't want to hear. He wanted to hear from the people on the back benches who were keeping quiet. He was not locked in to any particular ideology. He was very pragmatic, which may have disappointed some of his liberal supporters. Why would you pick Rahm Emanuel to be your chief of staff if your whole concept is "I'm an outsider," given that Rahm was the ultimate insider? You say, "I'm not going to be naïve about this. If you want to get Washington to do things, you have to get somebody who understands Washington, and Rahm is a guy who can do that." Obama wasn't going to let what he said in the campaign stop him from doing what he thought in the end was the right way to go.

DR: Many presidents fall in love with foreign policy, because you get criticized a little less by foreign leaders than you do by congressional leaders. Did Obama fall in love with foreign policy and want to make it his signature issue?

PB: I never got the sense that he really loved foreign policy. He was more driven by or interested in domestic policy. That became more frustrating for him after the first two years when the Republicans took the House with a decisive midterm election victory, which Obama called a "shellacking." His domestic legislative agenda therefore essentially died. He did then focus a bit more on foreign policy, where he could make a difference, and there were things he was really proud of. He was proud of, in his view, showing that diplomacy can work again, with the Paris Climate Accord, the Iran nuclear agreement, the opening to Cuba, the Trans-Pacific Partnership, which was the Asian trade deal that ultimately didn't go through. He saw them as examples of how, on the international stage, a practical person willing to negotiate could make a difference, whereas in Washington, in his view, the whole process was not on the level and rank partisanship made progress so hard. But his passion was still domestic policy.

DR: He decided to exit Iraq, but he did not decide to exit Afghanistan. In fact, he put more troops in there, a so-called surge. Why did he decide not to get out of Afghanistan?

PB: During the campaign, he had talked about the good war and the bad war. Afghanistan was the good war, mainly as a way of trashing Bush on Iraq, the bad war. We forget today, but back in that era, Afghanistan had more support, because it was seen as a righteous response to 9/11, even though the war wasn't going great. It didn't have the same political liability that Iraq had, because there weren't as many casualties or nightly images of bombs blowing up in Afghanistan. There was room to give it another shot, to see if we could do something there. We talked about his keeping people from the Hillary Clinton and Bush camps: he did the same thing on national defense by keeping Bob Gates, the Bush defense secretary, and some of the other military folks around him. They convinced Obama to give it a shot, arguing that it was worth trying a surge in Afghanistan in the same way that Bush tried a surge in Iraq. But Obama decided that he wasn't going to do it like Bush, so he had a two-year time limit on the surge. He was saying, "I'm willing to try this, but only for so long."

DR: Was the capture of Osama bin Laden a real priority for him? How did it come about?

PB: Leon Panetta, who was his CIA director and later defense secretary, says that Obama was regularly pressing them: "What's the latest on this? Have you gotten any leads?" I don't know that it was obsessive, but he was rigorously pushing the CIA for progress. That would be something he could show to the American public, if he could do what Bush failed to do and bring to justice the person who had perpetrated 9/11. What Leon Panetta would tell you is he was a regular prod when it came to that.

DR: President Biden was in the Senate for more than 30 years, and obviously enjoyed the Senate. President Obama was in the Senate for just four years. Did he respect members of Congress as much as President Biden seems to, or did he really not like the back-and-forth that congresspeople and senators like to engage in?

PB: President Obama did not like Congress. He didn't like the people or the process. The phrase he used all the time was "It's not on the level." He could sit down and make a deal with them, and then they would retreat from something they had said they wanted, because they decided it was politically in their interest to do so. He became quite jaundiced about them. He also didn't have the touch. He didn't see the benefit of schmoozing. Maybe the schmoozing didn't work as well as it did, say, during LBJ's time, but he hated the comparison. When people said, "LBJ did it. How come you don't do it as well?" he'd say, "LBJ had a two-thirds Democratic Congress and I don't." Fair. But LBJ also had a lot of Southern Democratic members who were not in favor of what he wanted either, and he still worked the program. Obama thought it was all fake and had little patience for the process.

DR: As the first African American president, did he spend a lot of time on civil rights or was that expected of him?

PB: It certainly was not a high priority, at least in the first term. He wanted to be thought of as a president who happened to be Black, not a Black president. He did not want to be defined by that. Especially in his first term, a lot of his Black supporters were disappointed that he didn't do more. He would argue that his health care plan would disproportionately help Black Americans. That wasn't very convincing to a lot of people who thought he was going to be more active on that front. Only in his second term did he begin to take on the issue of race to try to lead the country toward better understanding, after he was safely reelected. When we started having some of these horrific events with police shootings, he spoke out more, most memorably in Charleston after the killing of nine Black parishioners in a church, where he later sang "Amazing Grace" so movingly.

DR: Why did he pick Joe Biden to be his vice president?

PB: Biden was a safe choice. He was somebody who would reassure the public that this freshman senator who didn't know much about Washington had somebody at his side who knew everything about Washington and had experience with foreign affairs. Biden also could reassure working-class whites who might be nervous about Obama, because that's Biden's identity. I don't think that they necessarily were superclose, at least before taking office. In fact, during a committee meeting, when Obama was listening to Biden, who was the chairman, drone on, he slipped a note to an aide saying, "Shoot me now." So there were some struggles at the beginning. They are very different personalities and it took a while for Obama to appreciate Biden and vice versa. But they formed a personal bond especially when Biden's son Beau died. It was a personal moment for Obama. He was the only person outside the family who Biden really confided in at first that Beau was even that sick. Biden said he had to sell his house in order to pay the medical bills, and Obama offered to lend him the money instead. Which is an extraordinary thing, if you think about it. So there was this moment when they became quite close for a while. But there was some souring toward the end when Obama gently nudged Biden not to run for president in 2016 and Biden was disappointed or even a little resentful.

DR: Did President Obama ever doubt that he would get reelected? Why did he not seem to prepare much for his first debate with Mitt Romney?

PB: Incumbent presidents have a disease called overconfidence. Most of them seem to think that they don't need to prepare for a debate because they've been dealing with these issues day in and day out. They know the territory a lot better than a challenger could. But what they forget is that they haven't been challenged much to their faces. The media is going to ask you some tough questions, but your staff isn't. Most people who see you in the Oval Office are telling you how great you are. He was overconfident, like a lot of them are.

DR: Most second terms have problems. Experienced people leave. Fatigue sets in. How would you rate Obama's second term?

PB: There's not a big differential between his first term and second term except on the issue of race. Most of the diplomatic things we were talking about happened in the second term. He went through staff like other presidents do. People do get exhausted and leave. His second-term team was effective. What is underrated, or not mentioned a lot, is that Obama went through eight years without any real personal scandal, which is not typical of presidents these days. He never had an independent counsel looking at him. He never had anybody accuse him of anything with regard to personal corruption or infidelity or anything like that. He had a strong, clean eight-year record. Critics say, "There was this or that," but those were relatively small things, and they didn't involve him personally. Even in a second term where scandals tend to be more prevalent because people get a little too comfortable, he managed to keep that from happening. That's important for history.

DR: Why do you think that President Obama supported Hillary Clinton as his successor rather than his vice president, Joe Biden?

PB: For one thing, Biden hadn't indicated that he was going to run or wanted to run until late in the game. If he had said more openly "I'm thinking about it" early on, before Obama began embracing Hillary Clinton, then Obama would have probably stood back more. I think he thought the vice presidency was the peak of Biden's career because of his age, because of his long history.

Obama thought that Hillary was a strong candidate. He had come to respect her during her time as secretary of state. He thought she could do it. He had spent the 2008 campaign telling us that Hillary Clinton shouldn't be president, because the Clintons were done, they were the old Democrats, and we needed to move on to the future. Then he turns around six, seven, eight years later, and says "The person I beat and told you that you shouldn't consider to be the next president actually should be my successor." He didn't groom a next-generation successor. A lot of Democrats criticize him for that, saying he should have looked for somebody else to spend time bringing up, and instead went to the default setting.

DR: Do you think he encouraged Donald Trump to run for president by making fun of him at the White House Correspondents' Dinner?

PB: It didn't discourage him, that's for sure. It's probably too simplistic to say that Donald Trump decided on that very night to run, because he had wanted to be president going back to the '80s. But I think there's a certain personal animus that Trump developed, especially that night, when Obama humiliated him in front of a ballroom full of people and a national television audience. I think Obama just couldn't conceive that Donald Trump would or could ever be a serious candidate.

DR: When Trump then got the nomination of his party and ran against Hillary Clinton, did Obama ever think that Trump would be his successor?

PB: It was only very late that Obama recognized that Trump could win. He, like everybody, assumed that Hillary was a strong candidate, that of course she would win. The polls all showed her way ahead. How could the country possibly elect this guy he considered to be a buffoon, a cartoon character, a carnival barker? He said as much at various moments during the campaign. I think it shocked him when it happened, because it told him that the country was not what he thought it was. He then spends the next couple of months during this transition period grappling with why this happened and what it says about him and his presidency.

DR: Presidents usually have a meeting in the Oval Office with their successor: What was it like when Donald Trump came to the Oval Office to meet Obama?

PB: Obama had never actually met Trump in person, ironically, until they sat in the Oval Office following the election in 2016. It would turn out to be a more congenial meeting than either one of them might have expected, but he was definitely not impressed by Trump. He understood that Trump didn't understand anything. He wasn't really listening to what Obama was trying to tell him in terms of how to be president or what was going on in the world. Obama tried to be a good sport about it and to be the outgoing president that George W. Bush had been for him. Bush went out of his way to try to help Obama as he came in, to do whatever he could to make him a successful new president. Obama was determined to follow that example, and then found that Trump didn't want it. Trump's people were completely uninterested in listening or having any real communication at all.

DR: Final question: What has President Obama done in his retirement to continue his legacy?

PB: His presidential center has done some work on mentoring and issues like voting rights. He has focused a lot on writing his memoir, which is two volumes, and on his business ventures with Netflix. I think he pulled back from the stage, because he didn't want to give Trump a target. He knew that if he was too visible, too public as an oppositional figure, Trump would relish that. He would love to be able to run against Obama for four years. Then, once Biden came in, Obama likewise didn't want to do anything to overshadow or get in Biden's way by being too public. There's kind of a cost to that, right? We don't see Obama offering a lot of leadership to the country right now, with the exception of the immediate campaign cycle, when he goes out and campaigns for Democrats. He keeps quiet and lets things happen without being too vocal. He had his time at the top and thinks it's now time for others.

20

PRESIDENT
DONALD J. TRUMP

(b. 1946; president from 2017 to 2021)

W hen Donald Trump came down the escalator at Trump Tower in 2015, preparing to announce his candidacy for the Republican nomination for president, few political experts took his candidacy seriously.

Trump had never held any government or military positions—unlike every one of the 43 individuals who preceded him in that position. He was in an already crowded field of Republican candidates (ultimately 16 others). He was planning to self-fund his entire campaign. He had no obvious political base. His business career had seen a fair number of failures; his personal life had seen two divorces and a *Page Six* social life. And he had been a Democrat for much of his life.

But, as is often the case, the pundits had to eat their words.

Donald Trump won the Republican nomination somewhat handily, changed the course of the country's political dialogue, and ultimately defeated the early odds-on favorite, the former First Lady, Senator, and Secretary of State, Hillary Clinton.

Governing turned out to be a more complicated undertaking. President Trump tried to change the ways of Washington (the "swamp"), and there was clear pushback. He also faced Justice Department and congressional investigations, two impeachments, large White House and cabinet turnover, strong Democratic opposition in Congress (especially to the attempted repeal of Obamacare), resistance from traditional European allies, trade tensions with China, and largely unfavorable media reporting and analysis.

President Trump did get his large tax cuts through Congress, developed closer relations with many Middle East countries, strengthened relations with Israel, and oversaw a reasonably strong U.S. economy (with no appreciable inflation) until COVID-19 dominated the country's focus, when the pandemic essentially closed many parts of the country and economy.

And while vaccines for COVID were successfully developed in record speed, few Americans were inoculated before President Trump—who was seriously infected with the virus—left office.

Leaving office did not occur in the traditional manner. President Trump contested the results of the 2020 election, claiming that there had been fraud in many of the states he lost. No challenges by President Trump or his supporters could prove fraud to the satisfaction of any court, though that did not stop him from working to rally his supporters to challenge the outcome.

The violent events around and in the Capitol on January 6, 2021, shocked Americans and others around the world. That violence did not change the election's outcome, and President Trump left office peacefully on January 20, on schedule, and without any personal contact with his successor (though he did leave the traditional welcoming letter).

I have known President Trump for a number of years, but not as a business partner or political supporter. When my parents retired and moved to what I have called a suburb of Baltimore—West Palm Beach, Florida—I would often host family celebrations at a private club, Mar-a-Lago, though I was not a member. (The food and service were good, and it was convenient.) At those times, I saw Donald Trump, who was frequently at the club, often taking pictures with the club's guests, including mine. On one occasion, he said he knew of my investment firm.

A few months later, near the end of 2014, when I was looking for someone to interview at the Economic Club of Washington, a few members suggested Donald Trump, whose television show *The Apprentice* was popular and was likely to help draw guests to the club's dinner event. (I had never watched the show.)

Donald Trump accepted the invitation, and I found myself with him in the green room right before the interview. He said that I could ask him if he was going to run for president. I later did, and he said that he was seriously thinking of doing so, to my surprise.

When Donald Trump did become president, I saw him from time to time in my role as chairman of the Kennedy Center or as chairman of the Smithsonian Institution. And once, during COVID, I did a Zoom interview with him for the Economic Club of Washington.

Since he left office, I did not have much contact with him, other than to see him in an effort to get an interview for this book. Getting an agreement to do the interview was less of a challenge than finding a time.

Ultimately, on May 2, 2024, before his trial appearance date that day, I did have a chance to do an interview by phone in the time allotted. But I did not want that interview, and my own thoughts, to be the sole material in this book on President Trump. So I have included as well an interview that I did with Maggie Haberman, a *New York Times* reporter who covered Donald Trump in his New York career and in his presidency.

Maggie Haberman managed to cover Trump for the *Times* in an unusual way. For personal reasons, she decided to continue living in New York and report remotely, coming to Washington on occasion. That formula would seem to be a difficult one for developing sources, but she seemed to have no trouble doing so. And while she does not, like any good reporter, reveal her confidential sources, it would appear that she had no problem getting direct access to President Trump.

While her *New York Times* stories could rarely be said to be favorable to the image that he was trying to convey, President Trump seemed more than willing to talk to her. President Trump—unlike some presidents—seemed willing to talk to those who were not likely to write stories he would like. Why did he do the interviews—and even allow some to be taped? There are many theories. Mine is that Donald Trump deeply believes in what he says and feels he can convince even the most skeptical of reporters and journalists. My interview with Maggie Haberman was done at the New-York Historical Society on May 13, 2023.

Since my interview with President Trump and my interview with Maggie Haberman, he was convicted on 34 felony counts in a New York State court. The impact on the upcoming election is clearly unknown, but it is already clear that President Trump's supporters do not seem deterred by the convictions, viewing them to be the results of a "political" prosecution.

*   *   *   *

DAVID M. RUBENSTEIN (DR): When you ran for president in 2016, did you honestly expect to get the nomination? Or did you think a more traditional candidate would actually prevail?

DONALD J. TRUMP (DT): As a student of history, you assume that it can't be done, because there's never been someone other than a general or a politician elected president. So there's never been anything like this. Bottom line, did I expect to win? I guess so, or I probably wouldn't have run. I'm a positive person. I don't like doing things that aren't doable. I felt there was a good chance that I could win. I was very well-known, had a tremendously successful television show for many years. I thought I had a good chance.

DR: For a long time in New York, you had been a Democrat. What led you to become a Republican?

DT: I was a Democrat and not loving the policies, but in New York everybody was a Democrat, not that much different from what it is now, but somewhat different. As I started to go out and look at the world, I started not liking the policies of Democrats.

DR: When you met President Obama in the Oval Office after your election in 2016, was that the first time that the enormity of the job and the responsibilities really hit you? Or did you realize how significant the job was well before that?

DT: I would say I realized it when they announced that I had won, because as you know, Hillary was favored to win. I felt we were doing very well. I'll never forget, I had a big rally in Michigan that night, the night prior to the election. The level of enthusiasm was incredible, as it is now. I felt that. The big thing was when I heard the words "Donald Trump will be the next president of the United States." I was working so hard. I did rallies that were so packed and so enthusiastic, and I said: "Why would I lose?" Michigan hadn't been won by the Republicans in many years. And I won. I did a rally there where we had so many people who turned up, I said, "why would I lose Michigan? Why would I lose?"

DR: What about the job of being president did you most enjoy, and what did you least enjoy?

DT: There's so much you can do. It's just incredible. It's a powerful presidency. If you know what you're doing, there's so many things that you can do: the rebuilding of the military, which you do just with a magic wand. The trillions of dollars that can be spent on doing things that are good things, very good things, not wasteful things like we're doing now. It's horrible.

But there are so many things you can do. I could give you a list, but one of the things I felt very strongly about were the tax cuts. I actually think that regulation cuts were more important than the tax cuts. They were both important. They worked beautifully together.

DR: How did you find dealing with members of Congress?

DT: There were some that were an absolute pleasure to deal with. They wanted things to happen. There were others—and even in my own party, dealing with certain people was really not fun—they were people that didn't want to get things done, or didn't know how to get things done. Dealing with the other side, from day one, it was an obstacle, and it has been that way ever since.

DR: Did you have people you thought would be good role models for you as president?

DT: I was a fan of Ronald Reagan, except on trade. He was not good on trade. He really allowed Japan to come in and take over the auto industry, and various other things. But overall the one that I felt most strongly about was Ronald Reagan. I thought he was very good. I thought he created the picture of a president. He was under siege. I was under siege, I think, more than any other president. But Ronald Reagan was under siege for seven years, with the gun situation and Oliver North. It went on for years. It's like quicksand. Some of those things, you get into them and they're like quicksand. I'm sort of a student of a lot of presidents.

DR: As you look back on your presidency, do you have any regrets or things you wish you had done differently?

DT: No, except for people. I ended up working them out through mere force of personality, but I had some people that I would have never put in if I had known them better. I was never into Washington. I was not a member of Washington society. I knew very little about Washington, the mechanics for the people. I relied on other people to give me people. Now I know. I think I know everybody about as well as anybody. I know the good, the bad, and the ugly. But I was not somebody that would walk in and say, I really like this one. Now I know everyone. That's a tremendous advantage, because I had to rely on a lot of people. Some of them, RINOs

[Republicans in name only], are people that I learned not to respect too much as time went by, and I was relying on them to put people in charge of intelligence and lots of other things.

The big thing that I would say would be that it worked out because we had such a great economy, such a great military, we largely defeated ISIS, we got into no new war—so many different things, we could go on forever. But I did that through force. I had some people that were bad. That happens with all presidents, no matter what. You know about people, you can choose a person, you can guarantee that person is going to be great, and that person turns out to be a disaster. And somebody else that you didn't think would be so good turns out to be a superstar. I had a lot of great people, phenomenal people that will come back with me if I'm re-elected, but there were some people that were absolutely terrible. I got rid of them. Look, many of the people in the Biden administration should be fired immediately. How do you not fire the generals and the various people that were in charge of Afghanistan, as an example?

DR: One of the things you wanted to do was end Obamacare. The Republicans on Capitol Hill never came up with a plan to do that. Do you think it's realistic to try to change it now?

DT: It's lousy. It's not good. John McCain was a disaster. He campaigned on getting rid of Obamacare. Then he cast the vote against ending it. The famous thumbs down. McCain gave it a thumbs down. And everybody was stunned. We had a lot of good things, much better than Obamacare, but we didn't really put a lot of time into it until we got it terminated—what's the use? McCain did the country a tremendous disservice when he turned it down.

DR: Were there things you learned the first term that would make your second term better?

DT: I had a tremendously successful first term, but the one thing that I would say that I learned was people. I would put different people in certain positions. I pretty much already know the people that I'd be going in with, and they're fantastic people. Most of these people were tested under fire. It's all about people. If you put a good person at the top of whatever agency, these big behemoths—you put somebody good in charge, it'll run well. It's not much different from business, if you have somebody good in charge of a specific business, if you own a series of businesses, and you have somebody great at one, and not so good at another—it's all about the person. That's what it's about, and I know great people, which we didn't know before.

DR: Why do you really want to be president for another four years? You could spend your time playing golf, enjoying your grandchildren, being at Mar-a-Lago.

DT: I wanted it in 2016, and nobody much complained. The Republicans aren't allowed to complain, but I had a great victory in 2016. I think it's been marked down as an excellent presidency, really excellent, sometimes better than that. The people say some great things. I had a great four years, a very successful four years, despite opposition. Very few people could have lasted, I will tell you.

DR: You don't seem to tire out. As a young person, were you a good athlete? How do you get this physical strength to keep doing this?

DT: I had parents that lasted a long time. They were great. I have one friend whose mother died at 49 of a heart attack and the father died at 49 of a heart attack. That's not a good sign.

DR: Is the presidency as lonely a job, as many people have said?

DT: It's a very lonely job. I love the White House, but the White House has been called many things by many different presidents, some of them not very complimentary. I think the White House is incredible. But it is a lonely job. You're all by yourself up there. Two Christmases and New Year's Eves together, I didn't leave, I stayed in the White House. I was in the White House almost alone, other than massive numbers of security. You look outside, and you see the number of security people in trees, with rifles at level, which you've never even seen before, these rifles. It was sort of wild. But I'm in there, and I'm saying, wow, that had to be there because of certain things that were happening in other countries. Like when you look at what's happening right now with the campus protests, the president should be out there. You've got to be there. I had a couple of occasions where holidays came and I was there. It can be a very lonely job, absolutely.

DR: Did you expect that getting the nomination this second time running for president to be as easy as it was?

DT: Normally, if you were like a normal guy running for president, the campaign would be going on right now. I'd be talking to you as a candidate for the nomination, because it still would have a long way to go. Were you surprised that I was able to get it and get it that quickly?

DR: I didn't think it would happen that quickly.

DT: Did you think Ron DeSantis had a good chance of winning?

DR: Based on his having been elected governor in that overwhelming way, I thought he had a better chance than he turned out to have. But he made some big, fatal mistakes. He tried to run to the right of you. And there was no room to the right of you.

DT: There wasn't much.

DR: What are you most worried about in the country and in the world over the next four years?

DT: I think the radical left is a big threat to our country, far greater than China or Russia. When you hear the FBI report that they're worried about the right, they should not worry about the right. They should worry about the left, the radical left.

DR: Is running for president while dealing with various lawsuits a big challenge?

DT: I'm leading. That's an indication that I'm doing the right thing.

I seem to be handling it quite well, let me put it that way, because I'm winning. It's very unfair. But I think so far, and that's only so far, it's backfired right in their faces.

You know what does help me, really? Being the leading candidate in the Republican Party. There's great popularity. What really does make me angry—when I watch these lunatics on television, and they say "two unpopular candidates." I'm not unpopular.

21

MAGGIE HABERMAN
on Donald J. Trump

* * * *

DAVID M. RUBENSTEIN (DR): You spent four years covering Donald Trump as president. Why did you want to relive that and write a book?

MAGGIE HABERMAN (MH): I thought there were still things to say. What nobody had done in all of the books there are about Donald Trump is talk about the world he came from and how much that informed his time in the White House, which I really felt like I was seeing every day that I was covering him.

DR: When you covered Donald Trump, you were the White House correspondent for the *New York Times*. You did it in a very unusual way. You were based in New York for family reasons. Was it hard to develop sources when you were living in New York, or you figured out a way to do it?

MH: I figured out how to do it. I already knew a lot of people in Washington because I worked at *Politico*. I had covered Washington for a while in various ways, and I had covered the campaign, so I knew a lot of people who were going into the White House.

DR: I enjoyed reading your articles in the *New York Times*. I always wondered how you managed to get interviews with Donald Trump, because your articles weren't that favorable to him, I would say. Why did he keep giving you interviews?

MH: He is uniquely obsessed with the *New York Times*, and I just happened to be the person who covered him more often for the paper. The place the paper holds in his psyche as the outer-borough guy from Queens who always wanted to be approved of by elites, it's hard to overstate.

DR: When Donald Trump first began saying he might run for president, did you think, "There's no businessman in New York who is going to get elected president of the United States"?

MH: I definitely questioned (a) whether he would actually run and (b) whether a businessman from New York could win, especially one with the social positions that he had taken. He had been pro-choice for many years, pro abortion rights. I started covering him in earnest in 2011 from *Politico* when he was considering running. We actually treated it pretty seriously because he was rising in the polls and he was striking a chord, mostly on this lie about President Obama's birthplace. But then he didn't run. And so in 2015 I was very skeptical.

DR: Where did the birther idea come from? Trump didn't invent it, but why did he latch on to it? Why was he so obsessed with Obama's birthplace?

MH: I think a couple of reasons. It was provided to him by a few people around him. I frankly have never been able to pinpoint exactly who brought it to him. I know he was talking to a fringe activist named Jerome Corsi about it. He was talking to other folks who had been hanging on to it. His longest-serving advisor, Roger Stone, talked publicly about how this was helping Trump. A lot of what happens with Trump or what he talks about often boils down to race. I believe this is part of why he seized on it. And he saw it was getting attention.

DR: There's a famous White House Correspondents' Dinner that Donald Trump went to where Barack Obama, then president, made a lot of jokes about Donald Trump. He supposedly got red in the face. Was that what really propelled him to run for president—the idea that he would get revenge, in some sense?

MH: It was certainly a big part of it. I actually wrote that story for the *Times*. I was in the room that night for that dinner, and the energy was really something. Obama was making fun of Trump over the birth certificate issue, in part, and Obama had released his birth certificate, and everyone around Trump was laughing and Trump sat stone-faced. Trump does not like to be laughed at. And I think this always stayed with him.

DR: When you covered Trump and you got to know him better, how influential was his father in creating the personality that we now know as Donald Trump? What can you tell us about that?

MH: There are two main influences in Donald Trump's life. One is Roy Cohn, and one is his father, Fred Trump. And Fred Trump really was a self-made man. Fred Trump was the son of German immigrants. He built up this local real estate empire. But it was very successful. He was involved in local politics. He worked the Brooklyn political machine, but he was, in the words of Ivana Trump, a brutal father.

He was very, very tough on his children. He was curt, he was brusque. He instilled in his son this need to win at all costs and promoted his son as the heir, and was very undermining in things that he would say, and was very tough on his kids. And I think Donald Trump always has his father in his head.

DR: Donald Trump was sent to a military academy. Why did he go to a military academy? Did he want to be in the military?

MH: I don't think so, since he didn't end up in the military. It's funny that you raised this, because this came up in a conversation I had just the other day with somebody who grew up with him in Queens. There are various explanations offered for why he got sent to the military academy, but the overarching consensus is there were behavioral reasons his father sent him away for.

DR: Behavioral reasons? I don't believe it. So how did he do? He was a good athlete there?

MH: A very good athlete. He really was. He didn't perform the way he claims he performed, the best on the baseball team and so forth. I don't think he was a stellar student. He talked with you in an interview about getting knocked around by the head of his unit and punched and slapped and so forth. I think that left as big a mark on him as anything, but he was known among the other students as somebody whose father was bailing him out with the school a lot.

DR: He went to Fordham initially for two years. Why did he transfer out of Fordham? He went to the University of Pennsylvania subsequently?

MH: He went to Wharton. His sister Maryanne has told people in the past of Fordham that that's where he got in. I think that was the honest answer as to why he went there. And I think he did not consider Fordham to be up to the credentialist nature that he has for himself.

DR: And how did he do at Wharton?

MH: We don't know. It has been impossible to get his transcripts from his various schoolings. It has been very difficult to get people to speak with candor about how he actually did. There have been all kinds of stories about him having people take the SATs for him or help study for him. Look, academics is not his thing. So if I had to guess how he did, I doubt he was an A student.

DR: So after he graduates from Wharton, he goes to work for his father, and then ultimately he decides to go to the big part of the big city, which is Manhattan. His first project is a redevelopment of a hotel, and that made him famous at a relatively young age. I think he was in his late 20s.

MH: It did. I want to add one caveat in there. He had toyed with going to film school, and then ended up not doing that and going to work for his father. He has told people privately that his father didn't want him doing that. I think he said in his interview with you that he was bringing glamour to the real estate business. His first project was the Commodore Hotel, this decrepit hotel on the East Side on 42nd Street, which he remade into the Grand Hyatt. It's not a massive real estate project, but it was coming at a moment when New York City was on its heels fiscally. It helped him seem as if he was this larger-than-life figure. He got a ton of press around it.

DR: Subsequently he tried to build other buildings. Did he build a lot of buildings in New York other than the Trump Tower? That's his major building?

MH: That's his major building. There are a couple of smaller projects around. There's a UN-area building. There's another one on the East Side. He spent years focused on a West Side project that just never came to fruition in the way he had hoped, where he'd envisioned a television city. He's a very small-level builder.

DR: The people in the real estate community regard him as a major real estate player in New York?

MH: No. But that doesn't mean that they ignored him. Some of them, like Harry Helmsley, at least until Trump started attacking Leona Helmsley, treated him with some level of deference.

DR: What was Trump's seeming obsession with telling people he was worth $6 billion, $10 billion, or whatever the number might be?

MH: This is something that I do believe he learned from his father, which is essentially describe yourself as bigger than you are at all times for press purposes, that it helps you in various projects. But Donald Trump does nothing without doing it to excess. And so everything just became much grander than it needed to be and much more exaggerated than it needed to be.

DR: Did Trump have a lot of friends in the New York real estate community? Who would you say his closest friends are?

MH: For a time, Tom Barrack, who is an investor and philanthropist, was one of his closest friends. He met him during when he acquired the Plaza hotel. It's a pretty small group. Richard LeFrak, whose father knew Fred Trump, was some level of friend, maybe still is. He treats his customers in Mar-a-Lago as if they're friends. But these are not friends the way that most people would think of them.

DR: A lot of financial problems arose when we went through some recessions in late the '80s and so forth. Did Donald Trump come close to filing for bankruptcy? How did he avoid it?

MH: Donald Trump in the 1990s filed for bankruptcy related to his casinos. He didn't file for personal bankruptcy. It was something he was seeking to avoid at all costs. The banks bailed him out because they decided, particularly because he was such an employer in Atlantic City, that it was more in their interests to keep him going than to have him go under.

DR: Let's go to the campaign. We talked about Obama's making fun of him at the White House Correspondents' Dinner. But to run for president, you have to be organized, you have to raise money, typically.

MH: You don't have to do either of those things, it turned out, because he didn't do either one of those things.

DR: He said he would be a self-funder. Did he really have that much cash to be able to self-fund? How did he do it?

MH: I don't know how much cash he actually had. He put in very little cash. Something like $10 million was all he put in initially. But he claimed that he was going to be supporting this endeavor. Instead, it was something that everybody else supported through donations. I believe he got reimbursed on the loan, because that's generally how campaigns work. But no, a lot of what he said he was going to do when he kicked off his campaign in June of 2015, he did not end up doing. But that having been said, he was so ingrained in pop culture, he was so known to Republican voters, that he was able to do things another candidate just simply wouldn't have been able to.

DR: He was known to Republican voters. He became a Republican at some point, but had he not been a Democrat earlier?

MH: And a Republican too, and an independent. He switched his registration over and over and over, which is sort of fitting. He gave primarily to Democrats in New York because there are primarily Democrats in New York, but his personal politics were always much more a Nixonian law-and-order sort of 1968 variety.

DR: In the famous ride down the escalator at Trump Tower, did he intend to get as much attention as he did by talking about people coming from Mexico and how they're not the best people, or did that just happen by happenstance?

MH: I think it was pretty organic. He had a prepared speech that he threw aside when he got down there. Then he was off to the races and he saw that he was getting a reaction. But I will say his advisors had been talking to him about immigration. When he was looking at running in 2011, immigration was not something he was really talking about. This was instilled in him by Roger Stone and an aide named Sam Nunberg, because that's where the Republican electorate was.

DR: When he announced his campaign for president, did he really think he was going to be president, or did he think it would be a good publicity effort?

MH: I think he thought that it was going to be a good publicity effort and it would be something that would be fun to try because he had been talking about it since the 1980s.

DR: He starts running and then he has debates. I think there are 16 other Republican candidates ultimately. Did he really think that he could stand on the stage with all these more experienced political figures and debate these issues? Did he bone up on these issues or he didn't think he needed to do that?

MH: He looked at it as some other media event that he was going through. He had bluffed his way through so many before that he didn't see a reason to be different. As it turned out, he wasn't wrong, because the debates are a big part of why he won that primary.

DR: At what point did he say, "Wait a second, I could be the nominee of the party"? Did he realize that this was going to happen at some point and say, "Maybe I'm not really interested in this"?

MH: That's a great question. I think that at a couple of points he realized he could actually win the presidency. And I think he was torn between his desire not to be a loser and his possible disinterest in the job. I don't think he spent much time, if any, really thinking about what being president would be like before he won.

DR: Let's go to the campaign. The campaign is floundering a bit and is maybe running out of money. At some point he decides to have a reset and he brings in Steve Bannon and others. Who convinced him that he needed a reset? How did that come about?

MH: He was souring on Paul Manafort for a number of reasons. Paul Manafort was the campaign chairman at that point. Paul Manafort basically helped oust Corey Lewandowski, who had been the campaign manager until then. It was a crazy three-month period. But it was a couple of donors. It was Trump's own children. It was the fact that Manafort was getting a lot of bad headlines. Trump did not need a ton of convincing, but Bannon is also a very effective salesman, and he was in Trump's ear at that point too.

DR: Steve Bannon comes in and he's not the campaign manager, but he is a senior advisor. Was he really running it?

MH: I think he was the CEO of the campaign. Kellyanne Conway was the campaign manager, and she did do a lot.

DR: So it's moving forward, and Trump gets the campaign shipshape from his point of view, and he gets the nomination. Was he surprised he actually got the nomination when you talked to him?

MH: No, he was not surprised he got the nomination. That actually happened before Bannon came in. What he was surprised by was that he had basically clinched it, mathematically, on May 5th with the Indiana primary, but because of the arcane delegate rules within the party it wasn't totally sewn up. There was a window for allies of Ted Cruz to try to stop him at the convention.

DR: So he's going to be the nominee of the party. Who does he want to pick as vice president and how did he come to pick Mike Pence?

MH: I don't think he wanted to pick anyone as vice president. I don't think he understood the concept or why he needed one. He joked that Ivanka at one point could be it. He looked at Newt, he looked at Chris Christie, he looked at Mike Pence. Mike Pence was the choice of Paul Manafort and some of his children, because he could help with evangelical voters, and he was never going to upstage Trump. If it had been Newt Gingrich and Donald Trump, they would have fought the whole time. There was some risk or concern that that would be the case with Christie too. It was always going to be Mike Pence, but Trump played this game as if it wasn't going to be.

DR: How did he prepare for the presidential debates? Did he sit down and have people grilling him, or he just didn't do that?

MH: The prep sessions would generally turn into BS sessions. It was really him telling old war stories and people would drop in and out. They did try to work on him. They did try to do some traditional debate prep, but the traditional trappings of a campaign don't work with him.

DR: How do you think he did in the debates, or how did he think he did in the debates?

MH: There are two different questions. There's how the media thought he did and how the public thought he did. The media all thought that Hillary Clinton succeeded in those debates against him. I don't think the public thought that.

DR: As the election's moving forward, Hillary Clinton is pretty much in the lead consistently in the polls and in the electoral count that is projected. Did Donald Trump actually think a couple of weeks before the election that he was going to win?

MH: I believe he thought he could win, and the thought of losing was upsetting to him. But that doesn't mean that he was thinking about it the way a normal person would in a close race. But he did work very hard that final month in terms of going around.

DR: So he wins the election. Is he shocked that he wins that night?

MH: Yes. He will say he wasn't, but yes, he was.

DR: The next day, does he say, "The stars have fallen and I now have the burden of the world on my shoulders"? Is he worried about it or not worried?

MH: No. He says, "How cool is this? Look at this thing that just happened. Look at what I won. All these people are calling me. The leader of this country is calling me, the leader of that one is calling me." The Japanese prime minister calls. "Here, talk to Ivanka." That literally happened. He wasn't looking at it the way somebody else would.

DR: Two days or three days later, he has a meeting in the Oval Office, a traditional meeting that the new president gets with the outgoing president. What was that like? He looked like he was a little bit intimidated.

MH: Obama came away struck by how little Trump knew. I think Obama was trying to impress upon him what the challenges were. They talked about North Korea in particular. And Trump was completely jarred by what he heard and by realizing the enormity of this job.

DR: We had never had a president before who had not served in the government, either in the military or in some civilian part. So he had a lot of learning to do in the transition. Who ran the transition for him?

MH: Initially the transition was run by Chris Christie. It was a sort of a consolation prize after not being picked to be running mate, or was in concert with that moment in time. Christie got fired from the transition within two days of the election.

DR: Why was that?

MH: Because Bannon and Jared and Reince Priebus wanted Christie out and they wanted to run what the jobs were going to be and who was being put in certain places. It was the three of them.

DR: What was the cabinet selection process like there? Was there a pre-election transition effort that had a lot of potential names?

MH: Some of the names had been in rotation previously, but then they ended up in different jobs. Jeff Sessions would be a good example. A lot of names were being offered to Trump by various people he knew in New York or he knew in Republican Party circles. Mitch McConnell was making suggestions. It was not a formal, typical process, and Jared was running his own process at the same time.

DR: So the transition moves forward and ultimately Trump is ready for the inauguration. Who wrote that inaugural address? It didn't seem like a traditional one.

MH: The "American Carnage" inaugural address? It was a bunch of people, but Steve Bannon and Steven Miller, who was Trump's hard-line policy advisor, had the biggest hands in it.

DR: So Trump's inaugurated and has the various inauguration parties and so forth. When he gets in the office, does he say, "I really am not quite ready for this"?

MH: I'm sure he said that to himself in all seriousness, but that was certainly not something that he said to other people. The way that he tends to deal with anxiety or moments of pressure is to scream at people and to lash out. And he did a lot of that.

DR: White House staffs always leak, but there seemed to be, in the beginning of the administration, a lot of leaking, more than normal.

MH: More than ever.

DR: Were there people leaking against each other? Was it various factions? The Bannon faction and the Jared faction? Was that a great time for reporters because you got all these leaks coming?

MH: We definitely favor more information than less. It was a chaotic time. Jared and Bannon went to the White House as allies. They ended up having a split as time went on in the first few months. There were definitely people who were leaking against each other for factionalized reasons. There were a lot of people who were brought into that administration as what one advisor to a mayor I knew used to refer to as government auto mechanics. These were government auto mechanics around Republican circles, and they knew how things functioned, and they were brought in, but they didn't like Trump, and they were very disturbed by what they were seeing. A lot of times they were talking to reporters just to try to process what they were learning about.

DR: President Trump had four chiefs of staffs. The first was Reince Priebus, who had been the head of the RNC. Why did Trump pick him as chief of staff initially?

MH: Paul Ryan suggested that he would be a good person because he knew Washington and because some of the other names that were being suggested seemed unwise.

DR: And how did that relationship work?

MH: Not well. Reince Priebus was gone by August of 2021. The idea of Trump and a chief of staff is hard to process. You have to be willing to defer to your chief of staff, let them handle certain things. Trump just undid everything Priebus did all the time. And Jared Kushner did too.

DR: Normally you have a process in the White House where you go through a chief of staff or a scheduler to go in to see the president. You have to get an appointment and so forth. Was Trump's White House a little different? Did anybody just walk into the Oval Office?

MH: It wasn't quite like that, but he would invite people in without telling other aides that he had. We forgot to mention where Jared Kushner and Ivanka Trump joined him in his government as his top advisors.

DR: Did he want them to be in government?

MH: Initially he did want Jared Kushner there. He was more agnostic about his daughter. But he was very happy to have Jared Kushner running certain pieces for him. Then Jared Kushner started assuming more and more power. He also got enmeshed in the Mueller investigation into possible collusion with Russia, and started getting negative headline attention. Trump did not like that, and then wanted him to go.

DR: Under our laws, the president of the United States has no financial constraints. He can have a blind trust, as President Kennedy did, or not have a blind trust. How did Trump keep his business operations separate from what he was doing in the government? Did his two sons really run the business then?

MH: His two sons, but particularly Eric Trump, were at least the figureheads of the business. We're still learning exactly what Trump was doing in terms of his business in office. And I think we're going to be learning about that for some time. At minimum, he tried doing things like use his ambassador to the U.K. to get a golf tournament at one of his Scottish clubs. He was not unaware of what was taking place. He would host events at Mar-a-Lago. Everybody within the Republican Party started hosting events at his clubs. Maybe some of it happened organically, and I think in some cases it did, but in other cases it didn't.

DR: Go through a typical day. When did Trump get up in the morning? Is he an early riser, a late riser?

MH: He's a bad sleeper. You would sometimes see 3 a.m. tweets. There was a famous tweet that he fell asleep while sending, where he typed the word *covfefe*, where I think he was trying to type "coverage." But he would be up by 6 a.m. usually watching morning television. He would claim that he didn't watch *Morning Joe* or CNN. He would watch both. He would start calling people that early. Paul Ryan had to train him. "Can you just wait until I'm done with my morning workout before we start talking?" They tried having him calm down in part to keep him from tweeting in the residence around 9 a.m. But it started sliding back later and later.

DR: Did he actually do the tweets himself, or did he have a person who did it for him?

MH: There were times the tweets were done by committee, that they were drafted. Aides were often proposing them. But at that time of the morning it was generally him, or at night it was him himself.

DR: Some other presidents get up in the morning, they exercise and have a routine. Was he an exerciser?

MH: He was not an exerciser, no. He famously said that he thinks exercise saps your energy. "You have a limited amount of energy in your body, and exercise depletes it."

DR: What time did he typically get into the Oval Office?

MH: By the end, it was between 10 and 11 a.m. It was quite late.

DR: A lot of people, when president of the United States, feel that you observe the traditions of the Oval Office. You wear a suit and tie all the time and so forth. He always did that?

MH: Yes, he's a big suit-and-tie wearer, especially in front of people he doesn't know, which was much of the White House.

DR: Many presidents have worked out of the Oval Office, but some presidents just use it for ceremonial purposes, and there's a room off the side where they actually do the work. Where did he do his work?

MH: Mostly in the room off to the side. He liked being behind the Resolute Desk. That's where he would be when people would come in for presentation meetings. But he did a lot of his meetings in that private room, in part because that's where he had a huge big-screen TV put in. And he would watch TV constantly.

DR: Most presidents have a schedule that's set well in advance. They have a scheduler. Did Donald Trump keep to the schedule that he was set?

MH: No. He did have a scheduler. His scheduler had a tough job. Lots of presidents, as you know, can make their scheduler's lives hard, but he was just so willing to throw things out that it was complicated.

DR: Let's say at noon, did he go back to the residence for lunch as some presidents have done?

MH: No, he would generally stay down in the Oval Office area.

DR: How long did he typically stay in the Oval Office before he would go back to the residence? Until 5 or 6?

MH: Yes, it was usually about 5 or 6.

DR: And then he would go back and have dinner, typically in the residence?

MH: He would have dinner in the residence. Sometimes they would have dinner as a family. Sometimes he would host people for dinner and the

First Lady and their son would not be there. It was a couple of nights a week that he would host dinners.

DR: What were his relations like with the members of Congress? Did he treat them with respect? How did he deal with them?

MH: That's a really good question. He was very effective with Republican House members. He was not with Democratic House members because everything became split by party with him, and he didn't understand the need to woo the other side of the aisle. But with Republicans, he was very good at using the White House, Air Force One, and Marine One. These were toys to keep them on his side. And he was very good at working the phones. This is something that he did throughout his time at the Trump Organization in New York too. He was good at it.

DR: What would you say Donald Trump would say were his biggest accomplishments as president?

MH: What he would say are his biggest accomplishments would relate to expanding the military, which he overstates. He would say that a big accomplishment, and this one really was something he did, was moving the embassy from Tel Aviv to Jerusalem in Israel. He would talk about building a border wall, which they only built about 500 miles' worth of.

DR: He had a very popular line in the campaign: "I'm going to build a wall and I'm going to get the Mexicans to pay for it." Where did the idea of the Mexicans paying for it come from?

MH: It was all Roger Stone and Sam Nurnberg. That whole idea of the border wall in particular was initially done as a mnemonic device to get him to remember to talk about immigration, and then it morphed into something different.

DR: In foreign policy, he dealt with all the heads of state you're supposed to deal with. His trips overseas were generally well scheduled and organized? Did he enjoy going overseas to meet heads of state?

MH: He did. And they were well organized, but they often did not go off well because he would go off script or because he would get angry at world leaders, or he would tweet something as he was flying into the U.K. and insult the prime minister. The foreign trips were real struggles for his staff.

DR: He seemed to not like NATO. Why was he so upset about it?

MH: Why NATO in particular has never been entirely clear to me, other than the fact that he sees it as an institution that's ripping us off, the broader us, which is something he's been saying since the 1980s.

DR: What about Russia? He seemed to have a real fondness for Putin. What was the reason for that?

MH: I don't think we've ever established exactly why he was so praising and often fawning about Vladimir Putin. I can come up with a couple of reasons. He generally likes strong men. He has autocratic instincts. His children have talked about doing business with Russians. I think, just generally speaking, he admires the behavior of Putin and admires the fact that Putin is not constrained by something like a constitution.

DR: President Trump had a number of investigations. The first one was the Mueller investigation. In the end it didn't produce anything that changed anybody's habits or anything. Was he obsessed with the Mueller investigation?

MH: He was beyond obsessed. It ate into his presidency for the first two years. Now, it didn't produce anything that quote unquote changed minds, but it did lead to a lot of indictments of a lot of people around him, including Paul Manafort. It was never going to lead to an indictment of a president, regardless of whether the evidence actually led there or not, because of a Justice Department advisory opinion, dating back to the Nixon days, that you don't indict a sitting president.

But what it did do was it told a pretty complicated story, and a Senate Intelligence Committee report that looked at the same issues did the same thing. So Trump likes to say, "This report exonerated me." It is, as it often is with him, a lot more complicated than that.

DR: He was the only president we've had who's been impeached twice. Let's go through those. The first impeachment dealt with a call that he made to the president of Ukraine. What was that all about, and why was he so obsessed with Ukraine?

MH: Giuliani got in his head. There's lots of talk that Giuliani and Trump are old friends. They're not old friends. They're people who knew each other for a long time in New York, and had a transactional relationship, as are many of Donald Trump's relationships. Giuliani saw Donald Trump as a way to stay relevant, and he started pushing on him this tale about the Bidens, particularly Hunter Biden and Joe Biden making money from a corrupt energy company in Ukraine.

DR: Was he worried that he would actually be impeached and convicted, or he knew he would never be convicted by the Senate?

MH: He believed that he would never be convicted by the Senate because of his relationship with Mitch McConnell at that point and the other senators.

DR: Giuliani became a closer and closer advisor as the administration went on?

MH: I don't know about closer and closer, but he certainly stayed in, despite the fact that a lot of Trump aides blamed him for that impeachment. Giuliani was right there when the election was going on in 2020 and Trump wanted to claim that it was rigged.

DR: Some of the accomplishments Trump supporters would cite would be the Abraham Accords.

MH: Definitely.

DR: How did that come about?

MH: I should have mentioned that in the list of accomplishments, that was largely Jared Kushner–run, in all seriousness. It was a real accomplishment. Its effectiveness is debated. Not everyone agrees that it was as significant as they claim, but it was a big achievement. It did change the region. Trump again was sort of along for the ride on that, as he was with many policy pieces, but that was really Jared Kushner's baby.

DR: He also developed a relationship with China. He had an agreement with China that was designed to get China to buy more products from the U.S. Did that work out well? Was that an accomplishment, you think?

MH: I think that getting the trade deal was, although the tariffs that he put initially on China and were part of what paved the way for that were controversial. He was very happy with them. The trade deal was never quite what he claimed it was. Neither was his reworking of NAFTA, but for what his policy aims were, it was significant. However it happened, he wanted to preserve it as the coronavirus was emerging.

DR: Of his four chiefs of staff, which one was the most effective, or which one was he the closest to?

MH: He was personally the closest to Mark Meadows, who was not the most effective chief of staff. Mark Meadows presided over the worst period of time in that administration, and had a direct hand in problems with the COVID response and with the postelection behavior. John Kelly was the most effective.

DR: John Kelly was the former Marine who came in. He had been the head of Homeland Security and was brought in as chief of staff. But he was fired without a direct confrontation?

MH: They had had conversations about Kelly leaving. That one was a more of a drawn-out process, but ultimately Trump just laid it out in public.

DR: When President Trump was given national security secrets, were people and the government worried that he might disclose them?

MH: They were very worried, and those worries were born out in their minds at a point in 2019 when he tweeted out a picture that was classified of an Iranian facility that had been destroyed. They were constantly worried about what they were telling him.

DR: One time the foreign minister of Russia came to the Oval Office with the ambassador from Russia. It was said then that Trump disclosed some secrets that maybe he shouldn't have. Is that fair or not?

MH: That is an accurate description. It was intelligence either from the Israelis or related to Israel. It was the same meeting in which he started bragging about having fired James Comey. It was a very news-significant meeting.

DR: Let's talk about his reelection campaign. Did he ever have any doubt in his mind he wanted to be reelected? Or did he say, "Four years is enough and I want to go do something else"?

MH: He was definitely worn out by the job by 2020, but he wanted to win reelection.

DR: Who did he want to have run the campaign for him? Was it Jared or somebody else?

MH: That's a good question. He left it to Jared. I don't know whether he thought much about who he wanted. I don't think he thinks that way.

DR: Did he take Joe Biden seriously as an opponent?

MH: No, he did not. And he should have.

DR: He didn't take him seriously because he didn't know him, or because of his age?

MH: I think his age. He bought into the line of Biden making gaffes and all of the things known about him before.

DR: I've observed over the years that incumbent presidents of the United States don't prepare for debates that much because they know the issues well. When I worked for Jimmy Carter, he didn't really prepare for the only debate he had with Reagan. I think Barack Obama said he didn't prepare as much as he maybe should have. In his first debate, George W. Bush the same. So did Donald Trump prepare for the first debate with Joe Biden?

MH: He did not, and that was something that his folks had been upset with him about. You are correct. There's a long tradition of that. There was something else with that first debate, which is that Donald Trump may have had COVID and was onstage very animated and red and sweating.

DR: He seemed to interrupt Joe Biden a lot. Was it planned that way, or did it just happen?

MH: It was planned that way, but it was not supposed to be quite as vigorously done as it was. He was coached by Giuliani to interrupt a lot.

DR: There was one very serious thing about his health with respect to COVID, and a major part of his administration dealt with COVID. How close did he come to having a very serious health problem when he got COVID?

MH: He was much sicker than they ever said publicly. We found out later, my colleagues and I, six months later, that he had what was known as COVID pneumonia, infiltrates in his lungs. The public health officials in the administration believed that if he had not been given monoclonal antibody treatment, he would have died.

DR: Did he ever get told that?

MH: They were pretty clear with him how serious his health was. He knew he was sick.

DR: During the COVID period of time, initially the press briefings at the White House were done by the vice president, then Donald Trump came in and started doing them. Why did he replace the vice president and start doing those when the vice president seemed to like doing them?

MH: There were a couple of reasons. Some of Trump's advisors, seeing that Pence was getting a lot of coverage, encouraged Trump to step in and do this so that he didn't look like he was being outshined. Then Trump discovered it could be just like another rally setting. He would stand up there for two hours. These were not informational. He would argue with reporters.

DR: He didn't seem to get along with Tony Fauci that much toward the end. What was the reason for that?

MH: He considered Tony Fauci to be a showboat is what he would say to aides. But he didn't like that Fauci was offering information that contradicted Trump's narrative that everything was fine.

DR: Let's talk about the reelection campaign. He thought he would win. Is that right?

MH: He thought in 2020 that he was going to win, yes.

DR: When the election came forward that night, and Arizona was declared by Fox for Biden, did that really upset him? Did he ask Jared to do something about it?

MH: It was a seismic moment. When Fox News called Arizona for Biden, Trump said, "Get that fixed." Kushner called Murdoch. It caused all kinds of chaos within Fox News, but Fox stuck to it, and then the AP did it a few hours later.

DR: Did Trump go to bed that night thinking he was reelected?

MH: It's a really good question. I don't know whether he thought that he was reelected or not. I think he went to bed thinking he was going to convince everyone he was, no matter what.

DR: When he wakes up, people say Biden is going to be president. Does he immediately think that the election is stolen from him? Who convinces him the election is stolen?

MH: For the first few days, the campaign's own data was showing that Trump could make up votes in Arizona and in a couple of other states. By Friday, it was clear that was not the case. Saturday is when the networks called the race for Biden. Trump had already started suggesting the election was going to be stolen from him months earlier when there was widespread by-mail voting because of COVID. So I don't think Trump needed convincing. This is something Trump's been saying for years.

DR: Who was his closest advisor trying to convince him to challenge it? Was that Rudy Giuliani?

MH: Giuliani.

DR: There were, I think, 65 cases filed alleging voter fraud of some type or another. And 65 cases were thrown out of court. That didn't convince Trump that maybe there wasn't fraud?

MH: There may have been one that went a little further, but yes, almost 99 percent of them were gone. Trump sees everything as an ongoing negotiation, and so he wasn't looking at that and saying, "Oh, you know what? I might not be right." Narrative is all, artifice is all. This was no different.

DR: Did people come to him, Republican leaders or others, and say, "You're hurting the country. You should just concede and go about your business"?

MH: Most people were terrified and afraid of going near him. I do know that Tom Barrack, whom I mentioned earlier, had a meeting with him on November 16th, saying to him, "You are hurting yourself." Which is really the main way to get through to him, not about the country. "You should just stop this." And Trump refused.

DR: Did his family go to him and say, "You didn't get reelected"?

MH: What his family has claimed in private about what they did is very different than what was actually happening. First, his oldest two sons, in the days after the election, did everything they could on social media to whip up Republicans. "Go fight for my father." Inside, Jared Kushner and Ivanka Trump were not doing a whole lot to try to convince him otherwise.

DR: He made some calls to the secretary of state in Georgia. It's amazing to me, when I watch TV today, I see people have telephone tapes of people calling them. I don't tape it when people call me. Do people regularly tape these things? How come he seems to have tapes of calls he's made? Did the Georgia secretary of state tape all of his calls?

MH: Because by January of 2021, people had figured out that Donald Trump will get on the phone with you and then say that something entirely different was said. People in the White House had started taping him. It's not a surprise others did too.

DR: Was there any plan by Donald Trump to not leave the Oval Office, as has been suggested?

MH: I have reporting on this in the book. He had started saying to people within two weeks of the election, "I'm just not going to leave." I don't think it was a plan, but it was in his mind. "I'm not leaving, we're never leaving. Why would you leave when you won an election?" I don't know what would have happened if January 6th, 2021, didn't happen.

DR: Let's talk about January 6th. What was his plan on January 6th? It was to rally people and march to Capitol Hill and protest in a civil way? Is that what you think he wanted?

MH: His aides always point to how he said, "March peacefully and patriot-ically," to his allies. I don't think that he had a grand thought of what might happen. He was so angry and so riled up that it was just "Stop this some-how," "this" being the certification of Joe Biden's Electoral College win.

DR: When the Capitol was overtaken, there were calls made by leaders of the Congress to Donald Trump to call this off. Did he not take the calls on purpose? Why did he wait a couple of hours?

MH: He did speak to Kevin McCarthy, who told Trump that people were breaking into McCarthy's office. What we heard at the time and what we reported at the time was that Trump was watching on television and was happy with what he saw.

DR: Did he say to McCarthy, "Some of these people take this more seri-ously than you do"?

MH: Yes. "They're angrier about the election than you are, Kevin."

DR: When the violence occurred on January 6th, eventually Donald Trump issued a statement. How long was it before he actually issued it? Did he write that statement, or did people force him to give that statement?

MH: At around 2:20 or 2:24 — I have the time stamp wrong, I think — he tweeted essentially, and I'm paraphrasing, "This is happening because Mike Pence didn't do what he should have done," meaning reject Joe

Biden's win. That was his first statement. Aides spent time begging him to say something. He finally issued another statement saying, "You know, be peaceful." It was an emerging process.

DR: Do you think in truth Donald Trump thinks he won the election, that it was stolen from him?

MH: It's a great question. I don't know how to answer it. I think he's convinced himself of it at this point. I don't know whether he thought it at the time.

DR: Since he did leave office, has he ever talked to Joe Biden?

MH: No. He did leave Joe Biden a traditional letter, and what Biden said to people who work with him, after he got it — it was in Trump's familiar scrawl — he said he was more gracious than he'd expected he would be.

DR: Donald Trump has subsequently been indicted in New York. He's lost a civil trial in New York on a sexual abuse allegation. Would these things deter him from running for president again?

MH: No. In fact, these events made him more dug in on wanting to run, because the campaign becomes a shield.

DR: If Donald Trump runs for president again, as he says he's going to, and he's elected, what does he want to do in another term?

MH: There's been a lot of attention on the CNN town hall and some criticism of how it was conducted. He made a lot of news, and he made very clear what that second term would look like, including reinstating the child separation immigration policy. He promoted the idea of debt default. He wouldn't commit to aid to Ukraine. He wouldn't say whether he wants Ukraine to win the war. It would be, and he has said this in his own words, a term of him serving as people's retribution.

DR: One of the issues that's arisen with you and Bob Woodward and others is when you're a journalist and you have a scoop, do you give it to your newspaper or do you put it in your book? How did you deal with that conundrum?

MH: This comes up a lot. The process of reporting for a book is very different than the process of reporting for the daily newspaper. I found it takes time. It takes time to get information confirmed in a way that I could use in the book. My goal is always to get stuff in print in the newspaper as quickly as possible, and I gave a significant amount of information to the paper in real time.

DR: You've enjoyed your connection with Donald Trump over the years, would you say?

MH: I wouldn't think of it that way. He's a subject I cover. We're going to be talking about the Donald Trump era for decades, long after you and I are gone. It has been a privilege to be able to report on this moment in history, but this is an ugly moment in history, and it has been for journalists too.

22

PRESIDENT JOSEPH R. BIDEN JR.

(b. 1942; president from 2021 to present)

I n the country's nearly 250-year history, no individual who became president was likely talked about as a possible president for as long as Joe Biden.

At the age of 29, he was elected to the U.S. Senate, defeating an incumbent Republican, Caleb Boggs, who was thought to be unbeatable when Biden entered the race, after having served just a few years on the New Castle County Council in Delaware.

But then tragedy struck. A month before Biden was to be sworn in, his wife and young daughter were killed in a car crash; his two sons survived but were badly injured and needed extensive medical help. Biden considered abandoning the Senate seat, instead focusing on taking care of his family and living his life fully in Delaware, rather than spending time away from his sons in Washington.

But many senior Democratic senators spent time with Biden and convinced him to be sworn in and assume the position. He agreed to do so but resolved to come home every night, via the Amtrak train from Washington, D.C., to Delaware. And he did—and continued doing so long after his sons were grown. He stopped these daily train trips only when he became vice president under Barack Obama, a position that ended Biden's 36-year Senate career.

Prior to becoming vice president, Biden had run for president twice—once in the 1988 election cycle, though he pulled out early due, in part, to a desire to lead the U.S. Senate Judiciary Committee hearings on Supreme Court nominee Robert Bork; Biden was then the committee chair. In 2008, he made another run at the presidency, but did poorly in the Iowa caucuses and pulled out of the race. (Biden seriously considered running in 2016, but the death of his oldest son, Beau, from brain cancer made that a difficult time to focus on a campaign. President Obama counseled Biden not to run because of it and to support Hillary Clinton, which he did.)

When he left the vice presidency, Biden spent time building a think tank at the University of Pennsylvania, the Penn Biden Center, and working to keep his extensive political network alive. At the age of 76, he decided to run for president. Despite his name recognition, Biden did poorly in the first two contests, coming in fourth in the Iowa caucuses and fifth in the New Hampshire primary. As a result, he was seen potentially as someone destined to drop out in the near future. But James Clyburn, the dean of the South Carolina congressional delegation and the House majority whip, decided to support him before that state's primary, which was enough for Biden to win the primary. Shortly thereafter, most of the other Democratic candidates dropped out of the race and supported Biden, giving him a much easier path to the nomination than many had once thought possible.

The path to the presidency was not quite as easy. Donald Trump, despite his many challenges—a special counsel investigation, an impeachment, frequent staff and cabinet turnovers, frayed relations with longtime European allies, difficult press and media relationships—had maintained, if not strengthened, his support among his base. For most of the campaign, Biden seemed ahead in the projected popular vote, though the projected Electoral College vote seemed likely to be closer. When the voting was completed, former Vice President Biden prevailed, winning the popular vote by seven million votes and the Electoral College vote 306 to 232, capturing five states (Pennsylvania, Michigan, Wisconsin, Arizona, and Georgia) that President Trump had won in 2016. But in a nearly unprecedented series of actions and statements, President Trump refused to concede the election, and had his lawyers and supporters challenge the results. He also sought to have Vice President Mike Pence, as president of the Senate (and the official presiding over the official Electoral College vote), declare Trump the winner of the election.

As the world now knows, none of the sixty-plus lawsuits prevailed, Vice President Pence declared Joseph Biden the winner, and ultimately, after the attack on the Capitol on January 6, 2021, President Trump left the White House without meeting his successor or attending the inauguration. Former President Trump was later indicted by a Justice Department special counsel and a Georgia prosecutor for a number of actions surrounding the election aftermath. Neither of those cases have yet been resolved.

While the transition was truncated, for President Trump did not authorize the governmental transition process to proceed until late November, President Biden did start his administration on time on January 20, 2021, and was able to achieve his nearly 50-year dream of becoming president (and in so doing became the oldest person, at 78, inaugurated as president). And, in that position, he worked to get vaccines, developed under the Trump administration, distributed throughout the country, and to get additional spending approved by Congress to keep the economy going during the COVID period. (Early in the administration, Congress passed legislation to inject $1.9 trillion into the economy; President Trump had earlier persuaded Congress to inject $2.2 trillion into the economy when it became clear that COVID was dramatically weakening the economy.)

I have known President Biden for many years, in part because he was the first senator to endorse Jimmy Carter for president, and he worked with the Carter administration on many initiatives. Because I have stayed out of elective politics and campaigns since the Carter days, I have not been a political supporter of or contributor to any of President Biden's campaigns, but over many decades I got to know him through interactions at the Smithsonian and Kennedy Center. Because of that relationship of many years, I did offer to let him use my Nantucket, Massachusetts, home for Thanksgiving when he casually told me, during a Kennedy Center reception at the vice president's home, that he needed to find a home for the annual Thanksgiving visit of his family to that island (the house he normally used was not available). He actually did not know at the time that I had a home there. He used it twice as vice president and several times as president. (I am not there when he visits; I prefer warmer weather that time of the year.)

For this book, I asked President Biden's staff if I could interview him about the presidency itself, as opposed to the specifics of his administration, and he agreed to the interview, which follows. My interest in doing the interview was designed principally to hear his views on the office itself and the way he conducts it.

My own views on his presidency are not fully formed, for it is not over, and any real assessment will take time once it has been completed. But preliminarily, I think he won the election in part by being the anti-Trump, seen as a safe option who would restore some normalcy to Washington and would be able to reset relationships with international allies and be able to get some bipartisanship in Congress to get his agenda passed.

As of this writing, some of that has happened, though he was not able to eliminate the divisiveness that has taken over Washington in recent decades. And President Biden's approval ratings, like President Trump's, tended to stay below 50 percent. As a result, he had a difficult time getting his initial agenda through Congress. That was made even more difficult when Democrats lost control of the House of Representatives following the 2022 midterm elections.

But President Biden was able to get through some of his domestic agenda, at times much scaled back from the initial goals. For instance, his signature Build Back Better, a multitrillion-dollar Democratic wish list of enhanced economic, social, and environmental programs—containing many pent-up Democratic objectives—could not gain enough support in the Senate to pass, but a revised bill, largely crafted by West Virginia senator Joe Manchin, did pass, renamed as the Inflation Reduction Act. President Biden was able to get two signature programs approved with a good deal of bipartisan support: an infrastructure bill and a bill to support semiconductor manufacturing in the U.S.

Outside the U.S., President Biden improved relationships with our traditional European allies, though the relationships had started poorly when he decided to pull all U.S. troops out of Afghanistan without consulting or notifying the allies. (Also, the deaths of thirteen U.S. soldiers, due to a suicide bomb, during the withdrawal was clearly an early misstep in his foreign policy.) But the Biden team regained its footing when Russia invaded Ukraine. The president was able to convince European allies and the U.S. Congress to strongly support Ukraine, including significant financial and military resources; this undertaking became Biden's signature foreign policy achievement, for he was able to gain U.S. and European military and economic support of the Ukrainian effort to repel the Russian invasion (and that effort far exceeded early predictions of a quick Russian victory). However, as of this writing, support for Ukraine in the U.S. has waned, and the outcome of that war is unclear.

Other traditional allies actually did not see an improvement in their relationships with the U.S. Relations with Israel and the Persian Gulf countries were arguably stronger during the Trump years and deteriorated somewhat during the Biden years. President Biden was strongly critical of the Israeli government's desire to enact legislation that would weaken the authority of the judiciary, and later he came to disagree with Israeli prime minister Benjamin Netanyahu's insistence on continued bombing of Gaza in order to destroy Hamas's capabilities and control over Gaza. The split with Netanyahu's decision to proceed with an invasion of southern Gaza placed the U.S.-Israel relationship in a troubled state, despite President Biden's strong, lifelong support of Israel.

Also, early in the administration, Biden did not think he should be engaging directly with the crown prince of Saudi Arabia, believing that the prince had been responsible for the murder in 2018 of *Washington Post* journalist Jamal Khashoggi; that view moderated in time as Saudi Arabia's influence on Gulf matters of interest seemed to strengthen. But generally relations with the leading Arab countries in the Gulf were not as warm as President Biden would have preferred.

The challenges in the Middle East were not the only ones that weakened U.S. ties in certain areas. The war in Ukraine led Biden to essentially end any relations with Russia, imposing enormous sanctions on it and on prominent Russian oligarchs. The relationship with China certainly did not improve, and perhaps actually worsened, as the Biden administration (more than the Trump administration) continued to be quite supportive of Taiwan, which upset China. President Biden objected to practices in China that he sees as violating human rights norms, and that was not a major concern of President Trump.

The biggest economic challenge that President Biden has had to handle was the high rate of inflation—the U.S. inflation rate for the prior 25 years was essentially 2 percent. But because, in part, of the enormous amount of fiscal stimulus put into the economy by legislation passed under President Trump and President Biden to deal with the effects of COVID, inflation spiked to 8 percent. For a while, the Biden administration and the Federal Reserve thought the high inflation was "transitory," and few countersteps were taken at the outset of the rising inflation. But, in time, the Fed recognized the inflation in the economy was more enduring than once thought and began to raise interest rates steadily in 2022 and 2023, resulting in slower growth in the stock and real estate markets than might have been desired. But the economy did not dip into a recession in 2023 or 2024, despite many economists' predictions to the contrary, as consumer spending fueled economic growth and a tight market drove unemployment to near-record lows.

Any real assessment of the Biden administration, though, will depend on events subsequent to this writing. It does seem fair to say that presidents who get reelected tend to have more favorable reputations than those who do not, even though second terms are often quite troubled. So if President Biden ultimately wins reelection, it is likely history will treat him more kindly than if he were to lose.

I requested an interview with President Biden for this book, though not so much to review the events of his life and presidency, but more to hear his thoughts on the job of being president. And I was able to do such an interview in the Oval Office alone with him on April 2, 2024. That interview follows this introductory section.

As with President Trump, I did not want this book's assessment of the Biden presidency to be dependent just on my own observations and interview. So I also interviewed Franklin Foer, a journalist at *The Atlantic* magazine, about his very detailed book on the first two years of the Biden administration. That interview occurred at the New-York Historical Society on February 20, 2024.

* * * *

DAVID M. RUBENSTEIN (DR): From the time you were elected to the Senate, people have said "This man should be president." You were first elected to office when you were 29. You became president when you were 78. So for a longer period of time than anybody in our country's history, you've been talked about as a future president. Now that you are president, is it as much fun as you thought it would be when people told you should be president all those years?

PRESIDENT JOE BIDEN (JB): "Fun" maybe is not the right word. First of all, it's an incredible honor. I love these biographies which say "I knew I was going to be president since whatever." I didn't even know I was going to run for the Senate.

There are certain inflection points in world history where things change in a relatively short period of time, the outcome of which, how you deal with it, dictates what the next four, five, six decades are going to look like. The postwar period is over. The world is changing—everything from global warming to leadership to shifts in allegiances around the world.

I wasn't going to run this time around in. I just lost my son Beau in 2015, and they're talking about the presidency. I was a professor at Penn. It was a good job, and I actually enjoyed it. They gave me a couple million dollars to hire staff to set up the Penn Biden Center up there.

But what happened was when those folks came out of the fields, carrying torches, down in Charlottesville, with Nazi banners, and that young woman was killed, and the president was asked what he thought, and he said he thought there are good people on both sides—that's when I decided that I was going to run. Because I really do think, speaking of inflection points, that democracy is at stake—literally our democracy. It's not just here in the United States, it's happening around the world as well. But Donald Trump comes along, with his America First policy, undermining our foreign policy agreements around the world. His economic policy I felt was a disaster. The guy uses phrases like now he's going be a dictator in the second term, the first act if he's re-elected, etc.

What I did was, I went out and I made the speech on democracy. Because he didn't do a thing. He just sat there. He didn't do a goddamn thing. I shouldn't say that, but he didn't. The whole idea of what happened down in Charlottesville, all that occurring, and he had been asked what he thought of what was happening and he said, "There are good people on both sides"—I thought to myself, what the hell is going on? That's when I decided to run. I meant to reestablish the value system that was consistent with who the hell we are.

DR: You were vice president for eight years. Is the presidency a different job than it was under Barack Obama or other presidents because social media is different now, or because bipartisanship is completely gone? When you were in the Senate, there was bipartisanship, to some extent. It seems like it's gone now. Has the presidency changed a lot over the last couple of years, or is it pretty much the way it was when you were vice president?

JB: I think it's changed. It's changed for a couple of reasons. One is that Trump has, to the surprise of most people, taken over the heart and soul of the Republican Party. This is not your father's Republican Party, for God's sake. I've had five—and I promised I'd never say their names, so I won't—five Republicans that I served with when I was a senator, personally saying,

"I agree with you, but I can't be with you, because if I am, I'll get defeated in the primary." It amazes me, his hold on otherwise decent, honorable men that I've worked with. I don't know what the hold is. They believe, when he threatens retribution, that he means it.

But I think what's changed is the notion that the Republican Party has disintegrated. There's no center to it anymore. When I got elected, remember I said I ran for three reasons: to restore the middle class, to bring back a sense of honor and decency to the office, and to unite the country. They said, "That was the old days, Biden. You used to be really good at doing that with the Senate. You can't do it anymore." But I still was optimistic. Look, we got a hell of a lot done.

DR: What would you say you're most proud of what you've done as president?

JB: What I would say I am most proud of was dealing with the Inflation Reduction Act, which was really about being able to take on prescription drugs, take on pharma, take on these interests. There was a debate back in the '30s with regard to whether unions were legit or not legit; an element of that said that when the president is given money by the Congress to do something, to spend that money for the U.S. interest, he should hire American workers and use American products. I didn't know that existed. So I decided that in order to get stuff done that we needed to get done, we should invest in America, with American products—not unfair trade practices, but just invest in America. You may remember the criticism, understandably, that I got when I went to South Korea to try to get the chip manufacturers to come here. Well, guess what, they couldn't. $50 billion worth—it would have created thousands of jobs. I just don't want to be the end of the supply chain again. As long as we have a beginning of the supply chain, other countries can as well, but I don't want to be at the end.

The other thing I'm really proud of, I'm really proud we were able to move in the direction of getting the infrastructure bill passed. Infrastructure was weak for four years. We got $1.2 trillion, and there's a lot being built, a lot happening, a lot moving. I'm also proud of the fact that we were able to focus on a policy that focused on building the economy from the middle out, bottom up. There's so much more to do, though. There's so much more to do.

DR: It's said to be the loneliest position in the world, and the most responsibility. Is it enjoyable? Or is it just something you feel you need to do, but you don't jump up every morning and say, I can't wait to get in the office?

JB: It's a little of both. It's not like I can hardly wait to get over there and make those decisions about what I'm going to do about the fact that the Israelis just killed innocent civilians who were trying to bring food to the Gaza Strip. But part of it is I get a chance to change things. You can kind of taste it—if we do the following, we can make it better, we can move. Even the staff, as they'll tell you, sometimes will say to me, I'm not sure we can do that.

But for example, when I went to South Korea to get the chips act moving forward and semiconductor manufacturing, how the hell can we be the leading nation in the world while being a second rate chip manufacturer? My going to South Korea to meet with President Yoon and Samsung and saying, why don't you invest in America? We invented those damn chips— the end result was he decided to do it, and I said why? He says, You've got the best workers in the world, and it's the safest place to invest.

So I get an overwhelming sense of satisfaction when what we're trying to do begins to work. The frustrating part—and I knew it would be—is that it's hard as hell for this to trickle down to the American public, to understand how it's working for them. I knew this would take time.

DR: The Founding Fathers came up with a system, and they invented the presidency. If you could speak to one of them and say, "Look, you should have done this differently, or you should have gotten rid of the Electoral College, or you should have done something different," is there something you would say that would make the presidency even better for the country than the way it is now? Or basically it's okay, the way it's structured now?

JB: One of the best things they did that has been taken advantage of is the amendment process to add provisions of the Constitution. I'm not a big fan of the filibuster. I'm not a big fan of some of the things that the Congress has done to limit the ability of the majority to speak, and so I think the most important thing I would do is put us in a position where the Congress does not require supermajorities to get basic things done, like a budget, or supermajorities to be able to get decent things done, like civil rights, civil liberties.

DR: The Founding Fathers didn't require that.

JB: No, the Congress did it. They gave us the option. I think we've chosen some of the wrong options.

DR: As you look forward, what are you most interested in doing in a second term? More of the kind of things you've done in the first term? Is there any one thing you would love to do in a second term?

JB: There's several things that I would love to do. The reason why we have to win is that if Trump wins, he's going to wipe out everything we've done. I mean it—everything. For example, for all the talk about the big-spending Democrats, we've actually lowered the deficit. We've actually lowered it, the money we spent on what we brought in. I think we need a fairer tax system. Look, I know you're a very successful man, but the tax system is not fair the way it's running now. For example, we've got nearly a thousand billionaires in America. I'm a capitalist. That's wonderful. Just pay a frigging fair share of tax. If they just paid 25 percent, that generates $400 billion over 10 years. Imagine what we can do.

One of the things I'm proudest of having done is I met with the Business Roundtable about 18 months ago, and they were criticizing me about why I talk about labor. And I said, you know, when I was vice president, the secretary of commerce and I interviewed close to 350 CEOs of Fortune 500 companies, and said, what do you most need? They said a better-educated workforce. And I said, but you aren't educating your workforce anymore. I said, the DuPont company used to be one of the largest companies in the United States. I said, what happened was, when they bought a new enterprise, they trained their own workers to run it. You guys don't do that anymore. And at the end of the conversation, I said, so why are you opposed to me providing for better education and more training and apprenticeships? The end result was they sort of backed off and said, yes, we need that. What I'm saying is that it takes a while, when the world changes in terms of technology, when the way in which you communicate changes, to grasp hold of what it is you really want to do with what you have.

DR: Do you have any regret that your parents didn't live to see you be president of the United States? Just imagine what it would be like to say to your parents, "I've been elected president of the United States."

JB: Yes, I do, especially my dad. My mom lived to see me be vice president. I'm going to tell a quick story. When I got my ass kicked in the primary by Barack, my mother called me and asked me, what kind of guy is he? I said, he's honest, he's bright as hell, I think he's an honorable man. Growing up, my mother was everybody's mother confessor. My friends would always come to my mom for advice. She never let us know who she was advising, never violated anything. She wouldn't.

I was riding home on the train, I guess it was in early August, when Barack became the de facto nominee. And he said, I want to do a background check on you. I'm on the phone, on the train. And I said, background check? I said, Barack, I don't want to be vice president. I can help you more as a senior senator. I can really help you. He said, do me a favor. Go home and talk it over here with your family and get back to me in maximum 48 hours. I said okay, all right, but I don't want to be vice president. Next thing, I'm on the phone, between Baltimore and Wilmington. I call and I say, let's have a family meeting. I get home, and my wife, my three children, Ted Kaufman—he's the only non-Biden—and my mother, they all started off, and they all thought I should be vice president. Jill said, Joe, you should be vice president. If you don't do that, they're going to ask you to be the secretary of state, you'll be away all the time. I'll never forget that. We go through the whole thing. My mother was living with us. My dad had just passed away.

She was sitting against the railing on the front porch. And I said, Mom, you haven't said anything.

She said, let me get this straight. The first Black man that has a chance to be president says he needs you to get elected, and you told him, No? I said, Son of a bitch. That's exactly what happened.

And the night we're walking out, we are about to be announced, my mother saw the look on his face and she grabs his hands and says, "Come on, honey, it's going to be okay."

DR: What did she call you—Joe? Or Joey?

JB: Joey. My father called me Joe or Joey.

DR: Do you like to make decisions based on reading materials that your staff gives you or in oral meetings? I know some presidents only like to do oral meetings. Some like written things. Barack Obama liked to read a lot.

Jimmy Carter liked to read a lot. What's your style—to get meetings with people, or to read, or both?

JB: I think it's fair to say both. I am at home with a book like that every night, for real. But I also very much like to look people in the eye. It surprised me, the response to checking with the staff. I'm looking for detail. I don't want generic assertions. I want someone to tell me in detail why you think such and such. For example, I just had a meeting on the whole issue of what's going on in Israel and what I should be doing, and what's going on in Iran. I want to know the details before I make a decision.

I used to kid Barack. I'd sit in that chair, and he'd sit in this one in front of the fireplace, and the deal he and I made was that I literally got to be the last person that he worked with, the last person in the room, before he made his decision. I'd give him my advice, my opinion in detail why I thought he should do A, B, C, or D. He probably only disagreed 30 percent of the time, but he always said thank you. I said, don't thank me. I get to give you the advice, and I get to leave. You've got to make the decision. That's the biggest difference.

You know that Harry Truman deal about if you want a friend in Washington, get a dog? Well, it's not that so much, it's that it's very different when you know no one else is you.

DR: One of the most emotional things I've ever seen you be involved with was when Barack Obama surprised you by giving you the Presidential Medal of Freedom with Distinction. You were choked up, and you turned around to kind of get your emotions under control, and you came back and faced the crowd? You were truly surprised.

JB: I was. I was totally surprised. There are things you never think of. I never thought I could qualify for that.

DR: When I worked here, I was 27 years old. I was the youngest person in the White House. Now, in many cases, I am in rooms where I'm the oldest person. I'm now 74 years old. I say I'm too young to be president. I couldn't be president, I'm only 74. But you were nearly the youngest person ever elected to the Senate. You were elected when you were not even 30.

JB: There was one younger.

DR: All right. So now people say you're old. How do you deal with that? Because I deal with it all the time. People look at me, like, "You're kind of old to be doing this. Why are you still working?" And I say, " I feel young, and I'm still happy doing this." And if I'm happy, why do anything else? So how do you address that question that people ask you—are you too old to do this job or not?

JB: I don't think that. For the longest time I was too young for the job. The guard used to stop me getting on Senate elevators.

DR: They thought you were a staffer?

JB: They thought I was a staffer. Yeah. "No, this is for senators only."

DR: You have a trainer that helps you?

JB: Yes, I have a trainer.

DR: Does a trainer say to the president of the United States, you've got to work harder? Or they don't tell the president of the United States, you've got to work harder?

JB: Actually, they work me pretty hard. He works me pretty hard. I don't feel anything less in my stamina, or my intellectual curiosity, or in my ability. I'm going to say something about you. You have enormous experience. It's not like you were just doing business for all these years and decided you want to be engaged in the larger issues.

DR: I'm trying to give back to the country in some way.

JB: Bingo. Bingo, bingo, bingo.

DR: That's what life is about, right?

JB: I think it is. You think it is. But how many people want to give back or take? I think there are too many people today—maybe it's always been this way—who look at it in terms of how it can enhance or better their financial or physical circumstances.

DR: Some people measure their self-worth as a person by their net worth. I don't do that.

JB: Because you and I come from a similar background.

DR: I have a blue-collar background. My father worked in a post office. I've given away a good deal of money for various things in Washington, and we're going to redo the Lincoln Memorial, we're redoing the Jefferson Memorial, and hopefully you'll come there when we'll dedicate them.

JB: My dad used to have an expression on repeat—he repeated it a million times—Joey, a job is about a lot more than a paycheck. It's about your dignity. It's about respect. It's about being able to look your kid in the eye and say, "Honey, it's going to be okay."

DR: I agree.

JB: But how many people in your circumstances or in my circumstances think that way?

DR: To me, the greatest thrill is making your parents proud.

JB: Bingo.

DR: My parents are no longer alive, but they lived to see a lot of what I did. They always said to me, David, you're doing something good for the country, and that's what made them proud.

JB: Same. My mother used to say, as long as you're alive, you have an obligation to strive. You're not dead and you've not seen the face of God. And she meant it. My mother was a five-foot-one little Irish woman who had a backbone like a ramrod. But it was about principle.

DR: She lived to be 90?

JB: She was 92. She was born in 1917.

DR: 92. You've got a ways to go to catch up there.

JB: Yes.

DR: I appreciate your giving me this time. The book is coming out in September and it's about the presidency. I've interviewed a lot of great presidential scholars, and former presidents. President Clinton I've interviewed, and I've interviewed President George W. Bush. He's got a quite a sense of humor, as you probably know.

JB: He does. He's a decent guy.

When I said "Restore the soul of America," I was talking about decency. I have great faith in American people. American people are decent. They're decent. We're on the verge, God willing, of making enormous progress in this country.

DR: What keeps people young is a sense that they have an obligation to do something. They feel like they're doing something that makes their life worth living.

JB: Bingo.

DR: And that's what makes it possible for people to keep living.

JB: I couldn't agree more.

23

FRANKLIN FOER
on President Joseph R. Biden Jr.

*   *   *   *

DAVID M. RUBENSTEIN (DR): Why did you pick Joe Biden as a subject for a book?

FRANKLIN FOER (FF): My publisher came to me and asked me to do a book about the first 100 days of the administration. I was reluctant because I was never really connected with Joe Biden as a political figure. The first time I spoke to him was when I was a 24-year-old reporter and I got him on the phone. I was really excited to get Joe Biden on the phone, and five minutes into the conversation, it was clear to me that I was not going to be able to get him off the phone.

DR: Biden was elected to the United States Senate when he was 29. He couldn't take the job until he was 30. How did he get elected to the Senate at such an early age? He had only been a county councilman or something like that. Was he a great politician at the age of 29?

FF: He was a charismatic guy. He was riding on the coattails of the Kennedys. His family campaigned as an Irish Catholic clan in Delaware. They held coffee klatches in the style of the Kennedys. And he was a good public speaker, which is an interesting fact about him, because he'd had this stutter that was a defining fact about his childhood. His eloquence on the stump was something that he was quite enamored with because it showed how he'd overcome his fundamental disability.

DR: When his wife and young daughter were killed in a tragic car accident, he thought about not taking up the Senate seat. Senators came to him and persuaded him to take the seat. Whose idea was it to commute every night back from Washington to Delaware, which he did for thirty-some years?

FF: He was despondent at that moment. He lost his faith in God. He describes walking the streets of Wilmington spoiling for a brawl. And the Senate really gathered around him. Mike Mansfield, Hubert Humphrey, all of these names from another generation of American politics got together, and they told him that he had to do this. That's why he's always considered himself a Senate man. He's fetishized the institution because, in a way, it saved him from the depths of despair.

DR: From the time he got elected at the age of 29, people were saying he should be president. He's spent 48 years of his life, the longest period of time of any American in our country's history, trying to become president. Why did he want to be president?

FF: He thought of himself as a great man. One of the defining features of his personality is that there's this sizable chip on his shoulder. He was a guy who came from Scranton, Pennsylvania, who identifies with the blue-collar working class but grows up within a party that sociologically becomes something different. It's run by Ivy League meritocrats, so he feels somewhat out of place. He grew up being bullied for his stutter. He was always trying to prove himself. And what's the best way to prove yourself to the world but to become president of the United States?

DR: He's elected to the Senate in 1972. In 1988, he starts running for president, and then all of a sudden pulls out. Why?

FF: He was accused of plagiarizing a speech given by Neil Kinnock, a British Labour politician. It was one of the great humiliations of Biden's life. For a guy defined by his eloquence, the notion that it was inauthentic—and because oratory was a way of proving himself and overcoming his stutter—it really cut to the core of him. It was another moment of darkness where he fell into a pit of despair.

DR: I always wondered about that, because he didn't write the speech. Most politicians don't write their speeches. He had an advisor, Pat Caddell, a pollster and friend, who was the one who thought of the speech. Why didn't Biden just say, "I didn't write the speech"?

FF: I think in the moment he just got carried away. The speech nominally acknowledged Neil Kinnock, but he just took on this other guy's biography in the course of delivering this oratory.

DR: At the time, he said he was pulling out not so much because of the alleged plagiarism but because he wanted to concentrate on the Senate confirmation of Robert Bork. He was then the chair of the Senate Judiciary Committee. Did he lead the effort to kill Bork's nomination?

FF: In Washington, there are show horses and there are workhorses. Biden went from trying to be a show horse, who gave electrifying speeches, to becoming a workhorse. One way of proving he was able to do this was to throw himself into the stuff that the Senate did.

DR: He became famous for blocking Bork from becoming a Supreme Court justice. Later, he had another nominee sent up to him when he was chairman of the committee. That was Clarence Thomas. In hindsight, does he regret the way he handled that?

FF: No. Joe Biden is somebody who doesn't experience many regrets. What he experiences are grievances. He's still very angry at a lot of the women's groups who he felt characterized his performance in those hearings unfairly.

DR: Later he becomes chairman of the Senate Foreign Relations Committee and makes himself into a bit of a foreign policy expert. Did he enjoy that even more than being the head of the Judiciary Committee, because he's running around the world and gets to talk to heads of state?

FF: He enjoys them both considerably. He thinks of himself as the world's leading constitutional scholar. He also really does love foreign policy, more than almost anything in life. Speaking with foreign leaders on the phone is his happy place. And if his staff doesn't manage his schedule in the right way, it expands to blow up the entirety of his day.

DR: He decides to run for president again. This is the year that Hillary Clinton and Barack Obama are running. We don't talk much about the Biden campaign for that year. Why?

FF: Because it was a pretty stunted venture that went almost nowhere.

DR: Did he even get to Iowa or New Hampshire?

FF: It was such a footnote to the rest of his career. I think he made it through Iowa, but I don't think he made it to New Hampshire.

DR: Obama becomes the Democratic nominee for president that year, and he picks Joe Biden as vice president. Why did Obama pick him when he didn't know him that well?

FF: Obama sent some aide a note while Biden was speaking in the Senate Foreign Relations Committee, complaining about this blowhard who was going on forever. But what Obama needed was that weight, that resume. Joe Biden had the foreign policy experience. He had these relationships on the Hill. It was proof to the world of Obama's seriousness about governance.

DR: They were partners for eight years. How did they get along?

FF: There's an arc to the relationship. When Biden comes in, Obama needs him, and he gives him important tasks to perform, but at the same time, there is this cultural temperamental disconnect between the two of them. Joe Biden's tendency to go on to, to engage in these soliloquies where he references all of these characters from his past and from Scranton, annoyed Obama, who would roll his eyes at him. That essentially gave the green light to the rest of Obama's staff to turn Joe Biden into the punch line. And you know who knew that he was the punch line of all those jokes? Joe Biden, which only made him want to speak even more to win over the audience.

DR: When Obama runs for reelection, did he ever consider replacing Biden?

FF: No. Over the course of his presidency, Obama, who had campaigned against Washington politics and against politicians, came to have greater respect for the likes of Harry Reid, Nancy Pelosi, and Joe Biden. These tasks that Obama treated with such disdain, like negotiating with Mitch McConnell, he came to respect Biden for performing adequately.

DR: He gives Joe Biden a Presidential Medal of Freedom with Distinction, the highest honor a civilian can get, and kind of says, "You've done a great job as vice president, but Hillary's going to be a stronger candidate, and Beau Biden's death gives you a very good reason why you shouldn't be running." Is that essentially right?

FF: That's right. He doesn't say to Biden, "You're my anointed successor," but tells him that they need to clear the field for Hillary Clinton. Part of this has to do with Beau Biden's death and the trauma and grief and mourning that Joe Biden was experiencing, but it was also that Barack Obama clearly thought that Hillary Clinton was the better candidate. There's also an interesting counterfactual: if we went back to 2016, if Joe Biden had been the candidate then, in my opinion, he would have stood a much better chance of beating Donald Trump, because he neutralized a lot of the attacks that Trump would ultimately lob against Hillary Clinton.

DR: Trump is elected president. Biden is out of office, and for the first time since he was 29 or 30 years old he is out of government. What does he do?

FF: He sets up the Biden Institute. He takes a gig at the University of Pennsylvania. It's a period where he is a bit at loose ends, because he's a professional politician. It's the thing he's done for the entirety of his life.

DR: He leaves the vice presidency when he's roughly 73 years old. For those four years, for the first time in his life, he's making some money speaking, consulting, writing books, and so forth. Does he think that he should run for president again or his time is over?

FF: Very soon into the Trump presidency, Biden begins to think about running. The Charlottesville "Unite the Right" moment in 2017 is something that has a profound effect on his thinking about his political prospects and that maybe he's the one to stop Donald Trump.

DR: Was there a groundswell of support in the Democratic Party for Biden or not?

FF: I would say no.

DR: He has a shoestring campaign. He doesn't raise that much money. He comes in fourth in Iowa. But that's better than New Hampshire, where he comes in fifth. Why did he think he should continue? Did he have enough money to continue?

FF: One of the more admirable qualities Biden possesses is this incredible resilience that goes back to his stutter, continues through the tragedy that he suffers with his family in the car crash, continues through the collapse of his 1988 and 2008 campaigns. He has this ultimate faith in himself, in his ability, and he could see toward the South Carolina primary, where there was a different demographic and a chance to rebound.

DR: He wins the South Carolina primary, and then the people he's running against suddenly say, "We're giving up now." Why did they leave the field so quickly?

FF: The two other leading candidates came from much further to the left and were potentially riskier general election candidates. The pandemic was crashing. So the idea of having somebody who was a safe bet, a sober person who had governing experience, seemed like the wise political strategy.

DR: Biden gets the nomination. Why did he pick Kamala Harris as vice president?

FF: He promised to pick a woman as his vice president. He was never enamored with Kamala Harris as his leading choice for number two. Biden varies from being somebody who is extremely decisive, who has strong gut instincts, to somebody who struggles to make a decision. And this was a decision he struggled to make.

DR: The campaign was waged largely from his house. He didn't campaign that much physically because of COVID. Who was running the campaign?

FF: Joe Biden usually is his own most important campaign advisor, his most important foreign policy advisor, his most important economic advisor. He has strong instincts about how to conduct things based on his many years. This was just what events imposed upon the campaign. The pandemic shut everything down, and he was campaigning as the candidate of prudence in the middle of it.

DR: I've seen a lot of presidential debates but I'd never seen one like the first debate with President Trump. Was Biden prepared for that kind of interruption? What did he think of his performance afterwards?

FF: You can be intellectually prepared for Donald Trump, but then to actually experience it in that kind of setting, especially for somebody who was raised in the Senate with its genteel traditions—I think it kind of rocked Biden's world.

DR: The general election is held. President Trump doesn't agree with the outcome. What did Biden think? No transition was authorized, so what did he do after he won?

FF: The transition is fascinating for many reasons, but among them is this. Joe Biden's best friend is a guy named Ted Kaufman, who had been his chief of staff in the Senate and who, when Biden became vice president, got appointed to the Senate for a brief period, then was Biden's emissary to the Obama transition. Kaufman is an engineer who worked at DuPont. He looked at the transition process and said, "This is cockamamie. Everybody's focused on the wrong things. It's very inefficient." And so, when he was a senator, he wrote an act to remake the presidential transition.

He and Biden began talking in March of 2020 about what the transition would look like. It's one of the most impressive things, organizationally, that Biden did. It was a human resource operation that was extremely efficient.

DR: Jeff Zients, now chief of staff, ran the transition. Eventually, Biden is sworn in as president. Does he have his cabinet picked out in advance? How long would it take to get those people confirmed?

FF: One of the things Ted Kaufman understood was that the president has all this power to appoint people below the cabinet level. The goal was to have more than a thousand of those people in place on day one. Then they were very efficient about picking the cabinet.

DR: Their priority was dealing with COVID. When Biden took office, we were developing the vaccine, but there was no plan to distribute it.

FF: Biden had two big problems. The first was that the government had made this bet on Operation Warp Speed, but Pfizer, which made the vaccine that hit first, had not taken federal money because they didn't want the government involved in their business. There was a very broken relationship with Pfizer, which didn't have the manufacturing capacity to produce the amount of vaccine that was needed. So they needed to use the government to engage in, essentially, industrial policy to ramp up Pfizer's production. The other problem was that when the Biden team came in, they kept asking, "Where is the plan to take this vaccine and stick it in people's arms?" And they couldn't find that plan despite asking for it everywhere.

DR: Because there was no plan.

FF: There was no plan.

DR: Ultimately, Jeff Zients and his team developed a plan. Did it work?

FF: It did. It was a commonsense plan for utilizing pharmacies as a primary way to distribute the vaccine, correcting for not just inequities but the lack of a delivery mechanism for poor communities. I think it was one of the most successful government programs of all time, because within six months of Biden coming into office, it was possible to stroll into your neighborhood pharmacy to get a shot that would save your life.

DR: As part of getting the economy going again after being hurt by COVID, President Biden proposed an enormous stimulus package. We'd already had a stimulus package passed under President Trump. How large was the Biden stimulus package?

FF: It was $1.9 trillion. Some of that was not just stimulus. It was money that was needed to fund the pandemic efforts. But in between the time the stimulus was conceived and then passed, the Democrats won two special elections in Georgia, which gave them control of the Senate.

They had originally intended to create a stimulus that was $1.2 trillion, approximately, in size, but the Senate Democrats had this long wish list of programs. Usually, in an instance like that—this is what happened with

Obama—you get negotiated down, but in this instance, they got negotiated up.

DR: Of the $1.9 trillion that they wanted, what actually passed?

FF: There was a big expansion of the Child Tax Credit. There were programs that were essentially forms of reparations to Black farmers. There was the pandemic relief. There was money that got plowed into state and local governments. A lot of this was a correction for the failures of the Obama stimulus in 2009. The conventional wisdom within Democratic circles was that that bill was too small and this time they had to err on the side of going too big.

DR: Larry Summers, head of the National Economic Council under President Obama, said later that he made a mistake in not having a big enough stimulus. This time, he said the stimulus was too big and would cause inflation. Did that upset President Biden?

FF: It did. Larry Summers is the type of person who would gnaw at President Biden, because he comes from this elite that Biden believes looks down on him. This was in the middle of Biden's honeymoon period. Nobody in the Democratic Party was criticizing him. Summers was the skunk at the garden party. And Biden called him up and unloaded on him.

DR: Did Larry Summers ever get an appointment under President Biden?

FF: No, but he served a fairly important role. Biden continues to talk to him. I think there's something a little bit strategic in their symbiotic relationship. Summers knows that he can influence Biden, and Biden keeps Summers close so that he doesn't criticize him from outside.

DR: President Biden gets this piece of stimulus legislation passed. What's his next priority with respect to Congress?

FF: He unveils two big pieces of legislation, known at the time as the jobs plan and the families plan. The jobs plan was what would become the infrastructure bill. The families plan is what became the expansion of the social safety net. The climate plan became known as Build Back Better, a phrase that Biden had used.

DR: For the Inflation Reduction Act, part of Build Back Better, a major effort was made to pass the Democratic Party wish list, more or less. At just over $3 trillion, did everybody agree that was the right number?

FF: The Democratic Party is a coalition in which there are progressives. A lot of the policy, in terms of campaign promises and what became the stuff of those bills, was hammered out in confabs, where they had representatives of the Bernie Sanders and Elizabeth Warren camps meet with representatives of the Biden camp and come up with some sort of consensus policy, which became the basis for these bills. The fundamental fact of the Biden presidency is that he has this one-vote edge in the Senate, which means that any senator essentially has a veto over legislation, and there was a raft of senators who didn't like the price tag.

DR: Build Back Better was thought to be maybe too expensive by some Democrats, particularly the senator from Arizona and the senator from West Virginia. So they became very powerful. How did we go from Build Back Better to the Inflation Reduction Act? Was that Senator Joe Manchin basically dictating what was going to pass and Biden going along with it?

FF: There was this fascinating dynamic where Joe Manchin, a fairly conservative senator from West Virginia, becomes the primary negotiator on this bill. He's willing to go along with things that he doesn't actually believe in, because he wants to help Biden get a deal done. But at a certain point, as this stretches on, his desire to help the president and do what he considers to be the right thing come into tension. And it all blows up over a press release, of all things, at the end of the first year that Biden's in office. Biden had thought he was getting this deal done with Manchin and that he almost had Manchin's sign-off. He puts out this press release saying that they're still negotiating. Manchin was taking all this heat from the left, and the fact that he was singled out in this press release made him feel like he was being targeted by the president. So he goes on Fox News, and he pulls the plug.

DR: Ultimately, the bill got passed. Then somebody came up with the name "Inflation Reduction Act," which people laughed at. Who came up with the name?

FF: It was the product of several hands, but Joe Manchin especially liked the title.

DR: After the initial stimulus package, they focus on the infrastructure bill. How did they get a bipartisan infrastructure bill through Congress when President Trump hadn't been able to?

FF: The moderates in the Senate began to feel their oats. They saw Joe Biden coming in. They thought he was one of their own, and that they were going to be the ones bossing the institution. They felt there was this opportunity to get something done in a bipartisan way. For Biden, this was a commonsense political deal to hatch.

DR: After a couple of weeks, the infrastructure bill passed. Who's orchestrating this for Biden?

FF: A lot of that deal with the infrastructure bill was hashed out by the Senate. Then Biden sent in Steve Ricchetti, another former Biden chief of staff, who did a lot of negotiating back and forth. But Biden, who loves talking to foreign leaders, also loves talking to other senators. And there was a point where his chief of staff Ron Klain had to come into the office and say, "Mr. President, you're not the majority leader. You're not prime minister. I know that you love these negotiations, but you can't be the one conducting them."

DR: So President Biden pulls back from the day-to-day negotiations. Is he enjoying the job in the first year or so? The job he wanted for 48 years, he finally has it.

FF: One of the underrated aspects of Joe Biden, and probably one of the reasons why he's running for reelection, is that he does love his job. There are moments where he hates the fact that the world doesn't appreciate the great job he thinks he's doing, but dealing with senators and foreign leaders is his happy place.

DR: Let's talk about foreign policy. Initially there's a concern that the Chinese are not going to be as friendly as we once had thought. President Trump had been tough on the Chinese. The Chinese thought that

President Biden might be easier, like Obama. Why did the administration go toward a tough policy on China? Was that Joe Biden or his advisors?

FF: I think that's Joe Biden. In the middle of the Obama administration, he's at the vanguard of a revised policy toward China that becomes the consensus within the Democratic Party. He'd pull people aside and he'd start to talk about how China was engaged in unfair labor practices, unfair trade practices, how they had a poor human rights record.

Trump comes in and says all these things in a very impolitic sort of way, but he helps clear out some old conventional wisdom. Biden takes some of Trump's populism and implements it in a more responsible, moderate sort of way.

DR: The Chinese are surprised. They thought President Biden was going to have a much easier policy. What is Biden's policy now?

FF: He's trying to increase the pressure on China, trying to treat them in a more adversarial way without having the whole relationship run off the rails and culminate in something very dangerous.

DR: Let's talk about what many people would say is one of his biggest failures, which is Afghanistan and the retreat from it. He might not say that.

FF: He sure wouldn't.

DR: The Pentagon is saying, at the beginning of the Obama years, "We need more troops in Afghanistan if we're going to be able to do what we want to do." In your book, you point out that Biden thinks that the Pentagon is taking advantage of a new president. And he tells Obama what?

FF: He says, "Don't let the military jam you."

DR: In the beginning of the Biden administration, the issue arises of whether we should get out of Afghanistan. What does Biden say?

FF: First of all, there was a 2021 deadline imposed by negotiations, a deal that the Trump administration had cut with the Taliban. If the Taliban met various conditions by then, the U.S. promised it would get out. In a way, this deadline was a gift to Joe Biden, who wanted to get out of Afghanistan.

This timeline imposed pressure to make a decision. He begins to structure a decision-making process in order to avoid the bureaucratic pitfalls that stopped Obama from doing what he wanted.

DR: Despite the agreement that President Trump and his people negotiated, didn't many people in the Pentagon think that since we had 3,000 or 4,000 military people there, we should keep them there for a variety of reasons?

FF: That is true, but there's also an interesting dynamic happening in parallel to this. Mark Milley, the chairman of the Joint Chiefs of Staff, had just survived the Trump years. He was eager to prove that the civilians were in charge, that it was his job as commander of the military to submit to whatever democratically derived decision the president came up with.

DR: President Biden says, "I want out. No more troops. Everybody's gone." And preparation was made for an airlift to get everybody out. What went wrong that resulted in American soldiers getting killed?

FF: Very practical things went wrong, almost too boring to talk about. But the big-picture thing was that Biden never elevated the humanitarian evacuation to be one of the top concerns of the whole bureaucratic process. It became something of an afterthought. And there was an intelligence failure, where we thought that the Taliban would take over but that it would happen after we were gone.

DR: The Taliban obviously made greater progress than we anticipated. Then a bomb was set off and killed 21 American soldiers. Biden is not happy with this. Does he say, as Kennedy did with the Bay of Pigs, "I take the responsibility. I made a mistake"?

FF: We see these terrible images transpiring at Hamid Karzai International Airport. The president pivots and changes strategy in a dramatic fashion. He says, essentially, that every C-17 leaving Afghanistan needs to be filled with civilians.

In the end, the State Department and the military improvised the evacuation of 125,000 Afghans. In that respect, Biden deserves credit for changing policy. As it relates to the broader failure in Afghanistan, his response is to say that this was always going to be messy, which is probably true. But he never said that to the American people in advance of the messiness.

DR: What is his relationship with Vladimir Putin? Did he know Putin pretty well as VP and senator?

FF: He did. He got sent in for some of the reset discussions the Obama administration had. He tells the story about how he stared into Putin's eyes and told him afterwards, "You have no soul." At which Vladimir Putin laughed.

DR: The U.S. gets intelligence saying that the Russians are massing on the Ukraine border. We declassified this intelligence and start telling our allies. Did President Biden want to make sure the allies knew this was going to happen?

FF: That, and also he wanted Russia to be morally culpable for what was about to happen. He didn't want them to be able to plan any false-flag actions that would have shifted blame to the Ukrainians.

DR: President Biden rallies the European allies to support this effort to help Ukraine. He regards this as one of his most important accomplishments, to help Ukraine fight Russia, even though we haven't figured out the end of that war yet. If our European allies had believed our intelligence, would we be in a stronger position? The allies didn't initially believe that the invasion was going to happen.

FF: The biggest problem was that Volodymyr Zelenskyy didn't acknowledge the intelligence and he didn't act on it in the fullest sort of way. There were tough conversations that Tony Blinken, Kamala Harris, and Joe Biden all had with him, saying, "Your country is about to be invaded. You need to take all of these steps."

Zelenskyy was in disbelief. He said Russia was just conducting coercive diplomacy. Meanwhile, he was acting on it in measured ways. But there were things that he could have done at the beginning of the war.

DR: There is a war going on in Gaza as a result of what happened on October 7th, 2023. Something similar had happened before, earlier in the Biden administration, when rockets from Gaza were fired into Israel. What was

Biden's view on how to handle that? And what is his relationship with Benjamin Netanyahu?

FF: He has a relationship with Netanyahu that goes back to the 1980s. He has a relationship with Israel that goes back much further. His father was a Zionist. He grew up with the sense that if Israel didn't exist, it should be invented, that the Jewish claim to a state there was extremely strong, both because of the Holocaust and because of the larger history. He likes to boast about conversations he had with Golda Meir during the Yom Kippur War.

In May 2021, there are the rocket attacks from Gaza, and Israel begins to plan for a response. And Biden's attitude was, "What I need to do is bank emotional trust with the Israelis, because they have very good reasons for feeling anxious. Then, when the moment comes, I'm going to spend down that capital in order to shorten the length of this war."

DR: Let's talk about the way he operates the presidency. Some presidents, like President Obama, prefer to read memos and then send notes back to the staff. Is Biden that way, or he likes to have the team come in and talk about it?

FF: He processes everything verbally. He takes binders home with him at the end of the day and scrawls notes, but he's not an interior person. He can't sit in his study late at night, like Obama did, and think everything through. He needs to talk it through. Those sessions can be quite lengthy, and he tends to conduct them with his various small group of advisors, most of whom have been with him for a long time.

DR: Who are his advisors? At the beginning, it was Ron Klain, who had been his chief of staff when he was vice president, with him for over 20 years. He left at the end of two years. Who replaced him?

FF: Jeff Zients.

DR: Who are the other senior people in the White House now, the most influential people?

FF: There are several other people who had been Biden's chief of staff during the vice presidency. There's Steve Ricchetti, who had worked with

Clinton before then, who has this legislative responsibility. Bruce Reed had also worked in the Clinton White House, and had been Biden's chief of staff. There's Anita Dunn, his communications guru. Then there's a guy named Mike Donilon, who's worked with him since the 1980s. He's kind of Biden's alter ego, writes his big speeches.

DR: Two other people are very influential—two women. One of them is his wife. How influential is she on political matters?

FF: My sense is that she's extremely influential. Everybody will assert her influence, but then struggles to come up with examples. I think that's because she wields her power in the quiet of a family dinner or the bedroom. She's not vocal about asserting herself in public.

DR: What about his sister? She managed all of his campaigns until the most recent presidential campaign. Is she still influential?

FF: She'll play a role, especially in the construction of big speeches. But she's not a day-to-day policy advisor.

DR: You write about the first two years, but we're now past that. Is he enjoying the job?

FF: I think so. That's a complicated question to pose to anybody, let alone somebody who has the vast portfolio that he does. I think one of the things that he dislikes about his job is that he feels some sense of responsibility for the way in which his son Hunter has had his reputation tarnished, his career opened up by Republicans.

DR: Biden is the oldest person ever elected president of the United States. He was elected when he was 78. He has served as president at the age of 82. Do you have any insights about why at that age he would say, "Yes, I want to do this for four more years"?

FF: He comes from this other generation, and a lot of his techniques and theories of politics are antiquated by the standards of today. That's the thing that makes him interesting, and to an extent it makes him successful. The flip side of the age conversations we're having now is that there's wisdom that comes in.

But we need to disaggregate the age question into two separate questions. The first is a question of governance. Does he have the mental acuity to do the job now? The fact that in a press conference he confuses Egypt and Mexico, that's not shaping American policy in any sort of meaningful sort of way. When it comes to the way in which he governs, there are a lot of people who are very motivated to walk out of the Oval Office and say, "He's out to lunch." But you never heard Kevin McCarthy or Benjamin Netanyahu or Vladimir Putin saying, "This guy isn't up to the task."

There's a separate question of the energy and the stamina and the oratorical skills that are required to be a commanding political figure. That's the place where I see age taking the greatest toll on him. He doesn't have the ability to barnstorm across the country giving speeches. These big set speeches take a lot of concentration and effort for him, in part because of age, in part because of the stammer. In the last two years that has become a really big deal, because American voters say it's a really big deal.

DR: There's a great tradition of White House leaking. But in this administration, unlike the Trump administration, you don't see much leaking. Why?

FF: Because you have a group of people who've worked with him for so long, and they understand the way that he processes information. They don't react to anything that he says in a meeting with him because they've heard it all before from him. They know how he thinks. He needs to think aloud, and they're not going to punish him for that. He's a father figure to them in many respects. They feel this intense loyalty to the man.

DR: Today there are very few fresh faces working for him. Is that fair to say?

FF: Yes. Even the fresh faces, somebody like Jake Sullivan, his national security advisor, actually worked with him in the Obama White House. Brian Deese, the economic advisor who played a significant role in the first two years, was somebody Biden also knew from the Obama White House.

DR: Let's talk about his environmental policy. He appointed John Kerry to serve as a special ambassador for climate change. How has that effort worked, and why did he pick Kerry for that job?

FF: He and Kerry have the senatorial bond. They're also both liberal Catholics who have taken a lot of heat from their church because of their positions on abortion. And there was this real camaraderie. Kerry is one of the people Biden can go to as an outside advisor on many things. His job was to revive American climate diplomacy, which has been modestly successful. But the biggest reason that there's any hope for it is because we passed the Inflation Reduction Act, which for the first time takes significant steps to reduce our reliance on carbon.

DR: What would you say is Biden's major accomplishment during his first term as president?

FF: That he's presided over America's entry into a new age of political economy. It's not disconnected from the Trump administration. You had an orthodoxy that prevailed for 30 or 40 years, you could argue going back to Jimmy Carter, who began the process of deregulation, through the Reagan Revolution, through the Clinton and Obama administrations, which in different ways ratified the Reagan approach to the political economy.

Then Trump and Biden start to go in a different direction, with the tariffs on China, a more aggressive position on monopoly. Biden helps to revive trade unions. And then, primarily, there's this changing role for the American government in the management of the market. The government has become an investment banker that's made big bets on the economic future of the country through the CHIPS Act, through the Inflation Reduction Act, through the infrastructure bill. The state is shifting the trajectory of the economy in a way that I think will define economics for the next generation.

DR: What does President Biden like to do most?

FF: He enjoys negotiation. Joe Biden's strength is his empathy. It's something he tries to apply to senators and to foreign leaders. He really loves the process of sitting down beforehand and saying, "Okay, what is this person's self-interest? How am I going to be able to get them to yes?" Then he loves being able to talk about how he got that person to yes, after the fact, with his advisors.

DR: If President Trump decided not to run for election again, do you think Joe Biden would still run for reelection?

FF: It would complicate his decision. In a way, Trump's running made it easier for Biden to tell himself this story that he was the person who stopped Trump the last time, and a bet on any other Democratic politician was going to be risky. It wasn't worth it, given the stakes of this election.

DR: Sometimes he curses privately. Does he have a big temper? Or is he always even-keeled?

FF: He likes to talk about his Irish temper. The thing about Joe Biden is that the moments of grace with him are more intense than with your normal politician. When he's able to look into your eyes, or to call you when you've lost a parent, those are intense moments.

Then he has these flashes of anger. Some of them occur when he feels like people are talking down to him. If an aide comes in and starts talking to him as if he's a junior member of the House of Representatives, he'll get his back up.

DR: In your book, you never actually quote an interview you've had with Joe Biden. Is that because you can't talk about whether you got an interview with him or because you didn't get an interview with him?

FF: Joe Biden is not a fan in general of books about the presidency. He didn't cooperate with Bob Woodward. But I was able to talk to him off the record on two occasions with groups of other journalists. Which for me was helpful, because you hear all the stories about the guy. The difference between the public Joe Biden and the private Joe Biden, the Joe Biden that people describe to you and the Joe Biden that actually exists, is very narrow. He kind of is "what you see is what you get."

DR: What do you think most people don't know about Joe Biden?

FF: In the context of this debate about his age, you hear people talk about Joe Biden as if he's this guy who can't find his way around the White House and needs aides to steer him this way or that. But the Joe Biden who I saw, especially in those first two years, is somebody who is deeply engaged in the weeds of policy. Almost too engaged. Obama hated to prepare for a press conference or an interview. Joe Biden, who's been described as the gaffe machine, certainly feels like he has this need to prepare, and he tends to overprepare. The insecurity that grew out of the

Neil Kinnock speech and all the stuff that we described earlier is very real, and it's still with him.

It's almost a conspiracy theory that people have where they assume somebody else is running this presidency. But so far as I can tell, from what I have reported and what I've heard from everybody who's deeply involved, it's unmistakably Joe Biden's presidency.

DR: Sometimes people say you have to wait 40 years after a president's term to know if he did a good job. But let's suppose 10 years from today, if Biden just has the one term, what do you think historians would say he did that was really impressive?

FF: The problem with writing history is that the endpoint for your narrative dictates everything that comes before. For Joe Biden, his legacy suddenly hinges on one event, which is the result of the 2024 elections. Everything that he's done to this point becomes irrelevant if he loses to Donald Trump.

CONCLUSION

The United States has been fortunate to have had a number of extraordinary individuals serve the country in its "Highest Calling." After World War II and through the end of the twentieth century, we became the undisputed economic, financial, military, geopolitical, technological, and cultural global force, and that is likely to continue to a large extent well into the twenty-first century. Of course, the many strengths of the U.S. during this period cannot be attributed solely to the quality and effectiveness of a number of those who served their country as president of the U.S., but surely a number of them had a real impact in strengthening the country.

Stated differently, the country (and in my view the world) is surely better off when strong, competent, honest individuals attain the presidency and work their will on behalf of the American people.

How, though, do we get these kinds of people to want to serve, want to sacrifice a bit of their financial and physical well-being, their privacy, their reputations, and potentially their lives for the good of the country? How do we attract the country's most talented individuals, with some of the requisite political skills needed to get and do the job? In attracting top-tier talent, political parties should try to encourage individuals with broad experience in business, philanthropy, education, or nonelective government positions to consider becoming presidential candidates. Unfortunately, in attracting these individuals, the political parties are limited to native-born Americans, which is a requirement of the Constitution. While constitutional amendments are time-consuming and hard to achieve — as noted below — an amendment in this area would be a welcome change.

There are, to be sure, several proposed changes to the current campaign and election process that would help encourage more people to run, though these changes would no doubt be difficult to achieve. First perhaps is changing the way we elect presidents. The Electoral College, the result of a secret deliberation during the Constitutional Convention, was designed to ensure that reasonably informed citizens—the electors—selected the president rather than the presumably less-informed and less-educated masses (which, then, included only white Christian property-owning men, for only they could vote). In virtually every other election in the United States, the majority popular vote prevails. That is, presumably, the essence of a representative democracy. Unfortunately, the Electoral College runs counter to that notion. In five elections, the candidate with the second-most popular votes had the most Electoral College votes and became president. (These were John Quincy Adams in 1824, Rutherford B. Hayes in 1876, Benjamin Harrison in 1888, George W. Bush in 2000, and Donald J. Trump in 2016.)

The Electoral College is part of the Constitution, and an amendment to abolish it would require two-thirds approval by the Senate and the House and a ratification by three-quarters of the states. That is unlikely to occur. The smaller-population states have more influence in the Electoral College system than they would under a direct election system, and it is inconceivable that enough of the smaller states would approve of any change to the Electoral College. Indeed, more than seven hundred bills to change or abolish the Electoral College have been introduced in Congress since its inception in 1788, and none have won the approval of the Senate or the House.

However, a modified change to the Electoral College system has gained some momentum recently. Under the National Popular Vote Interstate Compact, each state agrees to have its electors vote for the popular-vote winner in the country. Sixteen states (and Washington, D.C.) with 205 Electoral College votes have approved such a plan, which would go into effect when states with 270 Electoral College votes approve of the plan. But the states that have approved this tend to be "blue" (Democratic) states, and the prospect of "red" (Republican) states joining it seems highly remote.

Another major obstacle to attracting the country's most talented individuals for presidential elections is the enormous, unrelenting time it takes to campaign. Through the early days of the twentieth century, presidential candidates did not personally campaign for the position. In recent decades, though, personal and constant campaigning has become a necessity. It has expanded from about a year before the general election to two years. President Trump announced his campaign for 2024 in November of 2022. No other country in the world has campaigns of this duration, and it is hard to believe that such long campaigns are an inducement to talented individuals to want to run and spend two years or so on the road campaigning, much less having to also raise the funds to do so. And the money now needed to run is staggering.

Today, no real limits exist on what an individual or corporation can give to a campaign. Prior to the campaign finance legislation reforms of 1971 (and the additional post-Watergate reforms of 1974), there were no federal limits on what could be given to a presidential general election campaign. With those reforms, a $1,000-per-person limit was established for individual donations. But in 1976 the Supreme Court in *Buckley v. Valeo* effectively overturned that limit. And in 2010, in the *Citizens United* case, the court allowed corporations to make contributions as well, which previously had been more or less prohibited, and also eliminated limits on "independent" campaign contributions. As a result, it is tempting for campaigns to seek large million-dollar-plus contributions, and they typically come from those who want something from the federal government—access, favorable legislation, contracts, appointments, and more. While that is hardly a new phenomenon in politics, or in presidential elections, today the sums involved are so large as to make the appearance of favoritism for large donors unavoidable, resulting inevitably in perceptions of less than a desired "clean" or wholly honest government. In 2020, the various entities supporting President Trump and then former vice president Biden spent more than $5 billion on the campaign. And few, if any, individuals who would like to run for president really want to spend time asking friends and strangers for the money currently needed to run.

In short, the biggest problems with the current presidential election system—in having a truly "democratic" election and in attracting talented individuals to run for president—are the method of voting, the length of the campaign, and the unlimited amount of money which can be given and which is spent. Unfortunately, as noted, none of these problems can really be changed without constitutional amendments, and in these areas, those amendments are all but impossible. Thus in the near term the meaningful changes that can be made to the way we elect presidents or pay for their campaigns will not occur.

But there are some lesser changes, which do not require constitutional amendments, that around the margin might be a way to improve some aspects of the presidency.

Disclosure. Presidential candidates (or presidents) are not required to make meaningful financial or health disclosures. The public would be served better, in my view, if presidential candidates were required to make public their income tax returns. Today no such requirement exists, though many candidates in recent years, and many presidents, have voluntarily made such disclosures. The Federal Election Commission does require candidates to file financial disclosure forms, but these forms are far short of what might be disclosed in an income tax filing.

Presidential candidates, or presidents, also do not need to disclose their health—physical or mental—and the disclosures that are routinely supplied by candidates do not contain any independent assessments, presumably due to the desire to protect the privacy of a candidate. But it seems reasonable that a certain level of privacy about the state of their health should be waived by someone seeking the highest office in the land, and some independent assessment would thus seem desirable. That seems particularly true for an incumbent president, although they routinely use government doctors to assess their health, and that assessment is likely to be slightly more balanced than a candidate's personal doctor's assessment. Of course, government doctors do seem, in time, to bond with their presidential patients, and rarely provide any information not favorable to their president.

Conflicts of interest. There are extensive conflicts-of-interest rules for presidential appointees. They may well have to sell many, if not most, of their assets if there could be a perception of a conflict. But, interestingly, there are no rules or requirements relating to a president's conflicts of interest. Typically, a president will not have that much in the way of financial resources as to which a conflict would really arise; but to avoid even the appearance of a potential problem, some have entered binding blind-trust arrangements. President Carter did this, as did President Kennedy. The wealthiest person to serve as president, Donald Trump, turned over his major business operations to his oldest sons to

oversee, though there was no binding blind trust. Legislation requiring blind trusts or some similar mechanism would seem to
make clear that a president's decisions are not designed for personal financial gain.

Transitions. Presidential candidates should be required to have
transition teams working at least three months before the November election, to ensure a relatively smooth change of power if the
incumbent party loses the election. And the incumbent president
should not be able to thwart a transition by refusing to permit a
transition to occur. Congress has addressed this problem, which
arose in 2020, by passing legislation in 2021. But the legislation
does not require either the outgoing or incoming president to take
transitions seriously, and put their best talent on the undertaking.
That cannot be legislated, but more media and public attention
on the pre- and post-election transition, as they occur, would be
helpful.

Pardons. The presidential power of pardon is granted in the Constitution, and that power seems absolute—no criteria for a pardon
are set forth in the Constitution, and there are no requirements
for explanation. Typically, presidents grant pardons throughout
their term, but many of the more controversial pardons seem to
be granted when the term is almost over, there generally being no
political consequences for a president who is leaving office. As his
administration was ending, one president, Bill Clinton, granted a
pardon to Marc Rich, who had been convicted of violating federal energy trading laws but fled from the U.S. prior to sentencing.
This pardon became highly controversial because of the circumstances that may have led to it being granted—gifts made before
the pardon from Rich's former wife to the Democratic Party and
the Clinton Presidential Library. President Trump also received
considerable adverse attention from some pardons granted at the
end of his term, such as to the father of his son-in-law Jared Kushner and to longtime political supporters Roger Stone and Paul
Manafort.

Pardon power is unlikely to be changed or modified by a
constitutional amendment or by the courts. But a law might be
upheld by the courts if a president were simply asked to explain

the reason for a particular pardon. An explanation would provide greater public understanding about why a pardon was granted, and that should serve the public's interest in knowing why a president has acted—though I recognize that a president, particularly one about to leave office, is unlikely to forgo granting a pardon because of such a requirement.

Press interviews/conferences. There is no requirement in the Constitution or any law that a president answer press questions or speak to any member of the press ever. A law requiring press appearances also seems hard to pass in Congress, but it would be desirable if presidents met regularly with some members of the press to answer questions, or to do a full-scale press conference from time to time. Some presidents have done this regularly, like President John F. Kennedy, who had a press conference nearly every two weeks. Others have been less willing to hold press conferences regularly, though they do talk to a few reporters (generally those who are friendly) from time to time.

The suggestion here is simply that it might be advisable to have some standard of a president meeting with a few or a full set of press members to respond to questions on a somewhat regular basis. Responding to press questions regularly does not mean that a president is necessarily doing a good job, but being forced to prepare for such conferences—and then answering questions—does seem to give the public a sense of what is in the mind of the person leading the country's government.

Debates. There is also no requirement that presidents or presidential candidates debate. The first such debates occurred in 1960, when Senator John F. Kennedy and Vice President Richard Nixon held four debates. The next presidential debates occurred in 1976, when President Gerald Ford and Governor Jimmy Carter had three debates.

Since that time, there have been debates in each presidential election. But there is no legal requirement to debate, and it is clear that the skill needed to do well in a debate is a bit different than the skill needed to be an effective president.

But debates do increase interest in the election, and generally are a plus for democracy. No law is likely to pass requiring presidential debates, but public and media pressure to ensure debates occur would be a welcome plus for presidential elections.

Former presidents. In some countries, leaders seem to make a fair amount of money while in office. In the U.S., presidents seem to make a fair amount of money after they leave office. Former presidents are now busily engaged in writing memoirs, building presidential libraries and museums, making speeches, and (depending on their popularity) campaigning for other political figures in their party.

Until the time of President Ford's retirement, the concept of making significant sums of money for speeches (or corporate appearances or board positions) was generally nonexistent. Presidents did make money writing their memoirs, but that was their principal source of postpresidential income for those who did so. In more recent years, most former presidents have managed to make a fair amount of money not only on their books, but also on speeches, business opportunities, or related investment activities. My former boss, Jimmy Carter, generally shunned making money on speeches or business projects and supported himself principally from royalties from his dozens of books, but he was a bit unusual. To be sure, he did seek to raise large sums from corporations and individuals to fund his center's activities, though that money did not accrue to him personally.

Former presidents have a wealth of experience, and there would probably be some benefit to having them work together from time to time on matters of national interest when asked by a current president. In recent decades, President Carter tried, with the approval of President Clinton, to settle a dispute in Haiti and, separately, to ease relations with North Korea. When former presidents can use their contacts and experience to work cooperatively, or even individually, with an incumbent administration to solve national or international problems, that would seem to be a positive outcome for the country.

Popular former presidents also tend to provide advice to their successor, as President Obama seems to have done with President Biden. Hopefully, presidents will try to take advantage of one or more of their predecessor's experiences, when appropriate. Of course, some former presidents do not get along with each other, and thus it may be difficult at times to get them all to work together on a project of great public importance. But any measure that all former presidents could support would be likely to actually occur or go into effect.

In the end, though, the responsibility for getting presidents who are highly qualified and able to lead the country effectively cannot be left solely to political parties. The real responsibility falls to the American citizen, who has an obligation to vote. Sadly, even in presidential elections, less than two-thirds of eligible voters actually vote. In 2020, about 66 percent of eligible voters actually voted. Stated in different terms, about 80 million Americans who could have voted did *not* vote. In few other Western democracies do so many eligible voters—percentage-wise—*not* vote.

The U.S. government and civic groups and others need to encourage every eligible voter to vote. Millions of Americans have died over the past nearly 250 years fighting to protect our freedoms, and that includes the right to vote. Every vote can make a difference, as we have seen in elections like 2000.

This book has tried to show how different the U.S. presidents can be in background, personality, and approach. And those differences can dramatically affect how a president governs, and thus how every American is impacted by a particular president. My wish is that every American who reads this book will feel a greater civic—and patriotic—obligation to learn as much as possible about a president before he—or no doubt soon, she—will govern, and affect thereby each American's life. And hopefully, every reader eligible to vote will be certain to vote.

POSTSCRIPT

Biden vs. Trump: Election 2024

As this book goes to press, it appears that the 2024 presidential election will be a re-match of the 2020 election, except that President Biden is now the incumbent and President Trump is now the challenger. (And there is an independent candidate, Robert F. Kennedy Jr., who could take away enough votes from one major-party candidate to enable another major-party candidate to win a state).

The outcome of the election between Biden and Trump is unclear at this moment. Just a few days ago, President Trump was found guilty by a jury in a New York Court on 34 felony counts relating to a payment designed, in the prosecutor's view, to keep private an apparent extramarital encounter, thereby helping Donald Trump win the 2016 election.

The verdict will be appealed by President Trump, but whether the appeal will be successful before the November 5, 2024 election is unknown. Also unknown at this time is the impact of the guilty verdict on President Trump's election prospects. Immediately after the verdict, his campaign seemed to have a large influx of campaign donations. Too, the immediate polling data does not seem to reflect any measurable loss of support for Trump among his supporters.

The guilty verdict was, of course, major news in the United States, for no former president has ever been found guilty of a felony by the U.S. legal system. But it was also major front-page news throughout the world.

And the reason is, as noted at this book's outset, the president of the United States has been, for at least a hundred years, the dominant political government figure in the world. And the world rightly recognizes that one person—the U.S. president—can determine the economic, financial, military, geopolitical, and cultural fate of so much of the world.

In this particular election, as in the previous two, the views and policy priorities of the candidates are completely different. And the U.S. electorate, and billions of people around the world, realize that their futures can be very different depending on who is elected.

So the American voter in 2024 truly stands in the docket of history, with the opportunity to change the country's, and the world's, course, making even more important the exercise of the right to vote.

To illustrate the impact of a single vote, one need only look at the 2000 and 2020 elections.

In 2000, George Bush won Florida and the presidency by just 537 votes. In 2020, Donald Trump would have won the election—without any real dispute—if roughly 43,000 voters (out of about 165 million voters) in Georgia, Arizona, and Wisconsin had voted for him rather than Joe Biden.

The 2024 election is likely to be equally dependent on the votes of a relatively small number of voters in the "swing" states (ones that voted for Trump in 2016 and for Biden in 2020) of Georgia, Arizona, Pennsylvania, Michigan, and Wisconsin. So everyone's vote will be extraordinarily important, and voters should exercise their right to vote, on Election Day or earlier, to help ensure that as large a percentage of eligible voters as possible reflect their views on who should be the next president of the United States. Every vote really does count.

ACKNOWLEDGMENTS

I reached an agreement with Simon & Schuster about eighteen months ago to write a book on entrepreneurship, a subject of real interest to me. I had intended to interview many of the country's leading entrepreneurs and distill the key traits that made them so successful.

As I prepared to begin those interviews, I found I could not resist writing a book on a subject of nearly lifelong interest to me, the U.S. presidency, and to have that book published before the 2024 presidential election. My hope (a bit naïve no doubt) was that some insights might better inform voters about the presidency as they assess their choices in the election. (I recognize that no one book is likely to really sway how voters assess their choice for president, but hope springs eternal for all authors that their books will have some impact on readers' thoughts and behavior. I am no different.)

Because Simon & Schuster was willing to accommodate my change of plans, I am very grateful, and particularly want to thank the company's gifted president and publisher, Jonathan Karp, and my editor, Stephanie Frerich, a real pro at taking overwritten prose and distilling it into a readable text.

I would also like to thank Presidents Bill Clinton and George W. Bush (and First Lady Hillary Rodham Clinton), Donald J. Trump, and Joe Biden for agreeing to let me interview them, and to have the interviews included in this book. I would also like to thank the many presidential scholars who allowed me to interview them and to also have those interviews included in this book. I did interview a number of other scholars on particular presidents and on the presidency, but space limitations prevented me from including all interviewees, though some of them are included in the audio version of this book.

I would also like to thank Jennifer Howard, who worked tirelessly to help edit the interviews, working closely with the interviewees and the publisher, and made certain that all consents were obtained and all interviews were accurate. Jennifer has worked closely with me on all my books, and her unflagging commitment to these books and to the requisite accuracy is much appreciated. I also want to thank my friend, and outstanding writer and editor, Marie Arana, for recommending Jennifer to me as I began writing books a few years ago.

This book could not have been completed on time or with the desired accuracy without my personal staff. My three-decade-plus chief of staff, the indefatigable and superefficient MaryPat Decker, made certain that all the desired interviews could occur when needed, and ensured that the others on the staff did what was needed to help get the book completed on time and with the required skill and diplomacy needed in interacting with the interviewees. In particular, I appreciate the efforts of Laura Boring and Amanda Mangum, who have also worked for me for, respectively, nearly two decades and one decade. A new addition to my personal staff, Jack Bertuzzi, also worked tirelessly to do the required research for my interviews and to fact-check my own writing (not an always easy task).

I would also like to thank Mandeep Singh Sandhu and his team for their skill in recording and transcribing many of the interviews in this book.

And I want to express my appreciation to Chris Ullman, who has worked tirelessly in helping to deal with the various public relations opportunities for this book (as he did with my prior books).

As with all my books, Bob Barnett, my friend of nearly half a century (dating back to law school), and now one of the country's leading representatives of authors in all genres, not only encouraged me to write this book but worked closely with Simon & Schuster to secure a contract for it. Without Bob's support and encouragement, this book, and all my previous books, would not have ever been completed or published.

I would also like to thank my colleagues at Carlyle, especially my cofounders, Bill Conway and Dan D'Aniello, and Carlyle's current CEO, Harvey Schwartz, for their willingness to put up with my need, from time to time, to miss Carlyle events to complete interviews for this book. Similarly, I appreciate the support of Brian Frank, who leads Declaration Partners, a family investment vehicle, for tolerating my need to reschedule meetings periodically to complete this book.

A number of the interviews occurred at places where I do public interviews from time to time, and I appreciate the leaders at those organizations for allowing me to use interviews which occurred at their forums: Carla Hayden, the Librarian of Congress, who facilitated my interviews at the Congressional Dialogues series at the library; Louise Mirrer, president and CEO of the New-York Historical Society, who made possible a number of interviews as part of its various history programs; and the 92nd Y's president, Alyse Myers, and program director, Susan Engel, for their help with one of the interviews done there.

I would also like to thank my new partner in purchasing the Baltimore Orioles, Mike Arougheti, for tolerating my need to miss or reschedule some meetings and calls as we moved to purchase the team earlier this year.

All author proceeds will be directed to the Johns Hopkins Children's Center and the Harlem Park Elementary/Middle School, both in Baltimore.

I am certain there are some errors in this book. No book is perfect, and this one is no different. For any such mistakes, I bear full responsibility.

— *David M. Rubenstein*

INDEX

THE HIGHEST CALLING
ADDENDUM

The goal of this book is to educate readers about the importance of the presidency and how those who served as president—while focused on doing what they thought was best for America—have been so different from one another in their backgrounds, skills, personalities, and accomplishments. My hope is that readers will recognize the importance of the office and the stark differences between presidents (and presidential candidates) and then exercise their important right to vote in presidential elections.

The book was never designed to be solely about the 2024 election, yet as of this writing, in late July 2024, several seismic events have occurred over the past six weeks, any one of which is enough to impact the election significantly. Together, these events make it dramatically different from what might have been anticipated in early June of 2024, when I finished writing, and a brief addendum seemed appropriate.

First, the June 27, 2024, debate between President Joe Biden and former president Donald Trump resulted in a widespread perception that President Biden had aged significantly and did not appear to have the mental acuity needed for a president who would serve from 2025 through the beginning of 2029, when Biden would be 86. That view, widely held by Republicans as well as many Democrats, led to calls from many of his closest supporters that he withdraw from the race.

Those calls initially led the president, his family, and his closest advisors and supporters to insist that he indeed had the requisite mental acuity. But, bowing to the growing political pressure (and the seeming drying up of donor support), President Biden announced on July 21, 2024, that he was withdrawing from the 2024 campaign and would support his vice president, Kamala Harris, to be the Democratic nominee. In the immediate aftermath of that announcement, Vice President Harris gathered sufficient political and financial support to in fact secure that nomination at the Democratic Convention in mid-August.

As if these circumstances were not enough to change the trajectory of the election, significant events on the Republican side occurred as well. On July 13, 2024, former president Trump was wounded in the ear by a would-be assassin's bullet at a rally near Butler, Pennsylvania. That he escaped with a superficial wound was seen by him, and many of his supporters, as a sign from God that he was being saved for the higher purpose of getting elected again.

On July 15, 2024, ahead of the Republican Convention that nominated Trump as its presidential nominee for the third time, Trump announced Senator J.D. Vance as his running mate. The potential VP is a 39-year-old, first-term senator from Ohio, who came to national attention as the author of the bestselling memoir *Hillbilly Elegy*. The selection of Vance was widely seen as an effort not only to bring youth to the ticket—with President Trump being 78—but also to lock in the future of Trump's Make America Great Again (MAGA) movement, of which Vance was an ardent proponent (after having earlier been an outspoken Trump critic).

Serving the U.S. as president, with its enormous national and global impact, is surely the nation's Highest Calling, but it is followed closely by the calling to every eligible citizen to actually vote in a presidential election. Hopefully, this book will inspire citizens to do so.

KEEP THE PIGS OUT

DON DICKERMAN

HOUSE

A STRANG COMPANY

Cover design by Justin Evans
Design Director: Bill Johnson

Copyright © 2010 by Don Dickerman

Library of Congress Cataloging-in-Publication Data:

Dickerman, Don.
  Keep the pigs out / by Don Dickerman.
      p. cm.
  Includes bibliographical references.
  ISBN 978-1-61638-139-4
  1. Spiritual warfare. I. Title.
  BV4509.5.D53 2010
  235'.4--dc22

                       2010021127

First Edition

10 11 12 13 14 — 9 8 7 6 5 4 3 2 1
Printed in the United States of America

*To my wife and two sons, who have
supported me and shared me.*

CONTENTS

INTRODUCTION

DURING MANY YEARS of ministry I have personally preached in more than eight hundred fifty different institutions. I have attended two executions, one in Mississippi and one in Florida. Karla Faye Tucker was my friend. I had seen dramatic changes in the lives of David Berkowitz, Mark David Chapman, and many other well-known inmates. I ministered to Ted Bundy on Florida's death row. I corresponded for years with Kenneth Bianchi (the "Hillside Strangler") and Charles "Tex" Watson of the Manson family. I was deeply entrenched in prison ministry.

But I began to understand that God was preparing me for a different level of ministry. I had no idea what it was, but I knew there was more—and I hungered for it. In 1995, after twenty-one years of prison evangelism, the Holy Spirit spoke to me through a federal prison officer. His words forever changed me—and our ministry.

After that experience I began to see people not only saved but also *healed and delivered*. It has been exciting. I suppose I have ministered deliverance either personally or corporately to nearly thirty thousand people—real people, all of them Christians. I have seen that there are many absolutely consistent spiritual principles about deliverance. I have learned by experience that deliverance is not difficult. I have seen many miracles. I wrote my first book about deliverance, *When Pigs Move In*, to help people see that deliverance from demonic oppression and possession is possible—and something God desires for all His children. I was prompted by the Holy Spirit to write this follow-up book to help people discover how to *maintain freedom*, because I have found that one of the greatest problems in this area is *ignorance.*

Maintaining freedom is easy. It involves not doing things that open doors to demonic powers. It is more of *not doing* than it is doing. This book is about knowing our limitations. It is about recognizing our boundaries. It is intended to help believers remain free and to not open doors to demon powers. You will find it helpful whether you are struggling to remain spiritually free of demonic oppression, or whether you are longing to be able to lead others through the principles for God's miracle gift of deliverance.

CHAPTER 1

A VISION WITHIN
A DREAM

URING A NIGHTTIME dream, I saw a huge winged creature hovering in the sky. It was more like a vision within a dream than a dream. The sky itself was bright and clear, and there were no clouds. The scene was somewhat tranquil. The bird-looking creature was brilliant in its appearance. It had a neon glow to it. The best way I could describe this creature is that it looked very similar to the mythical griffin—a legendary creature with the body of a lion, the head of an eagle, and the wings of a dragon. It was huge, white with a green-and-gold glowing outline. This was a splendid creature with great beauty, somewhat majestic in its appearance. It was so magnificent that it almost seemed expressive of worship. It appeared that either someone was seated on the creature or was part of his being. He had a bow in his hand.

Now, before I proceed with this vision within a dream, I feel I must qualify what I am sharing with some personal knowledge about myself. I am a conservative Christian. I am a licensed and ordained minister through Southern Baptist churches. I would say that I'm a pretty normal guy. I dream every night, but generally not about spiritual things. I dream about life happenings, you know, just regular *stuff*—high school, sports, or not being able to find where I parked my car. Like most dreams, that's all they are, just entertainment as we sleep. I don't try to figure out if a dream has some significant meaning. I'm a very basic guy, and what qualifies someone to be a *dream interpreter* anyway?

I proceed with careful forethought and biblical analysis in these areas. I guess I've seen and heard too many false prophecies and false words. I would say I am spiritually cautious, and I "try the spirits" to see if they are of God (1 John 4:1, KJV). I desire Holy Spirit discernment, and I despise deception. Often I reverently say, "God, if You are going to speak to me, give me something clear. Don't ask me to figure it out or to make some kind of spiritual application. Just make it plain for me."

This particular enlightenment came like a vision within a dream. It was like a flash amidst other things I was dreaming about. I could not tell you what else I dreamed about that night, but I could draw you a picture of this vision—it was so vivid. It is difficult to tell how high in the air this creature was, perhaps fifty feet. It was somewhat low in relation to where clouds may be.

On the ground beneath this *celestial* creature was a herd of sheep. The sheep were huddled together on the side of a hill. The hillside was a beautiful green color, and the rolling hills somewhat reminded me of Ireland. The sheep were near a fence, and it was as if I were viewing this from across the fence. There seemed to be acres and acres of rolling pasture, almost like a golf course, but it was pasture. The sheep were all together near the fence. It was not a great number of sheep, maybe twenty-five to thirty.

The sheep had the faces of men; I hope I can describe this so that you get a glimpse of it. I realize as I'm sharing this that it may sound like I think I'm Ezekiel or a prophet of God. I am neither. I'm just a regular guy. However, in this vision each one of the sheep had the face of a man. Each face was different; it was like I was gazing into a small crowd of people. All of the sheep seemed very sad, some of the faces were bleeding, and some had tears in their eyes. They just stood there.

The creature from the sky pointed his bow at them and shot what seemed to be hooks or barbs into their flesh. The sheep appeared not to know where this attack was coming from, and they put up no defense. They only looked at each other. They all seemed to be bruised in different ways. They just stood there and took it. Each of them had the countenance of having been beaten and bruised. They seemed to have no leader among them. There was no shepherd in the vision. They were vulnerable and ignorant of the assault.

The vision was brief but indelible.

The Dream Come to Life

The following night I was a guest preacher at a church in rural Fort Worth. I had actually forgotten the dream until I made a turn on a country road to get to the church. I saw a small herd of sheep huddled near the roadway fence. Immediately the dream came alive. Tears came to my eyes as I recalled the dream.

As I think about that dream today, I think how difficult it is for our modern society to relate to biblical accounts of sheep and shepherds. I don't know if I've ever even touched a sheep, and I know I've never met a real shepherd. It is clear, however, that God's Word compares believers and true followers as sheep, sheep of His pasture.

> Then Jesus said to them again, "Most assuredly, I say to you, I am the door of the sheep. All who ever came before Me are thieves and robbers, but the sheep did not hear them. I am the door. If anyone enters by Me, he will be saved, and will go in and out and find pasture....I am the good shepherd; and I know My sheep, and am known by My own. As the Father knows Me, even so I know the Father; and I lay down My life for the sheep."
> —JOHN 10:7–9, 14–15

The words of Jesus in John 10 say that believers are the sheep of His pasture and that He is the Good Shepherd. Man can only come to God through a door, and that door is Jesus. Actually, the proper way to enter any place is through a door. God's Word unmistakably compares believers to sheep. Psalm 95:7 says we are the "people of His pasture, and the sheep of His hand." Again in Psalm 100:3 it says, "We are His people and the sheep of His pasture."

In my dream all of the sheep were bruised, and the hurt was visible in their painful expressions. That is such a picture of the church today. Virtually all of the sheep in the church today are carrying wounds. Most don't know how to defend themselves and are really not sure how the wounds got there. Having a shepherd that does not lead is like having no shepherd at all. Sheep know how to follow, but they don't know how to fight. Jesus did not leave us defenseless. He left us with His Spirit and His Word. It is the call of the shepherd to equip us to stand.

I want to expose some of the "wiles" of the demons and how they access our lives. We cannot responsibly act upon things we do not know. Having no knowledge makes us extremely vulnerable. Ignorance gives great advantage to the demons. For the most part, Christians do not know because the demons have done a good job of keeping the information out of the pulpits and classrooms. It always amazes me at how Christians retreat when the *D* word is mentioned. Why is deliverance so difficult to discuss?

Why are people so quickly offended or intimidated by the subject of demons? Why can't you talk about it? Why is the subject so unapproachable? I believe it is because of ignorance, or because of nonteaching and false teaching. Those Christian leaders who do talk about it have often made it to be something it is not, and that does great damage.

It is difficult for me to understand how a preacher can open his Bible and preach fifty-two Sundays in a year and never mention the deliverance and healing message of the Gospels. I don't see how that can happen. I don't see how a seminary can instruct their Bible students for three years and never prepare them for dealing with sickness or for engaging demon spirits. I honestly don't get that. How can you sit in Sunday school and Bible classes most of your life and not be taught the reality of demonic activity in the life of believers? Would you agree that the demons have done a good job of keeping Christians in darkness? How can this be? Is it willing ignorance?

Second Peter 3:5 talks about deceived people who "willfully forget." Willing ignorance—I believe that is what it is. It is a conscious choice not to preach or teach the scriptural truth concerning the work of demons. What else could it be? Why else would it be? Isn't that like being dumb on purpose? I don't mean that in an unkind sense; we have been and are being duped by a message with a lack of truth and power.

In the walk of spiritual freedom, there are things we need to do to remain free. As important, maybe even more important, are things we should not do.

BASIC PREVENTION 101

CHAPTER 2

WHO LET THE PIGS OUT?

RECENTLY RECEIVED AN e-mail from a pig farmer in Australia. I knew he was referring to my book *When Pigs Move In*, but he said, "I just finished your book, *Who Let the Pigs Out?*" He went on to compliment me and tell how the book had helped him in ministry there. I have been thinking about his e-mail. Who did let the pigs out?

Obviously, the reference to pigs in this book is talking about unclean spirits. If you, as a believer, are the house, how do you keep the pigs out?

Pigs go in and out through gates. Once the pigs are kicked out, the question becomes, How do we keep them out? The simple answer is, *keep the gate closed.*

Gates are for closing and opening. They are for keeping things in and keeping things out. *Gate* and *gatekeeper* are fairly common words throughout the Bible. The function of the gate has not changed since Bible times. It still is what it always has been.

> And he set the gatekeepers at the gates of the house of the LORD, so that no one who was in any way unclean should enter.
>
> —2 CHRONICLES 23:19

Gates are doorways; very simply, they are entry points. It is common to walk into a building and see signs on or about the doors that may say Entrance or Exit. Most often, the signs point out the obvious. In essence they say, "Here's the way in, and here is the way out." Do you know that demons must have an entryway? Spiritual access to our life comes only through a doorway that we control. No one else can open these doors or the gates—just the owner.

When Jesus comes into our lives, He not only comes through a door but also by way of *our invitation*. He never comes uninvited, and He would never use forceful entry.

> Behold, I stand at the door and knock. If anyone hears My voice and opens the door, I will come in to him and dine with him, and he with Me.
>
> —Revelation 3:20

The choice is left to us. This is also the case with open doors for demon spirits. They can never enter against our will. Once a person has received Jesus Christ, that person has received eternal salvation. However, through the similar process of opening doors, one can choose to have demon spirits. It is rare that someone would consciously make that choice; however, it is all about granting legal permission, such as we do when we allow unforgiven sin to remain in our lives. I tell you, pigs will track down the smell of garbage and feast on it.

Throughout this book you will read that demons are empowered when we believe a lie. The lie, of course, is generally wrapped in an attractive package filled with partial truths. My friend Sid Roth, whose ministry now spans the world, speaks about being entangled in a New Age lie that offered him supernatural power but was filled with darkness and disconnection. After Sid Roth's salvation, he had to find a deliverance minister to cast out the evil spirits that had come through his New Age encounter.

> When you come into the land which the LORD your God is giving you, you shall not learn to follow the abominations of those

nations. There shall not be found among you anyone who makes his son or his daughter pass through the fire, or one who practices witchcraft, or a soothsayer, or one who interprets omens, or a sorcerer, or one who conjures spells, or a medium, or a spiritist, or one who calls up the dead. For all who do these things are an abomination to the LORD, and because of these abominations the LORD your God drives them out from before you. You shall be blameless before the LORD your God.

—DEUTERONOMY 18:9–13

Often the lie that demons use to gain access is nothing more than convincing you that a particular person or teaching is a better way than what is written in God's Word. It may involve coming into agreement with New Age thinking or some Eastern mystical religion, which, however sincere you might be, are doorways for demons.

Any teaching that denies the deity of God the Father, God the Son, and God the Holy Spirit is, when embraced, a doorway for demon powers. That is one gate that lets the pigs in. Secret orders and fraternities that point people to God but do so by bypassing the death, burial, and resurrection of Jesus Christ are absolute doorways to demon powers. These fraternal or sorority-type organizations generally boast of the good works they do in communities, but they will not proclaim Jesus Christ as Lord. Often they have good people as members, and their organizations do good works. But the important issue is that there is only one way to God, and that is through Jesus Christ.

False religions or false teachings within the church are always potential gateways for demons. Embracing any teaching that offers a way to God apart from Jesus Christ is a lie of demons. It is important to know that demons are liars; they kill, steal, and destroy. It is their objective to war against the saints. They are subtle and slick. They manipulate much through false gifts.

After many years of deliverance ministry, and multitudes of personal experiences, I can tell you that it is not difficult to walk in freedom. It is simple, and it involves yielding your life to truth. Remember, in

His prayer for the saints to His Father, Jesus said, "Your word is truth" (John 17:17). Jesus also told His disciples, "And you shall know the truth, and the truth shall make you free" (John 8:32). Virtually every doorway for demons is hinged upon a lie. These may be thinly veiled lies—and often are.

Simon Peter and Satan

There are several biblical accounts of how this happens. It appears to be the plan of demons always to wreak havoc. Jesus gave warning directly to Peter:

> And the Lord said, "Simon, Simon! Indeed, Satan has asked for you, that he may sift you as wheat. But I have prayed for you, that your faith should not fail; and when you have returned to Me, strengthen your brethren."
>
> —LUKE 22:31–32

I wonder, how many times is this true in our lives? How often are Satan and his demons looking for a way to *sift* our lives—to toss and turn us one way then the other? What I do know is that without legal consent, they cannot do their dastardly deeds.

I also wonder how Jesus knew that Satan desired to have Peter to sift him as wheat. Apart from being omnipotent, how did Jesus know this? Did Satan come before the Father and inquire about Peter, as he did about Job? Did he make an official request? Did Satan talk privately with Jesus about Peter? It is clear that Satan had already attempted to use Peter to hinder God's plan. Look at the discussion involving the three of them.

> From that time Jesus began to show to His disciples that He must go to Jerusalem, and suffer many things from the elders and chief priests and scribes, and be killed, and be raised the third day. Then Peter took Him aside and began to rebuke Him, saying, "Far be it from You, Lord; this shall not happen to You!"

But He turned and said to Peter, "Get behind Me, Satan! You are an offense to Me, for you are not mindful of the things of God, but the things of men."

—MATTHEW 16:21–23

Jesus said, "Get thee behind me, Satan," while talking to Peter. These are the same words He spoke directly to Satan during the wilderness temptation. Satan was already strongly associated with Peter's life and was influencing his thinking when Jesus told him that what Satan would like to do with him was sift him as wheat. Satan wanted to bring chaos to Peter.

Judas and Satan

Satan had success with Judas that he did not have with Peter. He actually "entered" into Judas.

And the chief priests and the scribes sought how they might kill Him, for they feared the people. Then Satan entered Judas, surnamed Iscariot, who was numbered among the twelve. So he went his way and conferred with the chief priests and captains, how he might betray Him to them.

—LUKE 22:2–4

Satan himself entered into Judas; he actually possessed him. It didn't seem that difficult and is described in just one sentence in God's Word. What doorway did he have? We could all guess, but it is obvious that there was a doorway through unconfessed sin and that he was likely a thief. Jesus even said, "Did I not choose you, the twelve, and one of you is a devil?" (John 6:70).

It is interesting that Jesus did not say that Judas *had* a devil; He said, "[He] *is* a devil." Maybe Judas was a secret agent of Satan. Look at John 13:2:

> And supper being ended, the devil having already put it into the
> heart of Judas Iscariot, Simon's son, to betray Him...

Look at this—he was at the Lord's Supper. Not just Judas...Satan
was there! It was there that he entered into Judas in the most solemn
of moments. After they had prayed together and given thanks, Satan
went into Judas. You see, demons are spirits. I don't think anyone saw
this happen. It wasn't visible; it was not even apparent. The other disciples were not even sure that it wasn't one of them who would betray
Jesus. Other than the heaviness of the moment, and words from Jesus,
do you think there was an evil presence? Did anyone sense it? I have
often wondered about this; was Judas so under a generational curse
that demons could go in and out through that door? Had he *made a
deal* with the devil? Certainly he was capable of that, for he made one
with the authorities to betray Jesus. People still make deals with the
devil today.

As foolish as it sounds to me, I know that, in their frustration and
foolish thinking, some people try to make bargains with Satan. Often
they seek power and favors through demonic means. I don't think
Judas was doing any of that, but I do believe Satan had something on
him and, perhaps because of his pride, Judas couldn't confess it.

Judas was a devil from the beginning. That's what God's Word says.
Satan entered into Judas. That's what God's Word says.

Closing the Doors

It is clear that Satan uses key people in order to interfere with God's
plan and to create demonic havoc in the affairs of men. In the passage
mentioned earlier in Deuteronomy 18, God tells the Israelites many
things not to do, but the bottom line was to be blameless before the
Lord. Freedom is maintained by being blameless—which means
keeping sin confessed and not giving a gateway to demons. To be
blameless is to have character that is without reproach, which can

only be attained as an individual keeps himself or herself covered and clothed in the righteousness of Christ.

Paul enlightens us more about it in Ephesians 4.

> Put on the new man which was created according to God, in true righteousness and holiness. Therefore, putting away lying, "Let each one of you speak truth with his neighbor," for we are members of one another. "Be angry, and do not sin": do not let the sun go down on your wrath, nor give place to the devil. Let him who stole steal no longer, but rather let him labor, working with his hands what is good, that he may have something to give him who has need. Let no corrupt word proceed out of your mouth, but what is good for necessary edification, that it may impart grace to the hearers. And do not grieve the Holy Spirit of God, by whom you were sealed for the day of redemption. Let all bitterness, wrath, anger, clamor, and evil speaking be put away from you, with all malice. And be kind to one another, tenderhearted, forgiving one another, even as God in Christ forgave you.
>
> —EPHESIANS 4:24–32

Clearly, he says anger that lingers gives a place for demons. Look at the flesh list here: lying, stealing, corrupt communication, grieving the Holy Spirit, bitterness, anger, malice, evil speaking, and clamor. These things, unforgiven, are demon doorways!

After these gates or doorways have been closed, a way to keep them closed is being tenderhearted and forgiving. These things are clearly written by the Holy Spirit. These things are easily understood.

After a believer has become free from demonic intrusion, one of the giant doorways for demons to gain a new entry point is revisiting the past. It's like probing a wound that is almost healed. It's re-aggravating a nagging injury so that it cannot heal. This is another "Don't go there." Learn to live in the moment. Sometimes there is a conscious effort involved to do this. The apostle Paul seemed almost to gloat in his victory over the past. He says (paraphrased), "I still have a lot of work to do. I'm not where I need to be in Christ, but one thing I have conquered; my past is no longer an obstacle. I am moving forward."

> Brethren, I do not count myself to have apprehended; but one thing I do, forgetting those things which are behind and reaching forward to those things which are ahead, I press toward the goal for the prize of the upward call of God in Christ Jesus.
> —Philippians 3:13–14

When you relive a past failure or an unpleasant time in your life, you are allowing demons another opportunity to use the incident once more against you. Don't go there. You must control that part of your thinking, or the demons will. You can choose to not think about the past, and when you do this, you seize any opportunities that demons may have had to torment you. You must take those thoughts captive! By faith, apply the blood of Jesus to the part of your mind that seems to be in replay mode. Speak your choice to dwell on pleasant and hopeful thoughts.

This is something that only you can change, *but you can change it.* Don't engage in conversations with others that dwell on the past. It is an absolutely fruitless exercise to talk about the painful past, absolutely fruitless. Learn to recognize when your thought patterns drift toward entertaining regret of yesterday. Don't participate in *what if* and *if only* conversations. Change the subject, and focus on things that are true, honest, and of good report. Remember that *Fret* and *Regret* are two bad dogs; don't let them in. Also remember that self-pity and desire for attention because of your past do not work to your benefit. Don't go there.

Disobedience Opens the Doors

In my experience with deliverance ministry and maintaining freedom I have discovered that it has a lot more to do with what not to do. Don't open doors. That's the way to keep demons out. Obedience to the Lord is not what keeps them out; it is disobedience that lets them in.

When Christ delivered individuals from demonic possession in the Bible, His ejection of unclean spirits was final. He barred a reentry. In Mark 9:25 we find Him charging the evil spirit to go out and enter no more.

> When Jesus saw that the people came running together, He rebuked the unclean spirit, saying to it, "Deaf and dumb spirit, I command you, come out of him and enter him no more!"

Casting out in the name of Jesus is final. In another illustration, Christ encountered a man possessed by an entire legion of demons. (See Mark 5.) When Jesus commanded the demons to leave the man, they pleaded to stay in circulation (v. 10). But Jesus commanded the demons to leave the man and allowed them to enter into a herd of pigs nearby. The Bible says, "Then the unclean spirits went out and entered the swine (there were about two thousand); and the herd ran violently down the steep place into the sea, and drowned in the sea" (v. 13). There would be no reentry in this man!

For the believer today who has been set free, the way to remain free, to maintain freedom, is to maintain a confessed relationship with God through Jesus. Practicing disobedience is a certain doorway for demons. Don't go there.

In Matthew 12 we have the story of an unclean spirit leaving a man and then returning with seven more demons. We read:

> When an unclean spirit goes out of a man, he goes through dry places, seeking rest, and finds none. Then he says, "I will return to my house from which I came." And when he comes, he finds it empty, swept, and put in order. Then he goes and takes with him seven other spirits more wicked than himself, and they enter and dwell there; and the last state of that man is worse than the first.
>
> —MATTHEW 12:43–45

I believe that the demons love to play havoc with these verses. The demons love this teaching. It instills fear into prospective deliverance candidates and prevents some pastors from even teaching about demons at all. It has been the subject of much mis-teaching about the casting out of demons. Many times I have heard well-intentioned but uninformed preachers talk about filling the house to keep the "cast out" demons from returning in greater numbers.

We must remember the examples of Jesus in Mark 9:25. His instruction to the demons was, "I command you, come out of him *and enter him no more!*" (emphasis added). Demons that are cast out do not have an option to return. There are plenty of other demons that can take their place, but when cast out into the abyss, they no longer have access to that life.

We must look closer at the scripture in Matthew 12 to understand what is happening in that example. Read those verses again. The illustration Jesus is using does not use the phrase "cast out" but rather "gone out." Matthew 12:43 reads, "When the unclean spirit is gone out of a man..." (KJV). The implication is that the demon goes out on his own, not at the command in the name of Jesus Christ. The demon *goes out* a door, looks for a better dwelling place, communicates with other demons, and *goes back* to *his* house: "I will return to my house" (v. 44). It is still his house. He will go back in the same door he came out. The door is still open. Not only that, but he also invites his demon friends that he encountered in the dry places to come with him.

He went back to see if the door was still open in *his* house, and it had nothing to do with the house being full of the Holy Spirit. The house was in good condition, clean and decorated. One can be so full of the Holy Spirit that they are overflowing, but there can still be an open doorway because of unconfessed sin. Unconfessed sin—disobedience—is what gives the demons permission to reenter the house. As long as there is disobedience in the house, that house is still *his* house. He still has an open doorway.

Demons must be "cast out." I don't know why the demon left in this scriptural illustration, but he was not cast out and doorways were not closed. The rights the demon had to the life had not been removed, and as long as the legal rights remained, he could come and go as he pleased.

For months after I first read this scriptural portion, I explored an answer to this question: If demons can come back in greater force, what's the point of casting them out in the first place? I could find absolutely no indication anywhere in Scripture that God operates like this. This, I believe, would be an insult to God's character—to think that He would honor someone's efforts to be free from demon powers in Jesus's name and then permit the demons to come back and torment that person to an even greater degree. Since 1995 when I first started doing deliverance ministry, I have never seen this happen.

Now, I will add that if more doorways are opened, more demons will come, but once doorways have been closed and demons are cast out, *those* demons cannot return. So it is not a matter of reading your Bible enough or praying enough that keeps demons out—it is disobedience that allows them in.

Don't Open the Doors

The bottom line is, clearly don't open doors! Throughout God's Word we find this principle: Don't go there; don't do things that open doors. Don't allow sin to linger. If you think that living a holy life will keep you demon free, that is only partially true. Living a holy life helps you not to open doors. It helps you to recognize sin and confess it in order to receive forgiveness. However, the most righteous person you know is subject to opening doorways to demons.

I have read a few books on this subject and have heard many comments from believers concerning staying free. While virtually all of the information is good instruction for building Christian character and establishing a strong foundation, reading so many chapters a day does nothing to get rid of demons. Certainly it makes them uncomfortable, but demons don't leave because you read the Bible.

Going to church whenever the church doors are open is likely a good thing to do, but that is not what keeps demons out.

Clearly, simply, their legal rights must be removed. You can read your Bible all day, but if you carry any unconfessed sin, then legal permission has been granted. That should not trouble you; it should encourage you. God's grace will always be sufficient. He will always forgive. It pleases Him when we can confess a sin and receive His cleansing. Demons are looking for an opening—unconfessed sin is an opening. Jesus is looking to cover our sin. Demons are looking for what is not covered.

It is staying forgiven that keeps us free. It is not in living without sin, for that is not possible. Rather, it is recognizing sin and admitting it to God.

You see, what's good about this is that anyone can do it. It is not about having to measure up all of the time; it's more about admitting it when we don't. Recognize who Jesus is. Staying free doesn't depend upon you living a perfect life but in knowing that you have a perfect Savior.

CHAPTER 3

DEMON RANK AND FILE

In the years that I have been ministering in the area of deliverance and healing, I have noticed that the most common questions I am asked concern not only the reality of demons but also what they are: If they are real, what are they, and what do they do? Can a Christian have demons? Doesn't the Holy Spirit protect us?

I receive questions like this all the time. The Holy Spirit leads us and guides us into all truth. He does not compel us to receive truth or to obey truth—nor does He prevent the consequences of disobedience. We, as believers, can "quench" the Spirit, and we can also "grieve" the Spirit (1 Thess. 5:19; Eph. 4:30). Believers can and do open doors for demonization.

Remember that the Bible does not attempt to explain the existence of God, nor does it try to prove it. Neither does the Bible explain or attempt to prove the existence of demons. The reality of demons was not questioned by Jesus or by those to whom He ministered. It was a reality that was understood and recognized. Jesus spoke to demons. He commanded their obedience. They recognized Him, and He recognized them. The work of demons was understood by others, and there was no attempt to explain their existence—and certainly no attempt to *explain it away.*

Somewhere in the beginning, perhaps in the predeterminate counsel of God, angels were created. The Bible declares that they are all ministering spirits sent forth to minister for the heirs of salvation—that would be you and me (Heb. 1:14). The myriads of created angels, an "innumerable company" (Heb. 12:22), worship and serve God. There are obviously angelic ranks, a hierarchy to be sure. The angels were given names and had various functions and assignments. Some have six wings and are called *seraphim*; some have four wings and are called *cherubim*; others have two wings with various assignments. Doubtless, there are ranks of angels we do not know about.

The angels had names, and their names had significance. They still have names. Michael is undoubtedly the angel with the highest rank and power. Gabriel is an angel of high rank, and Lucifer was the "anointed cherub" with radiant beauty (Ezek. 28:14). It seems that Michael is in charge of warring angels, Gabriel perhaps over messenger angels, and Lucifer must have been in charge of praise. He was adorned with an elaborate musical system with the created purpose of praising God. He apparently desired the praise for himself.

So magnificent was the created being Lucifer that at some point in history he rebelled and opposed God. This is important for understanding *what demon spirits are*. Lucifer wanted to be worshiped; he wanted to be like God, so he opposed God. He rallied a third of the angels, and there was a war in heaven. Lucifer, Satan, the serpent, the old dragon, was cast down to the earth with all of the angels that joined in the opposition. He was cast out of heaven. Interestingly, "cast out" is the term Jesus uses when He gave authority to believers. He told us to "cast out demons" (Matt. 10:8).

Fallen Angels in Opposition to God

I used the word *opposed* several times in the sentences above: Satan *opposed* God. To *oppose* another, you must stand in opposition to that person—you cannot oppose something without being the opposite.

That's the point here. In order for Satan to war against God, he had to do so with opposites.

Demon spirits are fallen angels who took on the opposite characteristics of God. The created became the enemy of the Creator, of all that God is. God is love. Hence, a demon spirit cannot operate in love but must, by its very nature, be the opposite of love. Satan is the opposite of the fruit of the Spirit and the opposite of the character of Jehovah God.

Satan, who was reduced to the god of *this world*, the world where we live, still wars against God through mankind. That's why Jesus came; God so loved...*this world* (John 3:16). Demon spirits are as real as the holy angels. They are spirits and are active in the affairs of mankind. They certainly can and *do* inhabit the lives of believers.

I mentioned a few of the angels' names—Gabriel and Michael. The names *Lucifer* and *Satan* are used interchangeably to identify the devil. *Beelzebub* is the name of a ruling demon power; the Jews and Jesus recognized his work. Baal, Moloch, Diana of the Ephesians, Jezebel, Apollyon, and Abaddon are a few of the names of demon spirits recognized and worshiped throughout Scripture. There are many. Angels have names and assignments; demons have names and assignments.

Remember the man Christ delivered in Mark 5 who lived among the tombs and was possessed by demons? Jesus commanded the strongman, the prince of the demonic kingdom inside the man, to identify himself. The demon's name was Legion. He ruled a kingdom of demon spirits that destroyed a herd of two thousand swine. The tormenting spirits caused the pigs to be out of control and to commit suicide. Demons have names and assignments and are part of a sophisticated hierarchy opposing all of God's creation.

You cannot fully realize your potential as a believer until you understand the opposition. That is an absolute truth. That's why I talk about it. We are being opposed; there is an opponent. Hordes of evil spirits circle where there is unconfessed sin and willing disobedience to God. They are like buzzards zeroing in on what is dead. Their legal ground is man's disobedience. Right now as you read this, there are eyes watching; you may even feel their intimidation as you read. Do you ever have the sense of being watched? The angels watch, but they *watch over* you as your defense and support. The demons watch, but they are looking for opportunities to gain access to your life. Their work is torment. They are your opponents.

If God is love—and He is—then demon spirits work in the area of hate, envy, selfishness, lust, bitterness, and other death-producing emotions. If love forgives—and it does—then demon spirits work in the area of unforgiveness. If God is truth—and He is—then demon spirits lie, and the truth is not in them.

What area do you struggle with in your Christian life? Could it be a demon spirit? Do you know how to defeat your opponent? Know your opponent—recognize the simple truth that demon spirits are fallen angels and they are actively opposing the body of Christ and individual believers. Ignoring the truth gives them the advantage. Calling it something else will not win the battle.

Demon Hierarchy

Demons are fallen angels, and they operate in a very sophisticated, structured hierarchy. It is important to know this in order for us to know our position in dealing with them. They are a government at war with God and against His saints, a highly organized system in varying ranks of administration solely in opposition to all that is holy. Their system and structure, of course, are of the same pattern that God established with the holy angels. It is a *copycat* government.

Look at Daniel 7:21–22. In the great vision that Daniel had, he states that Satan is making war against the saints. He says the war will continue until the Ancient of Days comes. The Second Coming of Jesus Christ is when the saints shall judge the world. The dominion of Satan will be shut down. The saints will sit down with Him on His throne and bask in the complete triumph and full downfall of the demonic kingdom. What I want to emphasize here is that in the meantime, war from the demonic powers is against the saints.

> I was watching; and the same horn was making war against the saints, and prevailing against them, until the Ancient of Days came, and a judgment was made in favor of the saints of the Most High, and the time came for the saints to possess the kingdom.
>
> —DANIEL 7:21–22

Revelation 12:17 reinforces this reality. The dragon, Satan, and his legions of demonic powers are at war with the remnant seed—those who keep the commandments of God and have the testimony of Jesus Christ: "And the dragon was enraged with the woman, and he went to make war with the rest of her offspring, who keep the commandments of God and have the testimony of Jesus Christ."

Demons at war with the saints; fallen angels are now a part of Satan's army. They are working with "that serpent of old, called the Devil and Satan, who deceives the whole world" (Rev. 12:9). He was cast out into the earth, and his angels were cast out with him. He "went to make war with the rest of her offspring, who keep the commandments of God and have the testimony of Jesus Christ" (Rev. 12:17). They are making war against the saints.

The Battle Is the Lord's

Believers are the focal point of the battle—BUT the battle is not ours; it is the Lord's. Our prayers to God through Christ Jesus summon angels to minister in our behalf. The war in the heavenly realm is between demons and angels. They are at war in the celestials. Michael the archangel did not challenge Satan. Rather, he said:

> Yet Michael the archangel, in contending with the devil, when he disputed about the body of Moses, dared not bring against him a reviling accusation, but said, "The Lord rebuke you!"
>
> —JUDE 9

Take a peek with me into some of the battles that occur in the heavenly realm. Read Daniel 10. Daniel was in mourning for three full weeks because of a "thing...revealed" to him (v. 1, KJV). Daniel knew that the vision he received was true, and he knew the meaning of it. He knew it was for the future. His heavenly encounter was virtually more than he could bear in his human strength.

He was apparently walking by "the side of the great river, that is, the Tigris, I lifted my eyes and looked, and behold, a certain man clothed in linen" appeared (vv. 4–5). Daniel was in Babylonian captivity. He was in modern-day Iraq, next to the Tigris River, in the area near the original Garden of Eden. While there were attendants there with him, he was the only one who saw this vision.

It is interesting that even though the others did not see the vision, they certainly sensed a holy presence. They trembled and ran for cover. Daniel says the voice of the words were like the voice of a multitude. Many believe it was most likely Jesus Himself who appeared and that the angel Gabriel was with Him. Clearly, Gabriel spoke to Daniel.

Daniel was so overwhelmed by what he saw and heard that he became ill; he had no strength. He was on his hands and knees with his face to the ground. He was earthbound, as we are, and he saw a glimpse of the heavenly realm.

The angel who spoke to Daniel assured him that from the first day that he prayed, his prayers were heard. He said: "I have come because of your words" (v. 12). Then startling words followed:

> But the prince of the kingdom of Persia withstood me twenty-one days; and behold, Michael, one of the chief princes, came to help me, for I had been left alone there with the kings of Persia.
> —DANIEL 10:13

Wow. The angel said that he would have been there sooner, but he had been delayed by a demon prince of the kingdom of Persia. God's plans and purposes can be delayed—but they can never be stopped. Gabriel told Daniel, "Michael, one of the chief princes [angels], came to help me."

When Daniel heard this, again, it was too much for him to endure. Our human strength is not sufficient for heavenly activity. Daniel became physically weak and again was on his hands and knees with his face to the ground. He couldn't speak. It was literally breathtaking. He had no breath left in him. He was in the presence of holy angels and had gotten a glimpse of warfare in the heavens. He felt the great heaviness of the inadequacy of his humanity. So should we.

Once again, God's messenger touched Daniel and restored his strength. Gabriel said to Daniel, "Do you know why I have come to you? And now I must return to fight with the prince of Persia; and when I have gone forth, indeed the prince of Greece will come. But I will tell you what is noted in the Scripture of Truth. (No one upholds me against these, except Michael your prince)" (vv. 20–21).

The kings of Persia had done much damage to the Jews, and the Persians' tyranny against God had given much authority to the demon prince of Persia. People empower demons by their actions and misdeeds.

The prince of the kingdom of Persia tried to prevent Daniel's prayers from being answered, but his prayers were heard from the first day, and heaven was responding to his fasting and praying. For twenty-one days the demonic princes withstood, but all that was needed was another angel. Demons may impede at times, but they never prevent the purposes of God. Never.

Gabriel and Michael. Wow, I wonder if Daniel had a clue what he had been privileged to experience? Think about it. When the demon powers of Persia resisted, God sent Michael, one of the chief princes, and the battle was secured. They continued in the warfare until it was certain that the Persian Empire would fall. Then Gabriel warns Daniel that the prince of Greece will come to fight against Israel.

While there is intense warfare in the celestial realm between angels and demons, and while the battle is for men's souls and testimonies, we are not to enter that battle except in prayer. Never are we instructed to challenge heavenly realm principalities and powers. Our battle with demons is upon this earth, not in the heavenlies. I believe that warfare in the heavenly realm is out of our spiritual authority—way out. There are clearly two levels of spiritual encounters: one in the heavens, fought by heaven's angels, and one on the earth. We will learn more in the chapters that follow about our preparation to do spiritual warfare here on the earth.

CHAPTER 4

WHERE IS THE HEAVENLY REALM?

WHERE DO THE heavenly beings dwell? The apostle Paul waited fourteen years to tell of a glorious visit to the "third heaven." He wasn't sure he was supposed to talk about this because of the possibility of appearing to be something that he was not. I guess if anyone had a cause to boast, it would have been Paul. He reveals the genuine humility that comes with real association with God. He cautiously tells of the experience.

We are not capable of knowing, nor is it needful for us to know all of the details about the heavenly realm. Rather, we should give thanks that we have a place because of Jesus. Paul was not even sure where he went. He didn't know if it was an in- or out-of-body experience. What he did know is that he could not explain it adequately. He heard words that he felt compelled not to speak.

This third heaven is called paradise.

> I know a man in Christ who fourteen years ago—whether in the body I do not know, or whether out of the body I do not know, God knows—such a one was caught up to the third heaven. And I know such a man—whether in the body or out of the body I do not know, God knows—how he was caught up into Paradise

and heard inexpressible words, which it is not lawful for a man
to utter.

—2 Corinthians 12:2–4

There are "realms" in the spirit world. We are earthbound; angels
and demons can travel and live in these heavenly realms. We cannot.

It was the understanding of ancient Israelites that there are three
heavens. Obviously they wrote in terms with which they were familiar.
The Jews spoke of three heavens. The first heaven consisted of the
earth's atmosphere, where the clouds and birds were. The second
heaven was where the sun, stars, and moon were. The third heaven was
the dwelling place of God. When Paul said that he was caught up to
the third heaven, he was referring to the very dwelling place of God.

In the Book of Job we can see the level of spiritual power that came
against him. The angels of God had come before God to give an account
of their ministry to man upon the earth—and Satan came with them.
"Now there was a day when the sons of God came to present themselves before the Lord, and Satan also came among them" (Job 1:6).

Satan had been banished from God's presence. Maybe he came
with God's permission based upon a request. He is the accuser of the
brethren. Regardless of why he came, he is there, and God asked him
for a *report*: "And the Lord said unto Satan, Whence comest thou?
Then Satan answered the Lord, and said, From going to and fro in
the earth, and from walking up and down in it" (v. 7, kjv). Up and
down? Does that include some heavenly realm-checking as well?

He had been looking for those whom he may devour. Surely he had
investigated Job. When God asked him about Job, in essence, Satan
called Job a mercenary. He said Job only served God because God
blessed him and his family. Satan tried to tempt God to do harm to
Job: "Stretch out Your hand and touch all that he has, and he will
surely curse You to Your face!" (v. 11). God granted Satan permission
to do that.

Read the incredible account in Job 1.

> So the LORD said to Satan, "Behold, all that he has is in your power; only do not lay a hand on his person." So Satan went out from the presence of the LORD.
>
> —JOB 1:12

Note the swiftness and severity of the attacks once Satan and his host of demons began their work. They used people on the earth (the Sabiens). They stole the oxen and the donkeys and killed the servants. No sooner had the messenger informed Job than word came that fire from heaven (lightning?) had consumed all of the sheep and servants. Demonic power in the heavenly realm was being unleashed.

Scripture says that while the first messenger was still speaking, another message came that the Chaldeans had taken all of the camels and killed the servants. Again, demons used people to carry out their mission of hate and hurt. The worst news of all was what Job had already suspected could happen.

> So it was, when the days of feasting had run their course, that Job would send and sanctify them, and he would rise early in the morning and offer burnt offerings according to the number of them all. For Job said, "It may be that my sons have sinned and cursed God in their hearts." Thus Job did regularly.
>
> —JOB 1:5

Job's children were protected because of Job's life and prayers. It appears that what he imagined could be the case likely was. His children were perhaps giving some legal permissions to Satan's attacks. Now the news comes:

> Another also came and said, "Your sons and daughters were eating and drinking wine in their oldest brother's house, and suddenly a great wind came from across the wilderness and struck the four corners of the house, and it fell on the young people, and they are dead; and I alone have escaped to tell you!"
>
> —JOB 1:18–19

The demons had caused a storm and directed it to destroy his children. The house was flattened by the strong, *tornadic* type of wind. The demons not only had power to use people against Job, and also the weather against him, but we see they also had the power to torment with sickness.

> So Satan went out from the presence of the LORD, and struck Job with painful boils from the sole of his foot to the crown of his head. And he took for himself a potsherd with which to scrape himself while he sat in the midst of the ashes. Then his wife said to him, "Do you still hold fast to your integrity? Curse God and die!"
>
> —JOB 2:7–9

It is interesting to note that even though Satan had been granted permission to take all that Job had, he did not take his wife. I can't give you the reason for this, but it appeared that it was part of the plan to use his wife against him. Most of us know the story of Job and his victories in the end. God had a complete hedge around Job and his family because of Job's life. It was impossible to penetrate, although Satan had tried and could not find an opening. There is a hedge of protection around me too. Why would I want to venture outside of it or shake my fist at demons?

The Territorial Prince of Texas

After being in deliverance ministry for several years I began to learn, by experience, that there were some demons associated with people that I could not send into the abyss. I began to understand, to some extent, the hierarchy and ranking position of demons. I learned to command demons to identify themselves by name. I had little success commanding spirits out according to their *function*—such as a *spirit of fear*, *spirit of rejection*, and so forth. I found that there might be multiple spirits that had similar functions. I began to understand why Jesus demanded the name of the demon in Mark 5.

I could also see that while He commanded them not to speak in *public*, He demanded their God-recognized name in *private*. I began to understand that the demons were all given a name when they were created. Being created first as holy angels, the names they were given were significant; they had meanings that described the creative function for each angel. I could see that since the demons rebelled against God, they were now opposites of what they were created to do. For example, an angel created to minister health is now a demon that brings sickness.

I began to command demons to reveal their creative names, names given by God before they fell from their first estate. The demons still have names today; that has not changed. They are created beings. I also found that they did not like this. Once they are identified, they cannot hide behind generalities. As I progressed in this simple revelation, I began to see increased success in deliverance. I also began to see that for every demon on the inside of a person, there is a counterpart in the heavenlies. It is as though the territorial spirits place a part of themselves on the inside. It is a *cell* or *seed*, if you will, and it enables the spirits to run their kingdoms by *remote control*.

When a demon is cast out, I learned to command that spirit in the individual to go into the abyss and not return to the heavenly realm, making a clear distinction that not only is he cast from the individual, but he is also separated from his principality. I also make it clear to demons that they cannot return to circulation. They do not like this. In essence, when this happens, the territorial spirit is weakened; he has lost some territory. I never command demons to go to *dry places*, for that seems to be where they congregate and make decisions. I don't command them to go to the *feet of Jesus* so that He can determine their fate. They have already been there; He has already decided. I send them into the abyss and out of circulation.

I will tell you that I have learned much more by experience than by trying to analyze a scripture. Experience that brings scripture alive is invaluable. I have enough classroom hours in deliverance to enable me to speak with some confidence. I figure that I must have ten thousand hours of personal experience and learning from the Holy Spirit's presence and teaching in the area of deliverance. That is certainly not a boast, but I hope that it reinforces some of what I am saying.

My first encounter with territorial spirits was many years ago when a lady to whom I was ministering said, "He [the demon] says you don't have the authority to send him into the abyss."

I responded with, "It's not my authority; the authority is in the name of Jesus."

"Still," the demon responded, "you can't send me there. I'm not on the inside. I came to help the inside kingdom."

I said, "Well, I can make you leave in the name of Jesus."

The evil spirit responded with, "Yes, you can do that, but you cannot take me out of circulation."

I began to see this on a regular basis. Outside territorial spirits will come to assist the minions on the inside. They come to bring confusion, doubts, and fears to the deliverance candidate. Since they have some legal rights to the person, they don't want to lose their kingdom. I have found that they will retreat to the heavenly realm when commanded to, and then the inside demons can be dealt with accordingly. This is a consistent pattern. It is always the same.

Not long after I began to understand this area of their working, I also learned to recognize the presence of outside spirits. I learned to *sense* their presence. Typically it may be a slight headache, some blurred vision, or momentary confusion. One day while ministering to a lady, there was an unusual encounter. Bill Allen, one of our ministry workers, was also in the session with me. At the same time we both *felt* a strong evil presence. It was so intense that I became dizzy. I asked, "Is there a territorial spirit present?"

I had hardly spoken the words when the demon spoke through the lady, "Can't you feel me?"

"Who are you?" I demanded.

"I am the prince of Texas. I am…" (I will not give you his name, because I don't want it in print. I also don't want anyone speaking his name.) I have since encountered this demon many, many times.

Everyone in our ministry knows him by name; other demons know who he is. Other demons know he is the prince of Texas. He is but one of millions of demons. I want you to see there is a very organized government of demons with varying rank and power. This particular demon is a "big shot," but in a global structure he would be similar to the governor of Texas—many demons above him and many below him. Sometimes I even give him a *military* type respect as a high-ranking spirit, but not as the enemy of Jesus Christ.

Still, he is just a demon, just a spirit, and he always obeys the command to leave once it is determined that he has no legal right to be here. He has no choice. He knows the rules, and so do all of the others. However, until we understand their workings, we cannot know how to engage in the battle. He is but one. It is the Lord who rebukes these ranking spirits as we stand in the name of Jesus and in the truth of His Word. I never challenge a demon.

You can be sure that there is a territorial spirit over your state, your county, your city, your neighborhood, your block, and your house—a sophisticated government of rule and reign in the demonic spirit realm. For you to know who they are holds no value. For you to know their primary function does nothing for you.

Demons are not named as functions; they have individual names. My name is not *preacher*; that's what I do. Even if you think you know a spirit over a locale, what would be the advantage of knowing it? It has no advantage. For you to *go there* in so-called spiritual warfare is a wide-open door for you to be tormented by those very spirits. Don't pick a fight with principalities and powers. Leave them alone.

Keep your focus where your authority is, and that is limited to you and what is yours. Venturing outside this realm is very dangerous. It is a fight you cannot win.

CHAPTER 5

PROTECTIVE BOUNDARIES FOR THE FREED

Have you ever heard anyone say, "God, let me out of the box"? In an effort to experience more of God, some people get out from under sound doctrine and have allowed their itching ears to be scratched by preachers and teachers of unsound doctrine. I am not referring to the host of people who left good, solid, but incomplete doctrine and traditional teaching that was denominational and restrictive for new churches that teach doctrine that is not limiting to the working of the Holy Spirit. I am talking about others who have ventured out, perhaps venturing too far out.

Some of these people have entertained their own lusts in order to be recognized by others as being *spiritual*. Just as Paul wrote to Timothy, the time will come, and I believe it now is, when people will not endure sound doctrine, but they will, after their own lust, heap to themselves teachers, having itching ears. (See 2 Timothy 4:3.) If the *box* we want to get out of is the Bible and sound doctrine—then get back in. The things that we believe and speak must line up with sound Bible doctrine. The apostle Paul addressed this issue and advises believers, "That we should no longer be children, tossed to and fro and carried about with every wind of doctrine" (Eph. 4:14). If we allow ourselves to step out of the box of sound doctrine, we will become empty and without satisfaction in our Christian experience—and we will open wide the doorway for demonic intrusion.

Remember that when Peter got out of the boat, it was at the invitation of Jesus. (See Matthew 14:22–33.) He experienced a great moment—a miracle—but then he got back in the boat. He was out because Jesus was there, but he got back in when Jesus did. The miracles you seek will happen because Jesus is there, not because you got out of the boat, or the box.

I believe that most people have gotten out of the box because they sincerely desire more of God and more from God. Most have realized that it is not happening, and not likely to happen, where they are presently worshiping. Sound doctrine will stand the test. Let your box be God's Word. There is security and safety in the box because God stands behind His Word.

> All Scripture is given by inspiration of God, and is profitable for doctrine, for reproof, for correction, for instruction in righteousness, that the man of God may be complete, thoroughly equipped for every good work.
>
> —2 Timothy 3:16–17

> But as for you, speak the things which are proper for sound doctrine.
>
> —Titus 2:1

We do harm to ourselves when we go against God's law and His spiritual principles. As some have said, we don't really break God's commandments; we break ourselves against His commandments. We don't break the commandments; the commandments break us. When we try to change what God has put into place, we find ourselves fighting against God.

God's Protection

God protects what is His. Remember how God protected the patriarchs in their unsettled condition. When they came as strangers to Canaan and were sojourners in it, they were but few and could have easily been defeated and swallowed up. There were many who wanted them destroyed, yet no man was allowed to do them wrong. God held back the hand of the Canaanites, Philistines, and Egyptians.

Kings were reproved and plagued for their sakes. Mighty Pharaoh was unable to resist God. God had called leaders for His people. They were the anointed of the Lord. They were sanctified by His grace and glory. They had received the unction of His Spirit. They were His prophets and preachers, instructed in the things of God by God. They were commissioned to instruct others. They were called and separated out by God. Therefore, if any touched them, they touched the apple of God's eye; if any harmed them, it was at their own peril.

I have experienced this godly protection without even being aware that there was an attempt to harm this ministry. Many years ago, not long after I had started going into prisons, I received a check from the Texas Department of Corrections Inmate Trust Fund for more than $600. The check was an offering from more than five hundred inmates at a particular prison in Texas. They had collectively drawn a dollar or so from their accounts to send me as a love offering for being faithful in coming to their prison. The chaplain called me to explain what an act of love it was from the inmate congregation. That just overwhelmed me. It still does when I think about it.

I didn't even know at the time how the inmate trust fund worked, didn't even know it existed. Basically, it is like a bank account for inmates. If a loved one sends them money, it goes into this fund. Through paper transactions, an inmate could draw from his account at the commissary or could even ask that a check be sent to someone on the outside. Most inmates have little or nothing in their accounts. During a prison church service, the congregation had decided they wanted to help support our ministry for being faithful in coming there. I didn't know anything about it.

Naturally, five hundred inmates sending individual withdrawal slips designated to go to me caused some attention in the prison system. A few weeks after I had received the check, the chaplain called again, almost crying, and his voice was broken. He proceeded to tell me that the warden of the prison had *banned* me from coming there. He was convinced that I must be bringing in drugs or something illegal, which is why the inmates were sending me money. The chaplain apologized and told me the men would be praying. I really didn't know what to do, so I did nothing.

About three weeks after this took place, the chaplain called again and told me that the warden had experienced a bad heart attack and died. He informed me that I was once again welcome on the unit.

I received a similar phone call from the prison director in New York State. This was many years later. In a very kind conversation, he told me that a particular prison ministry in New York had made a complaint about me. The complaint was that I only came to New York prisons to find out which inmates had money. The director said, "We don't believe that, and we have great appreciation for what you do. However, we have to investigate this woman's complaint, and until we have completed our investigation, you will no longer be able to minister in New York State prisons."

I did not know this lady, nor did I have any idea why such a charge would be made. It's very expensive to make a trip from Texas to New York. I don't know that I had ever received any money from a New York inmate. Knowing that someone had lied about me and our ministry caused me great pain. I didn't know what to do, so once again I did nothing. I still don't know who this woman was.

A couple of months passed, and I received another phone call from the director. He was very apologetic and professional. "Don, there is no problem with you or your ministry, and you are welcome to come here anytime." He further said, "By the way, the woman who made this complaint has since lost her family and her ministry."

I consider myself the "apple of God's eye." I know that I am called by Him, and I know I am anointed. That's not boastful to say that; I didn't have anything to do with it. My job is to be faithful.

There are some boundaries that we should not cross. There are some places we should not go. In the next section we will look at how to recognize and avoid demonic strongholds that could be sources of demonic oppression and intrusion. Whether you have already been delivered from demonic interference and are now seeking to understand how to "keep the pigs out," or are needing teaching to help you understand and recognize where you may have opened a doorway allowing demons to rush in, you will discover some of the strongholds that need to be eradicated from your life, and you will learn to stay within the Father's protective boundaries in the future.

RECOGNIZE AND AVOID THE STRONGHOLDS

CHAPTER 6

DON'T GET SNAGGED BY STRONGHOLDS

I N THIS SECTION of the book we are going to take a closer look at how to recognize *and avoid* the demonic strongholds that will quickly take hold in the life of the person who has not successfully locked and bolted the doors shut by confessing all known sin, walking in obedience to the Word of God, and focusing on only those things over which God has given His children authority through His righteousness and salvation.

Messed Up and Passed Up

The Bible contains a story that highlights the difficulties we can get into when we open a door and step out of God's boundaries. Read the biblical account of this parable about the good Samaritan, and allow me to review for you the hazards of getting messed up and passed up.

> Then Jesus answered and said: "A certain man went down from Jerusalem to Jericho, and fell among thieves, who stripped him of his clothing, wounded him, and departed, leaving him half dead. Now by chance a certain priest came down that road. And when

he saw him, he passed by on the other side. Likewise a Levite, when he arrived at the place, came and looked, and passed by on the other side. But a certain Samaritan...

—LUKE 10:30–33

Oh, you know this story. You've heard this message. If you've been to church just a few times, you know about this. This is a familiar story to everyone, called the parable of the good Samaritan. This may have been more than a parable; it may have been a report from a recent event that was in the news in Jericho and Jerusalem. It was a likely story. Priests who lived in Jericho but ministered in Jerusalem often traveled the road from Jericho to Jerusalem. The Levites, who served the priests, were also common travelers on the road. Perhaps Jesus was recounting an incident, but either way, He is illustrating a greater truth through the story. (See Luke 10:30–37.)

A certain man was attacked, beaten, robbed, and left for dead. Who were the thieves? Arabian highwaymen? Whether they were Arabians, plunderers who lived by spoil, some criminals from his own nation, or some of the Roman soldiers who, despite the strict discipline of their army, did this harm is not clear—but they were *hard up*. Virtually always those who *beat up* are the *hard up*. They are most often the ones who were first victims of life's hardships. In today's situation, it is likely this would have been a gang-related crime. Indignation rises within us when we hear of such crimes. The calloused hatred of such people stirs a righteous anger within us.

Regardless, the man needed help. He was likely a Jew, and it would have been helpful to him if someone of his own nation and religion would have come by.

A priest came by. He saw him and could not help but discern his desperate need. Seeing his bloody body and hearing his groans, the priest had to know. What a *messed-up* heart the priest had. He was supposed to be a man of public character and religious prominence, a man who professed sanctity, whose office obliged him to tenderness and compassion. (See Hebrews 5:1–2.) It is likely that he is one who taught others how to react in cases such as this. Yet this injured man was *passed up* by the *messed up*.

What an empty, disgusting feeling he must have had if he was conscious—a priest turned away from him. I'm sure that as the priest passed by, he was justifying his actions. He was tired…was on his way home…no one was looking…his reputation was not at stake. In reality, he was *messed up* in his relationship to God and to himself and others. Listen…there are some *messed-up* hearts in the lives of so-called *fixed-up* people.

Now comes the Levite. Not only did he see the hurting man, but also he "looked on him" (Luke 10:32, KJV). He made an assessment. He surveyed the damage and possibly made eye contact. But quickly he got as far away as possible, as if to say, "I did not know." Maybe he was too important; he was part of the *dressed-up* society, knowing better but doing it anyway. Compassion was also part of his daily learning and teaching. The *beat up* by the *hard up* was now *passed up* by the *messed up* and the *dressed up*.

The Bible says the wounded man was half-dead. I'm guessing that the priest and the Levite perceived that the situation required more than they were willing to give. It would be more than just helping him to his feet. It would mean time, effort, and money. It is interesting that whenever Jesus is asked *difficult* questions, He simply says, "Love Me, and then love your neighbor as yourself." (See Matthew 22:37–40.) The Word emphasizes that this *sums up* the commandments of God.

Next comes the good Samaritan. Who is this so-called *good Samaritan*? He could have been *dressed up*, but he wasn't *messed up*. A *good* Samaritan, in reality, would have been one who kept the Law and obeyed the commandments. Today there are only a few hundred Samaritans located in Nablus, about forty miles north of Jerusalem. Of course, you know of the Samaritan woman in John 4. The issue here is not that the man was a Samaritan but that he obeyed God's law and that his heart had a connection with God's heart. He could not help but show compassion. God is love.

This man *picked up* the *broken up*. He loved the unlovely. It is obvious that this man already had a relationship with God. He was *fixed up*. A good sign of a *fixed-up* heart is compassion. Not caring is an obvious sign of a *messed-up* heart.

Not only did the Samaritan *pick up* the wounded man, but he also *gave up* his own comfort; he put the man on his own beast. He *gave up* his own time and money and *paid up* the wounded man's medical needs and his room and board.

Often we feel that we don't *measure up*. But in reality, God has not asked much of us. He asks merely that we love Him with all of our mind, heart, and soul and that we love others as we love ourselves. Anyone who has been *cleaned up* by the blood of Jesus Christ can *step up* and be obedient.

Love the Lord your God with all your heart and with all your soul and with all your strength and with all your mind, and your neighbor as yourself. This is just my way of asking, Which one of the conditions in this section best describes you and your life today?

Preparation for Deliverance

Whether you are dealing with demonic interference and are looking for the steps to take for deliverance for the first time, or you have been delivered and freed from Satan's hold earlier and are now wanting to help others become free—or dealing with demons again for a second or third time—there are basic preparations that you must make to be ready to be set free.

Let's begin this section with an overview of the steps you must follow to experience deliverance.

Some time ago a lady completed a deliverance request form for our ministry and was eventually scheduled for an appointment. Before we see anyone in our office, we have found it very important for the individual to be as prepared as possible to experience deliverance. We send information explaining the process and ask the candidate to pray certain types of prayers before coming. We include a DVD that we call an "Introduction to Deliverance." We do our best to make the person feel comfortable about coming, knowing the demons will do their job of intimidation. We ask that the person deal with many things before coming to our office.

These are the same issues any individual must be willing to deal with before receiving deliverance.

1. Get rid of all unforgiveness.

In order for deliverance to be successful, there can be *no* unforgiveness in your life. Unforgiveness is legal permission for demons to torment believers. Read Matthew 18:23–35. Do not neglect the area of forgiveness for yourself—you must forgive yourself in order to be free. A typical prayer might be as follows:

> *Father, because You have forgiven me, I choose to forgive others. I forgive everyone who has hurt me, lied to me, or disappointed me. I confess unforgiveness as sin and repent of it. I receive Your forgiveness and apply it to my life by forgiving myself. Thank You for Your grace and mercy. In Jesus's name, amen.*

2. Renounce all satanic activities.

If there was ever any involvement (however innocent) in satanic activities, witchcraft, cults, or occult activities, they must be renounced. Here is a typical prayer:

> *Father, I renounce any bond or agreement I ever made with Satan and the kingdom of darkness. I know there can be no valid contract with a liar, and I renounce any words, oaths, or pledges made to Satan. I choose to be totally free from them. I choose to be cleansed from any ties with Satan. In Jesus's name, amen.*

3. Renounce soul ties.

Sexual relationships outside of marriage are called soul ties, and each one could be an entry point for demon spirits. The ties must be broken by confessing them as sin and then choosing to be free from them. I will include a prayer you can pray. It would be best if you could do so by denouncing each one by name; do the best you can with that. The deliverance process involves canceling permission of evil spirits to be in our lives. This prayer and renunciation will cancel consent that was granted through soul ties. The prayer can be something like this:

> *Father, I confess the sin of sexual relations outside of marriage. I renounce that sinful activity in Jesus's name. I call back that part of me that was given to another, and I refuse that part of another that may have come to me. I denounce soul ties with [SAY NAME] and choose to be free in Jesus Christ's name. Amen.*

4. Confess and renounce false religions.

False religions must also be confessed and renounced. Pray this prayer:

> *Father, because of my relationship to You through Your Son Jesus Christ, and in His name, I renounce all associations with pagan worship, false gods, false deities, and any involvement with them. I forgive my ancestors for their involvement, and I break any ties to any religion that denies the deity of the Lord Jesus. He alone is Lord. He alone can forgive sin and give man eternal life. I fully trust Jesus Christ, and I separate myself from the sins of my ancestors, in Jesus Christ's name. Amen.*

These are the requirements of anyone who comes to us for ministry. These are basic requests prior to the deliverance session. The suggested prayers we send are very general. Obviously, there may be other areas of permission that can open the door to satanic attacks and strongholds.

5. Avoid stepping out of the authority God has given to you.

One area that seems to be problematic with many people is stepping out of the boundaries where you do not have warfare experience or authority.

At one time I was in Houston taking a lady through deliverance. We were in the home of some ministry friends. The lady going through deliverance was a beautiful young lady and a graduate from a high-ranking university. We all sat around the dining room table. As we started the process, she became very fidgety, which is fairly normal.

For five hours, she gave me the names of demons as the commands were given. There must have been a hundred demons identified. Finally, about midnight, I said, "Something is wrong. There is a wide open door. It's a revolving door, and as soon as one demon is cast out, another comes in." I addressed obvious possibilities, such as unconfessed sin, anger, unforgiveness, and so on.

With each possibility, she was certain there was no unconfessed sin in her life. Finally I said, "Have you attempted to do any spiritual warfare against demons that have a territorial assignment—who have external assignments and are not demons you are struggling with inside your own life?"

"Oh, every day," she said. "I walk around my neighborhood and bind spirits over certain houses and over my city."

Immediately I knew that was the problem. I talked with her at length about the authority that God had given to believers. I reminded her that the Bible is very clear that these kinds of battles belong to God and the angels—not to her. I asked if she could confess that she had gone beyond her realm of authority, and she said, "Yes." Very simply, she did that. Just confessed. After she did, I went back to the deliverance process and commanded that the territorial spirit identify himself.

She looked stunned as she gave me his name and then said, "That's the name of my subdivision." In the name of Jesus, I commanded that the demon spirit confess to her that he would leave her and not bother her again. From her lips came these words, "If she'll leave me alone, I'll leave her alone."

There are many stories I could tell you like this. Don't start a fight you cannot win. Our authority does not extend into the heavenly realm. We have no rights in the heavens. Think about it. Why would you want to venture there? Don't go there.

In the remaining chapters of this section of the book we will take a close look at some of the satanic strongholds we need to avoid to remain free.

CHAPTER 7

THE MOST COMMON STRONGHOLD

THE MOST COMMON legal stronghold I have encountered is unforgiveness. We see this all the time. The lie demons use here is causing a person to feel justified in his or her anger and bitterness toward someone else or toward self, and sometimes even anger toward God.

> And whenever you stand praying, if you have anything against anyone, forgive him, that your Father in heaven may also forgive you your trespasses. But if you do not forgive, neither will your Father in heaven forgive your trespasses.
> —MARK 11:25–26

Forgiveness is not an option; it is a must. The closing words in the powerful parable about unforgiveness says, "…delivered him to the torturers.…So My heavenly father also will do to you if each of you, from his heart, does not forgive his brother his trespasses" (Matt. 18:34–35).

When Peter questioned Jesus about how many times a man had to forgive, he argued that seven times seemed to be enough, but Jesus said, "I do not say to you, up to seven times, but up to seventy times seven" (v. 22). After speaking these astounding words to Peter, Jesus completed the emphasis with a parable about the consequences of not forgiving.

He told of a man who had a great debt but could not pay it. His debt was insurmountable, and he was about to lose his wife and children. He owed $101 million, and foreclosure was imminent. (See Matthew 18:23–35.) The man went to his debtor and begged patience and forgiveness. "Then the master of that servant was moved with compassion, released him, and forgave him the debt" (v. 27). He had a debt he could not pay, and he was forgiven. That debtor is a picture of us.

But then this man who had received great grace and forgiveness went to one of his peers to collect a debt of about forty dollars. The man who had received great forgiveness pursued a small debt with vengeance. He put his hands on the man's throat and threatened him with prison. Even though his debtor pleaded for patience and made a promise to pay, he had the man cast into prison.

This is a vivid picture of how heaven sees our acts of unforgiveness. We have received grace beyond measure, unconditional love, and forgiveness for a debt we could not pay. Yet so often we refuse to forgive someone on our same level.

The one who had forgiven the great debt had these words for this man: "'You wicked servant! I forgave you all that debt because you begged me. Should you not also have had compassion on your fellow servant, just as I had pity on you?' And his master was angry, and delivered him to the torturers until he should pay all that was due to him" (vv. 32–34).

This parable that Jesus shared is sad. No one would treat someone else that way…would they? The picture is clear; forgiveness is not an option if you want to be free. Look at the strong words of Jesus after He spoke the parable.

> So My heavenly father also will do to you if each of you, from his heart, does not forgive his brother his trespasses.
>
> —MATTHEW 18:35

Unforgiveness is like the ultimate insult to God, and it carries a severe penalty for believers. God turns the unforgiving believer over to the torturers, to evil spirits. No, not in losing one's salvation, but many believers live in torment today because they refuse to forgive. Unforgiveness grieves the Holy Spirit of God.

> And do not grieve the Holy Spirit of God, by whom you were sealed for the day of redemption. Let all bitterness, wrath, anger, clamor, and evil speaking be put away from you, with all malice. And be kind to one another, tenderhearted, forgiving one another, even as God in Christ forgave you.
>
> —EPHESIANS 4:30–32

Unforgiveness is sin. Sin can only be removed by confession and repentance. I will tell you without blinking that if you have unforgiveness in your life, you have demons in your life.

Forgiveness is not an act of the will, nor is it an agreement that it is the right thing to do. You cannot *will* forgiveness. Unforgiveness must be repented of before God. It is a sweet-smelling fragrance to God, and He always receives our forgiveness of others. Healing comes through forgiveness.

Unforgiveness is torment. God turns those who refuse to forgive over to the tormentors. He looses those from bondage who forgive. Forgiveness is what we received at salvation. Forgiveness is honored by God. We are being Christlike—like God's Son—when we forgive. Once the unforgiveness is gone, the demons that came by that permission must be cast out. They don't necessarily leave just because you repented. Cast them out.

One of the things we see healed on a regular basis when this is done is fibromyalgia. We also see levels of arthritis healed. Here is a simple thought: If pleasant words and a cheerful heart are health to the bones, what is anger and bitterness to the bones? If repentance and departing from evil is health and marrow to the bones, what is holding on to unforgiveness?

Pleasant words are like a honeycomb,
Sweetness to the soul and health to the bones.

—PROVERBS 16:24

A merry heart does good, like medicine,
But a broken spirit dries the bones.

—PROVERBS 17:22

Do not be wise in your own eyes;
Fear the LORD and depart from evil.
It will be health to your flesh,
And strength to your bones.

—PROVERBS 3:7–8

What Forgiveness Is Not

Some people don't forgive because they misunderstand what it is. It is not saying that what happened is OK. It will always be painful; the deeds that hurt and offended you will always be wrong and always be painful when you remember them. When Jesus forgave me, He did not say sin was OK. Sin is ugly; it took Him to the cross. What He said was, "I love you anyway, in spite of the sin and the ugly, painful deeds." You can do that. You can look at the person(s) who has offended you and say, "I wish no harm for you. I want God to love you as He loves me." If vengeance is in order, I turn that over to God. I did not deserve forgiveness when God forgave me. The person who offended you may not deserve your forgiveness either, but because it is God's way, and God's instruction to do so, you do it.

I was in a meeting in Tomball, Texas, a suburb of Houston. I'll never forget this meeting; neither will our team members who were there with me. At the altar call that I gave, a lady stepped from her seat and came forward. Many others had also come, and our ministry associates were praying with various individuals. However, when this lady came, others came with her. I didn't know it at the time, but it was her family—grown children and spouses. The woman was so large she could hardly stand. She also had become very rigid as I talked to her. I invited her to sit in the first chair next to the aisle.

As I bent to talk with her, she told me that she knew she had demons because she could not forgive. I said, "Sure, you can forgive. You just choose to do it." She insisted that she could not. She also said that many times she had pledged that she would never forgive. She had a few tears in her eyes. "It's my mom," she told me. "I'll never forgive her. Even though she is dead, I will not forgive her."

I talked with her some more and told her that she could not be free from her torment until she forgave.

"I can't say it; I can't even say the words."

"Yes, you can; just say these words after me." I kept insisting that she look at me, and I encouraged her, "Just speak the words, 'I forgive my mother.'"

"I can't do it," she said. "If I forgive her, then she wins." Her family circled her seat and held hands.

"No," I said, "if you forgive her, you win, and your family wins."

She struggled and mumbled but just couldn't get the words out. Finally, she did, with words that seem to bolt from her mouth: "I forgive my mother!" When she spoke those words, her family fell to the ground in unison, and she burst into tears. Her family lay silently on the floor as I very simply and softly, in the name of Jesus, commanded the demons to go. They did; their right to her and to her family was broken in that moment.

James 3:14–17 gives some warnings about possible gateways similar to unforgiveness.

> But if you have bitter envy and self-seeking in your hearts, do not boast and lie against the truth. This wisdom does not descend from above, but is earthly, sensual, demonic. For where envy and self-seeking exist, confusion and every evil thing are there. But the wisdom that is from above is first pure, then peaceable, gentle, willing to yield, full of mercy and good fruits, without partiality and without hypocrisy.

If you have recognized the presence of unforgiveness—or any of these related strongholds mentioned in the verses above—in your life, and you want to be free of the demons who inhabit these strongholds, pray this prayer:

> *Heavenly Father, I ask You to forgive me for not forgiving. I acknowledge that unforgiveness is sin, and I repent before You and ask You to give me peace. I forgive all those who have hurt me, and I thank You for forgiving me for harboring bitterness and anger toward them. I choose to forgive myself, and I receive and apply Your forgiveness to my life. I want the peace that You give. I thank You for Jesus and the forgiveness provided at the cross. In Jesus's name, amen.*

CHAPTER 8

SPIRITUAL AGGRESSION

I'M A HIGH school football fan. I mean I don't miss a Friday night game. I suppose that at every high school game there are people who come to see the game, and there are people who come to see the band. I'm the football guy. I'm not much of a band guy, even though the school I support has a national championship band. I didn't even know there were marching band contests until a few years ago. I never thought about band competition. There's a lot of marching going on these days, you know—marching for women's rights, political candidates, gay rights, animal rights, minority rights...You'd be surprised what you can march for—just about anything you can think of.

Marching has even become popular in some church circles. Some are marching to "take our neighborhoods, cities, counties, countries, and world for God." This sounds very good. But there are way too many Christians who are engaging in this spiritual aggression. Sometimes there is an intimidation that comes from Christian leaders who say that if you don't engage in the warfare, you have not yet arrived.

Just what is *spiritual warfare* anyway? Actually the term is not even mentioned in God's Word. The principles, however, are found in the following verses:

Behold, I give you the authority to trample on serpents and scorpions, and over all the power of the enemy, and nothing shall by any means hurt you.

—LUKE 10:19

Finally, my brethren, be strong in the Lord and in the power of His might. Put on the whole armor of God, that you may be able to stand against the wiles of the devil. For we do not wrestle against flesh and blood, but against principalities, against powers, against the rulers of the darkness of this age, against spiritual hosts of wickedness in the heavenly places. Therefore take up the whole armor of God, that you may be able to withstand in the evil day, and having done all, to stand. Stand therefore, having girded your waist with truth, having put on the breastplate of righteousness, and having shod your feet with the preparation of the gospel of peace; above all, taking the shield of faith with which you will be able to quench all the fiery darts of the wicked one. And take the helmet of salvation, and the sword of the Spirit, which is the word of God; praying always with all prayer and supplication in the Spirit, being watchful to this end with all perseverance and supplication for all the saints.

—EPHESIANS 6:10–18

This charge I commit to you, son Timothy, according to the prophecies previously made concerning you, that by them you may wage the good warfare.

—1 TIMOTHY 1:18

Fight the good fight of faith, lay hold on eternal life, to which you were also called and have confessed the good confession in the presence of many witnesses.

—1 TIMOTHY 6:12

For God has not given us a spirit of fear, but of power and of love and of a sound mind.

—2 TIMOTHY 1:7

No one engaged in warfare entangles himself with the affairs of this life, that he may please him who enlisted him as a soldier.

—2 TIMOTHY 2:4

But recall the former days in which, after you were illuminated, you endured a great struggle with sufferings.

—HEBREWS 10:32

You are of God, little children, and have overcome them, because He who is in you is greater than he who is in the world.

—1 JOHN 4:4

And they overcame him by the blood of the Lamb and by the word of their testimony, and they did not love their lives to the death....And the dragon was enraged with the woman, and he went to make war with the rest of her offspring, who keep the commandments of God and have the testimony of Jesus Christ.

—REVELATION 12:11, 17

As you examine these scriptures, you will see that biblical spiritual warfare centers on the battle between the individual Christian and demons for the believer's *faith*. The primary battle each believer is called upon to fight is against *personal* attacks from demon powers. We are to stand against temptations, accusations, and lies. We are to resist fears, lusts, hindrances, curses, and such. There is clear teaching from God's Word that it is God who overcomes our enemy. It is the personal application of truth and the name of Jesus Christ concerning each individual. There is not one indication in the entire Bible that teaches the church to overthrow Satan's dominion over this world.

It is interesting that often when spiritual warfare is discussed, whether in print, in the pulpit, on TV, or in a private conversation, the idea is put forth that the church is to be spiritually aggressive in fighting, that we are to fight against principalities and powers, against the rulers of darkness and spiritual wickedness in high places.

In reality, that is not what Scripture teaches us at all. The spiritual armor Paul talks about is so that we are covered and are able to stand and to block the "fiery darts" of the wicked. There is no instruction to seek out the demons. The admonition is to be protected by what Jesus has already provided. We don't fight; we follow. It is in the power of *His might* that we stand. We are to pray, watch, and stand—not seek and destroy.

Don't pick fights with demons. We are to resist the devil and his demons, and we do that by humbling ourselves before God, not by shaking our fist at the demons. When demon powers have gained legal ground, we must remove their rights by confession of truth and repentance, not by yelling at them. Often all this does is give them more legal rights.

We are to stand. We stand upon the Word. Principalities and powers have already been defeated. Our victory is in being clothed in His righteousness and truth. It is exercising the truth of God's Word against the trickery and deception of the demonic lies.

> For I am persuaded that neither death nor life, nor angels nor principalities nor powers, nor things present nor things to come, nor height nor depth, nor any other created thing, shall be able to separate us from the love of God which is in Christ Jesus our Lord.
>
> —ROMANS 8:38–39

Our persuasion is in the truth of God's Word and the completed works of Jesus Christ—not in the aggressive warfare that we might attempt to do. Jesus destroyed principalities and powers through His shed blood, death, burial, and resurrection. He spoiled them and made a show of them openly, triumphing over them. Our aggression toward this unseen army of celestial realm demonic powers is standing in truth. It is always a truth encounter; never is it about power.

> For by Him all things were created that are in heaven and that are on earth, visible and invisible, whether thrones or dominions or principalities or powers. All things were created through Him and for Him.
>
> —Colossians 1:16

> Having disarmed principalities and powers, He made a public spectacle of them, triumphing over them in it.
>
> —Colossians 2:15

The power of the demon is the lie, plain and simple—twisted truth, tainted truth, partial truth. The father of lies and deception is Satan. His demons are like him. They cannot handle the truth. When you believe a lie, you empower demons. Telling them to go is no good until you repent of the lie and embrace the truth.

Any false belief exalts itself against the knowledge of God. It does not matter what events framed and formed the lie. It can only be fixed by truth. The spiritual wounds that we carry are generally from some trauma in the flesh. However, we do not war or fix those wounds with acts of the flesh. We cover the wounds with forgiveness. The demonic powers that lie to us about ourselves and tell us we are unworthy and unlovable must be resisted with truth. There is no other way. To ignore truth is to embrace the lie.

That's how you cast down imaginations. What is the truth? Then believe it and apply it. Our weapons are mighty through God... period!

> For though we walk in the flesh, we do not war according to the flesh. For the weapons of our warfare are not carnal but mighty in God for pulling down strongholds, casting down arguments and every high thing that exalts itself against the knowledge of God, bringing every thought into captivity to the obedience of Christ.
>
> —2 Corinthians 10:3–5

You see, the sword of the Spirit is the Word of God. We cast down imaginations and lies by the truth of His Word. His Word is alive. It is powerful. It is like a surgeon's knife for the soul.

> For the word of God is living and powerful, and sharper than any two-edged sword, piercing even to the division of soul and spirit, and of joints and marrow, and is a discerner of the thoughts and intents of the heart.
>
> —HEBREWS 4:12

Using Discernment

It is important in *today's* Christian walk that we are discerning disciples—not only followers of truth but discerners of truth. The *Word* of God is a discerner.

Frank Hammond, who wrote the classic book *Pigs in the Parlor,* told me a story of a man who stood up in a meeting and disrupted it greatly with an outburst. Brother Frank said he leaned over to another speaker on the platform and said, "That man has demons."

The man who sat next to Frank said, "You must have the gift of discernment."

To which Brother Hammond responded, "I don't know what I've got, but I know what he's got."

Seems everyone wants to *hear* from God; everybody wants a *word.* If you want to hear from God, you must hear His Word. God has already spoken through His Word, and His Word "is a discerner of the thoughts and intents of the heart" (Heb. 4:12). Simply put, your thoughts—your *thoughts from God*—must line up with the already spoken Word of God. We must come into agreement with the Word of God.

It is interesting that Hebrews 4:12 tells us that the Word of God is able to invade our entire being—spirit, soul, and body. An absolute key for genuine freedom is spiritual alignment; that is, our spirit agreeing with what God says in His Word, our soul—mind, will, emotions, and personality—believing and speaking what God's Word says, and our flesh agreeing in obedience to the truth of God's Word.

There is an interesting verse of Scripture written by James to believers:

> Do ye think that the scripture saith in vain, The spirit that dwelleth in us lusteth to envy?
>
> —JAMES 4:5, KJV

What? The spirit that dwells in us? "But if I'm a believer, only the Holy Spirit can dwell in me." Is that what you are thinking? What spirit do you suppose James is referring to here? Our human spirit most likely, but maybe evil spirits that dwell in our soul and body. Evil spirits must be cast out; our human spirit must be cast down. There must be agreement in our being for there to be healing and fullness of God's presence.

You see, the Word gets into even the "joint and marrow," and the Word brings healing. Coming into agreement with truth that God has already spoken allows us to receive and apply the promises of the Word.

Whenever God speaks, whatever He says automatically becomes law. In His legal system, alignment with truth brings freedom. Now, the opposite is true as well. Rebellion, refusal to receive His Word as truth, means to believe a lie, and the lie empowers demons. Empowered demons bring destruction, death, disease, and further deception to the believer. The job of every demon is to steal, kill, and destroy. The problem is that believers don't believe. More accurately, our belief is often tempered with conditions. The Word of God is alive. It is alive and powerful. How can that be?

> In the beginning was the Word, and the Word was with God, and the Word was God.... And the Word became flesh and dwelt among us, and we beheld His glory, the glory as of the only begotten of the Father, full of grace and truth.
>
> —JOHN 1:1, 14

The Word of God is *alive* because Jesus is the Word. It is powerful because Jesus is the Word. *What an incredible truth.* When you speak the Word, you actually speak His presence right into your life and your situation. "Your word is truth" (John 17:17). Discerning disciples must weigh *words* against God's Word. It is truth that liberates, and His Word is *truth*.

When Mary was holding the baby Jesus in her arms, I wonder, did she know that she was holding the one who was holding all creation in His grip? Maybe she knew, but I doubt that she could possibly comprehend that He was *in the beginning with God and that He was and is God*. Could she have known that while she was holding Him that He was actually holding her? Could she have known that He spoke everything into being and that when He speaks, all of creation obeys?

I think also that we are not able to receive the magnitude of power and authority that is ours in His name. I believe it is a little more than simply speaking His name; it is believing that His name is above every name. It is living daily, moment by moment in that amazing truth. His Word is truth. We are empowered by the truth of His Word, the presence of His Holy Spirit, and exercising His name in our lives.

CHAPTER 9

MENTAL DISORDERS AND DEMONS

WITHOUT DOUBT, THE most difficult individuals whom we deal with are those who have been diagnosed with mental disorders. I do not believe that all mental disorders are the result of mind-tormenting spirits; if that were true, then we could just make prayer circles around the mental institutions and bind all those spirits.

This is a tough one for several reasons. I am somewhat acquainted with it. My mother was diagnosed as *paranoid schizophrenic*. She attempted suicide nine times in a six-week period. She was tormented in her mind. This was before I knew about deliverance as I do now. Since her death, I have many times tried to discover what may have happened in her life that could have allowed this. I don't know. Her two sisters committed suicide. If they were abused as children, I don't know about it; none of my relatives know about it. While I suspect that may have been the problem, I don't know.

I can't find anything in her ancestry that helps me to answer the mystery—but there was a source. It was the work of demons. My friend Frank Hammond was convinced in his ministry that *rejection* is at the root of paranoia and schizophrenia. I have had many experiences to confirm that; however, there may be multiple things that come together to bring this about. Delusion is maximum deception.

Paranoia is defined as "a mental condition characterized by delusions of persecution, unwarranted jealousy, or exaggerated self-importance. It is unjustified suspicion and mistrust of others." "Exaggerated self-importance"—I see this a lot in the ministry, unfortunately, among ministers.

For the person affected with a mental disorder, the paranoia is real. That person sees something and hears something. Something is going on.

The question is really not whether it is caused by demons; rather, it is how the demons cause it. Without doubt, many people in this condition need medical help. Often the individual needs both spiritual and physiological help. Sometimes the person needs some medical attention to be ready to be delivered. It is virtually always different with each case.

The Lie Must Be Denounced

When a lie has been believed, it is very difficult to deal with demons until the lie has been denounced. The problem here is that the deception is so powerful that individuals do not perceive it to be a lie. They become so fully blinded by the lie that they are unable to see the truth. They are convinced that the government is persecuting them or that secret agents are assigned to spy and gather information against them. They are so convinced that it is very difficult for them to confess it as a lie. They often become suspicious of you because you don't believe their story.

It is always the same and never the same. It is the neighbors plotting against them, sometimes co-workers telling false stories about them, hearing people outside of their house or in the house. It may be they believe witches and warlocks have put curses on them. The torment they are in is real. There is no doubt that what they perceive is likely very real to them. So the dilemma is how to bring freedom to those suffering from disorders of the mind.

I assure you that it is more than simply commanding demons to go in the name of Jesus. If it were that simple, I would be at the mental hospitals right now. I have been there; I have prayed for institutionalized people. I have spent many hours in the psychiatric wings of the prisons. I have heard the demons react when I would walk down the halls or come by their cells. I have heard the screams down the corridors as the sounds from the chapel services spilled into the prison. It is more than just speaking the name of Jesus over a mentally ill person. It is complex, and until the legal rights of those demon powers have been removed (by the individual or parents), freedom does not come.

The name of Jesus will stir them, regardless. Demons hate and fear that name. Some people with mental disorders cannot even read the Bible because of the torment that comes. Some read it and are only able to see condemnation and judgment. The thing I know is that there is always a root, sometimes many roots. The problem is finding the root and removing permissions that demons have gained.

One of the things we have experienced in this area is that there is a common need for attention. Sometimes it is the only way a person knows to gain sympathy and importance. Over the years we have encountered *many* SRA victims. SRA is satanic ritual abuse. We have also learned that in most cases the supposed abuse never happened. The individual may *believe* it happened, but generally it is a lie. There are some instances where the abuse really happened, but not nearly to the extent people claim it happened.

We used to see of a lot of these people. We found limited success, and we also discovered that there was seldom any evidence to confirm the stories. This became all too common—no names, no addresses, no crime reports, no way to verify any of it.

A pastor of a church in a nearby city called me one night. He was distraught. He said, "Don, maybe you can help me; we are at our wit's end in knowing how to deal with a young lady. We have taken her into our home to try to help her. We have tried casting out demons, and it just seems to go on and on. We don't know what to do."

He began to tell me her story, and as he did, I knew I had heard it many times. It's the SRA story, and I don't want to minimize what may be a very real problem for some. As he told me her story, I said, "The reason you can't help her is because it didn't happen."

There was a silence on the other end of the phone. After a moment, he said, "You mean she's lying?" Part of her sad story was that when she stayed at a motel the church was paying for, her father had busted open the door and brutally raped her. I said, "Take her to the police; I'm betting she won't go."

Again there was silence. "You're right" he said. "We tried to take her there, but once we arrived, she wouldn't go in."

Of course there are demons involved, but the demons have permission because she is believing and perpetuating the lie. I always seem to end these stories with the same thing. It is truth that enables us to be free. Lies empower the demons.

You can avoid this stronghold by recognizing the power of a lie. If you are struggling with emotional and mental confusion or distress, close the door before a stronghold can be established in your life. Confess any known sin, and get rid of any lies in your life. If you are still struggling and cannot find the freedom for which you sincerely are seeking God's help, commit yourself to solid spiritual counsel from your pastor or a trusted Christian intercessor; seek also the expertise of a trained Christian psychologist to rule out any medical imbalances. You may well need medical help.

CHAPTER 10

THE TOUGHEST
OF ALL SPIRITS

THIS SCRIPTURE CLEARLY teaches that deliverance is part of Jesus's job description.

> The Spirit of the LORD is upon Me,
> Because He has anointed Me
> To preach the gospel to the poor;
> He has sent Me to heal the brokenhearted,
> To proclaim liberty to the captives
> And recovery of sight to the blind,
> To set at liberty those who are oppressed;
> To proclaim the acceptable year of the LORD.
> —LUKE 4:18–19

"Because He has anointed Me to...He has sent me to..." Jesus was sent to be:

- The breaker of the bondage
- The bearer of the burden
- The blesser of the bruised
- The binder of the brokenhearted
- The beacon to the blind

That's included in His anointed duties, for He came for the purpose of destroying the works of the devil.

Satan stripped Job. He shamed Peter. He slammed Paul. He buffeted Paul with "a thorn in the flesh" (2 Cor. 12:7). But Jesus is also the grace giver. He is the righteous restorer. The bottom line in all deliverance is Jesus.

Why does the subject of demons create so much controversy? Have you ever given much thought as to why no one is comfortable when the subject of *demons* comes up? What's the problem? Can you talk about it with your friends? How about with your pastor or church leaders? Since Jesus spent approximately one-third of His ministry dealing with demons and healing, why do we only talk about the other two-thirds? Have you ever given this any thought?

Do you suppose He was just speaking on the level of understanding of the poor, unintelligent people of *His time*? What a prideful assumption and insult to Jesus. Would the Creator of all things deceive us into believing that demons existed only in the thinking of an unenlightened generation? Is it realistic to think that now that man has become *so smart*, we know that demons really don't exist? Can we truly classify all our problems into categories other than spiritual causes? Does this seem a bit strange to you? Did demon spirits just go away? Did they ever really exist? What do you do with the scriptural accounts of them and Jesus dealing directly with them? How do you account for this? Most choose to ignore it. What about you?

What I know is that if you don't recognize this as biblical truth, you can't deal with evil spirits as the source of many problems.

I have seen, personally, about thirty thousand Christians freed of demonization—believers healed of demonic oppression. The atoning work of Jesus included: "to heal the brokenhearted...deliverance to the captives... recovering of sight to the blind...to set at liberty them that are bruised" (Luke 4:18, KJV). I have experienced this happening; there are hundreds of testimonies.

The Holy Spirit has shown me that it is not my job to *convince or persuade* people about the reality of demonic spirits that oppress believers. Rather I am just to present truth. So I am comfortable in presenting truth and leaving the results to Him.

Often I have been asked if there was a particular spirit that was more difficult than others. The strength of the spirit depends upon the amount of permission it is given. However, there is one spirit that I have encountered that is tougher than all of the others.

The Unteachable Person

The unteachable person is perhaps the most frustrating. I don't know if there is an unteachable spirit involved, but the person who will not accept teaching is a very difficult person to bring to deliverance. These people will not submit to truth, and it is often because they think they already know the truth. They have believed a lie for so long that it is virtually impossible to show them truth.

This person reverts to the lie. Some people have erroneous teachings about deliverance in their minds, and that in itself becomes bondage. That is why we spend so much effort in getting an individual prepared for deliverance. The unteachable spirit is virtually impossible to minister to because of the choice to remain in darkness.

Homosexual spirits are often difficult, because there are also, generally, some genetic problems along with learned habits. Other demon powers of fear and rejection, anger and pride give strength to this spirit. But homosexual spirits are not the toughest.

As I mentioned, mental disorders often present a whole set of problems. Disorder spirits with all of the confusion, fear, and doubt are difficult. *However, the most trying spirit of all is the human spirit.* You see, the human spirit it is not subject to the name of Jesus. It can resist Jesus or it can yield, whichever it chooses. It has free will. It is when the demon spirit becomes so ingrained with the human spirit that it becomes extremely hard.

The human spirit must surrender in order for demon spirits to be dealt with. The human spirit must desire to be free from the influence and misdirection of the demon spirit. When the human spirit becomes too comfortable with a situation to yield it to God, the demon spirit is strengthened. We have learned that it is fruitless to try to cast out demons against someone's will. The human spirit is you, and it is me.

That's why deliverance and healing are called "the children's bread" (Matt. 15:26). That's what Jesus called it. It is for believers. In this verse, Jesus told the Gentile woman who asked for healing and deliverance for her daughter, "It is not good to take the children's bread and throw it to the little dogs." It was reserved for the children of Israel. It was when she worshiped Him and expressed faith that she qualified. It is for believers.

The human spirit must be surrendered. Deliverance is not for those who *choose* to live in darkness. The choice to remain in sin disqualifies one for freedom. Refusal to denounce and confess sin is a choice to obey the human spirit in rebellion against God.

The most difficult spirit is not the *prince of Persia*, it is not the *king of the bottomless pit*, and it is not some high-ranking, ruling spirit in the heavenlies. It is your human spirit. It is the only spirit I have encountered that does not tremble at the name of Jesus. Until the human will is surrendered and by grace and through faith is born again, it is a very difficult spirit with which to deal.

People who are born again, Spirit filled, and zealous for God still have a human will and spirit. They can still disobey; they can and often do yield to the desires of the flesh. Disobedience is a doorway. Pride is an entry point—just go down the list of sins; they are gateways for demon spirits into the lives of believers. The toughest spirit you will deal with is your human spirit.

CHAPTER 11

"HANG-AROUND" DEMONS

WHAT I CALL *hang-around demons* are like the line from the hundred-year-old "Boll Weevil" song sung by Tex Ritter: "He was looking for a home; just looking for a home." They are like floaters, demon spirits that look for a place of activity in this world.

I had a friend tell me of a house in Louisiana that had some strange happenings. He described it to me and told me of the little girl who once lived there. He said sometimes she would levitate, and you could see it through the windows at night. The piano would play—you could even see the keys move—but no one was at the piano. He said everyone in that neighborhood knew there was something going on there. This house was a few houses from where he grew up.

I told him that I'd like to go there sometime. I've never seen or felt anything like that. Well, one day we did go there. We actually went to fish in a lake that was not too far from his old neighborhood, near Jena, Louisiana. I asked him to take me to that house. There was a different family there now. The house he grew up in had been destroyed by fire. His wife and sister were with us as we drove to the house where the "hauntings" had taken place. They all remarked about feelings they were having as we got near—goose bumps, hair standing up on the back of their neck, and so forth. I felt nothing.

I don't know what may have taken place at that house, but the memories of them being in that neighborhood reignited some fear in their lives. Being there stirred something; I don't think I can explain that. Maybe there were some hang-around spirits in that neighborhood from past events.

Recently I received the following e-mail from a medical doctor in another part of the country.

> Good morning, Don:
>
> I have recently read your book *When Pigs Move In*. It has been one instrument in opening up a whole new world to my spiritual eyes. One thing I have been curious about that I don't think was covered in your book is the idea of demons laying claim to, persisting in, or occupying land or a building. I acquired a new office about a year ago. I had always had some sense that something bad had happened there. Through the eyes of others with a variety of spiritual gifts, I am certain that abortions took place there. Likewise, there might have been something else on that land that predated the building. Have you had any experience with demons occupying a place, land, etc.? We have taken steps to rid this place of such forces. There is one who is still obstinate, and we will deal with him this weekend, but I would like to hear your take. God's Peace.

The e-mail is signed with the doctor's name. This is a good question—and one we get often. Thank God for this doctor and his sensitivity to God's Word and to the work of demons.

Cancel the Rights of Hang-Around Demons

There are demons that are not necessarily territorial spirits that *hang around* because of legal rights that were attained there. I don't believe this is territorial warfare. Spirits walk the earth looking and seeking. This is supported by Scripture in 1 Peter 5:8: "Be sober, be vigilant;

because your adversary the devil walks about like a roaring lion, seeking whom he may devour."

The Book of Job records Satan reporting to God that he had been walking to and fro and up and down in the earth. Looking; they are always looking. They look for opportunities to steal, kill, and destroy. God's holy angels are also looking; they watch over us. It is interesting to read how Satan described his activity to God:

> And the LORD said to Satan, "From where do you come?" So Satan answered the LORD and said, "From going to and fro on the earth, and from walking back and forth on it."
>
> —JOB 1:7

Once the demons obtain a right, they tend to want to retain it. For example, I don't know what may have taken place in any given motel room before I occupy it—likely many things that might give rights to demons to hang around. My approach is simply this: I paid for the room, and for that night it is mine. I declare this when going into the room. "I don't know who owns this building or what has gone on here. What I do know is tonight it is my room, and I declare it to be the headquarters of the Holy Spirit."

No demon has a right to me because of what someone else did. Maybe they have rights to be there, but they have no legal access to me. I told this to the doctor: "Whatever took place there before is now under your covering in Christ. It is your building, and you have the right to give it to the Lord. You don't really need another person to do this for you. God will honor your words and your claims to the property. Command in Jesus's name that any unclean spirits attached because of previous owners and their misdeeds have no legal rights there now. Make your office building the headquarters of the Lord Jesus where healing takes place in Jesus's name."

When you are in Christ Jesus, you have rights to make Him Lord over whatever is yours. Perhaps better said, you have the choice of giving Him lordship. Demons become squatters until their rights have been removed and they are commanded to go.

I don't go through my house and anoint things, but I know what is here and what shouldn't be here. I know when hang-around demons may have gained some access. It is important that we stay spiritually alert to what may grant a legal right.

I have people who ask me to come and pray over their property. The property owner should be doing this. How many times I have heard stories about *unusual hauntings*. "There's something in my closet." "I hear footsteps in the hall." "I feel like something is behind me." "There is something always watching me." There may be demon spirits involved; there may be a permission that has been given. You can deal with it; you're the one who needs to take authority.

What about the ghost stories and documentaries on TV about houses and buildings? There can only be one answer; it can only be deceptive demons. They certainly are not spirits of dead people—maybe demons that lived in a deceased person, but not the spirit of the dead. When someone dies, that person's spirit is immediately separated from the body and is no longer earthbound.

What you can know in the unexplained phenomena of the paranormal is that it always falls in the area of demonic deception. I have never seen anyone levitate. I have never seen objects move or fly across the room. My advice is to not think too much about these things. We always do better when we focus on what we know to be truth.

CHAPTER 12

DELAYED HEALING

WHAT MUST IT have been like to be in the actual presence of Jesus? What about just in the hours and days following His miracles? It is hard for me to conceive of what it must have been like in that area at the northwest corner of the Sea of Galilee. Scores, maybe hundreds, were receiving miraculous healings. The testimonies and excitement are hard to imagine. The Bible doesn't say much about that, the aftermath of His presence, but I would like to know.

> And when they came out of the boat, immediately the people recognized Him, ran through that whole surrounding region, and began to carry about on beds those who were sick to wherever they heard He was. Wherever He entered, into villages, cities, or the country, they laid the sick in the marketplaces, and begged Him that they might just touch the hem of His garment. And as many as touched Him were made well.
>
> —MARK 6:54–56

The pages of the New Testament are filled with His miracles of healing and casting out of evil spirits. Why do our churches remain so silent about it? Why don't we experience these things? In the Book of Luke, these passages give us some insight as to why.

> Great multitudes came together to hear, and to be healed by Him of their infirmities.
>
> —LUKE 5:15

> …a great multitude of people from all Judea and Jerusalem, and from the seacoast of Tyre and Sidon, who came to hear Him and be healed of their diseases.
>
> —LUKE 6:17

Our responsibility is in the area of expectation. The people came not only to *hear* Him but also to be *healed* by Him. It seems today we only go to hear Him. I believe the responsibility for expectation is missing in the church. It is the fault not only of the preachers but also of congregants who don't want their preachers to preach and practice healing and deliverance. Demon powers are doing a good job of keeping this out of church—think about it; this is what Jesus did and what He told us to do.

During a recent "Night of Ministry," a lady came at the altar call and handed me a note. She could not hear, and she could not speak clearly. But she came expecting. That's what we do at our ministry nights—we pray for the sick and cast out demons. As I prayed for her, she gently fell to the ground and lay on the floor throughout virtually the entire altar call time. When she was helped to her feet, she looked around in amazement and spoke, "I can hear you; I can hear you!" That's really exciting! We had many people healed that night; we always do.

One man told me that he was healed as he came into the parking lot. "I have had this condition in my right cheekbone for years, but the pain left when I pulled into the parking lot." That's pretty incredible.

As I looked over the people in attendance at the meeting, I noticed something common in their eyes—expectation and need. I believe that in most congregations *need* is common, but *expectation* is not. Someone needs to pump up the expectation level among believers. God is a faith God—God honors faith.

Expectation is not more than what it is. It is simply believing to receive based upon what God has said. There are at least seven biblical accounts of scriptural methods revealed for healing.

Scriptural Ways to Be Healed

1. The elders of the church can anoint with oil and pray for the people, and they may be healed.

> Is anyone among you sick? Let him call for the elders of the church, and let them pray over him, anointing him with oil in the name of the Lord. And the prayer of faith will save the sick, and the Lord will raise him up. And if he has committed sins, he will be forgiven. Confess your trespasses to one another, and pray for one another, that you may be healed. The effective, fervent prayer of a righteous man avails much.
> —JAMES 5:14–16

2. God's people can lay hands on each other in prayer and ask God for healing, and people may be healed.

> In My name they will cast out demons...they will lay hands on the sick, and they will recover.
> —MARK 16:17–18

3. God may grant someone the gift of healing with the authority to minister healing to others.

> To another faith by the same Spirit, to another gifts of healing by the same Spirit.
> —1 CORINTHIANS 12:9

4. God may grant healing in response to the faith of the person who desires healing.

> But Jesus turned around, and when He saw her He said, "Be of good cheer, daughter; your faith has made you well." And the woman was made well from that hour.
>
> —MATTHEW 9:22

5. God may grant healing to someone on behalf of the faith of others.

> They let down the bed on which the paralytic was lying. When Jesus saw their faith, He said to the paralytic…"I say to you, arise, take up your bed, and go your way to your house."
>
> —MARK 2:4, 11

Forgiveness of sin hits at the very root of all diseases and either cures them or alters their property. The way to remove the effect is to take away the cause. Perhaps there are other ways, but the common denominator is always Jesus. Mark 6:55 says, "[They] began to carry about on beds those who were sick to wherever they heard He was." They heard that Jesus was in the area, and not knowing how long He would be there, they hurried to get the sick to Him. As they knew He would be passing through a certain village or city, they laid the sick in the streets. All they wanted was just to touch His garment; by faith they knew that would be sufficient.

Everyone who touched Him was made completely well. What a remarkable account in Scripture. That's not asking much—"Just let me touch your clothes"—but it is expecting and receiving much. Everyone wants to be healed. Their investment in this healing miracle was enough faith that they made an effort to touch Jesus. They went to where He was, even though in some cases loved ones carried them there. They believed He could do it, they believed He would do it, and they made a move. Jesus disappointed no one. As many as touched Him were made whole.

Demons could not help but leave in His presence. Sickness and disease still bow to His name. The problem is that it is often more complicated than just speaking His name. What we don't know about sickness and disease is much greater than what we do know. Everyone would be healed if just speaking words would do it. The truth is that it is often very difficult to know what needs to be undone and if it is within our scriptural rights to undo it.

There may be numerous legal rights that demons have to someone's life. They likely include a combination of rights from several generations, and simply denouncing those rights will not necessarily fix the person or the problem. It is certainly part of the solution. It needs to be done; confession is easy. It's just something you do. Removing the permissions that demons have acquired is a part of the process. God will not cover our sin until we uncover it to Him. As long as we keep it hidden, it remains exposed to demons who seize upon the legal right of unconfessed sin.

6. God often heals through medical treatment.

> Use a little wine for your stomach's sake and your frequent infirmities.
> —1 Timothy 5:23

> So he went to him and bandaged his wounds, pouring on oil and wine.
> —Luke 10:34

> Then Isaiah said, "Take a lump of figs." So they took and laid it on the boil, and he recovered.
> —2 Kings 20:7

7. God performs sovereign acts of mercy to heal. He takes the initiative. He does the work.

Admit It and Quit It

> Now a certain man was there who had an infirmity thirty-eight
> years. When Jesus saw him lying there, and knew that he already
> had been in that condition a long time, He said to him, "Do you
> want to be made well?" The sick man answered Him, "Sir, I have
> no man to put me into the pool when the water is stirred up; but
> while I am coming, another steps down before me." Jesus said
> to him, "Rise, take up your bed and walk." …Afterward Jesus
> found him in the temple, and said to him, "See, you have been
> made well. Sin no more, lest a worse thing come upon you."
> —JOHN 5:5–8, 14

This section of Scripture confirms that sickness is in the world because
of sin—not necessarily our sin, but it is always directly or indirectly
related to unconfessed sin. Jesus certainly indicated that when He
spoke the words to the healed man: "Sin no more, lest a worst thing
come upon you." Change your lifestyle. Don't do what you did before,
or the results next time could even be worse.

The Book of Psalms indicates the same. Look at Psalm 107:17: "Fools,
because of their transgression, and because of their iniquities, were
afflicted." One version reads like this: "Some were fools through their
sinful ways, and because of their iniquities suffered affliction" (ESV).

Now, that is not to say that if anyone is sick it is because of unconfessed sin in his or her life. It is implied by Jesus, but the sickness could
also be from ancestral sin that has not been dealt with. It could be that
we live in a sinful world and have been exposed to sickness. We can't
always know why. That is the case here in the account of the man who
had been sick for thirty-eight years. None of the methods involving
human participation were used; it was a sovereign act of God. It is
beyond speculation to think that a childhood sin had caused his sickness, but to me, it is clear that ancestral sin likely brought about his
disease. It is also clear that this man was a believer; moments after he
was healed he was in the temple, where Jesus saw him and gave the
admonishment. Perhaps he was there to give thanks for his healing.

I have seen people receive deliverance and healing and then return to a lifestyle that brought on the conditions initially. This is unacceptable to God. Opening a door for demons is what this is all about—they are the tormentors; they bring about sickness and disease. Jesus basically said to this man who had been *sovereignly* healed: "Whatever allowed this into your life before, don't do it again."

Remember, He initially asked this man, "Would you like to be healed?" He gave him the opportunity to confess his need. Confession always precedes receiving from God. Confess it and address it. Stop it and drop it. The five-word summary of this story is *admit it and quit it.*

God's Sovereign Healing Still Works Today

I want to share one other situation showing how God sovereignly heals today. Several years ago I filled the pulpit quite often whenever our pastor would be gone or simply when he wanted me to preach. I was glad to do so. There was a member of that congregation named Donna who had been plagued with headaches and fainting spells. She had been to five neurologists and two neurosurgeons. The conclusion was that she had a brain tumor, a pituitary adenoma. They all concluded that it must be surgically removed.

Several people had been praying for Donna. She was scheduled to have surgery the Thursday following the Sunday I was to preach. All week long as I studied for the message, she was continually on my heart. I kept "hearing" the Holy Spirit tell me to lay hands on her and pray for her—in the service. I wanted to resist this because I had never seen it done at this church. I didn't know how they would receive it. But I knew God had spoken to me, so the only thing that mattered was being obedient to Him.

I preached, and at the close of the message, the music director got up to lead the congregation in an invitation song. "No," I said, "I don't want any music now. I am going to do what the Holy Spirit is urging me to do. I don't know what anyone will think about this, but I'm going to do it anyway. I am going to ask Donna and Mike [who were seated on the back row] to come forward, and I am going to pray for Donna's healing." Virtually everyone in the church knew about her condition. "I am going to lay hands on her and ask the Lord to heal her, and I want everyone who believes that God is still healing people to come and gather around her also to pray." The entire church came; there was no hesitation.

My wife and I left after the service to drive to Tennessee to visit with our son and daughter-in-law who lived in Nashville. Donna was to see her neurosurgeon the next day for a presurgery MRI and then to have her surgery on Thursday. She wore a T-shirt to her doctor that day with words across the front that said, "My God is an awesome God." Donna said that after they performed the MRI, she and her husband, Mike, waited to see the neurosurgeon. She said it was an unusually long time, and she was wondering what was taking so long.

Finally, the doctor emerged, and Donna said he had a perplexed look on his face. He said, "We have made a mistake. You don't have a brain tumor; there is nothing there."

Donna had believed all along that she would be healed and had told her unbelieving doctor that. After the doctor continued to try and explain how seven doctors could be wrong, Donna said, "Doctor, the mistake you have made is not giving God the glory for my healing." She now has in her possession MRI films that show a brain tumor before prayer and films that show *no* tumor after prayer. Our God is an awesome God!

You can trust our awesome God with your healing—or that of a loved one. Determine now to stand in faith that He will not delay your healing.

CHAPTER 13

KEEP THESE DOORS CLOSED

CURSE WITHOUT A cause—don't the demons wish they could torment believers without legal rights. Don't they wish they had more than the power of a lie. We'd all be sick or dead if it worked like that. If demons could do whatever damage whenever they chose, we would be in big trouble. However, they are limited by the truth of God's Word and the principles set forth by God Himself. Look at the scriptural truth tucked away in Proverbs 26:2.

> Like a flitting sparrow, like a flying swallow,
> So a curse without cause shall not alight.

There will be no causeless curse. That is, curses just can't happen because demons want them to; there must be a legitimate cause—no consent; no curse.

Identifying the Cause

Of more importance than recognizing the *curse* is discovering the *cause*. I believe that if you can receive this truth, it will help you greatly in your spiritual walk. Demons must have legal rights, rights that are recognized by Jehovah God, to gain access to believers. Here are some obvious causes that can bring a curse, opening the door to demonic strongholds in your life.

Ancestry

> I, the LORD your God, am a jealous God, visiting the iniquity [absence of moral or spiritual values, morally objectionable behavior] of the fathers on the children to the third and fourth generations of those who hate Me.
>
> —EXODUS 20:5

Iniquity of the ancestors may be a cause for a curse. It is our job to denounce it—to separate ourselves from generational sins that may have brought demons into the family.

Lying

If you tell a lie, you might get a demon. If you live a lie, you have a demon. What you attempt to cover, God will expose. What you expose and confess to God, He will cover. Believing a lie *is the* power of the demon. Victory as a believer hinges upon truth. Lies—telling them, living them, believing them—are cause for curse.

Unforgiveness

> ...delivered him to the torturers until he should pay all that was due to him. So My heavenly Father also will do to you if each of you, from his heart, does not forgive his brother his trespasses.
>
> —MATTHEW 18:34–35

Unforgiveness. It would be helpful to research everything the New Testament has to say about this sin. Sometimes it is more involved than merely confessing it. Often the demons that came through the sin have likely built themselves a kingdom, and they must be cast out. Refusing to forgive is cause for curse.

Of course, this includes forgiving yourself. Many times I have had deliverance candidates insist that they had no unforgiveness for anyone—anyone else, that is. Often they hold great resentment and unforgiveness for themselves.

Anger, bitterness, hatred, and related sins

> Be angry, and do not sin: do not let the sun go down on your wrath.... And do not grieve the Holy Spirit of God, by whom you were sealed for the day of redemption. Let all bitterness, wrath, anger, clamor, and evil speaking be put away from you, with all malice.
> —Ephesians 4:26, 30–31

Virtually all of the sins in this category are easy to justify. Because we make excuses for harboring these sins, it seems OK to continue in them. "Well, you'd be hurt too if you had experienced what I have." These are all causes for curses.

Rejection, perception, dejection

These are very tough root causes for curse. Rejection is horrible. Whether it is real or perceived, it is still one of life's most intense feelings.

> He is despised and rejected by men, a Man of sorrows and acquainted with grief. And we hid, as it were, our faces from Him; He was despised, and we did not esteem Him.
> —Isaiah 53:3

Jesus certainly understands rejection. He relates to all of our feelings. He was tempted in all points like as we are yet without sin. I believe issues of rejection are responsible for many of today's disorders. To be acquainted with grief; to be despised and to know and feel it; to have feelings of no self-worth, no esteem; to feel unaccepted; to have strong feelings that you simply cannot measure up in the eyes of others—these can be the vilest of painful emotions. These are not only unspeakably painful feelings, but when they are based upon a perception, they are cause for curse. In many of these cases, the cause becomes the curse. All of these lies must be resisted with truth.

I am not listing *all* of the causes for curse, just a few of the most common that I encounter. *Cause* is a legal right that demons have to torment believers. Any and all causes *can* be removed through repentance, confession, and renunciation and denunciation. Receiving and applying the work of the cross and coming into agreement with what God says in His Word bring freedom.

Here are more commonly encountered causes.

Trauma

Everyone has experienced some trauma at some time in his or her life. The way we manage the trauma generally determines whether demons get access or not. Disappointment is a big door opener for demons. Remember, the Word tells us to stand, not to fight. Often the best thing we can do is the only thing we can do. We can always stand on truth; we can always choose our thoughts.

Irrational fears

Irrational fears are obvious doorways to fear demons. Sometimes they are evidence that demons are already there. It is so easy to magnify the wrong thing; to focus on the *what ifs* in certain situations is needless exasperation of a virtual nonissue. I see that people who fear air travel have an extreme issue with focus. The more they focus on the *what if* and the more they think and talk about it, the more real the fear becomes to them.

What you can always know about fear is that it is a *spirit*, and God didn't give it to you. You can always know that. So, irrational fear is indication of a demon that is already there. To prevent giving strength to a demon already present or possibly opening a door to a new one, resist lies with truth and stand on that truth. Simply put, the truth is that airline travel is safe.

I heard about a lady traveling to Seattle to visit her daughter. She was very calmly reading a book. Suddenly there was a loud noise, and the plane shook violently. In a moment the plane leveled off somewhat, but the pilot spoke to the passengers, saying, "We have encountered some problems, but it looks like we are going to make it OK." The lady continued reading her book. However, the passenger seated next to her was about to have a nervous breakdown. She asked, "How can you be so calm? We might crash, and you just sit there reading a book."

The lady smiled and said, "Well, I have a daughter in heaven and a daughter in Seattle, and I'm gonna see one of them today."

Other Door Openers

There are so many things that we experience that could be door openers for demons. Generally, it is based upon how we respond to the experience. *Dejection* and *disappointment* are neighbors to *depression*. *Betrayal* can be there too, with all the questions of "Why me?" and "How could this happen?" Again, Jesus understands these feelings. Emotional wounds as well as physical wounds were included in the price He paid.

Abandonment is definitely a possible doorway for demons. These traumas have to be covered with the blood of Jesus, and that often—most often—involves forgiving. *Childhood abuse*—abuser or abused—is a cause for curse.

Sexual impurity—there is really no need to comment on this issue. You know if it applies, and you know what needs to be done. Admit it and quit it. Stop it and drop it. Confess it and address it. Call it and uninstall it. Sexual addiction is a demon. Sexual impurity opens the door. Often this is rooted in the ancestry, or perhaps some abuse in the early childhood. Receiving or causing sexual abuse, perversions, sexual relations outside of marriage, pornography, and births out of wedlock are all causes for curses.

Without much comment, there are a few others.

Dishonoring your body—alcohol, drugs, nicotine, body piercings, tattoos, vanity enhancements. Any and all could be cause for curse.

Occult/secret organizations—pledges, oaths, vows, and ceremonies; Freemasonry, Eastern Star, Rainbow Girls, Oddfellows, Rebecca Lodge, and others are included, along with many fraternities and sororities. Any organization that offers a way to God without salvation through Jesus Christ is a cause for curse.

Doubt is a choice. *Unbelief* is what people decide to do. It certainly not only opens doors for demons, but it also empowers demons who are already present. *Pride* generally is the prop that holds up doubt and unbelief. Not only have I found this to be scripturally true, but I have also seen that often the same type of demon power runs these kingdoms. He is generally a leviathan in his creative nature. This will likely mean little to you, but the demons all have a creative nature. The leviathan is not the name of a demon, but rather a type. You can read about him in Job and Psalms. We find that all demons have a creative identity like a serpent or a scorpion, as Jesus indicated in Luke 10:18–19. Similarly, I hear people say, "Oh, they have the python spirit." Python is not the name of a spirit. It is another type of spirit; it is a serpent spirit. Doubt, unbelief, skepticism, and pride all are cause for curse.

Cause for curse is simply legal permission that demons have gained through either the decisions made by our ancestors or the experiences of our own life. Remember, there are no curses without cause. While our lives may be affected indirectly by demons that torment other individuals, we maintain the security of what comes and goes directly in our lives. We stay in control by confessing open doorways and casting out demon spirits. There is no cause that cannot be canceled through Christ.

Removing the Cause

I have briefly discussed causeless curses. God's Word says there are none. So, if one does have demon spirits, the key is removing the cause. Here's a simple step-by-step procedure that is always true. It is a simple way to examine and proceed.

- *Cause*—What event(s) gave legal permission for demons to torment?

- *Curse*—What is the result from that root cause? All demons kill, steal, and destroy. What is being stolen from you? What is damaged? What is dying?

- *Consequence*—This is tied to the curse; the curse is tied to the cause. You can't remove the curse until you have dealt with the cause.

- *Choice*—God always honors our choices. Choosing to hold on to a legitimate cause for curse extends the consequences. I have seldom seen a demon leave without being cast out.

- *Confess*—Until there is confession of sin and agreement and alignment with truth, demons do not have to leave. Confession cancels permission.

- *Confront/cast out*—Demons must be cast out; they cannot be counseled or medicated out. Jesus said, "Cast out demons."

- *Cure*—Once the demon spirits have been removed, often physical healing takes place and emotional wounds begin to mend. That is God's process, and it always works.

Sometimes it sounds too simple. But I tell you, it is no more complicated than this.

CHAPTER 14

SOME SON OF SAM MEMORIES

A FEW YEARS AGO I took some friends with me to visit David Berkowitz, aka *the Son of Sam*. David is serving 365 years in the Sullivan Correctional Facility in Fallsburg, New York. You may be familiar with his testimony of salvation. There is such an incredible amount of information about his crimes and his incarceration that it is very difficult to condense. He was, without doubt, a demon-possessed young man. He was in a satanic cult called the Brotherhood. The killings were orchestrated. His group had designs on *bringing New York to its knees*.

I have heard the stories firsthand from David himself. I will include his brief testimony at the close of this chapter. He told me about the meetings of the Satanist group—where they met and some of the depraved occult nature of the meetings. They met at various locations over the months, including Van Cortlandt Park in the Bronx and, one of the favorites, Untermyer Park in Yonkers.

David told me about the locations, and I have visited them many times to understand a little of what was going on. At the park in Yonkers, there are a thousand steps that go down to reach an old building that once housed the maintenance man for the property. The park overlooks the east bank of the Hudson River. Spray-painted graffiti on the abandoned white stone caretaker's house is still visible. SOS, a symbol for Son of Sam, was likely put there by David himself and is found in various places in the park. The abandoned house, if still there, was the place of much evil and summoning of demons.

As you clear the trees after a literally breathtaking uphill climb into the main area of the park, you cannot fail to notice what appears to be a rather bizarre-looking rock formation. There is still much attraction to devil worshipers. There is a large structure more than forty-feet high at its west face. It was the *Eagle's Nest* and was built about eighty years ago as a cascading fountain. There is a gazebo at its summit that overlooks the Hudson River and the New Jersey Palisades. It is down the stairs from this gazebo that a satanic altar was used by the group. The park was once the estate of multimillionaire Samuel Untermyer. He had large stones from Great Britain incorporated into the fountain he built for his daughter's wedding. There is reason to believe that the wealthy lawyer had an interest in mysterious spiritual beliefs. Across a side street north of the park is St. John's Hospital. At the south end of the park and on a lower level there once stood a large pumphouse. For reasons never made public, it was knocked down in the early nineties, and not even a trace of its foundation can be seen today. It is rumored that former employees of nearby St. John's Hospital say they can still recall nights when chanting and torch flames were seen and heard in the depths of the woods, especially from the area of the now-demolished pumphouse, or "devil's cave."

Over Christmas 1976, dead Alsatian (also called German Shepherd) dogs, with their ears carefully excised, were found on the aqueduct just south of Untermyer Park. David told me of the blood that was put on the altar as a sacrifice. He says they chose German Shepherds because of their strength. Pretty gruesome, huh? I took my friends to this park after we had visited with David in his prison. They were curious.

As we walked to the area where the sacrifices were made, the so-called *satanic altar*, both friends expressed uneasy feelings. I stood on the altar and said to them both, "There is no need to fear."

One of them said, "I'm leaving. I'm going back to the top of the hill." As I got closer to my other friend, I could see that he was breaking out in red whelps on his neck and arms. I prayed for him, and they left immediately. Were there demons there? Absolutely. Did they have permission to be there? Yes. I share this with you as information. I didn't go there to fight with the demons, and they did not fight with me. I believe understanding our rights, and their rights, is huge. It's really not that difficult.

In 1976 and 1977, New York City was terrorized by a series of satanic murders. The entire nation was riveted to those bizarre occult-related crimes attributed to the Son of Sam. In time, David Berkowitz, age twenty-four, was arrested for this historic crime spree. Much evidence has revealed that David was steeped in Satanism and participated in rituals in which members of a devil worship cult helped to commit those crimes. David Berkowitz and other cult members were calling on demons to come into them to empower them to kill. The testimony of David Berkowitz is the account of God's more-than-amazing grace reaching into the depraved, dark world of David Berkowitz, freeing him from his torment, giving him forgiveness and eternal life, and bringing him into God's wonderful family.

Samhain is an ancient Druid name for one of the highest-ranking demons. This demon demanded human sacrifices, especially at certain times of the year, such as Halloween. This is where the moniker *Son of Sam* came from. David, in his delusion, believed he was a soldier for this demon.

> I will give thanks to the LORD with my whole heart;
> I will recount all of your wonderful deeds.
> I will be glad and exult in you;
> I will sing praise to your name, O Most High.
>
> —PSALM 9:1–2, ESV

If the Son sets you free, you will be free indeed.

—JOHN 8:36, ESV

David's Testimony

Like the psalmist says in one of the above passages, I must truly thank my wonderful God for His abundant love, grace, and mercy. You see, since my childhood I have been tormented and victimized by demons. During all of my childhood, and for much of my adult life, cruel demons had control of me. But thanks be to Jesus Christ, I was able to be restored to my right mind. There was a time in my life when I was living in complete rebellion against God. I was so wicked that I was actually worshiping the devil, and I was involved with Satanism.

Looking back at all that has happened to me, it is no surprise that I fell into such depravity. Let me tell you what some of my life was like when I was just a small child. When I was little, I would often have fits in which I would roll on the floor and knock over furniture. My mother (who has long since passed away) would have no control over me. I was so vicious and destructive that I often caused considerable property damage.

When I was in public school, I was so violent and disruptive that a teacher once grabbed me in a headlock and threw me out of his classroom. I was so much trouble that my parents were ordered by the school officials to take me to a child psychologist every week. But this had no effect. When I was young, I would get so depressed that I used to hide under my bed for hours. Then at other times I would lock myself in a closet and sit in total darkness from morning until afternoon. I craved the darkness and felt an urge to flee from people.

Other times I would wake up in the middle of the night, sneak out of the house, and wander the streets. I recall a force that would drive me into the darkened streets, even in inclement weather, where I roamed the streets like an alley cat in the darkness. Sometimes at three or four in the morning I would sneak back into the house the same way I left, by climbing the fire escape. My parents would not even know that I was gone.

I continually worried and frightened my parents because I behaved so strangely. At times I would go an entire day without talking to them. I'd walk around our apartment talking to myself. My parents knew that I lived in an imaginary world, but they could do nothing about it. From time to time I would see my parents break down and cry because they saw that I was such a tormented person. Thoughts of suicide plagued me continually. I was so depressed and haunted that I would also spend time sitting on the window ledge of my bedroom with my legs dangling over the side. My parents would yell at me to get in, but I seldom listened to them. I would feel such an urge to push myself out the window that my body would tremble violently. And we lived on the sixth floor.

My mom and dad tried to bring me up as best as they could. They loved me and gave me everything that good parents would give to their only child. But I was so wild, mixed up, and crazy that I could barely hang on to my sanity. Even when I would walk down the streets there always seemed to be a force that would try to make me step in front of moving cars.

I was overwhelmed with thoughts about dying, and I wasn't even a teenager. I had no idea what to do, and neither did my parents. They tried to raise me in the Jewish faith, but they knew nothing about Jesus, the Messiah of Isaiah 53.

Many of the things that happened to me might shock some people. But none of this was a shock to the Lord. In His day, when our Savior walked among humanity, cases of children being victimized and possessed by evil spirits was very common. (See Mark 7:24–30; 9:17–29.) In fact, childhood possession cases still happen today. But modern psychology tends to dismiss these disturbed children and blame their problems on some type of organic brain damage, family problems, something within the child's environment, etc.

There were a few times in my life when I was at a stage of equilibrium. I managed to finish high school even though most of the time I was truant or in trouble. I also spent three years in the army. I was honorably discharged in 1974. But even in the service I had problems.

In 1975 I had become heavily involved with the occult and witchcraft. Looking back I cannot even begin to explain how I had gotten involved. It seemed that one day everything magically fell into place. Books about witchcraft seemed to pop up all around me. Everywhere I looked there appeared a sign or symbol pointing me to Satan. It felt as if a mighty power was reaching out to me.

I had no peace of mind. I felt as if I was being pulled along by a powerful force. I had no idea how to fight it, and to be honest, I didn't try to. Why? Because things just seemed to be falling into place in a supernatural way. To someone who has never been involved in the occult, this could be hard to understand. But for people who have been involved, they know full well what I am referring to. The power leading me could not be resisted, at least not without Jesus. But I had no relationship with the Lord Jesus at this time, and so I had no defense against the devil.

Jesus said about Satan, "He was a murderer from the beginning, and has nothing to do with the truth, for there is no truth in him. When he lies, he speaks out of his own character, for he is a liar and the father of lies" (John 8:44, ESV).

Well, he certainly lied to me, for during the years 1976 and 1977, I had been lied to and deceived. And, as a result of listening to him, I wound up in prison with a sentence of more than three hundred fifty consecutive years. I was charged with six murders and a number of other shootings and crimes. [David was guilty of three of the thirteen shootings.]

When I first entered the prison system I was placed in an isolation cell for a while. Then I had been sent to Marcy Psychiatric Center. Eventually I went to Attica and Clinton prisons, and finally ended up where I am now, at the Sullivan Correctional Facility. As with many inmates, life in prison has been a big struggle. I have had my share of problems and hassles. At one time I almost lost my life when another inmate cut my throat. Yet through all this, God had his loving hands on me.

Over the years I have met a number of men who had accepted Christ. Many of them tried to witness to me. But because of the extent to which the devil had me bound, it was very hard for me to truly understand the gospel. However, about 1987 I did accept Jesus as my Lord and Savior. And today I cannot thank Him enough for all He has done for me.

Presently the Lord is using me to teach Bible studies in the chapel, as well as to give words of encouragement during our services. In addition, I have the authorization to work with the men whom the Department of Correctional Services has labeled *mentally disturbed* or who are *slow learners*. I have been able to counsel these troubled people and help them with some of their spiritual and physical needs.

CHAPTER 15

STAY WITHIN YOUR AUTHORITY

ONE OF MY best friends is Jay McCarley. I met Jay in Colorado Springs, Colorado, a few years ago. He and his beautiful family now live in the Dallas-Fort Worth area. Jay is especially gifted in the area of words of knowledge. He has also learned to stay within his spiritual authority and to not venture into the heavenly realm of warfare with demon powers. Staying within the authority God has given to you is one of the important lessons to learn if you want to avoid demonic intrusion and strongholds.

Some believe that if we know the events that took place at a particular time and location that allowed legal permission for demons to take possession of that region, we can simply speak the name of Jesus and thereby break that legal permission and cause the demons to flee. Armed with that knowledge, you can then denounce it or repent for someone else and cancel the rights of demons. In this chapter I want to help you understand the spiritual authority that God has given to you as an individual—and the spiritual position God has placed you in. The Bible gives us principles for spiritual warfare, and if we stay in the borders of God's authority, we will not open doors to demonic strongholds.

Let me illustrate this with an example from Jay McCarley. As a young minister, Jay accepted a call to a church in Youngstown, Ohio.

He and his family were trying to follow the call of God in their life. With spiritual zeal, Jay was following what he had been taught and was out to stop the territorial demons in their tracks. He recalls that a particular intersection in the city of Youngstown had an unusual amount of bad car accidents.

He passed that intersection daily going to and from his church. He said that one day as he went through the intersection, he decided to command the demons to stop their activity of violence there. He tells of this incident with some awe in his voice. He said, "I began to bind the demons that caused the wrecks and created the actions that brought so much damage and hurt to people. I was giving commands right and left. Suddenly I felt a presence so strong that I had to pull my car over, and I was becoming sick to my stomach. I heard the Holy Spirit speak to my mind, 'I'm going to protect you this time, but don't ever do that again.'"

He was trembling from the experience. He wasn't sure what this was all about. As he prayed, he said it became clear that in ignorance he had stepped out of his spiritual realm of authority. As he continued to learn from this experience, he found that at that very intersection there had been a history of violence. Union and nonunion workers had clashed on several occasions. There also had been murder committed in other situations. He learned that particular demons had gained rights because of what had happened in the past.

Jay says, "I learned that I should never enter into warfare with demon powers in the heavens. I pray for God's protection and intervention in situations, but I don't go after territorial spirits...ever."

In Revelation 13 there are two mentions of war concerning demon powers and saints. This is obviously during the Great Tribulation, but take a look at what is in the heavenly realm already.

> They worshiped the beast, saying, "Who is like the beast? Who is able to make war with him?" And he was given a mouth speaking great things and blasphemies, and he was given authority to continue for forty-two months. Then he opened his mouth in blasphemy against God, to blaspheme His name, His tabernacle,

and those who dwell in heaven. It was granted to him to make war with the saints and to overcome them. And authority was given him over every tribe, tongue, and nation.

—REVELATION 13:4–7

What human being is able to make war against heavenly creatures? I'm not saying this to cause you to fear but rather to cause you to be spiritually wise. That is our equipping—to stand against the wiles of the devil, not to track him down and start a fight. Jesus is our covering. Jesus didn't leave us with a battle cry against principalities but rather compassion for people.

The Battle Is the Lord's

A glimpse is often all we need to make spiritual assessments. Just a peek can bring fear or faith. What we see with our fleshly eyes often will produce immediate fear and dread. The things we see by faith can dismiss those fears and allow us to procure victory.

In 2 Kings 6 we have the account of Elisha being hunted by the king of Syria. You are likely familiar with the account.

> And when the servant of the man of God arose early and went out, there was an army, surrounding the city with horses and chariots. And his servant said to him, "Alas, my master! What shall we do?" So he answered, "Do not fear, for those who are with us are more than those who are with them." And Elisha prayed, and said, "LORD, I pray, open his eyes that he may see." Then the LORD opened the eyes of the young man, and he saw. And behold, the mountain was full of horses and chariots of fire round about Elisha.
>
> —2 KINGS 6:15–17

The king of Syria had sent soldiers to seize Elisha. He had discovered Elisha was likely the reason Syria could not defeat Israel. He found out where he was, at Dothan, which was not far from Samaria.

Hundreds of soldiers were dispatched to pursue and destroy Elisha. Create, if you will, a mental image of this attempt. By night the king sent an army to capture Elisha and bring him to him dead or alive. It seems that the king of Syria knew that he was fighting against God, but he did not know how to do it.

He thought, like so many, that great numbers or great wealth or an abundance of virtually anything in this world would bring the victory, so he sent a multitude of soldiers. What he failed to realize was that fire from heaven will consume fifty—or fifty thousand. The host of heaven is always sufficient—no matter the odds.

Elisha was not in a fortress; he had no guards or military presence around him. Yet an army was sent against him. Those who fight against God and His people don't know what they are doing. The appearance of the situation caused great trepidation for Elisha's servant. He was consumed by consternation, and he saw no way out. However, Elisha's faith was not diminished because he could see with spiritual eyes. The eyes of our faith are often opened through believing what God has already spoken. "Faith comes by hearing, and hearing by the word of God" (Rom. 10:17).

You know, if his servant had only a knowledge of God's Word, had he just recalled some of the psalms that he doubtless had read, he would have known that he did not need to be afraid of ten thousands of people. He did not need to fear a surrounding multitude or host against him.

> I will not be afraid of ten thousands of people
> Who have set themselves against me all around.
>
> —Psalm 3:6

> Though an army may encamp against me,
> My heart shall not fear;
> Though war should rise against me,
> In this I will be confident.
>
> —Psalm 27:3

One of the great things I have learned in my spiritual walk is that the battle is the Lord's. Genuine faith embraces the unseen hand of God. The spiritual battles in the celestial realm are beyond my abilities to enter into, beyond my ability to comprehend, and beyond my authority. It is my duty to stand on the truth and promises of God's Word. This involves knowing by faith that I can trust God.

When the enemies' armies surround us, there are likely fears within us. We must recall the Word of God and past victories. When the odds seem daunting and it appears that there are more who fight against us than those who are with us, "Fear not." For in reality, those who are with us to protect us *are more than those who are against us* to destroy us. The holy angels are unspeakably more numerous and our God infinitely more powerful.

We should never magnify the cause of our fear, but rather we must express our great and high thoughts of God through His Word. It is interesting to contrast the faith of Elisha and that of his servant; they both were followers of God. Elisha saw himself safe. His servant saw impending danger and surrender. One had insight to the spiritual realm by faith and by experiences of faith. The other could measure only by what he saw through his fleshly vision.

Elisha saw a guard of angels round about him. He understood by faith that the very gates of hell would not prevail against him. What he saw were "horses and chariots of fire all around" (2 Kings 6:17). He saw angels of God. Not only are angels God's messengers, but they are also His soldiers.

When Jacob met God's angels, he said, "This is God's host" (Gen. 32:2, KJV). Jesus said, "Or do you think that I cannot now pray to My Father, and He will provide Me with more than twelve legions of angels?" (Matt. 26:53). God's angels are all ministering spirits sent forth to minister for us (Heb. 1:14).

Elisha knew; his servant didn't. Those of us who know must help others to see.

Calming the fears of others is perhaps the greatest kindness we can show. The fearful and fainthearted are those who still do not see with their spiritual eyes. The clearer sight that we have of the sovereignty and power of God, the better we can pray for them. I see the darkness of demon powers both here and in the heavenlies, but I do not focus upon them. I focus on the greatness of God.

A magnifying glass does not change the object you are viewing, but it changes your perspective of the object. Magnify the Lord; focus on light and truth. Introduce darkness to light. The opening of our eyes by faith in what God has said will also be the silencing of our fears. The darkness can be frightening; we must choose to live in the light. Calamities and threats of this earthly life will always be lessened by a clearer vision of God through His Word.

Elisha had already seen God's Hand. He had felt and known His presence. He had already heard God's familiar words of "Fear not."

It is interesting that when the disciples feared they would perish in the storm at sea, they did not fear that Jesus would perish; they knew He was Master. All they could see was the threat that the storm was to them. That's all Elisha's servant could see. The overwhelming number of enemy soldiers captivated his thinking. Elisha asked God to allow him to see in the spirit realm. He said, "Do not fear, for those who are with us are more than those who are with them" (2 Kings 6:16).

There is a lot going on in heavenly places. We participate in prayer. We know by faith. But we have no God-given authority to challenge demon spirits in that area. Don't go there.

Restricted Territory

The heaven, even the heavens, are the LORD's;
But the earth He has given to the children of men.
—PSALM 115:16

I have already mentioned that our ministry has gathered some invaluable information in dealing with demons. Through countless hours of one-on-one sessions we have gathered not only names of demons afflicting damage on the inside but also the names and territories of their counterparts as rulers in the celestial realm.

The heavens, the spirit world, or the unseen world in the heavens is restricted territory to us as human beings. One of the obvious truths to us is that if the heavens were not restricted to us, we'd be able to see, hear, and talk with the spiritual beings that exist in this spiritual world. We can't, and Jesus never taught us to seek out these ruling principalities. The heavens are off limits except through prayer. God's angels are on one side; the fallen angels, including Satan, are on the other side.

We are terrestrial beings, and our authority in Christ extends to this earth and to people. We, as believers, are sent to people to evangelize, cast out demons, heal the sick, raise the dead, and cleanse the lepers. Our commission does not include casting *down* kingdoms.

Not only is it not our battle, but also it should not be a battle at all. Our job and our commission are to stand. We are to love God with all our mind, heart, and soul. To do those things that are pleasing in His sight. To resist Satan and his demons. Our commission is not to tear down a heavenly structure of rule, nor is it our job to challenge principalities that have earned their kingdom status by the sins and disobedience of God's people. It is ours to preach and teach the gospel through love to get these people saved. Once people belong to Christ, they can choose to make Him Lord. Once that is done, demonic powers with rights to that individual can be cast out. A wrong approach can lead to spiritual, emotional, and physical disaster.

Remember, Zacharias the high priest was struck mute by the angel Gabriel. The high priest had spoken presumptively and simply questioned the angel (Luke 1:11–20). Our present state remains a little lower than the angels. It is very unwise to presume to command those spiritual beings that are higher ranking in the created order.

Since Scripture is clear that angels only follow commands from God, why would we think that demons would obey ours? Remember, even the archangel Michael, when he was disputing with the devil about the body of Moses, did not dare to bring a slanderous accusation against him but said, "The Lord rebuke you!" (Jude 9).

Think about it; we operate outside the will of God by trying to confront these celestial beings ourselves. God's setup in His heavenly government is that He is the one to deal directly with the spiritual forces, while we mind our business here on the earth, living the Christian life.

Though we are in Christ, in this world we are still "a little lower than the angels" (Heb. 2:7), and we deceive ourselves when we assume authority that has not been given. Scripture says these beings are higher ranking in the created order than we are.

> This is especially true of those who…despise authority. Bold and arrogant, these men are not afraid to slander celestial beings; yet even angels, although they are stronger and more powerful, do not bring slanderous accusations against such beings in the presence of the Lord. But these men blaspheme in matters they do not understand. They are like brute beasts, creatures of instinct, born only to be caught and destroyed, and like beasts they too will perish.
>
> —2 PETER 2:9–12, NIV

Only God has power and authority over the celestial beings in the heavenly realms of the spirit world. Satan's territory in the celestial realm is therefore outside our given area of authority. Ours is on the earth, and that is limited to what is ours. Laying claim to such authority makes a person subject to demonic delusion and demonic strongholds.

KEEP YOUR SPIRITUAL WEAPONS READY

CHAPTER 16

COURTROOM OF DELIVERANCE

THE PRINCIPLES IN this chapter are a critical component in understanding the deliverance process and recognizing how to remain free.

Try to imagine this spiritual picture: a courtroom where Jehovah God is seated at the judge's bench. He is the Judge of all truth and righteousness. It is His legal system. Law is what He has spoken. Whatever God speaks becomes law. You can't see His face, just His glory. Holy angels encircle the bench and proclaim His holiness. God is not only the Judge; Scripture calls Him "the righteous Judge."

> Now there is in store for me the crown of righteousness, which the Lord, the righteous Judge, will award to me on that day—and not only to me, but also to all who have longed for his appearing.
> —2 TIMOTHY 4:8, NIV

Already we see that this is no ordinary courtroom. This courtroom is different. Only truth will be recognized here. You see, deliverance is not about power; it is not just about authority, though we certainly have it in Jesus Christ's name. It is about truth. All demons are liars, and their rights to a believer's life come through deception—it is in causing us to believe a lie. Their rights are obtained through sin and disobedience, either in our lives or those of our ancestors. An element of their deception is to make us believe that we can never be free.

What is a typical legal right that a demon may have? This would include unforgiveness, believing that it is OK to hold on to anger, resentment, or bitterness. These are common examples of what gives demons access to believers. It may be a conviction that there is justification for holding on to unforgiveness, or that bitterness is justified because of the level of hurt or disappointment. These must be confessed as sin before the righteous Judge. Forgiveness through the blood of Jesus Christ must be received. Once this is done, the demon no longer has a legal right to the life. Confessing the sin cancels the demon's rights to one's life, but it does not necessarily mean that the demon leaves. The demon must be commanded to go in the name of Jesus Christ. Demons must be cast out.

Prosecuting demons is what I do. In this courtroom, I represent the deliverance candidate. I am part of the firm—Father, Son, and Holy Spirit. I am a legal representative of Jesus Christ. Visualize that I am the defense attorney for the deliverance candidate. I am the prosecuting attorney against demons. I am defending the believing candidate and protecting his or her rights in the name of Jesus Christ. As His ambassador and by the authority given me in His name, I will be the deliverance candidate's attorney.

I will prosecute demon powers based upon the truth of God's Holy Word. All demons are liars, so what they say must be challenged with this question: Will that stand as truth before Jehovah God? I have found that demons will not lie to Jehovah God.

The line of questioning is simple. "State your name and occupation, demon." Jesus commanded this of the demoniac in Gadara. "What's your name? Who are you?" Demons have names given them by their Creator, Jehovah God. They have personalities, rank, and particular functions. And demons have job assignments.

Their jobs will always fall into four categories: rob, steal, kill, and destroy. Some are principalities and powers, some are rulers of darkness, and others are demons of spiritual wickedness. Some are serpents; some are scorpions, rats, octopuses, leviathans, beetles, and creatures of darkness; and some have other creative identities. Their assignments are against the purposes of God and against believers.

Once their name and job assignment are established, always as truth before Jehovah God, one main question remains: "Do you have any legal rights to remain in this person's life?" Permission, consent, legal rights must be from Jehovah God or from the individual. If the person wants to remain in bondage, the demons have permission to stay. But when confession is made, and it has been established that the demons have no legal permission, then we have absolute authority in Jesus Christ's name to cast these demons from the individual and into the abyss.

Holy angels are the *bailiffs* in this courtroom. They are there to enforce the commands and minister to the believer. There is always victory in this courtroom when righteous justice is the goal of the believer. What is righteous justice? In this case, it is desiring to be free from any lies of the demons—not having any secret deals with the enemy, not participating or cooperating with the opposition.

I believe there are four basic deliverance principles. Obviously, there are some foundational truths and basic rules or standards that apply to deliverance. At the risk of oversimplifying these principles, I will list them again; they always apply.

1. Either a believer has demons or he does not.

2. If one has demons, it must be that the demons are there by some kind of legal consent.

3. The believer must have a sincere desire to be free from demonic powers. The human will is absolutely recognized in this process. There is no consent that cannot be removed through Christ.

4. Once the consent, or legal right, has been removed, the demons can be cast out in Jesus Christ's name.

The removal of legal rights takes place in the courtroom of God's recognized legal system. Rights can only be removed through confession and repentance through Jesus Christ. It is His redemptive work on the cross and His miraculous resurrection that make this possible. Because we are believers, heirs of God, and joint-heirs with Jesus Christ, we can be represented *legally* in Christ's name. Unfortunately, some do not really want to be free.

One More Night With the Frogs

> Moses said to Pharaoh, "I leave to you the honor of setting the time for me to pray for you and your officials and your people that you and your houses may be rid of the frogs, except for those that remain in the Nile." "Tomorrow," Pharaoh said.
> —Exodus 8:9–10, NIV

Tomorrow! Read that verse again. **TOMORROW?** How about right now? The plague of frogs had brought Pharaoh to his knees, so he bargained with Moses to get rid of the frogs. Moses said, "You set the time," and Pharaoh said, "Tomorrow."

Incredible. Think about it. Why do we delay the blessings of God? Why do we choose to spend one more night with the frogs? Why don't we say, "Enough! I'm ready right now"?

In a day when *time* seems to be more important than anything, I was wondering how long it takes to get right with God. How long does it take to be born again? We all have been allotted the same amount of time: 24 hours each day, 1,440 minutes every day. Yet the excuse that is most offered for not getting something done is, "I just didn't have time." Most often that is not correct. Perhaps more proper would be, "I just didn't use my time wisely."

How long does it take to be saved? It takes .003 of a second to pop a balloon; how long does it take to be saved?

How long is forever? That's how long salvation lasts. Eternity is forever. Let me answer that first. How long does salvation last? Jesus said, "Whoever believes in Him should not perish" (John 3:16).

Many know the way and choose not to go. Pharaoh had his time, and he chose to stay with the frogs.

Here's how long eternity is. One of the slowest birds I am aware of is the pelican. His ten-foot-wide wings just seem to move in slow motion as he struggles into the air. Suppose he is to take each grain of sand from every desert in the world to the sun, one grain at a time; then every grain from every beach in the world, one grain at a time; then every drop of water from every river, stream, lake, sea, and ocean, one drop at a time. When he finishes all of that, thirty minutes of eternity has expired. Does that give you some inkling of how long it lasts?

The eternal life that God gives to believers through Jesus is for the same length a nonbeliever will spend eternally separated from God. Eternally separated—don't postpone salvation.

OK, here's how long it takes to be saved. Got a stopwatch? How long does it take to read the following?

God, I'm a sinner, and I need You. I know I can't go to heaven as I am. I need to be saved. I believe Jesus died on the cross and shed His blood for me. I believe He lives today, and He loves me. Come into my heart, Lord Jesus, and save me.

Did you time it? What was it, eight to ten seconds? That's not very long. What a sad, sad, discourse for our world. Don't stay with the frogs.

Some just will never bring themselves to the point of praying that prayer. Many will spend forever eternally separated from God in a place called hell because they refuse to call on the name of Jesus. There is no other name that brings salvation.

Actually, salvation does not even take eight to ten seconds. However long it takes you with your heart to reach out by faith and receive God's grace is how long it takes.

Would you suppose that *not having enough time* is a ridiculous excuse to offer God? Could it be that we just want one more night with the frogs—unwilling to repent and turn from sin?

A blue shark can swim one mile in one hundred forty seconds.* You can write a letter in eight to ten minutes. You can pray the prayer for salvation in eight to ten seconds. Now, most likely those of you reading this are already saved, but are you still in bondage to demons? So, I ask you, why spend one more night with the frogs? Why not determine in your life to be free and to live free?

---

* Elasmo-Research.org, "How Fast Can a Shark Swim?" Biology of Sharks and Rays, http://www.elasmo-research.org/education/topics/p_shark_speed.htm (accessed May 14, 2010).

CHAPTER 17

OVERCOMING OPPRESSION

I WAS PREACHING IN a West Texas prison a few years ago. I had preached many times in this prison located between Lubbock and Amarillo. I had services scheduled in four different prisons. The first was at Dalhart at the top of the Texas panhandle, then at Tulia, and then two prisons in Amarillo. There are many prisons in Texas, and quite a few in the panhandle area. Dalhart is almost four hundred miles from my home. That weekend I would fly to Amarillo, rent a car, and drive eighty-seven miles on to Dalhart.

I have preached in more than eight hundred fifty different prisons, so this was a typical ministry trip. In the four prisons I would preach to about a thousand men. This was a weekend trip, four prisons in three days. My wife took me to the airport on Friday morning. I'll never forget this trip. I was about to learn something more in the deliverance ministry that God was birthing in my life.

The moment I walked into the airport it started. I could feel a heaviness and oppressive presence, but I didn't necessarily attribute it to demons. Sometimes it is just a hassle to travel. The airline took my bag, which was not much, but it had my clothing, shaving kit, Bible, and everything else for the weekend. Then, while waiting for a boarding call, it was announced that the flight had been canceled and the next flight was three hours or so later. Uh oh, that wouldn't work; I could not make it to the prison on time.

I got little help from the customer service counter. Finally they agreed to put me on a different airline. Naturally, it was going to be out of another terminal, and they could not retrieve my bags. They promised to deliver them to the motel when the next flight arrived in Amarillo. I finally arrived in Amarillo with just the clothes I had on—tennis shoes, jeans, golf shirt. Inwardly I knew that I was dealing with some *spiritual opposition*. I just said silently to myself, and any demon listening, "I am going to the prisons, and I am going to preach."

I obtained a rental car and headed toward Dalhart. On the way I checked into the motel and picked up the Bible from the room. As I drove out of Amarillo on Highway 87, I set the cruise control on seventy miles an hour and had driven but a couple of miles when the road narrowed to two lanes due to construction. Just as I came over a slight hill, there was a stalled car. Highway safety cones marked the lane I was in. I recall hitting the brakes to avoid the collision, and my car veered to the right into the lane that was shut down. It made a complete 360-degree skid, did not touch one cone, and came back onto the highway headed for Dalhart. My heart pounded a little bit, but I remember saying, "I laugh at you, demons! I will preach tonight, and God will be glorified." You see, I happen to know the territorial spirit over the panhandle. I know his name; I have encountered him numerous times. I know him, and he knows me.

It seems that as soon as I arrived at the prison unit, the spiritual attack lifted. Anointing came. Many were saved, delivered, and healed that night. I preached in my jeans and golf shirt, using a Gideon Bible. However, when I went back to Amarillo, I could sense the oppression again. I had no appetite. I couldn't sleep. The next day I was scheduled to be at the Tulia transfer prison facility a few miles north of Lubbock.

I had not eaten all day, and I was tired from lack of sleep. I had decided I would get to Tulia a little early and stop at the Pizza Hut before going to the service. I recall this so well. After being seated, the waitress took my order and never came back. She walked near many times, but it was like I had become invisible. I waited and waited. Finally I said to myself, and to any demons that might be listening, "I have bread that you don't know about, and I will preach tonight." I left without being served and headed for the prison.

The oppression again seemed to lift when I went into the prison. This time I was dressed for church—you know, slacks and tie. I always did dress the same for church in prison as out of prison. I had *my* Bible. Again the anointing was strong, and God blessed in the service. At the close, a Hispanic inmate who had been sitting on the back row came up to me. I had noticed that his eyes seemed to affix to me as I preached. He said, "Sir, while you were preaching I felt the Holy Spirit tell me to tell you something. Satan has assigned a high-ranking demon to you. Do you know what that means?"

I assured him that I did know, and we had prayer. I left the chapel and walked down the hallway. I remember thinking, "Oh no, here we go!" I also remember the Holy Spirit whispering to me, "Same authority. Same authority."

When I got to the front door of the prison, an officer was at the door talking on his two-way radio. There was loud thunder, and lightning flashed across the West Texas sky. The clouds were very dark. The officer said to me, "Sir, which way are you headed?"

"Amarillo," I said.

"Listen, man, be careful; we just got word that there is a tornado on the ground between here and Amarillo."

I'm thinking again, "Here we go."

If you are familiar with the plains area, you know that water can rise very quickly and *washes* can become raging rivers. It was raining very hard, you know, cats and dogs. As I drove, I could hardly see the road. Interstate 27 was covered in the blinding rainstorm. Then it seemed out of nowhere I could feel the wheels of my car raise up from the road and the car drift to the left. I was almost swept off of the road, but the wheels soon touched on the other side. Again I whispered to whomever might be listening, "Your schemes will not work."

The oppression again seemed to intensify when I arrived back at the motel. Again, I could not sleep. I was so tired, and I had two more services the next day. I preached at the Clements and Neal Units in Amarillo and then went to the airport to make my return flight. It was late afternoon. I turned in my rental car, got my boarding pass, and was anxiously awaiting my return home. I almost knew what was about to happen. I was so weary. The announcement came. The flight had been canceled, and the next flight would be in three hours or so.

When I did eventually arrive at DFW airport and headed to my car, the oppression lifted. Obviously (to me) there had been a high-ranking demon assigned to me. It was a weekend I won't forget, and I just told you some of it.

I don't blame things on demons. I usually don't try to figure out when or how they might be involved. I don't overestimate them. I don't give them too much credit. I don't think about them much. I really do try to keep my focus on the truth of God's Word. I also know the reality of living in a sinful world. When demons are involved from the outside, from the heavenlies, and when it is directed at us, our authority is the same. It is the name of Jesus. For me and my ministry and life, the name of Jesus is *absolute authority*.

There is a big difference in *standing* when demons come after you and you deciding to go after them—a big difference. Don't pick any fights.

What Languages Do Demons Speak?

This is a legitimate question and is but one of a handful that have been asked of me about what language is used in the heavenlies. A woman told me about her curious question.

> When I was a little girl, I lived in India with my missionary parents. However, one day one of my aunts took me to a Hindu temple, and she put her hands on me and did some type of chant. I will never forget that day. I believe she gave me to one of the Hindu gods. I am now grown and live in America. I am

married, and I am saved. I know about spiritual warfare, and I have experienced a measure of deliverance. However, I feel there is something still there from that experience in India. I seem not to be able to cast these demons out. Could it be that they don't understand English? They are from a different culture, a different country, and maybe they have never heard English. Could they be hiding behind that or some feigned ignorance?

I took a young man through deliverance a few years ago, and he spoke perfect English with no foreign accent even though he grew up in Russia. What I found to be very interesting is that when we prayed and confessed before God, his language was pure. But as I began to bind the evil spirits and command them to reveal their names and functions, the tone of his voice changed, and he spoke with a heavy Russian accent. This happened every time the demons were addressed. However, he was not aware of it. When we finished the session and told him about it, he tried to emulate the accent that we described to him, and he could not do it.

He laughed because it seemed very strange to him that this could happen. He experienced great freedom that day, and I went away with some more Holy Spirit learning from on-the-job training. Here it seemed that the generational spirits that had been in his family so long certainly knew both English and Russian. To me it is clear that demons speak the language of the individual to whom they are attached. Do they speak to each other in a common demonic language?

I have heard them curse me in other tongues. They can certainly know other tongues. I have heard these hundreds of times. While I did not understand it, I certainly knew it was directed at me. Whenever the command is given that only the Holy Spirit can speak, they always stop.

You can feel the threat and absolute hatred when the tongues begin to speak. My educated guess is that demons communicate with each other simply through their minds. When they give you something to think about, it will be words that you understand in a voice that is believable.

This question came to me via the Internet.

> I would really like to know, when summoning a spirit (angelic or demonic), they usually speak the language of the person who summoned them, but what is their original language? And please don't say "Hebrew" or "Latin" or "Aramaic." It would be impossible for them to speak any of those languages originally because those languages didn't exist until humans came along—and if angels and demons predate the human race, it would be impossible for them to originally speak a human language. So does anyone know what language angels and demons ORIGINALLY speak?

Well, I don't know if anyone can answer the question, but it's a legitimate issue. Obviously God is the Creator and designer of all beings. That there is a language in the heavenly realm is documented all through Scripture. If they were speaking to you, they would merely be heard in your language. When speaking to each other or God, one may assume they have their own. We would assume this since everyone who has seen or spoken to angels understood them in their own language.

That they have a higher, more sophisticated form of communication is a given. Remember when Paul was caught up into the third heaven, he said, "…how he was caught up into Paradise and heard inexpressible words, which it is not lawful for a man to utter" (2 Cor. 12:4). Paul heard and saw things he could not describe or even try to put into human understanding. It's different, way different, and better, way better.

So, do Hindu demons understand commands given in English? Absolutely they do. Recently a medical doctor traveled to our office for deliverance. She lived on the East Coast and was from India originally. This doctor had been saved only a short while and had an unusual understanding about the deliverance process. She said, "I've been dealing with these things all my life, and it has intensified since I have been saved. They know that I know." She radiated with the new life of Christ in her. I predict she will be doing deliverance shortly. God will send people to her. She had a wonderful deliverance session. The Hindu demons understood in English in the name of Jesus. This doctor came back the next day to sit in one of our sessions to learn more about the simplicity of the process. She will be used of God, and I expect her to be successful.

One other note on this subject: God understands your language, and He will translate it to the demon if necessary. The name of Jesus Christ is understood by every demon everywhere.

CHAPTER 18

WHEN PIGS FLY

WHEN WILL THE name of Jesus not be sufficient? When pigs fly. When will the believer have no hope of being free? When pigs fly.

I want to share some simple truths in helping you to maintain freedom. The following steps are suggested for daily use to help you as you grow in Christ and continue in your spiritual authority to walk in freedom and exercise power over the enemy.

Confess sin immediately. Don't allow sin to linger. Memorize the verse below and keep it in your mind and heart. Stand in the awesome truth of God's promise to forgive.

> If we confess our sins, He is faithful and just to forgive us our sins and to cleanse us from all unrighteousness.
> —1 JOHN 1:9

Apply this, not so much by begging for forgiveness, but more so in thanking Him for it and receiving it by faith. Sin must be forgiven, and you must be cleansed immediately. Deliverance is only as good as our obedience!

When negative thoughts come, you must rebuke them and replace them with positive thoughts. Make sure the thoughts that remain in your mind fall in this category:

> Finally, brethren, whatever things are true, whatever things are
> noble, whatever things are just, whatever things are pure, what-
> ever things are lovely, whatever things are of good report, if there
> is any virtue and if there is anything praiseworthy—meditate on
> these things.
>
> —PHILIPPIANS 4:8

Premeditated sin will invite demons. Keep your plans holy and
pleasing to God. Anticipate increased freedom as you walk in
obedience.

> For this is the love of God, that we keep His commandments.
> And His commandments are not burdensome.
>
> —1 JOHN 5:3

There is an awesome promise that goes with keeping His commandments and doing those things that please Him.

> And whatever we ask we receive from Him, because we keep His
> commandments and do those things that are pleasing in His sight.
>
> —1 JOHN 3:22

Focus on Pleasing God

Focus on pleasing Him. Anticipate increased freedom as you walk
in obedience. You must learn to dismiss, immediately, the painful
memories of your past and live in anticipation and appreciation of life
without bondage. Keep this verse alive in you.

> Brethren, I do not count myself to have apprehended; but one
> thing I do, forgetting those things which are behind and reaching
> forward to those things which are ahead, I press toward the goal
> for the prize of the upward call of God in Christ Jesus.
>
> —PHILIPPIANS 3:13–14

Never forget that Satan and all of his demons are liars. Learn to recognize the lie. "When he speaks a lie, he speaks from his own resources, for he is a liar and the father of it" (John 8:44).

One of the favorite ploys of demons is to try to convince you that deliverance—your freedom experience—was only emotional and that you are still in the enemy's grip. "Submit to God. Resist the devil and he will flee from you" (James 4:7).

Trust God daily to help you makes correct choices, and He will.

> Having begun in the Spirit, are you now being made perfect by the flesh?
> —GALATIANS 3:3

Use the name of Jesus, the blood of the Lamb, and your confession of faith against all the demons' temptations and condemnation. All condemnation comes from Satan. Never believe him. You have been cleansed by the blood, and through the name of Jesus Christ, you are blood protected.

> And they overcame him by the blood of the Lamb and by the word of their testimony, and they did not love their lives to the death.
> —REVELATION 12:11

> There is therefore now no condemnation to those who are in Christ Jesus, who do not walk according to the flesh, but according to the Spirit.
> —ROMANS 8:1

Give Control to the Holy Spirit

Allow the Holy Spirit to control your life—all of you all the time. Make a conscious choice to make Jesus Lord of every day and every situation.

I beseech you therefore, brethren, by the mercies of God, that you present your bodies a living sacrifice, holy, acceptable to God, which is your reasonable service. And do not be conformed to this world, but be transformed by the renewing of your mind, that you may prove what is that good and acceptable and perfect will of God.

—Romans 12:1–2

Be filled with the Spirit.

—Ephesians 5:18

Therefore He who supplies the Spirit to you and works miracles among you, does He do it by the works of the law, or by the hearing of faith?

—Galatians 3:5

God's Holy Word must have a predominant place in your life. Sometimes this may mean not doing something that would take you away from it.

Let the word of Christ dwell in you richly in all wisdom, teaching and admonishing one another in psalms and hymns and spiritual songs, singing with grace in your hearts to the Lord.

—Colossians 3:16

This Book of the Law shall not depart from your mouth, but you shall meditate in it day and night, that you may observe to do according to all that is written in it. For then you will make your way prosperous, and then you will have good success.

—Joshua 1:8

Take a Stand in God

All of what you hear about the *armor* has to do with standing, not engaging in a battle. You can stand and be victorious as the promise of protection and victory comes from the Word of God. The armor is Jesus Christ; we are clothed in Him. You can stand in Christ!

> Finally, my brethren, be strong in the Lord and in the power of His might. Put on the whole armor of God, that you may be able to stand against the wiles of the devil. For we do not wrestle against flesh and blood, but against principalities, against powers, against the rulers of the darkness of this age, against spiritual hosts of wickedness in the heavenly places. Therefore take up the whole armor of God, that you may be able to withstand in the evil day, and having done all, to stand. Stand therefore, having girded your waist with truth, having put on the breastplate of righteousness, and having shod your feet with the preparation of the gospel of peace; above all, taking the shield of faith with which you will be able to quench all the fiery darts of the wicked one. And take the helmet of salvation, and the sword of the Spirit, which is the word of God; praying always with all prayer and supplication in the Spirit, being watchful to this end with all perseverance and supplication for all the saints.
>
> —Ephesians 6:10–18

Remind yourself of who you are in Christ, and stand in faith instead of wavering in fear. You must sever ties with old unhealthy friendships—this is a must.

The Bible asks, "Do you not understand that friendship with the world is enmity with God? Whoever therefore wants to be a friend of the world makes himself an enemy of God" (James 4:4). That's pretty plain. You can count on the demons to try to use *whatever worked before* to get access to your life again. You must avoid old patterns and break former habits that led to sin.

Be serious in your efforts to glorify the Lord Jesus. Look at the Word in Colossians 3:1–3:

> If then you were raised with Christ, seek those things which are above, where Christ is, sitting at the right hand of God. Set your

mind on things above, not on things on the earth. For you died, and your life is hidden with Christ in God.

Don't get distracted. Keep your focus on Jesus and on things above. This battle is one of dependency; be careful to not get confident in the flesh.

Admitting you can't do it all by yourself is not weakness; it is strength. Do things with His help. The lie of demons is to tell you that you can do it without God. Yet the Lord Jesus clearly says in John 15:5:

> I am the vine, you are the branches. He who abides in Me, and I
> in him, bears much fruit; for without Me you can do nothing.

Remember the wiles of the devils. Stay aware of the sneaky traps and trickery. Act in your God-given authority; it will always be honored by the Father, who gave it to Jesus to give to you. Praise invites God's presence and causes the enemy to run. Praise Him because He deserves it; give thanks to God for His continuous goodness. "The LORD executes righteousness and justice for all who are oppressed" (Ps. 103:6).

Be ready to receive what is given liberally by the Spirit of God. It is from the glory of Jesus Christ, who is at the right hand of His Father, who is also your Father. Remind the demons that you are an heir of God and a joint-heir with Jesus Christ. You are!

Receive what the Word of God describes as the fruit of His Spirit— "love, joy, peace, longsuffering, kindness, goodness, faithfulness, gentleness, self-control" (Gal. 5:22–23). Never forget that Jesus said, "As the Father has sent Me, I also send you" (John 20:21).

It seems there are certain things that require diligent attention. Criticism, negativity, grieving over the past, oversensitivity, doubt, selfishness, putting feelings before faith, and lack of genuine prayer are all on the list. Be an outgoing person and help others. Helping others will bring blessings. You cannot allow self-pity a place in your life.

> Now the works of the flesh are evident, which are: adultery,
> fornication, uncleanness, lewdness, idolatry, sorcery, hatred,

feel justified in picking up unforgiveness or bitterness. You may find yourself tempted with old habits or behaviors that do not fit in with the Christian life. The devil has a way of making the old times seem rosy to us, just as he tricked the Israelites in the desert into missing the melons, cucumbers, leeks, onions, and garlic that they had left behind in Egypt (Num. 11:5).

Of course Satan forgot to mention the misery and slavery that went along with those tasty fruits and vegetables. The demons have a way of bringing to mind only the pleasure of sin, not the misery that accompanies it.

Do not become nostalgic about the past, but keep your eyes on the future as you prepare to enter God's promised land. Jesus Christ did not come to take good things away from you but rather to bring you real life.

> The thief does not come except to steal, and to kill, and to destroy. I have come that they may have life, and that they may have it more abundantly.
>
> —JOHN 10:10

> Delight yourself also in the LORD,
> And He shall give you the desires of your heart.
>
> —PSALM 37:4

Recognizing the enemy's strategy is helpful, but it does not win the battle for us. It is more important that you learn and practice some positive principles that will enable you to gain ground quickly and hold it. It is important to develop a new way of thinking based upon truth from God's Word. Focus your attention on Jesus Christ. His blood is the most powerful protection in the universe. Moreover, Jesus Christ came and shed His very blood because He loves you. Confess the fact that He loves you. Talk to Jesus throughout every day, sharing the good things and the bad with Him. You can be sure He will not leave you. Allow the Holy Spirit to have His way with you. Pray throughout the day. Let the Holy Spirit show you negative attitudes, habits, feelings, and behaviors that need to be changed. The Holy Spirit is God's power given in order for you to become like Jesus Christ. He will show you things through the Bible, through other people, and through your experiences.

> Then Jesus said to those Jews who believed Him, "If you abide in My word, you are My disciples indeed. And you shall know the truth, and the truth shall make you free."
> —JOHN 8:31–32

Command the devil and demon powers, in the name of Jesus Christ, to go away and leave you alone. Make it clear that you intend to follow Jesus Christ no matter what. Above all, do not argue with the enemy and entertain his thoughts; you cannot beat him that way. Instead, clear your mind by gently praising Jesus Christ.

> Therefore submit to God. Resist the devil and he will flee from you.
> —JAMES 4:7

My advice is to not think much about demons. Don't dwell on them, don't think about them at night, and don't give them too much credit. Keep your focus on Jesus. Surround yourself with like-minded Christians. The Christian walk is not intended to be a solo performance. We need other people in the Christian fellowship to support us. This is nothing to be ashamed of, but rather it is God's preferred way. Jesus Christ ministers through His body.

> Bear one another's burdens, and so fulfill the law of Christ.
> —GALATIANS 6:2

Thank the Father for sending Jesus Christ and anointing Him with the Holy Spirit to bring us out of the kingdom of darkness into the kingdom of light. The late Dr. E. V. Hill, the great black pastor from Los Angeles, used to say, "Thank God for Jesus!"

"The Spirit of the LORD is upon Me,
Because He has anointed Me
To preach the gospel to the poor;
He has sent Me to heal the brokenhearted,
To proclaim liberty to the captives
And recovery of sight to the blind,
To set at liberty those who are oppressed;
To proclaim the acceptable year of the LORD."

Then He closed the book, and gave it back to the attendant and sat down. And the eyes of all who were in the synagogue were fixed on Him. And He began to say to them, "Today this Scripture is fulfilled in your hearing."

—LUKE 4:18–21

When will God's Word fail? When pigs fly!

So shall My word be that goes forth from My mouth;
It shall not return to Me void,
But it shall accomplish what I please,
And it shall prosper in the thing for which I sent it.

—ISAIAH 55:11

And the God of peace will crush Satan under your feet shortly. The grace of our Lord Jesus Christ be with you. Amen.

—ROMANS 16:20

CHAPTER 19

PIGS FROM THE PAST

YOUR MEMORY IS one of the very remarkable parts of your complex being. It serves as a news system for the brain; it is like the brain's history book. It is a think bank containing millions, perhaps billions of memoranda. It stores feelings and impressions, experiences, things seen, things heard, and things felt.

It is amazing that our memory can recall so many things just at the impulse of desiring to recall a past event. We are able to dwell on that happening and bring to our memory even more details than we want. At times, unfortunately, the memory can serve us or enslave us, a choice that each individual makes. In each person's memory bank are both positive and negative events. I can recall whichever I choose. I can make them dominant parts of my memory by dwelling on them more often than others.

There are multitudes of people who feel they can never survive the hurts of the past. They think there are things they can never get over. They think and speak of them constantly, which tends to reinforce the negative feelings. They say there is someone they can never forgive for a hurt or horror brought into their life. Many of these *dark* memories come out of our youth, when we were delicate and impressionable. It may be a sorrow that so crushed us that we feel we can never turn it loose. Many feel they can never forgive someone who mistreated them. These dark memories can cause maladjustment in our lives and can often be doorways for demons.

Lingering bruises may come from the workplace or with associates. Perhaps you feel you were cheated or wronged in such a way that you feel justified in holding on to anger and unforgiveness. Dark memories from painful experiences in your marriage or relationships with the opposite sex may haunt you. The source of painful memories is limitless.

The bottom line is this: it is not what happened to you; it is how you responded to what happened!

You can be humiliated, lied about, deceived, betrayed, and can even suffer bodily harm and still get over it. Your response to the problem determines the magnitude of the problem.

> No temptation has overtaken you except such as is common to man; but God is faithful, who will not allow you to be tempted beyond what you are able, but with the temptation will also make the way of escape, that you may be able to bear it.
>
> —1 CORINTHIANS 10:13

The problems you have experienced in life may be greater than what others have experienced, even though others have had bitter, unpleasant experiences as well. Though they may be very different in nature from yours, perhaps not as severe as yours, everyone has had problems that have left scars and painful memories. You must continually be aware that you have not been singled out for suffering and that in this world problems are normal.

Dealing With the Past

In prison ministry, we meet the extreme cases of *painful pasts*, but the problem is not the painful past; it is the way the individual chose to deal with the problem. Some have sought to justify their wrong actions because of wrong done to them in the past. When demon powers gain access to our memories, it is likely the doorway they used was through our thoughts.

You must come to grips with the fact that crisis is normal, problems are common, and unpleasant memories of the past are in everyone's life, not just yours. How you handle the past will depend pretty much on how you handled yourself while you were in the problem. Crisis is normal to the growth process; it is necessary for maturity to happen. It is pointless to measure our problems with the experience of others.

In genuine deliverance, it is not just *escaping from* but also *escaping to*. The first step in dealing with the past is acknowledging that it is over. It is the past! Unfortunately, for many people the events of yesterday have too much control on the events of today—and for some, tomorrow.

In spiritual life, panic blinds the eyes to being receptive to God's Word. It depresses the spirit, robs the prayer life, impairs faith, and inhibits the receipt of God's answers. When memories bring panic to your spirit, you can be sure demon powers are influencing your thoughts with lies. The torment that the evil spirits bring often includes thoughts of quitting.

David called this the "terror by night." Psychologists who specialize in sleep disorders recognize *night terrors* as a real phenomenon. But they don't know what causes it, and they don't know the cure.

David said:

> You shall not be afraid of the terror by night,
> Nor of the arrow that flies by day,
> Nor of the pestilence that walks in darkness,
> Nor of the destruction that lays waste at noonday.
> A thousand may fall at your side,
> And ten thousand at your right hand;
> But it shall not come near you.
> Only with your eyes shall you look,
> And see the reward of the wicked.
> Because you have made the LORD, who is my refuge,

Even the Most High, your dwelling place.

—PSALM 91:5–9

When you feel overcome by the panic of memories from the past, or panic in any form, I suggest that you put on some praise music or CDs or tapes of Bible reading, and praise God from your spirit. This is the time to renew your mind with the washing of the water of the Word!

Choose to be productive. Do something that honors God and others. Make a decision and do it. It is a favorite tool of demons to overwhelm you with thoughts of something bad happening. The demons use it to bring about defeat and destruction. When these feelings approach you, recognize their source, and resist them in the name of Jesus! Absolutely refuse to submit to the negative thoughts and depressive feelings that come as old painful memories are aroused. Learn to reject them and identify them as from Satan with intentions of destroying you!

The lies of demonic spirits are used to persuade you to withdraw from others. Don't stop communicating with people or with God. Don't cut yourself off by isolating yourself! Loneliness and isolation will only pervert your thinking. Good advice is not the same as godly action. The gospel is the good news, not good advice. Act upon it, speak the truth, and agree with what God says.

Keep your conversation positive. Don't allow self-pity and *poor-me thinking* to influence your talk. Always move forward; always anticipate victory. Make sure your conversation will energize angels to minister for you. Pay attention to what you say, and speak as though you know heaven is listening.

Don't be ashamed to tell God the truth and everything that your heart is feeling. Get rid of all the negative feeling by pouring your heart out in confession. You are committed to what you confess. What? You are committed to what you confess. What you confess, what you say, is what you believe. What you believe is what you will do. Negative confession produces negative feelings and a negative lifestyle. It often is legal permission for demons to operate in your life.

Confess the positive promises of God's Word. Believe them to materialize in your life, to become reality in your own life, and you will commit yourself to them. Build faith. Don't allow negative confessions to limit what you are building. Build your faith through prayer, God's Word, and an attitude of praise from your heart. Know this: faith attracts the positive; fear brings about the negative. Refuse to dwell on negative thoughts. When you feel inclined to complain about someone, about an injustice or trauma that was apparently caused by another person, take it up with the Lord. Don't take your murmurings to another person, and don't allow murmurings to live inside of you! Confess sin, confess your hurts and release them, and ask to be cleansed. Admit what your conscience convicts you about; don't cover it up. The Holy Spirit will be truthful; when you are convicted, confess it.

Base your conversation upon your trust in God, not your trust in your feelings. Remember this: God always builds on a positive. He is a faith God, and without faith it is impossible to please Him. God will use your own words to create a new life for you. God inhabits the praise of His people—not their complaints and criticisms. Begin to make positive communication; persist in conversation that is positive.

Stuck With Yesterday

Part of the problem of dealing with the past and the pain of it is that you know you can never go back and do it over. You are stuck with the events of yesterday. Everyone is. Sometimes you feel that life is unfair. Usually when we feel this way it is because we have used the wrong measuring stick. I'm pretty sure that you are more blessed than others. Don't complain about life; be thankful for it. Don't dwell on past failures or bruises that others caused. Trust it to Him and go on. He will vindicate for wrongdoing. It's not your job; it's His.

If you feel you can never be satisfied until the person who wronged you is punished, then you have a bigger problem. Why do you want someone else to hurt when you know how painful it is? You call it justice? Do you really want justice? Have you ever wronged anyone? Justice is not what I think we cry for when we are hurt; we just want the pain of the past to go away. Somehow we feel that if the perpetrator is punished, we will feel better. That's not the way it works. However, if that feeling dwells in you, you must remember, vengeance belongs to God. Revenge is not our friend. It is, instead, a great enemy and tool for Satan to use for further destruction. Trust God to vindicate you. See Him involved in all of your circumstances, past, present, and future.

> Let the peoples praise You, O God;
> Let all the peoples praise You.
> Then the earth shall yield her increase;
> God, our own God, shall bless us.
>
> —PSALM 67:5–6

The stronghold of the past, the grip of a grudge, the anvil of anger require prayer and praise! Praise is a statement to God and Satan. After you pray, while you pray, praise God with thanksgiving.

> Let them sacrifice the sacrifices of thanksgiving,
> And declare His works with rejoicing.
>
> —PSALM 107:22

Praise when the heart is bleeding and torn? Praise when the pressure is so great? Praise when walking through the valley of the shadow of death? Should I not weep instead? There is no shame in weeping, but don't weep too long. Replace the tears with praise and the sacrifice of thanksgiving. Give Him the sacrifice of praise. You will soon see that when you are mindful of your blessings and thank Him, the peace of God will manifest in your soul.

You can praise your way out of anything, even the pain of the past. While you may grow weary of hearing this, perhaps in much hearing it will sink home. It is a choice you must make; no one can do it for you. You must decide if you want to be free from the past. If you want healing, there are some things that you must do. Forgiveness and praise are not options; they are absolutes!

Praise has wonderful lifting power. First Samuel records a time when King Saul was tormented by an evil spirit. When David played on his harp, the evil spirit left Saul, and he was well. What a wonderful way to get rid of the enemy when he attacks with mental torment. Praise.

Praise God; praise the people you love. Never condemn or criticize—doing so is like throwing spiritual boomerangs. Martin Luther said, "When I cannot pray, I always sing!"

What you focus upon will ultimately consume you. Focus on God. Try the glance and gaze principle—just glance at the problem and the circumstances, and gaze upon Jesus.

In 2 Chronicles 20 there is the account of Jehoshaphat. He was told there was a great multitude coming against him from beyond the sea. He fully realized the difficulty, and he went to the Lord with the problem that he knew was too great for him: "We have no power against this great multitude that is coming against us; nor do we know what to do, but our eyes are upon You" (v. 12).

Word came to Jehoshaphat through one of the young men: "Do not be afraid nor dismayed because of this great multitude, for the battle is not yours, but God's.... You will not need to fight in this battle....Do not fear or be dismayed" (vv. 15, 17). Jehoshaphat appointed singers to go before the army singing, "Praise the LORD, for His mercy endures forever" (v. 21). Without one visible sign of victory they sang praise—right in the face of the enemy! Praise God, right in the face of the enemy!

"When they began to sing and to praise, the LORD set ambushes against the people of Ammon, Moab, and Mount Seir, who had come against Judah; and they were defeated" (v. 22). Two of the opposing armies began to fight the third, and when they had demolished it, they turned on each other until the valley was filled with dead bodies of the enemy, and "no one...escaped" (v. 24). The praise brought not only victory but also great reward.

> When Jehoshaphat and his people came to take away their spoil,
> they found among them an abundance of valuables on the dead
> bodies, and precious jewelry, which they stripped off for them-
> selves, more than they could carry away; and they were three
> days gathering the spoil because there was so much.
>
> —2 Chronicles 20:25

They had added riches and reward they never dreamed of, and "the
way of the wicked [was turned] upside down" (Ps. 146:9).

There were two songs in this great battle—a song of praise before
and a song of deliverance afterward! Remember, if you choose to deal
with your pain and your past God's way, the battle is the Lord's, and
you can know both victory and reward by praising Him.

> He also brought me up out of a horrible pit,
> Out of the miry clay,
> And set my feet upon a rock,
> And established my steps.
>
> —Psalm 40:2

The past is a pit—and "a horrible pit" at that! But the following
verses say:

> He has put a new song in my mouth—
> Praise to our God;
> Many will see it and fear,
> And will trust in the Lord.
> Blessed is that man who makes the Lord his trust,
> And does not respect the proud, nor such as turn aside to lies.
> Many, O Lord my God, are Your wonderful works
> Which You have done;
> And Your thoughts toward us
> Cannot be recounted to You in order;
> If I would declare and speak of them,
> They are more than can be numbered.
>
> —Psalm 40:3–5

David certainly knew calamity. He knew a painful past. Saul did not treat him very well! When someone hates you enough to try to kill you, I'd say that qualifies as a painful memory. When you are reminded by God's prophet that you have committed adultery and murder, and your sin is open before all of heaven, that qualifies as mental torment. When your children refuse to serve the Lord and seek all that God has given you, that must qualify as troubling thoughts.

There was a time when David was *greatly distressed* in his early life. He led his men in battle and returned to find himself in the midst of *calamity.* The people spoke of stoning him. They wept till they had no power to weep. Their wives, their children, and their belongings had been taken captive.

David inquired of the Lord, saying, "Shall I pursue this troop? Shall I overtake them?" The simple answer to his simple prayer was: "Pursue, for you shall surely overtake them and without fail recover all" (1 Sam. 30:8).

One of the most challenging—and rewarding—words in all of Scripture is found in this story: "But David encouraged himself in the Lord his God" (v. 6, kjv).

Encourage yourself in the Lord. Don't wait for others. It may never come; they have problems of their own. Likely, if you wait, others won't encourage you anyway; they may criticize and condemn you. Encourage yourself in the Lord. The responsibility for recovery and healing lies in your hands. In calamity—encourage yourself in the Lord—pursue! Take charge of your life, or someone else will. You make the choice to be healed. The pain of the past is only pain because you allow it to be. Pursue tomorrow. Pursue today. Forget yesterday. It's gone. Don't go there!

CHAPTER 20

BE READY ALWAYS

IN LUKE 5, we read the story of the disciples washing their nets. "So it was, as the multitude pressed about Him to hear the word of God, that He stood by the Lake of Gennesaret, and saw two boats standing by the lake; but the fishermen had gone from them and were washing their nets" (vv. 1–2). Fishermen wash their nets at the end of the fishing trip. It means they have quit fishing.

In life there are many opportunities to quit or keep going. Sometimes the things we deal with in life can be overwhelming. Whether it is demons or people or a set of circumstances beyond our control, sometimes we have to make decisions we never thought we would face. This is true for everyone.

We all know that when you are frustrated and weary, it's not the best time to make decisions. The best time is after properly evaluating and praying about them. Incorrect determinations come most often when our minds are weary and our emotions are weak. It was at this time that Jesus came by.

I am sure thankful to God that Jesus comes by in just such moments as these. I am thankful that it is possible to focus on Him and His Word in those *give up* moments. Look at how Peter, James, and John had their lives forever changed. These guys were professional fishermen. They knew what they were doing and obviously were good at it. However, this time things weren't going very well. They had been out all night and had nothing to show for it. Nothing. They had decided to quit, and they were washing their nets.

Lessons From the Fishermen

Have you ever been there? You know, things are not going as you planned. You have done the best you can, and it seems like everything has failed. You feel like a failure, and you really don't see how things can change for the better. Have you thought about quitting? Are you ready to *fold your tent? Throw in the towel, clean out your desk?* Have you felt as if you did your best and still have no hope for anything better? Have you had your wasted nights? What about a weary nature? Read Luke 5:1–11. There are seven truths that we can learn from this great section of Scripture.

1. Wasted nights

Peter and his partners, James and John, had fished all night and had nothing to show for it. They had done their best. They had put forth their best fishing efforts and skills but had no fish. They were in the right place for fishing, they had given themselves the best opportunity to succeed, they had the right equipment—but they had no fish.

I think they must have summed up their efforts as just a *wasted night.* Boy, I've heard that a few times in the prisons and out. Wasted days, wasted nights, wasted years. I'm also thinking that most people view their pasts that way, at least portions of them.

I like to fish. I have fished for hours and caught nothing. I sort of enjoy it anyway. However, these guys supported their families by fishing. It was their livelihood. The hours passed and the darkness faded to dawn. Nothing.

2. Weary nature

Now they are tired and frustrated. They had a *weary nature,* and they made a decision to call it quits. Tired and frustrated is not the condition you want to be in when you decide to quit.

3. Washing nets

They had decided to wash their nets and head back home. They had put forth a good effort, probably did everything they knew to do, but they were empty-handed and were calling it quits. It's difficult when you have done all you know to do and have nothing to show for it. Not only did it seem like a wasted night, but also now they had a weary nature. They were washing their nets when Jesus came by. Wasted night, weary nature, and now washing nets. There was a word needed.

4. Word needed

It seems that He still walks by when we reach this point in life. Maybe that is where you are right now. Don't wash your nets! Jesus got into Peter's boat and began to teach the throng of people that followed. They pressed upon Him; they all wanted a word from Jesus. I would like to have heard that message. At the close of His message to the people, Jesus had a word for Peter: "Don't wash your nets. Go farther out; let down your nets again. Try it again, and do it My way. Let Me help you. Don't quit; I can help you with this."

I'm sure Peter was shaking his head a little and maybe mumbling under his breath, "I know how to fish. I'm a pro. I have given my best effort here and applied my best knowledge." That was likely what he was thinking, but what he spoke changed his life forever.

5. Willing nevertheless

In spite of what he thought he knew, he decided to believe Jesus. He offered a willing "nevertheless." This is really where life-changing events take place. When all odds seem to be against you and God's Word seems so hard to believe, sometimes logic and reason must take a back seat to faith. It is important to hear God's Word amidst the opinions of the world and our human impressions.

There was a *word needed*. What we need most is to hear from God. Jesus had been teaching from the boat, and His words bring faith. Faith comes by hearing the Word. They didn't need a word from another fisherman; they needed a word from Jesus. Peter said what we say many times when we have experienced wasted nights and have a weary nature: "We have toiled all night and have taken nothing." I can almost hear the frustration in Peter's voice. He was virtually saying that Jesus didn't fully understand their situation.

Still, Peter offered a willing nevertheless. Even a reluctant, cautious step in faith is rewarded by God. Peter said what we say many times: "It just doesn't make sense." "I've already tried it my way, but because you say so, *nevertheless*, at Your word, I will let down the net." James and John had heard Jesus as well, and they went with Peter into the deeper waters.

6. Wonder nearby

When they believed Him and obeyed Him, when they acted upon His Word, what they could not do by their own skills and knowledge was done. They enclosed a great multitude of fish, so much so that the net they were washing broke. They filled both of the ships with so many fish the boats began to sink. Wow! The blessing for persevering is bigger than you think it is. The rewards of obedience and faith are beyond your expectations. Keep on fishing! There is a *wonder nearby*.

Often the thing we need most to happen seems beyond our grasp. It seems that only a miracle from God could change things. The miracle here was closer than they thought. They had already done their best, and they were good at what they did, but they had nothing to show for it. Even the words spoken by Jesus were difficult for them to believe, but they acted upon them anyway.

Simple acts of obedience can make or break a situation. The very thing you need is closer than you think. In spite of their experience as fisherman and their human logic, Peter offered a willing nevertheless.

7. Worship necessary

The last point of this story is *worship necessary*. What would you do? Think about what Peter and the others had just experienced. Empty nets now full, wasted night now fulfilled. A weary nature now revived, and *worship was necessary*. How could you not fall at Jesus's feet? How can we not give Him first place in our life all of the time? When we see ourselves and how limited we are, and we see God and how limitless He is, worship is necessary.

Don't wash your nets. You need a word from God. There is a wonder nearby; full nets and fulfillment are closer than you think. Can you look at your situation in light of God's Word? Can you *launch out* a little farther because of God's promises? Can you stand on His Word regardless of circumstances? I am not talking about foolish decisions; I'm talking about obeying His Word and moving upon what God has spoken to you through His Word. I believe I can tell you with assurance that there is a wonder nearby; don't wash your nets.

Remember these important principles from the fishermen:

- Wasted nights
- Weary nature
- Washing nets
- Word needed
- Willing nevertheless
- Wonder nearby
- Worship necessary

Do You See What I See?

"In the year that King Uzziah died..." That is how Isaiah dates the time of his heavenly vision. Uzziah had been one of the most prosperous kings of Judah and reigned longer than fifty years. Kings come and kings go, but our eternal King remains; He will reign forever.

> In the year that king Uzziah died I saw also the LORD sitting upon a throne, high and lifted up, and his train filled the temple. Above it stood the seraphims: each one had six wings; with twain he covered his face, and with twain he covered his feet, and with

twain he did fly. And one cried unto another, and said, Holy, holy, holy, is the LORD of hosts: the whole earth is full of his glory. And the posts of the door moved at the voice of him that cried, and the house was filled with smoke. Then said I, Woe is me! for I am undone; because I am a man of unclean lips, and I dwell in the midst of a people of unclean lips: for mine eyes have seen the King, the LORD of hosts. Then flew one of the seraphims unto me, having a live coal in his hand, which he had taken with the tongs from off the altar: And he laid it upon my mouth, and said, Lo, this hath touched thy lips; and thine iniquity is taken away, and thy sin purged. Also I heard the voice of the LORD, saying, Whom shall I send, and who will go for us? Then said I, Here am I; send me.

—ISAIAH 6:1–8, KJV

It is believed that King Uzziah died under a cloud of leprosy and that his kingdom faded. Our God lives, and His kingdom will never diminish. Isaiah saw some of God's glory, just a glimpse of it. He saw Him high and lifted up, seated upon His throne. Isaiah saw some of the magnificence of God's eternal glory in the same year that his earthly king was buried. God allowed this prophet to catch a brief glimpse of His holiness. Was this the third heaven that Paul speaks about? How can you have an accurate vision of God's throne and not be bowed in humility? How can reverence not consume you? Is this some of what Paul called "unspeakable"? There is more, because Paul said, "Eye has not seen, nor ear heard…the things which God has prepared for those who love Him" (1 Cor. 2:9). He is quoting from Isaiah. This is just a bit of what Isaiah saw. No man has seen God at any time. What Isaiah saw was His glory.

For since the beginning of the world men have not heard, nor perceived by the ear, neither hath the eye seen, O God, beside thee, what he hath prepared for him that waiteth for him.

—ISAIAH 64:4, KJV

What Isaiah saw is what we must see with our eyes of faith: the eternal Ruler. He is seated on a throne, His throne. No one has ever sat on that throne, nor will they. It is a throne of grace to which we may come boldly through Christ Jesus. This throne is high and lifted up. It is above all and over all. It is a throne of glory where we come to worship. It is one of holy and heavenly government under which we must be subject.

When Isaiah caught just a glimpse, he immediately cried, "Woe is me!" Wow! Isaiah saw "the King, the LORD of hosts" and immediately he recognized his own humanity. He saw all of his weakness and sin, all of his inadequacies. Can you imagine his feeling when one of the seraphim flew toward him? This angel was coming at him, coming to him. What emotions must have stirred within him. Can you also imagine a human being on this earth doing spiritual combat with a demon that perhaps once stood in the presence of God?

This particular six-winged creature also had hands. He flew to Isaiah and had a coal from the altar in his hand. With a touch from the altar of God, Isaiah was declared clean. Nothing less is sufficient to cleanse us than something from the altar of God. God Himself, incarnate through Jesus Christ, is our cleansing and our only cleansing.

What a scene this must have been. What humility must have enveloped Isaiah, and what surrender to the splendor of God. Isaiah says, "Also I heard the voice of the Lord, saying, Whom shall I send, and who will go for us? Then said I, Here am I; send me" (Isa. 6:8, KJV). He heard the voice of the Lord. Isn't it interesting that faith still comes by hearing the Word of the Lord? It may be a reference to the Trinity when He asked, "Who will go for us?"

God need not consult with others, for He Himself knows. As I believe, this is always the case. A willing, consenting messenger does most to bring God glory. Volunteering to answer God's call is honoring to God: "I'll do it."

I can relate to Isaiah's response. I am sometimes like a little kid when I sense God's call: "I'll do it; let me go for You. Let me participate." With all of the angels under God's command, why did He need a *man* to go for Him? Seems He could dispatch any of the angels to do His work. However, God in His sovereignty has chosen to use men to deliver His message to men. Jesus took upon Himself the form of a man. Man is why God so loves this world. We are the focal point of ministry from angels, and we are the center of attention for war from fallen angels. There doesn't seem to be a clear understanding of this.

Can you see our smallness in engaging in spiritual warfare in the heavenlies? Why would we dare go there? We are ambassadors of the King of glory, but we are not soldiers in a battle against heavenly realm demons. When they pick a fight with me, I will stand, and I will resist in His righteousness. But I will not start a fight with them.

I'm thinking that if we saw what Isaiah saw we would keep our eyes upon the throne of God.

Who Died and Left You in Charge?

And Jesus came and spoke to them, saying, "All authority has been given to Me in heaven and on earth."

—MATTHEW 28:18

So Jesus said to them again, "Peace to you! As the Father has sent Me, I also send you."

—JOHN 20:21

In the above verses, Jesus says, "I am sending you the same way the Father sent Me."

I know that you have heard someone ask this question sarcastically: "Who died and left you in charge?" Well, Jesus died and left us as believers in charge. When He was in the world, He was the light of the world. But now He says that we are the light of the world. We are what He was. He said that *all* authority had been *given* to Him, both in heaven and on the earth.

Who gave it to Him? The Father. Jesus also told us, "As the Father has sent Me, I also send you." How did the Father send Him? With all authority. That is clearly stated and clearly taught in Scripture. It is not boastful to believe that; it is scriptural. Jesus died and left us in charge. If that is not true, then what is? Think about it. If we are not *in charge* as His ambassadors, who is? If we don't have authority, who does?

There are at least three basic belief categories among Christians. There are some Christians who believe Jesus never did miracles and that He does no miracles today. Sadly, that is a much larger group than it should be. These are the "He didn't and He doesn't" group.

The second group believes that Jesus did miracles, but they no longer happen today. This is doubtless the largest group. This category is fueled by human logic and fear of being seen as spiritually ignorant. This is the "He did, but He doesn't" group.

The third group believes that Jesus did miracles and that they are still happening today. I am in that group. He did, and He does. When you have experienced miracles, is very difficult not to believe in them. When you read the New Testament, and God's Word says they will continue, how then can you not believe and yet say you believe the Word of God?

We see miracles in our ministry on a regular basis. There are hundreds of testimonies. I suppose if you do not believe miracles happen, then most likely you will not experience any, because God is a *faith* God, and it is impossible to please Him apart from faith.

> But without faith it is impossible to please Him, for he who comes to God must believe that He is, and that He is a rewarder of those who diligently seek Him.
>
> —Hebrews 11:6

So, clearly, if you cannot place faith in Him and in His Word, then it is not possible to please Him. But He rewards faith. You see, I believe there is authority in the name of Jesus and that my faith in that name is rewarded by God. I believe He did, and He does. I believe He died and left us in charge.

Remember the Roman centurion who wanted Jesus to heal his servant (Luke 7:1–10)? Jesus said He had never seen such faith in all of

Israel. The man told Jesus that he understood authority. He comprehended that Jesus could simply speak the word, and the sickness would have to go. Jesus called that "great faith." Understanding authority is great faith.

The name of Jesus is recognized authority in heaven and on the earth. It is in His name that every knee will bow. It is in His name that men might be saved. It's the only name given among men that will bring salvation.

> Nor is there salvation in any other, for there is no other name under heaven given among men by which we must be saved.
>
> —Acts 4:12

> Far above all principality and power and might and dominion, and every name that is named, not only in this age but also in that which is to come.
>
> —Ephesians 1:21

It is *His* name, and His name alone, that is above every name.

In John 16, Jesus said, "Until now you have asked nothing in My name" (v. 24). "Up until now," He says, "it was that you looked for the Messiah, but now I am here, now My name is exalted. My name will be honored by God the Father. Ask in My name; act in My Name."

I believe that an absolute key to seeing this scriptural truth come to life is this: "Act in My name!" It is more than just asking; it is acting upon His name.

> Believe Me that I am in the Father and the Father in Me, or else believe Me for the sake of the works themselves. Most assuredly, I say to you, he who believes in Me, the works that I do he will do also; and greater works than these he will do, because I go to My Father. And whatever you ask in My name, that I will do, that the Father may be glorified in the Son. If you ask anything in My name, I will do it.
>
> —John 14:11–14

The name of Jesus Christ is authority that is far above any principality, power, might, or dominion. It is far above all sickness and disease, disorders, fears, and works of demon powers. I believe He did, and He does! I believe He died and left us in charge. When legal rights have been removed, it is absolutely recognized authority in heaven and earth.

However, please follow this truth carefully—it is not authority where demon powers have been granted legal rights. Where there is unconfessed sin, there is also a legal right, and that must be removed. It must be canceled through confession. The cleansing blood of Jesus must be applied in order to remove the legal consent of demons, including sickness and disease. (No, not all sickness is caused by demons.)

There are also many legal rights that a demon may have to someone's life, but none that cannot be canceled through confession, denunciation, and renunciation. Generational sins, oaths, vows, pledges, ceremonies of secret societies, spoken words, and believing a lie are also rights that evil spirits may have in our lives. Jesus died and left us in charge. If you don't take charge, someone or something else will.

Don't step outside your realm of authority. Our authority has to do with what is ours and never extends to other people. Take charge of your life, your family, your *stuff.* "Therefore do not worry about tomorrow, for tomorrow will worry about its own things. Sufficient for the day is its own trouble" (Matt. 6:34).

Don't live in the past, and don't fear tomorrow. These are also doorways for demons. Speak truth. Agree with God's Word. Jesus died and left us in charge.

CHAPTER 21

WALK BY FAITH, NOT BY SIGHT

OVER THE YEARS I have heard many people give their opinion of what faith is—what they *think* it is. I wonder, what is your definition of faith? The Bible gives us a definition and then proceeds to give numerous examples to clarify the definition. The eleventh chapter of Hebrews is called the faith chapter of the Bible.

> Now faith is the substance of things hoped for, the evidence of things not seen....Without faith it is impossible to please Him [God].
>
> —HEBREWS 11:1, 6

That is the biblical definition, but what does it mean? I believe one of the most damaging doctrines being taught today is the idea that faith is believing God for miracles that *may* fall in the area of *flesh* instead of faith. I have been a minister for more than thirty years and have witnessed a handful of miracles. However, most people never see miracles, or perhaps they never recognize a miracle. If you believe faith is receiving miracles from God, you may be disappointed. That may be *part* of what faith is, but that's not all that faith is.

Based upon the examples of faith given in Hebrews 11, I believe an accurate scriptural description of faith is this: "a commitment to God that does not waiver, regardless of circumstances." Look at these examples.

Boat Today—Float Tomorrow

"By faith Noah..." (Heb. 11:7). Did Noah have the best of this world's goods? Was he in the elite of the community? Was that his desire? No, he just found grace in the eyes of the Lord, like any believer, and he faithfully lived out a commitment to God. Do you suppose that in the one hundred twenty years that Noah worked on the ark he may have become discouraged? Do you suppose his family ever questioned his commitment? Do you suppose they ever questioned the call of God on his life? Did he have the support of the community? You know that after ten...fifteen...twenty years he must have wondered, "Is it ever going to rain?"

You know his wife must have asked, "Are you sure God spoke to you?"

You know his children must have asked, "Come on, Dad, we've been working on this for fifty years; are you sure?"

God spoke to Noah *one time*. Faith can only be placed in what God has said. Anything apart from that is not faith. God spoke to Noah about the flood and the ark one time. One time is enough. God places something in your heart when he speaks. For one hundred twenty years Noah *faithfully* did what God called him to do. He did not waiver. He may have had questions; he may have had frustrations and persecutions and very little encouragement from others, but he did not waiver. God had placed something in his heart, and I believe it was something that allowed him to say in the face of all opposition, "Yeah, it's boat today, but *it's float tomorrow!*"

If God has not spoken it to your heart, then it is not faith that you are exercising; it may just be wishful thinking.

Roam Today—Home Tomorrow

Abraham was asked to leave his home and go to a strange land, not even knowing where he was to go. He just obeyed. Though he became a sojourner, he did not live in uncertainty. God had let him see a city "whose builder and maker is God" (Heb. 11:10).

Faith supercedes human reasoning. When God has spoken, only then can faith be activated. If what you do to please Him is based upon what your opinion of God is, that is not faith. The only way you can exercise faith is to place it in God's spoken word. Abraham's decision to obey God was not based upon anything he could perceive in his human understanding; rather, it was based solely upon believing what God spoke to him. Even though Abraham did not have the details, he was able to say, even though in a strange land, "OK, it's roam today, but *it's home tomorrow.*"

Pit Today—Palace Tomorrow

Joseph must have had some questions when his own family forsook him and even tried to kill him. You know the story of Joseph didn't take place in a few days or a few weeks. This is about his life. Surely some frustrations must have built when he survived the pit only to end up in the prison.

Joseph had a relationship with God bigger than the circumstances he faced. God had put something in his heart that allowed him to keep on walking. He was able to say, "Uh huh, it's pit today, but *it's palace tomorrow.*" Many times our journey from the pit to the palace is by way of a prison. Faith is commitment to God that is not based on good conditions—it *is* regardless of circumstances. Only God can put something in your heart that allows you to see that what He has spoken will come to pass.

Bricks Today—Tracks Tomorrow

Look at the examples of Moses's faith. He had a faith that allowed him to choose to suffer affliction, forsake Egypt, and not fear the consequences. Something in his heart was saying, "Yes, we're making bricks today, but *we're making tracks tomorrow.*" He had a commitment to God that does not waver. I believe that faith keeps on believing regardless of circumstances. That's what I believe faith is. Consideration of consequences and circumstances won't quench a genuine commitment of faith.

Faith does not consider the desires of the flesh in fulfilling a commitment to God. Moses must have thought he was doing something wrong when Pharaoh continually refused to *let his people go.* He surely must have become frustrated as the months passed and his people were hurting with seemingly no hope of deliverance. However, he had God's promise, and God had placed something in his heart that allowed him to discount the flesh. Bricks today, tracks tomorrow. Faith is believing God's Word. Faith can only be placed in what God has said.

I tell you that I have seen more disappointment in the Christian life by those who believed they *heard* from God, but what they *heard* was not in accordance with God's Word. Faith must be in what God has said, not in what someone said that God said. Do not place your faith in what others tell you that God told them about you or for you. Faith *must* be in what God said; otherwise it is not faith at all.

Headache Today—Head Home Tomorrow

Do you think Stephen had any questions about faith? Based on what is called *faith* by many of today's preachers, Stephen must have thought he had failed. As he was being *stoned to death*, did he wonder why his faith wasn't *working*? Of course not, because his faith was a commitment to God regardless—not dependent upon things going according to his fleshly feelings. God had put something in his heart that would allow him to know that it maybe it was headache today, but *it's head home tomorrow.*

Banish Today—Vanish Tomorrow

The faith of the apostles saw them suffer greatly for the gospel's sake—crucified upside down, shot to death by arrows while in prayer, stoned to death, heads chopped off—sounds like something may have been wrong with the apostles' faith. No, that is what faith is—an unwavering commitment to God regardless of circumstances! How can we be so gullible as to believe that faith is something that fulfills our fleshly desires? Could it be that we are selfish? Could it be there is something desperately lacking in our commitment? The apostles were faithful in their commitment unto death. John was the exception, and though he was not martyred, he was sentenced to die on the lonely island of Patmos. God had placed something in his heart that would allow him to say amidst all of the persecution, "Yeah, it's banish today, but *it's vanish tomorrow.*"

Beat Up Today—Beamed Up Tomorrow

The truth of the gospel is that real faith often invites persecution. Paul said, "Yes, and all who desire to live godly in Christ Jesus will suffer persecution" (2 Tim. 3:12). Did Paul live in a big house? Did he have the best in accommodations? Did he have a travel agent who saw to his transportation desires? He might have been more efficient if he did, but he didn't.

Rather, he evangelized regardless. He spent most of his nights in the city jails. He was beaten (195 stripes); he was stoned, mocked, ridiculed, and threatened. He had a physical problem he could not get removed through prayer. Yet God promised sufficient grace and had placed something in his heart that allowed him to continue so that he could say, "Sure, it's beat up today, but *it's beamed up tomorrow.*"

Cross Today—Crown Tomorrow

Paul wrote Timothy from death row. What had he done wrong that his *faith* did not work? No wealth, about to be executed. He did his job, he fought a good fight, he finished his course, he had no complaints. He was ready to go. He was able to tell young Timothy to "endure afflictions" (2 Tim. 4:5). Afflictions? Afflictions! I can hear some preachers now: "If you just had the right kind of faith, you wouldn't have afflictions."

I pray you are not being deceived by what the Bible calls "another gospel," one that appeals to your flesh. Faith endures afflictions. Faith continues in spite of afflictions, because faith is a commitment not dependent upon pleasant circumstances.

In 2 Corinthians 4:17 Paul tells us that "our light affliction, which is but for a moment, is working for us a far more exceeding and eternal weight of glory." Paul was also able to tell us all that there is a crown laid up for those who love Him. Yes, it is cross today, but *it is crown tomorrow.*

The commitment of faith is impossible without the grace of God. Faith keeps on walking because it does not depend upon circumstances. It does not bend when we see the problems mounting, when dark clouds get darker, because faith does not walk by what we see. Troubles in this world, according to Scripture, will continue to mount. The greatest minds have no solutions. Perplexity grips the hearts of many.

With each day, increasing possibilities for world pressures mount. Our world appears to be close to erupting with problems, about to explode from the dynamite of difficulties. But real faith will allow you to keep on walking in God's calling and will let you say, "Sure, it's rupture today, but *it's Rapture tomorrow.*" I believe that's what faith is. Faith doesn't keep records; it keeps walking...regardless.

Why Is It So Hard to Believe?

Believe Me that I am in the Father and the Father in Me, or else believe Me for the sake of the works themselves. Most assuredly, I say to you, he who believes in Me, the works that I do he will do also; and greater works than these he will do, because I go to My Father.

—JOHN 14:11–12

Jesus is talking to His disciples about "believing." Why is it so hard to believe? He says, "You believe in God; likewise, in the same manner, believe in Me." The above verses are strong, emphatic words from Jesus for us to believe—simply believe.

I want to give you three of many reasons to believe.

1. Believe Him for His world's sake.

2. Believe Him for His Word's sake.

3. Believe Him for His work's sake.

Believe Him. Can you honestly look at the world and the miracles of creation and not be stirred in your belief? Can you read the miracles throughout God's Word and remain in unbelief? He told His disciples, "Believe Me then for the works' sake, but believe Me."

Unbelief is an insult to all three—the creation, the infallible Holy Word of God, and the miraculous works of Jesus. To live in doubt is to live in opposition to God.

We cannot receive what God has for us aside from belief. It is really not complicated. God is a faith God. He always has been. Abraham, through faith, became the "father of all those who believe" (Rom. 4:11). His faith was counted for righteousness (v. 3). Abraham "did not waver at the promise of God through unbelief, but was strengthened in faith, giving glory to God, and being fully convinced that what He had promised He was also able to perform" (vv. 20–21). Unbelief robs you of God's blessings and of God receiving glory. Our access to God is through faith (Rom. 5:2).

Jesus rebuked the disciples for having *no faith* and *little faith*. He praised two Gentiles for having *great faith*—the woman of Canaan in Matthew 15, and the Roman centurion in Luke 7.

Jesus cried, "O Jerusalem, Jerusalem, the one who kills the prophets and stones those who are sent to her! How often I wanted to gather your children together, as a hen gathers her chicks under her wings, but you were not willing!" (Matt. 23:37).

I believe it was unbelief that caused Jesus to weep over the city. Our unbelief doubtless grieves the heart of God, and it limits the blessings of God. Unbelief binds the hands that bless. It grieves the giving, compassionate heart of God.

I believe it was unbelief that caused Jesus to weep as He went to the tomb of Lazarus. Instead of believing Jesus could and would raise Lazarus from the dead, Mary and Martha blamed Jesus for not being there.

Jesus chided Thomas for not believing: "Do not be unbelieving, but believing.... Thomas, because you have seen Me, you have believed. Blessed are those who have not seen and yet have believed" (John 20:27, 29).

Does *believing* make you vulnerable? Is it the *what if* involved that causes you to hold back? Is it pride? I believe it is both.

I ministered at the Agape International Church in Plano, Texas, which is a Chinese body of believers. The pastor, Dr. Chen, is also a medical doctor. He said to me over lunch, "When my daughter was three and a half years old, three-quarters of her heart muscle was deteriorated. Other doctors told me she would need a heart and kidney transplant and would need medication for the rest of her life if she survived. I prayed for seven days. God healed my daughter completely without any help from doctors. Today she is nineteen and a student at Stanford University. She scored 1550 on her SAT, and her brother scored 1600." Jesus Christ is still healing people. It is not hard for me to believe.

His world. His Word. His works. Jesus gave us three reasons to believe. Isn't creation itself reason enough to believe? Look around; God so loved the *world*. Look at His Holy *Word* that is tried and true; isn't that sufficient? Jesus said, "If you can believe Me for no other reason, believe Me for the *work's* sake." It seems as if frustration might have accented His words…BELIEVE ME.

> Verily, verily, I say unto you, He that believeth on me, the works that I do shall he do also; and greater works than these shall he do; because I go unto my Father.
>
> —John 14:12, kjv

"Because I go unto my Father"? What does that mean? It means that the same authority that God had given to Him, He was going to give to the church. Later He said, "As my Father hath sent me, even so send I you" (John 20:21, kjv).

This is hard for some to believe. Hence, not many mighty works are seen. The Word also says that Jesus could not do many mighty works in Nazareth because of their unbelief. Unbelief will prevent us from receiving all that God has for us, for, without faith, it is impossible to please God.

Does it require a lot of faith? It involves taking a step, making a move. It requires getting out of the boat. Peter walked on water with a "little faith," but had he stayed in the boat with others who doubted, he could not have even exercised "little faith." Peter got out of the boat. Abraham started walking. What step do you need to take to express your faith in God and His Word? I think it also involves getting back in the boat when Jesus is in the boat.

Recently I had an unsuspecting medical need arise. I discovered I had three herniated disks in my neck. I saw four different doctors plus my son, who is a neurosurgeon. (One of his partners did the surgery.) I'm not sure how the injury occurred.

I believed God for my healing and received it through the hand of God and four very skilled doctors. May I say to you that believing

God has nothing to do with not trusting Him to use people? God uses people to bring about His miraculous works. His healing and delivering power can be seen throughout His Word—and people are involved.

We don't need a Moses, a David, an Elijah—we need some vessel God can use to bless His people. The father of the demonized boy said to Jesus, "But if You can do anything, have compassion on us and help us" (Mark 9:22). Look at Jesus' response: "'If you can believe, all things are possible to him who believes.' Immediately the father of the child cried out and said with tears, 'Lord, I believe; help my unbelief!'" (vv. 23–24).

The issue remains the same—not if He can do it, but if you can believe He will do it! Your faith is not any stronger if you believe He will do it apart from medicine and doctors. The father would have been happy if the disciples had cast out the demons. See God at work in your life and in His world, and thank Him for it.

CHAPTER 22

YOU ARE THE TEMPLE OF GOD

ow can a Christian have demons?" "If the Holy Spirit of God lives in me, how could evil spirits get into me as well?" "How can sin and evil thoughts live in the temple of God?" Defining the temple is necessary in order to understand how the temple is defiled and defended. The temple in which God lives on the earth today is the body of a born-again believer. This is such an overwhelming thought. God actually indwells the believer with His Holy Spirit. This can become confusing to some who ask the question, How can a Christian have demons? Evil spirits can get in the temple, just like evil thoughts and sinful actions, by choices we make and gates that we open.

My now-deceased friend Frank Hammond used to say, "A Christian can have anything he wants." Our will is still intact when we are saved. Our body is a trinity; we are three in one. We are a *spirit* that has a *soul* that lives in a *body*. The best comparison I know is to look at our body or, more correctly, our being as a temple or tabernacle, as Paul calls it in 2 Corinthians 5:1: "For we know that if our earthly house, this tent, is destroyed, we have a building from God, a house not made with hands, eternal in the heavens." Do you recall the Old Testament tabernacle? It was three parts—an outer courtyard, then the actual structure of the tabernacle (which included the holy place), and the holy of holies. The holy place was twice as large as the holy of holies.

The Old Testament tabernacle is a picture of our being. The court-yard represents our flesh, the holy place our soul, and the holy of holies our spirit. The holy of holies is where the Spirit of God dwells. This is important in understanding how the temple is defiled. Where does the Spirit of God dwell in the believer? In our spirit. Not in our soul and flesh—that is the part of us that we can yield to God or to disobedi-ence. Our soul is made up of our mind, will, and emotions. Our flesh is that which can be seen, touched, and felt; it has substance. The spirit has no substance; it is intangible. It is our spirit that is born again, and it is in our spirit that the Holy Spirit of God takes up residence.

Perhaps the spirit is also the "inner man." It is very important to understand that we are a trinity, a three-part being. The spirit has been born again; the soul and the flesh are "being saved" as we yield ourselves and conform to the image of Christ. It is the soul and the flesh that can be inhabited by demon powers. It is the soul where spir-itual battle takes place, and often it manifests in the flesh.

The mind is the battlefield. The mind and the brain are sepa-rate, but I cannot scientifically prove to you how I know this. The brain is physical; the mind is soulish. The seed of sin is in the mind, while the fruit of sin may be manifested in the flesh. Demons do not—cannot—*possess* a believer, but they can and do *oppress* believers, and the oppression takes place in the body and soul. Remember, possession implies ownership. We are clearly owned by God. We are purchased with a price. We are redeemed. Genuine possession cannot take place. There are many words that can be appropriately used to describe demons in or attached to Christians. Perhaps the clearest term would be *demonized*.

Do you recall how angry Jesus became when He entered the temple and saw it *defiled* by those buying and selling and by the money changers?

> Then Jesus went into the temple of God and drove out all those
> who bought and sold in the temple, and overturned the tables of

the money changers and the seats of those who sold doves. And He said to them, "It is written, 'My house shall be called a house of prayer,' but you have made it a 'den of thieves.'"

—MATTHEW 21:12–13

How was the temple of God defiled? The things of the world had been brought into the temple. That's how it is defiled today. It happens when *we* invite things of the world into our lives. This also becomes an invitation for demon spirits to inhabit the temple. Just as rats are attracted to garbage, when our life has unconfessed sin, unbroken curses, or unforgiveness, the demons come, and they defile the temple.

They must be *driven* out. Medicine may cover the symptoms of demons, but they cannot be medicated out. Counseling may help a person deal with the consequences of demons, but it will never make them leave. They cannot be counseled out. You can never reason with a demon or train your flesh so that the demon leaves. Neither can they be removed by you *willing* them to be gone. All Christian activity is helpful in keeping the demons somewhat *in check*, but to be rid of them, they must be *cast out*. They must be driven out in the name of Jesus Christ. Jesus said, "In My name they will *cast* out demons" (Mark 16:17). Can the temple be defiled? Absolutely! Just as Jesus saw the holy temple of God defiled, He sees ours defiled by things we have permitted in our lives.

The lie we have believed is that once we have confessed our sin, the demons leave. Not necessarily so. Repentance and confession of sin cancel the penalty of sin. We are certainly cleansed of sin, but have the demons been commanded to leave? The *permission* of the demon spirit to be there has been canceled, but I have found they often do not leave until they are commanded to do so. Notice that healing came after the temple was cleansed (Matt. 21:14).

No sin could enter the holy of holies; it meant certain death for the high priest to come into God's holy presence with sin in his life. Just as sin could not enter the holy of holies, neither can demon spirits enter the spirit of a believer. The temple polluters that Jesus chased from the temple were not in the holy of holies; they were in the outer court. So you see, possession is not the issue. The Holy Spirit possesses our spirit; He is the owner. We are purchased, redeemed, bought with a price. Defiling the temple involves the soul and the flesh. Our mind, our will, our emotions, and our flesh—this is where the tormentors do their damage. A defiled temple is a troubled temple. A troubled temple must be cleansed by the Lord Jesus. *Cleansed*, in this case, is more than being forgiven. It is driving out the source of the defilement.

So, how do we get them out and keep them out? If demon spirits are present, we must determine if they have consent to be there. Consent must be from Jehovah God or from ourselves. Demons could be present by permission of generational sin of the forefathers, and if that is the case, then these spirits have consent to be there. Generational sin, or ancestral sin, is consent given by God according to Exodus 20:5: "For I, the LORD your God, am a jealous God, visiting the iniquity of the fathers on the children to the third and fourth generations of those who hate Me." This is a scriptural principle or law, if you will. It is legal permission for evil spirits to pass from one generation to another.

Remember, it is not possession; it is oppression, and Jesus went about doing good, healing all those who were oppressed of the devil. Do they have consent to stay? That's the issue. Have you confessed the curse-breaking power of Jesus Christ's name over generational sin? Has anyone commanded the spirits to leave? Have you not only repented of unforgiveness, anger, bitterness, and similar sins but also have commanded spirits that may have come by that doorway to leave?

It is important that you know. My experience has been that evil spirits do not leave until they are commanded to leave. Repentance cancels their permission to be there, but they leave when they are commanded to leave. Jesus *drove* out those who defiled the temple with great authority. He has given us authority over all the power of the enemy. Keeping the temple cleansed is keeping doorways closed that allow demons entrance. Read carefully this statement: the presence of the Holy Spirit does not keep demon spirits out; keeping doorways closed by the leadership of the Holy Spirit does. Man has a choice to *quench* or to *grieve* the Holy Spirit. The Holy Spirit does not fight our battles; He leads and guides us, but our will is always honored.

What Is Holiness?

It is written, "Be holy, for I am holy."

—1 PETER 1:16

For I am the LORD who brings you up out of the land of Egypt, to be your God. You shall therefore be holy, for I am holy.

—LEVITICUS 11:45

Does the word *holy* bring pleasant or unpleasant thoughts to your mind? Does it conjure up images of people who have claimed to be representatives of a *holy God*, but their personal lives were stained with iniquity? Do you see people dressed in black and being extremely legalistic about who God is and how He must be served? What comes to your mind when someone makes reference to *holiness*?

Is it *religious fanatics* with plain faces and unattractive dress? Is it some human being in Rome who carries a title? What exactly comes to your mind when the Bible says, "Be holy, for I am holy"? When the Word of God tells us to be like Him and that He is holy, what do you think God expects?

For our life to be Christlike, it means to be holy because God is holy. What is holiness? Let me draw a very simple parallel.

If we are to be like Christ...if we are to be like God...if we are to show Christ to others through our life...how are we to do it? God is love! An absolute necessary quality of a believer's life—if that believer is to be like Him—is to show love. It is the first of His commandments: to love Him and to love others as we love ourselves. God's likeness is His Holy Spirit. God is a Spirit and must be worshiped in spirit and truth. So to be like Him, His Spirit must live in and through us. You see, His Holy Spirit is Him. Love is produced by His Spirit; we can limit it or release it in fullness.

To be holy is to be like Him. To be like Him, His Spirit's fruit must live through us. So, then, God is not only love but also joy, peace, longsuffering, kindness, goodness, faith, meekness, and temperance (Gal. 5:22–23). These are characteristics of God, and they should be of those of us who believe—not by our power but by His Holy Spirit living through us.

God is joy. Joy is holiness. The opposite is depicted in society as a characteristic of God. Holiness is seen as long-faced and with no sense of humor. Black robes and a somber countenance have been portrayed as holy. Not so! The contrary is true. Laughter and smiles reflect joy. God is joy, as God is love. It is a clear picture of how we should be in order to be like Him. There is no gloom in Christ, no darkness at all in God. God is joy. Holiness must include joy, even joy that is unspeakable.

So, to be holy as He is holy involves the other fruit of His Holy Spirit. Don't complicate this. God is love. God is joy, and God is peace.

Troubled, chaotic, disturbed, dark, hopeless—these are not and cannot be part of who God is and what God expects from us. God is peace. He does not simply give peace; He is peace. God is what the fruit of His Spirit describe. There is one Spirit with *nine flavors*. Fruit can only be the product of its source. Peace is who God is, and to be like Him and to show Him to others, peace must be displayed, because that's who He is. He is love, He is joy, and He is peace.

This peace is peace with God and peace with people; it is a positive peace, filled with blessing and goodness—not simply the absence of fighting. We could say that this peace is a peace of the Holy Spirit, because it is a higher peace than just what comes when everything is calm and settled. This is a peace of God, which surpasses all understanding.

God is longsuffering or patient. *Longsuffering* means that you can have love, joy, and peace, even over a period of time when people and events annoy you. God is not quickly irritated with us (Rom. 2:4; 9:22), so we should not be quickly irritated with others.

Patience itself is a work of the Spirit. Martin Luther said:

> Longsuffering is that quality which enables a person to bear adversity, injury, reproach, and makes them patient to wait for the improvement of those who have done him wrong. When the devil finds that he cannot overcome certain persons by force he tries to overcome them in the long run.... To withstand his continued assaults we must be longsuffering and patiently wait for the devil to get tired of his game.*

God is love. God is joy. God is peace, and God is patient. So, to be holy is to be like Him; His Spirit must abide unrestricted in our life.

God is kindness and goodness: These two words are closely connected. About the only difference is that goodness also has with it the idea of generosity. Can you imagine God being anything other than *kind* and *good*? Unfortunately, the image many people have of God is that of an unkind judge. To be like God, His Holy Spirit of kindness and goodness must live through us.

God is love. God is joy. God is peace. God is patient. God is kind. God is good.

And God is faithful. In order to be like Him we must have faith and be faithful. The Holy Spirit of God works in us faithfulness, both to God and to people. Reliability must be a quality of a man who is yielded to the Holy Spirit of God. It cannot be otherwise. A man can be found faithful and full of faith by being like the Holy Spirit of God who lives in him.

---

* Martin Luther, "Galatians Five," Blue Letter Bible, June 25, 2005, http://www.blueletterbible.org/commentaries/comm_view.cfm?AuthorID=23&contentID=4758&commInfo=27&topic=Galatians (accessed March 13, 2010).

So, then, to be like God we must know that God is love. God is joy. God is peace. God is patient. God is kind. God is good. God is faithful.

God is meek. He is gentle. What a great image this brings to our holy God. In His mercy and grace we see His gentleness. The fruit of His holy presence can only produce gentleness. God anoints the humble and the lowly of heart. The assertive, demanding, abrasive personality is a warning flag of the absence of the likeness of Christ. His greatly honored gift is humility. The desire for flattery and recognition of men is not what God has in mind when He says to be holy. We are to be holy because He is holy and His Holy Spirit lives in us.

God is love. God is joy. God is peace. God is patient. God is kind. God is good. God is faithful. God is gentle.

To be like God we must know self-discipline that always benefits others. "Temperance" is the word used by the King James Version for this fruit of God's Holy Spirit. God is never out of control. Self-control involves a yielding to God's Holy Spirit and an agreement with God's Holy Word.

The world knows something of self-control, but almost always for a selfish reason. It knows the self-discipline and denial someone will go through for self, but the self-control of the Spirit will also work on behalf of others. God is temperate. His presence strengthens the will to do what is right. It is the enemy of the glutton and addict.

So, to be holy because He is holy requires simply yielding to His presence in us through Christ Jesus. His Spirit causes us to be like Christ. Other spirits cause us to be unlike Christ.

God is love. God is joy. God is peace. God is patient. God is kind. God is good. God is faithful. God is gentle. God is temperance. The Holy Spirit is God.

> Yours, O Lord, is the greatness,
> The power and the glory,
> The victory and the majesty;
> For all that is in heaven and in earth is Yours;
> Yours is the kingdom, O Lord,

And You are exalted as head over all.
Both riches and honor come from You,
And You reign over all.
In Your hand is power and might;
In Your hand it is to make great
And to give strength to all.
Now therefore, our God,
We thank You
And praise Your glorious name.

—1 CHRONICLES 29:11–13

CHAPTER 23

THE WORD OF KNOWLEDGE

My FIRST ENCOUNTER with *words of knowledge* was in October of 1995. I was preaching at the Federal Correctional Institution in Three Rivers, Texas. The medium-security prison is located about halfway between San Antonio and Corpus Christi, just off Interstate 37. This is a medium-security complex of about fourteen hundred inmates. But there is also a federal camp there. My friend David Pequeno served as the chaplain there.

There was something very unusual in the chapel service that evening: a uniformed correctional officer was seated among the inmates and worshiping with them. That just never happens. If there is an officer present, it is because he has been assigned to the chapel. It is very unusual for an officer to mingle with the inmates. I had never seen this before. I found out later that he was off duty and was studying to become a federal prison chaplain. His name was Warren Rabb. After the service, he told the officer on duty that he would escort me to my car because he wanted to talk with me.

He came up to me and shook my hand, and we made small talk as we left the main building. Walking across the prison grounds, I recall the evening was brisk and the sky was so clear and crisp. It was one of those *perfect evenings*. Officer Rabb told me of his call to the ministry and of his desire to become a federal prison chaplain. We visited some more after reaching the prison parking lot, and after we prayed together, I headed back to Corpus Christi to the south. Officer Rabb headed toward his home in Beeville to the east. I stopped at a convenience store for a soft drink and a snack before getting on Interstate 37. I was to be in four prisons on this trip, and I was staying in Corpus Christi.

As I pulled up at the convenience store service station, Officer Rabb pulled in right behind me. Before I could get out of my car, he came running over and told me, with great excitement, that God had given him a vision about me and he *had* to share it with me. He said, "I would have followed you all the way to Corpus to tell you about the vision." He was so excited that I could feel and sense that God had spoken to him. This is what he told me:

> I saw you standing in this big black pot, and there was oil bubbling all around you, not boiling, just bubbling. All around the pot there was a sea of people, as far as you could see, and they were all sick. The stench of their sickness was nauseating as it went up to the heavens. Then the oil began to bubble up and cover you, and as it ran from your head and down your arms and touched the people, they were healed. Get ready, brother; God's fix'in to pour it out on you!

I cannot adequately describe what I felt. It was like I had just been bathed in God's glory. While he was sharing the words with me, I sensed the presence of God's Spirit stirring in me. I knew these words were from God. But I didn't know what to do with the words from the vision. As I drove back to Corpus Christi, tears continually moistened my eyes. There was subdued excitement in my spirit. I thanked God many times and gladly received the anointing. I honestly didn't know how to process all of it. My seminary training had not covered this. I knew how to preach; I had seen thousands receive Christ as Savior, perhaps one hundred thousand or more, but I had never seen anyone healed or delivered of demons.

Actually, what I had been taught was contrary to the word given to me by Officer Raab. I had been taught that the gifts of the Spirit had died out with the apostles. I had been taught that the gifts would cease "when that which is perfect has come" (1 Cor. 13:10), and that this meant God's Word. Since we have God's Word, then there is no need for the gifts of the Spirit to operate—that's what I had been taught. I am ashamed today that I was so blinded to scriptural truth and that I was so heavily influenced by religious tradition that I had missed some of the greatest truths. I didn't know how to make this happen. I didn't know how to give altar calls except for salvation. I would find out that I didn't need to know.

If you have read *When Pigs Move In*, you have already read this account. I realize, however, that many have not heard the story at all. That was a life-changing event in my life, and I can't tell you that I understand it. I can tell you, however, that it began to happen and has not stopped.

Not long after this incredible experience, I was back in that same area of the state preaching at a state prison in Beeville. The unit of the Texas Department of Criminal Justice is named the Garza West facility. About five hundred inmates were in the gym that night, and perhaps as many as two-thirds of the men had answered the altar call. When the service was over, the men returned to their seats and were called back to their housing area by dorm location. As they filed out in single file, one of the men stepped from the line and approached the chaplain.

I had noticed this young man during the service. He sat on the front row, and he stared at me as though he *saw something*. There was sort of a look of wonderment on his face as I ministered. The chaplain brought him over to me and said, "This inmate has a word for you from the Lord, something the Lord showed him as you preached."

He still had this look on his face. He said, "Sir, while you were preaching, I saw something, and I feel God told me something to tell you." He moved beside me and asked me to stretch my arm forward, straight out toward the now empty seats. He placed his arm on top of mine and said, "God told me to tell you that as you extend your hand, so will He extend His." He seemed puzzled, as if he was just passing a message to me. "Do you know what that means, sir?"

"Yes," I told him, "yes, I do. Thanks for sharing that with me." When I left the prison that night, again, the Holy Spirit of God just seemed to cover me. It is so holy that it is very difficult to share. Tears again filled my eyes simply from the glory of His presence. I knew God had spoken to me again, and I am just unable to describe how humbling this was and is to me.

I have experienced genuine words of knowledge. No one has to convince me of the reality of this gift. The need for discernment was not too great in either of these *words*. I knew. My assignment was, and still is, just keep preaching. Just keep being faithful to His Word.

God's Gonna Give You a House

Jay McCarley, whom I mentioned earlier, is one of the most accurate men I have known in the area of words of knowledge. I suppose I have had hundreds speak what they called "a word from the Lord" to me or over me. Most have been inaccurate, shallow, or so general it could apply to anyone. I have learned through receiving hundreds of empty *words* from *the Lord* through others to test the spirits. Although many of the words I received were false words, and I have seen many false words for and from others, there is a genuine Holy Spirit gift that is legitimate in the body of Christ. This story about Jay is one example of that legitimate gift.

A few years ago Jay had asked me to accompany him on a business trip to Las Vegas. He didn't want to go there by himself, and he said he would pay my way just to come along with him. When he agreed to take his golf clubs, I said I would go. We played golf one day when it was 114 degrees. Obviously, that's not my point.

On the plane ride up there, we had a row to ourselves. Jay was next to the window, and I was in the aisle seat. About halfway there he leaned over in the empty seat between us and said, "Don, God is going to give you a house." He said with a big smile on his face, "It's going to be beyond your expectations and will be within two years."

OK. I actually don't remember what I said, but I remember thinking, "How is that going to happen?" Do I get all excited? Do I start to try to make that happen? What's my responsibility in that? I just filed it away.

Less than two years later, Jay was ministering with me in Houston. We had a "Night of Ministry" in Tomball, Texas, on a Saturday night. Before the service started, he walked over to me and said, "Remember that word I gave you on the plane to Las Vegas? It's starting tonight!"

I thought, "Is someone here in Houston gonna give me a house?" I just filed that *word* away also. We stayed in Houston on Sunday to minister deliverance to many people and drove back to Dallas-Fort Worth on Monday.

On Tuesday, our youngest son and his wife came over to visit from Plano. He had just begun his practice as a brain surgeon, after many years of preparation. He was thirty-eight and had been in school since he was five years old. Now he had his own office and was beginning his practice as a neurosurgeon. We had lived in our home for forty years. He was born there. He and his brother had grown up there. During our visit, he said, "Dad, before Paula and I buy us anything, we want to buy you and Mom a new house!"

We live in that house today. It is nice. We live in a small, gated community with three fishing ponds and walking trails, and directly behind is a park. It's perfect. We are blessed. I share that with you to encourage you. The gifts of the Spirit are genuine, valid gifts. Please don't be guilty of imitating and confusing others, and don't be duped by false words.

Spiritual Balderdash—"C'mon, Man"

One of my favorite board games is called Balderdash. A game that can produce many laughs, it is played with words written on game cards that have dictionary meanings, but virtually no one knows the definition. I won't explain the game; you likely know about it anyway. The game involves a lot of deception, just like the one I'm about to discuss. The word *balderdash* is actually defined as "senseless talk or writing." I think there is a fringe element of Christianity that has embraced doctrines of the flesh that could well be described as *spiritual balderdash*—nonsense.

Let me give you an example. A preacher says, "God has told me that one hundred people are supposed to give one thousand dollars." That's absurd; it's poppycock; it is nonsense; it is balderdash; it is wrong. Now, here is the truth: if one hundred people send me one thousand dollars each, I will have one hundred thousand dollars. That is truth. A preacher may have come to the conclusion that a way to raise one hundred thousand dollars is for one hundred people to donate one thousand dollars each. But to say it as it is generally presented is spiritual balderdash. Preachers need to repent of this. That's just wrong.

What do you mean when you say, "God told me…"? Do you understand what a huge statement that is? *God* told me. Did He summon you to His presence? Were you escorted into the heavenlies? Did He call you by name? Did He send an angel with a special message? Did He call you on the phone? Did He come to your room and give you some words apart from the Word of God? Many of the "God told me…" statements that you can hear in the church today are simply pretentious and presumptuous.

The Holy Spirit lives in every believer, and part of His work is to lead us and guide us into all truth. He walks beside us and comforts and encourages us. God's holy angels minister for us. We can communicate with God through prayer, and we have an invitation to come directly to His throne. What a wonderful relationship we have, and what provision is made for us! The presence of God's Holy Spirit will convict us and overshadow us; often His very presence will bring tears and waves of peace. But please don't be pretentious and presumptuous. Don't be guilty of misleading others with "God told me…" Maybe a gentler, more accurate way to say this would be, "I sensed in my spirit that God was saying..."

I want only what is real, and I am very disturbed by what is phony. If you are a true prophet, then what you speak is true. But if you call yourself a *prophet* and what you speak is false, that would make you a *false prophet*. I would never sit down and argue with you, but I will put your words to the test.

> Beloved, do not believe every spirit, but test the spirits, whether they are of God; because many false prophets have gone out into the world.
>
> —1 JOHN 4:1

Is the gift of prophecy a genuine gift of God's Holy Spirit? The Bible says it is (1 Cor. 12:10). If it is a legitimate, valid gift, then it certainly would be part of the schemes of demons to counterfeit it and deceive through it.

> Having then gifts differing according to the grace that is given to us, let us use them: if prophecy, let us prophesy in proportion to our faith.
>
> —ROMANS 12:6

If you want to open your life to demonic deception, a sure way to do it is to abuse the gift of prophecy by saying that you have a "word from the Lord" when all you have are your own false words.

This just in—breaking news from heaven—don't go there. During football season, one of the ESPN pregame shows has a segment called "C'mon, man!" In reality they are just making light of some aspect of NFL football from the week before. I can't help but think about this when I think about the *spiritual balderdash* we can find today: "C'mon, man!"

CHAPTER 24

PUT PRAISE ON YOUR FACE

CHANGE THE WAY you look—the way you look at yourself. The way you look to yourself. The way you look to others. The way you look at God. The way you look to God.

> Why are you cast down, O my soul?
> And why are you disquieted within me?
> Hope in God;
> For I shall yet praise Him,
> The help of my countenance and my God.
>
> —PSALM 43:5

Would you agree that we take too much off of the devil? Look at the above verse. Why am I so cast down, depressed, anxious, and discouraged? Why do I take this when I know the source of it, and I also know who is my help and health giver? I know the One who changes my countenance, and I know that praise brings His presence. Why would I not do something to change things?

The King James Version reads, "For I shall yet praise him, who is the health of my countenance." The word *countenance* literally means "the way we appear to other people;" it is our face or facial expressions. Countenance is appearance conveyed by the face. Strangely, our countenance is a good indicator of what we are feeling on the inside. Depressed people generally look depressed.

Now, I am not saying that all depression is the work of demons, but I am saying that none of it is the work of God. There are situations and circumstances that bring depressed and hopeless feelings; there are likely physical, maybe even nutritional causes for depression. However, most often it is the work of demons, when we have believed their lie.

That is not to say that God cannot minister to you when you are depressed and that life-changing lessons cannot be learned, but I am saying we often just *take* it from the demons without fighting! Don't be a *taker*. Don't receive a *cast down, disquieted soul*. The word *disquieted* means "to be anxious;" it is irrational fear.

Rebuke, refuse, resist! All lies are canceled by truth. If you have believed the lie of demons, you must remove the power of that lie by speaking the truth, believing the truth, and acting upon the truth.

Don't be a passive taker; be a positive resister. If you have believed what appears on the surface, choose to believe what appears in the supernatural. Call that which is not as though it is and that which is as though it is not. Speak truth and faith into your situation.

It is interesting that God's Word tells us what kinds of thoughts we should entertain. The first mention is *truth,* as recorded by Paul in Philippians 4:8:

> Finally, brethren, whatever things are true, whatever things are noble, whatever things are just, whatever things are pure, whatever things are lovely, whatever things are of good report, if there is any virtue and if there is anything praiseworthy—meditate on these things.

Believing a lie or entertaining irrational fear is an invitation to a cast-down soul. It is permission for demons to torment. Choose to dwell on truth and things that are honest, just, pure, lovely, of good report, virtuous, and praiseworthy. Choose to think on these things, and the God of peace shall be with you.

One of the most remarkable things I see in deliverance ministry is *change of countenance.* Deliverance ministry is the most real aspect of Christianity I have ever experienced. The countenance change takes place when the demons are driven out by truth and the authority of Jesus Christ's name. I literally see people come in one way and go out another. I could tell you many stories; perhaps I will at another time.

The peace, power, and presence of the Holy Spirit are able to flow through the individual once the legal rights of the demons have been destroyed. By the way, it was "for this purpose the Son of God was manifested, that He might destroy the works of the devil" (1 John 3:8).

Denouncing their lies and believing God's truth is the process for deliverance that I use in my ministry, and it is always the biblical process wherever you are. That is how deliverance takes place. The cast-down soul and disquieted countenance are removed by the work of the cross and the resurrection power of the gospel.

Jesus is health to our countenance. Speak His Word, which is truth, into your life. Change the way you look—the way you look at yourself, the way you look to yourself, the way you look to others, and the way you look to God.

Praise is an invitation to the Holy Spirit to envelop and indwell you where you are.

> But You are holy,
> Enthroned in the praises of Israel.
>
> —PSALM 22:3

> Praise the LORD, for the LORD is good;
> Sing praises to His name, for it is pleasant.
>
> —PSALM 135:3

It is correct to say that praise produces a pleasant, healthy countenance. Don't take anything off of the devil and his demons. Praise sends them running. Christ's presence produces love, joy, peace, patience, kindness, goodness, faithfulness, and self-control. I promise you that His presence will change the way you look. His presence is health to your countenance.

Somebody said, "Give the devil hell." No, that's the demons work; give them heaven! Remind them of all that is holy, righteous, and true. That's what torments evil.

A "Fist Pump" by Jesus

> Then the seventy returned with joy, saying, "Lord, even the demons are subject to us in Your name."…In that hour Jesus rejoiced in the Spirit and said, "I thank You, Father, Lord of heaven and earth, that You have hidden these things from the wise and prudent and revealed them to babes. Even so, Father, for so it seemed good in Your sight. All things have been delivered to Me by My Father, and no one knows who the Son is except the Father, and who the Father is except the Son, and the one to whom the Son wills to reveal Him."
>
> —LUKE 10:17, 21–22

Look at the excitement in the above verses. The Seventy returned with joy! And Jesus rejoiced in the Spirit! This was like a team meeting after a great victory where the coach was praising his team for a good job.

When you read Luke chapter 10, you see that Jesus sent seventy men to go in His name. He appointed thirty-five two-man teams to go before Him into every city and place that He would come. The parallel account in Matthew 10:1 says, "He gave them power over unclean spirits, to cast them out, and to heal all kinds of sickness and all kinds of disease." He gave authority to His twelve disciples and then to seventy *rookies—babes*, if you will—to cast out demons and to heal all kinds of sickness.

Notice that when the thirty-five teams returned from their appointments, they returned with *joy* saying, "Lord, even the demons are subject to us in Your name." The Bible indicates they were exuberant.

It was unrestrained joy. It was *all over their faces.* I wonder how they expressed that joy.

I vividly recall how I expressed supernatural joy the first time I experienced it in Kingston, Ontario, Canada. I could take you right to the spot on the top step of the Kingston Ontario Federal Prison for Women. I had just ministered in my first deliverance. I commanded demons in the name of Jesus, *and they obeyed.* A tormented woman was set free.

I walked out of that prison, paused on the top step at the prison entrance, threw the Bible in my right hand high above my head, and said, "Yes, in the name of Jesus, yes!" I left with joy! I'm pretty sure I know what these men felt when they returned to Jesus.

I know the joy of participating with the Holy Spirit and exercising the name of Jesus Christ against demons, sickness, and disease. But I wonder what Jesus was feeling when Scripture says Jesus rejoiced in the Spirit at their report.

"In that hour Jesus rejoiced in the Spirit." Jesus is genuinely excited here. Literally, the ancient Greek says, "He was thrilled with joy." God delights in using the weak and foolish things of this world to confound the wise (1 Cor. 1:27–29).

The ancient Greek word for *rejoiced* means "referring to exceptional rejoicing and exultation." Do you think it might have been equivalent to an athlete's *fist pump* when experiencing victory? I think it was something like that.

Jesus's joy makes Him break out into prayer. He praises God the Father for His wisdom, for His plan, and for His own unique relationship with God the Father—"I thank You, Father!" How many times have I said, "Thank You, thank You, thank You!" because of the joy of seeing people delivered and healed by the authority of His name. It's the response that must come.

You see, I am ever aware that the things I see and experience in this ministry have simply been *revealed to me,* that I qualify not as wise and prudent but as a *babe* in His sight. I wouldn't want it any other way.

I believe today that Jesus rejoices when we act in His name and believe His Word. Maybe He gives a fist pump or a high five to the angels when Christians act upon faith in His Word. The angels do give high fives when people accept Christ; there is joy in heaven whenever one sinner repents.

Rejoice is too weak a word. It is *exulted in spirit. Exulted* means "to show triumphant joy." Jesus gave visible expression to His unusual emotions, and the words "in spirit" are meant to convey to the reader the depth of His emotions. This is one of those rare cases in which the veil is lifted from off the Redeemer's inner man. We, like the angels, may *look into it* for a moment (1 Pet. 1:12).

As we look on this with reverential wonder, and as we perceive what it was that produced this ecstasy, we will also find rising in our hearts a measure of exultation in our spirits. I think I see an unbridled smile and an expression of victory that could be seen as a fist pump by Jesus. *Exulted*, remember, is "to show or feel triumphant elation." The thirty-five two-man teams of rookies had obeyed His Word, and the demons had obeyed their commands. Jesus is not just pleased; He is exulted! He feels the triumph, and He shows it.

I like the picture I see here: Jesus exulted, and the Father exalted. It is my desire to bring exultation to Jesus and exaltation to the Father. One produces the other. This whole process, Jesus said, "seemed good to the Father." If it makes Jesus rejoice and seems good to the Father, why are we not doing it in the church today?

Jesus made sure that the seventy men did not rejoice in the wrong thing. He basically said, "You have power over demons because I gave it to you; don't lose sight of why you have such authority." We are in Christ, and Christ is in us. We have been blood bought and Word taught. We are redeemed, and that is why we can walk in faith.

Rejoicing in our victories leads to "Thank You, Father," just as it did with Jesus in Luke 10:21. Does it confound the wise? You be the judge. Authority as a believer is not received or understood through education and accomplishment. Really, it is not even discovered; it is *revealed*. It is not hidden; it just cannot be seen through carnal eyes.

CHAPTER 25

GOD DISPATCHES ANGELS

TOWARD THE END of the apostle Paul's ministry, he would take his last recorded journey. This time he was the guest of the government; he was a prisoner of Rome. Some historians believe he may have traveled after his trip to Rome, but it is not mentioned in Scripture. It is believed that Paul was beheaded in approximately 64 or 65 during the reign of Nero. Without doubt, Paul is one of the great Bible heroes. He met what appears to be a minimum qualification to be called an apostle—he had personally seen the resurrected Christ. He was not self-appointed or self-promoted.

From the standpoint of historical evidence, the account of Paul's voyage and shipwreck found recorded in the Book of Acts is supported by a wealth of detail. After the apostle Paul's missionary journeys were completed, he was arrested in Judea, tried, and then transported as a prisoner to Rome. There is vast information aside from biblical accounts to substantiate this incredible journey. The storm and the ensuing shipwreck read like a Hollywood script.

I want to explore something else. Why didn't the apostle and his friends engage in spiritual warfare to stop the storm and threatening conditions?

Aristarchus and Luke were with Paul. They were allowed to travel with him, but Paul was in custody. They boarded a ship headed to Asia Minor, and undoubtedly the Roman custodians of Paul expected to change ships there and head to Rome. This was not a short journey, and it was not without much complication. However, it is interesting that there is no mention of Paul binding the principalities over the Mediterranean or anything similar on this harrowing journey. To be sure, they prayed, for Paul was certain in his spirit that danger was impending. He warned them against going into the storm.

> Now when much time had been spent, and sailing was now dangerous because the Fast was already over, Paul advised them, saying, "Men, I perceive that this voyage will end with disaster and much loss, not only of the cargo and ship, but also our lives." Nevertheless the centurion was more persuaded by the helmsman and the owner of the ship than by the things spoken by Paul.
> —Acts 27:9–11

Now this was a large vessel they were on. It was likely an Egyptian grain ship, perhaps the largest of ships at that time. Many believe it was comparable to nineteenth-century ships. There were 276 passengers, plus much cargo. Paul apparently was in on the discussion about whether or not it was safe to travel. He gave his advice and his perception; he warned that to sail would lead to danger. The centurion in charge weighed all of the advice and decided to ignore Paul's warning.

At this point it does not seem that Paul is speaking to them as from the Lord. His warning did not include "The Lord said..." Luke and Aristarchus had not given their opinions. Surely the three of them had prayed about the situation. They were about to be caught in a two-week storm at sea. Two weeks of life-threatening pounding by the wind and waves.

But not long after, a tempestuous head wind arose, called Euro-clydon. So when the ship was caught, and could not head into the wind, we let her drive.

—ACTS 27:14–15

Binding the Storm?

Was the weather bureau assigning names to storms back then? What is Euroclydon? Actually, it was a name describing a stormy wind from the north or northeast that occurs in the area of the Mediterranean where they were. Remember, they weren't on a rowboat, and the mariners were professionals. No ships sailed on the Mediterranean in the winter. They had an option to stay at Fair Havens on the island of Crete, which was not a good winter harbor, or try to make it to the Phoenix harbor farther west. They never made it and eventually ship-wrecked on the island of Milete, or modern-day Malta. This is about sixty miles south of Sicily, and the island is only seventeen miles long and nine miles wide. Their decision to try to make it on to Phoenix was not a good decision. Due to the lateness of the season, they faced the possibility that the ship could be wrecked by adverse winds.

This seems like the perfect opportunity to engage in spiritual warfare. Just bind Euroclydon; stop the activities in the heavens that may have negative effects on the earth. They didn't. I don't know any believer in Scripture more qualified to do this than the apostle Paul. Jesus stopped storms. Paul didn't. Paul did get assurance from an angel of God that they would be safe in the storm, but the angel did not stop the storm! I believe there is great information here for believers.

Some people say that in Mathew 8, Jesus rebuked His disciples for not having faith to stop the storm at sea. He said to them after He had calmed the wind and waves, "Where is your faith?" (Luke 8:25). Remember, faith can only be placed in what God has said. What could their measure of faith be? He had spoken earlier, "Let us cross over to the other side of the lake" (v. 22). That's the rebuke for no faith. He had told them they were going to the other side! Clearly He didn't scold them for not stopping a storm but for not believing they were getting to the other side.

> But He said to them, "Where is your faith?" And they were afraid, and marveled, saying to one another, "Who can this be? For He commands even the winds and water, and they obey Him!"
>
> —LUKE 8:25

During the storm on the Mediterranean Sea, Paul's faith had to be in the fact that he was going to Rome. Look at what he said: "'Men, you should have listened to me' (Acts 27:21); what a fine mess you've gotten us into now!" Generally our messes are created by our disobedience. Paul reminded them—and us—they wouldn't be facing the wrath of the storm if they had made godly decisions to start with.

I don't know what storms you may have been in. They can bring a lot of fear when the thunder and lightning are all about you. I'm talking about real storms, not a parable about life's difficulties. I'm talking about storms when the wind is so fierce that even the noise of the wind is frightening. Paul and those sailors had looked this storm in the face for fourteen days. No moon or stars. Just blackness and fierce threatenings. Two weeks of waves pounding the ship up and down on the storm-tossed sea. I'm sure many were seasick; I doubt there could have been much sleep or rest. There wasn't much hope of survival. Actually, the Bible says, "All hope...was finally given up" (v. 20).

Why didn't this great apostle just bind it all and command it to stop? Because it doesn't work that way! Knowing the truth in these situations is vital for getting through them. You will feel like a failure if you try to stop or tear down heavenly principalities and powers; you might even feel like God has failed you.

I don't know if there were demons directly involved with these storms; the storms happened every year and every time atmospheric conditions allowed it. The commanders made a bad decision, and now they were reaping the consequences. It was poor judgment to do what they did. They did not listen to the warning. While Paul did not say, "God told me to tell you not to go," his godly advice to them was, "Don't go." They got themselves in a mess by not heeding godly advice. Now they were doing all they knew to get out of it.

God Dispatches an Angel

We must have a biblical understanding to know when to pray and what our privileges are in prayer. God's Word tells us to pray *for* the peace of Jerusalem, not *against* the demonic principalities over Jerusalem. There is a big difference. If you face a genuine storm, not a figurative storm, your prayer should be for safety, not in binding demon powers that may be directing the storm. It's like praying against gravity or some other law that God has instituted. When the elements come together, they create something based upon God's laws. To be sure, demons know how to bring some of those things into being. Paul did not pray against any of this. He asked God about it, *and God sent an angel to him.* It is interesting that the angel was dialed in on Paul's location and came right to where he was.

The angel did not stop the storm. Instead, the angel came right through the storm and assured Paul that the angels would see to their safety. If we had authority to stop evil, why then don't we just do it?

How would you have prayed in Paul's situation? The next time the sky gets dark and the weather channel has identified a storm coming your way—I mean a heavy, dark, fierce-looking cloud—think about what Paul didn't do. He never stepped out of his realm of authority.

God dispatches angels. This angel came with a message of assurance and hope. Paul did not boast that he knew the coming events because he was a prophet. Rather, he encouraged them that in spite of it all they would be safe. In all of the despair of the situation, Paul could direct a prayer to God, and God could dispatch an angel to him.

The ship is tossed with winds and waves, bouncing and sloshing from the extreme violence of the storm, and yet the angel of God finds a way into it. God knows where you are and how to bring you to safety. I'm sure the demons involved in the individual lives of those on board were *revving up* the fear. No storm can hinder God's grace and mercy to His people, for He is a very present help in time of need. We are invited to come boldly into His presence. We pray best when we understand our helplessness and are able to express our dependency upon God. There is a vast difference in *standing* in His faithful Word and in acting foolishly bold. Paul never commanded the heavenly realm demonic powers. Paul knew he had been given no authority in that area. He trusted God and encouraged men.

Supernatural Journey

My earliest memories are good memories. I don't recall ever feeling lost or unloved. I always felt like I knew God, even though I knew nothing about Him. I always felt connected way before I was actually saved. I really don't know how to explain that. I just don't recall not feeling loved by God or me not loving Him. It was not until I was twelve years old that I invited Christ in my life, but even then I think it was the first time I realized I needed to be saved. I did it the moment the Holy Spirit convicted me.

I recall crying all day from the moment I was saved. I went back to church that night to be baptized, and the tears started again. I was not sure why, but I could sense something happening in my life. I guess I have never really been surprised when I see God working in my life. Amazed maybe, humbled always, but it's like I've always known Him.

Now, you could not have told me when I surrendered my life to preach that I would be preaching in prisons. I thought I would be the next Billy Graham! No way I would have believed that someday I'd be talking about angels and demons or that I would be allowed to participate in people being healed and seeing lives changed through casting out demons. The first experience I had with the supernatural was during my thirties.

My oldest son, Donnie, came to know Jesus when he was eight years old. He was exposed to the gospel more than the average eight-year-old, but he trusted Jesus because he realized he was a sinner and Jesus is the Savior. He came to Christ just as everyone else who is born again. Everyone who is saved today is saved the same way. I am proud of my son Donnie. He learned to love Jesus at an early age, and, as a third grader, he brought several of his friends and ultimately their families to know Jesus. I am happy that he grew up loving Jesus and sharing Him with others.

Both of my sons were typical boys, three years apart. They played football, baseball, basketball, and even fought with each other occasionally. What I want you to understand is that what I am about to relate to you happened to a perfectly typical seven-year-old boy, my youngest son, Robby. Robby is now a neurosurgeon, but when this experience took place he was in the second grade.

"I saw an angel, Dad, really!" Robby, our youngest son, had been saved about a year when this happened. He, like his older brother, trusted Jesus at an early age. They were not prompted. They came to Jesus, convicted by the Holy Spirit.

I recall a Wednesday evening that there were workers at our home, and I was preparing to leave for church. I excused myself, but before I left, Robby came to me and said, "Dad, can I go with you?" He had not had supper, and because of the circumstances, I told him to stay home with his mother and brother. He said, "Wait, Dad, I'm going to go out in the backyard under that tree and read my Bible. Where does it talk about my angels?"

I thought a moment and told him to read Matthew 18. He was only seven and could barely read, but he went out with his Bible as I left. After church, several people wanted to visit, some had problems, and others were just making conversation. It was past Robby's bedtime when I finally got home, but he was up and waiting. He had made arrangements with his mother to sleep with me because "he just wanted to talk."

It seemed that I could sense a very strong presence of God. Robby and I went to bed. The lights were out, and my wife and other son were asleep in another room. I asked Robby what he wanted to talk about. He said, "Dad, have you ever seen an angel?" I told him no, that I never had. He said, "I saw an angel, Dad, really! I saw two of them. While I was reading my Bible under the tree, I asked God if He would let me see *my angels*, and He did!"

This caught me by surprise, and I began to cautiously question him. He sensed the doubt in my questions, and he began to cry. Through his tears he said, "I knew nobody else in the whole world would believe me, but I thought you would." Then he said, "Dad, they are here, they are in the room right now, and they look sad."

I saw nothing, even though there was enough light to see the doors and windows. However, I did sense an awesome presence of God. I explained to Robby that I could not see them, but I assured him that I believed he did. I asked where they were, and he said that one was standing at the door and the other one right beside him. I was careful not to put words into his mouth, but I asked if they were small like little statues that he may have seen.

"Oh, no, Dad. They are bigger than you. They're bigger than the door."

I asked if they had long blond hair and looked like women, because I thought maybe he had seen paintings like this.

"No, sir, one of them has dark hair and one has blond hair, but it is short, and they're not girls; they're men."

I became increasingly more aware that God was letting him see what millions of Christians never get to see. Robby was not afraid, nor was he surprised. He told me, "I just knew God would let me see them 'cause He knows how much I love Him and how much I wanted to see *my angels*."

I asked him if he could describe them to me, and without hesitation or forethought he said, "The one at the door is big and has short blond hair and looks kinda like Uncle Dick in Georgia. He has either two big wings or six little ones; I can't tell for sure. It's sort of foggy, but I believe he has three wings on each side, they sort of cover up his arms, and he has a black book in his right hand. Nothing in his left hand." I asked if he had on a gown, and Robby said, "No, he has on really shiny white clothes, kinda like those [Roman] soldiers wear in pictures. His belt is shiny white." I asked if he could see the angel's feet. He rose up in bed and said, "Yes, sir, he has on sandals laced up around his legs."

I asked about the angel standing at his side, and he giggled a little in excitement. "He looks kinda like me, Dad, 'cept his hair is dark, and he is a man." He asked me if they would play with him, and I told him no, they were sent from God to watch over and protect him. I told him they only wanted him to worship God.

"Every time you say *Jesus* or *God*, they look at you and smile," said Robby. I asked if he would describe them further. "Yes, he has either two big wings, or four little ones." He just couldn't be sure. He said it looked like little lines on their wings, but it wasn't really clear. "He has a sword in his right hand and a little red Bible or book in his left hand. His clothes are the same. They are really shiny white, Dad, really white."

He asked me if he could go with them. "Go with them?" I could barely hold back my tears; had God sent His angels for my son? I asked him why he wanted to go with them. He said, "'Cause they're so pretty, and I want to watch over you and Mom and Donnie so no one will ever hurt you."

I explained to him that he could not be an angel, because God has something better prepared for His children. He said, "They're smiling again, Dad." Then he asked if he could talk to them. I really didn't know what to say because I had never seen an angel before, but I told him he could try. He turned to the one by his bedside and asked, so sweetly, "What's your name?" He said the angel replied either Judas or Jude. Robby seemed alarmed and asked if Judas wasn't a bad man. I explained to him that many other people were named Judas or Jude beside the one who betrayed Jesus. I knew my son would have never made up that name. This was very real.

He then asked the one at the door for his name and told me, even though he could barely hear, he was sure it was Daniel. This experience lasted for about three hours. He asked me if he could touch them; again I said, "Rob, I just don't know. If you want to try, I will go with you."

He said, "I think they will come to me if I ask." He asked in seven-year-old faith, "Daniel, will you come to my bed so I can touch you?" He was elated, and immediately he said, "Dad, feel how soft their wings are." He took my hand and directed it, but I felt nothing, nothing but God's presence in a way I had never known before.

Soon he said, "I don't need to see you any more tonight, but please stay and let me see you when I wake up." In a few minutes he was asleep, but not me.

I could not sleep. I had been bathed in God's love and grace. I had experienced something that made me aware of God's presence as never before. I listened for God to speak to my heart. It was as though He was saying, "Go and tell the world about My holy angels." I could not recollect hearing a message or preaching a message on God's supernatural beings. I was sure if I had seen angels, I could not speak or write of them. It was not necessary to my faith to see them, but how it increased as I witnessed them working in my son's life. I could tell of their activity and ministry today with great assurance even though I never have seen an angel.

The next morning as I arose to leave for work, I went to the bedside to kiss my sleeping son. I realized I was standing where one of his angels stood or was standing. He opened his eyes and said, "I love you, Dad." He looked around the room and said, "Dad, they're still here." He smiled and closed his eyes in the sweetest experience I have ever known since my walk with Jesus began.

In the following weeks and months, I read more about angels than ever before. I interviewed numerous people and checked every detail my son related with God's Word. There was no conflict but, rather, abounding evidence. He has told me, and only me (he would not talk about the angels to anyone else), of a few occasions where they have appeared to him since that night. Once as he was taking a test at school, he said he was getting confused and was about to cry. He said, "I knew the answer, but my mind wouldn't think." Just before tears came, he said Daniel appeared and said simply, "Now think, Robby," then the angel disappeared. "Dad, he didn't tell me any answers, but my mind got smart again."

He told me that once, as he ran outside to recess, there were two groups of kids playing. As he started toward one, Daniel appeared in front of him and said, "Don't go over there, Robby. You will get hurt." He said he has seen them a few times when his mother drove him home from school.

"Daniel always stands outside of Mom's [car] door, and Judas by mine. They don't fly; they just go beside the car." He would often see them on the school playground standing beside a tree watching him. For months he would tell me about the experiences. One day he asked if it was OK to tell God he didn't need to see them anymore. He was satisfied. It was becoming a little overwhelming to him.

Now, I know there will be some who read this who will not believe it. My purpose for sharing this is not for you to believe it but to believe God—believe Him, believe His Word, believe that His angels are ministering spirits sent forth to minister for them who are heirs of salvation.

Scripture says in Matthew 18:10, "Take heed that you do not despise one of these little ones, for I say to you that in heaven their angels always see the face of My Father who is in heaven."

I have written a book about this called *Protected by Angels*. This was many years ago, and it was the beginning of an incredible journey. I explored the Scriptures. For years I have been open to scriptural truth about God's supernatural world—not in a curiosity sense, but in a quest for truth. I have never been one to chase after signs and wonders; actually, I am quite the opposite. I believe God has revealed through Scripture and experience that angels and demons are very active in all of our lives. We are privileged to be in Christ. That angels minister for us is amazing. That we have been given authority in Jesus's name to cast out demons…Wow! It's just very important that we know our position in all of this.

CHAPTER 26

IT AIN'T OVER WHEN IT'S OVER

YOGI BERRA, FORMER major league baseball player, is remembered best probably for one quote. At least it is the one I remember best. He once said, "It ain't over 'til it's over." Well, obviously he was talking about baseball; one more strike, one more out, one more batter. Hey, we may win. You can never be sure until it's over, no matter the score. It ain't over 'til it's over.

When Dick Motta coached the Washington Bullets, and his team was down in the NBA finals, he said, "The opera isn't over until the Fat Lady sings." When things weren't looking good for the Bullets and the sportscasters were predicting doom, Motta would tell them to wait for the fat lady.* Everyone knew what he meant. You have to win four games to be NBA champs, and even though his team was down, there was still the fourth game to win. It ain't over 'til the fat lady sings.

I say sometimes we quit too soon—we give up too easily.

If you know Jesus Christ, don't quit. Don't even think about it; don't give place to the devil. Make it a part of your daily walk, and make

---

* NBA.com, "'Fat Lady' Sings Victorious Tune for Bullets: Game 7, 1978 NBA Finals," The 60 Greatest Playoff Moments: Honorable Mention, http://www. nba.com/encyclopedia/moments/60moments_hm_1-10.html (accessed May 18, 2010).

it clear to Satan and to those who are around you: "I will not quit!" Quitting is not an option. Satan's lie is to tell you that you are already defeated, that there is no use holding on any longer. He will remind you of every failure you have ever experienced. He is a liar. Understand that. He is a deceiver. He comes to you with only the power of deception. He is not in control; he never has been, and he never will be. God is in control.

Satan is a created being. He is not omnipresent; only God is. He is not all powerful; only God is. Satan can only be but in one place at a time; he likely doesn't even know your name. It is his demons, in the hierarchy of the kingdom of darkness, that trouble you. You need not be in bondage if Jesus has set you free. He has given you authority over the demons, in the name of Jesus Christ. Don't believe their lie. Rise up and declare that God is in control and He is your Lord (if indeed He is). The kingdom of darkness may be turning up the heat, but God has His hand on the thermostat. He will be the one to decide when enough is enough. Don't quit; don't even think about it.

God is faithful. Dwell on those three words for a moment; just roll them over in your mind and heart. God is faithful. Are you His child? Well, God is faithful. First Corinthians 10:13 says, "No temptation has overtaken you except such as is common to man; but God is faithful, who will not allow you to be tempted beyond what you are able, but with the temptation will also make the way of escape, that you may be able to bear it." God is faithful.

God in the Midst of Your Problem

If you are in the midst of a problem, bring God into the problem with you by repentance and genuine praise. That is, get right with God, and praise Him in the problem. Israel spent forty years in the problem because they refused to get right with God. Jesus spent forty days in the problem because He had God in the problem with Him. He fasted;

He prayed. He fought Satan with the Word. Get right with God, and God will get in the problem with you.

If you are saved, the very fact that there is a problem means there is an escape. Look at this scripture again: "God is faithful...but with the temptation will also make the way of escape." With the trial comes a way out. It matters not why you are in the problem. If Satan has turned up the heat in your life, it is with God's permission. He must have permission to touch God's property. It is possible, as in the case of Paul, that God has sent a messenger of Satan to buffet you. Perhaps He is pruning, breaking, shaping, molding, remaking you into the image of His dear Son. Regardless of the reason, what Satan means for evil, God intends for good in the life of His children. Praise Him in the problem.

The idea is not to get out of the problem, but to get God in the problem with you and see that He receives maximum glory. Now, here is a critical key for you if you are in a trial. Praise Him *in* the problem—not when you get out. Note again the last part of the verse we quoted earlier: "...that you may be able to bear it." I recall a female prison chaplain telling me about a problem she was going through, but she said, "I can praise my way out of anything!" The goal is not to get out, but to get Him in it to go through it with you. He will give you grace to bear it. He knows what you are able to bear. It may look like it's over. Circumstances may say to you that it's over. Satan will tell you in many different ways that it is over. *It ain't over!*

When Paul and Silas where imprisoned in Philippi, they had done nothing wrong. They engaged in spiritual war, and Satan got upset. They exposed the kingdom of darkness and cast a demon from a young lady. All hell broke loose...literally. The demons so stirred up the people that the two preachers were beaten openly and cast into the inner prison.

In the darkness and stench of the prison, feet in stocks, hands no doubt in chains, back bleeding, and somewhat humiliated, they did not question God. They did not ask God, "Where are You? Why have You allowed this?" They knew the entire jail would be listening to the conversation of these two who claimed to know God through His Son, Jesus Christ. You must always be aware that others are watching you demonstrate your faith when you are in the midst of the darkness. God is attracted to praise.

Instead of complaining and questioning, while still in their pain, they *praised Him*! God is attracted to praise. He will come right where you are when you praise Him. Not only will He come, but also Satan's demons will leave when you praise Him. At about midnight, I can hear the two weary, bleeding saints begin to cry out, "There is power, power, wonder-working power, in the blood of the Lamb!"* The demons began to tremble; they tucked their tail between their legs and ran like cowards. The earth began to tremble also. Prison doors fell to the ground, every man's shackles dropped to the floor, and instantly every prisoner was free from the bondage that held them. But they did not leave. There was a way out; had God not opened the door as a way of escape? No, *He was coming in*! He came in so that they would be able to bear it, so He may receive maximum glory. He came in so that every man would know the power and love of Jesus Christ. Stay in the problem until the jailer comes to his knees.

Satan is the jailer if you are in bondage. He is the one that holds you captive. If you will allow God to come into the problem with you, you will be able to bear it, and you will beat it! You can stay until the jailer says, "Uncle!" Stay until you are free and the demonic stronghold in your life is broken by the power of God. Don't even think about quitting or yielding. Stay in until the jailer comes to his knees. Don't look for the easy way out. Why go out if God is on the inside? Don't settle for second best. Stay until God is fully glorified. Proclaim to yourself, to your associates, to your enemies, to God, and to all of hell, "*It ain't over!*" God is bigger than over. No matter what the circumstances, if you are a child of God, get right with God. Get God

---

* "There Is Power in the Blood" by Lewis E. Lewis. Public domain.

in the problem with you, and you will be victorious! Don't focus on the circumstances.

You see, since Satan cannot create anything, he must use what is already there. Only God can create; that's why He can *make* a way of escape even if it looks impossible. Satan will use circumstances to lie to you. His only power over a believer is deception. He will lie because he is a liar. He will rob you of peace because he is a robber. He will steal your joy because he is a thief. He will kill your hope because he is a murderer. You must not focus on circumstances; they will eat you up. Focus on the God who can eat up the circumstances! Believe God regardless! The Word of God is where you must find strength.

Faith really does come by hearing, and hearing by the Word of God (Rom. 10:17). The Word is true, because Jesus *is* the *Word*—"And the Word became flesh and dwelt among us" (John 1:14). He is truth. His Word is true, because *He is* the Word. The Word, then, is personal. His promises are true because He *is* the promise. The Word of God is where you must find strength. "The eyes of the LORD are on the righteous, and His ears are open to their cry" (Ps. 34:15).

God promised Abraham and Sarah a son. God promised. Abraham looked at the circumstances and thought the circumstances too great an obstacle for God. He was a hundred years old; his wife was ninety. He was controlled by a lie of the devil that told him this was too big for God. I can hear him reasoning with God, "Lord, you must understand that I'm an old man; my wife is old. *It is over for us.*" It ain't over! When it's over is when God is in the problem. You don't have to help Him; you just have to trust Him. Abraham created a big mess by trying to help God fulfill His promise. He had two sons—one by his handmaid, a mistake, and one by his wife as God promised, a miracle.

Do you suppose Joseph may have had some questions when his own family turned their backs on him and cast him into a dark pit with intentions of leaving him there and then lying to their father? Do you think he may have had some deep pain when they decided to forsake him and sell him? The pain must have been intense. Do you think he may have had some doubts about God's hand on his life when he was imprisoned? He went from the darkness of a pit to the despair of a prison. Satan sent his best temptation, but God was *in the problem* with him, and Joseph was able to bear it. While Joseph was in the pit and in the prison, God had a palace in mind. He had blessing in store. He was in the problem with him, and He is bigger than the problem! It ain't over *when* it's over.

God was in the fiery furnace; He was in the lions' den—and He will come to you in your problem too if you will get your life right and praise Him. That's a pretty simple formula: repentance and real praise. He will come to your problem too.

In Mark chapter 5 there are three people who could not find help in this world. It was over for them, as it seemed. One man was so possessed of demons that he lived in a graveyard, cutting himself with stones, hassling people, out of control, without hope for help. He had been run out of town; no one could tame him or help him. He was sentenced to die in his bondage. It was over for him. But it ain't over when it's over. Jesus came and simply *spoke* his freedom to him. He *is* the Word, remember. Two thousand demons were driven from him in an instant, and a man who could not function in life or live in society immediately was made a missionary. Jesus Christ is bigger than the problem.

A woman who had an issue of blood for twelve years had spent all of her money on doctors and did not get better; she only got worse. She was without hope and under the sentence of a painful bondage that would grip her all the way to her grave. She just touched Him. *He is health!* He is *life*; He is the *Word*! Instantly she was free from the pain of her problem. Jesus got involved in the problem, and He is bigger than any problem—*any problem*! It doesn't matter how you got in the problem or what the problem is; you need God in the problem with you. Jesus did not come to get us out of problems; He'll get in the problem with you. He's not hard to find if you are searching for Him.

A man was told by a doctor that his little twelve-year-old daughter was going to die. There was no more medical help for her; she was going to die! He, in his pain, sought Jesus. Not only did he find Him (He's not hard to find if you are searching for Him), but also Jesus agreed to go home with him and touch the little dying girl. On the way there, word came that it was too late—the little girl was dead. "Don't bother Him anymore," they said. Oh, but Jesus said (my words), "Don't worry about it; it ain't over. I know it looks like it is. I know circumstances say it is. I know that in this world, death is over. But, I'm still going home with you. I'm still going to touch her, and she is still going to live. It ain't over." The man invited Jesus into the problem with him. Jesus is bigger than death itself. He is *life*; how can He not be bigger than death? Let Him in the problem with you, and know that it ain't over when it's over if you know Jesus Christ.

WHAT ANGELS DO

ANGELS WERE ACTIVE at the resurrection.

> And behold, there was a great earthquake; for an angel of the Lord descended from heaven, and came and rolled back the stone from the door, and sat on it. His countenance was like lightning, and his clothing as white as snow.
>
> —MATTHEW 28:2–3

One angel killed 185,000 enemies of God's people.

> And it came to pass on a certain night that the angel of the LORD went out, and killed in the camp of the Assyrians one hundred and eighty-five thousand.
>
> —2 KINGS 19:35

Holy angels shut the mouths of lions.

> My God sent His angel and shut the lions' mouths, so that they have not hurt me.
>
> —DANIEL 6:22

Angels were active at the birth of Jesus. Angels bring peace.

> And behold, an angel of the Lord stood before them, and the glory of the Lord shone around them, and they were greatly afraid. Then the angel said to them, "Do not be afraid."
>
> —LUKE 2:9–10

Angels are sent from God to minister to believers.

> Are they [angels] not all ministering spirits sent forth to minister for those who will inherit salvation?
>
> —HEBREWS 1:14

Angels escort believers into God's presence.

> So it was that the beggar died, and was carried by the angels to Abraham's bosom. The rich man also died and was buried.
>
> —LUKE 16:22

Angels minister strength in times of heaviness.

> Then an angel appeared to Him from heaven, strengthening Him.
>
> —LUKE 22:43

Angels obey His Word and praise Him.

> Bless the LORD, you His angels,
> Who excel in strength, who do His word,
> Heeding the voice of His word.
>
> —PSALM 103:20

Angels are ever watchful and keep His Word.

> For He shall give His angels charge over you,
> To keep you in all your ways.
> In their hands they shall bear you up,
> Lest you dash your foot against a stone.
>
> —PSALM 91:11–12

Angels surround those who trust the Lord.

> The angel of the LORD encamps all around those who fear Him,
> And delivers them.
>
> —PSALM 34:7

Angels will be active in judgment and the Second Coming.

> The Son of Man will send out His angels, and they will gather out of His kingdom all things that offend, and those who practice lawlessness, and will cast them into the furnace of fire. There will be wailing and gnashing of teeth.
>
> —MATTHEW 13:41–42

Angels are *special agents* sent by God.

> Then the high priest rose up, and all those who were with him (which is the sect of the Sadducees), and they were filled with indignation, and laid their hands on the apostles and put them in the common prison. But at night an angel of the Lord opened the prison doors and brought them out.
>
> —ACTS 5:17–19

Angels appear in many forms and fashions.

> But the Angel of the LORD called to him from heaven and said, "Abraham, Abraham!" And he said, "Here I am."
>
> —GENESIS 22:11

> An angel of the Lord appeared to Joseph in a dream.
>
> —MATTHEW 2:13

> This Moses whom they rejected, saying, "Who made you a ruler and a judge?" is the one God sent to be a ruler and a deliverer by the hand of the Angel who appeared to him in the bush.
>
> —ACTS 7:35

> About the ninth hour of the day he saw clearly in a vision an angel of God coming in and saying to him, "Cornelius!"
>
> —ACTS 10:3

> Do not forget to entertain strangers, for by so doing some have
> unwittingly entertained angels.
>
> —HEBREWS 13:2

Angels can guard, protect, and lead.

> Behold, I send an Angel before you to keep you in the way and to
> bring you into the place which I have prepared. Beware of Him
> and obey His voice; do not provoke Him, for He will not pardon
> your transgressions; for My name is in Him.
>
> —EXODUS 23:20–21

Angels can be God's enforcers.

> Then immediately an angel of the Lord struck him, because
> he did not give glory to God. And he was eaten by worms and
> died.
>
> —ACTS 12:23

Angels don't know the time of the end.

> But of that day and hour no one knows, not even the angels of
> heaven, but My Father only.
>
> —MATTHEW 24:36

Angels respond to God.

> Or do you think that I cannot now pray to My Father, and He
> will provide Me with more than twelve legions of angels?
>
> —MATTHEW 26:53

DEMONS OR NO DEMONS

D EMONS OR NO demons, here are some good things to consider.

> A wise man will hear and increase learning,
> And a man of understanding will attain wise counsel.
> —PROVERBS 1:5

Don't allow painful memories.

Tomorrow will take care of itself.

Always agree with God's Word.

Get proper rest.

Go to bed mad; wake up sad.

Worship regularly.

Live with a constant awareness of God's presence.

Have a purposeful routine.

Don't overdo it. Delegate wisely and learn to say no.

Trust others. Let them help you.

Yesterday is gone. Don't live in the past.

Regret is a "bad dog."

Choose your words carefully.

Take it easy, one day at a time.

Incur NO credit card debt—none.

Unclutter your life. Life is simple.

Purposely balance your life.

Golf is good.

Pace yourself.

Have a budget, and live within it.

Have a plan.

Learn to laugh.

Choose godly friends.

Eat right; be smart. Be disciplined.

Don't be late.

Pick up after yourself.

Write down thoughts and inspirations.

Go to bed on time.

The end of depression begins with doing things for others.

Choose your music wisely.

You learn by listening.

Make sure your presence makes others feel better.

Always have something to which you look forward.

Make friends with godly folks.

Make someone else laugh. Laugh some more.

Give your love to someone.

Exercise forgiveness.

Pride precedes failure.

The inside of your car is a tattletale.

Listen more; talk less.

Do things that are worthwhile.

Live thankful.

Encourage someone.

Practice receiving God's love and grace.

Don't be critical; people do the best they can.

Make your words energize ministering angels.

Don't sell "snake oil." Don't buy snake oil.

If cleanliness is not next to godliness, it is high on the list.

Your opinion is probably not that important to others.

Why not be the best you can be?

Have realistic expectations.

Faith comes by hearing the Word of God.

Take time to make decisions concerning others.

Be on time, always.

It is usually not necessary to give advice.

TV is not that important.

Learn to relax.

Don't condemn yourself.

Don't get even.

Bitterness must not find a place in your heart.

Practice joy.

Take pride in what you do—not in what you've done.

Be neat. Clutter reflects you.

Exercise faith. God is a faith God.

Keep your home ready for an important visitor.

Hope is in you; call on it when necessary.

Don't believe a lie.

Compliment someone.

Don't let anger linger.

Rest in truth.

Invest wisely.

Eat out sometimes; enjoy it, and be thankful you can.

Your loved ones need you in good health.

Keep your mind active.

If something needs to be done, you do it.

You have more than most people. Don't complain.

Don't procrastinate.

If you're forgiven, act like it; guilt is an unnecessary burden.

Check your conversation; don't talk about yesterday.

What if and *if only* should never be topics of discussion.

Concern requires action. Worry acquires headaches.

Medicine is OK if you need it; don't be "squirrelly" about it.

Don't mistake wealth for prosperity.

Faith may be life's most important ingredient.

Play games with others; fellowship with others.

No one makes you eat.

Don't look for blame.

Why not be the best you can be?

When you walk in the room, make it brighter.

Get out of debt.

Practice discipline.

Simplify life. Enjoy it.

Don't be in the position of having to make excuses.

Be on time—you disrespect others when you are late.

Get the speck out of your own eye,

Don't complicate simple things; let the government do that.

Tell God that you love Him.

Give something to someone.

Be wise as a serpent and harmless as a dove.

Everyone deserves a kind word.

Enjoy today.

Be the blesser.

Praise with thanksgiving invites God's presence.

Bodily exercise is overrated.

Don't show people pictures unless they ask; they usually don't care.

Blessings are in serving, not in being served.

Godly alignment is good.

Do what is expected of you.

Love people, and you become important to them.

If you don't take care of your body, who will?

Have realistic expectations.

Harmony is a good thing.

Disdain distraction.

Have something worthwhile to do.

Give from your heart.

You probably don't need to buy anything.

Three necessities:
    Someone to love
    Something to which you look forward
    Something worthwhile to do

FREE NEWSLETTERS
TO HELP EMPOWER YOUR LIFE

Why subscribe today?

☐ **DELIVERED DIRECTLY TO YOU.** All you have to do is open your inbox and read.

☐ **EXCLUSIVE CONTENT.** We cover the news overlooked by the mainstream press.

☐ **STAY CURRENT.** Find the latest court rulings, revivals, and cultural trends.

☐ **UPDATE OTHERS.** Easy to forward to friends and family with the click of your mouse.

CHOOSE THE E-NEWSLETTER THAT INTERESTS YOU MOST:

- Christian news
- Daily devotionals
- Spiritual empowerment
- And much, much more

SIGN UP AT: **http://freenewsletters.charismamag.com**

8178